Adventure Guide™ *to the*

Pacific Northwest

Don & Marjorie Young

HUNTER

HUNTER PUBLISHING, INC.
130 Campus Drive, Edison NJ 08818
(732) 225 1900, (800) 255 0343, fax (732) 417 0482

1220 Nicholson Rd., Newmarket, Ontario,
Canada L3Y 7V1, (800) 399 6858

The Boundary, Wheatley Road, Garsington
Oxford, OX44 9EJ England
01865-361122; fax 01865-361133

ISBN 1-55650-844-1

©1999 Don & Marjorie Young

Maps by Kim André & Lissa K. Dailey
© 1999 Hunter Publishing, Inc.

Cover photo: *Crater Lake* (Oregon Tourism Commission)
Back cover photo: *Heliskiing, Vernon, BC*
(Keoki Flagg, TLH Heliskiing)

Cartoons by Joe Kohl

For complete information about the hundreds of other travel guides offered by Hunter Publishing, visit our Web site at:
www.hunterpublishing.com

All rights reserved. No part of this book may be reproduced, transmitted or utilized in any form or by any means, electronic or mechanical, including photocopying, recording, or by any information storage and retrieval system, without permission in writing from the publisher. Brief extracts to be included in reviews or articles are permitted.

Every effort has been made to ensure that the information in this book is correct, but the publisher and authors do not assume, and hereby disclaim, liability to any party for any loss or damage caused by errors, omissions, misleading information or potential problems caused by information in this guide, even if such errors or omissions are a result of negligence, accident or any other cause.

4 3 2 1

Contents

Westward Ho!	1
Geography & History	1
The Nature of Adventure	4
Information Sources	10
Northern California	13
The Northern California Coast	13
Getting Around	15
Touring	16
Adventures	20
On Foot	20
Beach Walking	20
Wildlife Viewing	23
Among the Trees & Flowers	25
On Horseback	26
On Wheels	27
Driving Tours	27
Biking	28
Off-Road Tours	28
Carriage Tours	29
Rail Tours	29
On the Water	29
Whales	29
Saltwater Fishing	31
Freshwater Fishing	32
Diving, Crabbing, Surfing, Boating	34
Outfitters on Water	35
In the Air	36
Cultural Excursions	36
Where to Stay	40
Crescent City	40
Eureka	40
Fort Bragg	41
Hoopa	41
Samoa	41
Scotia	41
Trinidad	41
Camping	41
Where to Eat	42
Crescent City	42
Eureka	42
Fort Bragg	43

Samoa	43
Information Sources	43

North-Central California 44
- Getting Around 44
- Touring 47
- Adventures 50
  - On Foot 50
    - Hiking Trails & Wildlife Viewing 50
    - Gold & Gemstones 55
  - On Horseback 56
  - On Wheels 57
    - Driving Tours 57
    - Off-Road Touring 58
    - Biking 58
    - Rail Tours 59
  - On the Water 60
    - Fishing 60
    - Boating 64
  - On Snow 66
  - In the Air 68
  - Cultural Excursions 69
- Where to Stay 74
  - Dunsmuir 74
  - McCloud 74
  - Mt. Shasta 75
  - Weaverville 75
  - Weed 75
  - Yreka 75
- Camping 76
- Where to Eat 77
  - Mt. Shasta 77
  - Yreka 78
- Information Sources 78

Northeastern California 79
- Getting Around 79
- Touring 80

- Adventures 84
  - On Foot 84
    - Hunting 84
    - The Bizz Johnson Trail 84
    - The Lost Captain Dick Mine 84
  - On Horseback 84
  - On Wheels 85
    - Driving Tours 85

Biking	86
On the Water	86
Fishing	86
On Snow	87
In the Air	88
Cultural Excursions	88
Where to Stay	89
Ravendale	89
Susanville	89
Camping	90
Where to Eat	90
Johnstonville	90
Susanville	91
Information Sources	91

Oregon 93
Coastal Oregon 95

Getting Around	95
Touring	96
Adventures	100
On Foot	100
Beachcombing & Rockhounding	100
Wildlife Viewing	101
Hiking Trails	102
On Horseback	105
On Wheels	106
Driving Tours	106
Biking	109
Off-Road Driving	109
Rail Tours	110
On the Water	111
Clam-Digging, Crabbing & Fishing from Shore	111
Offshore Fishing	113
Freshwater Fishing	114
Boating	115
Windsurfing & Waterskiing	116
Whale- & Storm-Watching	117
In the Air	118
Cultural Excursions	119
Where to Stay	122
Brookings Harbor	122
Cannon Beach	122
Florence	122
Gleneden Beach	123
Gold Beach	123
Orleans	123
Otter Rock	123

Contents

Winchester Bay	123
Yachats	123
Camping	124
Yurts & Rustic Cabins	124
"Traditional" Camping	124
Where to Eat	125
Astoria	125
Newport	125
Information Sources	125

Central Oregon 126

Getting Around	126
Touring	127
Adventures	135
On Foot	135
Hiking Trails	135
Guided Hikes	139
Gold & Gemstones	139
On Horseback	140
Rodeos	140
Wagon & Trail Rides	141
On Wheels	141
Covered Bridges	141
Wineries & Llama Farms	143
Driving Tours	144
Mountain Biking	145
Group Tours	146
Rail Tours	147
On the Water	148
Boating, Waterskiing & Windsurfing	148
Fishing	149
Rafting & Kayaking	151
Commercial Cruises	152
Competitive Swimming	153
Houseboating	153
On Snow	154
Skiing	154
Snowmobiling	157
Ice Skating	157
Dog Sledding	158
In the Air	158
Air Shows	158
Ballooning	158
Scenic Flights	159
Gliders	159
Hang Gliding	159
Cultural Excursions	160

Where to Stay	166
Ashland	166
Bend	166
Cave Junction	166
Hood River	167
Crater Lake	167
Diamond Lake	167
Newberg	167
Portland	168
Salem	168
The Dalles	168
Troutdale	168
Warm Springs	169
Camping	169
Where to Eat	171
Albany	171
Ashland	171
Eugene	172
Hood River	172
Portland	172
Salem	173
Information Sources	173
Eastern Oregon	**174**
Getting Around	174
Touring	176
Adventures	178
On Foot	178
Gold, Gems & Geodes	178
Wildlife Viewing	180
Hiking	181
Hunting	182
Guided Hikes	182
On Horseback	183
Rodeos	183
Horse Shows & Pack Trips	185
On Wheels	186
Ghost Towns	186
Off-Road Driving	188
Biking	188
Rail Trips	189
Auto Racing	189
On the Water	189
Rafting	189
Fishing & Boating	190
On Snow	194
Skiing & Snowboarding	194

Snowmobiling	194
In the Air	195
Cultural Excursions	195
Where to Stay	199
Halfway	199
Pendleton	200
Camping	200
Cabins	200
Covered Wagons	200
Tepees	200
"Traditional" Camping	201
Where to Eat	202
Haines	202
Pendleton	202
Information Sources	203
Washington	**205**
Coastal Washington	**207**
Getting Around	207
Railroads	209
Airlines	209
Ferries	210
Urban Transit	210
Touring	211
Adventures	215
On Foot	215
Hiking Trails	215
Maps & Guides	221
Wildlife Viewing & Nature Parks	222
Guided Hikes	225
On Horseback	227
Riding	227
Horse Shows	227
Rodeos	228
Races	229
On Wheels	229
Biking	229
Rail Tours	230
Off-Road Driving	231
Races	231
On the Water	232
Fishing	232
Catching Squid & Shellfish	236
Boating	237
Swimming, Windsurfing & Whale-Watching	240
Kayaking	240
Whitewater Rafting	241

Ferry Rides	242
Cruises	244
On Snow	245
In the Air	247
Shuttle Service	247
Air Shows	247
Charters & Tours	248
Ballooning	249
Kite Flying	249
Gliders, Paragliders & Parachutes	250
Cultural Excursions	250
Where to Stay	266
Island Lodgings	266
Bellingham	267
Blaine	267
Everett	267
Kirkland	267
La Conner	268
Ocean Shores	268
Olympia	268
Port Angeles	268
Port Townsend	269
Seattle	269
Sequim	271
Snoqualmie	271
Tacoma	271
Camping	271
Where to Eat	275
Anacortes	275
Bellevue	275
Black Diamond	275
Bow	275
Cosmopolis	275
Everett	275
Friday Harbor	276
Gig Harbor	276
Kirkland	276
La Conner	276
Port Townsend	276
Renton	276
Seattle	277
Sequim	277
Stanwood	277
Information Sources	278
Central Washington	**279**
Getting Around	280

Airports	281
Touring	281
Adventures	283
On Foot	283
Hiking Trails	283
On Horseback	287
Horse Shows	287
Riding	287
Rodeos	288
On Wheels	288
Rail Tours	288
Shuttle & Van Tours	289
On the Water	289
Windsurfing	289
Rafting & Kayaking	289
Fishing	290
On Snow	291
In the Air	292
Cultural Excursions	293
Where to Stay	298
Ashford	298
Leavenworth	298
Longmire	298
Packwood	299
Camping	299
Where to Eat	299
Leavenworth	299
Longview	300
Vancouver	300
Information Sources	300
Eastern Washington	302
Getting Around	303
Airports	303
Railroads	305
Touring	305
Adventures	308
On Foot	308
Hiking	308
On Horseback	310
Rodeos	310
Horse Shows & Races	312
Riding	313
On Wheels	313
Auto Racing	313
Biking	314
Wagons & Motorcycles	314

Rail Tours	315
On the Water	315
Rafting	315
Cruises & Ferry Rides	316
Fishing	317
Races	318
Houseboating	319
On Snow	319
Snowmobiling	319
Skiing	319
In the Air	321
Ballooning	321
Gliding, Hang Gliding & Paragliding	321
Kites	321
Air Shows	322
Cultural Excursions	322
Where to Stay	332
Kennewick	332
Moses Lake	332
Republic	332
Richland	333
Soap Lake	333
Walla Walla	333
Camping	333
Where to Eat	335
Cheney	335
Conconully	335
Goldendale	335
Newport	335
Omak	335
Spokane	336
Toppenish	336
Information Sources	337
Southern British Columbia	339
Victoria & Vancouver Island	341
Getting Around	341
Touring	343
Adventures	344
On Foot	345
Outfitters	345
Hiking Trails	345
On Horseback	348
On Wheels	349
Tours & Motor Home Rentals	349
Racing	349
Cycling	350

Rail Tours	350
On the Water	350
Diving & Whale-Watching	350
Fishing	354
Boating	356
Aquarium	357
On Snow	357
In the Air	358
Cultural Excursions	359
Where to Stay	363
Campbell River	363
Nanaimo	364
Parksville	364
Port Hardy	364
Victoria	364
Camping	365
Where to Eat	366
Chemainus	366
Duncan	366
Protection Island	367
Victoria	367
Information Sources	367
Vancouver & Environs	**368**
Getting Around	369
Airports	370
Touring	371
Adventures	371
On Foot	371
Hiking Trails	371
On Horseback	378
Rodeos	378
Horse Shows	378
Riding	378
Racing	379
On Wheels	379
Motor Home Rentals	379
Biking	380
Auto Racing	380
Railroads	380
On the Water	381
Rafting	381
Fishing	382
Cruising & Diving	387
On Snow	388
Skating	388
Skiing	388

In the Air	389
Cultural Excursions	390
Where to Stay	396
Harrison Mills	396
Langley	396
New Westminster	396
Richmond	397
Vancouver	397
Camping	398
Where to Eat	399
New Westminster	399
Richmond	399
Stevenson	399
Vancouver	399
White Rock	400
Information Sources	400
Inland BC	**400**
Getting Around	401
Airports	401
Touring	402
Adventures	404
On Foot	404
Hiking Trails	404
Rockhounding	409
Wildlife Viewing	409
On Horseback	410
Rodeos	410
Riding	411
On Wheels	414
Biking	414
Day Trips & Off-Road Trips	415
Races	416
Train Rides	416
On the Water	416
Fishing	416
Boating	419
Windsurfing	421
Cruising	422
Houseboating	423
Scuba Diving	424
On Snow	425
Skiing	425
Snowmobiling	427
Hockey & Dog Sledding	427
In the Air	428
Cultural Excursions	429

Where to Stay	435
Chilliwack	435
Jesmond-Clinton	435
Harrison Mills	436
108 Mile Ranch	436
Jandana Ranch	436
Kelowna	436
Penticton	437
Revelstoke	437
Vernon	437
Whistler	437
Camping	438
Where to Eat	439
Kelowna	439
Merritt	439
Penticton	440
Powell River	440
Information Sources	440

Maps

The Pacific Northwest	1
Northern California Coast	14
North-Central California	45
Northeast California	81
Regions of Oregon	93
The Oregon Coast	97
Central Oregon	128
Mt. Hood & the Columbia River Gorge	157
Portland	163
Portland Region	164
Eastern Oregon	175
Regions of Washington	205
Coastal Washington	206
Central Washington	282
Eastern Washington	304
Vancouver Island, BC	342
Vancouver Area	370
Inland British Columbia	403

About The Authors

Don Young

This is Don's third book for Hunter Publishing. His first was *Adventure Guide to Southern California*; his second, *Romantic Weekends: America's Southwest*.

Don is no stranger to travel. He has been throughout the North American continent, visiting each of the United States, the Caribbean, virtually all of the Canadian provinces, and much of Mexico. He also has seen much of Europe – England, Scotland, Wales, the Netherlands, Belgium, Luxembourg, France, Germany, Austria, Italy, Switzerland, and Liechtenstein. His most recent trip: an assignment in New Zealand and Australia.

Marjorie Young

In addition to being Don's co-author and traveling companion, Marjorie has enjoyed a marvelous career as both an elementary school teacher and as a mother.

A seasoned traveler in her own right, her "passport credits" include a couple of places that Don has yet to see, notably Japan and the Scandinavian countries. Marjorie's next "big adventure"? Who can say?

Westward Ho!

Geography & History

■ California

When most people hear the words "West Coast," the first thought that comes to their minds is California.

Indeed, California is the West Coast's largest and most populous state, and the length of the California coastline far exceeds that of both its neighbors, Oregon and Washington.

From our earliest days as a nation, it was determined that the United States had a "manifest destiny" to become a country whose borders reached "from sea to shining sea." If that promise was to be fulfilled, it was essential that California had to become a part of the Union.

At first, the Far West, including California, was deemed to be a part of Mexico, and that claim was supported by the strength of the Spanish crown. But other than to establish a string of missions extending from San Diego to Carmel, neither Spain nor Mexico did very much to explore and develop their West Coast holdings.

The United States offered to buy the territory from Mexico, but were rebuffed. Then in May 1846, the United States and Mexico waged a brief war. When it ended less than two years later, Mexico disavowed all claims to California.

In September 1850, California became our 31st state.

■ Oregon

Spanish and English sailors landed in the region of modern-day Oregon as early as the 1500s. Capt. James Cook charted some of the Oregon coastline in 1778, and Capt. Robert Gray began visiting the region in 1787. Gray later discovered the Columbia River, which he named for his ship.

The Columbia River, which forms much of the border between Oregon and Washington, contains one-third of the potential water power in the United States.

In the winter of 1803-04, President Thomas Jefferson directed Merriwether Lewis and William Clark to explore the Pacific Northwest. After a remarkable journey, chronicled in numerous books and movies, Lewis and Clark reached the mouth of the Columbia River, near the present city of Astoria, in 1805.

In 1843, the Oregon Trail opened the Northwest to settlers, bringing 1,000 pioneers into the area. That figure increased to 1,500 the following year, and 5,000 by 1847.

By 1848, the year that James Marshall discovered gold in California, thereby triggering the Gold Rush, Oregon had been organized as a territory. That territory encompassed not only what we now know as Oregon, but Washington, Idaho, and parts of modern-day Montana and Wyoming.

As civilization advanced, conflicts with the Native population increased. The Cayuse War was waged between 1848 and 1850; the Yakima War, between 1855 and 1858; and the Nez Percé War in 1877. Originally, 125 tribes throughout the Oregon Territory had a combined population of 100,000-200,000. Today, 38,500 Indians live on seven reservations throughout Oregon and 81,500 Indians live on 27 reservations throughout Washington. The reservations encompass a total of nearly three million acres.

The Washington Territory was created in 1853. It included not only Washington, but parts of modern-day Idaho and Montana. Ten years later (1863), the Idaho Territory also was spun away from Oregon.

On 14 February 1859, Oregon became America's 33rd state.

■ Washington

Smaller in size than Oregon but more populous, Washington encompasses 66,582 square miles and has a 157-mile coastline. Its western regions receive some of the highest rainfall totals in the country, while the center of the state is dominated by the Cascade Mountain Range. The eastern two-thirds of the state, largely agricultural, contain vast areas of desert.

It was Capt. George Vancouver of Britain who first explored the area while seeking a Northwest Passage. That was between 1792 and 1794.

In 1889, Washington entered the Union as our 42nd state.

■ British Columbia

Canada's westernmost province, British Columbia was one of the last regions in North America to be explored and settled.

Eventual control of the region was a major campaign issue in the election of 1844, when America's 'manifest destiny' was a dominant campaign issue. Having wrested California and much of the Southwest from Mexico in a short-lived 'war,' President James Polk turned his attention to the British, who controlled Canada. Polk's campaign slogan, "54-40 or Fight," proclaimed that he would settle for nothing less than a borderline above the 54th parallel, but negotiations ultimately placed it at the 49th parallel, thus ceding Vancouver to the British.

In 1871, British Columbia was admitted to the Canadian confederacy.

Today, British Columbia boasts a population of just over three million. It is one of the richest provinces in Canada. Its coastline is dotted with islands and perforated by fjords. Its largest city, Vancouver, is the third largest, and the largest seaport, in all of Canada. And its quaint capital, Victoria, is a tourist's delight.

The Nature of Adventure

Although some might argue the point, "adventuresome" does not mean "foolhardy."

True adventurers – those who engage in such activities on a regular basis – take very few risks. They study where they are planning to go and what they are planning to do; they go properly equipped; and they rarely go alone.

When you embark upon your next adventure, exercise good judgment and do the same.

Some of these pointers may help.

■ On Foot

- When hiking, wear sturdy shoes and carry an ample supply of water. Carry a map and a compass. Take a survival/first-aid kit. Travel with a buddy, so that you have someone to help in case of an emergency. Tell someone where you are going, when to expect you back, and don't forget to notify that person *as soon as you return*.

- Just as bikers should defer to hikers on the trail, both hikers and bikers should defer to those who are on horseback.

- If you decide to go caving, never go alone. Keep the group together. Take at least two sources of light per person (some cavers also carry a candle and a good supply of matches). Wear a hardhat, preferably with a lantern on it so your hands can be free.

If you encounter a bear or a mountain lion:

- Stay away from it. Give it a chance to escape.
- Do not run. The animal may think you are prey.
- Do not crouch or bend over. Make yourself look as large as possible by raising your arms or spreading your jacket.
- Wave your arms slowly.
- Do not turn your back on the animal.
- Do not scream, but speak in a firm, loud voice.
- Throw stones, branches, or whatever you can reach without having to bend over.

- If attacked, fight back. Use whatever you have available, including your fists, jacket, or cap.

■ On Horseback

- Unless you are accompanied by an experienced guide, do not go into unfamiliar territory without a map and a compass.
- Do not wander so far that, should the horse become injured or should you and the horse become separated, you cannot easily walk back to civilization.

■ On Wheels

- When traveling, check the weather forecasts before you head out. In the winter, allow plenty of time to reach your destination and drive more slowly.
- In California, drivers of off-road vehicles and all-terrain vehicles (ATVs) must wear helmets, be able to show registration, and be sure all juveniles have adult supervision. They may not carry passengers or exceed the 15 mph speed limit.
- Bicyclists should yield to walkers and horseback riders on the trail. They should not ride more than two abreast, and after dark the cycle or the rider must have a white light that is visible for at least 500 feet in front and a red light or reflector visible for at least 600 feet to the rear.
- Mountain bikers should wear headgear, gloves, knee pads, elbow pads, and thick clothing. Don't ride any farther out than you can walk back in case of a flat tire, a broken part, or an accident. Be very careful to control your downhill speed, especially if you do not know the road; a sudden curve can throw you.

■ On the Water

- Safe boating tips can be found in free booklets provided by the **US Coast Guard** and **Metropolitan Life Insurance Co.**, ☎ 800/METLIFE; by the **National Safe Boating Council**, PO Box 8510, Lexington, KY 40533, ☎ 606/244-8242; and by **United Safe Boating Institute**, 1504 Blue Ridge Rd., Raleigh, NC 27622, ☎ 919/821-0281.
- Jet ski safety is covered in a booklet published by **Personal Watercraft Industry Assn.**, 200 E. Randolph Dr., Suite 5100, Chicago, IL 60601, ☎ 312/946-6200.

- Canoeing and kayaking safety is discussed in a brochure from the **US Canoe Assn.**, 606 Ross St., Middletown, OH 45044-5062, ☎ 513/422-3739.
- Along the Pacific coast, be aware of bad weather approaching. Keep a safe distance from logs in the surf. Stay away from cliffs that are collapsing.
- Whitewater rafting is exciting, but first timers should be aware of the various classifications of wild water:

CLASS	SKILL LEVEL	WATER CONDITION
	WHITEWATER CLASSIFICATION CHART	
I	Easy	Calm, moving water with occasional riffles.
II	Intermediate	Little bursts of bouncing rapids in clear, wide channels between long stretches of calm.
III	Difficult	Irregular waves through narrower channels where maneuvering around rocks is required.
IV	Very Difficult	Rapids are intense, loud, and long, with complex, rocky obstacles in the way.
V	Exceptionally Difficult	Rapids are long, loud, narrow, and violent, following one after the other without interruption.

MARINE LIFE

If you are not familiar with the marine life found along the coast in the Pacific Northwest, you might want to familiarize yourself with these creatures:

Barnacle – A crustacean that "cements" itself to rocks and other surfaces.

Bay Mussels – If you gather some of these morsels, you should know that the daily limit is 10 pounds, including the shells.

Bull Kelp – A plant that grows 18 inches a day during the summer and is harvested for use as an ice cream thickener.

Clams – Local varieties include the geoduck (*gooey-duck*), the horse or gaper, the softshell, the native littleneck, the manila, and the butter clams. Geoducks, on which there is a harvest limit of three, are almost rectangular, can exceed 20 pounds, and can live more than 150 years. The limit on horse or gaper clams is seven, and that on softshell, native littleneck, manila, and butter clams is 40, though the catch cannot exceed 10 pounds.

Decorator Crab – Fastens pieces of seaweed to its shell with a sticky glue in order to camouflage itself.

Flatfish – A sole, flounder, or halibut.

Isopod – A creature that looks like a multilegged insect.

Jellyfish – A saucer-shaped creature with a gelatinous body and long tentacles studded with stinging cells.

Limpet – A crustacean with a low conical shell that clings tenaciously to rocks or timbers when disturbed.

Moon Snail – A large snail that eats clams.

Nudibranch (*noo-de-brank*) – Sometimes called sea slugs, these gastropods are found in shallow waters, where they feed primarily on sea anemones. Often brightly colored, they lack both a shell and gills.

Octopus – In Puget Sound, these creatures can grow up to 30 feet from arm-tip to arm-tip.

Oyster – In this region, the most common varieties are the Pacific oyster, which carries a daily harvest limit of 18, and the Olympia oyster, a mottled gray variety that grows no larger than a silver dollar and is not to be harvested.

Pacific spiny lumpsucker – A tiny fish that can stick to rocks or seaweed.

Pipefish – A green-to-brown fish that looks like eelgrass and is related to the sea horse. The male has an abdominal pouch in which it carries the young.

Sand Dollar – A flat, circular sea urchin that lives chiefly in shallow water on sandy bottoms.

Scallop – An edible bivalve mollusk with a radially ribbed shell.

Sea Anemone (*ah-nem-oh-nee*) – An animal that looks like an underwater flower.

Sea Cucumber – A soft animal capable of expelling its internal organs when threatened and escaping while the attacker feeds on those organs.

Sea Stars – Another term for starfish, an echinoderm that feeds primarily on mollusks. The body usually has five "arms," causing the creature to resemble a star.

Sea Urchins – Look like underwater pincushions.

Seaworms – Some varieties (ribbon worms) can stretch up to 80 feet in length.

Tube worms – Live in a leathery tube with their feathery mouth parts protruding.

■ On Snow

- Wear layers of clothing, warm gloves or mitts, boots, and a helmet. Avoid mountainous terrain after heavy snowfalls or prolonged periods of high winds, indicators of peak avalanche weather.
- Dress in layers, especially two pairs of socks. Carry an extra set of socks and gloves. Sunglasses can be very helpful. A visor is essential for clear vision and wind protection.
- Watch the weather reports!
- In case of trouble, strapping tape, a folding saw, a knife, and a flashlight can be extremely useful.
- When sledding, limit yourself to one person per sled, and stay off the runs when climbing the sled hills.
- If you intend to iceskate, take a shovel to remove snow.
- Frostbite can be recognized by a loss of feeling and a dead white appearance to the skin. Keep the affected area covered and restore your body temperature as quickly as possible, preferably in a water bath of up to 105 degrees.
- Hypothermia is a rapid and progressive mental and physical collapse resulting from lowering the *inner* temperature of the human body. Untreated, it can lead to death. Avoid exposure to cold, wind and moisture, and wear the proper clothing. Down-filled clothes are very effective; cotton gives little protection. Wear a waterproof windbreaker. Don't drink alcohol. Give first aid by raising the victim's body temperature with hot drinks, quick-energy foods, and a warm indoor environment or, if this is not possible, body contact in a warm sleeping bag.

Snowmobilers:

- In mountainous terrain, the safest routes are along the ridgetops and slightly on the side toward the wind, away

from cornices. Stay out of the valleys and away from the bottoms of slopes.
- Avoid driving on frozen lakes. Drowning is a leading cause of snowmobile fatalities.
- Don't travel so fast you cannot react in an emergency. A wire fence can be almost invisible from a distance, and it can be deadly when hit at high speed.
- Be careful when crossing a road of any kind. Come to a complete stop before going on.

■ Cultural Excursions

Equally as enjoyable as outdoor adventure are the many forms of adventure that can be experienced *indoors*. For example, you can watch an exciting Western movie, or attend an actual Western rodeo. You can go to a lecture to learn about the Native Americans, or attend some real Native American dances. You can watch an archaeologist search for clues that will unravel an ancient mystery, or help to search for clues by participating in a dinner-theater murder mystery.

Although all of these things can be done indoors, they are all adventures, and they are all fun. Give them a try.

■ Where to Stay

As a guide to how much the many hotels, motels, inns, and B&Bs mentioned in this book will cost, we have adopted the following price guide:

Accommodation Price Scale	
$	Rates up to $50 per night
$$	$50 to $100 per night
$$$	$100 to $175 per night
$$$$	Over $175 per night

■ Camping

Be careful with fires. Don't be a litterbug; leave a clean camp by packing out all bottles, cans, and unburnable refuse.

Generally speaking, river and creek water should be boiled before you drink it, even in areas that might seem to be pristine.

■ Where to Eat

As an indication of what meals cost in the various restaurants listed here, we have utilized this price scale:

Restaurant Price Scale	
$	Inexpensive
$$	Moderate
$$$	Expensive

■ Information Sources

Sports Etc., PO Box 9272, Seattle, WA 98109, ☎ 206/286-8566, a multisport magazine, is available free of charge at many sports-related facilities.

Cyclists might enjoy the free monthly tabloid newspaper *Bicycle Paper*, 1205 E. Pike, Suite 1A, Seattle, WA 98122, ☎ 206/323-3301, which covers cycling activities throughout the Pacific Northwest. The paper is published 10 times a year, from February through November.

> The free *Border to Border Bed & Breakfast Directory*, PO Box 1283, Grants Pass, OR 97526, lists B&Bs in California, Oregon, and Washington.

It should be noted that there are a number of ways to reduce expenses when you travel throughout the Pacific Northwest. Tourist Information Centers, Chambers of Commerce, and such tourist-oriented establishments as hotels, motels, and restaurants often distribute free publications containing coupons that can be used to discount your room rates, your meals, and the entrance fees to a variety of popular tourist attractions.

> Such publications include *Exit Information Guide*, published by Exit Information Guide, Inc., 4205 N.W. 6th St., Gainesville, FL 32609, ☎ 352/371-3948, Web site www.exitguide.com, and *Traveler Coupon Guide*, published by ExitInfo, Inc., PO Box 600650, San Diego, CA 92160-0650, ☎ 619/463-6800, fax 619/463-6805, Web site www.exitinfo.com.

📖 Another extremely valuable way to cut your travel costs is to acquire a copy of the *Entertainment* booklet for the area in which you will be traveling. The booklets are very area-specific and, although they are not free, they can save you enough money to easily offset their cost. The *Entertainment* booklets are published by **Entertainment Publications, Inc.**, 2125 Butterfield Rd., Troy, MI 48084, ☎ 800/374-4464.

Northern California

In 1775, a Spanish vessel captained by Juan Francisco de Bodega landed near Trinidad Head and left a crude cross to signify Spain's claim to the land.

Early on, the land was predominantly under the control of British and Russian interests, but following the highly publicized Lewis and Clark expedition, Americans from the central and eastern United States flooded into the region in great numbers, eventually leading to the Bear Flag Revolt for independent statehood in 1846. Although the revolt failed, the United States invaded the area that same year.

When the Mexican War ended in 1848, Mexican interests in California were ceded to the United States. That same year, the Gold Rush began, and two years later, on September 9, 1850, California was admitted to the Union, adding a 31st star to the American flag.

In terms of land mass, California, "The Golden State," is the third largest state in the nation.

The Northern California Coast

To many people – particularly "the locals" – Northern California begins somewhere in the vicinity of the Big Sur, well south of San Francisco. The distinction between "North" and "South" usually is far less geographical than it is sociological, economic, and political.

"Southern California" has traditionally represented the "sun-and-fun" attitude of those residing in Greater Los Angeles, in San Diego, and in the lands most immediately adjacent to the Mexican border, while "Northern California" has identified the business-oriented, politically motivated, often ultra-liberal people residing in Greater San Francisco and Sacramento, the state capital.

In point of fact, there is a *third* California – the true "Northern California," which begins somewhere north of San Francisco and its urban sprawl, well away from the condominiums, the traffic jams, and the frenetic lifestyle of the city and its satellites – somewhere, let us say, in the vicinity of Fort Bragg, halfway up the California coast between San Francisco Bay and the Oregon border.

From this point northward, the California climate is different, the scenery is different, and the people are different. This is not *urban* country, it is *outdoor* country, where adventure – in one form or another – waits just around the bend.

Getting Around

With the Pacific Ocean on one side and mountains on the other, the coastal region of California is fairly well channeled north and south. Only two roads – Route 36, which goes through the Shasta-Trinity National Forest from Alton to Red Bluff, and CA 299, which heads east out of Arcata, passes through the towns of Willow Creek and Redding, and then races almost unimpeded toward the Nevada state line – offer passage from east to west through the picturesque Coast Range of mountains.

Running north and south, CA 1 (the Coast Highway) parallels the ruggedly beautiful California coastline all the way from the Mexican border through Fort Bragg and into Leggett, where it merges with US 101 (the Redwood Highway). There are few alternate roadways until US 101 reaches Crescent City, where US 199 heads toward the east, then turns northward again, angling toward the Oregon border just 30 miles away.

Although an excellent highway, US 101 is a road to be taken at a leisurely pace. Beauty is the objective here, not speed, and those who take the time can find a limitless number of treasures to enjoy, both natural and man-made.

A WORD TO THE WISE

If you have reason to be concerned about the impact of weather, road maintenance, or some other road condition on your trip, ☎ *916/445-1534 or 800/427-7623 for current statewide road conditions.*

From the **Amtrak** station in Martinez, it is possible to connect with Caltrans Bus Route 7 for transportation along the Northern California coast. At this writing, the **bus** makes stops at the "Skunk Train" depot in **Willits**, the Park 'n Takit Market in **Laytonville**, Peg House in **Leggett**, Waterwheel Restaurant in **Garberville**, Scotia Inn in **Scotia**, the bus depot in **Fortuna**, Stanton's Coffee Shop in **Eureka**, Transit Plaza in **Arcata**, and the Arcata Airport in **McKinleyville**.

Although the region is served by a number of small airports, there are no major air terminals in the northernmost parts of California.

Touring

From Fort Bragg, just 156 miles north of San Francisco, CA 1 curves slowly inland, unites with US 101, and heads toward **Garberville**.

Movie Sets

So profoundly beautiful is this region that literally dozens of motion pictures have been filmed here.

In 1979, Warner Bros. used **Ferndale's** Main Street and the Ferndale Cemetery for scenes in a TV film, *Salem's Lot*.

Eureka has appeared in a number of films, starting with Paramount's earliest (1919) version of *The Valley of the Giants*. Then it appeared in the 1923 version of *Ruggles of Red Gap*, followed by a 1950 version of the same film called *Fancy Pants*, starring Bob Hope and Lucille Ball.

Subsequently, Eureka has appeared in the 20th Century-Fox film *Valley of the Redwoods*, the CBS-TV film *A Death in Canaan*, Universal's TV movie *The Immigrants*, Warner Brothers' TV film *Salem's Lot*, and Paramount's *Jennifer 8*.

Steven Spielberg filmed *The Lost World/Jurassic Park* in the Humboldt County State Parks and turned both Patrick's Point in **Trinidad** and Prairie Creek Redwoods State Park in **Orick** into a Costa Rican rain forest.

Edwards & Hunt: First American Road Trip contains scenes shot along Tish Tang Creek and the Trinity River near **Hoopa**, and **Trinidad State Beach** provided the background for a number of scenes. Some of Redwood Creek near **Orick** also appeared in the picture.

For *Green Dolphin Street* (MGM, 1947), a New Zealand Maori settlement and a timber operation were built along the Klamath River near **Weitchpec**.

Smith River National Recreation Area became the forest moon of Endor for Lucas Films' 1981 movie *Return of the Jedi*.

North of Garberville, in **Scotia**, can be found the largest redwood lumber mill in the world.

Fortuna

Fortuna (pop. 9,000) is the largest city in the Eel River Basin and "the northern gateway to the Redwood Empire." Due to the numerous springs in the surrounding hills, Fortuna was originally (1875) called Springville. It later became known as Slide.

Beyond Fortuna, a slight detour to the west takes you to the westernmost city in the continental United States: **Ferndale**. Ferndale's downtown area has changed little since the 1890s, and the entire community, founded in 1852, is recognized as a State Historical Landmark. (A free souvenir copy of *The Ferndale Enterprise* newspaper contains a map that enables you to take a self-guided walking tour of the town.)

Eureka

Just north of Ferndale, the coastline swings eastward and relocates itself alongside US 101 just south of Eureka (pop. 27,000), the largest coastal city between San Francisco and the Oregon state line."Eureka," meaning "I have found it," is the state motto of California.

Billing itself as "The Best Small Art Town in America," Eureka estimates that more than 8,000 artists live in the county.

Eureka also claims to have more Victorian buildings per capita than any other city in California – a considerable boast, as any visit to the state's northernmost communities will attest. And what is a Victorian home without a ghost? Eureka claims several, including a female who likes to play 1930s jazz on an antique phonograph, two mischievous children who run through the hallways at night, and Frank, a man who likes to follow women into the bathroom... but disappears as soon as he is seen.

Arcata

After Eureka comes Arcata, another community with a large number of old Victorian homes. Here, in 1860, a 24-year-old Bret Harte worked at *The Northern Californian* newspaper. He resided in a house at 927 J St.

California's First Railroad

Arcata had California's first and only (at that time) railroad – a tiny flat car, drawn by an old white horse named Spanking Fury, that transported freight and passengers over the two-mile wharf to the Town Plaza. The Arcata & Mad River ("Annie and Mary") Railroad suffered a tragic accident one Sunday in 1896 when the Mad River bridge collapsed and the train plunged onto the gravel bar below.

Arcata is located on Humboldt Bay, the largest harbor between San Francisco and Puget Sound. Its waters produce more than half the oysters grown in California.

Willow Creek

About 40 miles west of Arcata on CA 299 is the little town of Willow Creek, known as China Flat in the 1850s when it served as a distribution point for supplies being shipped to the various mining camps scattered throughout the hills.

Sasquatch

Long before white men came, Native Americans living in this heavily wooded area spoke of a huge manlike creature and his family, said to be living in the Bluff Creek area along the Klamath River. The Karok Indians called him *Ma' Ruk-'Ara-Ra,* meaning "Giant Mountain Person."

The first white settler to come across this gigantic creature reported his experience in Crescent City in 1886, and during the Gold Rush, numerous Chinese mine workers reported seeing the apelike man between Happy Camp and Thompson Creek. Others said they had seen the large creature – seven to eight feet tall, weighing 350-800 pounds, with a light covering of hair all over its body – in the area between Willow Creek and Happy Camp. All reports agreed on another amazing characteristic: the creature, whatever it was (or is), had enormous feet.

In 1935, huge footprints were found in the snow on a nearby mountain. In 1958, heavy industrial equipment was mysteriously moved about in the Bluff Creek area. Loaded drums were thrown around, gigantic footprints were sighted everywhere, and workers said some foul-smelling "thing" was following them through the dense underbrush. In 1960, otherwise reliable people reported numerous sightings of Big Foot (or Bigfoot) throughout the region.

Since 1930, more than 120 sightings of Big Foot have been reported in the town of Eureka alone, more than 50 of them since 1960.

Sometimes known as Sasquatch, and often compared to the Himalayan Yeti, or Abominable Snowman, Big Foot draws the curious from near and far, and Willow Creek, tucked away into the Six Rivers National Forest, is the "Gateway to Bigfoot Country." A large statue of Big Foot stands in the center of town. There is a Bigfoot Avenue, a Bigfoot Chevron station, a Bigfoot Golf & Country Club, and a Bigfoot Outdoor Company, which specializes in whitewater rafting trips and raft rentals. The residents of Eureka celebrate Big Foot Daze every August, and a Big Foot Jamboree is held every Labor Day weekend in Happy Camp.

Just north of Willow Creek lies a valley containing the Hoopa Reservation, tribal home of the Hupa or NaTiniXwe (*Na-tin-o-way*) Indians. The Hoopa reservation is California's largest (93,000 acres) and occupies about one-fifth of Humboldt County – a county roughly the size of Rhode Island.

DID YOU KNOW?

It is in the Hoopa Valley, according to Indian legend, that all rainbows have their beginning.

McKinleyville

Returning to the main highway (US 101) and continuing northward from Arcata, motorists soon enter the village of McKinleyville, which boasts the world's tallest totem pole. Standing 160 feet high and weighing 57,000 pounds, the totem is located in the McKinleyville Shopping Center on Central Avenue. Now paralleling the sometimes serene, sometimes rugged California coastline, the highway passes through **Trinidad**, a great place to stop for a picnic lunch or a stroll along the beach.

Orick to Crescent City

Another pleasant rest stop is the Redwood National Park Information Center, ☎ 707/488-3461, one mile south of **Orick**. Past that is **Klamath**, and then **Crescent City**, where the tiny crescent-shaped harbor shelters some 280 commercial fishing vessels. In a given year, Crescent City's fishing fleet harvests 500 tons of shrimp, 700 tons of Dungeness crab, 90 tons of salmon, and 9,200 tons of other fish.

20 ■ Adventures

DID YOU KNOW?

The oldest working lighthouse on the Pacific coast (1856) can be seen in Crescent City.

Smith River is the Easter lily-growing capital of the world.

Adventures

With so much outdoors around, the only problem facing visitors to Northern California is what to do next.

Had enough of the forests? Visit the mountains.

Tired of being tied to the land? Turn to the sea... or the air.

Sick of the salt water? Go to one of the countless freshwater rivers or lakes in the area and go fishing, boating, swimming, whitewater rafting, gold panning... or whatever else comes to mind.

■ On Foot

Beach Walking

Walking along the beach, perhaps combining the walk with a little beachcombing, is practically a state sport in California. Around **Fort Bragg**, some of the better places to walk the beach are Noyo Beach, Glass Beach, and Pudding Creek Beach. Farther north, around **Cleone**, try 10-mile-long MacKerricher State Park, Ten Mile Beach, or Seaside Beach. And in **Westport** there's Pete's Beach, Wages Creek Beach, Howard Creek Beach, and Juan Creek Beach. **Eureka** offers an unusual black sand beach at **Shelter Cove**.

Trinidad is surrounded by beautiful beaches. Trinidad Beach State Park, north of town off Stage Coach Road, offers excellent beachcombing and an attractive natural rock arch. **Big Lagoon County Park**, seven miles north of town, also provides good beachcombing, camping, and a boat launch. Both beaches are wide, and driftwood and seashells are plentiful.

At 625-acre **Patrick's Point State Park**, 4150 Patrick's Point Dr., ☎ 707/677-3570, five miles north of **Trinidad**, beachcombers search for surf-polished agates. (Agates also can be found on the beach near Crescent City, and the area around **Willow Creek** contains bloodstone, jasper, and petrified wood, as well as agates.)

At **King Range National Conservation Area**, ☎ 707/825-2300, west of **Garberville**, the 54,200-acre wilderness contains the largest stretch of untouched beach on the northern Pacific Coast.

The **Lost Coast Trail** runs for 24 miles. From US 101, drive west to Briceland and Shelter Cove Roads. Facilities include four campgrounds.

King Range, one of the most geologically active ranges in the United States, has risen 66 feet over the last 6,000 years. It also is the gateway to the **Sinkyone Wilderness Area**, which provides camping and whale-watching opportunities as well as hiking.

Crescent City is the heart of the Redwood National Park country (the redwood is the California state tree). There are 56 miles of hiking trails in the national park, and 108 additional miles in the adjacent state park. On **Crescent Beach**, two miles south of Crescent City off Enderts Beach Road, the beachcombing is excellent, and the whale-watching from the Crescent Beach Overlook is fantastic during the migration season.

If you would rather walk in the woods than walk along a sandy beach, **Richardson Grove State Park**, eight miles south of **Garberville**, ☎ 707/247-3318, is a 1,414-acre facility along US 101 that contains 10 miles of hiking trails, some swimming holes, some riverside beaches, and a chance to fish for trout and steelhead in the Eel River. The park also has a Visitors Center and a campground.

The 33-mile-long **Avenue of the Redwoods**, west of US 101 and two miles south of **Weott**, leads to **Humboldt Redwoods State Park**, the largest of California's several redwood state parks. Encompassing 51,315 acres, the park offers 100 miles of hiking trails, as well as fishing and swimming along the Eel River, horseback riding and mountain biking along the fire roads, and three campgrounds. Two miles south of town, the Visitors Center contains a natural history museum, provides valuable maps, and furnishes useful camping and hiking information. (For additional information, contact the **Humboldt Redwoods State Park Visitor Center**, Box 276, Weott, CA 95571, ☎ 707/946-2263.)

Grizzly Creek Redwoods State Park, ☎ 707/777-3683, is 18 miles east of **Alton** on Route 36 between Carlotta and Bridgeville, where Grizzly Creek meets the Van Duzen River. A 388-acre park, it encompasses five miles of hiking trails and offers camping, fishing, and swimming. Nature programs are often conducted, and the museum and a visitors center are open daily, 9-7, during the summer. **Van Duzen County**

Park, 12 miles east of Alton, has a pleasant nature trail that runs beside the Van Duzen River.

Russ Park in **Ferndale** offers three miles of hiking trails, as well as trails for horseback riding and birdwatching. No wheeled vehicles are allowed. From Main Street, turn left on Ocean and go past the cemetery to a gravel parking lot.

Arcata Community Forest & Redwood Park, ☎ 707/822-5953, is a 575-acre forest within the **Arcata** city limits that is accessed from East 11th Street or East 14th Street. A self-guided map to the park's 10 miles of trails is available at the local Chamber of Commerce.

If you detour eastward to **Willow Creek**, pick up a free copy of the pocket-sized *Horse Linto Creek Interpretive Trail* brochure produced by the US Forest Service at the Lower Trinity Ranger District, PO Box 68, Willow Creek, CA 95573, ☎ 530/629-2118. Then, while in the area, hike across **Ammon Prairie**, where you can pick fresh fruit from the old trees still standing there, abandoned. Also hike to **Grays Falls** or **Burnt Ranch Falls** on the Trinity River where, in the fall, you can watch the salmon jump the rapids.

The **Yurok Indian Loop Trail** in **Klamath** is a moderate 1.2-mile hike. Leaving the trailhead at the north end of the Lagoon Creek picnic area, the trail gradually climbs the coastal bluffs. A free brochure, available at the trailhead, describes the local Native American culture.

Turning inland from Crescent City, US 199 leads to the **Smith River National Recreation Area**, ☎ 707/457-3131, near **Gasquet**. The area offers 65 miles of trails, including **Doe Flat Trail**, which follows an old mining road along Doe Creek to a former mine site at the end of the road; **McClendon Ford Trail**, an easy two-mile hike through a Douglas fir forest and across Horse Creek, en route to a bouldered beach on the South Fork of the Smith River; and **Myrtle Creek Trail**, a moderate two-mile trail that begins across the river from US 199. (A self-guided hiking brochure available at the Smith River NRA headquarters contains some interesting mining, geologic, and cultural history associated with the Myrtle Creek Trail.)

A more ambitious route is the **South Kelsey Trail**, a 32.2-mile hike of moderate difficulty. Built by Chinese workers in the 1850s, the trail started in Crescent City and ended nearly 200 miles away at the Fort Jones Army post. Originally used by mule trains, the trail now begins near Horse Creek and follows the South Fork before it ascends 5,775-foot Baldy Peak, where it provides some outstanding views of the Pacific Ocean, the Siskiyou Mountains, the Marble Mountains, and Mount

Battery Point Lighthouse, Crescent City (Robert Holmes, CDT).

Shasta. The trail continues on to Harrington Lake and then enters the Klamath National Forest.

Those who like to combine sightseeing with their walking will enjoy a visit to **Shelter Cove**, where the colorful **Cape Mendocino Lighthouse** (☎ 800/262-2683) is in the process of being relocated and where they can climb **Kings Peak**, the highest point on the shoreline of the continental United States (4,086 feet). Nearby **Mal Coombs Park** offers boat launching, rock fishing, and tide-pooling opportunities, along with a chance to dive for abalone and do a little surfing, swimming, or jetskiing.

Battery Point Lighthouse, at the end of Front Street in **Crescent City**, has been called "the best lighthouse in Northern California" by *Sunset* magazine.

Wildlife Viewing

Enjoying the opportunity to see unusual birds and animals is one of the great rewards of hiking – or simply walking – through the woods.

Around **Fortuna**, deer and game birds are plentiful. In Loleta, the **Humboldt Bay** (Eel River) **Wildlife Refuge**, 1020 Ranch Rd., Loleta, CA 95551, ☎ 707/733-5406, can be reached by taking the Hookton Road exit off US 101 and traveling west for five miles. Park and then hike south along the beach.

Prairie Creek State Park near **Eureka** shelters a herd of 2,000 Roosevelt elk, and the nearby Humboldt Lagoons marshlands offer some excellent birdwatching. Also near Eureka is the **Six Rivers National Forest**, which includes a number of outstanding birdwatching areas. Among the best are Ruth Lake, the Lower Trinity River around Willow Creek, and the high mountains near Sange Peak, Bear Basin Butte, Whitey's Peak, North Trinity Mountain, Horse Mountain, Black Lassic, or Ant Point. Ask for a free copy of the pamphlet *Birds of the Six River National Forest*.

Across the harbor from **Arcata** is the 154-acre **Arcata Marsh & Wildlife Sanctuary**, 600 S. G St., Arcata, CA 95521, ☎ 707/826-2359. Once a city dump, the sanctuary now maintains a delightful Interpretive Center and 4.5 miles of trails. The best birding can be enjoyed from mid-July to early May. (A free map and a free brochure, *Birding in the Arcata Marsh & Wildlife Sanctuary*, are available at the Arcata Chamber of Commerce.)

Duck hunters might head for the mouth of the **Smith River** and/or **Lake Earl**, halfway between the mouth of the river and **Crescent City**.

The **Smith River National Recreation Area** around Crescent City (mentioned above) teems with wildlife such as blacktail deer, black bears, gray squirrels, blue herons, yellow-legged frogs, ospreys, raccoons, garter snakes, otters, martins, fishers, grey foxes, and (rarely) rattlesnakes.

Guided hikes and interpretive tours are often conducted in various parks and preserves along the California coast. At **Point Cabrillo Preserve** just south of **Fort Bragg**, for example, Sunday docent-led walks have been initiated during the summer months by the North Coast Interpretive Association, and a public access trail has been opened on a rugged bluff previously fenced off to sightseers. The access is 200 feet south of CA 1 and the Comptche-Ukiah Road.

Near **Arcata**, the **Lanphere-Christensen Dunes Preserve**, ☎ 707/444-1397, has sand dunes more than 80 feet tall, but access is available only to guided tours. The tours are conducted at 2 PM on the first and third Saturdays of every month from the Pacific Union School parking lot, 3001 Jones Rd. If you go, take a jacket and some soft-soled shoes. Also in Arcata, the **Redwood Region Audubon Society** conducts walks through the **Arcata Marsh** every Saturday morning at 8:30, rain or shine. The walks begin at the end of I Street.

Forest walks are regularly scheduled from Patrick's Point Drive in Trinidad, ☎ 707/677-3638.

Around **Orick**, summer interpretive programs are conducted at the south entrance of the **Redwood National Park** Information Center, ☎ 707/488-3461. Trail maps also are provided, and during the summer a ranger-guided shuttle bus operates between the Information Center and **Tall Trees Trailhead** for the benefit of those who prefer to walk alone.

Prairie Creek Redwoods State Park, also near Orick, offers summer interpretive walks and talks. **Fern Canyon** is a nice walk from the end of Davison Road with resident herds of Roosevelt elk (USE CAUTION AND DO NOT APPROACH). The park contains 70 miles of trails for hiking and mountain biking. Beachcombing and camping facilities are provided. A museum and a visitor center also are in the park.

At **Jedediah Smith Redwoods State Park** near **Hiouchi**, summer interpretive walks and talks also are conducted, and camping, hiking, fishing, swimming, and river floating are available.

Two-hour tidepool or seashore walks are conducted daily in the summer at **Enderts Beach** near **Crescent City**, but accessing the beach involves a half-mile hike-in. Summer interpretive walks and talks also are offered at nearby **Del Norte Coast Redwoods State Park**.

For those who enjoy professional guidance when they hike, **Adventure's Edge**, 10th & F Sts., **Arcata**, CA 95521, ☎ 707/822-4673, offers such services to backpackers, bicyclists, and cross-country skiers. River touring trips also can be scheduled. An interesting variation is provided by **Winged Boot**, 11 Glendale Dr., Arcata, CA 95521, ☎ 707/826-1054, E-mail heather@humboldt1.com., which specializes in arranging backpacking trips and other outdoor activities *especially for women*.

Among the Trees & Flowers

Along with the wildlife, many hikers enjoy seeing the broad variety of beautiful, often unusual vegetation that can be found while hiking in Northern California.

The **Lassics**, a government-designated geological area, on Route 36 a little more than an hour east of **Alton**, boasts 3,640 acres of Jeffrey pines, violet-flowered onions, golden fawn lily, burgundy lupine, and purple penstemon.

In the **Six Rivers National Recreation Area**, located an hour east of **Eureka** on CA 299, there are 1,077 acres of Jeffrey pines and Port Orford cedars, as well as magnificent views of the Trinity Alps.

Arcata Forest Nature Trails, a free booklet available from the City Manager's Office, 736 F St., Arcata, CA 95521, ☎ 707/822-5953, contains maps of two interesting trails near Arcata: **Trail 1 Loop** and **Campbell Creek Trail**. The booklet also describes the flora to be seen along those trails, which includes salmonberry, wild cucumber, thimbleberry, skunk cabbage, and red huckleberry.

On North Bank Road in **McKinleyville** is the **Azalea Park Reserve**, which has trails winding through acres of wild azaleas. Take the Central Avenue exit off US 101.

East of Crescent City near **Gasquet** in the Smith River National Recreation Area, the **Summit Valley Trail** starts along a mile of old jeep road, then travels through mountain meadows filled with spring wildflowers. A short side trail leads to an old fire lookout.

Craig's Creek Trail, a moderate 7.4-mile trail through the Smith River National Recreation Area, follows an old pack trail used by miners in the late 1800s. It passes through old-growth redwood, Douglas fir, knob cone pine, alder, tan oak, live oak, and chinquapin, and ends where Craig's Creek joins the South Fork of the Smith River.

■ On Horseback

 Very much a part of the western tradition, this part of the country revels in its rodeos. **McKinleyville** has its Pony Express Days & Rodeo during the first weekend in June. Also held in June is the Redwood Acres Fair & Rodeo held at the Redwood Acres Fairgrounds in **Eureka**, ☎ 707/445-3037; the Rodeo in the Redwoods, ☎ 707/923-2119, staged in **Garberville**; and Pro Rodeo Days, held on the Del Norte County Fairgrounds in **Crescent City**, ☎ 707/464-9556.

The **Fortuna** Rodeo is staged each July in the downtown rodeo grounds in Rohner Park, Fortuna, CA 95540, ☎ 707/725-3959 or 725-3726. This is America's most westerly rodeo, said by some to be the oldest in the West (started in 1921). The rodeo is accompanied by a week-long carnival, parade, and Wild West celebration.

Orick also stages a rodeo each July on the Orick Rodeo Grounds, ☎ 707/488-9827, 488-6755, or 488-2525.

Horseback riding takes many forms in this part of the country, from riding along the sandy beaches to scaling the forested mountains on trips that may last overnight or even longer.**Ricochet Ridge Ranch**, 24201 N. Hwy 1, **Fort Bragg**, CA 95437, ☎ 707/964-7669, Web site horse-vacation.com., offers both types of rides. The ranch, located two miles north of Pudding Creek Bridge, is open daily from 9 to 6.

Redwood National Park near **Crescent City** offers 41 miles of equestrian trails, and **MacKerricher State Park**, located on CA 1 three miles north of Fort Bragg, has been called "the best beach for horseback riding in Northern California."

In **Arcata**, **Clam Beach County Park,** north of the Arcata-Eureka Airport on the east side of US 101, has some excellent riding trails, and **Hammond Trail County Park** has a 2.2-mile hiking, biking, and equestrian trail that winds along the coast to McKinleyville.

Redwood Trails, 265 Idlewood Lane, **Trinidad**, CA 95570, ☎ 707/488-2061 or 800/443-5074, offers horseback riding, camping, and "prize-winning blackberry pie" amidst the world's largest elk herd. You can rent horses at **Sea Horses**, Clam Beach, **Trinidad**, CA 95570, ☎ 707/839-4615. **Tall Tree Outfitters**, PO Box 12, **Orick**, CA 95555, ☎ 707/488-5785, conducts horseback tours in the Redwood National and State Parks. Turn off US 101 onto Drydens Road at Orick School and go one mile to the end of the road. The firm also offers dinner rides, all-day tours, and extended pack trips along Redwood Creek.

■ On Wheels

Driving Tours

Avenue of the Giants is a 31-mile portion of old Hwy 101 that parallels the current US 101. It separates from the present freeway north of Fortuna and Ferndale, and meanders peacefully through 51,222 acres of redwood groves.

Another scenic motor route begins in **Willow Creek**. From Forest Service Road #1, it is possible to see Mount Shasta and the Pacific Ocean at the same time. During the spring, a drive along CA 299 from Willow Creek to Weaverville is highlighted by the beauty of blooming redbuds and dogwoods.

From **Hiouchi**, Howland Hill Road provides an alternate, more scenic route through the redwoods to Crescent City, but the road is unpaved and narrow.

Prairie Creek Redwoods State Park on US 101 north of **Orick**, ☎ 707/488-2171, is an excellent place to see herds of Roosevelt elk without having to leave the car. **Cal-Barrel Road** provides an unpaved but scenic drive. **Davidson Road**, also narrow and unpaved, goes to Gold Bluffs Beach, site of some one-time gold mining operations.

In the **Smith River National Recreation Area**, get a copy of *Smith River National Recreation Area Backroads Discovery*, which maps and describes four excellent motor tours of the region: **Forest Highway #15**, a 33-mile, three-hour, one-way trip along a paved road; **Ship Mountain Route**, which covers 45 miles one way and takes better than three hours over gravel and paved roads; **Camp Six Lookout**, which covers 22 miles in two hours over a gravel road, with a historic fire lookout and an interpretive stop along the way; and **Old Gasquet Toll Road**, a one-hour, 17-mile trip over a slow gravel road, with interpretive stops and great vistas along the way.

Biking

📖 While in the Smith River National Recreation Area, stop at Caltrans District 1, PO Box 3700, 1656 Union St., **Eureka**, CA 95502-3700, and ask for a free copy of *District 1 Bicycle Touring Guide*, which covers the California north coast.

📖 Another free brochure that will be helpful to bikers, *Mountain Cycling in the Arcata Community Forest*, is available from the City of Arcata, 736 F St., **Arcata**, CA 95521, ☎ 707/822-8184.

Good bike routes in the Arcata area can be found in the **Arcata Bottoms**, **Arcata Marsh**, **Arcata Community Forest**, and along the **Hammond Coastal Trail**. If you left your bike at home, you can rent one at **Revolution Bicycle Repairs**, 1360 G St., Arcata, CA 95521, ☎ 707/822-2562.

Around **Eureka**, **Humboldt Redwoods State Park** has been listed as one of the top 10 mountain biking areas in the country. A free trail map is available from the Eureka/Humboldt County Convention & Visitors Bureau, 1034 2nd St., Eureka, CA 95501, ☎ 707/443-5097, 800/338-7352 (inside CA), or 800/346-3482 (outside CA). There are 11 miles of mountain bike trails in the national park and an additional 40 miles of trails in the various Redwood state parks.

Off-Road Tours

A popular spot for off-road driving in the Redwood National and State Parks is **Freshwater Lagoon Spit**, where off-road vehicles are allowed to access the beach in three posted areas. Vehicles may be driven on the wave slope of the beach at or below mean high tide, but not in the dunes or on any vegetation.

Off-roaders should contact the **Off-Highway Motor Vehicle Recreation Division** of the California Department of Parks & Recreation, 1725 23rd St., Ste. 220, PO Box 942896, Sacramento, CA 94296-0001, ☎ 916/324-4442, fax 916/324-1610, E-mail pubinfo@calohv.com, which can provide a mountain of information about areas open to off-highway recreation as well as the state's off-road rules and regulations.

Also useful is a free pocket-size brochure, *Samoa Dunes Recreation Area*, which is available through the Bureau of Land Management, 1125 16th St., Room 219, Arcata, CA 95521, ☎ 707/822-7648, or at the Arcata Chamber of Commerce office. The **Samoa Dunes Recreation Area** is near the US Coast Guard station on Humboldt Bay and is popular for hiking, surfing, fishing, and beachcombing.

Carriage Tours

Care to see the area by an alternate means? Try **Old Town Carriage**, 2nd & F Sts., ☎ 707/442-7264, in **Eureka**, which offers regular horse-drawn carriage tours from the town gazebo.

Rail Tours

Railroading has always played an important role in this part of the country, and continues to stimulate the imagination of its citizens and visitors even today. One of the best-known rides on this part of the coast is the California West Railroad **Skunk Train**, Box 907, **Fort Bragg**, CA 95437, ☎ 707/964-6371 or 800/77-SKUNK, fax 707/837-9611. For over 100 years, the trains have covered the 40-mile "Redwood Route" carrying logs, loggers, freight, and passengers. Pulled by a 1924 Baldwin steam engine, the train has recently increased its runs 50% over previous years. Full-day trips, half-day trips, and one-way trips are offered. The train leaves the foot of Laurel Street in Fort Bragg and from US 101 in Willits. The line is closed on Thanksgiving, Christmas, and New Years Day.

■ On the Water

Whales

Of all the mammals on earth, the gray whale undertakes the longest yearly migration – a round trip of over 12,000 miles from the Bering Sea to the Baja peninsula of Mexico. The southward journey occurs every winter between September and February; the return trip, with the whales' newborn calves in tow, begins around mid-February and passes here between March and June. Weighing up to 45 tons and growing to 50 feet in length, the whales have been proclaimed the official marine mammal of California. Between 18,000 and 21,000 whales make the annual migration to Mexico, traveling in small groups or "pods" of two to six animals.

During their migration, the whales cover 70 to 80 miles per day, traveling at a rate of three to five miles per hour and surfacing every three to five minutes to breathe.

Your first glimpse of a migrating whale may be a "blow" – a burst of water up to 15 feet high. On a clear day, these spouts can be seen for miles, and the explosive "whoosh" of the whale's exhalation can be heard half a mile away.

"Breaching," or bringing the body above the surface, is rarely seen in the Northwest and is much more common in the warmer waters along the Southern California beaches. (See *Adventure Guide to Southern California* [Hunter Publishing] for directions to good whale-watching locations in that part of the state.)

Choice locations for whale-watching in Del Norte County include **Klamath Overlook**, about four miles off US 101 on Requa Road; **Endert's Beach Overlook**, about three miles off US 101; **Battery Point**, accessible only at low tide from the parking lot at the foot of A Street in Crescent City; **Brother Jonathan Vista Point**, on Pebble Beach Drive at Ninth Street in Crescent City; **Point St. George**, three miles northwest of Crescent City at the west end of Washington Boulevard; and **Castle Rock**, an island near Crescent City. In Humboldt County, look for whales at **Clam Beach** and **Moonstone Beach**, 12 miles north of Eureka; **Gold Bluffs Camp-ground**; **Luffenholtz Beach**; **McKinleyville Vista Point**; **Patrick's Point State Park**; **Redwood National Park** near Orick; **Shelter Cove**; **Table Bluff** and the bluffs just south of **Centerville Beach** in the Eel River Valley; and **Trinidad Memorial Lighthouse**.

California State Beaches, ☎ 916/653-6995, offer a number of programs during the whale migration, and the town of **Fort Bragg**, ☎ 707/961-6300 or 800/726-2780, fax 707/964-2056, celebrates an annual **Whale Festival** each March.

In addition, a number of companies charter boats to ride out among the whales as they pass. In Arcata, **University Center Activities**, Humboldt State University, Arcata, CA 95621, ☎ 707/826-6018, is such a company. In Eureka, contact **King Salmon Charters**, 1875 Buhne Dr., Eureka, CA 95503, ☎ 707/442-3474. In Fort Bragg, **Anchor Charter Boats**, PO Box 103, Fort Bragg, CA 95437, ☎ 707/964-4550; **Party**

Boat *Patty C,* PO Box 572, Fort Bragg, CA 95437, ☎ 707/964-0669; *Noyo Belle,* North Harbor Drive, Fort Bragg, CA 95437, ☎ 707/964-3104 or 964-1300; **Tally Ho**, North Harbor Drive, Fort Bragg, CA 95437, ☎ 707/964-2079; and **Telstar Charters**, North Harbor Drive, Fort Bragg, CA 95437, ☎ 707/964-8770, offer whale-watching excursions.

Saltwater Fishing

Naturally, fishing is one of the primary pursuits in this region. That includes freshwater fishing as well as saltwater fishing.

Anchor Charter Boats, Box 103, Fort Bragg, CA 95437, ☎ 707/964-4550, leaves Noyo Harbor on expeditions for salmon, albacore, and various bottom fish. The company operates daily from 7 to noon and from 1 to 6 during the summer; from 8 to 1 in the winter.

Noyo Belle, North Harbor Drive, Noyo Harbor, Fort Bragg, CA 95437, ☎ 707/964-3104 or 964-1300, can be chartered for fishing, for cruises, or as a party boat.

Farther north along the coast, **King Salmon Charters**, 3458 Utah St., Eureka, CA 95501, ☎ 707/442-FISH, operators of the 36-foot *Moku,* takes customers deep-sea sport fishing, bottom fishing, tuna fishing, crabbing, and birdwatching, or on bay excursions.

Other fishing charters can be arranged at **Woodley Island Marina**, off the north shore of Eureka in Humboldt Bay. Take the Samoa Bridge (Route 235) from US 101. In addition to fishing charters, boats can be rented for cruising, dining, and individual sailing.

Trinidad Bay Charters in Trinidad Harbor, ☎ 707/839-4743, 677-3625, or 800/839-4744, offers two trips daily to do some light-tackle rock cod fishing with Captain Tom Lesher. Sailing aboard the *Jumpin' Jack,* the first trip leaves at 6:15 AM and returns at 11:15 AM, while the second trip leaves at 12:15 PM and returns at 5:15 PM. Hourly rates are provided for evening trips. Half-day and full-day private charters can be arranged.

Shenandoah Charters, ☎ 707/677-3344, also operates out of Trinidad Harbor.

> 📖 In Crescent City, where the best salmon trolling occurs between June 1 and September 30, a useful free brochure, *Fishing in Del Norte County, CA*, can be obtained at the Chamber of Commerce, 1001 Front St., PO Box 246, Crescent City, CA 95531-4133, ☎ 707/464-3174 or 800/343-8300, fax 707/464-9676.

Of course, it isn't necessary to charter a boat to go saltwater fishing.

In California, fishing from a public dock or pier requires no license, which makes this form of fishing very popular with out of state visitors, who usually pay a premium for a fishing license whenever they are away from home.

In **Eureka**, fishermen find fish along the **Del Norte Street Fishing Pier** and the **Adomi Fishing Pier**. The latest fishing information is obtained over **The Fishphone**, PO Box 6751, Eureka, CA 95502, ☎ 707/444-8041.

The Crescent City fishing pier also is popular.

Around **Arcata**, chinook (king) and coho (silver) salmon are taken from small boats and from the harbor jetties. Redtail perch, shark, skate, sturgeon, halibut, and stingray are caught from boats, piers, and docks. Kelp bass, snapper, ling cod, perch, and cabazon are caught by rock fishing from the jetties.

The Arcata Boat Ramp is the only concrete ramp on Arcata Bay, but it is important to watch the tide tables. The ramp is inaccessible at tides lower than +3.0. **Mad River County Park**, five miles northwest of town, has a boat launch, and some excellent fish are taken right off the beaches, which also are popular with beachcombers.

In **Trinidad**, there is good fishing along **Agate Beach** between the ocean and the Big Lagoon.

Surf fishing can also be excellent around **McKinleyville**.

Freshwater Fishing

Freshwater fishing is as popular as saltwater fishing in this part of the state. Little wonder. During the spawning season, the rivers and streams are chock-full of salmon and steelhead trout, rushing upstream.

Around **Garberville**, the **Benbow Lake State Recreation Area**, two miles south of town off US 101, contains a 26-acre lake that is extremely popular during the steelhead and salmon run from October through March. Camping, swimming, and boating also are popular there.

Two miles southwest of Garberville, the Eel River in **Tooby Memorial County Park** provides good steelhead and salmon fishing, as does the portion of the Eel River that flows through Fortuna. The Klamath, Trinity, Van Duzen, Mattole, and Mad Rivers, as well as Redwood Creek, all contain salmon and steelhead, ready for the baited hook.

The **Klamath River**, third largest river on the West Coast, also boasts cutthroat, shad, and sturgeon. Salmon are the dominant species from July to November. Steelhead come into their own from June to February, and trout take over between May and November.

Shad also populate the **Trinity** and **Eel Rivers**.

On the **Mattole River**, the fishing is primarily for steelhead. **A.W. Way County Park**, 35 miles south of Ferndale, provides a campground and swimming as well as access to fishing on the Mattole River.

The region also has an abundance of freshwater lakes. In Arcata, for example, **Klopp Lake** has a good population of cutthroat trout. In the **Marble Mountain Wilderness Area** nearby, there are almost 90 high-elevation lakes. **Fish Lake**, on Route 96 between Weitchpec and Orleans, contains both brook and rainbow trout. **Big Lagoon**, off US 101, has cutthroat and steelhead trout, plus starry flounder. **Freshwater Lagoon** contains rainbow trout, while in the ocean across the highway, anglers can try their luck with the redtail perch. **Stone Lagoon** also features cutthroat trout, but they may only be taken on artificial lures with single barbless hooks.

In the **Smith River National Recreation Area**, the chinook salmon *average* 20 pounds, but can reach as much as 70 pounds! The steelhead trout *average* 10 pounds and can reach as much as 27 pounds! Steelhead, an oceangoing rainbow trout, are most readily caught from December through March. The cutthroat trout range from eight to 21 inches, and their season runs from late spring throughout the summer.

Access points to the Smith River include **Cedar** on Route 199 east of Patrick Creek, **Sand Hole** on Route 199 west of Patrick Creek, **Howard Griffin Bridge** on Route 199 east of Gasquet, **Mary Adams Bridge** on Route 199 west of Gasquet, **Hardscrabble Creek** near Route 199 west of Gasquet, **Coopers Flat** near the junction of Routes 199 and 427 east of Hiouchi, **Second Bridge** on Route 427 south of Route 199, and **Sand Camp**, **Redwood Flat**, **Rattlesnake Flat**, and **Goose Creek**, all on Route 427.

In the **Lower Smith River** (below the bridge at US 101), the tidewater at the river mouth has ling cod, black snapper, cabazon, flounder, perch, and smelt. In and above the tidewater, fishermen can catch sea-run cutthroat trout, steelhead trout, chinook salmon, and coho salmon. Any time of year is good for the tidewater fish; spring, summer and fall for the cutthroat trout; September to December for the salmon; and November through March for the steelhead.

In the Hiouchi and Gasquet area of the **Upper Smith River**, steelhead and cutthroat trout are taken from May to November from the forks and tributaries of the river. From mid-November to the first of March, cutthroat, salmon, and steelhead are taken from the main stream to Patrick's Creek and on the South Fork to Jones Creek on Big Flat.

A WORD TO THE WISE

Special Note To Hikers: **Stoney Creek Trail** *follows the North Fork of the Smith River 1.6 miles to its junction with Stoney Creek and is nicely shaded. The fishing is good, there is interesting flora in the area, and there are nice views of the river.*

Diving, Crabbing, Surfing, Boating

Of course, fishing with rod and reel is not the only form of water-related adventure along the Pacific coast. Diving for abalone, raking for clams, and casting a net for crabs also are popular diversions, along with surfing, diving, and boating.

Rock picking and free diving for abalone is productive around Eureka, especially near **Shelter Cove**, **Petrolia**, **Cape Mendocino**, **Trinidad**, and **Patrick's Point**.

Clamming is popular on the beaches around Fortuna and in McKinleyville's **Clam Beach County Park**, eight miles north of Eureka.

Crab fishing also is good around Fortuna, and in Crescent City between December and June.

In addition to the abalone and other "fruit of the sea," divers will enjoy a visit to **Sinkyone Wilderness State Park**, ☎ 707/986-7711, an underwater park that surrounds Bear Harbor in Humboldt County, where the 17-mile coastline includes California's northernmost giant kelp beds. There are no developed facilities in the park. Information and gear can be obtained at **Pacific Quest Dive Center**, 160 Marine Way, Crescent City, CA 95531, ☎ 707/464-8753, fax 707/465-1120, E-mail pacificquestdivecenter@juno.com.

Eureka offers some excellent surfing, and Crescent City has some outstanding tidepooling.

Rhyn Noll Surfboards, 1220-A Second St., Crescent City, CA 95531, ☎ 707/465-4400, rents surfboards, boogie boards, and wetsuits. It also has an unusual Surf Museum. Located on US 101 South, the store is open Monday through Friday from 10 to 6, on Saturday from 10 to 5, and on Sunday from noon to 4.

Worth a stop, particularly if you're traveling with children, is **Undersea World**, 304 Hwy 101 South, Crescent City, CA 95531, ☎ 707/464-3522. Here you can pick up starfish, tickle sea anemones, pet sharks, see stingrays "fly" through the water, watch sea lions perform, and view an octopus, wolf eels, and other creatures of the sea.

Inland, the Willow Creek area provides a number of pleasant beaches along the **Trinity River**, including **Sandy Bar**, popular for swimming and tubing (but use caution, because the access is steep and the road is rough, especially in wet weather); **Tish Tang**, north of town off Route 96, which offers a nearby campground, fishing, swimming, and 4x4 access to the river; **Big Rock**, where you will find swimming and, in the early morning, fishing; **Kimtu**, a popular fishing spot (no vehicles are allowed on the beach during the summer months); **Hawkins Bar**, which is popular for tubing, fishing, and swimming; and **Eel River**, which offers excellent canoeing and kayaking from Myers Flat to where the South Fork enters the main tributary. Boating conditions are best from November through mid-June, although the afternoons can be quite windy from March through April.

*Do not swim in the ocean at **Freshwater Lagoon Spit** in the Redwood National and State Parks due to swift currents, cold water, and a dangerous undertow, even on calm summer days.*

Outfitters on Water

Redwood Empire Outdoor Adventures, PO Box 757, Miranda, CA 95553, ☎ 707/943-3083, can furnish guides for hunting and fishing.

Hum-Boats, 2 F St., Eureka, CA 95501, ☎ 707/444-3048, rents kayaks and leads kayak tours, offers cruises on the bay aboard a small sloop, and rents sailboats.

M.V. Madaket, at the foot of C St. in Old Town Eureka, CA 95501, ☎ 707/445-1910, offers bay cruises that depart daily at 1, 2:30, and 5. Tuesday through Saturday, they also offer a 5:30 PM cocktail cruise. The ship, first used in 1910, is the oldest passenger-carrying commercial vessel still in use in the United States.

Electric Rafting Co., PO Box 4418, Arcata, CA 95521, ☎ 707/826-2861, features rafting trips on the Salmon, Trinity, Burnt Ranch, Klamath, Upper Klamath, Smith, and Eel Rivers.

Aurora River Adventures, PO Box 938, Willow Creek, CA 95573, ☎ 916/629-3843 or 800/562-8475, specializes in whitewater rafting, float trips, equipment rentals, kayak lessons, swimming, and hiking. **Kimtu**

Outdoor Adventures, operating out of the same office, also offers rafting and fishing trips, plus an unusual Native American historical tour that floats down the Trinity River, stopping at the Hupa Indian Museum, with lunch at the ancient Na Tini Xwe Indian village, where you see the village houses, sweat lodge, and ceremonial dance grounds.

Bigfoot Rafting Co., CA 299 and Willow Way, PO Box 729, Willow Creek, CA 95573, ☎ 916/629-2263 or 800/722-2223, features whitewater rafting on the Trinity, Klamath, Salmon, and Smith Rivers. Guided trips are available, as are raft and kayak rentals.

North Coast Adventures, PO Box 939, Trinidad, CA 95570, ☎ 707/677-3124, provides guided kayak trips both on Trinidad Bay and on the ocean.

Klamath River Jet Boat Tours, PO Box 947, Klamath, CA 95548, ☎ 707/482-7775 or 800/887-JETS, takes you on a wildlife tour to see bear, blacktail deer, elk, osprey, eagles, hawks, otters, mink, seals, and sea lions. Morning, evening, scenic, and dinner cruises also are available.

The Damm Drifter, 380 Terwer Riffle Rd., Klamath, CA 95548, ☎ 707/482-6635 (summer) or 464-7192 (winter), is a fishing guide service.

■ In the Air

For the aviation enthusiast, the **Arcata-Eureka Airport**, located at 3561 Boeing Ave., McKinleyville, CA 95521, is the only major airport on the coast between San Francisco and Portland. A substantial number of smaller airports are available, however.

Garberville, Shelter Cove, Samoa, and **Weaverville** have airports, and there is a 2,800-foot paved airstrip in **Terwer Valley** near Klamath.

Rohnerville Airport, south of Fortuna, has a 4,000-foot runway, and **McNamara Field** in Crescent City, ☎ 707/464-7311, a daylight airport, has a 3,400-foot runway.

■ Cultural Excursions

Arcata

Arcata's Chamber of Commerce, 1062 G St., Arcata, CA 95521, ☎ 707/822-3619, fax 707/822-3515, E-mail chamber@arcata.com, Web site www.arcata.com/chamber, has a free map outlining a 20-minute, self-guided walking tour of the town's Victorian homes.

During September's **Pastels in the Plaza**, ☎ 707/822-7206, hundreds of artists from throughout the county are drawn to Arcata to decorate the plaza sidewalks with chalk art.

Humboldt State University's **Natural History Museum**, 1315 G St., Arcata, CA 95521, 707/445-6567 or 826-4479, fax 707/826-4477, Web site www.humboldt.edu/~natmus/, operates an intriguing series of nature adventure programs for children. The museum is open daily from 10 to 4, except on Sundays and Mondays.

Arcata's **Minor Theatre** is one of the oldest continuously operating movie theaters in the United States. **Wildberries Marketplace**, 747 13th St., Arcata, CA 95521, ☎ 707/822-0095, fax 707/822-0211, E-mail phil@wildberries.com, Web site www.wildberries.com, is an unbelievably up-scale grocery. Open between 8 AM and 9 PM Sunday through Thursday (until 10 PM on Fridays and Saturdays), the market is a combination supermarket, juice bar, café, and bakery that deals in locally grown organic produce and natural foods.

Blue Lake

In Blue Lake, students study mask, mime, movement, clowning, and commedia at **Dell'Arte School of Physical Theatre**, ☎ 707/668-5663, the only professional training program of its kind in America.

Crescent City

Crescent City, now a county seat, was founded in 1852, one year after a band of treasure hunters discovered the tiny bay while searching for a hoard supposedly hidden by a legendary prospector.

St. George Reef, located off Point St. George north of town, is where the sidewheeler *Brother Jonathan* was wrecked in the 1860s.

Battery Point Lighthouse Museum at the foot of A St. in Crescent City is both a working lighthouse (with its resident ghost, of course) and a museum. Standing since 1856, the lighthouse is open between 10 AM and 4 PM Wednesday through Sunday from April through September, tides permitting.

Seal Rock Light, built in 1891, sits on a small reef seven miles off shore.

Main Museum, 6th & H Sts., Crescent City, is housed in the former County Hall of Records. It was used as the county jail until 1963, and some of the original jail cells remain on the second floor. The museum is open from 10 AM to 4 PM, Mondays through Saturdays from May through September.

Undersea World, 304 Hwy 101 South, Crescent City, CA 95531, ☎ 707/464-3522, features a tidal pool, sea lion performances, and the chance to see such creatures as a stingray, an octopus, and a wolf eel.

Eureka

Fort Humboldt State Historical Park, 3431 Fort Ave., Eureka, CA 95501, ☎ 707/445-6567, was the northernmost fort on the Pacific coast during the 1800s. Capt. Ulysses S. Grant, then known as Sam, was stationed there in 1853 and liked to go horseback riding through the redwoods. Fort Humboldt Days, ☎ 707/445-6567, which reenact life at the fort between 1853 and 1866, are celebrated each August.

> The **Eureka Chamber of Commerce**, 2112 Broadway, Eureka, CA 95501, ☎ 707/442-3738 or 800/356-6381, fax 707/442-0079, has a free brochure, *Walking Tour of Eureka's Murals*, that describes ten outdoor and three indoor murals that are located throughout downtown Eureka. Another interesting brochure is *Take a Victorian Architectural Tour of Eureka, California*.

Humboldt Bay Maritime Museum, 1410 2nd St., Eureka, CA 95503, ☎ 707/444-9440, is located in a replica of the oldest house in Eureka and is open daily from 11 to 4. The museum also offers harbor cruises. Call for the current schedule.

Eureka hosts **Redwood Coast**, ☎ 707/445-3378, "the best small-town festival in the West," a Dixieland jazz festival that is held every March. **North Coast Repertory Theatre**, 300 5th St., ☎ 707/442-6278, provides live theater, and **Humboldt Light Opera**, 406 14th St., ☎ 707/445-4310, furnishes musical entertainment.

The **Lost Coast Brewery** in Eureka is the first brewery in America founded and operated by women.

Ferndale

The Humboldt County Fair, the oldest uninterrupted county fair in California, is held every August at the Humboldt County Fairgrounds, Ferndale, CA 95536, ☎ 707/786-9511 or 725-1306.

Also held in Ferndale is the **California Indian Basketweavers Gathering**, ☎ 707/786-7511, a statewide gathering of the tribes also held on the Humboldt County Fairgrounds with demonstrations and exhibitions.

Fort Bragg

Mendocino Coast Botanical Gardens, 18220 North Hwy 1, Fort Bragg, CA 95437, ☎ 707/964-4352, occupy 47 acres. They are open between 9 AM and 5 PM from March through October, and between 9 AM and 4 PM from November through February.

Footlighters Little Theater, 248 E. Laurel St., Fort Bragg, CA 95437, ☎ 707/964-3806, presents a Gay 90s melodrama, and is open Wednesday and Saturday at 8 PM from May to September. **Gloriana Opera Co.**, 721 N. Franklin St., Fort Bragg, CA 95437, ☎ 707/964-7469, provides musical theater, and **Warehouse Repertory Theatre**, 18791 N. Hwy 1, Fort Bragg, CA 95437. ☎ 707/961-2940, offers a dramatic schedule from March to December.

Hoopa

In Hoopa, the native homes on the **Hupa Indian Reservation** are known as xonta (*hon-ta*), and the **Hoopa Tribal Museum**, located in the Hoopa Shopping Center on County Road 96, ☎ 916/625-4110, is the only Indian-owned and operated museum in the state. Redwood dugout canoes are displayed, and tours to ceremonial grounds, Indian villages, and the ruins of Fort Gaston, built in 1851, are available.

Klamath

Trees of Mystery, 15500 Hwy 101, PO Box 96, Klamath, CA 95548, ☎ 707/482-2251, 482-2005, or 800/638-3389, fax 707/482-2005, is on US 101 ("The Redwood Highway"), 16 miles south of Crescent City and 65 miles north of Eureka. Included is the **End of the Trail Indian Museum**, one of the largest private collections of authentic Indian artifacts; a **Nature Trail** through the redwoods; and the **Trail of Tall Tales**, which relates amusing stories about Paul Bunyan.

Myers Flat

On the Avenue of the Giants, **Drive Thru Tree**, PO Box 145, Myers Flat, CA 95554, is a favorite with children that includes a three-story tree house, a balance tree, a children's stump, the "rings of history," and a café.

Orick

For more than a quarter of a century, Orick has hosted the annual **Banana Slug Derby** in Prairie Creek Redwoods State Park, ☎ 707/488-2171. The event, held each August, features a parade, a bake sale, and more than 100 slithering slugs.

Trinidad

Trinidad's Patrick's Point State Park contains **Sumeg Village**, ☎ 707/488-2041, a recreated village to preserve the Yurok Indian lifestyle. Self-guided walking tours visit the Indian homes and sweat houses.

Where to Stay

Crescent City

Crescent Beach Motel, 1455 Redwood Hwy South, Crescent City, CA 95531, ☎ 707/464-5436, $$, two miles south of town, is the only motel on the beach.

Curly Redwood Lodge, 701 Redwood Hwy South, Crescent City, CA 95531, ☎ 707/464-2137, fax 707/464-1655, $$-$$$, across from the boat basin, has extra-large rooms, most of which have a view of the Battery Point Lighthouse and offer a great view of the sunset.

Eureka

Eureka Inn, 518 7th St., Eureka, CA 95503, ☎ 707/442-6441 or 800/862-4906, fax 707/442-0637, Web site www.humboldtdining.com/eurekainn, $$$-$$$$, is in a magnificent English Tudor structure built by the Chamber of Commerce in 1922. To get a badly needed local hotel, the chamber formed a company, sold stock, and bought the land on which the hotel now stands.

Carter House Country Inn, 1033 3rd St., Eureka, CA 95501, ☎ 707/444-3062 or 800/404-1390, fax 707/444/8067, E-mail carter52@carterhouse.com, Web site www.carterhouse.com, $$-$$$$, is a "B&B/hotel." The inn has lovely gardens, a 1958 Bentley limo, and actually occupies three buildings: the original Carter House ("the most photographed Victorian in the world"), the Bell Cottage, and the old Hotel Carter.

Fort Bragg

The Gray Whale Inn, 615 N. Main St., Fort Bragg, CA 95437, ☎ 800/382-7244, $$-$$$$, is a four-story inn with just 14 rooms and a buffet breakfast.

Surf 'n Sand Lodge, 1131 N. Main St., Fort Bragg, CA 95437, ☎ 707/964-9383 or 800/694-0184, fax 707/967-0314, $$-$$$, offers terrific ocean views.

Hoopa

Best Western Tsewenaldin Inn, off County Road 96 in downtown Hoopa, CA 95546, ☎ 916/625-4294 or 800/528-1234, $$, was built by an Indian tribe in 1989. All rooms have a view of the Trinity River.

Samoa

The **Samoa Airport B&B**, 900 New Navy Base Rd., Samoa, CA 95564, ☎ 707/445-0765, $$, occupies a building that was constructed to serve as a blimp base during World War II.

Scotia

Scotia Inn, 100 Main St., Scotia, CA 95565, ☎ 707/764-5683, $$-$$$, occupies an historic 1923 redwood inn and has an excellent restaurant.

Trinidad

The Lost Whale Inn B&B, 3452 Patrick's Point Dr., Trinidad, CA 95570, ☎ 707/677-3425 or 800/677-7859, fax 707/677-0284, E-mail lmiller@northcoast.com, Web site www.lost-whale-inn.com, $$$, has been called one of the 10 most romantic B&Bs in the nation by *American Historic Inns*. It encompasses four acres of gardens and has several wooded trails. Guests can listen to barking sea lions and watch for whales while enjoying a gourmet breakfast and an afternoon tea.

■ Camping

For **California State Park** campground reservations, ☎ 800/444-7275.

Adventure in Camping, Box 2188, Mammoth Lakes, CA 93546, ☎ 619/648-7509 or 800/417-7771, allows you to take your choice of the state parks. It then parks a trailer there for your use and takes it away after you leave. The company is open year-around from 9 AM to 5 PM.

Humboldt County's Parks Department, ☎ 707/445-7651, has public campgrounds at Big Lagoon, Clam Beach, the Samoa Boat Ramp, and Van Duzen.

In **Redwood National and State Parks**, ☎ 707/464-6101, Web site www.nps.gov, tent camping is allowed on the beach at the southern end of Freshwater Lagoon Spit, south of the southern beach access road, near Information Board G, or on the hard-packed dirt where the vehicles park. Campers may not park in the day-use parking area, but a parking area for tenters is located at the south end of the camping area, immediately adjacent to the southern day-use area.

There are four developed campgrounds in the **Smith River National Recreation Area**, ☎ 800/280-2267, in which campers can stay for up to 14 days: **Patrick's Creek** on US 199, 26 miles northeast of Crescent City, ☎ 707/677-3570, E-mail treerngr@aol.com; **Panther Flat**, US 199, the largest – and most expensive – Smith River campground, which affords seasonal pickings of huckleberries and blackberries; **Grassy Flat**, on US 199 between Patrick's Creek and Gasquet, which is open between May and September; and **Big Flat**, off Route 405 near its junction with Route 427.

Where to Eat

Crescent City

Near Crescent City in the northwest corner of the state, **Harbor View Grotto Restaurant & Cocktail Lounge**, Citizens Dock Road and Starfish Way, ☎ 707/464-3815, $$, enjoys a lovely harbor view. The restaurant is a survivor of the 1964 tsunami (tidal wave), caused by an Alaskan earthquake.

Eureka

There are several marvelous eating establishments in Eureka. **The Rib Room** in Eureka Inn, 7th & F Sts., ☎ 707/442-6441, $$-$$$, is complemented by a pleasant downstairs **Rathskeller Pub**. **Restaurant 301** in The Carter House, 1033 3rd St., ☎ 707/444-3062 or 800/404-1390, $$-$$$, has been featured in *Bon Appétit* and *Art Culinaire* magazines for serving such gourmet delights as Humboldt Bay Kumamoto oysters and fruit vinaigrette. And The Sea Grill, 316 E St., ☎ 707/443-7187, $$, has received the local Reader's Choice Award for "Best Seafood Restaurant in Humboldt County" five years in a row.

Fort Bragg

For lunch or dinner on the Fort Bragg waterfront, visit **The Wharf**, PO Box 1429, Fort Bragg, CA 95437, ☎ 707/964-4283, $$. To find it, take North Harbor Drive to Noyo Harbor.

Samoa

The community of Samoa, which sits on a tiny sand spit across the bay from Eureka, features **The Samoa Cookhouse**, ☎ 707/442-1659, $$. Founded in 1885, the restaurant is the last authentic logging camp cookhouse in the western United States and it still serves family-style meals seven days a week. From Eureka, take Samoa Bridge to the end, turn left on Samoa Road, and make the first left turn.

Information Sources

California Department of Fish & Game, 679 Second St., Eureka, CA 95501, ☎ 707/445-6493.

California Department of Forestry, 1025 US 101 North, Crescent City, CA 95531, ☎ 707/464-6493.

California Division of Tourism, PO Box 1499, Sacramento, CA 95812-1499, ☎ 916/653-6995, or 800/862-2543, ext. 200, Web site gocalif.ca.gov.

California State Parks, PO Box 942896, Sacramento, CA 94296-0001, ☎ 916/653-6995, Web site ceres.ca.gov/parks/. Camping reservations: ☎ 800/444/7275.

Klamath National Forest, Ukonom Ranger District, PO Drawer 410, Orleans, CA 95556, ☎ 916/627-3291.

Redwood National Park Visitor Information, 1111 2nd St., Crescent City, CA 95531, ☎ 707/464-6101. Hiouchi Ranger Station, open spring, summer and fall, offers summer interpretive programs.

Six Rivers National Forest Headquarters, 1330 Bayshore Way, Eureka, CA 95501, ☎ 707/442-1721, has ranger districts headquartered in Lower Trinity, ☎ 916/629-2118; Mad River, ☎ 916/574-6233; and Orleans, ☎ 916/627-3291.

North-Central California

Sparsely populated, heavily agricultural, the north-central part of California is a wide valley reaching from the Coast Range of mountains on the west to the mountainous forests on the east.

The Gold Rush of the mid-1800s played a prominent role in stimulating the development of this part of the state, and in many places abandoned mines and ghost towns still polka-dot the hillsides.

If the land has acquired a reputation as a travel destination, however, it is because of its majestic beauty – the beauty of its woods, lakes, rivers, and its singularly outstanding mountain, Mount Shasta.

Getting Around

As it does along the Pacific Coast, travel throughout this region of California flows principally north and south. Bisecting the area is the West Coast's major Interstate, I-5, which, like a river of concrete, transports traffic between the major metropolitan centers to the south and the Oregon border, Washington, and beyond to the north.

Getting Around ■ 45

North-Central California

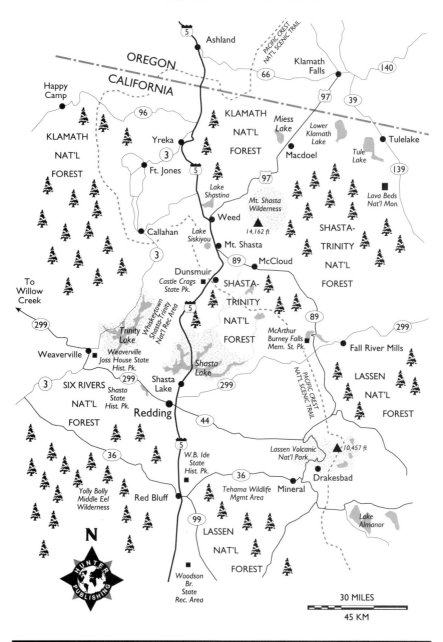

■ Getting Around

Like tributaries emptying into a mighty river, sizeable highways add to the flow of I-5 on three occasions. At Red Bluff, CA 99 introduces traffic headed to and from Fresno, Bakersfield, Los Angeles, San Diego, and as far south as the Mexican border. Traffic headed to or from Reno, Las Vegas, and other cities to the southeast connect with I-5 by way of CA 44 at Redding and CA 89 (a spin-off from CA 44) at Mount Shasta.

In Weed, not far short of the Oregon border, US 97 branches off to the northeast toward Klamath Falls, while I-5 continues on to Medford.

While the automobile is the undisputed king of travel in this region, aviation enthusiasts also will find the area pockmarked with small airfields: five miles northeast of **Montague**, **Siskiyou County Airport** has a 7,500-foot, paved and lighted runway, while **Rohrer Field**, PO Box 128, Montague, CA 96064, ☎ 916/459-3456, just a mile west of town on the Montague-Yreka Airport Rd., has a 3,360-foot, paved and lighted runway.

Both Chico and Redding have municipal airports: **Chico Municipal Airport**, Chico, CA 95927, ☎ 800/241-6522; and **Redding Municipal Airport**, 6751 Woodrum Circle, Ste. 200, Redding, CA 96002, ☎ 916/224-4321.

A 3,700-foot, paved and lighted airport is just four miles northwest of Weed.

Scott Valley Airport, ☎ 916/842-8250, three miles south of Fort Jones and nine miles from Etna, has a 3,700-foot long, 50-foot wide asphalt runway.

Mott Field, two miles north of **Dunsmuir** and four miles southwest of **Mount Shasta**, has a 3,100-foot, paved and lighted runway.

The airfield half a mile southwest of **Happy Camp** has a 3,000-foot paved runway, and in **Butte Valley**, six miles southwest of **Dorris**, there is a 4,300-foot paved and lighted airfield.

Nine miles southeast of **Tulelake** is a 3,600-foot field that also is paved and lighted.

The **Trinity Center** airport has a 3,000-foot strip.

Weaverville and **Burney** also have small airports.

At this writing, **Amtrak** continues to serve this region on a daily basis. The *Coast Starlight* train makes stops in **Chico**, **Red Bluff**, **Redding**, and **Dunsmuir**.

Touring

Dunsmuir

In Dunsmuir, take the Mott Road exit off I-5 and turn left onto Dunsmuir Ave. Across from the stop sign, you will see **Hedge Creek Falls**, which cascades 30 feet over the lip of a one-time lava flow.

On 25 October 1879, "Black Bart" (Charles E. Bolton) held up the Roseburg-Redding stagecoach just above these falls. It was one of three holdups that Black Bart committed in this area.

Mount Shasta

Mount Shasta, a dormant 14,162-foot volcano that last erupted in 1786, dominates the skyline. With a volume of 80 cubic miles, Mount Shasta is the largest volcano in the United States.

From a French word meaning "chaste," Mount Shasta lies in the Cascade range, a part of the infamous Pacific "Ring of Fire." The range extends from Mount Lassen in the south into British Columbia in the north, with a volcano situated every 50 miles or so along the route.

Mount Shasta (Robert Holmes, CDT).

The Indians say the Great Spirit lives in Mount Shasta. Others say that the crater houses an ancient white-robed brotherhood that descended from the Lemurians, inhabitants of a mid-Pacific continent called Mu. Much like the legendary continent of Atlantis, Mu is said to have disappeared beneath the sea over 400,000 years ago.

DID YOU KNOW?

The town of Mount Shasta was wild and wooly in the early days, frequented by such notorious stagecoach robbers as John and Charles Ruggles, "Shorty" Hayes, "Sheet Iron" Jack, and Joaquin Miller. Miller later gained fame as a poet and lived with the Indians, eventually siring a daughter called Cali-Shasta.

Today, the town of Mount Shasta is noteworthy for its "penny pine tree plantation," to which the local school children contribute their pennies in order to pay for the planting of new trees.

In the town of **Etna**, originally called Rough & Ready and later Aetna Mills, gold is still bought and sold in the local drug store.

Yreka

Yreka (*Wy-re-ka*) was named I-E-K-A, a word meaning "north mountain," by the Shasta Indians. It is a name they used when referring to nearby Mount Shasta.

The county seat of Siskiyou County, Yreka sprang up when gold was discovered in nearby Black Gulch Ravine in March 1851. An exhibit of gold is still displayed in the County Courthouse. Ask for a free copy of *Highways & Byways of Siskiyou County* and *Recreational Map of Scott Valley and Salmon River*, both useful road maps of the surrounding area that will direct you to the many things that there are to see and do here.

Traveling I-5 today, it may seem hard to imagine, but in November 1941, the roads in this part of the state, just 22 miles south of the Oregon border, were so poor that the residents protested with a mock "secession." The citizens proclaimed the region "The State of Jefferson, 49th State of the Union" (at that time, Alaska and Hawaii had not been admitted to the Union) and blocked travel on Highway 99 outside of Yreka each Thursday. The people's rebellion ended when the Japanese attacked Pearl Harbor just a month after the protests began.

Fort Jones, southwest of Yreka, was established in 1852 to protect the area from raids by the Rogue River Indians. At one time or another, William T. Sherman, Ulysses S. Grant, and Philip H. Sheridan were either associated with or assigned to the fort.

Weaverville

Weaverville, the seat of Trinity County, was named for John Weaver, one of the three men who built the area's first cabin in the 1850s. When the three men drew straws to determine who would name the town, Weaver won, but he left town shortly afterward and was never heard from again.

Hyampom, east of Weaverville, bears an old Wintu Indian name and has an unusual swinging mule bridge.

Trinity Center

Trinity Center rests at the north end of Trinity Lake, the third largest lake in California, which has 145 miles of shoreline distributed among three separate arms.

Tulelake

Ever wonder where horseradish comes from? Or how goose down pillows are made? Tulelake has both a horseradish factory (**Tulelake Horseradish Co.**, Box 636, 619 Main St., Tulelake, CA 96134, ☎ 916/667-5319) and a goose down pillow factory (**Tulegoose Pillow Factory & Gift Center**, 347 Modoc Ave., PO Box 548, Tulelake, CA 96134, ☎ 916/667-2728). Both of them offer tours.

Newell, just south of Tulelake, was a Japanese internment camp during World War II.

Happy Camp

Traditional Indian ceremonies (Pikiavish) are held each year at the mouth of Clear Creek near Happy Camp, and at Katimin above the mouth of the Salmon River. Happy Camp is the home of the Karuk Indian tribe, 632 Jacobs Way, Happy Camp, CA 96039, ☎ 916/493-5305, which is known for weaving beautiful basketry.

Adventures

■ On Foot

Hiking Trails & Wildlife Viewing

Chico

The recently opened **The World of Trees Independence Trail** in Bidwell Park, Chico, is the first trail in Butte County that is accessible to the physically and visually challenged. The trail highlights the changing sounds, smells, textures, colors, and shapes of nature, and 20 signed stations along the trail note each tree's name and gives a brief description of the species. Adjacent to the trail, the **Chico Nature Center** has maps that explain each variety of tree, plant, and type of wildlife found along the trail.

 An excellent publication for hikers, mountain bikers, and equestrians, *Northern California Trails*, PO Box 5048, Chico, CA 95927, ☎ 916/345-7315, fax 916/891-4463, E-mail emoore@observant.com, is produced in Chico.

Redding

The **Sacramento River Trail** is a six-mile-long riverside trail in Redding.

In **Lassen Volcanic National Park**, free ranger-guided nature walks are conducted during the summer and snowshoe hikes during the winter. A free visitor guide is available from the Shasta Cascade Wonderland Association, 14250 Holiday Rd., Redding, CA 96003, ☎ 916/275-5555, 800/326-6944, or 800/474-2782, fax 916/275-9755. Mount Lassen last erupted in 1917.

Dunsmuir

Near Dunsmuir, **Mossbrae Falls**, bejeweled by moss and wildflowers, can be reached by a trail that runs along the railroad tracks leading north out of town.

Mount Shasta

Mount Shasta, one of the world's most sacred mountains, is located six miles north of Dunsmuir. The 14,162-foot mountain has five glaciers and a series of hot springs near the summit. **Shasta Mountain Guides**, 1938 Hill Rd., Mount Shasta, CA 96067, ☎ 916/926-3117, can help arrange hikes of one day or longer.

At **Shasta Lake**, visitors frequently see blacktailed deer, Rocky Mountain elk, great blue herons, raccoons, black bears, and ospreys, and the area has the largest number of bald eagles in California.

Lake Shasta Caverns, Box 801, O'Brien, CA 96070, ☎ 916/238-2341 or 800/795-CAVE, first became accessible to the public in 1964, when a tunnel was constructed. Boaters can visit the caverns by going up the Eastside McCloud River Arm of Lake Shasta, where they can dock free at the Cavern Landing. Others must take a 15-minute cruise across the lake aboard a catamaran, then take a bus more than 800 feet up the mountainside to reach the caverns. The caverns are open every day except Thanksgiving and Christmas. Guided tours are offered.

McCloud

A visit to the **Three Falls of the McCloud River** makes a wonderful hike. From McCloud, take Highway 89 east and watch for the Fowler's Campground sign, then turn right. A trail from Fowler's Campground follows the river to the **Lower Falls**. Parking that provides access to the falls is available a mile past the campground. The **Middle Falls** are hard to find. Before reaching Fowler's Camp, take a road to the left for one mile, then look for a semicircular parking area with a pine tree in it. The fairly rough trail to the falls starts directly across the road from the parking area. To reach the **Upper Falls**, continue three-tenths of a mile down the road from the Middle Falls parking area, watching for a turn-off on the right. Take the turn-off and go two-tenths of a mile until the road forks. Take the right-hand fork, park, and you can access the river near the falls.

The cliffs are steep and there are no guardrails at the Middle or Upper Falls, so extreme care should be taken in both of those areas.

The Pacific Crest Trail

In **Klamath National Forest** (1312 Fairlane Rd., Yreka, CA 96097, ☎ 916/842-6131) near Etna, it is possible to access The Pacific Crest Trail, which extends 2,600 miles from Mexico to Canada, passing through 23 national forests and seven national parks. Established on 2 October 1968, the trail is used by equestrians as well as hikers. A campfire permit is required.

The trail enters Klamath National Forest at Scott Mountain on Highway 3, extends into the Salmon-Trinity Alps, and crosses Carter Meadows. It then runs through the Russian Peaks Wilderness; enters the Marble Mountain Wilderness, passing through Shelley Meadows above the Cliff Lake area; and moves on past the Sky High Lakes and Marble Valley. Before exiting the wilderness area, the trail passes Paradise, Bear, and Turk Lakes. The last main exit point before the Oregon border is on Highway 96 along the Klamath River in Seiad Valley.

The Klamath National Forest segment of the trail is 120 miles long and ranges in elevation from 1,400 feet at Klamath River to 7,648 feet near Smith Lake.

Watch for poison oak below the 3,000-foot elevation.

There are eight access points to the trail in this area of Northern California (inquire at a ranger station for a map): **Parks Creek**, 2.5 miles north of Weed; **Picayune** and **Gumboot**, both of which start from Lake Siskiyou; **Soda Creek**, 2.2 miles south of the Dunsmuir interchange off I-5; **Girard**, from the Soda Creek interchange off I-5; and **Squaw Creek**, **Ah-Di-Na**, and **Ash Camp**, all near McCloud.

The midway point of the trail between Canada and Mexico lies near Hamburg in Seiad Valley, northwest of Yreka. The Seiad Valley Post Office, ☎ 916/496-3211, and the Scott Valley Drug Store, ☎ 916/467-5335, in Etna serve as food supply points and will hold packages for hikers if they are plainly marked "HOLD," with the expected date of arrival clearly indicated, and are addressed as follows:

(Name of hiker)
Hold for PCT
Seiad Valley, CA 96086
or
Scott Valley Drug Store
511 Main St.
PO Box 610
Etna, CA 96027

Kelsey Creek

About 10 miles south of Hamburg, northwest of Yreka, the **Bridge Flat Campground** sits near the Kelsey Creek Bridge. Half a mile up a trail from the campground is an overlook that provides marvelous views of waterfalls in the creek. Kelsey Creek also affords good birding and is an excellent spot from which to view naturally spawning salmon and steelhead.

Another spot with lovely waterfalls and amazing flora is at the junction of **Ukonom Creek** and the **Klamath River**.

The Scott River

There are a number of places where it is possible to hike down to the Scott River south of Hamburg. Ask the Scott River Ranger District, ☎ 916/468-5351, or the Scott Valley Chamber of Commerce, PO Box 111, Greenview, CA 96037, for a free flyer *Take a Hike Along the Lower Scott River*. (If you go in person, the Chamber's office is at 1417 S. Main St. in Yreka, ☎ 916/842-4001.)

At **Goosenest** near Montague, there is a trail that leads to the crater of an extinct volcano.

*Burney Falls
(Robert Holmes, CDT).*

McArthur-Burney Falls State Park

McArthur-Burney Falls State Park is seven miles north of the junction of CA 299 and CA 89, 11 miles from the town of Burney. The 129-foot falls flow into scenic Lake Britton, and lovely nature walks are available beside the streams and falls.

Also near Burney, a quarter-mile north of the junction of CA 89 and CA 44, are the **Subways Caves**, a geological formation created 2,000 years ago by flowing lava. The caves can be explored for a distance of about 1,000 feet. Be sure to take a coat and a flashlight.

The Shasta Divide Nature Trail

The Shasta Divide Nature Trail begins at the Whiskeytown Lake Visitor Information Center on CA 299. Ranger-guided walks, gold panning demonstrations, and illustrated evening programs are offered in the **Oak Bottom Amphitheater** from mid-June through Labor Day.

The Canyon Creek Trail

The Canyon Creek Trail near Junction City is the most popular trail into the Trinity Alps. The trailhead is at the end of Canyon Creek Road north of CA 299.

Lava Beds National Monument

Lava Beds National Monument near Tulelake offers Captain Jack's Stronghold and over 300 lava caves, lava tubes, and ice caves to explore, much of it profusely "illustrated" with petroglyph rock drawings. It was at Lava Beds that America fought its most costly Indian War, the Modoc War of 1872-73. The Visitor Center at Lava Beds (☎ 916/667-2282) is open between 9 AM and 6 PM from mid-June to Labor Day and between 8 AM and 5 PM the rest of the year.

Weed

Near Weed, a popular 2.5-mile trail scales 6,343-foot **Black Butte**.

Excellent birding can be found in the **Shasta Valley Wildlife Area**, ☎ 530/459-3926, a 4,000-acre preserve eight miles east of Yreka off State Route 3. The best birding begins in February, when large flocks of bluebirds, ferruginous hawks, and pheasants are common. Some 274 species of birds frequent the area, and a free map and brochure help visitors to locate and identify them.

A two-mile loop known as **Eastside Road** provides good birding near Callahan, west of Weed, especially during the nesting season in April. Raptor viewing is good in October and November.

Yreka

Greenway Hiking Trail, a paved, handicapped-accessible trail that follows Yreka Creek through the town of Yreka is good for birding. Ask the Yreka Chamber of Commerce, 117 W. Miner St., Yreka, CA 96097, ☎ 916/842-1649 or 800/ON YREKA, or the Siskiyou County Visitors Bureau, 808 W. Lennox, Yreka, CA 96097, ☎ 916/842-7857 or 800/446-7475, fax 916/842-7666, for a free pamphlet, *Birding in Siskiyou County*. Happy Camp, west of Yreka, is surrounded by old-growth spotted owl habitat. There are many roads throughout the steep mountainous terrain from which to access the best birding and, in the fall, to go mushrooming. For guidance, contact the **Happy Camp Ranger Station**, ☎ 916/493-2243, or contact **Wilderness Packers**, PO Box 405, Happy Camp, CA 96039, ☎ 916/493-2793, who will arrange a trip for you.

Macdoel

Some of the best raptor viewing in the state is available around Macdoel. Bald eagles and Swainson's hawks are common. Ask for a map and a brochure at either the Chamber of Commerce office, ☎ 916/397-2397, or the Goosenest District ranger office, ☎ 916/398-4391.

Tule Lake

This area of Northern California does, in fact, attract the greatest number of bald eagles outside Alaska. **Tule Lake** is the winter home and breeding ground for hundreds of bald and golden eagles. The **Klamath Basin National Wildlife Refuges** in the area also draw a sizeable wintering of bald eagles. **Butte Valley** attracts both bald eagles and Swainson's hawks.

Birding brochures and maps are available for the Butte Valley, Iron Gate, Kelsey Creek, Seiad Valley, Shasta-Trinity Forest, Shasta Valley Wildlife Area, Tree of Heaven, and Tule Lake areas.

Gold & Gemstones

An area in which hikers can look for riches is around Happy Camp, a place noted for deposits of Californite, chalcopyrite, garnet, nephrite (some containing gold), pyrite, williamsite, rhodonite, and jade, some of it with gold inclusion. **Chan Jade Mine** near Happy Camp has gold, nephrite, idocrase (vesuvianite), and serpentine, while the east side of **Thompson Mountain**, nine miles north of town between East Fork and Thompson Creek, contains rhodonite.

The New '49ers, 27 Davis Rd., Happy Camp, CA 96039, ☎ 916/493-2012, will show you where and how to find gold; ask for their free information package.

Near Weaverville, people pan for gold in the **Trinity River**.

West of Yreka, actinolite is found in **Black Gulch**; agate, ammonites, bloodstone, cephalopods, jasper, and petrified wood are found at **Black Mountain**; agate, bloodstone, gold, jasper, and petrified wood can be found around **Cottonwood Creek**; and copper can be found in slate along **Humbug Creek**.

The Klamath River is the second largest gold-producing area in California, and gold can be found on the bars all along the river.

Somes Bar in the Scott River produces both gold and wollastonite, while **Cottonwood Creek** contains agate, bloodstone, gold, jasper, and petrified wood. **Grouse Creek** has chert, galena, and gold, and the gravels of **Hungry Creek** contain cassiterite.

The **Salmon River** contains gold and platinum. The gravels of the East Fork and the gravels, bars, and beaches of the South Fork also contain gold and platinum, while the head of the Little South Fork offers gold, platinum, and azurite.

Soapstone can be found south of **Hamburg**.

Big pale-pink crystals of axinite can be uncovered at Hornbrook Cut crossing the Klamath River, while agate, carnelian, jasper, petrified wood, and rhodonite can be found northeast of Hornbrook at **Jenny Creek**.

Onyx can be found six miles south of Mount Shasta. **Box Canyon** south of town contains dark green serpentine, and **Shasta Springs** on the Sacramento River has green travertine, known locally as "Shasta onyx."

Pyrope garnet can be uncovered at Dunsmuir, and a mineral spring near **Soap Springs Hotel** contains aragonite.

Mines around Callahan bear barite, chalcopyrite, chromite, erythrite, gold, pyrite, pyrrhotite, smaltite, and zaratite, and the **Martin McKean Mine** also contains chromite, kammererite, and unvarovite garnet.

■ On Horseback

Once again, rodeos are a popular diversion in this part of the country.

In Montague, southeast of Yreka, the **Montague Junior Rodeo**, ☎ 916/459-5280, is held every May, led off by a Sunday parade. That is followed in July by the **Siskiyou County Posse Rodeo**, ☎ 916/842-2888, and in September by the annual **Labor Day Rodeo**.

Etna hosts the **Scott Valley Pleasure Park Rodeo** in May, followed by the annual **Old Timer's Rodeo and Dance**, ☎ 916/468-5959, on the last Saturday in July.

During July, the annual **Redding Rodeo**, ☎ 916/225-4100, leads off a week of rodeo-related activities. The **CCA Junior Rodeo**, PO Box 10, McArthur, CA 96056, ☎ 916/336-5695, is held in McArthur, east of Burney, in the middle of the month, and the **Six Rivers Rodeo**, ☎ 707/574-6681, also is held during July.

In August, the **Siskiyou Golden Fair** is held on the Siskiyou Golden Fair Grounds, ☎ 916/842-2767. The fair not only has a rodeo, but also an art exhibit, food, carnival rides, and a horse show.

Other horse events are popular throughout Northern California, as well.

McArthur hosts the annual **McArthur Cutting Horse Show** in the fairgrounds, two weeks before Labor Day. The three-day event is free and there is a Saturday night BBQ. For more information, contact

George or Chris at McArthur Farm Supply, ☎ 916/336-6133. In Seiad Valley west of Hamburg, a **Horse Show and Rummage Sale** is held each May.

Those who feel the urge to slip their own leg over the back of a horse can rent an animal in Weaverville at **Beck's Historic Carr Creek Ranch**, ☎ 916/628-5486; at **Coffee Creek Guest Ranch**, ☎ 916/266-3346; or at **Trinity Alps Resort**, ☎ 916/286-2205.

In Montague, **TN Arabians**, Shelley Road, ☎ 916/459-3399, has a sizeable stable of Arabian horses, while **Bryan & Sherman Packing**, 5238 Pheasant Lane, Montague, CA 96064, ☎ 916/459-5417, not only rents horses, but also arranges packing trips into the mountains and woods for hiking, fishing, hunting, sightseeing, and photography. The company also operates a facility at 4125 East Side Rd., Etna, CA 96027, ☎ 916/467-3261.

El Capitan's Morgans off Walker Road in Horse Creek, ☎ 916/465-2355, provides a stable of Morgan horses.

Access to Adventure, 92520 Hwy 96, Somes Bar, CA 95568, ☎ 916/469-3322 or 800/552-6284, fax 916/469-3357, arranges horseback rides and wilderness pack trips as well as whitewater rafting trips. Somes Bar is located southwest of Happy Camp.

Wild Horse Sanctuary, PO Box 30, Shingletown, CA 96088, ☎ 916/474-5770, fax 916/474-5728, arranges two- and three-day pack trips on horseback to let riders participate in longhorn cattle drives or track wild horses and burros through the foothills of Mount Lassen. The company leads a nationwide program to protect wild horses.

Want somebody else to do the driving? **Surrey and Celebrations** in Six Rivers, ☎ 916/468-2681, will take two to four passengers on a horse-drawn surrey ride through historic Yreka.

■ On Wheels

Driving Tours

Everitt Memorial Highway provides a scenic drive up Mount Shasta from Mount Shasta City. The 14-mile trip ends at an elevation of 7,800 feet near Panther Meadow. Take the Central exit off I-5 in the town of Mount Shasta.

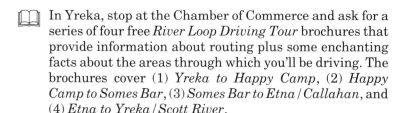

 From November through March, it is a good idea to carry chains when you drive through this region. Passes at the 4,000-foot elevation on I-5 and US 97 frequently are subject to chain use only or closure.

📖 In Yreka, stop at the Chamber of Commerce and ask for a series of four free *River Loop Driving Tour* brochures that provide information about routing plus some enchanting facts about the areas through which you'll be driving. The brochures cover (1) *Yreka to Happy Camp*, (2) *Happy Camp to Somes Bar*, (3) *Somes Bar to Etna / Callahan*, and (4) *Etna to Yreka / Scott River*.

The US Forest Service produces a free brochure, *Trinity Scenic Byway*, that lays out a wonderfully scenic drive along the Trinity River from Redding to Arcata.

Off-Road Touring

The first 86-mile segment of the **California Back Country Discovery Trail**, a trail for off-road vehicles, recently opened near the Mendocino National Forest east of Fort Bragg. The segment runs from Upper Lake to Covelo, but eventually will extend all the way from Mexico to Oregon. For up-to-date information, contact the **California Off-Highway Motor Vehicle Recreation Division**, PO Box 942896, Sacramento, CA 94296-0001, ☎ 916/324-1573, fax 916/324-1610.

Off-roaders will find it useful to get a free copy of the Shasta-Trinity Off-Road Vehicle map from the **Shasta-Trinity Forest ranger station**, ☎ 916/246-5222, or the McCloud Ranger District, ☎ 916/964-2184.

Biking

Cycling is very popular in this part of the country, and local agencies have done a great deal to encourage it.

📖 Cyclists will find the 46-page brochure *Northern California Mountain Bike Guide* very useful. The free brochure describes 40 of the best mountain bike rides in the region and indicates their rate of difficulty. A copy of the brochure can be obtained from the **Shasta-Cascade Wonderland Association**, 14250 Holiday Rd., Redding, CA 96003, ☎ 916/275-5555 or 800/474-2782, fax 916/275-9711, E-mail scwa@shastacascade.org., Web site www.shastacascade.org.

📖 The **Yreka Chamber of Commerce** has prepared *Yreka Bike Trips*, a free brochure that lays out six self-guided rides and day trips throughout the area.

Seventeen other bike routes are described in *A Cyclist's Guide to Great Mountain Biking Routes*, a free brochure available from the US Forest Service, 1312 Fairlane Rd., Yreka, CA 96097, ☎ 916/842-6131.

Klamath National Forest contains over 4,000 miles of roads and trails suitable for mountain biking. Two other popular mountain biking areas include **McCloud** and **Whiskeytown Lake**.

The Fifth Season, 300 N. Mount Shasta Blvd., Mount Shasta, CA 96067, ☎ 916/926-3606, fax 916/926-1337, rents biking, skiing, and climbing equipment. It also provides recorded weather, ski, and climbing information, ☎ 916/926-5555.

House of Ski, Everitt Memorial Highway at Ski Village Dr., Mount Shasta, CA 96067, ☎ 916/926-2359, and **Shasta Cycling Adventures**, 9404 N. Old Stage Rd., Weed, CA 96094, ☎ 916/938-3002, also rent bikes.

Shasta Cycling Adventures, 9404 N. Old Stage Rd., Weed, CA 96094, ☎ 916/938-3002, offers both hiking and mountain biking excursions.

Rail Tours

For railway fans, **McCloud Railway Excursion Rides and Sunset Dinner Trains**, ☎ 800/733-2141, operate out of McCloud during the summer, beginning in late May. The excursion train operates at 4 PM on Saturdays; the dinner train at 6:30.

Yreka Western Railroad, 300 E. Miner St., PO Box 660, Yreka, CA 96097, ☎ 916/842-4146 or 800/Yreka-RR, provides a three-hour *Blue Goose* excursion that operates in all seasons except winter. The train, pulled by a 1915 Baldwin steam engine, goes through Shasta Valley to the historic railroad/cattle town of Montague, where passengers can take a horse-drawn wagon ride, visit the 1887 Depot Museum, and tour the historic buildings. Established in 1889, the rail line came under new ownership in 1997.

■ On the Water

Fishing

Fortunate are the fishermen who have the opportunity to visit, much less live in, this part of the country. All they are required to decide are two things: (1) Should I fish on a lake, a river, or a stream? (2) What kind of fish shall I go after?

Near Redding, rainbow and brook trout can be taken out of **Lewiston Lake**. **Park Marina Water Sports**, 2515 Park Marina Dr., ☎ 246-8388, will rent you a canoe or a raft.

Gumboot Lake southwest of Mount Shasta City is well stocked with trout. The lake, located 13.3 miles past Lake Siskiyou on a paved road (Forest Road 26), sits at an elevation of 6,000 feet and is normally closed by snow until some time in May.

Hat Creek Park, along CA 299 between Burney and Fall River Mills, permits catch-and-release trout fishing and has a number of pleasant hiking trails.

Whiskeytown Lake, in the Whiskeytown National Recreation Area, has rainbow and brown trout, largemouth bass, smallmouth bass, spotted bass, and kokanee salmon. There are marinas at Brancy Creek and Oak Bottom, and a launch ramp at Whiskey Creek.

In the Weaverville area, the **Trinity River** has brown trout, steelhead trout, and salmon, and the popular **Clair Engle Lake** (locally called **Trinity Lake**) offers largemouth bass, smallmouth bass, rainbow trout, German brown trout, kokanee salmon, and catfish. The state record smallmouth bass came from this lake. The lake is 20 miles long, has 145 miles of shoreline, and is widely used for boating, waterskiing, swimming, hunting, and hiking.

Tangle Blue Lake near the base of Scott Mountain requires a three-mile hike-in; **Ruth Lake** offers rainbow trout, catfish, largemouth bass, and smallmouth bass; and **Mad River** can provide seasonal steelhead fishing.

Steelhead and salmon are caught in season at **Big Bar.**

Near Lewiston, an old Gold Rush town, angling is limited to fly fishing in the **Trinity River** from the Old Bridge (one of the oldest one-lane bridges in California) north to the fish hatchery. The portion of the river between the Old Bridge to the Klamath River to the south is good for chinook and coho salmon, and from late fall through winter, for steelhead. Brown trout and rainbow trout also are present. Aside from the excellent fishing, the Trinity River is noted for rafting, canoeing, tubing, swimming, cycling, hiking, camping, and hunting.

Little **Lewiston Lake**, with only 15 miles of shoreline, limits boaters to a 10 mph speed limit and offers some great fly fishing for trout. The lake can be reached on CA 3 (the Trinity Heritage National Scenic Byway) by heading north out of Weaverville, or from Redding turn north on Trinity Dam Road and drive through Lewiston.

Below **Lewiston Dam**, there is a two-mile stretch of stream in which nothing but fly-fishing is allowed. Brown and rainbow trout can be taken there.

In **Lake Siskiyou,** south of Mount Shasta, there are rainbow trout, (often large) brown trout, and bass. Crayfish work well on the bass; trolling is the best for trout. The lake covers 430 acres, is fed by five pure mountain streams, and bears a 10 mph speed limit. **Box Canyon Dam** often produces good fishing.

Lake Siskiyou Camp-Resort, PO Box 276, Mt. Shasta, CA 96067, ☎ 916/926-2618, rents boats and tackle. It also has a marina, a deli, a 600-foot beach, a 150-acre campground, and a BBQ restaurant under a geodesic dome.

Lake McCloud, east of Mount Shasta, provides both lake and stream fishing. From CA 89 in McCloud, turn onto Squaw Valley Road at the Shell station and go 9.2 miles to the lake. The banks are very steep, so fishing from a boat is recommended.

Southeast of Yreka, **Kangaroo Lake** is in the Scott River Ranger District of Klamath National Forest, 11263 N. Hwy 3, Ft. Jones, CA 96032, ☎ 916/468-5351. The 25-acre lake, one of the few high mountain lakes accessible by car, runs as deep as 100 feet. Brook, brown, and rainbow trout are available, and there is a platform on the edge of the lake for the benefit of the disabled. Motorless boating, camping (18 sites), and a trail around the lake are additional features of the area.

The **Klamath River** is famous for the fall run of "half-pounders" (steelhead and salmon weighing up to three pounds). Steelhead fishing is best from September through April, and salmon fishing is best from September through October. Drift boat fishing is very popular. Other possibilities along the Klamath include:

- **Dillon Creek** – From the mouth of the creek, work upstream about a quarter of a mile or downstream to the bridge over the Klamath River. Lures, bait, and the fly-and-bubble work best.

- **Presido Bar** – From the boat ramp, work upstream to a large boulder garden. The bar is good for wading and wet- or dry-fly fishing.
- **Ti-Bar** – From just above the boat ramp, work the large, slow areas downstream as far as possible.
- **Rock Creek** – Although there is a quarter-mile walk to the river, fish hold above and below the mouth of the creek.
- **Halverson Creek** – Walk half a mile upstream on the west side of the river for some excellent wet- and dry-fly fishing.
- **Stuarts Bar** – A steep road takes you to the river and the boat ramp. Start at the upstream end of the river bar and work downstream to just above the bridge.
- **Green Riffle** – The tail-out at the top of the river bar is good.

Do not go any farther downstream than Green Riffle by boat because Ishi Pishi Falls can be extremely dangerous.

- **Dolans Bar** – From the boat ramp on the upstream end of the river bar, work downstream to just below the large rock at the end of the bar.
- **Orleans Bar** – Over half a mile of slow, deep water makes this an excellent spot for bait and lure fishing. The tail-out below the boat ramp is good for fly fishing.

When fishing the Klamath, good fly patterns are the brindle bug, silver Hilton, Orleans barber, green mossback, and Royal Coachman. Among the baits, roe is good (fresh is better than processed), and nightcrawlers work well. Spinning lures in yellow, black, and brown are best, with brighter colors working better in murkier water. For best results, retrieve spinning lures in the bottom half of the river.

Fishing in the Klamath, Salmon, and Scott Rivers centers on salmon and steelhead. Tributaries such as Canyon, Elk, Grider, Shackleford, Ukonom, and Wooley Creeks contain rainbow trout and small salmon. Eastern brook trout may be present in the upper regions of many streams.

Wooley Creek is one of few in the Klamath flowage to contain summer steelhead *and* support a spring run of king salmon.

Bob Claypole's Fishing Guide Service, PO Box 38, Klamath River, CA 96050, ☎ 916/465-2370, and **The Oaks**, Klamath River, CA 96050, ☎ 916/465-2323, can provide knowledgeable local guide service, as can

W.O.A. Fishing Adventures, PO Box 29, Horse Creek, CA 96045, located east of Hamburg.

Marble Mountain Wilderness can be reached by many roads from Route 96 between Hamburg and Somes Bar, from Scott River Road between Scott Bar and Fort Jones, and from the Fort Jones/Etna/Sawyers Bar/Somes Bar Road. A map is available at any Klamath Forest Service office. A part of Klamath National Forest, the area has 89 lakes between 5,150 and 7,400 feet of elevation that range in size from half an acre to 67 acres. Eighty of the lakes are stocked with rainbow, brown, and eastern brook trout.

None of the lakes is accessible by road, but some can be reached by a hike of an hour or two from the end of a road. Others require packing in. A list of packers and guides can be obtained from the Forest Supervisor's Office, Klamath National Forest in Yreka or the California Department of Fish & Game in Redding.

To fish the lakes, a Wilderness Permit, available through the US Forest Service, is required. Some of the better lakes in the Marble Mountain Wilderness for fishing include: **Abbott's Lake** (8 acres, 20 feet deep) has brook trout, as do **Deadman Lake** (9 acres, 25 feet deep) and **Ethel Lake** (9 acres, 22 feet deep).

Green Granite Lake (4 acres, 11 feet deep), **Katherine Lake** (5 acres, 13 feet deep), **Lake of the Island** (13 acres, 25 feet deep), and **Ukonom Lake** (67 acres, 68 feet deep) contain brook and rainbow trout. **Campbell Lake** (33 acres, 30 feet deep) holds brook, rainbow, and brown trout. **Clear Lake** (6.5 acres, 62 feet deep) and **Hancock Lake** (44 acres, 56 feet deep), the third largest lake in the mountains, may contain the largest fish in the area. The two hold brook, rainbow, and brown trout, as do **Cliff Lake** (52 acres, 175 feet deep) and **Lost Lake** (8 acres, 30 feet deep).

Snowstorms can begin any time after mid-September, but generally do not occur until after October 1. The lakes are rarely accessible before June. Fishing is best in September and October.

At Tulelake, **Orr Lake** contains rainbow trout to five pounds, catfish to eight pounds, and largemouth bass to six pounds, but the lake is privately owned and there are some rules for its use. No motors over 12 hp are allowed, for example, but swimming, picnicking, and camping are permitted.

Avid anglers might enjoy a brief stop at the **Coleman National Fish Hatchery**, 24411 Fish Hatchery Rd., Anderson, CA 96007, ☎ 916/365-8622, where between 13 and 15 million chinook salmon and a million steelhead trout are reared annually. The hatchery sits beside Battle Creek, 11 miles southeast of town, and is open daily from 7:30 to dusk.

Boating

📖 Boating also is very popular throughout California. Visitors would be wise to obtain a free copy of *California Boating Tips*, available at many of the local tackle shops and marinas.

Medicine Lake, off CA 89 northeast of Bartie, provides boating, fishing, and camping in an area of exotic volcanic terrain.

Near Hornbrook, north of Yreka, **Iron Gate Lake** is popular for boating, trout fishing, water sports, and camping.

Copco Lake, also near Hornbrook, has cabins, a marina with boat and motor rentals, and a store. Fishing, hunting, and water sports are available.

Waterskiing is popular on **Iron Gate Lake**, **Copco Lake**, **Lake McCloud**, **Whiskeytown Lake**, and **Lake Shastina**, as well as **Lake Britton**, near Burney, and **Ruth Lake,** near Weaverville. Lake Britton also is popular for windsurfing and jetskiing, and Whiskeytown Lake is a favorite place for scuba diving, power-boating, sailing, and canoeing,

John Steiner's Ski Center, 19821 Califontana Way, PO 993711, Redding, CA 96099-3711, ☎ 916/275-6744, offers rentals as well as lessons in skiing and wakeboarding.

Shasta Lake bills itself as "the houseboat capital of the world." Some 400 houseboats ply the lake, rented for anywhere between $800 and $4,000 a week. (For more information: ☎ 916/275-5555.)

Among the houseboating suppliers: **Holiday Flotels**, 16814 Packers Bay Road, Lakehead, CA 96051, ☎ 800/331-3137; **Holiday Harbor**, PO Box 112, O'Brien, CA 96070, ☎ 800/776-2628, Web site www.shastacascade.org/holidayharbor; **Jones Valley Resort**, 22300 Jones Valley Marina Dr., Redding, CA 96003, ☎ 916/275-7950 or 800/223-7950, Web site www.houseboats.com; **Lakeview Marina Resort**, PO Box 992272, Redding, CA 96099, ☎ 916/223-3003 or 800/825-6850, Web site www.shastacascade.org/lakeviewmarina; **Packers Bay Marina**, 16814 GB Packers Bay Rd., Lakehead, CA 96051, ☎ 916/275-5570 or 800/331-3137, Web site www.shastacascade.org/packersbay/; **Lakeview Marine**, PO Box 992272, Redding, CA 96099-2272, ☎ 916/223-3003, 238-2442, or 800/825-6850, fax 916/238-8433; and **Silverthorn Resort**, PO Box 4205, Redding, CA 96099, ☎ 916/275-

1571 or 800/332-3044, Web site www.shastacascade.org/silverhornresort.

Antlers Resort & Marina, PO Box 140, Anders Rd., Lakehead, CA 96051, ☎ 916/238-2553 or 800/238-3924; **Bridge Bay Resort**, 10300 Bridge Bay Rd., Redding, CA 96003, ☎ 916/275-3021 or 800/752-9669, Web site www.sevencrown.com; **Lakeshore Marina**, 20479 Lakeshore Dr., Lakehead, CA 96051, ☎ 916/238-2301; **Shasta Marina**, 18390 O'Brien Inlet Rd., Lakehead, CA 96051, ☎ 916/238-2284 or 800/959-3359; and **Sugarloaf Resort**, 19671 Lakeshore Dr., Lakehead, CA 96051, ☎ 916/243-4353 or 800/223-7950, Web site www.houseboats.com, rent such things as patio boats, fishing boats, jet skis, Sea Doos, and ski boats, as well as houseboats.

Trinity Lake near Weaverville also is popular for houseboating.

Other popular spots to participate in various water sports include the **Sacramento River** near Dunsmuir, where rafting, tubing, rockhounding, and gold panning vie for attention with swimming, fishing, and hunting. The **Big Bar** area is popular for whitewater rafting, kayaking, inner tubing, and gold panning.

Near the town of Burnt Ranch, **Burnt Ranch Gorge** provides exciting whitewater rafting and kayaking on the Trinity River.

Lake Siskiyou, south of Mount Shasta, is the only lake in California developed solely for recreation. In addition to fishing and boating, the lake is widely used for camping and for its hiking trails. The summer wildflowers are exquisite, kayak and canoe rentals are available, and visitors can cruise the lake on the 36-foot voyager canoe *Spirit of Lake Siskiyou*.

Lake Shastina, just north of Weed, offers fishing, boating, whitewater rafting, windsurfing, lodging, a restaurant, and a lounge. The lake offers limited bank fishing for trout, bass, crappie, and catfish. Water levels may drop significantly in the late summer, but the area also offers tennis, hiking, and hunting, as well as an 18-hole Robert Trent Jones Jr. golf course at 5925 Country Club Dr., Weed, CA 96094, ☎ 916/938-3201 or 800/358-4653.

Medicine Lake, in the Modoc National Forest, PO Box 818, Tulelake, CA 96134, ☎ 916/667-2246, is a 600-acre natural alpine lake at an elevation of 6,500 feet. There are three Forest Service campgrounds on the north and south shores of the lake; picnic and swimming facilities are on the east shore. There is a boat-launch ramp and a loading dock, and a privately owned store rents cabins and boats.

Just north of Yreka at the intersection of Routes 263 (Main St.) and 96, is an area of the **Klamath River** that is popular for whitewater rafting, canoeing, and kayaking. The Klamath east of Hamburg is widely used for tubing.

Turtle River Rafting Co., PO Box 313, Mt. Shasta, CA 96067, ☎ 916/926-3223 or 800/726-3223, will arrange one- to five-day trips for whitewater rafting on the Klamath, Trinity, Rogue, Upper Sacramento, Salmon, Scott, or Owyhee Rivers.

Living Waters Recreation, PO Box 1192, Mt. Shasta, CA 96067-1192, ☎ 916/926-5446 or 800/994-RAFT, also arranges half-day, all-day, or two-day river trips, as does **River Dancers**, 302 Terry Lynn, Mt. Shasta, CA 96067, ☎ 916/926-3517 or 800/926-5002. **Osprey Outfitters**, 2033 Ti Bar Rd., Somes Bar, CA 95568, ☎ 916/469-3399; **Klamath River Outfitters**, 3 Sandy Bar Rd., Somes Bar, CA 95563, ☎ 916/469-3349 or 800/748-3735; and **Access to Adventure**, 92520 Hwy 96, Somes Bar, CA 95568, ☎ 916/469-3322, 800/KLAMATH, fax 916/469-3357, lead kayak and rafting trips as well as drift-fishing trips for shad and steelhead.

■ On Snow

Before going snowmobiling, get a free Shasta-Trinity Off-Road Vehicle map from the Mount Shasta Ranger District office. The office also prepares a useful general information tape that can be accessed at ☎ 916/926-3781.

A tape containing information about road, weather, and snow conditions can be accessed around the clock, ☎ 916/926-5555.

Northwest of Chico, a new $10 million, four-story, 43,000 sq. ft. condominium hotel, **Lodge at Kirkwood**, is the centerpiece for Kirkwood Mountain Village, a world-class skiing village located at the base of the resort's six major ski lifts. Contact Kirkwood Resort Co., PO Box 1, Kirkwood, CA 95646, ☎ 209/258-7339 or 258-6000, fax 209/258-8899.

Northeast of Chico at Butte Meadows, **Colby Meadows Cross-Country Ski Area** is on the western slope of the Sierra Nevada Range at an elevation of 4,800-6,000 feet. The area contains nine miles of ski trails.

North of Butte Meadows at Mill Creek, **McGowan Lake Cross-Country Ski Area** has 10 miles of trails at 5,020-6,200 feet of elevation. Parking spots are on CA 89, two miles north of CA 36, and at the junction of CA 36 and Nanny Creek.

During the summer, **Mount Shasta Ski Park**, 104 Siskiyou Ave., Mt. Shasta, CA 96067, ☎ 916/926-8610 or 926-8600, fax 916/926-8607, Web site www.skipark.com, is open Wednesday through Sunday for chairlift rides, paragliding, and mountain biking. It also features a 24-foot climbing tower and nature walks. But in the winter, downhill and cross-country skiing and snowboarding reign supreme. Facilities include two triple chairlifts, 25 ski trails, and 1,400 vertical feet of skiing on 425 acres. The park, Northern California's largest night skiing operation, allows night skiing from Wednesday through Saturday.

The park also provides three miles of marked cross-country ski trails ranging from less than a mile to nearly 1.5 miles in length. In an area of 2,000 acres, the trails are found at elevations of 6,600-7,000 feet. The cross-country skiing season generally runs from Thanksgiving to Easter. For current skiing conditions, contact the park's snow phone: ☎ 916/926-8686.

While in the park, be sure to check out an interesting exhibit that uses videotapes, photographs, charts, and aerials to demonstrate the way in which Mount Shasta was formed.

Castle Lake Nordic Ski Center, 10 miles southwest of Mount Shasta on Castle Lake Road (PO Box 660, Mt. Shasta, CA 96067), provides 31 miles of groomed cross-country ski trails for every ski level, beginner to expert. The trails traverse outstanding scenery and terrain.

Lake Siskiyou, south of Mount Shasta, is very popular for winter cross-country skiing and ice skating.

McCloud, which hosts the National Dog Sled Races every January (usually on the last weekend of the month), has a number of venues for winter sports including downhill and cross-country skiing, tobogganing, snowmobiling, and sledding. The most popular cross-country skiing areas are at **McCloud Flats** and **Snow Man's Hill**. Snowmobile fans frequent the **Pilgrim Creek Snowmobile Park**.

Around **Etna**, the dogsled season usually begins by Thanksgiving and runs through March. **Dogsled Express**, PO Box 15, Etna, CA 96027, ☎ 916/467-5627, will take you to Mount Shasta, the Trinity Alps, or the Marble Mountains, where you will operate one sled, pulled by huskies and Alaskan malamutes, while an experienced guide follows on another.

Around **Weaverville**, cross-country skiing is enjoyed in the Trinity Alps at **Scott Mountain**, **Coffee Creek Road**, **Weaver Bally**, and **Hayfork Mountain**.

Lassen Volcanic National Park is closed in the winter except in the Manzanita Lake area, where cross-country skiing is permitted. Take CA 44 east from Redding to the north entrance of the park or take CA 36 from Red Bluff to the south entrance.

In **Mad River** and in **Burney**, cross-country skiing and snowmobiling are as popular in the winter as hiking, horseback riding, and biking are in the summer.

Snowmobiling is the principal sport at **Deer Mountain Snowmobile Park** in the Goosenest Ranger District of Klamath National Forest. The park is located 17 miles from Weed on US 97, then four miles up Deer Mountain Road. It allows access to the north and east sides of Mount Shasta and has 250 miles of groomed trails to explore.

Snowmobile rentals and tours can be arranged at **The Fun Factory**, Lake Shastina, ☎ 916/842-8585.

In the northeastern corner of the region, just south of the Oregon border, **Four Corners/Medicine Lake Snowmobile Park** southwest of Tulelake provides winter sport for snowmobilers.

■ In the Air

Each June for more than 50 years, **Airport Day**, PO Box 475, Fall River Mills, CA 96028, has been celebrated with airplane rides, demonstrations, and a pancake breakfast.

Every May, an airshow is staged at **Redding** Municipal Airport, ☎ 916/222-1610. Each September, the Chico Airshow is held at **Chico** Municipal Airport. ☎ 530/898-2359.

Also in September, the annual **Siskiyou Balloon Faire** is held at Siskiyou County Airport, 800 S. Main St., Yreka, CA 96097, ☎ 916/842-8022. The event features hot air balloons, crafts, music, and food.

If you'd like an airplane ride of your own, you can contact **Hillside Aviation** at Benton Field in Redding, ☎ 916/241-4204, or **Horse Mountain Aviation**, Rt. 2, Box 23, Tulelake, CA 96134, ☎ 916/664-5391.

Montague Aviation, operating out of Rohrer Field, Montague-Yreka Airport Rd., PO Box 128, Montague, CA 96064, ☎ 916/459-3456, offers glider rides as well as scenic flights and biplane rides.

Been **bungy jumping**? Perhaps (like us) you're not interested but would just like to watch. **Box Canyon Bungy Co.**, located at Lake Siskiyou's Box Canyon Dam, ☎ 916/926-5867, is the place to go. Park off Cattle Lake Road in Mount Shasta City.

Or perhaps **hang gliding** is more to your liking. There's hang gliding off the Hat Creek Rim near Burney almost every afternoon between March and November. For a site guide, stop at Fireside Village in Hat Creek, ☎ 916/335-4505.

■ Cultural Excursions

Chico

Gold Nugget Museum (☎ 916/872-8722) is at 502 Pearson St. in Paradise, southeast of Chico. Open Wednesday through Sunday, noon to 4, the free exhibits include an old miner's cabin, a blacksmith shop, and a replica of a gold mine.

Errol Flynn filmed the epic *Adventures of Robin Hood* in Chico's **Bidwell Park** in 1937. The colorful **Honey Run Covered Bridge** and the **National Yo Yo Museum** also are in Chico.

Burney

In Burney, the **Glenburn Church**, built in 1886, is still heated by a potbellied stove. With Mount Shasta and the old Creighton flour mill in the background, the church is a photographer's favorite.

Dunsmuir

Cedar Lodge Exotic Bird Farm, 4210 Dunsmuir Ave., Dunsmuir, CA 96025, ☎ 916/235-4331, has cockatoos, African Greys, and Amazon parrots. It is the largest aviary of its kind in Northern California.

Etna

The **Etna Brewery**, 131 Callahan Rd., Etna, CA 96027, ☎ 916/467-5277, also makes *root* beer.

Sawyers Bar is 29 miles from Etna via steep grades to an elevation of 6,000 feet. The town has the oldest Catholic church north of San Francisco (1855) and sits atop an estimated $200,000 in placer gold. The one-street town, much damaged by fires over the years, is perhaps the most picturesque of the old mining towns in the region.

Fall River Mills

Fort Crook Museum in Fall River Mills features a three-story main building, an 1884 pioneer cabin, a 1900 one-room school-house, and the original 1930 Fall River Jailhouse.

Fort Jones

Over 125 bison roam the **Wild Rose Ranch**, PO Box 842, 4716 Mill Creek Rd., Fort Jones, CA 96032, ☎ 916/468-5967, fax 916/468-5968, and bison meat (lower in calories, fat, and cholesterol than turkey, beef, or chicken) can be purchased there.

North of Fort Jones, the McAdam Road turnoff marks the original stagecoach route to Oregon and leads to the ghost town of **Deadwood**, once a mining camp and Yreka's rival for the county seat. Cincinnatus Hiner (Joaquin) Miller, "The Poet of the Sierras," worked as a miner and a cook in Deadwood.

Happy Camp

Big Foot

During the mid-1800s, a group of Chinese were hired to dig ditches from Thompson Creek to the mines between Happy Camp and Seiad Valley. One day, a group of the men went running into camp saying that they had seen a big hairy man digging roots. The men were so frightened they never returned to the job. It was one of the region's first reports of Big Foot. (See *Sasquatch*, page 18)

Gold and jade mines are still operating in Happy Camp, which makes an excellent base for hunting, fishing, and camping excursions. The town has an annual **Big Foot Jamboree** (☎ 916/496-2300) on Labor Day weekend, with a salmon BBQ, food and craft booths, and dancing. **Equinox Ranch**, 6437 Indian Creek Rd., Happy Camp, CA 96039, ☎ 916/493-5395, raises llamas and grows mushrooms commercially. And the **Karuk Tribe** of California makes its headquarters here at 746 Indian Creek Rd., Happy Camp, CA 96039, ☎ 916/493-5305.

A WORD TO THE WISE

As you pass along the Klamath River in this area, watch for the water ouzel or "dipper," a bird that runs underwater along the river bottom in search of food. Look for them in the shallow rapids or near shore. Also keep an eye out as you pass any type of dump. Dumps are often frequented by black bears, particularly at dusk and at night.

Hornbrook

Near Hornbrook, north of Yreka, is the **Hilt Buddhist Community**.

Klamath River

Highlight of the year in Klamath River is the annual **Kornball Follies** melodrama (☎ 916/465-2224), sponsored by the Klamath River Fire Company Auxiliary. The October event is staged in the Klamath River Community Hall.

Quigley's Store in Klamath River was built in the mid-1920s by Willis "Moon" Quigley, who often guided Herbert Hoover on fishing trips. "Moon" is gone, but the store – and the name – remain.

McArthur-Burney Falls State Park

On CA 89, between Mount Shasta to the north and Lassen Park to the south, is McArthur-Burney Falls State Park, centered around a 129-foot waterfall that Theodore Roosevelt once called "the eighth wonder of the world." Camping is allowed and there is a boat ramp.

McCloud

Every August, McCloud holds its **Heritage Days** (☎ 916/964-3113 or 964-2626), a week-long event in which the entire community dresses in period costume, train rides are offered on the old McCloud Railway, mail is delivered by pony express, a melodrama is staged, and such things as wool spinning and quilting are demonstrated.

Red Bluff

At 135 Main St. in Red Bluff is a nondescript clapboard cottage with a shingled roof and porch. In 1864, sympathetic residents of the community took pity on the family of abolitionist **John Brown**, who had been executed five years earlier following his raid on the federal armory at Harper's Ferry. They invited Brown's family to live in this humble house, and the family remained here until 1870.

William B. Ide Adobe State Historic Park, 3040 Adobe Rd., Red Bluff, CA, ☎ 916/527-5927, was named for the first and only president of the Republic of California. The centerpiece of the park is his lovely and historic 1846 adobe home.

Red Bluff Roundup (Robert Holmes, CDT).

Redding

Turtle Bay Park and Museum, 800 Auditorium Dr., Redding, CA 96001, ☎ 530/243-8850 or 800/TURTLE BAY, fax 530/243-8898, is located on a bend in the Sacramento River. The 60-acre park has lush riparian habitat, vernal pools, trail systems, and considerable resident wildlife. The 3,800-square-foot museum, designed to resemble a turn-of-the-century sawmill, contains a giant log slide that transports children from the second floor to an outdoor play area. **Paul Bunyan's Forest Camp**, part of the park, has both indoor and outdoor activities and exhibits, plus a 200-seat amphitheater.

Equally intriguing for parents is **Carter House Natural Science Museum**, 1701 Rio Dr., Redding, CA 96001, ☎ 530/225-4125, which has an Animal Discovery Room in which children are encouraged to play with over 30 different species of animals.

The **Redding Convention & Visitors Bureau**, 777 Auditorium Dr., Redding, CA 96001, ☎ 916/225-4108 or 800/874-7562, fax 916/225-4354, has a number of useful (and free) brochures that will make your visit there more interesting. One is the pocket-sized *Redding's Historic Architecture*, which describes three self-guided tours of the town. Another is *A Glimpse of Times Past*, which is a guide to the museums throughout the county. A third brochure, *You'll Fall for Far Northern California*, describes eight magnificent waterfalls that are worth visiting, six in Northern California and two in southern Oregon.

Weaverville

The town of Weaverville has an interesting history, enchantingly illustrated in the **Joss House State Historic Park** (☎ 916/623-5284) on CA 299 in the heart of town. In 1852, Weaverville had a population of 3,000 people, half of whom were Chinese. Most of the Chinese belonged to some tong or secret society. At the encouragement of some of the town's non-Oriental miners, two of the tongs, the Young Wos and the Ah Yous, faced off in Five-Cent Gulch to fight "The China War." Armed only with knives and forks (firearms were forbidden to the Chinese in those days), 500 Young Wos routed 300 Ah Yous, resulting in two deaths. Few Chinese remain in Weaverville today, but the 1852 Taoist temple standing in the park is the oldest continuously operating Taoist temple in the country.

Weed

Near Weed is **Mount Eddy** (9,038 feet), which was named for the grandfather of movie singer/actor Nelson Eddy.

Callahan, west of Weed, is nearly a ghost town now, but it was one of the earliest stage stops in the region. The Catholic church dates from 1858, there is an 1859 Stage Stop Hotel and an old-time blacksmith shop, and the nickelodeon in the town's quaint old tavern was originally shipped around the Horn. Every August, the town celebrates its past with the **Callahan Days Wild West Show**.

Yreka

Yreka has been visited by a varied list of celebrities, including Bret Harte, Lotta Crabtree, Joaquin Miller, Zane Grey, and Herbert Hoover. Many of its Victorian homes (there are more than 75 restored 19th-century homes in town) are listed on the National Register of Historic Places. (A free self-guided tour map is available at the Chamber of Commerce.)

For anyone interested in the American Indian, the **Siskiyou County Museum**, 910 S. Main St., ☎ 916/842-3836, is truly noteworthy. Its Native American gallery contains exhibits from such local tribes as the Karuk, Shasta, Konomihu, Okwanuschu, Achomawi, and Modoc. Across the parking lot from the main museum in Yreka is a 2.5-acre outdoor museum – a collection of five original buildings dating from 1856 to 1920.

In the mid- to late 1800s, two sizeable Chinatowns existed along Miner Street in Yreka. There is an interesting old **Chinese Cemetery** just north of Montague Road between I-5 and the old railroad.

Also look into the **Klamath National Forest Interpretive Museum**, 1312 Fairlane Rd., Yreka, CA 96097, ☎ 916/842-6131.

Fort Jones, southwest of Yreka, was once called Wheelocks Post and was associated with such prominent military figures as William T. Sherman, John Bell Hood, Ulysses S. Grant, and Philip H. Sheridan. Although nothing remains of the original fort except a marker, the **Fort Jones Museum**, 11913 Main St., Fort Jones, CA, ☎ 916/468-5568, is of interest.

The old stone museum has an excellent collection of Indian baskets, and on the north side of the building is the famous **Rain Rock**, which weighs about two tons. The Indians once brought rain by pounding holes into this rock. To stop the rain, the stone was covered. The museum is open during the summer, but only by appointment during the winter. Admission is free.

Where to Stay

This part of the state generally does not offer a wide choice when it comes to accommodation. It helps if you like to stay in B&Bs.

Dunsmuir

Railroad Park Resort, 100 Railroad Park Rd., Dunsmuir, CA 96025, ☎ 916/235-4440, $$-$$$, provides motel units in authentic old railroad cabooses. The units include a color TV and a telephone, and there is a restaurant and a cocktail lounge on the premises. Creekside camping is also available (☎ 916/235-4611), plus on-site trout fishing.

McCloud

McCloud River Inn, 325 Lawndale Court, PO Box 1560, McCloud, CA 96057, ☎ 530/964-2130 or 800/261-7831, fax 916/964-2730, E-mail mort@snowcrest.net, $$, occupies a turn-of-the-century building that served, in turn, as the main office of the McCloud River Lumber Co., the town bank, and the community's telephone switchboard office. Now restored, the building houses an espresso bar, an art gallery, gift shops, and an old-fashioned candy shoppe in addition to the B&B.

Mt. Shasta

In Mount Shasta, you might look into the **Alpine Lodge**, 908 S. Mt. Shasta Rd., Mt. Shasta, CA 96067, ☎ 916/926-3145 or 800/500-3145, fax 916/926-5897, $-$$, or **Evergreen Lodge**, 1312 S. Mt. Shasta Blvd., Mt. Shasta, CA 96067, ☎ 916/926-2143 or 800/244-3039, $-$$.

Lake Shasta Camp-Resort, PO Box 276, Mt. Shasta, CA 96067, ☎ 916/926-2618 or 888/926-2618, $$, offers a bit more in terms of "fringe benefits." In addition to allowing overnight camping, the camp has a marina, a tackle shop, a fishing dock, a 600-foot beach, a launch ramp, and a store. It also rents patio boats, fishing boats, canoes, pedal boats, kayaks, sea cycles, and rafts.

Even more upscale is **Mount Shasta Resort**, 1000 Siskiyou Lake Blvd., Mt. Shasta, CA 96067, ☎ 916/926-3030 or 800/958-3363, fax 916/926-0333, Web site www.mountshastaresort.com, E-mail msresort@macshasta.com, $$-$$$, which has a 6,400-yard golf course, tennis courts, and a restaurant where a Sunday champagne brunch is served.

Mount Shasta Ranch, 1008 W.A. Barr Rd., Mt. Shasta, CA 96067, ☎ 916/926-3870, $-$$, is a two-story B&B built in 1923 as a thoroughbred horse ranch.

Weaverville

Weaverville Victorian Inn, 1709 Main St., PO Box 2400, Weaverville, CA 96093-2400, ☎ 916/623-4432, fax 916/623-4264, $-$$, is a two-story, 61-room motel.

Weed

At **Stewart Mineral Springs**, 4617 Stewart Springs Rd., Weed, CA 96094, ☎ 916/938-2222 or 800/322-9223, $-$$$$, you can pick and choose. Accommodation ranges from camping to dormitory units to apartment units to private one-room cabins and finally to an A-frame house with five bedrooms and three baths. In its 13 individual bathing rooms, the spa furnishes therapeutic mineral baths, massages, saunas, and purification sweats.

Yreka

Miner's Inn, 122 E. Miner St., Yreka, CA 96097, ☎ 916/842-4355 or 800/528-1234, fax 916/842-4480, $$, is a Best Western affiliate with 135 units, including some suites. There is an adjoining restaurant and a swimming pool.

■ Camping

Camping on public lands can be arranged rather easily in this part of the country. For reservations, contact **Biospherics**, ☎ 800/280-2267.

Lassen National Forest has campgrounds at **Alder Creek** on Route 32, **Battle Creek** on Route 36, **Black Rock** on Ponderosa Way, **Butte Creek** off Route 44, **Butte Meadows** off Route 32, **Cherry Hill** off Route 32, **Crags** off Route 44 on Route 89, **Elam** on Route 32, **Goumaz** on Route 36, **Gurnsey** on Route 36, **Hat Creek** on Route 89, **Hole-in-the-Ground** off Route 36, and **Juniper Lake** on Route 312, as well as campgrounds at **Manzanita Lake** on Route 89, **Potato Patch** off Route 32, **Roxie Peconom** off Route 36, **South Antelope** on Route 202, **Southwest** on Route 89, **Summit Lake** on Route 89, **Warner Valley** on Route 312, and **West Branch** off Route 31. Additional sites are available at **Big Pine**, **Bridge**, **Cave**, and **Rocky**, all on Route 89, but they are open only from late April to October. There is another site at **Honn**, but it has no drinking water and it is not recommended for trailers due to a limited amount of turn-around space.

The Bureau of Land Management operates a campsite at **Ramhorn Springs** off County Road 395. There is piped water, there is a corral for horses, and there is no fee.

Elk Creek Campground, PO Box 785, Happy Camp, CA 96039, ☎ 916/493-2208, has been rated the #1 rural RV park on the west coast. Rafting is available from June through September, along with jet boat rides, drift boating, fishing, and hunting. The campground is within Klamath National Forest.

Along the Klamath River Road, there are numerous campgrounds, including **Beaver Creek Campground**; **Sarah Toten Campground**, half a mile east of Hamburg; **O'Neil Creek Campground**; **Tree of Heaven Campground**, southwest of Hornbrook (named for the 100-year-old Allanthus trees from China that are found there); **Fort Goff Creek Campground** between Seiad and Happy Camp; **Sulphur Springs Campground**, famous for its Indian sulphur springs; **West Branch Campground** north of Happy Camp; and **Dillon Creek Campground** north of Somes Bar.

Many campgrounds also can be found along the Salmon River Road: **Camp Eden** west of Callahan; **Idlewild Campground** between Etna and Sawyers Bar; **Mule Bridge Campground** north of Idlewild, which is largely for parties of horse riders or parties with pack stock; **Little North Fork Campground** near Sawyers Bar (if you go, boil any water you take from the creek before you drink it); **Matthews Creek Campground** southeast of Forks of Salmon; **Red Bank Campground** southeast of Sawyers Bar; **Bacon Rind Campground** between Sawyers Bar and Cecilville; **East Fork Campground** east of Cecilville; **Shadow Creek Campground** near Callahan; **Trail Creek Campground** west of Callahan; and **Oak Bottom Campground** between Sawyers Bar and Somes Bar on the Salmon River.

On the Scott River Road, campgrounds include: **Spring Flat Campground**, **Bridge Flat Campground**, **Indian Scotty Campground**, and **Lovers Camp**, all west of Fort Jones.

Along Scott Mountain Road, campgrounds include **Scott Mountain Campground,** south of Callahan, and **Etna Campground,** within the Etna city limits.

On the Gazelle-Callahan Road, there is the **Kangaroo Lake Campground** east of Callahan.

Six miles past McCloud on Route 89 is the Forest Service's **Fowler Campground**, which has several well-maintained trails leading from the campground to the Lower Falls of the McCloud River and the base of Middle Falls. More primitive but spacious camping is available at **Cattle Camp** near the east end of the McCloud River Loop.

In Six Rivers National Forest, the Forest Service has campgrounds at **Grizzly Camp** near Willow Creek; **Boise Creek** and **East Fork** west of Willow Creek; **Tish Tang** north of Willow Creek; and **Grays Falls** and **Hoss Linton Creek** east of Willow Creek. Reservations are not required.

Where to Eat

Food, like housing, is limited in much of this region. A taste for solid home cooking is a genuine asset. Nonetheless, a few surprises can be found.

Mt. Shasta

How about a Mexican restaurant called **Poncho & Lefkowitz**? You'll find one at 310 W. Lake St., Mt. Shasta, CA 96067, $-$$. They're closed on Sundays.

Serge's Restaurant, 531 Chestnut St., Mt. Shasta, CA 96067, ☎ 916/926-1276, $$, serves French cuisine indoors and outdoors, but they're closed on Monday.

For California cuisine, there's **Highland House Restaurant**, 1000 Siskiyou Lake Blvd., Mt. Shasta, CA 96067, ☎ 916/926-3030, $$. They serve lunch, dinner, and a Sunday brunch. They also have a lounge.

Yreka

Yreka has **Ma & Pa's**, 102 Montague Rd., ☎ 916/842-5618, $$, and **Grandma's House**, 123 E. Center, ☎ 916/842-5300, $$. **The Peasantry Restaurant**, 322 W. Miner, ☎ 916/842-5418, $$, specializes in sourdough pancakes (an acquired taste) and omelets.

Information Sources

Clear Lake National Wildlife Refuge, Rt. 1, Box 74, Tulelake, CA 96134, ☎ 916/667-2231.

Klamath Basin National Wildlife Refuge, Rt. 1, Box 74, Tulelake, CA 96134, ☎ 916/667-2231.

Klamath National Forest, 1312 Fairlane Rd., Yreka, CA 96097, ☎ 916/842-6131, has numerous district offices in the area, including Goosenest Ranger District, 37805 Hwy 97, Macdoel, CA 96058, ☎ 916/398-4391; Happy Camp Ranger District, PO Box 377, Happy Camp, CA 96039, ☎ 916/493-2243; Oak Knoll Ranger District, 22541 Hwy 96, Klamath River, CA 96050, ☎ 916/465-2241; Salmon River Ranger District, Etan, CA, ☎ 916/467-5757; and Scott River Ranger District, 11263 S. Hwy 3, Fort Jones, CA 96032, ☎ 916/468-5351.

Lassen Volcanic Park, PO Box 100, Mineral, CA 96063, ☎ 916/595-4444.

Lava Beds National Monument, PO Box 867, Tulelake, CA 96134, ☎ 916/667-2282.

Mendocino National Forest, 825 N. Humboldt Ave., Willows, CA 95988, ☎ 916/934-3316, with district offices in Corning, CA, ☎ 916/824-5196, and Covelo, CA, ☎ 707/983-6118.

Shasta-Trinity National Forest, 2400 Washington Ave., Redding, CA 96001, ☎ 916/246-5222, and its ranger districts in Big Bar, ☎ 916/623-6106; Hayfork, ☎ 916/628-5227; McCloud, ☎ 916/964-2184; Mt. Shasta, ☎ 916/926-4511 or 926-3781; Shasta Lake in Redding, CA, ☎ 916/275-1589; Weaverville, ☎ 916/623-2121; and Yolla Bolla in Platina, CA, ☎ 916/352-4211.

Northeastern California

One of the most remote regions in "the lower 48" states is the northeasterly corner of California. There are no airports worth mention, there are no interstate highways, the largest city (Susanville) has a population of fewer than 7,500 people, and the second-largest city (Alturas) has fewer than half that number.

Still, it is beautiful country, checker-boarded with national and state forests, mountains, lakes, rushing rivers, and babbling streams.

Getting Around

Once more, the preferred mode of travel is the automobile.

The only federal highway, US 395, enters the area at Hallelujah Junction to the south and winds its way northward past Susanville, Alturas, and Goose Lake into Oregon.

Out of Susanville, Route 139 goes north past Eagle Lake, passes through Modoc National Forest, and moves on through Tulelake on its way to Klamath Falls, Oregon.

From Hallelujah Junction, a state highway (CA 70) wends a crooked trail northwest through Portola and Quincy, then abruptly bends to the southwest toward Lake Oroville.

Westbound, traffic from Susanville has a choice of taking CA 36 to Red Bluff via Lake Almanor and Chester en route, or taking CA 44 northwest to Redding through Lassen National Forest.

From Alturas, CA 299 snakes westward through Canby and Adin on the way to Burney and Redding in the central part of the state, or eastward to Cedarville near the Nevada state line.

Touring

Paxton

Paxton, once called Soda Bar because of all the mineral springs in the area, was once a thriving placer-mining town.

Rich Bar

Rich Bar (Barra Rica to early Mexican miners) once was so rich in gold that a single panful of "dirt" could produce from $100 to $1,500. In all, over $3 million in gold was removed from the area.

Lake Almanor

Chester, a lumber town, is built on the northwestern shore of Lake Almanor, which covers 45 square miles and is dotted with small islands. Although the name of the lake sounds like it is of Spanish origin, it actually was derived from the names of three girls – *AL*ice, *MA*rtha and Eli*NOR*e. The girls were the daughters of a pioneer family, and their father was president of the Great Western Power Company.

Standish

Standish was an experimental Utopian community when it was established in 1897. A wildlife refuge is nearby.

Johnstonville

Johnstonville, was once called Toadtown because thousands of toads would suddenly appear after a rain. It lies along the Noble Emigrant Route, a trail surveyed in 1852 that passed through Noble's Pass in the

Northeast California

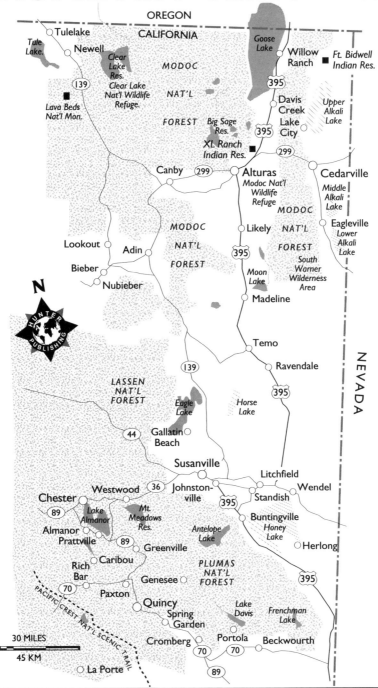

Sierra and followed the Susan River into Northern California. Within three years, the trail was the state's most heavily traveled immigration route, but it is little remembered today.

Susanville

Isaac Roop established a trading post in Susanville in 1854, and named the town and the nearby river for his daughter Susan. When a small gold rush got started in the area two years later, the residents of the town felt a need for some sort of government. Perceiving that the region belonged neither to California nor to Utah, the residents established the **Territory of Nataqua** and made Susanville the territorial capital. When a survey in the early 1860s indicated that the region actually was within the boundaries of Plumas County, California, the residents became angered, realizing that they would soon have to begin paying taxes. A two-day "Sagebrush War" was waged in Susanville in February 1863 between the citizens and the county tax collectors, and Isaac Roop's house became known as **Fort Defiance**. On April 1, 1864, the issue was resolved when the state legislature created Lassen County and proclaimed Susanville the county seat. Lassen County is approximately the size of Connecticut.

From 1880 to 1927, the narrow-gauge Nevada-California-Oregon Railway (a line often called the Narrow, Crooked and Ornery) operated in the Susanville area.

Eagle Lake (☎ 916/257-2151), the second largest natural lake in California, is 16 miles northwest of Susanville. The area is open from dawn to dusk daily from Memorial Day weekend to mid-October. During the summer, Wednesday campfire programs and Saturday slide presentations are featured.

From 1913 to 1956, the Red River Lumber Co. was the biggest pine lumber mill in the world and **Westwood**, 22 miles west of Susanville, was one of the largest lumber company towns in the West. A 25-foot redwood statue of Paul Bunyan stands in the town.

South of Susanville, flanking both sides of CA 70 from Cromberg to Storrie, is **Plumas National Forest**. **Honey Lake**, **Lake Almanor**, and the **Mountain Meadows Reservoir** ring the northern border of the forest; **Lake Oroville** sits on its southwestern corner; and **Frenchman Lake**, **Lake Davis**, **Antelope Lake**, **Little Grass Valley Lake**, and **Bucks Lake** lie within the boundaries of the forest itself.

La Porte

La Porte, once a mining town but now almost a ghost town, was one of the earliest ski-sport towns in the country. As early as the 1860s, La Porte miners used homemade skis to race each other down the slopes. **Lassen National Forest**, 55 S. Sacramento St., Susanville, CA 96130, ☎ 916/257-2151, encompasses a mountainous region of 1.1 million acres west and north of Susanville. **Lassen Volcanic National Park** lies within its borders.

Modoc National Forest

Modoc National Forest, 800 W. 12th St., Alturas, CA 96101, ☎ 916/233-5811, is inhabited by over 300 species of wildlife, including a substantial number of wild horses. Covering over 1.5 million acres, the forest is directly beneath the Pacific Flyway, a major migratory route for many kinds of birds. Also in the area are **Burnt Lava Flow**, an expanse of black lava that is dotted with islands of timber, and **Glass Mountain**, a huge mass of obsidian (black "volcanic glass").

Forming the eastern boundary of Modoc National Forest are the **Warner Mountains** and the **South Warner Wilderness**, which encompasses **Eagle Peak**, the highest mountain in the Modocs. The South Warner Wilderness covers 70,385 acres and offers 118 miles of trails, made accessible by eight trailheads. The area is popular for hiking, horseback riding, fishing, and cross-country skiing.

Indian Reservations

XL Ranch Indian Reservation, one of two reservations in this remote corner of the state, lies along US 395 just outside of Alturas. **Fort Bidwell Indian Reservation**, just a few miles from the point where California, Nevada, and Oregon come together, is the other, and was built as a Cavalry outpost in 1866. When Fort Bidwell was abandoned as an Army post in 1892, the fort became a school for Indian children, and although the old Army barracks were torn down in 1930, the Indians remain, living in little cottages clustered around a schoolhouse and a small hospital.

Adventures

■ On Foot

Hunting

Lassen County is outstanding hunting country. Mule deer can be found in the desert areas, and blacktailed deer in the higher Sierra habitats. Pronghorn antelope also frequent the area. Special tags are required.

All three of the county's state wildlife areas – **Ash Creek Wildlife Area**, occupying 13,000 acres near Bieber; the 7,800-acre **Honey Lake Wildlife Area**; and **Willow Creek Wildlife Area**, a 2,700-acre satellite of Honey Lake – offer waterfowl hunting on Wednesdays, Saturdays, and Sundays during the fall season.

The Bizz Johnson Trail

Although the Bizz Johnson Trail runs from Susanville to Westwood, an 18-mile segment that runs along the Susan River is the most scenic. It is an easy hike with a maximum grade of three percent, and is very popular for hiking, backpacking, and cross-country skiing. Birdwatching and rockhounding also are popular. Twenty-six miles of the trail run along an old Southern Pacific railroad line.

The Lost Captain Dick Mine

Somewhere around Alturas, near a high pass between Pine Valley and Owl Creek in the Warner Mountains, is the Lost Captain Dick Mine. According to legend, a small hole in the mountainside will lead the successful treasure hunter to a tunnel laced with veins of gold.

■ On Horseback

The **Bureau of Land Management** maintains corrals for wild horses and burros near Litchfield and Wendel.

The **Bizz Johnson Trail** from Susanville to Westwood makes an excellent equestrian trail. It crosses 11 bridges and passes through two tunnels, one 450 feet long and the other 800 feet long, both of which are passable on horseback. Riders who wish to avoid the tunnels can follow the riverside trails, which are provided as alternate routes.

■ On Wheels

Driving Tours

Using Susanville as a base of operations, some excellent side trips may be taken throughout this region of Northern California. Among the best are a visit to the **Black Rock** and **Smoke Creek Deserts**; a trip down Route 44 to **Hat Creek**, **Four Corners**, **Bieber**, and **Adin**, returning south on Route 139 to **Eagle Lake** and back to Susanville; a drive from Susanville to **Antelope Lake**, **Taylorsville**, **Greenville**, **Lake Almanor**, and back; a trip from Susanville to **Mineral**, **Lassen Park**, **Hat Creek**, and back; an evening drive to **Pine Creek Valley** to see the many antelope that frequent the area; and a trip along the Forest Service loop to **Hamilton Mountain**. Some of these trips involve driving on dirt roads. Study the map, inquire locally about road conditions, and drive carefully.

Accidents occur frequently in this area during storms, with the highway often blocked for long periods. I-80 and US 50 are particularly vulnerable to closures. Poor visibility can lead to closures during heavy storms along I-80. It is far better to wait at Applegate or Pollock Pines below the snow line than to sit in your car for hours in a snowstorm. During storms, Caltrans broadcasts information regarding road conditions on low-frequency radio transmitters with a range of two or three miles. Eleven such transmitters are located along I-80 between Dixon and the Nevada state line, with five along US 50 between Placerville and South Lake Tahoe. Contact Caltrans, District 3, PO Box 911, Marysville, CA 95901, ☎ 916/741-4571, 800/427-ROAD, or 800/735-2929, www.dot.ca.gov/hq/roadinfo, for winter driving information.

Those who enjoy backcountry driving on gravel and dirt roads will find a hundred miles of driving pleasure between **Goose Lake** and the **Clear Lake Reservoir**, just south of the Oregon border.

Turning west off US 395 at the crossroads town of **Davis Creek**, it is possible to drive up the western side of Goose Lake, join Route 140 north of the Oregon state line, and then return to US 395 in Lakeview, Oregon.

Alternatively, one can turn west at an intersection about midway up the western shore of Goose Lake, take a left (heading south) at the next intersection and, staying to the left, return to US 395 at Alturas, passing **Big Sage Reservoir** northwest of town.

A somewhat longer backroads loop will take you to a paved highway (CA 139) northwest of **Canby**.

Other possibilities include taking a right (heading west) at an intersection near Big Sage Reservoir to reach the tiny village of **Triangle**, deep in the Modoc National Forest; taking a long loop past **Dog Lake** and **Drews Reservoir** to Route 140 in southern Oregon; and continuing westward at the various intersections just mentioned, passing **Clear Lake** and the **Clear Lake National Wildlife Refuge**, and joining CA 139 in Newell, southeast of Tulelake.

Biking

For cyclists, the **Bizz Johnson Trail** near Susanville provides an interesting, sometimes challenging ride. The trail is best suited to wide-tired bicycles, and riders should use caution when crossing the planking on the decked bridges or when going through the unlighted tunnels.

Motorized vehicles are not allowed on the trail between Susanville and the last Susan River crossing, 2.4 miles west of Goumaz.

■ On the Water

Fishing

Eagle Lake, 16 miles north of Susanville, is the second largest natural lake located wholly within California. It contains rainbow trout that average about three pounds, although the size ranges from one to 11 pounds. Spring fishing is best along the rocky shoals of the southern and western shores. Wobblers and wet flies work best.

The lake also is popular for waterskiing, windsurfing, and sailing. **Eagle Lake Marina** (☎ 916/825-3454), on the south shore of the lake, offers swimming, docks, and boat rentals. **Mariner's Resort** (☎ 916/825-3333), on the north shore of the lake, has a store, a dock, a restaurant, and a lounge. There's good fishing, and party boats are available for rent. **Spaulding Marine & Resort**, 686-955 Spaulding Rd., Eagle Lake, CA 96130, ☎ 916/825-2118, which has docks and a tackle shop, also rents boats and provides a guide service.

Antelope Lake also offers good fishing.

A rolling plateau of 20,000 acres, the **Caribou Wilderness Area** in Lassen National Forest holds more than 20 lakes, which contain brook, brown, and rainbow trout.

Elsewhere in Lassen County, there are a number of good fishing sites. **Crater Lake** contains brook trout. **Caribou, Shotoverin Lake, Dodge Reservoir,** and **Little Bailey Reservoir** contain rainbow trout. **Silver Lake** and **Homer Lake** hold both rainbow and brown trout. **Long Lake** holds both rainbow and brook trout. **Blue Lake** and **McCoy Flat** contain all three species of trout: brook, rainbow, and brown. The **Honey Lake Wildlife Area**, **Moon Lake**, and the **Pitt River** have catfish. **Mt. Meadows Reservoir** and **Straylor Reservoir** offer good bass fishing.

For those who prefer to fish in streams rather than fishing on larger bodies of water, the **Pitt River** is noted for its catfish, but also provides some good trout fishing near Bieber.

In Lassen County, **Willow Creek** offers anglers a chance to vie for brown trout. **Ash Creek, Clear Creek, Goodrich Creek,** and the **Hamilton Branch** all contain rainbow trout.

In the spring and early summer, the **Bizz Johnson Trail** near Susanville provides access to good fishing in the **Susan River**. Rainbow trout are stocked in the river between Susanville and Devils Corral, 6.5 miles west of town, on a bimonthly basis from June through July. Brown trout, speckled dace, Lahontain redside, and Tahoe sucker also can be caught there.

■ On Snow

Coppervale (☎ 916/256-3866), 13 miles west of Susanville off Route 36, has four ski runs, two lifts, one rope, and one poma. The facility is open on Tuesdays, Thursdays, weekends, and holidays.

Stover Mountain (☎ 916/258-2193), one mile southwest of Chester along Route 36, is open on weekends and holidays. It offers four runs, one rope tow, and one poma.

Snowmobiling and cross-country skiing are popular in **Lassen National Forest**, particularly in such places as:

- **Fredonyer Winter OHV Area** in the town of Fredonyer, west of Susanville. The trail goes 10 miles south of town and 17 miles north and west of town to Swain Mountain. For more information, contact Eagle Lake Ranger District, 55 S. Sacramento St., Susanville, CA 96130, ☎ 916/257-2151.

- **Morgan Summit Winter OHV Area** in the Almanor Ranger District just off US 36. Almanor Ranger District, PO Box 767, Chester, CA 96020, ☎ 916/258-2141, can provide more information.

- **Jonesville Winter OHV Area** located two miles east of the Cherry Hill Campground on Butte Meadows Road.

- **Ashpan Winter OHV Area** in the Hat Creek Ranger District just off Route 44.

- **Swain Mountain Winter OHV Area** on County Road A21 between Route 44 and Route 36. From Susanville, go west on US 36 to US 44 and take US 44 northwest to Bogard. Trails interlace the region north and west of Swain Mountain. For more information, contact Almanor Ranger District, PO Box 767, Chester, CA 96020, ☎ 916/258-2141.

The **Bizz Johnson Trail** follows the old Fernley & Lassen Branch Line of the Southern Pacific Railroad, winding 25.4 miles from Susanville to Mason Station, and then follows existing roads for an additional 4.5 miles into Westwood. Snowmobiles are allowed west of Devils Corral, 6.5 miles west of Susanville. In addition, most of the forest is open to snowmobiling and cross-country skiing.

Check with a Forest Service office if in doubt.

■ In the Air

If you're looking for a place to land, you'd better aim for **Nervino Airport & Aero Services** along Route 70 in Beckwourth, ☎ 916/832-5042.

■ Cultural Excursions

Many of the quaint little towns in this portion of Northern California have interesting, albeit small, museums that can be rewarding.

Alturas

Modoc County Historical Museum, 600 S. Main, Alturas, ☎ 916/233-6328 or 233-2944, is open Tuesday through Saturday, May to October, from 10 to 4.

Quincy

Plumas County Museum, 500 Jackson St., Quincy, is open 8-5 Monday through Friday, 10-4 on Saturdays and Sundays from May to mid-October. There is no admission fee.

Susanville

Roop's Fort & Lassen County Museum (☎ 916/257-4584), on North Weatherlow Street in Susanville, occupies a building constructed in 1854. The exhibits include a lot of old photos and Indian artifacts.

Bieber operates the **Big Valley Museum**, and Westwood also has a small museum.

A series of eight murals decorates historic uptown Susanville, and it is claimed that the 1862 **Pioneer Saloon** is the oldest continuously operated business in Northern California.

The **Susanville Visitors Center**, located in a railroad depot dating from 1913, is open from June to September. During the off-season (October through May), trail conditions are posted outside the building for the benefit of travelers and outdoorsmen.

Where to Stay

Ravendale

A bit more posh and considerably more remote is **Spanish Springs Resort** on US 395 in Ravendale, ☎ 916/234-2050, $$$. Lodgings range from deluxe log cabins to suites, duplexes, and bunkhouse rooms. Three family-style meals are served each day, including prime rib on Saturday night and a champagne brunch on Sunday. A main lodge and a rustic Western bar are on-site. During the day, guests can participate in cattle drives and horse drives, go horseback riding, go hiking, shoot skeet, or try their hand at archery during the summer, or they can go cross-country skiing, ice fishing, or sleigh riding in the winter.

Susanville

Best Western Trailside Inn, 2785 Main St., Susanville, CA 96130, ☎ 916/257-2665 or 800/528-1234, $-$$, offers a free continental breakfast and a heated pool in which to relax after a hard day's drive.

■ Camping

Reservations to camp on public lands operated either by the Forest Service or the Bureau of Land Management can be made through **Biospherics**, ☎ 800/280-2267, fax 301/722-9802.

In the Lassen National Forest, such facilities include **Almanor** on Lake Almanor, **Christie** on Eagle Lake, and **Eagle** on Eagle Lake, all three of which are accessible to the disabled.

Aspen Grove and **Merrill** are at Eagle Lake, and part of the Merrill campground stays open until the end of the fishing season, weather permitting. **West Eagle Group #1** and **West Eagle Group #2** also are at Eagle Lake. At **North Eagle Lake** off Route 139, the season runs from mid-May to the end of November. **Rocky Knoll** and **Silver Bowl** are at Silver Lake, **Bogard** is on Route 44, and both **Domingo Springs** and **High Bridge** are off Route 36.

Several Lassen facilities charge no fee for camping. These include **Butte Creek** off Route 44 and **Benner Creek**, **Warner Creek** and **Willow Springs**, all off Route 36.

There are commercial camping facilities at Eagle Lake. **Eagle Lake Marina** (☎ 916/825-3454) is on the south shore of the lake adjacent to the Forest Service campgrounds. **Eagle Lake RV Park**, 687-125 Palmetto Way, ☎ 916/825-3133, has a grocery store and laundromat, but is only open from May through October. **Mariner's Resort** (☎ 916/825-3333) is on the north shore and has a store, a restaurant, and a lounge.

Camping is allowed on BLM and Forest Service land along the oft-mention **Bizz Johnson Trail**. Seven-day camping is permitted between trailheads unless otherwise posted. No camping is allowed, however, along South Side Road in the Susan River Canyon west of Hobo Camp, and unless authorized, camping also is prohibited at or within one mile of Hobo Camp or Devils Corral.

Where to Eat

Johnstonville

The Gables (☎ 916/257-7227) on US 395 in Johnstonville only serves dinner, but you can take your pick of seafood, beef, or chicken, and wash it down with a fine wine. The restaurant is open Tuesday through Saturday, 5-9 PM.

Susanville

St. Francis Hotel (☎ 916/257-4820) in downtown Susanville serves family-style Basque meals – an adventure in their own right. Lunch is served from 11:30 to 2 and dinner from 6 to 9:30. The restaurant is closed on Sundays. This is no place to "eat on the run"; plan to relax and enjoy yourself.

Information Sources

Bureau of Land Management, 705 Hall St., Susanville, CA 96130, ☎ 916/257-5381.

Lassen National Forest, 55 S. Sacramento St., Susanville, CA 96130, ☎ 916/257-2151, and the ranger district offices in Chester, ☎ 916/256-2141; Eagle Lake, ☎ 916/257-4188; and Fall River Mills, ☎ 916/336-5521.

Modoc National Forest, 800 W. 12th St., Alturas, CA 96101, ☎ 916/233-5811, and the ranger district offices in Adin, ☎ 916/299-3215; Tulelake, ☎ 916/667-2246; and Cedarville, ☎ 916/279-6116.

Plumas National Forest, 159 Lawrence St., PO Box 11500, Quincy, CA 95971, ☎ 916/283-2050, and the ranger district offices in Blairsden, ☎ 916/836-2575, and Quincy, ☎ 916/283-0555.

Oregon

Until the middle 1800s, none of the world's great nations seemed particularly interested in the region known today as Oregon.

Certainly, various explorers had made early visits. Each, it seemed, represented a different nation. Spanish and English sailors visited the region as early as the 1500s and 1600s. The Russians made their way as far south as Fort Ross, midway down the California coast. And Capt. James Cook charted some of the local coastline in 1778.

Sir Francis Drake, who sailed past Northern California and southern Oregon in 1579, called the place "New Albion." A.B. Rogers, a British major, was the first to use the name Oregon, which he spelled "Ouragon."

But little was really known about the territory when the United States acquired it from France as a part of the Louisiana Purchase. As a result, the Lewis and Clark Expedition was sent to check things out; they ultimately reached the mouth of the Columbia River in 1805. A few adventurers, principally the so-called "mountain men," then came along to explore the interior of the territory. Companies like the Hudson's Bay Co. (British) and John Jacob Astor's Pacific Fur Co. (American) established outposts to buy furs and market them throughout the world.

In 1819, the southern boundary of Oregon was set at 42° north by means of a treaty with Spain, but the United States and Britain contested the northern boundary for the next quarter of a century, until the border was finally set at the 49th parallel in 1844. The Oregon Territory, which encompassed not only Oregon but Washington, Idaho, and parts of Montana and Wyoming, was created by an act of Congress on 14 August 1848. The Washington Territory was spun off in 1853, and 10 years later, the Idaho Territory was created. Oregon was admitted to the Union on 14 February 1859, becoming the United States' 33rd state.

Having established its political control over the Pacific Northwest, the United States still had to establish its jurisdiction over another intransigent group of people – the Native Americans who inhabited the area. These people were unwilling to share their land amicably.

At one time, between 100,000 and 180,000 Indians lived in the region, organized into some 125 separate tribes. The first of those tribes to require the attention of the military was the Rogue Indians, against whom Maj. Philip Kerney first directed his troops in 1851. It would be five years before the last battle with the Rogues was fought, at Oak Flat on the Illinois River.

In 1872, the Modocs, led by Captain Jack, waged war against the government that had demanded that they leave their ancestral homeland and live among their enemies, the Klamath. Although the Modoc War lasted only a year, it was both bloody and expensive. Captain Jack ultimately was captured and hanged; his people were relocated to a reservation in Kansas. In 1877, 700 Nez Perce warriors led by In-Mut-Too-Yah-Lat (Chief Joseph) entered into battle with the United States. Although this too was a relatively brief conflict, the war was nonetheless wide-ranging, and ended with Chief Joseph's now-famous pronouncement: "From where the Sun now stands, I will fight no more forever."

Coastal Oregon

Our tenth largest state, Oregon enjoys a 296-mile coastline along the Pacific Ocean. Generally speaking, the coast is wilder and more rugged than most of that found in California, but it is ideally suited to the state's robust fishing industry, which is one of the world's largest.

Even larger is Oregon's timber industry, which supplies a fifth of the nation's softwood lumber, a quarter of its hard-board, and half of its plywood. Lumber and wood products produce $3.3 billion a year for the Oregon economy. Paper and allied manufacturing produces an additional $859 million a year.

Getting Around

Clinging to the water as it does throughout Northern California, US 101 (once known as the Roosevelt Highway) defines the Oregon coastline from north to south.

East-west links with the inland cities are shorter and occur more frequently than those in Northern California. From Bandon, OR 42 leads inland through Coquille and Myrtle Point to Roseburg.

At Reedsport, OR 38 provides another link with the east, connecting with Interstate 5 about midway between Roseburg and Eugene. From Florence, OR 126 provides a more direct route to Eugene, while in Waldport, motorists can take OR 34 northeastward to Corvallis. A more direct route to Corvallis from the coast is US 220, which intersects with US 101 in Newport.

Just north of Lincoln City, OR 18 heads east to McMinnville. Motorists can branch off OR 18 onto OR 22 near Willamina and head southeast into Salem. At Tillamook, OR 6 strikes inland toward the northeast and into the western suburbs of Portland. North of Cannon Beach, US 26 angles southeast into those same suburbs; and from Astoria, US 30 travels the southern shore of the Columbia River toward Kelso and Longview, Washington before turning south and into Portland.

 As you drive throughout Oregon, beware of the shoulders of the roads. All too often, the roadside drop-offs are abrupt, sharp and deep, and they can destroy your tires or even cause your car to roll over if you encounter them at high speed.

There are no self-serve gas stations in Oregon. As recently as 1997, the voters vetoed an amendment to the law that would have permitted self-service pumps.

Oregon Passenger Services is a large map that outlines the Greyhound, Trailways, and Amtrak routes throughout Oregon, as well as the other modes of public transportation. The State Department of Transportation, Transportation Building, Salem, OR 97310, ☎ 503/378-3432, offers the map free of charge.

Another useful publication is *Northwest Travel* magazine, 1525 12th St., PO Box 18000, Florence, OR 97439, ☎ 541/997-8401 or 800/348-8401.

Touring

Astoria

Astoria, the oldest American settlement west of the Rockies, was founded by John Jacob Astor in 1811, thereby creating the first American trading post in the Pacific Northwest. The War of 1812 encouraged Astor to sell his Pacific Fur Co. to the British North West Co., and the name of Astoria was changed to Fort George. In 1824, when Russia renounced all claim to the area, the British built Fort Vancouver on the opposite side of the Columbia River and moved the company's headquarters there.

Brookings

Brookings is the gateway to Oregon's "Banana Belt," a region with unexpectedly pleasant year-round weather.

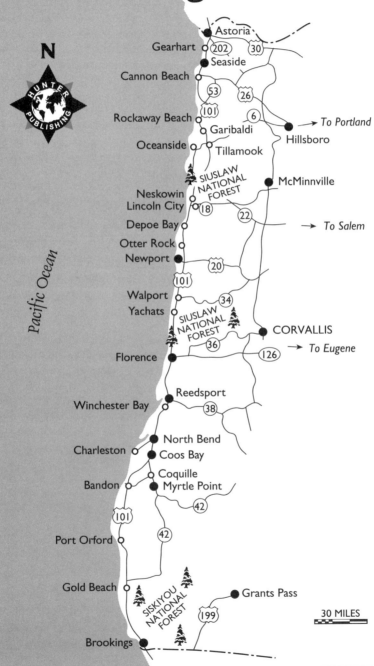

Depoe Bay

The name of Depoe Bay has an interesting history. In 1894, the US government allotted 200 acres to a Siletz Indian named Charles Depot (so called because he worked for a nearby US Army depot). In 1927, a modern townsite was planned and named for Charles, whose family had subsequently adopted DePoe as a fancier way to spell the family name. The present spelling has been in use since 1928, when a post office was established in the town.

Depoe Bay is noted for the gargantuan spouts of sea water that occur along the nearby coast.

Garibaldi

Garibaldi hosts annual crab races each February.

Gold Beach

The community of Gold Beach is said to be located on a huge gold deposit, 40 miles long, 10-20 miles wide, and 6-100 feet deep. "Beach mining" has continued here since 1852, when the McNameara brothers found gold in the beach sands and generated national attention.

Hiouchi

Hiouchi, a region popular with hunters and fishermen, is surrounded by the 300,000-acre Smith River National Recreation Area, formed in 1990.

Klamath

The town of Klamath was destroyed by a flood in December 1964, but has been reborn as a popular place to go camping or touring on a jet boat.

Lincoln City

Lincoln City has a 7.5-mile long beach, and each year 18,500 gray whales pass by there during their annual migration. The world's shortest river, the 400-foot Devil's River, also can be found there.

Newport

Newport, with its colorful Yaquina Bay bridge, has a haunted lighthouse. The ghost, named Muriel, is said to have mysteriously vanished from the Yaquina Bay Lighthouse while awaiting the return of her father, a sea captain.

Oregon coast near Lincoln City (Oregon Tourism Commission).

Port Orford

Port Orford, just 70 miles north of the California border, is the most westerly incorporated city in the US.

Reedsport

In Reedsport, the local radio station (99.5 FM) uses the call letters CRAB. The Antarctic research vessel *Hero* is stationed on the Reedsport waterfront.

Seaside

At Seaside, the end of the Lewis and Clark Trail is known as the "Seaside Turnaround." There is a two-mile promenade beach walk, and the town hosts the annual Miss Oregon Pageant.

Yachats

Yachats (*Yah-hots*) is from the Chinook Indian word *yahuts*, meaning "dark waters at the foot of the mountain." The tiny (pop. 560) community has some of the most dramatic surf action in the world during the winter storms of December, January, and February.

Adventures

As one moves farther north, the Pacific coastline becomes increasingly rugged. Soft, sandy beaches become scarcer, and the water temperature drops markedly, reducing the appeal of many water sports.

Residents of Oregon are notoriously fond of the outdoors, however, and the state offers an opportunity to engage in virtually any form of recreation that your heart desires. If the beachfront becomes too blustery, one simply moves farther inland.

The greatest diversity may be found in the center of the state, where the benefits of a "four-season" climate are most evident. There, spring, summer, fall, and winter sports can all receive their full measure of attention.

In addition to its climatic diversity, Oregon's geological diversity influences the various recreational opportunities that are available. Where the west provides access to the ocean and the center provides access to the forests and the mountains, the east is flatter and more arid – a marvelous place to go horseback riding and camping.

■ On Foot

Beachcombing & Rockhounding

Given the length of the Oregon coastline, it is no surprise that beachcombing is a very popular pastime. Beachcombing usually is best after an exciting winter storm.

Seven Devils Wayside and **Whiskey Run**, eight miles south of Charleston on Seven Devils Road, are good places to find agates, including flower jasper and agitated myrtle.

Cape Arago State Park and **Sunset Bay State Park,** near Coos Bay, are also good places to try your hand at rockhounding.

In **Lincoln City**, beachcombing for agates is popular in four places: along the Pacific Ocean north and south of the entrance to Siletz Bay, between 32nd and 35th Streets, off 15th Street, and north of Road's End State Beach.

Agate Beach, off Ocean View Drive north of Newport and south of the junction with US 101, is another good spot to go beachcombing for agates, as is the beach in **Port Orford**, also noted for the fossils often found there.

The **Yachats** area also provides good rockhounding.

A WORD TO THE WISE

Most agates are found in the winter or early spring. Do your collecting on an outgoing tide while the sand is still damp and the shiny agates will stand out more prominently. If the sand is dry, however, you can improve your luck by walking toward the sun as you search for treasures.

Wildlife Viewing

With 820,000 acres of state forests and 240 state parks, the opportunity to view wildlife is exceptional in Oregon.

There is a wildlife viewing deck in **Fort Stevens State Park** (☎ 503/861-1671), 10 miles west of Astoria off US 101.

The area around the **Coquille River Lighthouse** near Bandon is also noted for wildlife viewing, and there are two national wildlife refuges within the Bandon city limits: **Oregon Islands** and **Bandon Marsh**.

Around **Cannon Beach**, look for tufted puffins, and at **Cape Arago State Park** near Charleston, watch the whales, seals, and sea lions, as well as the birdlife. Cape Arago is a popular place to go hiking, tidepooling, and storm-watching also.

Good birdwatching can be enjoyed in **Port Orford**, where tufted puffins, porpoises, Steller's sea lions, and harbor seals are commonly seen on the offshore rocks. The area is referred to as the "Thousand Island Coast."

 The **Oregon Department of Fish & Wildlife**, PO Box 59, Portland, OR 97207, ☎ 503/229-5403, 229-5410, or 800/233-3306, has produced a free *Visitor's Guide to Oregon's Fish Hatcheries and Wildlife Management Areas*, a 68-page, pocket-sized booklet that contains maps, directions, offices to contact, and guidelines on what to see and do throughout the state. The department has regional offices in Corvallis, Roseburg, Bend, LaGrande, Hines, Newport, and Clackamas.

Also extremely helpful is *National Wildlife Refuges: A Visitor's Guide*, a free brochure/map provided by the US Fish & Wildlife Service, Department of the Interior. Another free pocket-sized brochure, *America's Elk Country*, is available from the USDA Forest Service.

A very useful booklet containing maps, listings of suppliers and guides, and other helpful references is published by **Oregon Outdoors Association**, PO Box 10841, Eugene, OR 97440, ☎ 503/683-9552 or 800/747-9552, fax 503/683-9517.

Animal lovers will enjoy a visit to **West Coast Game Park Safari**, Rt. 1, Box 1330, Bandon, OR 97411, ☎ 541/347-3106, located seven miles south of town on US 101. Over 450 animals and birds are exhibited in the park, which calls itself "America's largest wild animal petting experience."

Tidepooling, another way to examine wildlife close up, can be explored in Charleston's **Sunset Bay State Park** and **Cape Arago State Park**. For pointers on where to go and what you'll see, contact the **Oregon Institute of Marine Biology** at 4619 Boat Basin Dr. in Charleston, 97420, ☎ 541/888-2581.

Hiking Trails

Fort Stevens State Park, 10 miles west of Astoria, has a hiking/nature trail that makes a loop three-quarters of a mile long. Located where the Columbia River reaches the Pacific Ocean, the park contains two small lakes: Coffenbury Lake and Swash Lake. An interesting museum is on the park grounds. The wreck of the *Peter Iredale* can be seen on the beach.

In Astoria, **Shively Park** has some pleasant paved, forested trails, including one that connects **Astoria Column** with **Cathedral Tree**, a magnificent giant spruce.

Around Astoria, Clatsop County affords a number of hiking trails, such as **Oregon Coast Trail**, **Cape Falcon Trail**, **Neahkahnie Mountain Trail**, and a number of trails within both **Saddle Mountain State Park** and **David Douglas Park**.

A free program is conducted every Saturday afternoon during the storm-watching season (January through April) in **Bullard's Beach State Park,** just north of Bandon. Bandon also conducts tours of the local cranberry bogs (contact the Bandon Chamber of Commerce, PO Box 1515, Bandon, OR 97411, ☎ 503/347-9616, for details).

Loeb State Park, near Brookings, and **Harris Beach State Park**, just north of Brookings, offer some excellent hiking possibilities. The Brookings-Harbor Chamber of Commerce, 16330 Lower Harbor Rd., PO Box 940, Brookings, OR 97415, ☎ 541/469-3181 or 800/535-9469, fax

541/469-4094, can provide a free hand-out, *The Oregon Coast Trail in Curry County*, that includes an annotated map.

The Brookings Chamber also offers a free pocket-sized brochure called *Self-Guided Forest Ecology Tour* that directs you along the Chetco River and up the Bomb Site Trail (five miles paved and 13 miles on gravel). "Bomb Site" refers to the first US mainland site ever bombed by enemy aircraft. Japan's strategy on 9 September 1942 was to dispatch a plane, assembled and launched from atop a submarine, to drop an incendiary bomb. The bomb was to start a forest fire and thereby divert American resources from the war, at that time less than one year old. Wet conditions foiled the attempt, but two weeks later, three more incendiary bombs were dropped near Port Orford. They also failed to ignite.

> *Trail Opportunities on the Chetco Ranger District of the Siskiyou National Forest* details over 84 miles of trails in the area. The free brochure is stocked by many area chambers of commerce or can be obtained from the US Forest Service, Chetco Ranger District, 555 Fifth St., Brookings, OR 97415, ☎ 541/469-2196.

The hike over **Tillamook Head** traverses a cape between Tillamook and Cannon Beach, and passes through **Ecola State Park** (☎ 503/436-2844), which is just two miles north of Cannon Beach off US 101. Near the midway mark, there is a primitive hikers' camp and there are the remnants of a World War II radar base and bunkers. The one-day hike, which covers six miles each way, is navigable throughout the year.

Tillamook Rock, a 100-foot basalt sea stack, sits a mile offshore, and **Tillamook Rock Lighthouse** is now used as a columbarium (a place to store urns containing the ashes of the deceased).

Cape Meares State Park is just west of Tillamook, and the 1890 **Cape Meares Lighthouse** is no longer in use, but the unusual "Octopus" tree is nearby and worth a quick look.

The Tillamook area is a mecca for nearly every sort of outdoor activity. Hiking, beachcombing, birdwatching, hunting, camping, and biking are all popular there. **Cape Lookout State Park** is southwest of town, and **Munson Creek Falls**, the highest falls in the Oregon Coast Range (266 feet), is just seven miles south of town.

Oswald West State Park, which offers beach access and some wonderful hiking, is 11 miles south of Cannon Beach. The beach is known for a phenomenon known as "the singing sands," and is the venue for an annual spring contest for sandcastle builders.

In Charleston, **South Slough National Estuarine Reserve** (☎ 541/888-5558), on Seven Devils Road, has nature trails and is a marvelous spot for both canoeing and photography.

The trail in **Sunset Bay State Park**, just southwest of Cape Arago near Coos Bay, offers good views of the **Cape Arago Lighthouse**. Coos Bay's **Shore Acres State Park**, **Bastendorff Beach County Park**, and **South Jetty** are great places to do some storm-watching in the winter.

The Florence area has miles of ocean shoreline, and hiking trails that will lead you by lakes, streams, and waterfalls. **Cape Perpetua** (☎ 541/547-3289) is just 24 miles north of town; **Carl G. Washburne State Park** (☎ 541/547-3416), 14 miles north of town; and **Devils Elbow**, 12 miles north of town. **Jessie M. Honeyman State Park** (☎ 541/997-3641) is just south of town at 84505 US 101 South.

Humbug Mountain Trail, near Gold Beach, is a six-mile hike. The trail rises from the ocean to an elevation of 1,700 feet and provides magnificent views. The **Shrader Old Growth Trail** and the **Lower Rogue River Trail** are nearby.

Just north of Port Orford is **Cape Blanco State Park**. Off Cape Blanco, diving boats can be seen, their crews gathering sea urchins for the Japanese market.

There is an easy trail from Cape Blanco to Point Orford that affords panoramic views of the coastline. From Oregon Street (US 101), go west on 9th Street. The trailhead is on Coast Guard Road, two blocks to the left.

Devil's Lake State Park is just south of Lincoln City.

South Beach State Park (☎ 503/867-7451) and **Yaquina Bay State Park**, both popular for beachcombing, kite flying, and sandcastle building, are south of Newport, while **Beverly Beach State Park** is north of town.

Newport's **Mike Miller Park** winds through one of the few Sitka spruce forests in the world.

William M. Tugman State Park, south of Reedsport, is a nice place to hike.

In **Seaside**, the Chamber of Commerce, 7 N. Roosevelt St., PO Box 7, Seaside, OR 97138-0007, ☎ 503/738-6391 or 800/444-6740, fax 503/738-5732, E-mail seaside@aone.com, has prepared a brochure that describes several self-guided hikes.

Saddle Mountain Trail, a one-day hike that ascends the highest peak in the northern Coast Range, is open from March to December.

Oswald West State Park contains 15 miles of hiking trails through coastal rain forest, along the beach, and up some steep headlands. **Cape Falcon Trail** is a one-way, two-mile hike through an old-growth spruce forest where there are trees up to 12 feet in diameter.

Neahkahnie Mountain Trail, 2.6 miles south of Oswald State Park, provides good views of the coast and of the winter gray whale migration. Wildflowers line the pathway in late spring.

Seaside conducts regular "Volkswalks" along the beach during the spring, summer, and fall.

Warrenton Trail skirts a Columbia River estuary from Warrenton along old railroad beds, dikes, and roadways.

In Winchester Bay, a popular place to hike is the **Windy Cove Park,** along Salmon Harbor Drive.

In **Cape Perpetua**, a 2,700-acre scenic area three miles south of Yachats, hikers will encounter volcanic rock, wildlife, tidepools, and an ancient rain forest within two miles of the Visitors Center.

If straight hiking is too tame and you're into more strenuous forms of outdoor recreation, **AdventureSmith Guides**, PO Box 2241, Lake Oswego, OR 97035, ☎ 503/293-6727, can give you rock climbing lessons and take you on guided climbs.

■ On Horseback

Astoria (**Iverson Farms**), Cannon Beach (**Sea Ranch Stables**), Gearhart (**Gearhart Stables**), Seaside (**Faraway Farms**), and Warrenton (**Jim's Westlake Stables**), all in Clatsop County, are places to go when you wish to do a little horseback riding.

C&M Stables, 90241 Hwy 101 North, Florence, OR 97439, ☎ 503/997-7540, also rents horses, as does **Neskowin Riding Stables**, north of State Park in Neskowin, ☎ 541/392-3277.

Indian Creek Trail Rides, 94680 Jerry's Flat Rd., PO Box 194, Gold Beach, OR 97444, ☎ 541/247-7704, provides one-hour, two-hour, and lunch rides daily, from May to September.

Hawk's Rest Ranch Stables & Trail Rides, Box 6048, Pistol River, OR 97444, ☎ 541-247-6423, offers 1.5-hour ranch, beach, and sunset rides from 8 AM to 7 PM daily.

📖 Ranger stations in Waldport and Alsea can provide trail maps for horseback riders, and the Forest Service can furnish a free digest-sized brochure, *Horse Sense: Packing Lightly in Your National Forests*, that is very helpful for anyone planning a pack trip.

Rodeos? You bet! The **Tillamook County Rodeo** is held each June. In July, the **Curry County Fair**, 29392 Ellensburg Ave., Gold Beach, OR 97444, ☎ 541/247-4541, fax 541/247-4542, and the **Lincoln County Fair**, 633 NE 3rd St., PO Box 437, Newport, OR 97365, ☎ 541/265-6237, fax 541/574-9183, both have rodeos.

■ On Wheels

Driving Tours

The Oregon coast is dotted with colorful and historic lighthouses, which make excellent viewpoints for watching the whale migrations and the late fall, winter, and early spring storms – or simply a place to stroll and admire the beauty of the coastline almost any time of year.

A delightful weekend can be spent driving along the coast, looking at the lighthouses – perhaps touring a few – and taking some unforgettable pictures to put in "the memory book."

📖 A free brochure, *Oregon Coast Lighthouses*, is available from the Oregon Parks and Recreation Department, 1115 Commercial St. NE, Salem, OR 97310-1001, ☎ 800/452-5687. It describes the many Oregon coastal lighthouses.

Warrior Rock Lighthouse, at the northern tip of Sauvie Island, 64 miles upstream in the Columbia River, was built in 1888 and is still active. A runaway barge rammed the light in 1969.

Cape Blanco Lighthouse (1870) is still active in spite of the fact that it is the oldest, highest, and westernmost lighthouse in the "lower 48" states. The 59-foot tower, ☎ 503/332-6774, sits 245 feet above the ocean, and is open to visitors Thursdays through Mondays from April to the end of September. Located in a magnificent wildlife-viewing area, the lighthouse can be reached from the town of Sixes by turning west on Cape Blanco Road (clearly marked) and driving for five miles.

The **Cape Arago Light** (1866), still active, is located 100 feet above the ocean off Gregory Point, on an island three miles west of Charleston.

The 44-foot tower has a unique foghorn. Although closed to the public, the light can be seen from a trail in Sunset Beach State Park.

Umpqua River Light is the oldest (1857) lighthouse in Oregon still on active service. At Winchester Bay, near Umpqua Lighthouse State Park, ☎ 503/271-4631, the 65-foot tower overlooks the sand dunes near Reedsport from an elevation of 165 feet. The light and a museum are open for tours between 9 and 11:30 AM and between 1 and 3:30 PM Wednesday through Saturday, and between 1 and 4:30 PM on Sundays from May 1 to September 30. (NOTE: These times are subject to change). The facilities are closed on Mondays and Tuesdays.

Heceta Head Lighthouse (Michael Chafran, CVALCO).

Also still active is **Cleft of the Rock Lighthouse**, which is privately owned and operated by a retired Coast Guardsman who once was the keeper on Tillamook Rock. Located a mile south of Yachats, the light is not open to the public.

Desdimona Sands, active from 1902 until the late 1940s, marked a sandbar in the middle of the Columbia River adjacent to the town of Astoria. It once was almost destroyed by fire.

One stormy night, the **Coquille River Light** was nearly rammed by a ship. Active from 1896 to 1939, the light can be accessed from Bullards Beach State Park, two miles north of Bandon, on the north bank of the Coquille River, and is open to visitors year-around during daylight hours. Tours to the tower watch room can be arranged on request, ☎ 503/347-2209.

Heceta Head Light was built in 1894 and is still active. The light is on the west side of 1,000-foot Heceta Head, 205 feet above the ocean, and is an easy hike from the parking lot at Devil's Elbow State Park, 12 miles north of Florence. The light has a 56-foot tower, and its beacon can be seen 21 miles from land – the strongest light on the Oregon coast. The light is open for tours from noon to 5 daily, May through September. The keeper's house is said to be haunted. The assistant keeper's house (Heceta House, ☎ 503/563-3211) is open on the third weekend of each month during the summer. Off-season tours of the lighthouse can be arranged by calling Jessie Honeyman State Park, ☎ 503/997-3641.

Also said to be haunted is **Old Yaquina Bay Lighthouse**, 846 SW Government St., Newport, OR 97365, ☎ 503/265-5679 (the north end of the bridge across Newport Bay). Newport's oldest building, the lighthouse was used for only three years, from 1871 to 1874. Its 40-foot tower rises from a Cape Cod-style house in Yaquina Bay State Park on US 101, and is one of the few lighthouses on the Pacific Coast built with the lightkeeper's living quarters in the same building as the tower. The place is open as a museum from 11 AM to 5 PM daily, May through September, and on weekends from noon to 4 the remainder of the year.

The **Yaquina Head Light** (1873) is located on 100 acres just off US 101, three miles north of Newport. Its 93-foot tower, which stands 162 feet above sea level, is the tallest on the Oregon coast. The Yaquina Head Outstanding Natural Area, in which the lighthouse is located, provides close-up views of seabird nesting areas in the **Colony Rock** seabird rookery from an observation deck equipped with a telescope. Guided morning tours to the tower's watch room are offered daily from mid-June to mid-September and the lower portion of the light (☎ 503/265-2863) is open daily from noon to 4. The park is open daily until dusk, and trails to the **Quarry Cove** tidepools are accessible year-around.

Take care near the ocean. Large waves can sweep you off the rocks or the beach, especially when there is an incoming tide.

Cape Meares Lighthouse (1890-1985) can be found nine miles west of Tillamook, in Cape Meares State Park. Sitting 217 feet above the ocean, the 38-foot tower is the shortest on the Oregon coast. Trails lead from the main parking area to the lighthouse and to viewpoints overlooking a number of offshore islets that are inhabited by Steller's sea lions and nesting seabirds. The light is open to the public from 11 to 4 daily, May through September, and on weekends during October, March, and April. Tours can be arranged by appointment year-around, ☎ 503/842-4981.

Tillamook Rock Lighthouse (mentioned above) stands 1.2 miles out to sea on a basaltic islet off Tillamook Head between Cannon Beach and Seaside. Rising 133 feet above sea level, the 62-foot tower is known as "Terrible Tilly" because of its exposure to severe storm waves. There is no public access to the light, and the closest views available are from the Oregon Coast Trail between Ecola State Park and Seaside on Tillamook Head.

Other nice drives on the Oregon coast include the **Three Capes Scenic Loop** north of Pacific City, and the drive east from Port Orford on Elk River Road, which passes the salmon hatchery and offers some extremely scenic views of the **Elk River Canyon**.

Biking

The best bicycling in Coastal Oregon usually occurs from late August to early October.

> A free *Oregon Bicycling Guide* classifies Oregon's 7,600 miles of roads into four levels of suitability for cycling. That brochure and a free map, *Oregon Coast Bike Routes*, are available through the Oregon Department of Transportation. ☎ 503/378-4880.
>
> The Oregon Parks and Recreation Department, 525 Trade St. SE, Salem, OR 97310, ☎ 800/551-6949, offers a free booklet entitled *Cycle Sense in Oregon State Parks* that also is very useful.
>
> The Coos Bay Chamber of Commerce has prepared a free brochure describing 15 county bike trails, and there are a number of excellent sites for biking in Clatsop County, including **Fort Stevens State Park**, the southern part of **US 101**, **Young River Falls Loop**, **Walluski Loop**, **Seaside**, and **Cannon Beach**.

Bicycles are available for rent in Fort Stevens State Park, Seaside, and Cannon Beach. **Seaside Surrey Rentals**, 80 Ave. A, Seaside, OR 97138, ☎ 503/738-0242, also rents bicycles, pedal surreys, and roller blades.

Off-Road Driving

With the ocean close at hand, driving a dune buggy or a motorcycle among the coastal sand dunes is an extremely popular pastime in this part of the country.

> The US Forest Service, Siuslaw National Forest, 31525 Hwy 22, Hebo, OR 97122, ☎ 541/392-3161, offers a free *Off-Highway Vehicle Guide to Oregon Dunes National Recreation Area and Sand Lake* that can be extremely helpful. They also have two other free pocket-sized brochures that are useful: *Off-Highway Vehicle Recreation Opportunities in the Pacific Northwest* and *Getting Around on National Forest Roads*.

If questions still remain, contact the **Oregon OHV Association**, 34074 E. Peuebles Rd., Eugene, OR 97405, ☎ 541/747-5653, or the **Oregon Dunes National Recreation Area**, 855 Highway Ave., Reedsport, OR 97467, ☎ 541/271-3611.

Siuslaw National Forest has set aside four areas for OHV use, three in the **Oregon Dunes National Recreation Area** and one in the **Sand Lake Recreation Area**.

Rentals

- **Far West Rentals** (☎ 541/756-3491 or 756-2322), on US 101 five miles north of Coos Bay, rents four-wheel dune buggies and is open seven days a week.
- **Sandland Adventures**, 85366 Hwy 101 South, Florence, OR 97439, ☎ 541/997-8087, rents dune buggies and conducts tours on the dunes. **Buggy Express Rentals** (☎ 541/997-5363), four miles south of town on US 101, also rents dune buggies.
- **Far West 4-Wheel Rental**, 320 Sandy Way, Hauser, ☎ 541/756-3491 or 756-2322, is another place to rent dune buggies.
- **Pacific Coast Recreation**, 4121 Coast Hwy 101, North Bend, OR 97459, ☎ 503/756-7183, which is open from 9 AM to 6 PM daily, rents four-wheel ATVs and conducts sand dune tours.
- **Spinreel Dune Buggy Rentals**, 9122 Wildwood Dr., North Bend, OR 97459, ☎ 503/759-3313, is open seven days a week from 9 AM to sunset.

Every Labor Day weekend, Port Orford hosts the **Cape Blanco Grand Prix Sports Car Races**. The time trials are held on Saturday and the races on Sunday and Monday.

Rail Tours

Oregon Coastline Express, 4000 Hangar Rd., Tillamook, OR 97141, ☎ 503/842-2768 or 842-9344, provides two unusual railway excursions. The **Caboose Run** (*Lil' Toot Toot*) is a two-hour, 6.5-mile round trip from Tillamook to some blimp hangars in the area. The trip, which includes a tour of the hangars, leaves Tillamook daily at 10:30 AM and 1:30 PM. The **Rock Coast Route** is a four-hour, 44-mile round trip from Tillamook to Wheeler. It is offered from Sunday through Friday at 8 AM and 1 PM, and on Saturday at 10 AM and 5:30 PM.

■ On the Water

Clam-Digging, Crabbing & Fishing from Shore

Outdoor adventures often have an outstanding side-benefit: you can *eat* the birds or game that you shoot, the fish and crabs that you catch, or the clams that you dig from the ocean bottom.

Along the Oregon coast, clam-digging is a particularly popular pastime for both residents and visitors alike. The digging is always best at low or minus tides.

Free brochures that tell about digging for both softshell and littleneck clams can be obtained at the Charleston Visitor's Center, Boat Basin Drive, and Cape Arago Highway at the west end of the Charleston/South Slough Bridge, PO Box 5735, Charleston, OR 97420, ☎ 541/888-2311. The center is open daily from May through September and on weekends year-around.

Clamming is particularly popular near Bandon, Bay City, Tillamook, and Yachats.

Clams sometimes can be hazardous for human consumption when toxins are absorbed from periodic blooms of photoplankton. Check with the Oregon Department of Fish & Wildlife (☎ 503/325-2462) to inquire about the edibility of saltwater species and ☎ 503/338-0106 to ask about freshwater species.

Unlike clam-digging, where it is necessary to get out in the water and muck about in the mud, crabbing can be done from dry land, generally from a dock, a pier, or a jetty.

Crabs are found in the deeper channels of a bay and are most abundant on the slack tide of either incoming or outgoing tides. The best season is from October through February. Dungeness crab is particularly large and succulent in December.

Each crabber is allowed to keep 12 male crabs per day, but the crabs must measure at least 5.75 inches across the shell (*not* the wide span between the claws). No license is required for crabbing.

A WORD TO THE WISE

To cook the crabs, boil eight quarts of water in a large pot in which you have dissolved half a cup of salt. Put three live crabs in the boiling water, which will kill them instantly. Boil the crabs for 15-20 minutes and then immerse them in a pot of cold water to cause the crab meat to separate from the shell.

Tips on crabbing, like tips on clam-digging, are available in the form of free brochures at the Charleston Visitor's Center.

Crabbing is particularly good at Bandon, Bay City, Charleston, Depoe Bay, Fort Stevens State Park, Garibaldi, Hammond, Newport, off the dock in Port Orford, off the dock in Reedsport, in Seaside, in Tillamook, off Waldport's Port of Alsea docks on Port Street (☎ 503/563-3872), in Nehalem Bay in Wheeler, and off the dock in Winchester Bay.

Clamming and crabbing demonstrations are presented by the **Alsea Bay Bridge Interpretive Center**, 620 NW Spring St. (US 101), PO Box 693, Waldport, OR 97394-0693, ☎ 503/563-2002 (call for times). The center also conducts walks on the historic Alsea Bay Bridge at 2 PM daily from July 4 through Labor Day.

Crab rings can be rented on the dock at **Bay Marina** (☎ 503/563-2003) in Waldport.

Fishing off the beaches and jetties can produce rockfish, perch, flounder, and salmon – but be careful of incoming tides and large waves.

Bottom-fishing also can produce ling cod, sea bass, snapper, sole, cabezon, and halibut (in season). A special license is required for sturgeon fishing.

Good locations for saltwater fishing include Bandon, Charleston, Rockaway Beach, and Tillamook. Port Orford and Reedsport are noted for their surf fishing. Fishing is often excellent off the docks at **Port of Alsea** (☎ 503/563-3872), on Port Street in Old Town Waldport, and in **Carnahan Park**, eight miles north of Seaside off US 101.

The people of Yachats enjoy netting silver smelt *right off the beach*. The smelt spawn in the sandy coves near town between April and October, and the sport culminates with a huge community Smelt Fry each year.

Meanwhile, in Depoe Bay, people enjoy their annual September Salmon Bake. Freshly caught salmon are cooked over open fires in the time-honored Indian manner.

Offshore Fishing

If fishing from shore is too tame, boats can be chartered to take you fishing in the offshore waters.

Astoria Cruise & Charters (☎ 503/325-0990) in Astoria, the West Mooring Basin in Astoria, and the mooring basins in Hammond and in Warrenton all have places to charter a fishing boat.

Tiki Charters, 325 Industry, Astoria, OR 97103, ☎ 503/325-7818, charters fishing trips and also arranges ecotours and river cruises.

In Charleston, **Charleston Marina**, 4535 Kingfisher Dr., 97420, ☎ 541/888-2548; **Betty Kay Charters**, Charleston Boat Basin, PO Box 5020, ☎ 541/888-9021 or 800/752-6303; and **Bob's Sport Fishing**, Charleston Boat Basin, PO Box 5018, ☎ 541/888-4241 or 800/628-9633, all provide charters.

At the north end of the bridge on US 101 in downtown Depoe Bay, **Tradewinds**, PO Box 123, Depoe Bay, OR 97341, ☎ 541/765-2345 or 800/445-8730, can provide whale-watching and scenic cruise charters as well as fishing charters for halibut and salmon fishing.

Dockside Charters, on Bay Street at the Depoe Bay harbor, PO Box 1308, Depoe Bay, OR 97341, ☎ 503/765-2545 or 800/733-8915, Web site www.newportnet.com/dockside/htm, accepts charters to troll for salmon or to go bottom fishing. On whale-watching cruises, the firm *guarantees* that whales will be sighted.

Garibaldi/D&D Charters, 7th Street and US 101, PO Box 556, Garibaldi, OR 97118, ☎ 503/322-0007, 322-0381, or 800/900-4665, fax 503/322-2495, takes fishing charters, nature excursions, and whale-watching, birding, photography, and diving cruises.

In Hammond, charters can be arranged through **Corkey's Charter Fishing**, ☎ 503/861-2668; **Columbia Pacific Charter**, ☎ 503/861-1527 (May through October) or 861-3303 (November through April); and **Tiki Charters**, ☎ 503/861-1201.

Windsurfing off Warrenton (Astoria-Warrenton CC).

Sea Gull Charters, 343 SW Bay Blvd., Newport, OR 97365, ☎ 503/265-7441, schedules fishing, whale-watching, and scenic excursions.

Warrenton Deep Sea Fishing, ☎ 503/861-1233, and **Charlton Deep Sea Charters**, ☎ 503/861-2429, both in Warrenton, also book fishing charters.

Freshwater Fishing

One of the more interesting and pleasant aspects of the Oregon coast is its flexibility. If you would prefer freshwater fishing to saltwater fishing, you simply head east instead of west.

Florence, for example, has 26 freshwater lakes and two rivers nearby.

Tahkenitch (meaning "many arms") **Fishing Village**, 80135 Hwy 101, Gardiner, OR 97441, ☎ 541/271-5222, about halfway between Florence and Reedsport, offers 1,500 acres of freshwater fishing and boating, plus 100 miles of ocean shoreline. Guests can go hiking in the sand dunes and on nature trails, observe wildlife, fish from a dock, and rent a motor boat, paddle boat, or canoe. Rainbow trout, cutthroat trout, steelhead trout, largemouth bass, crappie, catfish, bluegill, perch, and coho salmon can all be caught there.

Devils Lake (once called Indian Bay) in Lincoln City contains yellow perch, largemouth bass, brown bullhead, rainbow trout, crappie, bluegill, and grass carp. (An old Indian legend has made night fishing on Devils Lake rather unpopular. According to the legend, an octopus-like monster occupies the lake and will ensnare any boat that crosses the moon's reflection at night in the center of the lake.) Port Orford enjoys fall runs of chinook salmon and steelhead trout on the **Elk River**, three miles north of town, and on the **Sixes River**, five miles north of town. **Garrison Lake**, which lies mostly in the town west of US 101, has boat ramps and freshwater fishing. **Floras Lake** lies off US 101 about 11 miles north of town, then four miles west.

> Freshwater fishermen should get a copy of the free brochure *Oregon's Top Rivers for Salmon & Steelhead*, prepared by the Oregon Department of Fish & Wildlife, PO Box 59, Portland, OR 97207, which contains a wealth of information about two of the area's most popular freshwater fish.

📖 Another publication containing loads of useful information is *Fishing Guide*, published by Angle Publications, PO Box 671, Tillamook, OR 97141, ☎ 503/812-1884. You can probably get a free copy in the Chamber of Commerce office.

Fishawk River Co., PO Box 1954, Brookings, OR 97415, ☎ 503/469-2422, arranges one- to six-day fishing trips.

The Oregon Angler, PO Box 489, Elkton, OR 97436, ☎ 503/584-2277 (summer), or PO Box 350, Sixes, OR 97476, ☎ 503/332-3450 (winter) and 800/428-8585, provides guides who can steer you to shad, smallmouth bass, stripers, and sturgeon in the summer, or chinook salmon and steelhead trout in the winter on your choice of the Umpqua, Rogue, Smith, Elk, or Sixes Rivers.

Rogue River Outfitters, PO Box 1078, Gold Beach, OR 97444, ☎ 503/247-2684, arranges camping trips and duck hunts in addition to fishing trips.

Umpqua River Guide, 3438 Ridgeway, Reedsport, OR 97467, ☎ 503/271-5583, conducts fishing trips.

Tim Marshall, PO Box 696, Tillamook, OR 97141, ☎ 503/842-5171, leads fishing expeditions for chinook salmon in the spring and fall, and for steelhead trout in the winter.

Salmon Harbor Marina, PO Box 1007, Winchester Bay, OR 97467, ☎ 541/271-3407, has a boat launch and campsites. It also leads fishing trips on the Umpqua River.

Boating

Of course, boating can be an adventure all its own, even without the fishing.

📖 Boaters would do well to get a free copy of *Oregon Coastal Harbors*, produced by the US Army Corps of Engineers, Portland District, PO Box 2946, Portland, OR 97208-2946. Also useful are three free booklets produced by the Oregon State Marine Board, 435 Commercial St. NE, Salem, OR 97310, ☎ 503/378-8587: *Oregon Boating Facilities Guide*, *Oregon Boater's Handbook*, and *Safe Boating Hints for Personal Watercraft*.

Boats can be rented at **Honeyman Park Lodge** (503/997-9143) in Honeyman State Park in Florence; in **Quatat Park** (☎ 503/717-0125) on the Necanicum River in Seaside; on the dock at Waldport's **Bay Marina** (☎ 503/563-2003); and at **Taylor's Landing** (☎ 503/528-3388), 10 minutes east of Waldport on Route 34. Taylor's Landing has a marina and a floating diner, and can furnish guide services. Quatat Park rents kayaks, canoes, pedal boats, and hydrobikes as well as fishing boats.

Canoeing is quite popular around Brownsmead, Knappa, John Day River, and Cullaby Lake in Clatsop County.

M&M Seaplane Operations, 83595 US 101, Florence, OR 97439, ☎ 503/997-6567, rents jet skis for use on Lake Woahink.

Rogue River Safaris, Box 225, Wedderburn, OR 97491, ☎ 541/247-2333 or 247-7497, offers 90-minute jet boat rides on the Rogue River between May 15 and September 15.

Rogue River Reservations, PO Box 548, Gold Beach, OR 97444, ☎ 503/247-6022 or 247-6504, fax 503/247-7714, outfits both rafting and jet boat trips, along with inland hiking trips.

From May 1 to October 31, **Jerry's Rogue Jets**, Box 1011, Port of Gold Rush, Gold Rush, OR 97444, ☎ 541/247-4571 or 800/451-3645, Web site www.roguejets.com., and **Mail Boat Hydro-Jet Trips**, 94294 Rogue River Rd., Box 1165, Gold Beach, OR 97444, ☎ 541/247-7033 or 800/458-3511, both offer 64-, 80- and 104-mile round trips through the whitewater.

Umpqua Jet Adventures, 423 Riverfront Way, Reedsport, OR, 97467. ☎ 541/271-5694 or 800/353-8386, fax 503/271-5127, provides two-hour cruises on the Umpqua River.

If you arrive on the coast with a boat of your own, you can launch it at the Bureau of Land Management boat ramp on North Spit or at **Empire Public Boat Dock**, both in Charleston. **Carnahan Park** north of Seaside also has a boat launch.

Or you can leave the driving to somebody else and charter a boat to take you on a cruise. **South Sea Charters**, PO Box 1446, Newport, OR 97365, ☎ 503/867-7200, for example, will take you sailing aboard the ocean racer *Battlecry*, winner of the 1975 Admiral's Cup.

Windsurfing & Waterskiing

Windsurfing (or sailboarding) is another popular sport along the Oregon coast.

In Bandon, you can windsurf on the lake, on the river, or in the ocean. Around Warrenton, windsurfing is popular in **Young's Bay** and in **Trestle Bay**. In Lincoln City, both windsurfing and surfing are common in **Devil's Lake** and from 35th Street south to the entrance to Siletz Bay.

Windsurfing also is popular around Charleston, around Florence, on **Floras** and **Garrison Lakes** in Port Orford, at **Hubbard Creek** in Port Orford, near Rockaway Beach, and in Tillamook.

Cleanline Surf, 171 Sunset Blvd., ☎ 503/436-9726, and 719 First Ave., ☎ 503/738-7888, both in Cannon Beach, rents surfing equipment and is open daily.

Rock Reef Surf Shop, 646 SE US 101, Depoe Bay, OR 97341, ☎ 503/765-2306, rents surfing gear.

Central Coast Watersports, 1560 2nd St., Florence, OR 97439, ☎ 541/997-1812 or 800/789-DIVE, can provide rentals for surfboarding, body boarding, snorkeling, scuba diving, and kayaking.

Gold Beach is a good area for surfing, as is Charleston.

Port Orford is preferred for scuba diving – beginners in the harbor and the more experienced divers in the kelp beds west of the harbor.

Charleston and Tillamook are also popular for scuba diving.

Waterskiiers seem to like Bay City and Rockaway Beach.

When you go windsurfing, be sure that the winds and the tides are headed in opposite directions. Also be aware that the water along the Oregon coast, unlike that in Hawaii or Southern California, is only 62° at most, even in the summer, so a wetsuit is necessary.

Whale- & Storm-Watching

Whale-watching in the winter can be enjoyed near Charleston, particularly at the **Simpson's Reef Overlook**, **Cape Arago State Park**, **Bastendorff Beach County Park Overlook**, and **Umpqua Lighthouse State Park**.

Around Reedsport, spectators like to whale-watch from **Lighthouse Viewpoint**.

In Port Orford and Rockaway Beach, people see the whales from late December, when they head south, to March, when they return to the north.

Depoe Bay has an annual "Celebration of the Whales" each spring.

Marine Discovery Tours (☎ 800/903-BOAT) in Newport takes spectators to the whales aboard the 65-foot *Discovery*. Literally dozens of other charter companies also offer whale-watching excursions during the migration season.

A similar pastime, storm watching, can be enjoyed at **Cape Arago** near Charleston.

■ In the Air

With so much water available upon which to land, floatplanes are common in Oregon, but heavy boat traffic on the water and unseen boulders or snags in the water can be dangerous to those who don't exercise the proper level of caution. Aviators should get a copy of the US Army Corps of Engineers' *Seaplane Operations at Corps Lakes* and study their regulations.

There are small airports in Dunes City, Florence, Gearhart, Gleneden Beach, Gold Beach, Lakeside, Nehalem, Pacific City, Powers, Sixes, Tillamook, Toledo, Waldport, Warrenton, and Yaquina.

M&M Seaplane Operations, 83595 US 101, Florence, OR 97439, ☎ 503/997-6567, specializes in scenic flights.

MK II Inc., PO Box 2176, Gearhart, OR, ☎ 503/223-5469, offers charter flights.

Tillamook Air Tours, PO Box 605, Tillamook, OR 97141, ☎ 503/842-1942, located next to the blimp hangar and the Naval Air Station Museum, can arrange private charters, tours of the coastline, and whale-watching trips in season.

The area around Tillamook is popular for hang gliding, while the sport of kite flying reaches Olympic proportions at various places on the Oregon coast. In April, Cannon Beach hosts the **Puffin Kite Festival**, and in June, Seaside holds a **Kite Festival**. In July, the venue changes to the **Southern Oregon Kite Festival**, staged in Brookings. In the fall, kite enthusiasts gather on the beach at the mouth of the Yachats River for another annual **Kite Festival**.

Kite flying also is a major sport in Bandon, at Fort Stevens State Park, on Gearhart's Little Beach, in Seaside, in Rockaway Beach, and in Tillamook.

Kites Northwest, ☎ 503/738-6850 or 800/KITESNW, and **Kite Factory of Seaside**, ☎ 503/738-5483, both in Seaside, and **Yikes! Kites** (☎ 503/997-1936) on the North Jetty in Florence can supply you with your choice of kite.

In LaGrande, the **Wallowa Lake Tramway**, ☎ 503/432-5331, provides a 15-minute ride up 8,200-foot Mount Howard – the steepest vertical lift for a four-passenger gondola in North America. The tram is open from 10 AM to 4 PM daily between late May and October.

■ Cultural Excursions

Museum fans should look for *Pocket Guide to Oregon Museums* at participating museums or from the Oregon Historical Society, 1230 SW Park Ave., Portland, OR 97205, ☎ 503/222-1741. It can help you avoid a lot of museums where the exhibits seem more like the contents of Grandma's attic than a serious collection of significant artifacts.

Astoria

Strolling through Astoria, stop by the 6th Street viewing dock and the 14th Street River Park before visiting the **Columbia River Maritime Museum**, 1792 Marine Dr., ☎ 503/325-2323, and its 24,000 square feet of exhibit space. The museum is open daily from 9:30 AM to 5 PM. Outside the museum is the *Columbia,* the last US Coast Guard Lightship to serve on the Pacific Coast.

Six miles south of Astoria off US 101 is **Fort Clatsop National Memorial**, Route 3, Box 604-FC, Astoria, OR 97103, ☎ 503/861-2471, fax 503/861-2585, a 1995 replica of the fort built by Lewis and Clark in 1805. From June through October, the staff dresses in period costumes of the early 1800s and gives demonstrations of candle-making, smoking meat, making clothing and canoes, and firing flintlocks. The main building houses a museum, which presents an interesting and informative slide show, and is open from 8 AM to 6 PM between mid-June and Labor Day, and until 5 PM in the winter.

Nearby, on the northernmost tip of the coast, is 37-acre **Fort Stevens State Park**, ☎ 503/861-2000 or 861-1470, which contains a military museum. Built in 1863, Fort Stevens is the only enclosed Civil War earthworks site on the West Coast – the first defense post on the Columbia River. Blacksmith demonstrations are given, along with Civil War reenactments. In the summer, visitors can tour Battery Russell, a 90-year-old underground gun battery that served as a command center during World War II – it was fired on by a Japanese submarine on 21 June 1942. It is the only military installation in the continental United States to be attacked during WW II and the first to be fired on since the War of 1812. Deactivated as a military post after World War II, the fort is open seven days a week during the summer, and Wednesday through Sunday in the winter. Guided tours in a 2.5-ton Army truck are available during the summer.

Near Fort Stevens, on the Pacific Ocean side of the peninsula, is the wreck of the *Peter Iredale,* a 287-foot, four-masted sailing ship that went aground in 1906.

Astor Column, atop Coxcomb Hill – 164 steps from the bottom to the top – is a different kind of "museum." Built in 1926 and patterned after the Trojan Column in Rome, the 125-foot tower is covered with murals depicting the colorful history of the region.

If you're in town overnight during July or August, stop in to see *Shanghaied in Astoria*, a melodrama about Astoria's colorful waterfront history. Check the newspaper for time and place.

Coast Theater Playhouse, 108 N. Hemlock, PO Box 643, **Cannon Beach**, OR 97110, ☎ 503/436-1242, offers live theater on Friday and Saturday evenings, and during the summer on Thursday evenings, too.

Shore Acres State Park & Botanical Gardens, 13030 Cape Arago Hwy in **Charleston**, ☎ 541/888-3732, has some lovely Oriental gardens.

Another lovely garden that parallels Rockreall Creek is the **Delbert Hunter Arboretum & Botanic Garden**, 631 Park St., PO Box 604, **Dallas**, OR 97338, ☎ 503/623-7359.

Coos Bay

Self-guided walking tours of Coos Bays' historical buildings, the Bay Area, the North Bend historical area, and local trails can be obtained, free of charge, at the Bay Area Chamber of Commerce, 50 E. Central, PO Box 1515, Coos Bay, OR 97420, ☎ 541/269-0215 or 800/824-8486.

If you've gained a taste for Native American food during your travels, you can get a sampling to take home by shopping in Coos Bay. Local stores sell the wares of **Blue Earth Food Products** (☎ 503/269-1647), a company operated by the Confederated Tribes of Coos, Lower Umpqua, and Siuslaw Indians.

Siletz Tribal Smokehouse (☎ 800/828-4269) in **Depoe Bay** also sells Native foods. You can top them off with a treat from one of the town's three colorful candy shops: **Depoe Bay Candy Shoppe** (☎ 503/765-2727) at Bay Street and US 101, **Fuddy Duddy Fudge** (☎ 503/765-2878) on US 101 north of Clarke Street, or **Ainslee's Salt Water Taffy** (☎ 503/765-2431), also on US 101, where caramel corn and chocolates are made, as well as taffy.

In mid-July, Coos Bay hosts the **Oregon Coast Music Festival**. (For specifics, contact the Festival offices at PO Box 663, Coos Bay, OR 97420, or the Oregon Coast Music Association, c/o Coos Art Museum, 235 S. Anderson, Coos Bay, OR 97420, ☎ 541/267-0938, fax 541/267-2333, E-mail ocma@mail.coos.or.us.)

Florence

Florence is bedecked with a series of murals that can be seen at 1436 Bay St., 1498 Bay Street, and 802 US 101. At the North Jetty, **Sea Horse Stagecoach** (☎ 503/964-3174 or 999-0319) will provide you with a horse-drawn coach ride along the beach, where you will see the *Westward Ho!* **Sternwheeler** (☎ 503/997-9691) docked by Mo's in Old Town.

Florence also offers two interesting museums: **Fly Fishing Museum**, 280 Nopal St., Florence, OR 97439, ☎ 503/997-6349, and **Siuslaw Pioneer Museum**, 85294 US 101 South, PO Box 2637, Florence, OR 97439, ☎ 503/997-7884. The Pioneer Museum is open from 10 to 4 daily except Mondays, but it is closed the entire month of December.

Eleven miles north of town, **Sea Lions Caves**, 91560 US 101, Florence, OR 97439, ☎ 503/547-3111, has a year-around colony of resident Steller's sea lions.

Oregon Coast Aquarium, 2820 SE Ferry Slip Rd., **Newport**, OR 97365, ☎ 541/867-3474, is open daily except Christmas between 9 AM and 6 PM in the summer and between 10 and 5 in the winter. It contains over 190 species, allows hands-on exploration at the Touch Pool, and features a Discovery Lab.

Visitors can feed the seals at **Seaside Aquarium**, 200 N. Promenade, **Seaside**, OR 97138, ☎ 503/738-6211. Built as a natatorium (an indoor swimming pool) in the 1920s, the facility was converted into an aquarium in 1937. It contains 35 separate viewing tanks.

In **North Bend**, you can watch oysters being harvested and packed at **Clausen Oyster Farms**, 811 North Bay Dr., ☎ 541/756-3600.

Prehistoric Gardens, 36848 S. Hwy 101, **Port Orford**, OR 97465, ☎ 541/332-4463, has created scientifically correct replicas of dinosaurs, displayed in an Oregon rain forest. The exhibit is located 12 miles south of town at Arizona Beach.

Umpqua Discovery Center, 409 Riverfront Way, **Reedsport**, OR 97467, ☎ 503/271-4816 or 800/247-2155, has a "hands on" museum and learning center.

Tillamook

Tillamook Naval Air Station Museum, 6030 Hangar Rd., Tillamook, OR 97141, ☎ 503/842-1130, is open daily. Housed in the world's largest wooden structure, the museum's exhibits include such World War II aircraft as the F4U Corsair, B-25 Mitchell bomber, German Messerschmidt ME-109 fighter, and American P-51 Mustang fighter.

Tillamook is noted nationwide for its cheeses, of course, so you should plan to stop at the **Tillamook Cheese Visitors Center**, PO Box 313, Tillamook, OR 97141, ☎ 503/815-1300. The center is open daily from 8 AM to 6 PM between mid-September and May 23 and from 8 AM to 8 PM between May 24 and mid-September. Although the emphasis is on their cheese, be sure to try the Tillamook ice cream too.

The Little Log Church by the Sea in **Yachats**, built around 1927 in the shape of a cross, is open to visitors.

Where to Stay

Brookings Harbor

Best Western Beachfront Inn, PO Box 2729, 16008 Boat Basin Rd., Brookings Harbor, OR 97415, ☎ 541/469-7779 or 800/468-4081, fax 541/469-0283, $$-$$$, sits on the waterfront 1.5 miles south of Brookings. The units are large and each has a balcony, but the three-story building has no elevator.

Cannon Beach

Stephanie Inn, just west of Beach Loop Road at the foot of Gower Street in Cannon Beach, ☎ 503/436-2221 or 800/633-3466, E-mail stephinn@seasurf.com, Web site www.ohwy.com/stephinn.htm, $$$-$$$$, offers the flavor of New England in an Oregon waterfront setting.

Florence

Driftwood Shores, 88416 First Ave., Florence, OR 97439, ☎ 541/997-8263, fax 541/997-5857, $-$$$, offers attractive ocean views and has a restaurant, lounge, and coin laundry.

Gleneden Beach

Salishan Lodge, US 101, Gleneden Beach, OR 97388, ☎ 541/764-3600, 764-2371, or 888-SALISHAN, $$$-$$$$, is a newly remodeled up-scale resort with a Scottish-style par-72 golf course. There also is a new 350-yard 18-hole putting course, three indoor tennis courts, hiking trails, 23 shops and galleries, and an excellent restaurant. The buildings are all connected with covered walkways and bridges.

Gold Beach

At **Paradise Lodge**, PO Box 456, Gold Beach, OR 97444, ☎ 541/247-6022, 247-6504, or 800/525-2161, $$$-$$$$, guests can enjoy whitewater rapids, waterfalls, wilderness walking paths, and fishing. Meryl Streep once made a movie there, and Zane Grey once had a cabin there, in which he wrote a novel called *Rogue River Feud* about the region.

Orleans

Klamath River Lodge, PO Box 145, Orleans, CA 95556, ☎ 707/444-5555, $$, is four miles downriver from the town and offers a swimming pool, hiking trails, and fishing, while **Sandy Bar Ranch**, Ishi Pishi Rd., PO Box 347, Orleans, CA 95556, ☎ 916/627-3379, $$, provides opportunities for hiking, biking, swimming, rafting, kayaking, and fishing.

Otter Rock

The Inn at Otter Crest, PO Box 50, Otter Rock, OR 97369, ☎ 503/765-2111 or 800/452-2101, $$-$$$, sits on a cliff above the ocean.

Winchester Bay

Salmon Harbor Belle B&B, F Charter Dock, Salmon Harbor Marina, Winchester Bay, OR, ☎ 541/271-1137 or 800/348-1922, is a floating B&B aboard a three-level sternwheeler.

Yachats

The Adobe Resort/Motel, PO Box 219, Yachats, OR 97498, ☎ 541/547-3141 or 800/522-3623, $$-$$$, sits at the ocean's edge, with tidepools and beach trails close at hand.

> The Oregon Lodging Association, 12724 SE Stark St., Portland, OR 97233, offers a free guide, *Where to Stay in Oregon*, and the Oregon Bed & Breakfast Guild, PO Box 3187, Ashland, OR 97520, also provides a free *Directory*.

Camping

Yurts & Rustic Cabins

Camping in Oregon is full of options. In addition to pitching a tent on their own, visitors are given an opportunity to stay in a yurt, a cabin, a covered wagon, a tepee, or a houseboat.

The finer cabins and the houseboats are restricted to central Oregon; the covered wagons and the tepees to eastern Oregon, but the Oregon state parks do equip the coastal region with yurts and with a rustic type of cabin.

One of the newest camping crazes is the yurt, a Mongolian-style structure 16 feet in diameter with a 10-foot high ceiling capped with a clear skylight. Sort of circular domed tent stretched over a latticed framework. Yurts are available for rent at several places along the Oregon coast. **Harris Beach** near Brookings has four, **Champoeg** has six, **Bullards Beach** near Bandon has six, **Valley of the Rogue** has six, **Jessie M. Honeyman State Park** between Reedsport and Florence has four, **South Beach** between Waldport and Newport has ten, **Beverly Beach** between Newport and Lincoln City has 14, **Cape Lookout** near Tillamook has four, **Nehalem Bay** between Tillamook and Seaside has nine, **Fort Stevens** near Astoria has nine, and **Wallowa Lake** has one.

The yurt provides inexpensive housing ($25 per night for as many as five people; $5 more for each additional person up to eight).

 A free four-color, pocket-sized brochure, *Yurt Camping*, has been produced by the Oregon Parks & Recreation Department, 1115 Commercial NE, Salem, OR 97310, ☎ 800/452-5687.

As to the "rustic" cabins available on the Oregon coast, they can be found in **Alfred A. Loeb State Park** on the Chetco River, near Brookings. The cabins have one bunk bed and one double bed, electric heat and indoor lights. Fee: $35 per night.

"Traditional" Camping

More traditional camping is available at **Bullards Beach Campground** in Bandon, at **Cape Perpetua** near Yachats, at **Bastendorf Beach Campground** and **Sunset Bay Campground** in Charleston, at **Sunset Bay State Park** (☎ 541/888-4902) in Coos Bay, at **Barview Campground** in Garibaldi, at **Fort Stevens Campground** in

Hammond, at **Neskowin Creek Campground** in Otis, at **Elk River Campground** (☎ 541/332-2255) in Port Orford, at **Circle Creek RV Park & Campground** (☎ 503/738-6070) in Seaside, at **Sea Perch Campground** (☎ 503/547-3505) in Yachats, and at three sites in Sandlake, **Cape Lookout Campground**, **Sand Beach Campground** and **Whalen Island Campground**.

> 📖 Campers might wish to obtain a free copy of *Guide to County Campgrounds, Parks & Recreation Facilities*, produced by the Oregon Parks Association, PO Box 366, St. Helens, OR 97051.

> 📖 Another free brochure, *Camping in Oregon & Washington*, is available from many chambers of commerce.

Where to Eat

Astoria

Pier 11 Feed Store, Restaurant and Lounge, 77 11th St., Astoria, OR 97103, ☎ 503/325-0279, $$, is on the pier at the end of 10th Street. The restaurant offers a rustic atmosphere and a river view.

Newport

The Whale's Tale, 452 SW Bay Blvd., Newport, OR 97365, ☎ 541/265-8660, $$, sits on the bayfront, is small and cozy, and serves good seafood and shellfish. It is open from 11:30 AM to 2:30 PM and from 4 to 10 PM, but closed on Wednesdays during the spring and winter and from January 2 to mid-February.

Information Sources

Oregon Tourism Division, 775 Summer St. NE, Salem, OR 97310, ☎ 800/547-7842.

Central Oregon

Between the ruggedly beautiful Pacific Ocean seacoast and the sparsely settled, largely agrarian counties in the eastern part of Oregon, the central part of the state contains the bulk of the state's population, the seat of its government, its largest cities, and its highest mountains. There is considerable development along the western side of the Cascade Range, but relatively little on the eastern side.

Along with the many stories about Big Foot that are told in this part of the country, a number of tales regarding the adventures of Paul Bunyan and his companion Babe, the Blue Ox, also are recounted.

Although a product of the Great Lakes states, legends tell us that Paul Bunyan did journey to the Pacific Northwest on at least one occasion. That time, Bunyan went for a walk and carelessly dragged his peavy (a stout, hooked lever used in handling logs) along the ground behind him, thus creating the Columbia River Gorge.

Some say Paul Bunyan never died. He just retired to the Alaskan bush, where he lives to this day.

Getting Around

As in Northern California, the principal traffic flow through Oregon runs north and south, and Interstate 5 is the main artery. Of the major cities in the state, only Klamath Falls and Bend are *not* located on I-5. Both of those cities are on the *eastern* side of the Cascades and both are located on US 97, Oregon's *second* most important north-south trafficway.

Interstate 84 swings into Oregon from Idaho, slashes across the northeastern corner of the state, encounters the Columbia River at Boardman, and then swings west along the south bank of the river until it eventually reaches Portland, where it connects with I-5 and I-205, the high-speed detour around city congestion.

Between US 97 and I-84, there is only one other major north-south highway traversing the state: US 395, which crosses the southern border of the state from the remote northeastern corner of California, then ambles northward toward Pendleton and Walla Walla, Washington.

East-west traffic is sparse, at best. Indeed, only two highways, US 20 and US 26, travel all the way across the state from the Pacific Ocean to the Idaho state line. US 20 passes through the Willamette National Forest and the city of Bend on its way east. US 26 enters the Portland metropolitan area from the Pacific coast, then wanders southeast through the Mount Hood National Forest and the Warm Springs Indian Reservation to Prineville, and onward through Ochoco National Forest and Umatilla National Forest to join US 20 just west of the Idaho border.

US 95 cuts off the southeastern corner of the state as it links northern Nevada with western Idaho. CA 140 travels from Medford through the Rogue River National Forest to Klamath Falls, and then into northwestern Nevada.

Klamath Falls, just north of the California border, has a commercial airport.

West of the Cascades, Eugene, Salem, and Portland also maintain commercial airports, while east of the Cascades, only Pendleton is easily accessible by commercial airline.

An airport shuttle (☎ 888/RIDE-VIP) flies daily between McMinnville and Portland. It leaves McMinnville at 8 AM, and leaves Portland at 1 PM.

Amtrak's Pacific Coast route travels north from Chico and Redding, California, stopping in Klamath Falls, Chemult, Eugene, Albany/Corvallis, Salem, and Portland before passing into the state of Washington.

Touring

Aurora

Aurora was established in 1856 as a Christian communal society. In the late 1800s, its community brass band traveled throughout the northwest presenting concertsh, though the communal society was disbanded in 1883.

128 ■ Central Oregon

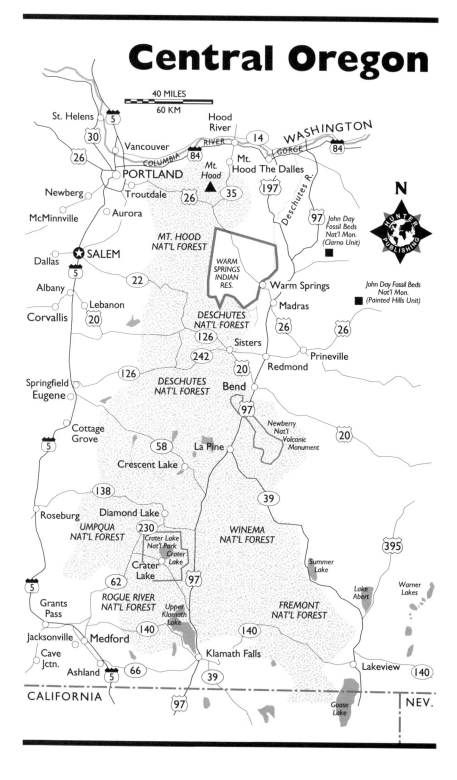

Mount Hood (Hood River CC).

Corvallis

Corvallis, originally called Marysville, was a candidate for state capital during the 1850s.

Columbia River Gorge

The state's northern boundary is formed by the picturesque Columbia River Gorge.

It was in 1775, a year before the American Revolution, that Bruno Heceta, a Spanish navigator, sighted the mouth of a large river along the coast of what is now northern Oregon. He did not enter it.

In 1788, Capt. John Meares searched for the river that Heceta had noted, but he mistook the wide mouth of the Columbia for a bay and named it Deception Bay.

On 11 May 1792, Capt. Robert Gray again found the river. He named it for his ship. Five months later, Lt. William Broughton, an English navigator, sailed 100 miles up the river, where he sighted and named Mount Hood and claimed the region for England.

On their historic venture west, Lewis and Clark reached the mouth of the Columbia River in 1805.

The second longest river in America, the Columbia runs 2,000 miles from its confluence with the Snake River near Oregon's eastern border to the Pacific Ocean.

Early travelers on the lower Columbia had to ride aboard sternwheelers. They would go ashore at the Cascades, transfer to a portage railroad, and ride to the upper landing, where they could board another sternwheeler. At The Dalles, they would disembark again and ride a horse-drawn wagon around Celilo Falls before they could board a third sternwheeler. The *Bailey Gatzert*, one of the fastest and most luxurious sternwheelers ever built, carried the passengers on the final leg of their journey. The need for such an arduous trip was eliminated with the removal of the hazardous John Day Rock in 1873, the construction of the Cascade Locks in 1896, and the construction of a canal around Celilo Falls in 1915.

The banks of the Columbia were opened to vehicular traffic when the Columbia River Highway was dedicated on 6 June 1916. That road has subsequently been updated, although not totally replaced, by Interstate 84.

> The drive along the Columbia River reveals an endless array of wonders. Before setting out from Portland, pick up a free copy of the US Forest Service map/brochure *The Columbia River Gorge National Scenic Area* and its companion *Lodgings & Activities Guide, Columbia River Gorge National Scenic Area*.

From Portland, take I-84 20 miles east to Troutdale and get off at Exit 17 – the waterfall loop, a remnant of the historic old Columbia River Highway. The road takes you past Corbett and Dabney State Park to **Crown Point State Park**, the centerpiece of which is **Vista House**. Sitting 733 feet above the river, the imposing stone building, which is open from April to mid-October, furnishes some marvelous views, and provides visitors with a great deal of helpful and interesting information about the river and the gorge.

Next, the old highway passes through **Latourell**, **Shepperd's Dell** and **Bridal Veil State Parks**, each of which contains its own waterfall, and then it enters the Mount Hood National Forest.

The **Wahkeena Falls** Picnic Area and **Multnomah Falls** follow. Multnomah Falls makes a 620-foot drop from Larch Mountain and is the fourth highest waterfall in the United States – the second highest *year-around* waterfall. A paved trail leads to the top of the falls, and a colorful stone lodge at the bottom contains restrooms, a restaurant, a visitor center with some interesting displays, a gift shop, and a snack bar.

Two miles farther to the east, the old Columbia River Highway reaches **Oneonta Gorge** and the **Oneonta Botanical Area**, where you can hike upstream during one of the low-water periods to see some impressive hanging gardens. Another half-mile takes you to **Horsetail Falls**, and soon thereafter the road rejoins I-84 as it continues eastward.

To reach **Bonneville Dam**, which offers free tours, take Exit 40 off the Interstate. The Visitor Center, Cascade Locks, OR 97014-0150, ☎ 541/374-8820, and a fish hatchery are open from 9 to 5. (Turning in the opposite direction at Exit 40 will take you to the **Wahclelle Falls** trailhead on Tanner Creek.)

By returning to the Interstate and continuing eastward, you will come to the **Bridge of the Gods**, Box 307, Cascade Locks, OR 97014, ☎ 503/374-8619. The toll bridge is the third oldest bridge across the Columbia River (1926), and if you wish to turn northward into Washington it will cost you 75¢. The Pacific Crest Trail crosses the Bridge of the Gods.

An example of the old sternwheelers that once plied the river is on display at the **Marine Park Visitor Center**, PO Box 307, Cascade Locks, OR 97014, ☎ 541/374-8619.

Passing **Viento State Park**, the town of Hood River comes into view. (For more information about the "Windsurfing Capital of North America," contact Columbia River Gorge National Scenic Area, USDA Forest Service, 902 Wasco Ave., Suite 200, Hood River, OR 97031, ☎ 541/386-2333). Another toll bridge (75¢) crosses the Columbia River into Washington at Hood River.

A second stretch of the old Columbia River Highway begins at Exit 69 in Mossier and loops to the top of Rowena Plateau on the way to The Dalles. The **Tom McCall Nature Preserve**, a wildflower refuge maintained by the Nature Conservancy, is atop the Rowena Plateau.

The Dalles (which rhymes with "gals") derived its name from a French word, "dalle," and refers to the rapids that flow swiftly through a narrow channel and over flat, basaltic rocks in the river. On 25 October 1805, Lewis and Clark camped on a high bank overlooking the river in this area.

While in the area, take the time to take a self-guided historical walk, see the Fort Dalles Historical Museum at 15th and Garrison, and enjoy a free tour of The Dalles Dam. At the Visitor Center, ☎ 541/296-9778, the old passenger train used to bypass the Cascades is on display.

The **Columbia Gorge Discovery Center**, 5000 Discovery Dr., The Dalles, OR 97058, ☎ 541/296-8600, opened at Crate's Point near The Dalles in 1997. The center complements another center located across the river in Stevenson, WA, and includes 48,000 square feet of indoor and 80,000 square feet of outdoor exhibits. It is open daily from 10 to 6.

Crossing the river on US 87 at this point enables you to return to the Portland/Vancouver area by a different route, WA 14.

Passing through Bingen and White Salmon, WA, you will arrive at the **Columbia River Interpretive Center**, 990 SW Rock Creek Dr., PO Box 1037, Stevenson, WA 98648, ☎ 509/427-8211 or 800/991-2338, fax 509/427-7429. The center is open daily from 10 to 7 in the summer and from 10 to 5 in the winter. Indian artifacts and the world's largest rosary collection are on display. A nine-projector slide show recreates the cataclysm that formed the gorge.

Beacon Rock State Park showcases the world's second largest monolith, overshadowed only by the Rock of Gibraltar.

> A free pocket-sized brochure, *Fort Cascade Trail Guide*, has been produced by the US Army Corps of Engineers, and is available at most visitor centers or chambers of commerce in this area. It describes, and will help you to locate, 14 historic sites between here and the city of Vancouver, 40 miles east.

If your visit happens to occur in mid-June, check out the annual "Gorge Hiking Weekend," sponsored by **Friends of the Columbia Gorge**, 319 SW Washington St., Suite 301, Portland, OR 97204, ☎ 503/241-3762. The weekend event includes nine easy, six moderate, and three strenuous hikes; horseback rides; and bike tours.

Cottage Grove

Cottage Grove, just 20 miles from Eugene, calls itself the covered bridge capital of Oregon, and has the only covered railroad bridge west of the Mississippi.

Dallas

The town of Dallas, east of Salem, should not be confused with The Dalles, a city on the banks of the Columbia River Gorge. Dallas is the home of Delbert Hunter Arboretum & Botanical Garden, 631 Park St., PO Box 604, Dallas, OR 97338, ☎ 503/623-7359, which parallels Rickreall Creek.

Crater Lake National Park

Crater Lake National Park is Oregon's only national park. Thirty-three miles around, the lake is 1,932 feet deep – America's deepest lake. The area contains waterfalls and provides some outstanding hiking and camping opportunities.

Hour-and-a-quarter cruises, conducted from mid-June to mid-September, weather permitting, take you past three landmarks: Wizard Island, The Phantom Ship, and Old Man of the Lake.

There are over 90 miles of hiking trails in the park, but there is only one way to reach the shoreline of the lake, the mile-long **Cleetwood Cove Trail** that drops 700 feet as you descend from the East Rim Shore to the water, making the return trip the equivalent of climbing 65 flights of stairs – definitely *not* something to be undertaken by the very young, the elderly, or the infirm. Bicycles are restricted to the paved roads and to the **Grayback** nature road.

Rim Drive and the park's north entrance are closed by snow from October through early June, so winter access is limited to Rim Village on Route 62 from Medford or on Route 97 from Klamath Falls.

Well south and west of Crater Lake are the **Oregon Caves**, 20000 Caves Hwy, **Cave Junction**, OR 97523, ☎ 541/592-3400, fax 541/592-6654. Discovered in 1874 by a hunter who was chasing a bear, the attraction consists of 480 acres of intricate marble caves, always a cool 42° inside. The caves, proclaimed a National Monument in 1909, are open every day but Thanksgiving and Christmas.

Galice

Indian Mary Park in Galice once was the smallest Indian reservation in the United States. It was given to Indian Mary in memory of her father, Indian Joe, in recognition of his aid to white settlers during the Indian Wars of 1855-56.

Grants Pass

In the 1860s, Grants Pass was a stage coach stop, named in honor of Grant's success at Vicksburg in 1863. It became a railhead in 1884, and the county seat in 1886.

Jacksonville/Medford

The entire town of Jacksonville, just 32 miles north of the California border, is listed as a National Historic Landmark by the US Department of the Interior. Years ago, Jacksonville was the county seat, but then the railroad asked the town for a $25,000 "bonus" to put a station there. The city refused, and the station was built in nearby Middle Ford on the banks of Bear Creek. Middle Ford later shortened its name to Medford, and Medford eventually took over as the county seat.

Lebanon

Lebanon is a colorful pioneer town with a restored one-room schoolhouse, an abandoned grist mill, a number of old houses, and the ruts of the old Santiam Wagon Road. Nearby **Sodaville** is now a ghost town.

Mount Hood

Each year, between 15,000 and 20,000 people climb 11,235-foot Mount Hood ("Wy'East" to the Indians), most of them by the southside route, but even experienced climbers are encouraged to exercise great care in making the trip. Rapidly changing weather and snow conditions can cause unexpected dangers.

Numerous sightings of Big Foot have been reported around Mount Hood.

Minor eruptions occurred in 1804, 1853, 1854, 1859, 1865, and 1907.

Mount St. Helens

After a series of ash eruptions that started in April, 1980, an earthquake measuring 5.1 on the Richter scale struck Mount St. Helens at 8:32 AM on 18 May. Much of the mountain slid into Spirit Lake, and after the avalanche, the equivalent of a 50-megaton explosion blew off the top of the mountain. A 240-square-mile stand of old timber, enough to build 640,000 three-bedroom homes, was leveled in minutes. For the next nine hours, hot gas and ash spewed 60,000 feet into the air. A 320-foot deep "grand canyon" was created. A "mat" of one million trees now floats on the surface of Spirit Lake. The 200-foot Harmony Falls is no more, but two new falls were created. Now "healing," an immense lava dome is building that should replace the original mountaintop within 150 to 250 years – if it doesn't erupt again first.

Oakland

Oakland boasts the first organized historic district in Oregon. Of the 136 properties in the district, almost half of them were built before 1900.

Portland

Originally called Stumptown and now known as "The City of Roses," Portland is Oregon's largest city. The Portland Rose Festival, 220 NW Second Ave., Portland, OR 97209, ☎ 503/225-5555, fax 503/227-6603, E-mail info@rosefestival.org, Web site www.rosefestival.org, is celebrated each June.

St. Helens

First named Plymouth and then called Casenau, after a prominent Indian chief, St. Helens, is a deep-water seaport just 29 miles northwest of Portland. The town became the Columbia County seat in 1903.

Salem

Salem, the state capital, had a chaotic history after a fire destroyed the Salem State House in 1855 and another fire destroyed the capitol building in 1935. The present capitol was completed in 1939.

Adventures

■ On Foot

There are over 50 ghost towns in Linn County near **Albany**. Also in the area are the unusual Jacob sheep, a 300-year-old strain that bears four horns, two pointing straight up and two curving downward.

Hiking Trails

Around Ashland, hike the **Rogue River National Forest** or the trails in **Howard Prairie Lake County Park**, which also offers a boat ramp, boat rentals, fishing, a marina, waterskiing, and horseback riding.

In **Banks/Vernonia State Park** (☎ 503/324-0606), along OR 47 near **Banks**, is a rail line that was built in the 1920s to haul logs, lumber, and passengers. The line was abandoned and the rails were salvaged in 1973, leaving a trail that is eight feet wide, paralleled by a horse trail that is four feet wide. The trail crosses 12 bridges and two trestles. The trail also offers good opportunities to see wildlife. A free pocket-sized brochure with maps is available from local chambers of commerce and Oregon State Parks offices.

From **Pilot Butte**, a cinder cone on the eastern edge of **Bend**, one can see Mount Hood, Mount Jefferson, Three-Fingered Jack, Mount Washington, the Three Sisters, Broken Top, and Mount Bachelor.

Take US 97 11 miles south of Bend, turn west at Lava Lands Visitor Center, and continue four miles along a cinder road to a picnic area. Go downstream to the right, cross the footbridge, and hike about a mile to reach **Benham Falls**.

From the western city limits of Bend, take Galveston Avenue for 11 miles and then travel 3.5 miles on a graveled forest road into Deschutes National Forest, where you will find **Tumalo Falls**, a 97-foot waterfall.

Twelve miles south of Bend and a mile south of Lava Butte, in Deschutes National Forest, is **Lava River Cave**, a spectacular lava tube that is nearly a mile long. The cave is thought to be longer, but it is blocked by a sand plug of undetermined size. You can rent a lantern to explore the interior, and there is a Lava Lands Visitor Center at 58201 S. Hwy 97, Bend, OR 97707, ☎ 503/593-2421.

Opposite the Sunriver turn-off on US 97 in Deschutes National Forest, turn east onto Forest Road 9720 and go nine miles to a trailhead that will lead to **Lava Cast Forest**, a "forest" of lava tree molds. A paved, self-guided nature trail also is in the area.

> Pick up a free copy of *Fort Cascades Trail Guide*, a brochure produced by the US Army Corps of Engineers, but available at many chambers of commerce. The guide will tell you about the Warren Fishwheel #3 (1894), the 1894 flood, the site of the Cascades townsite (1850-94), the Fort Cascades compound (1856-61), Indian petroglyphs, McNatt's barn, stable and hotel (1858), McNatt's grave (1861), Sutler's store and blacksmith shop (1859), the Portage Tramway that transported fish for the Warren Packing Co. cannery (late 1890s to 1930), and the former route of the Cascade Portage Railroad (1863), all in the Cascade Locks area.
>
> In **Eugene**, get a free copy of the *Lane County Oregon Road & Recreation Map*, produced by Lane County Parks, 3040 N. Delta Hwy, Eugene, OR 97408. It will guide you to **Row River Trail**, a multi-use hiking, biking, and horseback riding trail, and to other sites in the area. Near Falls City is the **Valley of the Giants**, a forest of huge Douglas firs. Before you go, contact the Salem office of the Bureau of Land Management, ☎ 503/375-5646, regarding road and bridge information.

Near **Glendale**, try your hand at finding the **Lost Soldier Mine**. In 1853, a five-man detachment of soldiers discovered the rich mine when they became lost in the Coquille Mountains. The site is supposed to be along a tributary not far from the west fork of Cow Creek, about 10 miles west of Glendale. Others, however, say that the mine is in the mountains north and west of Jump-Off-Joe and Graves Creeks.

The **McKenzie River National Recreation Trail** runs from Route 126 at the southwestern end of Fish Lake almost to the McKenzie Bridge. The trail passes the parking lot at Coldwater Cove on Clear Lake; Sahalie and Koosah Falls; Carmen Reservoir; the Tamoulitch Valley Special Interest Area; Deer, Frissell, Peggy, Boulder, Scott, and Lost Creeks; and the McKenzie Ranger Station (☎ 541/822-3381).

Orleans, near **Marysville**, is a ghost town that vanished in the flood of 1861. Only the cemetery remains.

In the **Medford** area, **The Table Rocks**, Upper and Lower, are separated by Sam's Valley. It is an interesting area for hiking. Inquire at the Bureau of Land Management, 3040 Biddle Rd., Medford, OR 97504, ☎ 541/770-2200, for a map. Also ask for the free brochure *Birds of the Medford District*.

Champoeg State Park (☎ 503/678-1251) is off US 99W, seven miles east of **Newberg**, on a townsite wiped out by floods in 1861 and 1892. The park offers hiking along the Willamette River, biking, and camping.

Oregon Caves contains 480 acres of marble caves and a number of trails, including **No Name Trail**, a 1.1-mile round trip past several streams; **Caves Creek Trail**, which follows Caves Creek for 1.8 miles; **Cliff Nature Trail**, a round trip of three-quarters of a mile; and **Big Tree Trail**, a 3.3-mile round trip to a Douglas fir that is 12.5 feet thick and some 1,200-1,500 years old.

> 📖 A free brochure entitled *Clackamas County Parks Guide* can be obtained at the Clackamas County Park Department, 902 Abernethy Rd., **Oregon City**, OR 97045. It will direct you to hiking trails throughout the region. A similar publication, the free pocket-sized *Guide to Portland Parks & Recreation*, has been produced by Portland Parks & Recreation, ☎ 503/823-2223. Available at the **Portland** Chamber of Commerce office, the publication lists 206 recreational sites throughout the city.

Tryon Creek State Park, 11321 SW Terwilliger Blvd., Portland, OR 97219, ☎ 503/653-3166, is the only state park within a major metropolitan area. Covering 645 acres, the park contains eight miles of hiking trails, three and a half miles of horse trails, and three miles of paved bicycle paths. There also is a nature center with three half-mile loop trails.

Portland Audubon Society, 5151 NW Cornell Rd., Portland, OR 97210, ☎ 503/292-6855 or 292-0304, has a bird sanctuary with four miles of hiking trails, a nature store, a nature center, and a wildlife care center. Field trips and tours are offered.

Timberline Mountain Guides, PO Box 23214, Portland, OR 97281-3214, ☎ 503/636-7704, will take you rock climbing.

Ten miles south of **Madras** and 17 miles north of **Prineville** on US 26, the **Rimrock Springs Wildlife Management Area** contains birds, deer, antelope, and coyotes. A 1.5-mile trail has two observation decks.

Ochoco National Forest, 3160 NE 3rd St., Prineville, ☎ 503/447-9647, covers 1,500 square miles and encompasses three wilderness areas that offer both hiking trails and camping. Maps and information are available at the Prineville Ranger Station on US 26, which is open from 7:30 to 4:30, Monday through Friday.

Smith Rock State Park, a few miles northeast of Redmond, has some hiking trails and some cliffs that are good for rock climbing. If you need a little help with the climbing, **First Ascent Climbing Services**, 1136 SW Deschutes, Redmond, ☎ 503/548-5137, can provide instruction and guide services.

> The Roseburg Visitors & Convention Bureau, 410 SE Spruce St. PO Box 1262, 410 SE Spruce St., **Roseburg**, OR 97470, ☎ 541/672-9731 or 800/444/9584, has a free hiking brochure as well as a map that will lead you on a self-guided walking tour of the town.

Near Roseburg, just off OR 138 at Glide, is **Colliding Rivers Viewpoint**, where the swift, deep waters of the North Umpqua River funnel into a whitewater chute, ramming head-on into the rapids of Little River, which come tumbling in from the south. From here, the combined waters churn directly westward. It is the only place in the world where such a phenomenon occurs. **Silver Falls State Park**, 20024 Silver Falls Hwy SE, Sublimity, OR 97385, ☎ 503/873-8681, is on OR 214, 26 miles east of Salem. **Trail of Ten Falls**, a seven-mile hiking trail through Silver Creek Canyon, passes 10 waterfalls ranging in height from 27 to 178 feet and actually passes *behind* three of them. The park also has a three-mile jogging trail, a four-mile biking trail, and 14 miles of equestrian trails, plus a campground and the Howard Creek Horse Camp.

Willamette Mission State Park (☎ 503/393-1172) on Wheatland Road, eight miles north of **Salem**, was settled by missionaries in 1834. The original mission was destroyed by a flood in 1861. Today, in addition to the hiking trails, the park has a boat ramp, equestrian trails, a fishing dock, and a wildlife viewing area.

Guided Hikes

Adventure Out, PO Box 1408, **Hood River**, OR 97031, ☎ 541/387-4626, arranges rock climbing, hiking, mountaineering, and skiing trips.

Hood River Trails, 2149 W. Cascade St., Suite 106 A-7, Hood River, OR 97031, ☎ 541-354-5888, E-mail hrtrailsgorge.net, Web site www.gorge.net/business/hrtrails, can handle hiking, mountain biking, skiing, snowboarding, windsurfing, horseback riding, and whitewater rafting excursions.

Gold & Gemstones

Oregon's state rock is the "thunderegg" (geode), which is created when a cavity is formed in a hardening volcanic flow by steam and gases and the cavity fills with mud largely composed of rhyolite. The mud adheres to the walls of the cavity as it dries, leaving an even smaller central cavity, and then water flows into the cavity, introducing silica. When the rhyolite solidifies and the central area hardens, a thunderegg measuring from one inch to several feet in diameter remains.

Geodes can be found in **Antelope**, which also is one of the best places in the state to find gem-grade agate. They can also be found in **Madras**, particularly on Richardson's Recreation Ranch (formerly the Priday Ranch) northeast of town.

Mitchell is another good spot to hunt for geodes, as well as gem-grade agate. **Bend** provides good hunting for agate, geodes, jasper, crystal nodules, and obsidian, and it is possible to pan for gold in **Cottage Grove**.

Prineville calls itself the "rockhound capital of the world" and stages an annual Rockhound Pow Wow each June. The **Limb Cast** area 55 miles east of town was once at the bottom of a large lake, and produces thundereggs from one inch to several feet in diameter, depending on the depth at which you dig. The geodes also are found in streams, under tree roots, on surfaces weathered by wind and rain, and in bedrock at all depths.

Lucky Strike Thunderegg Mine and **Valley View Mine** (☎ 503/462-3332), both 35 miles east of Prineville off Route 26, permit the public to dig for thundereggs for a fee during the summer months.

The **Murray Mountain** area near Prineville contains moss agate with some angel wing and plume, while the **Glass Butte** area has obsidian, including some silver sheen obsidian, most commonly found in Mexico. "Fire" obsidian found there possesses a "flame" as pronounced as any found in opal or agate. Crook County claims to have the best green jasper deposit in the northwest, with color ranging from blue to dark jade green. Other minerals found in the area include agates with dendrites, white plume agates, moss agates in various colors, green jasper, jasper interlaced with agate, Ochoco chalcedony, and petrified wood.

Elkins Gem Stones, 833 S. Main, PO Box 576, Prineville, OR 97754, ☎ 503/447-5547, can provide rockhounds with a great deal of helpful information. The hillsides and creekbeds north of **Warm Springs Indian Reservation** contain agate, jasper, and geodes.

While rockhounding, watch for rattlesnakes, especially around rock slides and damp areas during the warm months. Wood ticks, common in the spring, are another hazard because they often carry spotted fever and other infections.

■ On Horseback

Rodeos

Rodeos, rodeos everywhere! Starting as early as March, Oregon's action-packed rodeo season seems boundless.

In March, a rodeo is held in Corvallis. In May, they are held in Arlington, Salem, Tygh Valley (an All-Indian Rodeo), Spray, and Milton-Freewater. By June, the rodeo arenas have moved to Albany, Hermiston, the Warm Springs Indian Reservation, Sisters, and The Dalles.

As the 4th of July rolls around, the largest rodeo in western Oregon is held in St. Paul. Others soon follow in Hermiston, Central Point, Madras, St. Helens, Albany, Corvallis, Klamath Falls, Philomath, Prineville, Eugene, Haines, Halfway, Cottage Grove, Elgin, and La Pine.

Rodeo action in August is equally frenetic, with events scheduled in Redmond, Hillsboro, Philomath, Canby, Fossil, Hermiston, McNary, Rickreall, Sublimity, Tygh Valley, Lakeview, Brooks, Molalla, and Paulina.

Fossil, Hermiston, Moro, Portland, and McMinnville all hold rodeos during September.

Wagon & Trail Rides

Many other horse-related events occur in Central Oregon. In December, for example, Albany offers horse-drawn hay wagon tours on which you can sing Christmas carols.

In Bend, **C&G Farms** ☎ (541/383-2523) provides horse-drawn carriage rides.

Mountain Shadow Ranch, HC 66 Box 690, Cascade Locks, OR 97014, ☎ 541/374-8592, leads trail rides in the Columbia River Gorge.

Saddleback Stables (☎ 541/593-1000) at Sunriver Resort in Sunriver offers hay rides, sleigh rides, or guided trail rides, as does **River Ridge Stables** (☎ 541/382-8711) at Inn of the Seventh Mountain, 18575 SW Century Dr., in Bend.

Mountain Gate Stables, 4399 Hwy 66, Ashland, OR 97520, ☎ 541/482-8873, located between the town and Emigrant Lake, features pony rides and "kiddie trail rides." They also offer one-, one-and-a-half-, and two-hour guided trail rides for adults on their 2,000-acre range.

CJ Lodge, PO Box 130, Maupin, OR 97037, ☎ 503/395-2404, furnishes covered wagon trips and horseback trips, separately or in combination.

At **L Bar T Guest Ranch**, 193 N. Morrow Rd., Wamic, OR 97063, ☎ 503/544-3010, guests can rope, ride, and drive cattle. They also can take pack trips, covered wagon trips, or trail rides on the Oregon Trail.

Rock Springs Guest Ranch (☎ 541/389-1854) in Bend, **Mountain Shadow Ranch** (☎ 541/374-8592) in Cascade Locks, **Fir Mountain Ranch** (☎ 503/354-2753) in Hood River, and **Eagle Crest Resort** (☎ 503/923-2072) in Redmond all provide guided trail rides.

Too-Much-Bear Trails, 48370 Norquist Lane, Oakridge, OR 97463, ☎ 503/782-3900, arranges wilderness rides and pack-trips into the Willamette Wilderness.

■ On Wheels

Covered Bridges

Some of the more colorful bridges around Albany include **Gilkey Bridge** over Thomas Creek on Goar Road between Jefferson and Scio; **Larwood Bridge** over Crabtree Creek Fish Hatchery Road near Larwood; **Short Bridge** over the South Santiam River on High Deck Road near Cascadia; **Hannah Bridge** over Thomas Creek on Camp Morrison Drive south of

Jordan; and **Hoffman Bridge** over Crabtree Creek on Hungry Hill Drive north of Crabtree.

Some other old "kissing bridges" (so called because, in the days before automobiles, young swains found the covered bridges a convenient place to steal a kiss) are **Bohemian Hall Bridge** over Cox Creek on Price Road east of Albany; **Crawfordsville Bridge** over the Calapoosia River on Route 228 north of Crawfordsville; **Shimanek Bridge** over Thomas Creek on Richardson Gap Road northeast of Scio; **Weddle Bridge** over Ames Creek on 14th Avenue in Sankey Park, Sweet Home; and **Jordan Bridge** over Salem Canal, connecting Pioneer and Wilderness Parks in Stayton.

Cottage Grove calls itself the "Covered Bridge Capital of Oregon" for good reason. Within the immediate area are **Centennial Bridge**, **Chambers Railroad Bridge**, **Currin Bridge** on Row River Road, **Mosby Creek Bridge**, and **Dorena Bridge**, south of Dorena Lake.

The Eugene area also boasts a fair number of covered bridges, including **Belknap Bridge** on King Road West off McKenzie River Drive; **Cannon Street Bridge** in Greenway Park, Lowell; **Centennial Bridge,** adjacent to City Hall on Main Street in downtown Cottage Grove; **Chambers Bridge,** at South River Road and Harrison Street in Cottage Grove; and **Coyote Creek Bridge** on Battle Creek Road just off Territorial Highway, south of Veneta.

Some other covered bridges close to Eugene are **Currin Bridge** on Laying Road, 1.5 miles from town on Shoreview Drive off Garoutte Road near Cottage Grove; **Lake Creek Bridge** on Nelson Mountain Road, just off OR 36, 30 miles west of Route 99; and **Earnest Bridge** on Paschelke Road, just off Marcola Road near Marcola. The Earnest Bridge appeared in a scene in the 1964 movie *Shenandoah*.

Goodpasture Bridge, just off OR 126 at Leaburg Dam near Vida, has 10 Gothic louvered windows on each side and is the second longest covered bridge in the state. **Lowell Bridge**, just off OR 58 at the Lowell intersection, had to be raised six feet when Dexter Dam was completed and the reservoir filled in 1953. **Mosby Creek Bridge,** on Layne Road east of Cottage Grove, sits in a very picturesque setting and is the oldest covered bridge (1920) in Lane County. **Office Bridge**, which originally connected a mill and the mill office on the north edge of Westfir, has a covered walk running along the outside of the bridge.

Near Galice, the **Grave Creek** sits just east of I-5; near Pedee, there's the **Ritner Creek** covered bridge; and near Silverton, there's the **Gallon House Bridge**, built in 1917.

📖 A free brochure, *Covered Bridges of Oregon*, has been produced by the Oregon Department of Transportation's Bridge Engineering Section, Room 329 Transportation Building, Salem, OR 97310, ☎ 503/378-6551. The brochure spotlights covered bridges throughout Benton, Coos, Deschutes, Douglas, Jackson, Josephine, Lane, Lincoln, Marion, Multnomah, and Polk Counties.

Another free brochure, *Covered Bridge Country*, is available at the Albany Visitors Association, 300 Second Ave. SW, PO Box 965, Albany, OR 97321, ☎ 541/928-0911 or 800/526-2256, fax 541/926-1500, Web site www.tico.org/albany, or at many of the other central Oregon visitors bureaus and chambers of commerce.

Wineries & Llama Farms

Oregon has a great many wineries, too, and a tour of them can be as entertaining as a tour of the covered bridges.

📖 A slick brochure, *Discover Oregon Wineries*, has been published by the Oregon Wine Advisory Board and the Oregon Winegrowers' Association, 1200 NW Front Ave., Suite 400, Portland, OR 97209, ☎ 800/242-2363. The brochure is distributed free of charge and is a marvelous guide to the wineries throughout the state.

Another free booklet, the Washington County *Wine Country Scenic Loop*, is available free of charge from the Beaverton Area Chamber of Commerce, 4800 SW Griffith Dr., Suite 100, Beaverton, OR 97005, ☎ 503/644-0123, fax 503/526-0349. While you're there, you might consider picking up another free brochure, *Washington County Parks Guide*.

For some reason, the wine country around Newberg also abounds in llama ranches. If you would like to visit one, there's **Chehalem Valley Llamas**, 315 W. Columbia Dr., ☎ 503/538-4241; **Grand Oaks Farm**, 31150 NE Schaad Rd., ☎ 503/538-6830; **Hillside Llamas**, 15385 NE Kincaid Rd., ☎ 503/538-7512; **Ladd Hill Llamas**, 18155 SW Kramlen Rd., ☎ 503/625-0633; **Llamas de La Foresta**, 33895 NE Wilsonville Rd., ☎ 503/625-5019 or 538-4704; **Mountainside Ranch & Llama Yarns of Oregon**, 17771 NE Hillsboro Hwy, ☎ 503/538-7618; **Rain Dance Ranch**, PO Box 1060, ☎ 503/538-7053; **Spring Creek Llama Ranch**, 14700 NE Spring Creek Lane, ☎ 503/538-5717; and **Yamhill Llama/Kuvasz**, 16900 Yamhill Hwy, ☎ 503/538-5901.

If you're not into wines, but would like to see some llamas anyway, there are a number of llama and alpaca breeders in Grants Pass: **The Applegate Llama Stud**, 7980 New Hope Rd., ☎ 541/862-2170; **Apple Hill Ranch**, 17600 Hwy 238, ☎ 541/846-7577; **Bolt Mountain Llamas**, 4222 Midway Ave., ☎ 541/471-1019; **Odyssey Llamas**, 635 Ewe Creek Rd., ☎ 541/476-9782; and **Valley View Farm**, 1856 Dowell Rd., ☎ 541/474-2129.

In Hood River, **Riverside Llama** (☎ 509/493-1021) and **Double Dutch Farms** (☎ 541/386-7971) raise llamas and alpacas.

Other llama ranches can be found in Ashland, Cave Junction, Central Point, Eagle Point, Jacksonville, Medford, Rogue River, Shady Cove, and Williams.

Cascade View Llama Ranch at 63135 Dickey Rd., in Bend, ☎ 541/389-8204, will arrange for you to take a llama trek. So will **The Halligan Ranch** (☎ 541/389-6855 or 382-5758) in Redmond; **Wiley Woods Ranch**, 555 Howell Prairie Rd. SE, Salem, OR 97301, ☎ 503/362-0873 or 931-3978, E-mail mplozr@aol.com; and **Patterson Ranch**, 15425 McKenzie Hwy, Sisters, OR 97759. ☎ 503/549-3831. Some other nice day-trips in central Oregon include:

Driving Tours

From Bend, go west on Franklin Avenue past Drake Park and follow the signs to **Cascade Lakes Highway**, an 87-mile paved loop that provides beautiful views of **Mount Bachelor**, the **Three Sisters**, and **Broken Top**. The portion past Mount Bachelor is often closed during the winter.

To reach the 140-mile **Mount Hood Loop**, drive east on I-84 to Hood River, then turn south on OR 35 (Exit 64). The loop ends at Troutdale, where you rejoin I-84 for the return to Cascade Locks. The 110-mile **Lower Klamath Loop Tour** starts at the Klamath County Museum on Main Street in Klamath Falls and takes you past or through the **Klamath Wildlife Area** at Miller Island, a wonderful birdwatching area; **Bear Valley National Wildlife Refuge**, a winter roosting site for bald eagles; **Indian Lake**, just over the state line into California; **Skull** (or **Fire**) **Island**, site of past Indian ceremonials; **Lower Klamath National Wildlife Refuge**; **Laird's Landing**; remnants of a World War II German prisoner-of-war camp on Hill Road north of the US Fish & Wildlife Service headquarters; **Tule Lake National Wildlife Refuge**; **Lava Beds National Monument**; **Captain Jack's Stronghold**; and some Indian petroglyphs, then returns through the town of Tulelake, CA.

📖 A free pocket-sized brochure, *Lower Klamath Loop Tour*, describes the tour and is available at the Klamath County Department of Tourism, 1451 Main St., PO Box 1867, Klamath Falls, OR 97601, ☎ 503/884-0666.

Similarly, a free four-color pocket-sized brochure outlining the *Diamond Drive Tour* is available from the US Forest Service Ranger Station, 49098 Salmon Creek Rd., PO Box 1410, Oakridge, OR 97463, ☎ 503/782-2283.

If you need a Jeep to get where you want to go, **Jim Smolich Motors**, 2250 NE Hwy 20, Bend, OR 97708, ☎ 541/389-1177, rents 'em by the day, week, month, or year.

Mountain Biking

For those who enjoy mountain biking, there are a number of good trails available around Pendleton. Maps and information can be obtained at the Chamber of Commerce.

Umatilla National Forest has 1,000 miles of roads suitable for mountain biking. **Harris Park**, southeast of Milton-Freewater, is the beginning of a bike trail to **Blalock Mountain**, and the exciting **Lookingglass Trail** starts at the **Woodland Campground** in Elgin. **Lookout Mountain Loop** is accessed east of the **Jubilee Lake Campground**, 12 miles from Tollgate.

📖 A free brochure, *Biking in Washington County*, can be obtained from the Washington County Visitors Association, 5075 SW Giffith Dr., #120, Beaverton, OR 97005-8721, ☎ 503/644-5555 or 800/537-3149, fax 503/644-9784, Web site www.wcva.org.

A similar brochure, *Cycle Lane County Oregon*, is available at no cost from the Convention & Visitors Association of Lane County, 115 W. 8th Ave., Suite 190, PO Box 10286, Eugene, OR 97401, ☎ 503/484-5307, 800/452-3670 (in Oregon), or 800/547-5445 (outside Oregon), fax 503/343-6335, Web site www.cvalco.org.

The Bend Chamber of Commerce Visitor Center, 63085 N. Hwy 97, Bend, OR 97701, ☎ 503/382-3221 or 800/905-2363; and the Visitors Bureau in Roseburg can supply you with free maps of biking trails in their areas, as well.

There also is a *Clackamas County Bike Map*, but the county office in Salem (☎ 503/650-3708) doesn't give them away, it sells them.

Biking near Oakridge (Norm Coyer, CVALCO).

📖 Free biking brochures are plentiful in Portland, however. Ask for a copy of *Portland Bikeways* at the Chamber of Commerce; the *Bicycle Program* brochure at the City of Portland Bureau of Traffic Management, 1120 SW 5th Ave., Room 730, Portland, OR 97204-1972; the *Springwater Corridor Map* at the Portland Parks & Recreation office, ☎ 503/823-5127; and/or the Multnomah County bike map and brochure at the Multnomah County offices, ☎ 503/248-5050.

High Cascade Descent, PO Box 8782, Bend, OR 97708-8782, ☎ 503/389-0562 or 800/296-0562, and **Pathfinders**, PO Box 210, Oakridge, OR 97463, ☎ 541/782-4838 or 800/778-4838, E-mail pathfndr@efn.org., arrange mountain bike tours.

Pacific Crest Mountain Bike Tours (☎ 541/383-5058) in Sunriver Village sets up single- and multi-day biking trips, and **Sunriver Sports** (☎ 541/593-8369) rents bikes. **Discover Bikes**, 1020 Wasco St., Hood River, OR 97031, ☎ 541/386-4820, also rents mountain bikes.

Group Tours

Portland has two rather unusual "adventures on wheels" that are worth looking into.

SamTrak, 1945 SE Water Ave., Portland, OR 97214, ☎ 503/653-2380, operates an open-air excursion car or caboose that takes people on a sightseeing trip along the Willamette River, weather permitting, between **Oaks Park Amusement Center** and the **Oregon Museum of Science & Industry**, passing through the **Oaks Bottoms Wildlife Refuge**. There are three boarding points. The schedule varies according to season (call for the current departure times).

Portland BrewBus, 319 SW Washington, Suite 812, Portland, OR 97204, ☎ 503/273-9206 or 888/BIG-BREW, Web site www.brewbus.com, conducts a four-hour guided tour of the local breweries and brewpubs. The fee includes beer, snacks, and a souvenir diploma. From May through October, the Saturday tours leave the Red Lion-Lloyd Center at 2 PM and the Benson Hotel at 2:10 PM.

Rail Tours

Oregon also has its share of fun-filled rail tours.

Spirit of Oregon, 10285 NW Roy Rd., Cornelius, OR 97113, ☎ 503/324-1919, runs from Roy to Cochran: 27.5 miles, crossing two trestles. The dinner train leaves Saturdays at 4 PM from April through September and again in December. The brunch train leaves Saturdays and Sundays at 11 AM from April through December.

Mount Hood Railroad, 110 Railroad Ave., Hood River Depot, Hood River, OR 97031, ☎ 503/386-3556 or 800/872-4661, fax 541/386-2140, runs through the valley from Hood River to Parkdale. The company operates excursion, brunch, and dinner trains.

Vintage Trolley, 115 NW First Ave., Suite 200, Portland, OR 97209, ☎ 503/323-7363, operates an electric trolley through the city. From March through April, the trolley operates from 10 AM to 6 PM on Saturdays and Sundays only, but from May through New Year's Day, it also operates from 9:30 AM to 3 PM Monday through Friday.

Willamette Shore Trolley, 311 N. State St., PO Box 308, Lake Oswego, OR 97034, ☎ 503/222-2226, operates an electric trolley that runs seven miles along the Willamette River from Portland to Lake Oswego. First established in 1887 as the Portland and Willamette Valley Railroad, the line was purchased in 1893 by the Southern Pacific Railroad. In Portland, the trolley stops at Southwest Moody and Sheridan Street and at RiverPlace on Harbor Way. It skirts Willamette Park and Powers Marine Park, then enters a wooded area along the river. The line crosses two high trestles, one of which is the 686-foot Riverwood Trestle, and passes through the 1,396-foot Elk Rock Tunnel, making a gradual S-curve between the portals. After crossing another short bridge, the trolley arrives in downtown Lake Oswego, where the depot is in an old station on State Street between A Avenue and Foothills Road. The passenger cars have come from countries around the world; ask your motorman for the history of the car in which you are riding.

City of Prineville Railway, 185 E. 10th St., Prineville, OR 97754, ☎ 503/447-6251, is a steam railroad that has served the community since 1918.

Crooked River Railroad Co., 525 S. 6th St., PO Box 387, Redmond, OR 97756, ☎ 541/548-8630, fax 503/548-8702, E-mail dintrain@empnet.com, provides Western murder mysteries, dinner rides, Sunday champagne brunches, Friday night summer hoe-downs, and occasional mock train robberies. It takes a scenic 38-mile route through the high desert between Redmond and Prineville and operates on weekends year-around.

Windsurfing on the Columbia River (John E. Campbell, Hood River CC).

On the Water

Boating, Waterskiing & Windsurfing

Canoeing is extremely popular around Bend, particularly on Blue, Sparks, Hosmer, Irish, Taylor, Charlton, Davis, and Summit Lakes; on the Crane Prairie Reservoir; and on the Little Deschutes River from Wickiup Junction to the mouth near Harper Bridge.

Waterskiing also is popular around Bend on Cultus Lake, Lake Billy Chinook, Prineville Reservoir, Haystack Reservoir, Suttle Lake, Crescent Lake, and Odell Lake. In St. Helens, waterskiiers prefer the river, and have set up a slalom course less than a mile from the town docks.

The free booklet *Skiing Oregon Safely* is available from the Oregon State Marine Board (address above).

Hood River calls itself the "Windsurfing Capital of North America" and practitioners flit about the Columbia River there like a flock of multicolored butterflies nearly every day of the year. For information, contact the **Columbia Gorge Windsurfing Association**, ☎ 541/386-9225.

Both waterskiing and windsurfing are practiced on **Emigrant Lake** (☎ 541/776-7001), six miles from Ashland, and on six other mountain lakes within 25 miles of the city.

Hood River Windsurfing, 101 Oak Ave., Hood River, OR 97031, ☎ 503/386-5787, can help with the equipment and provide important pointers.

> A slick, 8 x 10-inch, magazine-style publication called *Boating Guide to the Lower Columbia & Willamette Rivers* has been produced by the Oregon State Marine Board, 435 Commercial St. NE, Salem, OR 97310-0650, ☎ 503/378-8587. The equally slick *Willamette River Recreation Guide* magazine and the *Oregon Boater's Handbook* can be obtained from the same source. All three are free of charge.

There's a free monthly boating newspaper, *Freshwater News*, 700 N. Hayden Island Dr., Suite 200, Portland, OR 97217-8172, ☎ 503/283-2733, readily available in tackle shops around Portland.

Fishing

In Oregon, fishing almost always is good for one species or another, at one place or another, using one technique or another.

Between January and June, steelhead trout and spring chinook salmon can be caught on the **Upper** and **Lower Willamette Rivers**, the **Rogue River**, and all coastal rivers. April to September is a good time to fly fish for trout on the **McKenzie River**.

May to December is good for largemouth bass, trout, bluegill, crappie, perch, catfish, and coho salmon on **Siltcoos Lake**, while June to September is good for smallmouth bass on the **Columbia** and **Umpqua Rivers**, and September to November is good for chinook on all coastal rivers and bays.

Trout fishing is good in the 1.8 million-acre **Deschutes National Forest**, 1645 Hwy 20 East, Bend, OR 97702, ☎ 503/388-2715, which has 500 miles of streams, 150 lakes, and six wild scenic rivers.

Popular trout waters around Bend include **Blue**, **Crescent**, **Cultus**, **Davis**, **East**, **Hosmer**, **Lava**, **Odell**, **Paulina**, **South Twin**, **Sparks**, and **Suttle Lakes**; the **Crane Prairie** and **Wickiup Reser-**

voirs; and the **Big** and **Little Deschutes, Fall,** and **Metolius Rivers**. Rainbow trout, smallmouth bass, mountain whitefish, channel catfish, chinook salmon (in the spring), and steelhead trout (in the summer) also are caught in the **John Day River**, the nation's third longest free-flowing river.

Around Redmond, north of Bend, **Billy Chinook** and **Haystack Lakes** and **Ochoco and Prineville Reservoirs** provide good trout fishing. Along the **Columbia River Gorge**, winter steelhead are taken from the **Sandy** and **Clackamas Rivers** from mid-November to March, while spring chinook are dominant in the **Sandy, Clackamas,** and **Willamette Rivers** between March and June.

The **Columbia River** offers walleye from May to November, shad from May to June, and sturgeon, steelhead, and fall chinook from May to August. **Sandy River** near Gresham offers some excellent salmon and steelhead fishing, as well as rafting, kayaking, and canoeing.

Diamond Lake on OR 138, seven miles north of Crater Lake National Park, is open to fishing only. There is boat access on the north and south sides of the lake, and boat rentals are available. The Visitors Bureau in Roseburg can provide a variety of free fishing brochures.

Around **St. Helens**, the early months are best for sturgeon, March to June for runs of salmon, June to August for summer steelhead, and fall for chinook and coho salmon. During February and April, the residents dip for smelt from the city or county docks behind the courthouse or from a boat.

Lake Selmac in Selma is a 160-acre man-made lake containing trout, bass, and crappie. It has a boat ramp and provides good boating, swimming, and camping in addition to the fishing.

South Umpqua River near Winston provides good fishing for smallmouth bass. In **Tillamook Bay**, the catch of fall chinook is best from mid-September to December.

Fishing on the Fly, PO Box 9486, Bend, OR 97708, ☎ 503/382-1264 or 800/952-0707, and **The Fly Box** (☎ 541/388-3330) arrange fly fishing float trips on the Deschutes River and walk-in trips to other fishing locations.

Fly By Nyte Guide Service, PO Box 24, Rufus, OR 97050, ☎ 503/739-2770, will help you fish the Columbia River for walleye, sturgeon, bass, or steelhead from a 22-foot jet boat, with all gear provided.

Don Schneider's Reel Adventures, 57206 E. Marmot Rd., Sandy, OR 97055, ☎ 503/622-5372 or 789-6860, makes half-day, all-day, and over-

On the McKenzie River (Shirley Petersen, CVALCO).

night fishing excursions for salmon, steelhead, sturgeon, shad, walleye, or bass aboard a jet sled, drift boat, raft, or kayak.

Rafting & Kayaking

Whitewater rafting and kayaking are practically a state sport in Oregon, particularly in the northern part of the state, where there are literally dozens of companies with the experience and the equipment to handle the rugged local conditions. Among them: **Noah's World of Water**, 53 N. Main, PO Box 11, Ashland, OR 97520, ☎ 541/488-2811 or 800/858-2811, Web site www.noahsrafting.com, runs rafting trips three times a day, seven days a week from April through September.

Blazing Paddles, PO Box 7855, Bend, OR 97708-7855, ☎ 541/388-0145, Web site wwwbendnet.com/blazingpaddles, handles all-day, 17-mile whitewater rafting trips on the Lower Deschutes River.

White Water Warehouse (Wilderness Water Ways), 625 NW Starker Ave., Corvallis, OR 97330, ☎ 541/758-3150 or 800/214-0579, provides whitewater rafting trips as well as float and fishing trips.

Wild Water Adventures, Box 249, Creswell, OR 97426, ☎ 541/895-4465 or 800/289-4534, offers rafting trips on the Willamette, Lower McKenzie, North Santiam, Rogue, Upper McKenzie, McKenzie, North Umpqua, Deschutes, and Klickitat Rivers.

Hellgate Jetboat Excursions, 953 SE 7th St., Grants Pass, OR 97526, ☎ 541/479-7204 or 800/648-4874, will take you jetboating on the Rogue River, or **Orange Torpedo Trips**, PO Box 1111, Grants Pass, OR 97526, ☎ 503/479-5061 or 800/635-2925, fax 503/471-0995, will take you down the river in an inflatable kayak.

White Water Cowboys, 210 Merlin Rd., Merlin, OR 97532, ☎ 541/479-0132 or 800/635-2925, guides whitewater trips that range from two hours to four days in length. The company also rents rafts and kayaks.

River Drifters, 13570 NW Lakeview Dr., Portland, OR 97229, ☎ 503/645-6264, conducts rafting trips on the Upper Clackamas, White Salmon, Deschutes, North Santiam, and three other rivers.

Portland River Co., 50 SW 2nd Ave., Box A-8, Suite 400E, Portland, OR 97201, ☎ 503/229-0551, E-mail prc@network13.net, conducts whitewater rafting trips and sea kayak tours on the Willamette River. The two-hour guided trips leave Portland's Riverplace Marina.

For those who like to tear up the water on their own, **SK Watercraft Rentals**, 3409 NE Marine Dr., Portland, OR 97211, ☎ 503/284-6447, rents stand-ups, one-seaters, two-seaters, three-seaters, and jet boats for use on the Columbia River.

Commercial Cruises

At a more leisurely pace, the historic **Canby Ferry** (☎ 503/650-3030) still transports passengers across the Willamette River. So does the **Wheatland Ferry**, which crosses the Willamette just south of Dayton off Wallace Road.

The *Columbia Gorge* sternwheeler, ☎ 541/223-3928 or 541/374-8427, leaves the dock at the Visitors Center in Cascade Locks at 10, 12:30, and 3 throughout the summer months for two-hour cruises on the Columbia River. The ship goes downriver to Bonneville Dam, then back upstream to Stevenson, WA, before it returns to Cascade Locks.

Between October and June each year, the *Columbia Gorge* cruises the Willamette River, with the passengers boarding at SW Front Street and Stark Avenue in Portland. Then, at the end of June, Hood River's "Sternwheeler Days" celebrate the return of the ship to her home port for the summer (for details, contact the Port of Cascade Locks, ☎ 541/374-8619).

Cascade Sternwheelers, 1200 NW Front Ave., Suite 110, Portland, OR 97200, ☎ 503/223-3928, fax 503/223-4013, operates the *Columbia Gorge* as well as another sternwheeler, *Cascade Queen*. The *Cascade Queen* takes narrated excursions up the Columbia River Gorge each weekday. Different excursions receive different narrations. One is about Lewis and Clark, another is about The Oregon Trail, and a third is called "Steamboat'n USA." Dinner dances with live music are held on Friday nights from 7 to 10. Brunch and dinner cruises are offered on Saturdays and Sundays.

In Portland Harbor, **Rose City Riverboat Cruises** (☎ 503/234-6665) takes harbor tours and moonlight cruises.

Portland Spirit, 842 SW First Ave., Portland, OR 97204, ☎ 503/224-3900 or 800/224-3901, conducts lunch, brunch, and dinner cruises, as well as sightseeing cruises and dance cruises. Passengers board at Tom McCall Waterfront Park in downtown Portland. The same company operates *Willamette Star,* a 75-foot yacht that offers the area's newest dinner cruise.

Great River Cruises & Tours, 2511 N. Hayden Island Dr., Portland, OR 97217, ☎ 503/228-6228 or 800/720-0012, offers 3.5-hour "Night Sights and City Lights" sunset dinner cruises on the Willamette River plus cruises through the Columbia River Gorge, lunch cruises, five-hour sightseeing cruises, and a combination cruise/tour to Mount St. Helens. **Adventure Cruises**, 2206 SE 141st Ave., Portland, OR 97233-2415, ☎ 503/762-0939 or 800/613-2789, offers seven-day voyages on the Columbia River.

Bubba Louie's West Wind Sailing, ☎ 541/386-4222 or 800/880-0861, is located in the Mid-Columbia Marina, Port Marina Park, near Hood River. They'll take you sailing on the Columbia River or rent you a boat to sail yourself.

Competitive Swimming

Every September, Hood River hosts the annual **Cross Channel Swim**, Oregon's equivalent to swimming the English Channel. Over 400 swimmers make the mile swim across the Columbia River. For details, contact the Hood River County Chamber of Commerce, 405 Portway Ave., Hood River, OR 97031, ☎ 541/386-2000 or 800/366-3530, fax 541/386-2057.

Houseboating

With a houseboat, the water is your home. **Chinook Water Chalets**, ☎ 503/546-2939, rents houseboats on Lake Billy Chinook. The company is based at Three Rivers Marina on the Metolius arm of the lake.

On Snow

Skiing

To provide up-to-the-minute information on winter conditions, numerous regions operate a "snow phone." These include: **Anthony Lakes**, ☎ 541/856-3277; **Copper Spur Ski Area**, ☎ 503/230-2084; **Hoodoo**, ☎ 541/822-DEEP; **Mount Ashland**, ☎ 541/482-2754; **Mount Bachelor**, ☎ 541/382-7888; **Mount Bailey**, ☎ 800/733-7593; **Mount Hood Meadows**, ☎ 503/227-SNOW; **Mount Hood SkiBowl**, ☎ 503/222-BOWL; **Summit Ski Area**, ☎ 503/272-0256; **Timberline Ski Area**, ☎ 503/222-2211; and **Willamette Pass Ski Area**, ☎ 541/345-SNOW.

> The useful *Winter Travel Guide: Clackamas County, Oregon* can be obtained free of charge through Clackamas County Tourism Development Council, 621 High St., Oregon City, OR 97045, ☎ 800/647-3843.

Snow in the High Cascades may keep many of the hiking and cross-country trails closed until June or July. Maps and general information are available at the Deschutes National Forest Office, 1230 NE 3rd St., Bend, OR 97709, ☎ 541/388-5664.

Anthony Lakes, 61995 Quail Rd., La Grande, OR 97850, ☎ 541/963-4599 or 856-3277, Web site www.anthonylakes.com, offers one double chairlift, one poma, and a backcountry Snowcat. There are eight miles of cross-country trails. Snowboarding is allowed. Rentals are available. The facility is open from 9 to 4.

Hoodoo Ski Bowl, Box 20, Hwy 20, Sisters, OR 97759, ☎ 541/822-3799, Web site www.hoodoo.com, just 45 minutes west of Redmond, has three chairlifts and a rope tow. Night skiing, lessons, and skiing on 10 miles of trails cross-country also are available. **Mount Ashland**, PO Box 220, Ashland, OR 97520, ☎ 541/482-2897, Web site www.mind.net/snow, is 15 miles outside of town. Facilities include four chairlifts, 23 downhill runs, and over 80 miles of trails for

Cross-country skiing, Mount Bachelor.

cross-country skiing. Lessons and rentals are available. The season normally runs from November to April.

Mount Bachelor, 335 SW Century Dr., PO Box 1031, Bend, OR 97709-1031, ☎ 541/382-2442 or 800/829-2442, fax 541/382-6536, Web site www.mtbachelor.com, is open from 8 to 4 daily during the winter and from 10 to 4 after June 13. The largest ski resort in the northwest, the facility is located 22 miles west of town on the Cascade Lakes Highway, provides 3,100 feet of vertical skiing, a summit lift to 9,065 feet, and views into three states. There are six detachable express quads, one detachable express triple, three triple chairlifts, one double chairlift, and two surface airlifts. The US Ski Team has trained here for the past 30 years.

Snowboarding, dog sledding, hiking, and mountain biking are all popular at Mount Bachelor, but alpine skiing is king from November into July. Over 35 miles of trails permit cross-country skiing over 3,200 acres of glades, bowls, and groomed trails. The Cross Country Center rents equipment. There also is a cafeteria and a day care center.

Mount Hood Meadows Ski Resort, 6420 SW MacAdam, Suite 216, Portland, OR 97201 (or PO Box 470, Mt. Hood, OR 97041), ☎ 503/246-1810, 337-2222, or 800/9292-SKI, E-mail skiatmhm@aol.com, Web site www.skihood.com, is just 67 miles from Portland. The resort offers 2,150 skiable acres with 2,777 feet of vertical skiing. The longest run covers three miles, and a new Heather Canyon chairlift raises the total number of lifts to ten, including three high-speed detachable quads, one fixed-grip quad, six double chairs, one pony lift, and a complimentary tow rope. Night skiing is provided on 22 runs with four lifts, and over nine miles of cross-country trails are available. Snowboarding and Snowcat skiing also are permitted.

Mount Hood Ski Bowl, 87000 Hwy 26, Government Camp, OR 97028, ☎ 503/222-2695, is America's largest night ski area and has the northwest's only half-mile dual alpine slide. Open from Memorial Day to mid-October and from mid-November to mid-April, the site has 65 day runs and trails, and 34 lighted night runs. There is a ski school and a snowboard park. During the summer, sky-chair rides are offered, there are 40 miles of mountain biking trails, and there is a bungy tower. **Timberline Ski Area**, Timberline Lodge, OR 97028, ☎ 503/231-5400 or 800/547-1406, E-mail timlodge@teleport.com, Web site www.teleport.com/~timlodge, sits on the south slopes of Mount Hood. The facility provides six chairlifts – two detachable quad chairs, one triple chair, two double chairs, and one double beginner chair – and 31 trail runs cover more than 1,000 skiable acres. Night skiing is available, but there is no ski patrol and no snow control.

Timberline Lodge, Mount Hood (Hood Rover CC).

Willamette Pass, PO Box 5509, Eugene, OR 97405, ☎ 503/484-5030 or 800/444-5030, is off Route 58 between Eugene and Bend, north of Odell Lake. Night skiing is available each Friday and Saturday from December 30 through March 25, and there are 12.5 miles of trails for cross-country skiing.

The Inn at Hood River Village Resort, 1108 E. Marina Way, Hood River, OR 97031, ☎ 800/828-7873, offers two-party ski packages to either Mount Hood Meadows or Timberline Ski Bowl.

Cross-country skiing is popular in any of the Sno-Parks along Route 35 near **Hood River**. **Crater Lake National Park** also is popular with cross-country skiers.

Diamond Lake Resort, Diamond Lake, OR 97731, ☎ 800/733-7593, can provide Snowcat skiing, cross-country skiing, inner-tubing, snowboarding, ice skating, snowmobile rentals, and guided snowmobile tours. In the summer, the resort offers chuckwagon and buggy rides. Fishing charters aboard a 25-foot cabin cruiser capable of accommodating six leave at 7 AM and 1 PM for four-hour trips. Horseback riding, ☎ 541/793-3337, is available by the hour, half-day, or all-day. There is an RV park, a campground, and a marina that rents boats, motors, canoes, and paddle boats.

Skiing equipment is available for rent at both Diamond Lake Resort, ☎ 541/793-3333, and Crater Lake Lodge, ☎ 541/594-2511.

Mt. Hood & the Columbia River Gorge

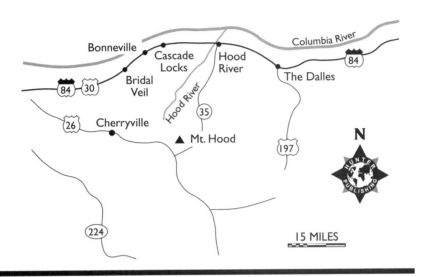

Near Roseburg, downhill skiing is popular at **Mount Bailey**, although there are no chairlifts to date. Instead, a Snowcat transports skiers up the mountain.

Warner Canyon Ski Area, ☎ 503/947-5001, is 10 miles northeast of Lakeview, just north of the California state line. It has 14 runs, with a vertical drop of 730 feet, and is open from 1 to 4 PM on Fridays and from 9 AM to 4 PM on Saturdays, Sundays, and legal holidays. Ski rentals are available. In the same locale, there are snowmobile trails at **Warner** and on **Quartz Mountain**.

Snowmobiling

People like to go snowmobiling along **Mid-Cascade Lakes Highway**, at **Dutchman's Flat** and in the high country around Bend. Maps are available at the Chamber of Commerce office.

Fantastic Recreation Rentals (☎ 541/389-5640) rents snowmobiles and conducts guided snowmobile tours on Mount Bachelor.

Ice Skating

If you want to go ice skating, **Inn of the Seventh Mountain**, 18575 SW Century Dr., Bend, OR 97702, ☎ 503/382-8711 or 800/452-6810, fax 503/

382-3517, has an outdoor rink that is open from November to April. The inn also arranges snowmobile trips, horse-drawn sleigh rides, sleigh ride dinners, horseback rides, and hiking.

Shevlin Park Hatchery Pond, ☎ 541/389-PARK, on Shevlin Park Road, four miles west of Bend, also has an outdoor pond that is used for ice skating.

Lane County Ice Arena, 796 W. 13th Ave., Eugene, OR 97402, ☎ 541/687-3615, offers ice skating, lessons, and skate rentals.

Dog Sledding

For something a little bit different, try dog sledding. **Oregon Trail of Dreams**, ☎ 541/382-2442 or 800/829-2442, at Mount Bachelor Sunrise Lodge near Bend, will give you a ride in a dog sled.

■ In the Air

Air Shows

A large airshow associated with Portland's annual **Rose Festival** is held at the Hillsboro airport in June.

In Troutdale, the Experimental Aircraft Association and the local Chamber of Commerce host an annual Summer **AeroFair**, and in September there is an annual **Fly-In** at the Prineville airport, ☎ 541/447-1118.

Ballooning

A **Hot Air Balloon Classic** is held in Tigard's Cook Park during Portland's big **Rose Festival** each June.

Those who attend Beaverton's annual **"The Taste of Beaverton"** celebration, also held in June, can go aloft in a tethered hot air balloon.

Albany hosts the **Great Balloon Escape**, ☎ 541/928-0911, each year filling the skies with over 30 hot air balloons and lots of excitement. In September, the **Northwest Hot Air Balloon Championships** are held in Salem.

If you would like to experience a hot air balloon flight yourself, **Oregon Adventures Aloft** (☎ 800/238-0700) in Medford, **Vista Balloon Adventures** (☎ 503/625-7385 or 800/622-2309) in Portland, **Morning Glory Balloon Co.** (☎ 503/389-8739) in Redmond, or **Vista Balloon**

Adventures (☎ 503/625-7385 or 800/622-2309) in Sherwood will be happy to oblige.

Scenic Flights

If a plane ride is more to your liking, they are available too. **The Flight Shop** (☎ 541/382-3801 or 800/261-0019) at Bend Municipal Airport offers charter flights and scenic tours. **Hillsboro Aviation**, 3565 NE Cornell Rd., Hillsboro, OR 97124, ☎ 503/648-2831 or 800/345-0949, also furnishes aerial tours.

Mid-Columbia Water Sports, Port Marina Park, Hood River, OR 97041, ☎ 503/386-3321, takes scenic flights over the Columbia River Gorge. **Jim's Biplane Rides**, PO Box 919, North Plaines, OR 97133, ☎ 800/FLY-1929, will take you aloft in a bright blue and orange open-cockpit 1929 biplane.

C&C Aviation, 14430 SE Center St., Portland, OR 97236, ☎ 503/760-6969, 306-8938, or 800/516-6969, E-mail chad@ccavn.com, Web site www.ccavn.com, flies out of Evergreen Airport on Mill Plain Boulevard in Vancouver, WA, across the Columbia River from Portland, and takes flights over Mount St. Helens.

Precision Helicopters, 17770 NE Aviation Way, Newberg, OR 97132, ☎ 503/537-0108, fax 503/538-2414, takes scenic flights, arranges charters, and gives lessons in flying planes or helicopters. If you're already a licensed pilot, they'll even rent you a plane.

Rainbow Helicopters, 705 SE Salmon, PO Box 863, Redmond, OR 97756, ☎ 503/548-3255, features helicopter rides and an air taxi service. **Conquest Helicopters**, 1123 NW Graham Rd., Suite 300, Portland-Troutdale Airport, Troutdale, OR 97060, ☎ 503/661-1452, 260/0350, or 260-0349, fax 260/661-0266, also furnishes helicopter rides.

Gliders

Aircraft engines too noisy? **Cottage Grove Aviation**, 78833 Airport Rd., Cottage Grove, OR 97424, ☎ 503/942-0663, will take you on a sailplane flight. So will **Cascade Soaring**, PO Box 369, Dayton, OR 97114, which flies out of the McMinnville Airport, ☎ 503/472-8805.

Hang Gliding

Or you can watch people do it *without a glider!* Go to the **Hang Gliding Festival in Lakeview**, ☎ 541/947-6040, held in July.

Skydive Oregon, 12150 S. Hwy 211, Molalla, OR 97038, ☎ 800/934-5867, will take you parachuting. So will **Pacific Parachute Center** (☎ 503/843-3616) at the airport in Sheridan.

■ Cultural Excursions

Ashland

Ashland is a theater-oriented city. The **Oregon Shakespeare Festival**, 15 S. Pioneer, Ashland, OR 97520, ☎ 541/482-4331, has an international reputation. It presents 11 plays in three unique theaters from February through October. Backstage tours and lectures are available, and there is an interesting museum.

While in Ashland, you also might wish to attend **Oregon Cabaret Theatre**, **Rogue Valley Symphony**, **Rogue Opera**, or **State Ballet of Oregon** if you're in a musical mood, or **Southern Oregon State College Theatre**, **Studio X**, **Actor's Theatre of Ashland**, **Ashland Children's Theatre**, or **Lyric Theatre** if you're in the mood for drama.

Should the suspense of a thrilling play become too much, Ashland also has a plethora of spas. **A Beach House**, 368 Otis St., Ashland, OR 97520, ☎ 541/482-0196; **Atrium**, 51 Water St., Ashland, OR 97520, ☎ 541/488-8775; or **The Phoenix**, 2425 Siskiyou Blvd., Ashland, OR 97520, ☎ 541/488-1281, can fix you up with a massage, a facial, or perhaps an herbal wrap. **Spa Lithia** (☎ 541/552-0144), the town's newest spa, is located in the historic railroad district.

Miss Mella's Drama Theater, 628 SE Jefferson, **Dallas**, OR 97338, ☎ 503/623-4120, presents some hilarious melodrama.

Bend

The world's largest commercial reindeer ranch, **Reindeer Ranch Operation Santa Claus**, is located 18 miles northwest of Bend at 4355 W. Hwy 126. Bend also has its share of local theater. **Community Theatre of the Cascades**, 148 NW Greenwood, ☎ 541/389-0803, and **Magic Circle Theatre**, 2600 NW College Way, ☎ 541/383-7575, both feature live theater productions. For more to do in town, a map to follow on a self-guided historic walking tour of Bend is available at the Chamber of Commerce.

Sunriver Nature Center and Observatory, ☎ 541/593-4394 (Nature Center) or 593-4442 (Observatory), is open year-around. The center is located 18 miles south of Bend, while **Osprey Observation Point** at

Crane Prairie Reservoir can be found 45 miles southwest of town. Well signed, the latter is one of few such nesting sites in the United States. Try to visit it in the summer, when the best viewing is available.

Another treat for the nature-lover is **High Desert Museum**, 59800 S. Hwy 97, Bend, OR 97702, ☎ 541/382-4754, Web site www.highdesert.org. Located 3.5 miles south of Bend on US 97, the center is open daily from 9 to 5. There are 20 acres of trailside exhibits, and every half hour from 10 to 4, live animal talks are presented. The museum is open daily.

For something of a more fanciful nature, visit **The Funny Farm at Buffet Flat**, located seven miles north of Bend on Route 97 at the Deschutes junction. The private five-acre park, which is open daily, takes a whimsical look at re-use and recycling by means of totem poles, the Love Pond, a Bowling Ball Garden, the Yellow Brick Road, an Electric Kaleidoscope, goats, pigs, sheep, and a dog that lives on the roof.

Chiloquin/Warm Springs

There is a wonderful display of Native American artifacts in the **Klamath Tribes Museum** (☎ 800/524-9787) in Chiloquin, and in **The Museum at Warm Springs** (☎ 503/553-3331), on US 26 in Warm Springs.

For authentic Native American souvenirs, shop **Inter-Tribal Sports Clothing & Gifts**, ☎ 503/553-1141; **L & L Red Dog, Fine Arts**, ☎ 503/553-6607; **Thunder Hawk Indians Arts & Crafts**, ☎ 503/553-5833; **Traditional Treasures**, ☎ 503/553-6448; **Warm Springs Clothing Co.**, ☎ 503/553-3210; or **Wy-East Beads & Gifts**, ☎ 503/553-5009, all in Warm Springs.

Eugene

Eugene is the home of the **University of Oregon**, where the **Museum of Natural History**, 1680 E. 15th St., Eugene, OR 97403-1224, ☎ 541/346-3024, bills itself as "The 13,000-Year-Old Tourist Trap," and its **Museum of Art**, East 14th and Kincaid Sts., Eugene, OR 97403-1223, ☎ 541/346-3027, the largest state-supported art museum in Oregon, is known for its outstanding collection of Asian art.

Momokawa Sake, 920 Elm St., **Forest Grove**, OR 97116, ☎ 503/357-7056, is the only sake (*sa-kay*) brewery in the northwest.

Hood River holds free concerts in **Jackson Park** on Thursday nights throughout August.

You can tour **Jacksonville** in a horse-drawn carriage, and afterwards visit the **Children's Museum**, 206 N. Fifth St., which occupies the old (1910) Jackson County Jail. The museum is open from 10 to 5 between Memorial Day and Labor Day. The rest of the year, it is open from noon to 5 on Sunday and Tuesday, and from 10 to 5 from Wednesday through Saturday. The museum is closed on Monday.

Every August, **Junction City** hosts a **Scandinavian Festival** with crafts, music, and dances. Swedish pancakes, Danish pastries, open-faced Norwegian sandwiches, and Kransekage (an authentic Danish wedding cake) generally are on hand.

Fort Klamath Museum & Park, ☎ 503/381-2230, located at the north end of Agency Lake in **Klamath Falls**, contains the gravesite of the Modoc Indian rebel Captain Jack and three of his braves. The park is open between 10 AM and 6 PM Thursday through Monday between June and Labor Day.

Jensen Arctic Museum, 590 W. Church, **Monmouth**, OR 97361, ☎ 503/838-8468, is the largest Arctic museum west of Maine. It is located on the campus of Western Oregon State College and is open from between 10 AM and 4 PM Wednesday through Saturday.

The **Mount Angeles Abbey**, ☎ 503/845-3030, founded in 1882 by Benedictine monks from Switzerland, sits on a 300-foot butte 18 miles northeast of **Salem**. **Queen of Angeles Monastery**, Benedictine Sisters, 840 S. Main St., Mt. Angel, OR 97362-9527, ☎ 503/845-6141, is open Saturday and Sunday afternoons, and on other days by appointment.

Hoover-Minthorn House, 115 S. River St., **Newberg**, OR 97132, ☎ 503/538-6629, was the boyhood home of President Herbert Hoover. Dr. Henry John Minthorn was Hoover's uncle, the brother of Hoover's mother Huldah. When Hoover was 11, his uncle lost a son and invited Hoover (who had earlier lost both of his parents) to live with his family.

Oregon Caves National Monument, PO Box 128, Cave Junction, OR 97523, ☎ 541/592-3400, fax 541/592-6654, offers 75-minute guided tours between 8:30 AM and 5 PM during the spring (May 1 through May 31) and the fall (the Monday after Labor Day to September 30). The tours also are offered between 8 AM and 7 PM during the summer (June 1 through Labor Day); and at 9:30, 11:30, 1, 2:30, and 4 during the winter (October 1 through April 30). The caves are located 20 miles southeast of town on OR 46. The final eight miles of road are narrow and winding, so towing a trailer is not recommended. The caves are chilly, and a jacket is advisable.

Adventures ■ 163

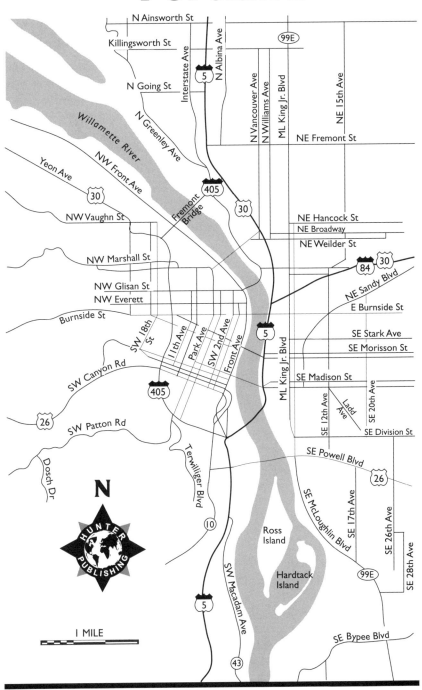

End of the Oregon Trail Interpretive Center, 1726 Washington St., **Oregon City**, OR 97045, ☎ 503/657-9336, Web site www.teleport.com/~sligard/trail.html, is located on Abernethy Green, 20 minutes southeast of Portland (Exit 10 off I-205). The center resembles a row of three covered wagons and is open year-around. Guided tours are available.

Oregon Fever, PO Box 68, Oregon City, OR 97045, ☎ 503/657-0988, Web site www.teleport.com/~norrisa/otp_home.shtml, is an outdoor musical presentation given at 8 PM nightly from mid-July through early August at the Oregon Trail Interpretive Center. The show is preceded by some old-time fiddling, clogging, folk music, and pioneer history talks by historians or authors.

Portland

You'll be greeted by a 70-foot talking tree at **World Forestry Center Museum**, 4033 SW Canyon Rd., Portland, OR 97221, ☎ 503/228-1367.

The museum is located in Washington Park next to the zoo, and is open daily from 9 to 5.

Naturalists from **EcoTours of Oregon**, 1906 SW Iowa St., Portland, OR 97201, ☎ 503/245-1428, lead scenic minivan tours to Mount St. Helens, the Columbia River Gorge, the northern coast, to study Indian culture, on whale-watching expeditions, to wineries and microbreweries, skiing, and more. Similar services are performed by **Scenic Minivan Tours**, ☎ 503/255-5558 or 888/846-2240, and **Northwest Tours**, ☎ 503/665-5585.

Portland's **Nob Hill** is a great place to go people-watching. Located on NW 23rd Avenue between NW Everett and NW Northrup, the area has a number of unusual shops and restaurants.

> Pick up a free copy of *Portland's Colorful Nob Hill* walking guide, prepared by the Nob Hill Business Association, PO Box 10025, Portland, OR 97210, ☎ 503/274-6888.

Oregon Museum of Science & Industry, 1945 SE Water Ave., Portland, OR 97214-3354, ☎ 503/797-4000, 797-4600, or 800/955-6674, bills itself as a "playground for the mind." It is open year-around.

Portland's **Chinatown** is located north of NW 3rd Avenue and east of NW Couch Street.

From June through September, the local sawmills in **Roseburg** open their doors for free tours. For a schedule and reservations, contact the Roseburg Visitors & Convention Bureau, ☎ 541/672-9731.

DID YOU KNOW?

*According to Indian legend, a skookum (evil spirit) lives in **Skookum Lake** in **St. Paul** and "will swirl in an eddy to drag down anyone venturing upon its waters."*

Salem

In Salem (originally called Chemeketa, meaning "place of peace"), the **Oregon State Capitol**, 900 Court St. NE., ☎ 503/986-1388, offers free admission along with two hours of free visitor parking. The building is open between 7:30 AM and 5:30 PM Monday through Friday, between 9 AM and 4 PM on Saturday, and between noon and 4 PM on Sunday. Free guided tours are provided (contact Capitol Use Services, ☎ 503/986-1388, fax 503/986-1131).

Three ferries, each with a six-car capacity, cross the Willamette River near Salem: the **Buena Vista** ferry near Buena Vista, south of Independence; the **Wheatland** ferry near Hopewell, just off Route 221; and the **Canby** ferry in Canby.

Willamette University, 900 State St., Salem, OR 97301, ☎ 503/370-6818 or 370/6340, is the oldest university in the West. Guided tours of the 61-acre campus include visits to three immaculately kept flower gardens.

Silver Falls State Park, 20024 Silver Falls Hwy SE, in **Silverton**, ☎ 503/873-8681, is Oregon's largest state park. Within its 8,706 acres are ten waterfalls ranging from 27 to 178 feet in height. The park is 26 miles east of Salem.

A block south of **The Dalles** Chamber of Commerce, off 3rd Street, the 1859 two-story frame county courthouse still stands as a reminder of the days when Wasco County covered an area greater than the British Isles and was the largest county ever created in the United States.

Where to Stay

Ashland

Lithia Springs Inn, 2165 W. Jackson Rd., Ashland, OR 97520, ☎ 541/482-7128 or 800/482-7128, $$-$$$$, is a B&B with private entry, in-room whirlpools, and naturally occurring mineral water in your own room.

Bend

Inn of the Seventh Mountain, 18575 SW Century Dr., Bend, OR 97702, ☎ 503/382-8711 or 800/452-6810, fax 503/382-3517, $$$, is the closest resort to Mount Bachelor. Biking, hiking, riding horses, skiing, golf, swimming, snowmobile trips, horse-drawn sleigh rides, and outdoor ice skating are among the amenities. **The Riverhouse**, 3075 N. Hwy 97, Bend, OR 97701, ☎ 800/547-3928, $$-$$$, sits on the banks of the Deschutes River. It has three restaurants, and will arrange ski packages.

Cave Junction

For something really different, **Out'n'About Treehouse Treesort**, 300 Page Creek Rd., Cave Junction, OR 97523, ☎ 541/592-2208 or 800/200-5484, E-mail treesort@magick.net, $$-$$$, enables guests to stay in one of five treehouses: the Deluxe for Two; the Swiss Family Complex, a pair of treehouses connected by a swinging bridge; the Luxury Cabintree; or the Treeroom Schoolhouse Suite. Guests also may stay in a conventional cabin (with an adjoining tree-fort), a tipi that is 18 feet in diameter and can sleep four, or a "treepee" that is nine feet across and has a deck area. Guests at the Treesort are called the "Tree Musketeers" and can buy souvenir "treeshirts" ($15-$75). Activities include swimming, horseback riding, trail riding, rafting trips (spring and summer), and craft trips.

Hood River

Best Western Hood River Inn, 1108 E. Marina Way, Hood River, OR 97031, ☎ 541/386-2220 or 800/828-7873, $$-$$$, sits on a bluff overlooking the Columbia River Gorge. Use Exit 64 off I-84 to reach the inn.

Columbia Gorge Hotel, 4000 Westcliff Dr., Hood River, OR 97031, ☎ 503/386-5566 or 800/345-1921, fax 541/387-5414, E-mail cghotel@gorge.net, Web site www.orge.net/lodging/cghotel, $$$$, also is on a bluff overlooking the Columbia River. Built in 1921, it serves its guests a complimentary five-course "Honey from the Sky" breakfast.

Crater Lake

Crater Lake Lodge, PO Box 128, Crater Lake, OR 97604, ☎ 503/594-2511 or ☎ 541/830-8700, fax 541/830-8514, $$-$$$, has 71 rooms. Located in Rim Village overlooking the lake, it is open from mid-May to mid-October. (Alternate address: 1211 Ave. C, PO Box 2704, White City, OR 97503.)

Diamond Lake

Diamond Lake Resort, Diamond Lake, OR 97731, ☎ 541/793-3333 or 800/733-7593, $$$, has a free *Trail Map* that shows the hiking, snowmobiling, and all-terrain vehicle trails in the area.

Grants Pass

Wolf Creek Inn, an historic stagecoach stop 20 miles north of Grants Pass, has been restored as an eight-room hotel with a dining room. The rates range from $55 to $75, and reservations are made through the Oregon State Parks office.

Newberg

At **Spring Creek Llama Ranch B&B**, 14700 NE Spring Creek Lane, Newberg, OR 97132, ☎ 503/538-5717, $$-$$$, you can experience life on a llama ranch. Another llama ranch B&B is **Llast Camp Llamas B&B**, 4555 NW Pershall Way, Redmond, OR 97756, ☎ 503/548-6828, $$.

Portland

Fifth Avenue Suites Hotel, 506 SW Washington, Portland, OR 97205, ☎ 503/222-0001, $$$, is homey and has large, comfortable rooms. There is ample parking and the hotel has a pleasant restaurant.

Portland's **Mallory Hotel**, 729 SW 15th Ave., ☎ 503/223-6311 or 800/228-8657, $$, also features a nice restaurant and is across the street from a parking garage that can be accessed with your room key.

Salem

Bethel Heights Farm, 6055 Bethel Heights Rd. NW, Salem, OR 97304, ☎ 503/364-7688, fax 503/371-8365, $$$, occupies 20 acres atop a hill outside of town. The B&B affords lovely views of the surrounding vineyards and the valley below, and the complimentary cooked breakfasts are exceptional.

Marquee House, 333 Wyatt Court NE, Salem, OR 97301, ☎ 503/391-0837, $$, is a B&B on the banks of Mill Creek. The rooms bear names that have a Hollywood flavor: Auntie Mame, Blazing Saddles, Pillow Talk, Christmas in Connecticut, and Topper.

Sunriver Resort, PO Box 3609, Sunriver, OR 97707, ☎ 541/593-1000 or 800/547-3922, Web site www.sunriver-resort.com, $$$, sits at the riverside and offers horseback riding, cycling, whitewater rafting, hiking, fly fishing, tennis, and in the winter, skiing.

The Dalles

Shilo Inn, 3223 Bret Clodfelter Way, The Dalles, OR 97058, ☎ 503/298-5502 or 800/222-2244, $$, is next to The Dalles Bridge that crosses the Columbia River to Washington.

Troutdale

McMenamins Edgefield B&B Resort, 2126 SW Halsey, Troutdale, OR 97060, ☎ 503/669-8610 or 800/669-8610, E-mail edge@mcmenamin.com, $-$$$$, is another excursion into the unusual. The hotel-like lodge was once the county poor farm. Some of its rooms have a private bath, but many of the guests must share a bath – the experience is made less intimidating because there are separate facilities for men and women in each wing of the building. The Black Rabbit Restaurant is enjoyable, as are the resort's three pubs. The resort has its own brewery and its own winery, plus 25 acres of gardens. On-premises glassblowers and potters demonstrate their skills, and there is an on-site theater that shows full-length feature films at 6 and 9 nightly – for a $1 admission fee. Tours of the lodge are conducted daily at 1, 2, and 5 PM.

Warm Springs

Kah-Nee-Ta Resort & Lodge, PO Box K, Warm Springs, OR 97761, ☎ 503/553-1112 or 800/554-4-SUN, $$-$$$, is owned and operated by the Indians. Horseback riding, swimming, volleyball, tennis, rafting, golf, and mountain biking are available, and guests should not miss the salmon bakes and the Indian fry bread.

■ Camping

Forest Service campgrounds normally are open from May 1 through mid-October. Reservations can be made via the National Campground Reservation System: ☎ 800/280-2267.

Reservations Guide for Oregon and Washington State Parks, ☎ 800/551-6949 or 858-9659 (for Oregon) and 800/233-0321 or 833-6388 (for Washington), lists 8,000 campsites in more than 70 state parks, and *Oregon State Parks Directory*, produced by Oregon State Parks, 1115 Commercial St. NE, Salem OR 97310, ☎ 503/378-6305 or 800/551-6949, is available at most Oregon visitor centers and chambers of commerce.

The cabins in Oregon's state parks have a bedroom with an unusual bunk bed – a single bed above a double bed. They also have a futon couch that makes into a double bed, a bathroom with a shower and a sink, and a kitchen with a refrigerator, a microwave, and a gas BBQ. Cabins are available at **The Cove Palisades,** near the shore of Lake Billy Chinook east of Madras, and at **Prineville Reservoir**. They cost between $45 and $65 per night.

Four air-conditioned houseboats are available between May 1 and October 31 from Oregon State Parks on **Lake Billy Chinook**. A 10-passenger boat rents for $580 on a weekend and $1,485 for the week, while a 12-passenger boat rents for $650 on a weekend and $1,590 for the week. In the **Rogue River National Forest** near Ashland, campsites are available at **Fish Lake/Doe Point**, just off Route 140, 35 miles east of town; **North Fork,** on Road 37, 23 miles from town; **Beaver Dam**, on Road 37, 23 miles from town; and **Daley Creek,** also on Road 37, 23 miles from town (they are across the road from one another).

The **Columbia River Gorge** area has campsites at **Cloud Gap** on Cooper Spur Road, 20 miles south of Parkdale; **Eagle Creek**, ☎ 541/386-2333, eastbound off I-84 at Exit 41 or westbound at Exit 40 and then circle back east; **Eight-Mile Crossing**, 10 miles west of Dufur on Road 44; **Lost Lake**, ☎ 541/386-6366 or 352-6002, on Lost Lake Road in Hood River; **Rock Creek Reservoir**, seven miles west of Wamic off Road 48; **Tilly Jane**, 20 miles south of Parkdale on Cooper Spur Road; and **Wyeth** east of Cascade Locks.

In **Deschutes National Forest** (use the National Campground Reservation System), there are campsites in **Whitefish Horse Camp**, **Simax Beach** and **Windy Group Site** on Crescent Lake; at **Odell Lake Campground** on Pebble Bay; and at **Summit Lake Campground** on Summit Lake.

Northwest Land Management, PO Box 57, Crescent Lake, OR 97425, operates Crescent Lake Campground, Spring Campground, Contorta Point Campground, Tandy Bay Campground, and Tranquil Cove Campground on **Crescent Lake**; Trapper Creek Campground, Princess Creek Campground, Sunset Cove Campground, and Odell Creek Campground on **Odell Lake**; East Davis Campground, West Davis Campground, and Lava Flow Campground on **Davis Lake**; and Crescent Creek Campground on **Crescent Creek**, all in Deschutes National Forest.

Fishing on the Williamson River (John Abbott, Klamath County DT).

In **Winema National Forest**, there are Aspen Point Campground and Sunset Campground at **Lake of the Woods**; Williamson River Campground at **Williamson River**; and Digit Point Campground at **Miller Lake**.

Camping is available at **Valley of the Rogue State Recreation Area**, ☎ 541/582-1118, on I-5, 12 miles east of Grants Pass. **Laurance Lake/Kinnikinnick Campground**, ☎ 541/352-6002, in Hood River is a Forest Service park. **Willow Lake**, **Rogue Elk**, and **Cantrall-Buckley County Parks** near Medford have provisions for camping. **Scaredman Campground**, ☎ 503/440-4930, 40 miles east of Roseburg on Route 138, is a Bureau of Land Management campground.

Champoeg Campground, ☎ 503/633-8170, seven miles east of Newberg off US 99W, was a town with 30 buildings and a population of 200 in the mid-1850s. The town was twice wiped out by floods (1861 and 1890) and was abandoned in 1892.

Where to Eat

Albany

Flinn's Living History Theater, 222 First Ave. West, Albany, OR 97321, ☎ 541/928-5008 or 800/636-5008, $$, is a dinner theater that serves breakfast, lunch, and dinner from 8 AM to 8 PM daily. **Valley Conference Center**, 9368 SW Beaverton Hillsdale Hwy, **Beaverton**, OR 97005, ☎ 503/297-3153, $$, presents a murder mystery during dinner. **Eddie May Murder Mysteries**, 1414 SW 6th Ave., **Portland**, OR 97205, ☎ 503/524-4366, $$, also stages murder mystery dinners.

Ashland

The Black Sheep, 51 N. Main St., Ashland, OR 97520, ☎ 541/482-6414, E-mail flock@theblacksheep.com, Web site www.theblacksheep.com., $$, is styled along the lines of a British restaurant/pub and is open daily from 11 AM to 12:30 PM.

Burger time? Try **Beetle Bailey Burgers**, 1st Ave., **Culver**, OR, ☎ 503/546-8749, $-$$, which is open daily from 7 AM to 9 PM.

Eugene

Oregon Electric Station, 27 E. 5th Ave., Eugene, OR 97401, ☎ 541/485-4444, $$, has been rated one of America's 100 busiest restaurants. Customers dine in antique railway cars. A National Historic Landmark, the restaurant has three lounges and specializes in prime rib.

Hood River

Stonehenge Inn, 3405 Cascade St., Hood River, OR 97031, ☎ 541/386-3940, $$, occupies a turn-of-the-century house in a beautiful wooded area.

Portland

Dining in Portland can be outstanding. It also can be fun. How else can you explain restaurants bearing such names as **Walter Mitty's**, 11830 Kerr Pkwy., in Lake Oswego, ☎ 503/246-7153, $$; **Henry Ford's**, 9589 SW Barbur Blvd., in Portland, ☎ 503/245-2434, $$; and **Rickenbacker's**, 3355 NE Cornell Rd., in Hillsboro, ☎ 503/640-9601, $$

McCormick & Schmick's Harborside, 10309 SW Montgomery, ☎ 503/220-1865, $$-$$$, is an institution in Portland. The firm owns four other restaurants in Portland, three in Seattle, one in Denver, six in five different cities throughout California, and one in Washington, DC. Seafood is their specialty. Try the whole oven-roasted Dungeness crab with garlic butter and lemon.

Huber's, 411 SW Third, Portland, OR 97205, ☎ 503/228-5686, $$-$$$, is the city's oldest restaurant (1879). Ornamented with an arched stained glass skylight, Philippine mahogany paneling, a brass cash register, a brass ship's clock, pewter wine buckets, and silver wine stands, the restaurant today belies the time when, during the flood of 1894, the chef sat in a rowboat behind the bar and served steamed clams and turkey sandwiches to the clientele that rowed in from the other side. Dinner is served daily except Sunday; lunch only during the week.

You can laugh a little at **Harvey's Comedy Club**, 436 NW 6th, Portland, OR 97210, ☎ 503/241-0338, $$.

Want to enjoy "the finer things" in Portland? Then try these: an appetizer of brie and grape quesadilla with cherry tomato salsa and Cilantro creme fraiche, followed by an entree of grilled steelhead with berry vinegars and pepper oils at **Esplanade at Riverplace**, 1510 SW Harbor Way, ☎ 503/228-3233, $$; sturgeon braised with dry cider and sweet apple at **L'Auberge**, 2601 NW Vaughn, ☎ 503/223-3302, $$-$$$; Cornish game hens with an apricot stuffing or "Steak in a Bag" – top sirloin coated with egg bread and cheddar cheese – at **Falcon's Crest Inn**, 87287 Government Camp Loop Hwy, ☎ 503/272-3403, $$-$$$, in suburban Government Camp; and for dessert, white bean brettone soup with blueberry mousse in vacherin cups at **Western Culinary Institute**, 1316 SW 13th Ave., ☎ 503/223-2245.

The Sternwheeler *Rose*, 6211 N. Ensign, Portland, OR 97210 ☎ 503/286-7673, serves you dinner on the river. Their specialty is slow-roasted prime rib. ***Portland Spirit,*** 842 SW 1st Ave., Portland, OR 97205, ☎ 503/224-3900, also offers a dinner cruise.

Salem

You can enjoy a fine Italian meal at **Alessandro's**, 325 High St. SE, Salem, OR 97301, ☎ 503/370-9551, $$-$$$. To sample Native American foods, try **Deschutes Crossing Restaurant**, ☎ 503/553-1300, in Warm Springs.

Information Sources

Tourism Division, Oregon Department of Economic Development, 775 Summer St. NE, Salem, OR 97310, ☎ 800/547-7842.

Oregon Department of Parks & Recreation, 1115 Commercial St. NE, Salem, OR 97310, ☎ 503/378-6305 (publications), 800/551-6949 (parks information), or 800/452-5687 (reservations).

US Fish & Wildlife Service, Region I, 911 NE 11th Ave., Eastside Federal Complex, Portland, OR 97232-4181, serves California, Oregon, and Washington.**Crater Lake National Park**, PO Box 7, Crater Lake, OR 97604, ☎ 541/594-2211.

Mount Hood National Forest, 16400 Champion Way, Sandy, OR 97055, ☎ 503/668-1771; **Rogue River National Forest**, 333 W. Eighth St., PO Box 520, Medford, OR 97501, ☎ 503/858-2200; **Siskiyou National Forest**, 200 NE Greenfield Rd., PO Box 440, Grants Pass, OR 97526, ☎ 503/471-6500; **Siuslaw National Forest**, 4077 Research Way, Corvallis, OR 97339, ☎ 503/750-7000; **Umpqua National For-

est, 2900 NW Stewart Pkwy., PO Box 1008, Roseburg, OR 97470, ☎ 503/672-6601; **Willamette National Forest**, 211 E. Seventh Ave., PO Box 10607, Eugene, OR, ☎ 503/465-6521; and **Winema National Forest**, 2819 Dahlia St., Klamath Falls, OR 97601, ☎ 503/465-6714.

Eastern Oregon

There are two separate and distinct parts to eastern Oregon: the northern portion, which is considerably more populous in spite of a heavy concentration of national forests, and the southern portion, which lacks as much as one significant population center.

The northern part has a number of counties; the southern part, just two.

The biggest reason for these differences is the quality of the soil. The lush Snake River valley in the north is rich in agriculture and abounds in wheat fields and truck farms.

The semiarid south has little more than sandy soil, great expanses of porous lava, sage plains, and alkali flats. The Jordan Valley is populated principally by sheep and Basques, the intrepid shepherds imported from the European Pyrenees during the 19th century to tend to the flocks.

Without a substantial amount of rain, the short rivers and shallow lakes in southeastern Oregon often shrink into nothingness. The major exception is the Owyhee River that separates itself from the Snake River near Nyssa and closely parallels the Idaho state line for some 200 miles.

Paradoxically, Lakes Harney and Malheur in the southeastern part of the state sometimes overflow their banks, join in the middle, and form Oregon's largest inland body of water.

Getting Around

Where there are no people, there is not much need for a complex network of roads and highways. In the southern part of eastern Oregon, there are but a handful. US 95 crosses the Nevada state line at McDermitt, drives almost due north for 55 miles to Burns Junction, and then strikes out for the Idaho border to the northeast.

Eastern Oregon

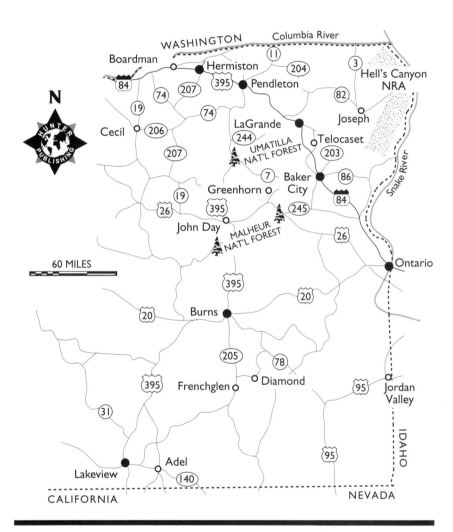

OR 78 extends northwest from Burns Junction to Burns – a distance of almost 100 miles – passing through towns that are so small their populations aren't even noted on the official state map.

Roughly paralleling US 95/OR 78 on the route to Burns is OR 205, which enters Oregon at Denio on the Nevada state line and crosses the Burns city limits 140 miles later.

US 20 passes through the region going east and west.

In northeastern Oregon, things are different. True, there is no metropolis there (Pendleton has a population of just over 15,000), but the increased density of the cities and towns makes the area seem considerably less barren. There's even an interstate highway: I-84, which roughly follows the path of the old Oregon Trail. Fresh from its eastward journey along the southern shore of the Columbia River, I-84 bends inland at Boardman, passes Pendleton, and then streaks southeastward toward Boise on the other side of the Idaho border.

US 26 provides another east-west corridor, while US 395, northbound out of Burns, links up with the Interstate in Pendleton, where OR 11 provides a direct link with Walla Walla, just across the Washington state line.

Touring

Adel

The town of Adel has Oregon's only spouting geyser.

Baker City

In light of what you have just read about eastern Oregon, it may surprise you to learn that Baker City, which sits on the Powder River and is backed by the Elkhorn Mountains, was larger than either Boise or Spokane just 100 years ago. According to the US Census, Baker City had a population of 6,663 in 1890; today, a century later, its population is just 9,585.

Baker City was named for Col. Edward Dickinson Baker, a Civil War hero, a friend of Abraham Lincoln, and the first US Senator from Oregon. Once known as the "Queen City of the Mines," the town of Baker is now surrounded by ghost towns.

Burns

Burns is located just south of a Paiute Indian Reservation and 26 miles north of the 185,000-acre **Malheur National Wildlife Refuge**, ☎ 541/493-2612. The refuge is noted for its birding, the season for which peaks between mid-March and mid-June. **Malheur Lake** and **Benson's Pond** on Central Patrol Road lie within the boundaries of the refuge.

Cecil

Cecil, ☎ 541/989-8188, was founded by a pioneer who stopped to repair his wagon and stayed on to repair the wagons of others. A 125-year-old post office still stands.

Goose Lake

Goose Lake, in the southern part of the region, is a vestige of the prehistoric Lake Chewaucan; the old shoreline can be seen along the side of the adjacent mountains.

Greenhorn

Greenhorn, once a famous mining camp, is the highest and smallest city in Oregon.

Hells Canyon National Recreation Area

Near the town of **Halfway** is the Hells Canyon National Recreation Area. Pick up a copy of the free brochure *Look Into Hells Canyon National Recreation Area* and two US Forest Service brochures, *Hells Canyon Scenic Byway* and *Heritage Hells Canyon National Recreation Area*. **Hells Canyon Scenic Byway**, which runs for 314 miles, including a 208-mile loop through the Wallowa Mountains, is called the nation's longest Scenic Byway.

Indian Villages & Reservations

Pittsburg Landing, in the Hells Canyon area, was once an Indian village. The **Umatilla Indian Reservation** is snuggled between the towns of Pendleton and **Elgin** (pop. 1,775), while the **Fort McDermitt Indian Reservation** straddles the Nevada state line.

Jordan Valley

Twelve miles past Jordan Valley and three miles past the turnoff to Rome on Route 95, is the burial place of trapper John Baptiste Charboneau, the son of Sacajewea.

Joseph

Joseph, named for the famous Nez Perce Chief Joseph, has a substantial arts community. Bronze foundries there cast statuary for sculptors all across America.

LaGrande

The **Grande Ronde River** once flowed on both sides of Island City, creating an island eight miles long and half a mile wide, isolating **Island City** from the neighboring community of LaGrande. Today, the river flows along only one side of the town and only a highway separates the two communities. LaGrande is the seat of Union County and the LaGrande/Union County Visitor & Convention Bureau, 1912 Fourth St., #200, La Grande, OR 97850, ☎ 541/963-8588 or 800/848-9969, fax 541/963-3936, has a map and guide, *Turns of the Brick*, that enables visitors to take a self-guided walking tour of the town.

Telocaset

Telocaset, near **Union**, lies in the exact center – north and south, east and west – of the 50 United States.

Adventures

■ On Foot

Gold, Gems & Geodes

In 1845, a wagon train headed west crossed the Humboldt River at Gravelly Ford near present-day Beowawe, NV. There, it split into two parts, one group to continue along the Humboldt and the other to head due north along the Black Rock Mountains.

Sighting on the Twin Sister peaks, the latter party started down the steep west side of the mountains. By a spring in the canyon below, some members of the party, gathering wood for the campfire, picked up some "pretty yellow rocks" and filled their little blue buckets with them. One of the women died beside the spring and was buried under a pile of rocks, and one of the little blue buckets was left hanging on a branch as a marker.

Crossing the Deschutes River, most of the yellow rocks were lost, but a few, used by the children as playthings, remained. Eventually, the band reached northwestern Oregon, settled on homesteads, and began farming. It was several years later before a few of the settlers recognized the "yellow stones" as gold.

A party of 90 people returned to the area where the gold had been found, hoping to recognize the area by the little blue bucket that had been left hanging there. More than half the party were killed by hostile Indians, and only two returned safely to Yreka, California, without finding the Lost Blue Bucket mine. Some experts put the location of the mine on Canyon Creek near Canyon City.

Gold is only one of the natural treasures to be found in the eastern part of Oregon. Geodes are common throughout the southeastern region, especially in **Succor Creek Canyon** on the north side of US 95 at the Idaho border.

Fossil beds are located next to the baseball field behind the **Wheeler County High School**, and are open to the public. No special tools are needed. Most rocks will contain impressions of leaves, as well as those of fruits, cones, seeds, and occasional flowers. Also found there so far: an unidentified bat, a new species of salamander, and numerous insects.

Near John Day is the **John Day Fossil Beds National Monument**, HCR 82, Box 126, Kimberly, OR 97848, ☎ 541/987-2333, E-mail joda_interpretation@nps.gov, Web site www.nps.gov/joda/index.html, which covers 14,000 acres and consists of three units: **Clarno**, between Fossil and Shaniko on the north side of Route 218; **Painted Hills**, three miles from Mitchell in Wheeler County; and **Sheep Rock** near Dayville. The monuments' headquarters are in John Day, and the main (Cant Ranch) visitor center is located on Route 19 in the Sheep Rock unit.

Rockhounding is good on **Hart Mountain** near Lakeview, where geodes, sunstone, obsidian, cinnabar, petrified wood, jasper, agates, and opals are often found. Rockhounding also is outstanding near **Vale**. **Succor Creek State Park** offers excellent hunting for thundereggs and agates, but the trip down an all-season gravel road generally requires a high-clearance vehicle. Petrified wood can be found at **Cow Valley, Jamieson, Hope Butte**, and **Jordan Valley**. Agate is found at **Jamieson, Warm Springs Reservoir, Riverside, Leslie Gulch Canyon**, and **Jordan Valley**.

From the Mosby Creek covered bridge east of Cottage Grove, **Row River Trail** crosses Row River just east of the Currin covered bridge, then parallels the river and Dorena Lake to a point just northwest of where Row River Road meets Sharps Creek Road. The trail is open from half an hour before sunrise to half an hour after sunset, and no motorized vehicles are allowed. (For further information, contact the Bureau of Land Management, 2890 Chad Dr., Eugene, OR 97408-7336, ☎ 503/683-6600.)

In **Elgin**, explore the Rockwall escarpment and the ice caves north of town. Twenty miles northwest of **Jordan Valley** are the Jordan Craters and Lava Beds.

Wildlife Viewing

Hart Mountain National Antelope Refuge, on 241,104 acres 68 miles northeast of Lakeview, is a great place to see pronghorn antelope, California bighorn sheep, mule deer, or sage grouse, and some stream fishing also is available.

LaGrande offers many outdoor adventures afoot. **Ladd Marsh Nature Trail**, six miles west of town off Foothill Road, is a good spot for birding and wildlife viewing. The trail makes a one-mile loop through the 3,208-acre marsh, one of the largest remaining wetlands in northeast Oregon. For photographers, a photo blind is provided.

Spring Creek, 12 miles west of LaGrande off I-84 following Forest Road 21 south for about three miles, is a nesting site for the great gray owl. The courtship period begins in February, making the birds very vocal at night. Incubation runs from mid-March to early April, and the young remain in the nest for about four weeks. The young will then remain near their nest for two or three weeks after fledging. The area is usually closed by snow in the winter, often making it difficult to reach during the peak nesting season. (For more information, contact LaGrande Ranger District, 3502 Hwy 30, LaGrande, OR 97850, ☎ 503/963-7186.)

Visitors can see a buffalo ranch, deer, elk, and more by doing the **Boise Cascade Scenic Driving Tour & Nature Hike**, Hurricane Creek Highway west of Route 82, across from the Rodeo Grounds, ☎ 503/432-2011.

Leslie Gulch Canyon, near **Vale,** has some spectacular rock formations and bighorn sheep can often be seen at dawn or dusk. In the **Three Fingers** area nearby, wild horses frequently frolic. Hunters look for deer around **Ironside Mountain**, **Bully Creek**,

Castle Rock, **Succor Creek**, **Cedar Mountain**, **Three Forks**, and the **Trout Creek Mountains**. Elk are hunted around **Ironside Mountain** and **Castle Rock**, while antelope are found at **Antelope Flats** and in the **Trout Creek Mountains. High Lonesome Hunts**, 4733 John Day Hwy, Vale, OR 97918, ☎ 541/473-2916, fax 541/473-9150, organizes big game and bird hunts.

The 25,000-acre **Starkey Elk Project**, 25 miles southwest of LaGrande on Route 244, ☎ 541/963-7122, is open for hiking, mountain biking, and horseback riding from late April to mid-December.

Hiking

Oregon Trail Adventures, 66716 State Route 237, LaGrande, OR 97850, ☎ 541/963-2583, 534-5393, or 800/527-8787, will cater to your fishing, hunting, and whitewater rafting needs.

Oregon Trail Interpretive Park at Blue Mountain Crossing (Exit 248 off I-84 west of LaGrande) has a five-mile paved path and discovery trails. The park is open from 8 AM to 8 PM between Memorial Day and Labor Day.

Gangloff Park, on Adams Avenue (Route 30) northwest of Island Avenue in LaGrande, has a nature trail and a historic cabin on 2.5 acres. The nearby **Blue Mountains** provide plenty of opportunities for hiking, backpacking, camping, fishing, and swimming.

Eagle Cap Wilderness, a 360,000-acre area in the Wallowa Mountains, is popular for hiking, backpacking, camping, and fishing. The range has 15 peaks over 9,000 feet high – more than any other range in the state – and there are 76 lakes, most of them filled with brook and rainbow trout. Hundreds of miles of trails are accessible from more than 20 trailheads for hikers and horsemen, but no motorized vehicles are allowed and no camping is permitted within 100 feet of a stream or lake. A free permit is required (contact LaGrande Ranger District, 3502 US 30, La Grande, OR, ☎ 541/963-7186).

Oregon Trail Interpretive Park is at Blue Mountain Crossing, 12 miles from LaGrande. Take I-84 west to the Spring Creek exit, then travel 2.5 miles to the park. "Living history" presentations are offered on weekends during the summer. There is a half-mile paved path with descriptive signage, and the facility, which is open from May to October, is wheelchair accessible.

Cove Hot Springs Pool, ☎ 541/568-4890, 17 miles east of LaGrande in the community of Cove, is open only during the summer months.

In **Pendleton**, you can take a self-guided walking tour with the aid of a map provided by the Pendleton Chamber of Commerce, 501 S. Main St., Pendleton, OR 97801, ☎ 541/276-7411 or 800/547-8911, fax 541/276-8849, Web site www.pendleton-oregon.org.

Wallowa-Whitman National Forest, PO Box 907, 1550 Dewey Ave., Baker City, OR 97814, ☎ 503/523-6391, provides 1,700 miles of hiking trails.

*Eagle Cap Wilderness
(Phil Bullock, Oregon Tourism Comm).*

For hiking, camping, and biking, the **Elkhorn Mountains** and the **Wallowa Mountains** are a good choice. The Wallowa Mountains Visitor Center, ☎ 503/426-5546, which is open from Memorial Day to Labor Day, is in Enterprise, near mile post #64. **Halfway** also is a good area for sightseeing, hiking, boating, fishing, hunting, and camping.

Hunting

For hunting, the **Eagle Cap Wilderness Area** near **Elgin** is good for elk, deer, and bear.

LaGrande is also good for deer, elk, and antelope. You can camp on the banks of Grande Ronde River in **Hilgard State Park**, eight miles west of town off I-84 at Exit 252, and you can camp and fish in **Red Bridge State Park**, 16 miles southwest of town on Route 244 (take the Hilgard Exit).

Thompson-Krein Outdoor, Rt. 1, Box 3346, Heppner, OR 97836, ☎ 541/676-5005, are two private hunting preserves where you can take pheasant and chukar.

Milton-Freewater is noted for its hiking and camping as well as its deer, elk, and upland game bird hunting. **Anderson River Adventures**, Rt. 2, Box 192-H, Milton-Freewater, OR 97862, ☎ 503/558-3629 or 800/624-7583, arranges whitewater rafting trips, jet boat tours, fishing charters, drop camps, and bird-hunting trips.

Guided Hikes

Hurricane Creek Llama Treks, 63366 Pine Tree Rd., Enterprise, OR 97828, ☎ 541/432-4455 or 800/528-9609, will arrange an outing with a llama. So will **Wallowa Llamas**, Rt. 1, Box 84, Halfway, OR 97834, ☎ 503/742-4930.

Hell's Canyon Bison, 120 N. Main St., Halfway, OR 97834, ☎ 503/742-6558, conducts buffalo tours from the Halfway Library, Wednesdays through Saturdays from 10 AM to 3 PM.

Eagle Cap, 59761 Wallowa Lake Hwy, Joseph, OR 97846, ☎ 800/681-6222, leads pack trips by horse into Eagle Cap and the Snake River Wilderness. It also conducts combination float and horseback trips, summer fishing trips, and sightseeing trips. Spring bear hunts are organized, as well as hunts for deer, elk, cougar, and bighorn.

High Country Outfitters, PO Box 26, Joseph, OR 97846, ☎ 503/432-9171, provides hunting guides, sets up drop camps, and conducts trail rides by the hour, two hours, half-day, or all day. Combination float/horseback trips also can be arranged.

Cornucopia Wilderness Pack Station, Rt. 1, Box 50, Richland, OR 97870, ☎ 503/893-6400 or 742-5400, handles hunting trips, drop camps, summer wilderness trips, pack trips, horse rentals, remote downhill or cross-country ski trips, and combinations thereof.

Salt Creek Summit Recreation Park, near Wallowa Lake and Joseph, is popular as a hiking trailhead in the summer and as a winter sports center as well. **Catherine Creek State Park**, 14 miles southeast of Union on Route 203, is a nice place for camping and fishing, and the Eagle Cap Wilderness is nearby.

■ On Horseback

Rodeos

Eeeeee-hahhh!!! Let's go to the rodeo! Out here, the rodeo doesn't come for one week a year; it often lasts all summer long. The **Oregon Trail Stampede Open Rodeo**, held on the County Fairgrounds in Baker City, ☎ 541/562-5664 or 853-2335, takes place in April, July, and August. The **Milton-Freewater High School Rodeo** takes place during the last weekend in April, while the town's **Pioneer Rodeo Days**, ☎ 541/938-5563, are observed in late May or early June.

Joseph stages the **Junior Rodeo** and Spray presents the **Spray Rodeo**, ☎ 541/468-2442, in May. John Day's **Grant County High School Rodeo**, ☎ 541/575-1900, and LaGrande's **Eastern Oregon State College Rodeo**, ☎ 800/848-9969, are held in mid-May, and on the third weekend in May, Jordan Valley hosts the **Big Loop Rodeo**, ☎ 503/586-2460.

The **Eastern Oregon Livestock Show, Rodeo & Parimutuel Horseracing**, 760 E. Delta, PO Box 434, Union, OR 97883, ☎ 541/963-8551 or 800/848-9969, the oldest continuously run rodeo in the northwest, kicks off in early June. Lakeview hosts a **Junior Rodeo**, ☎ 503/947-4486, in mid-June. Nyssa holds its **Nyssa Nite Rodeo**, ☎ 503/372-3657, which draws the largest number of amateur contestants in the northwest, on the last Thursday, Friday, and Saturday in June.

Vale's **4th of July Rodeo**, ☎ 503/473-3800, an amateur, four-day event, begins on the first and winds up on the fourth. One of the highlights is the "Suicide Race" in which the cowboys gather atop a steep slope and race their horses down the slope and into the arena.

In Elgin, the **Elgin Stampede PRCA Rodeo**, ☎ 541/963-8588, in July includes a carnival, a rodeo, dances, a flea market, parades, a horse-pulling contest, and a suicide race, all rolled into one. Also held in July is the **Haines Stampede Rodeo** in Haines, ☎ 800/523-1235, where the festivities include horse races and wild cow races; the **Catherine Creek Junior Rodeo** at the Stock Show Grounds in Union, ☎ 541/562-5055 or 800/848-9969; and the **Catherine Creek Junior Rodeo** in LaGrande.

Chief Joseph Days, Box 13, Joseph, OR 97846, ☎ 541/432-1015 or 432-4363 (The Sports Corral), also fall in July. Events include a PRCA rodeo, a carnival, a golf tournament, dances, and a parade.

The week-long **Harney County Fair, Rodeo & Race Meet**, S. Egan St., PO Box 391, Burns, OR 97720, ☎ 541/573-6166 or 573-2636, fax 541/573-8387, takes place in mid-September, shortly after the **High Desert Team Roping** competition that is held in August.

Also held in August are the **Gilliam County Fair**, Route 19 & Cottonwood, PO Box 701, Condon, OR 97823, ☎ 541/384-4139, where the activities always include a rodeo; the **Wheeler County Fair & Rodeo**, 702 Third St., PO Box 362, Fossil, OR 97830, ☎ 541/763-4560, fax 541/763-2026; the **Oregon Trail Pro Rodeo**, Morrow County Fairgrounds, ☎ 541/676-5157 or 676-9711; the **Morrow County Fair & Oregon Trail Rodeo**, Route 74, PO Box 464, Heppner, OR 97836, ☎ 541/676-9474, fax 541/676-5590; the **Umatilla County Fair**, 425 W. Orchard, PO Box 94, Hermiston, OR 97838, ☎ 541/567-6121 or 567-6151, fax 541/567-8115; the **Grant County Jackport Rodeo & Horse Races**, 409 NW Bridge, PO Box 7, John Day, OR 97845, ☎ 541/575-1900, fax 541/575-2248; the **Blue Mountain Rodeo** in LaGrande; and the **Malheur County Fair Rodeo**, ☎ 503/473-3431.

The **Baker County Fair & Rodeo**, ☎ 800/523-1235, is held in late August or early September in Halfway, while the **Panhandle Rodeo** is held there on Labor Day weekend. LaGrande hosts the **Eastern Oregon High School Rodeo** during September in the city's Maverick's Arena, also the venue for the **Tri-County Roping** competition that same month. The **Lake County Round-Up & Fair** in Lakeview also is held in September.

During the second full week in September, the famous four-day **Pendleton Round-Up**, PO Box 609, Pendleton, OR 97801, ☎ 503/276-

2553 or 800/457-6336, Web site www.ucinet.com/~roundup, is linked with the **Happy Canyon Indian Pageant**. The **Pendleton Round-Up Hall of Fame**, ☎ 541/278-0815 or 276-2553, which is open between 1 to 4 PM Mondays through Fridays, is located under the grandstands on the Round-Up Grounds.

Horse Shows & Pack Trips

Eastern Oregon presents other events involving horses, too.

Milton-Freewater holds a **Junior Horse Show**, ☎ 541/938-5563, in May. The **John Day Valley Draft Horse & Mule Classic** is held on the second weekend in June. **Grande Ronde Polo & Hunt Club** stages annual matches in LaGrande in June and July, and in Cove each July. The annual **Bar C Bar** cutting horse competition, ☎ 541/523-3356, takes place in Baker City, and the **Eastern Oregon All-Breed Horse Show** is held in Maverick's Arena in LaGrande each July.

Large black Clydesdale work horses are raised outside the town of Enterprise. Look for them in the fields around Mile Posts 66 and 67.

Enterprise and John Day both stage **Open Horse Shows** in August, and the **Oregon Trail Days/Rendezvous** is held in LaGrande that same month. **Hells Canyon Mule Days** are celebrated in Joseph in mid-September.

Horse packing in Baker County (Baker County VCB).

Steens Mountain Packers, Route 205, Frenchglen, OR 97736, ☎ 541/495-2315 or 800/977-3995, arranges wilderness pack trips, authentic horse drives, trail rides, river trips, and photo workshops.

Outback Ranch Outfitters, PO Box 269 or PO Box 384, Joseph, OR 97846, ☎ 503/432-9101 or ☎ 503/426-4037, puts together pack trips in Oregon and in Washington that include fishing, sightseeing, and big game hunting. Combination horseback and float trips can be arranged, as can stays on a working cattle ranch, where guests can engage in roundups, drives, and branding.

Eagle Cap Wilderness Pack Station, 59761 Wallowa Lake Hwy, Joseph, OR 97846, ☎ 800/681-6222, sets up pack trips, drop camps, and one-hour, two-hour, or full-day rides.

From **North Powder**, a horse-drawn wagon will take you on a narrated elk-viewing excursion through the **Elkhorn Wildlife Area** on weekends and holidays between 11 AM and 2:30 PM from December through February.

Cornucopia Wilderness Pack Station, Rt. 1, Box 50, Richland, OR 97870, ☎ 541/893-6400 or 742-5400, sets up big game hunting trips, fishing trips, recreational horse-pack trips, and day rides in the Eagle Cap Wilderness and in the Hells Canyon area.

On Wheels

Ghost Towns

Around Hells Canyon, the **Pittsburg Landing Road** (Forest Road 493) is a narrow, steep gravel road that leads to the Snake River at the bottom of the canyon.

Baker City, host to the **Oregon State Gold Panning Championships**, ☎ 541/523-3356, each July, is virtually surrounded by ghost towns.

Auburn, which had a population of over 5,000 during the 1862 gold rush but today is marked only by a descriptive marker and a small cemetery, is located 10 miles southwest of Baker City. **Bourne** is seven miles up Cracker Creek from Sumpter. **Copperfield**, 75 miles northeast of Baker City, was such a notorious place that it once was closed by martial law.

Granite, 15 miles west of Sumpter, was the site of a gold strike in 1862 and the home of the long-producing Cougar-Independence and Buffalo Mines. The present town, a ghost town since most of the old buildings were razed in the 1940s and 1950s, is a mile and a half north of the original town.

Homestead turned into a ghost town when a 1928 slump closed the copper mine there. **Pondosa**, 20 miles from Baker City on Route 203, once was a busy lumber mill town. An interesting old hotel remains. The ghost town of **Richmond** is located between Service Creek and Mitchell.

Rye Valley, another gold rush town, retains the Hanging Tree and the old cemetery. To reach it, go through the upper Burnt River Valley or take the Rye Valley exit off I-84 east of Baker City.

Sparta, 20 miles northeast of Baker City, once was a gold town and a stage stop. An old stone store building (1872) is all that remains. Take Route 86 to the Sparta turnoff, then drive north for five miles on a gravel road with an uphill grade. **Sumpter**, 30 miles west of Baker City, was an old gold-mining town. Between 1899 and 1903, the town had a brickyard, sawmill, smelter, electric lights, a water system, miles of wooden sidewalks, baseball and basketball teams, a race track, an undertaker, a brewery, a dairy, two cigar factories, an extensive Chinatown, a hospital, 16 saloons, livery stables, blacksmith shops, five hotels, a clothing store, three general stores, a school with 200 students, an opera house, two banks, four churches, a phone system, three newspapers, and a fire department – 81 businesses to serve a population of 3,000. The town was destroyed by fire in 1917.

Whitney, 14 miles west of Sumpter, was a logging town located on the Sumpter Valley Railway line. Only a few dilapidated buildings remain.

Other ghost towns in this part of Oregon include **Galena**, where gold was discovered in 1862. Hardly anything remains today. To get there from John Day, take US 26 east to Austin Junction, then turn left onto State Hwy 7 for one mile. Turn left onto County Road 20, cross the meadow, then take the Middle Fork of the John Day River into Galena.

Susanville, a neighbor of Galena, is also a ghost town today. **Granite**, 15 miles west of Sumpter, is a ghost town that retains a population of 20 hardy souls and has several old buildings dating from the 1800s. **Richmond**, located off Route 207 between Mitchell and Fossil (watch for the signs), has several old buildings that are still standing.

Lonerock has the look of a ghost town, although 35 people continue to live there. The church, dance hall, post office, jail, and store remain from the town's pioneer days. From Condon, head east on Route 206 for five miles, then branch right on Lonerock Road and drive 15 miles to a gravel road that will take you into the town.

📖 Look for a free copy of *Drive the Adventure*, which contains descriptions of 14 of Eastern Oregon's best driving tours.

Off-Road Driving

Southeastern Oregon is a good place to go off-road driving, but it is important to check the road conditions in the area you plan to visit before setting out.

The sand dunes in **Christmas Valley** are great for ATVs.

Dug Bar Road (Forest Road 4260) in the Hells Canyon area is recommended only for high clearance or 4WD vehicles. The steep, narrow, one-lane dirt road makes for an all-day trip between Imnaha and the Snake River.

Honeycombs, a 12,000-acre region between Succor Creek and Owyhee Reservoir in Jordan Valley, has some magnificently beautiful rock formations. A high-clearance vehicle is needed, as well as a good map.

Indian Rock Overlook, 15 miles from La Grande, is a nice day's drive, but requires a 4WD vehicle. Take Fox Hill Road.

West of **Ukiah** is the **Winom-Frazier Off-Highway Vehicle Complex**, 100 miles of scenic trails on over 63,500 acres of the Wallowa-Whitman and Umatilla National Forests. The trails also are used by hikers and horseback riders.

📖 Get a free *Winom-Frazier OHV Complex Trail Map & User Guide* from the North Fork John Day Ranger District, Umatilla National Forest, Box 158, Ukiah, OR 97880, ☎ 541/427-3231.

Biking

📖 *Oregon Cycling Magazine* (actually more of a tabloid newspaper) is a free monthly publication produced by the Center for Appropriate Transport, 455 W. 1st Ave., Eugene, OR 97401-2276, ☎ 541/686-9885, fax 541/686-1015, E-mail ocycling@efn.org, Web site www.efn.org/~cat]. Biking is also well covered in *Women's Sports Northwest*, a bimonthly pulp-paper magazine published at 935 SE Bidwell St., Portland, OR 97202, ☎ 503/233-5917, E-mail sbott503@aol.com.

Spout Springs in the Blue Mountains near Elgin provides trailers for mountain bikers during the spring and summer.

In the **Hells Canyon** area, the **Wallowa Mountain Road** (Forest Road 39) is a five-hour scenic tour between Baker City and La Grande along a paved, two-lane road. An all-day trip along **Hat Point Road** (Forest Road 4240) begins at Imnaha and climbs the sheer cliff of the Imnaha River canyon along a narrow, steep, single-lane gravel road to the Hat Point Overlook. A half-day trip along the **Imnaha River Road** (Forest Roads 3960 and 3955) follows a two-lane gravel road along the wild and scenic river. A two-lane paved road, the **Snake River Road,** between Oxbow Crossing and Hells Canyon Dam, goes deep into the canyon.

Hells Canyon Bicycle Tours, 102 W. McCully, PO Box 483, Joseph, OR 97846, ☎ 503/432-2453, rents bikes and arranges one- to four-day tours of the Hells Canyon National Recreation Area.

Pedaler's Place Cycle & Ski Shop, 318 S. Main in Pendleton, ☎ 503/276-3337, rents bikes.

Rail Trips

Eastern Oregon does not neglect its opportunities for adventure on the rails. **Sumpter Valley Railroad**, PO Box 389, Baker City, OR 97814, ☎ 541/894-2268 or 800/523-1235, makes a five-mile trip from the old train depot in Sumpter through the Oregon Wildlife Game Habitat Preserve on a narrow gauge railroad. The rides are offered on weekends and holidays, from Memorial Day through September.

Auto Racing

Stock car races are held at the fairgrounds in **LaGrande** during June, July, and August.

■ On the Water

Rafting

Near **Baker City**, **Hells Canyon** is the continent's deepest river gorge. At the bottom, the **Snake River** is widely used for whitewater rafting, jetboating, fishing, and exploring.

Also near Baker City, **Anthony Lakes** provide camping and fishing opportunities, and **Phillips Reservoir** is popular for fishing, boating, swimming, and camping.

Cascade River Adventures, PO Box 771, Bend, OR 97709, ☎ 541/382-6277 or 800/770-2161, arranges whitewater rafting trips.

White water rafting in Hells Canyon (Baker County VCB).

Wapiti River Guides, 69748 Lantz Lane, Cove, OR 97824, ☎ 800/488-9872, plans fishing, hunting, eco-river running, and nature trips on the Grande Ronde, Owyhee, and Salmon Rivers. Of their guides, the owner boasts: "We have Robert Redford and Julia Roberts lookalikes... from the knees down."

T.R.T. Raft & Rentals, Box 893, 1610 Alder, Elgin, OR 97827, ☎ 541/437-9270 or 800/700-RAFT, rents rafts and kayaks, as well as chartering trips.

Peer's Snake River Rafting, PO Box 354, Halfway, OR 97834, ☎ 546/742-2050 or 800/555-0005, schedules whitewater rafting trips through Hells Canyon, which also is noted for its fishing.

Hells Canyon Adventures, 4200 Hell Canyon Dam Rd., Box 159, Oxbow, OR 97840, ☎ 541/785-3352 or 800/422-3568, fax 541/785-3353, plans two-hour, three-hour, and all-day jetboat tours and one-day rafting trips through Hells Canyon.

In **Weston,** camping, backpacking, rafting, and climbing trips are planned by **Oregon Backwoods**, 101 E. Main St., ☎ 541/566-9309.

Fishing & Boating

The **J.S. Burres Wayside** off Route 206, 20 miles northwest of **Condon,** is on the John Day River and provides access to good fishing, as does the **John Day River Wayside** off State Route 218, 20 miles west of Fossil.

Two lakes near **Cottage Grove** provide excellent opportunities for engaging in water sports. **Dorena Lake** is east of town. **Cottage Grove Lake** is south of town.

In the **Elgin** area, water sports fans visit **Jubilee Lake**, the **Big Canyon Fish Hatchery**, the **Snake River Canyon**, **Wallowa River**, and **Wallowa Lake**.

The **Snake River** near **Halfway** is supposed to have some of the best catfish water in the state.

Willow Lake, near **Heppner,** is popular for its fishing.

The **Umatilla** and **Irrigon Fish Hatcheries**, ☎ 541/922-5732, 922-2762, or 922-5659, can be reached by taking Paterson Ferry Road north from Route 730 to the river or taking Eighth Street west out of Irrigon. The Umatilla hatchery raises fish for the Umatilla River, and the Irrigon hatchery raises fish for the Wallowa and Imnaha Rivers.

At mile post #5 outside of **Imnaha**, look for a fish weir, which is staffed from mid-June to late August. By the time a salmon reaches here, it already has passed eight dams and climbed nine fish ladders en route.

The **Pacific Salmon Visitor Information Center**, ☎ 541/922-4388 or 922-3211, is at McNary Dam, near Umatilla.

Clyde Holliday State Park, on the John Day River seven miles west of John Day, offers camping, hiking, biking, and fishing. The John Day River holds trout.

Trout fishing and boating are popular on **Antelope Reservoir**, 10 miles southwest of **Jordan Valley.**

Lehman Hot Springs, west of **LaGrande**, has a 9,000-square-foot swimming pool. It also offers camping, hiking, and fishing in the summer, and cross-country skiing and snowmobiling in the winter.

LaGrande has a number of other choice spots to engage in water sports. **Morgan Lake**, five miles up Morgan Lake Road from Walnut St., offers fishing, swimming, and nonmotorized boating, and there are private jetties to provide access for the handicapped. The **Grande Ronde River**, the state's second longest free-flowing river, runs 180 miles, contains steelhead and rainbow trout, and provides opportunities for fishing, camping, hiking, and rafting. **Wolf Creek Reservoir**, 24 miles southeast of town, can accommodate fishing, camping, waterskiing, and boating, while **Pilcher Creek Reservoir** nearby affords camping and wildlife viewing.

Lake Billy Chinook was created in 1963. It has 72 miles of shoreline and is on the **Warm Springs Indian Reservation**, so a Tribal fishing license is required. **Perry South Campground**, farthest west on the Metolius River arm of the lake offers camping, fishing, and a boat launch. **Three Rivers Marina**, about four miles east of the Perry South Campground, provides camping, swimming, fishing, a boat launch, a marina, boat rentals, and supplies.

Cove Palisades State Park is located south of Round Butte Dam. **Cove Marina**, which is on the Crooked River arm of the lake in the park, rents boats and can provide supplies. The **Crooked River** day-use area, which features swimming, a boat launch, fishing, and waterskiing, is just off the marina. **East Loop Camp**, a campsite, is on the south end of the park.

On a peninsula opposite the Cove Palisades State Park is the **Lower Deschutes** day-use area, which provides a boat launch, swimming, waterskiing, and fishing. The **Upper Deschutes** day-use area is south of the other area on the Deschutes River arm of the lake and provides swimming, fishing, waterskiing, and boat launch facilities. The lake also offers houseboating and sailing opportunities.

Anderson River Adventures, Rt. 2, Box 192-H, **Milton-Freewater**, OR 97862, ☎ 503/558-3629 or 800/624-7583, charters whitewater rafting trips on the Snake River in Hells Canyon and on the Grande Ronde River. The firm also conducts jet boat tours, fishing charters, bird hunting charters, and from September through December, steelhead trout fishing.

Lake Owyhee, 35 miles south of **Nyssa**, stretches for 52 miles behind the Owyhee Dam, the longest lake in Oregon and the third highest manmade dam in America at the time it was built. Two state parks, camping facilities, and a restaurant/lounge are on the lake. On the third weekend in May, Nyassa hosts a **Catfish and Crappie Festival** for the benefit of local college scholarships.

Southeast of **Oakridge** on County Road 6178 is 2,710-acre, eight-mile-long **Hills Creek Lake**, completed in 1961. There is a paved road along the western shore and a gravel road along the eastern shore, and there are five US Forest Service parks around the lake. **Lookout Point Lake**, another lake in the area, is located northwest of Oakridge.

In **Richland**, there are the **Brownlee** and **Oxbow Reservoirs** for boating and fishing. **Springfield** also has two substantial bodies of water for watersport enthusiasts, **Dexter Lake** and **Fall Creek Lake**, both of which are southeast of town off Route 58.

Umatilla National Wildlife Refuge, ☎ 541/922-3232, near **Irrigon** at Route 730 and I-82, sustains a large population of 180 species of birds, including geese, ducks, long-billed curlew, bald eagles, pelicans, burrowing owls, and great blue herons. Mule deer, coyote, raccoons, porcupine, and beaver also can be found there, and portions of the refuge are open to fishing, hunting, horseback riding, and boating.

Indian Lake, 19 miles southeast of **Pilot Rock** on East Birch Creek Road, is on the southern tip of the Umatilla Indian Reservation, ☎ 541/276-3873. Just 15 miles south of Pendleton on Route 395, the 80-acre lake offers opportunities for trout fishing, camping, hiking, and biking.

Thief Valley Reservoir, 12 miles south of **Union**, is popular for fishing and windsurfing.

Around **Vale**, bass, crappie, catfish, and perch can be taken from **Buylly Creek Reservoir**, **Lake Owyhee**, **Warm Springs Reservoir**, and **Cow Lakes**. For trout, look to **Warm Springs Reservoir, Beulah Reservoir**, and **Malheur Reservoir**, all of which have difficult boat launches; **Antelope Reservoir**, which has a gravel boat ramp; and the North Fork, South Fork, and main section of **Malheur River**.

Wallowa Lake, ☎ 541/963-7186, at the end of State Route 82 a few miles from **Joseph**, is four miles long, a mile wide, and almost 300 feet deep at the south end. It is one of the state's most beautiful lakes.

The Legend of Wallowa Lake

An Indian legend tells about a brave who disturbed the solitude of an enormous, horned monster far up in the mountains. The monster fled and the brave followed, until they reached this lake. The monster plunged in, and the brave followed. The two swam to the middle of the lake... and the monster sank, never to be seen again. The brave swam about for a few minutes and then he too disappeared beneath the surface, never to rise. Ever since, says the Indian legend, sure death has awaited anyone who ventures near the center of the lake.

Warrenton Deep Sea Inc. in **Warrenton**, ☎ 503/861-1233, charters sturgeon-fishing trips from May through September and salmon-fishing or bottom-fishing throughout the year.

On Snow

Skiing & Snowboarding

Spout Springs Ski Resort, Rt. 1, Box 65, **Weston**, OR 97886, ☎ 541/566-2164, is located in the Blue Mountains northwest of Elgin, on State Route 204. The resort has a small Alpine ski area and trails for snowmobilers and cross-country skiers. Other activities include snowboarding, summer hiking, and mountain biking. **Andies Prairie Sledding and Winter Camping Area** is just off Route 204, 14 miles northwest of town. Sno-Park permits are required.

A **Snow Festival** is held in **Halfway** on the Martin Luther King Jr. holiday weekend. The event includes ice sculptures, Nordic ski events, and snowmobile runs.

Anthony Lakes Ski Resort and Recreation Area, 61995 Quail Rd., **Island City**, OR 97850, ☎ 541/963-4599 or 856/3277, Web site www.anthonylakes.com, is in the Elkhorn Mountains. It has a lift and caters to downhill skiing (16 runs), cross-country skiing (10 kilometers of trails), Snowcat skiing, and snowboarding in the winter. Camping, fishing, and hiking are popular in the summer. Equipment is available for rent and there is a restaurant on-site. Take the North Powder exit off I-84 and travel west on Route 285 for 18 miles. The resort is open from 9 AM to 4 PM daily.

Vale also makes a marvelous base of operations for skiers. Within two to two-and-a-half hours of town are **Bogus Basin** in Boise (ID), **Brundage** in McCall, and **Anthony Lakes** near Baker. Within a four-hour drive, there is skiing at **Sun Valley** (ID) and **Bend**.

Snowmobiling

Area chambers of commerce have a pocket-sized map/brochure prepared by the Sumpter Valley Snowmobilers and Oregon State Snowmobile Association that describes the snowmobile areas around **Sumpter**. There are 340 miles of groomed snowmobile trails, including those that run from Sumpter Valley to Granite Mountain, from Whitney Valley to Beaver Meadows, from Desolation Meadows to Greenhorn, and from Granite to John Day River along Crawford Creek. Snowmobiles can be rented from **Sumpter Snowmobile Rental & Tours**, ☎ 541/894-2522 or 800/390-2522, and from **Stage Stop Service Station**, ☎ 541/894-2304.

■ In the Air

There are small airports in **Baker City, Boardman, Cottage Grove,** and **Creswell. Pendleton** has a commercial airport.

Plane rides can be arranged at **Baker Aircraft,** ☎ 503/523-5663, in Baker City, and **LaGrande Aviation,** ☎ 541/963-6572, in LaGrande, operates a charter service to Portland.

Ballooning can be experienced in **Burns,** which offers balloon rides during the annual **Rock & Rise Reunion** in July. **High Wallowas Balloon Adventures,** 81922 Fish Hatchery Lane, Enterprise, OR 97828, ☎ 503/426-3271, specializes in balloon flights over the Wallowa Valley seven days a week. Enterprise also hosts the **Wallowa Mountain High Balloon Festival,** ☎ 503/426-3271 or 426-4622, in mid-June.

Heli-Steens, Route 205, Frenchglen, OR 97736, ☎ 541/495-2315 or 800/977-3995, E-mail info@steensmountain.com, Web site www.steensmountain.com, provides scenic helicopter tours, heli-hiking tours, and heli-fishing trips.

Lakeview calls itself the "Hang Gliding Capital of the West" and hosts a **Hang Gliding Festival,** ☎ 503/947-6040, in late June.

Hang gliding also is popular along **Abert Rim,** a 2,000-foot escarpment near **Valley Falls,** on US 395.

Wallowa Lake Tramway, Wallowa Lake Hwy in Joseph, ☎ 541/432-5331, has a gondola ride that carries passengers to an elevation of 8,300 feet up Mt. Howard above Wallowa Lake.

■ Cultural Excursions

Baker City

Baker City was founded in 1862 a few miles east of the gold fields and at the foot of the hill where the **Oregon Trail** entered the valley. The **Visitors & Convention Bureau** has a *Historic Baker City Walking Tour* map that will help you to locate the most interesting sights. The city's newest museum, **Adler House Museum,** 2305 Main St., opened in 1998, while the town's new **Sports Complex** includes a 28-acre athletic park with two baseball and two softball fields, three soccer/football fields, parking lots, a concession stand, restrooms, and a jogging trail. The **Oregon Trail Trolley** conducts horse-drawn, rubber-tired coaches on narrated tours of the town on Fridays, Saturdays, and most holidays, leaving at 3, 4, and 5 PM.

Oregon Trail Regional Museum, 2480 Grove St., Baker City, OR 97814, ☎ 541/523-9308 or 523-3449, houses the Cavin-Warfel Collection of rocks, minerals, fossils, and semiprecious stones; the Wyatt Cabochon collection; and a fire obsidian collection. The building, built in 1920 as a natatorium (swimming pool), is open between 9 and 5 from May 1 through late October.

The not-to-be-missed **Oregon Trail Interpretive Center**, PO Box 987, Baker City, OR 97814, ☎ 541/523-1843, is located on Flagstaff Hill, seven miles east of Baker City on Route 86. The center is operated by the Bureau of Land Management.

Working Cowgirls, 2205 3rd St., Baker City, OR 97814, ☎ 541/523-1039 or 523-5555, is a show in which Entertainer, a working cowgirl, and Sagebrush, her sidekick, relate some real-life experiences covering a span of three generations. The show is interlaced with poetry and traditional music.

Burns

Once a major cattle center, Burns retains a great deal of the atmosphere of the Old West. **Glass Buttes**, 50 miles west of town, is one of the largest known outcroppings of iridescent obsidian, widely used by the early Indians for making spearheads and arrowheads. **Alvord Desert**, at the eastern base of Steens Mountain, was a prehistoric lake and is full of sand dunes – the truest desert in all of Oregon. **Harney County Historical Museum**, 18 W. D St., PO Box 388, Burns, OR 97720, ☎ 503/573-2636, is open between 9 AM and 5 PM Tuesday through Friday and from 9 AM to noon on Saturday from May through mid-October.

Canyon City

Joaquin Miller's cabin is located by the post office in Canyon City, next to the museum.

Echo

In **Ft. Henrietta Park,** on the Umatilla River in Echo, wagon ruts along the Oregon Trail are still visible and there is a replica of an old blockhouse. During the annual **Fort Henrietta Days** in September, festivities include musket-firings, frying pan throws, and tomahawk throws. There are hay rides and demonstrations of the old-time crafts, such as quilting. The men wear trapper's gear from the 1850s, and all the townspeople eat "Fort Henrietta Cannonballs," a pastry prepared from a secret recipe known only to the men of the Methodist Church.

Elgin

Just east of Elgin lies **Cricket Flat Fort**, and the **Elgin City Hall & Opera House**, ☎ 541/437-2520, built in 1912, shows classic and foreign movies on Friday, Saturday, and Sunday nights. The Opera House also is used for live plays on occasion.

Frenchglen

In Frenchglen, an eight-room hotel held over from the cattle days has been preserved as a monument.

John Day

Kam Wah Chung & Co. Museum, adjacent to the city park in John Day, represents the local culture during the late 1800s. The 1879 census listed 960 Anglos and 2,468 Chinese miners living in eastern Oregon. One personality you will learn about, Ing ("Doc") Hay, was a merchant, an herbalist, a "doctor," a priest, the postmaster, and a spiritual adviser. During Prohibition, he sold whiskey. He was a master of "pulse diagnosis," a means of detecting illnesses simply by taking the patient's pulse. Exhibits in the museum include ground tiger bone and rhino horn, whole dried rattlesnakes, bear paws, deer hooves, and whole dried Chinese lizards. The museum is housed in an 1868 stone building that, at one time or another, also served as a gambling parlor and an opium den. The town of John Day celebrates Kam Wah Chung Days with a **Chinese Festival** on the third weekend in September.

Picture Gorge, at the junction of Routes 19 and 26 near John Day, is a 500-foot chasm containing colorful palatial formations and ancient Indian writings and drawings.

Jordan Valley

Jordan Crater, one of the youngest volcanoes in the continental United States, is in Jordan Valley. The last eruption occurred 2,500 years ago.

Joseph

The 1896 robbery of the First Bank of Joseph is reenacted every Wednesday at 1 PM on Joseph's Main Street from July to September. During the robbery, one bandit (Jim Brown) was killed, another (Dave

Tucker) was injured and captured, and a third (Cy Fitzhugh) escaped with the loot. Fitzhugh was never caught, but Tucker served his time in prison and returned to Wallowa County to become a prominent stockman – and vice-president of the bank that he had helped to rob. The old bank is now the Wallowa County Museum, where admission is free, but the town's "dance hall girls" pass the hat.

The Columbine Players, ☎ 541/519-5720, provide live entertainment at the **Mainstreet Theatre** in Joseph.

Ontario

Four Rivers Cultural Center, 676 SW 5th Ave., PO Box 980, Ontario, OR 97914, ☎ 541/889-8191 or 888/211-1222, E-mail frcc@micron.net., opened in mid-1997. The center celebrates the confluence of cultures (Native American, Basque, Hispanic, European, and Japanese-American) at the confluence of four rivers (the Snake, Malheur, Owyhee, and Payette). An authentic Japanese garden is on the grounds.

Pendleton

In Pendleton, stop at the Chamber of Commerce for a free pocket-sized map, *Step Into the Past*, showing how to take a self-guided walking tour of the downtown district. **Pendleton Underground Tours**, 37 SW Emigrant, Pendleton, OR 97801, 541/276-0730 or 800/226-6398, takes 90-minute guided tours through a once-busy hive of speakeasies and bordellos built by the Chinese in the late 1800s. At one time, as many as 90 passageways honeycombed beneath the downtown area. The tour passes through the Shamrock Cardroom, a laundry, a meat market, the Chinese jails, living quarters, and bordellos, which were called "cozy rooms." Conducted year-around, the hour-and-a-half guided tour is offered between 10 AM and 4 PM Monday through Saturday.

Vert Museum, at SW Fourth and Dorion Streets in Pendleton, ☎ 541/276-8100, presents Native American exhibits. The **Children's Museum of Eastern Oregon** is located at 400 S. Main St., ☎ 541/276-1066, in Pendleton, and the legendary **Pendleton Woolen Mills**, 1307 SE Court Place, ☎ 541/276-6911 or 800/568-3156, offers tours.

Coyote Creek Ranch, ☎ 541/276-5455, stages a barn dance and presents Western melodramas. From Pendleton, leave I-84 at Exit 216 and follow the signs.

Indian Lake Recreation Area Recreation Area (Hump-Ti-Pin, or "grizzly bitten" to the Indians) is on the south tip of Umatilla Indian Reservation near Pendleton. Camping is allowed from May 15 to September 30 and there is an 80-acre lake stocked with rainbow trout (a Tribal fishing permit is required), but boats are allowed to have electric motors only.

Ukiah

Lehman Hot Springs, PO Box 247, Ukiah, OR 97880, ☎ 503/427-3015, is near Milepost 17 on Route 244 in the Blue Mountains. Water gushes from the ground into the mineral springs at 140-157°, but the large pool is kept at 88-92° and the smaller pools are maintained at 100-106°. Swimming, hiking, camping, and fishing are popular pastimes. There is a new, 9,000-square-foot natural hot mineral pool.

Umatilla

In Umatilla, the **McNary Lock and Dam**, at Routes 730 and 395, offers self-guided tours year-around and guided tours throughout the summer. The 5,009-acre **McNary Wildlife Park**, built and maintained by the area's Boy Scouts, stretches along the Oregon side of river with ponds and a man-made stream stocked with fish.

Vale

Murals depicting life on the Oregon Trail adorn the town of Vale. *The Crossing*, depicting wagons crossing the Snake River, adorns the Grace Lutheran Church (the site of the crossing is still visible near Old Fort Boise from the Oregon Trail kiosk south of Nyssa); *The New Arrivals*, a tribute to the state's pioneers, is on Malheur Drug Store (the site depicted in the mural can be seen on Lytle Boulevard, two or three miles south of town); and *The Short Cut*, depicting the hardships of wagon train travel, decorates the TVCC Outreach Center (the blue bucket held by a girl in the mural represents the Lost Blue Bucket Mine supposedly discovered on the Meek Cutoff to the Willamette Valley). New murals are commissioned each year.

Where to Stay

Halfway

Clear Creek Farm B&B, PO Box 737, Rt. 1, Box 138, Halfway, OR 97834-0676, ☎ 800/742-4992, $$$, provides "cookie jar privileges." Children and "well-behaved pets" are welcome. The 160-acre grounds contain gardens, ponds, orchards, and a wooded creek. Buffalo tours and dinners are provided Mondays through Fridays at 4:30 PM.

Pendleton

Doubletree Hotel Pendleton, 304 SE Nye Ave., Pendleton, OR 97801, ☎ 541/276-6111, fax 541/278-2413, $$, is a three-story inn with 170 rooms, a dining room, and a coffee shop.

■ Camping

Cabins

Looking for something different? **Oregon Parks & Recreation Dept.**, 1115 Commercial NE, Salem, OR 97310, ☎ 800/452-5687, rents cabins, covered wagons, and tepees for camping. Ask for brochures.

Cabins are located in **Cove Palisades State Park** near Culver, **Smith Rock State Park** near Terrebonne, and the same locations as the covered wagons (listed below). Rustic cabins with four single beds and mattresses also are available in **Emigrant Springs State Heritage Area** in the Blue Mountains for a fee of $20 per night.

Covered Wagons

Covered wagons are located in the **Emigrant Springs State Heritage Area** (two sites), on the **Blue Mountain Forest State Scenic Corridor** between Meacham and LaGrande (two sites), in the **Hilgard Junction State Recreation Area**, at the **Red Bridge State Wayside**, and at **Farewell Bend** (two sites). Each "wagon" has indoor lighting, two full-size beds with mattresses, a table, a smoke detector, and a fire extinguisher. Outside there is running water, a picnic table, a fire ring, an old-fashioned tripod with coffeepot, hot showers, and modern restrooms. Visitors must bring their own sleeping bags or other bedding, flashlight, matches, water container, hatchet, cooking utensils, and eating utensils. The fee is $25 per night.

Tepees

Tepees contain carpeting, lighting, and foam mattress pads. Outside there is running water, a stack of firewood, hot showers, a picnic tables, and modern restrooms. Visitors must bring the same equipment as those who are staying in one of the covered wagons. The tepees are located in the **Farewell Bend State Recreation Area** near Huntington, and **Ontario State Recreation Site** at Ontario. There are four tepees at the latter site, one that sleeps eight, one that sleeps 12, and two that are capable of sleeping five people each. **Lake Owyhee** has two tepees, each capable of sleeping five. The fee is $25 per night.

"Traditional" Camping

Around **Baker City**, campers might like to try **Travel-L-Park**, 2845 Hughes Ln., Baker City, OR 97814, ☎ 541/523-4824 or 800/806-4824, or **Union Creek Campground** in the Wallowa-Whitman National Forest, HCR 87, Box 929A, Baker City, OR 97814, ☎ 541/894-2260.

Thirty-five miles northwest of **Elgin** off Route 204, **Jubilee Lake Campground**, ☎ 509/522-6290, has camping facilities on a beautiful lake that is open to nonmotorized boating. Off OR 82, 15 miles northeast of town, **Minam State Park**, ☎ 800/452-5687, has camping facilities.

Shelton State Park, ☎ 800/452-5687, on State Route 19, 10 miles southeast of **Fossil** has campsites and two miles of foot trails. Nearby is the John Day River Scenic Waterway for fishing, swimming, and innertubing and the John Day Fossil Beds.

To reach **Willow Creek Campground** in **Heppner**, ☎ 541/676-9618, take Route 207 south for one mile and then head east for one mile on Willow Creek Road.

Indian Lake Campgrounds, ☎ 503/276-3873, near **Pendleton,** is on the Umatilla Indian Reservation and is operated by the Indians.

Ollokot Campground in **Salt Creek Summit Recreation Park** was once used by the Nez Perce Indians and is named for Chief Joseph's brother.

Ukiah-Dale Forest State Park on US 395, three miles southwest of **Ukiah,** has a number of campsites.

There are a number of campsites in **Umatilla National Forest**, including a number that charge no fee. These include

Penland Lake Campground, 26 miles southeast of Heppner off Forest Road 21, which provides access to fishing; **North Fork John Day Campground**, 10 miles west of Granite on the Blue Mountain Scenic Byway (Forest Road 52), where horse-handling facilities are available at the adjacent trailhead; **Bear Wallow Campground**, on Route 244 between Ukiah and LaGrande, which has a quarter-mile of interpretive trails; and **Umatilla Forks Campground**, between the North and South Forks of the Umatilla River, which accesses fishing and hiking in the North Fork Umatilla Wilderness.

A couple of additional campgrounds in the park *do charge a fee*, and these include **Bull Prairie Campground**, three miles off Route 207, which allows fishing, nonmotorized boating, and hiking; and **Jubilee Lake Campground**, the largest and most popular campground in the forest, which is adjacent to a 2.8-mile trail.

Maps, rules and generally useful information about camping is contained in a brochure entitled *Camping on the Umatilla National Forest*, which is available from Umatilla National Forest Headquarters, 2517 SW Hailey Ave., Pendleton, OR 97801, ☎ 503/276-3811.

Catherine Creek State Park, on OR 203 eight miles southeast of **Union,** offers campsites. **Union Creek Campground**, HCR 87, Box 929A, Baker City, OR 97814, ☎ 503/894-2260, which is located on Phillips Lake, has a boat ramp and good fishing is available. **Wallowa-Whitman National Forest** provides 60 campsites.

Where to Eat

Haines

Haines Steakhouse, ☎ 503/856-3639, $$, is on US 30, the old Oregon Trail, in Haines. Voted the best steakhouse in Oregon for two years running, the restaurant is open Sundays from 1 to 9 PM, Mondays from 5 to 10 PM, Wednesdays through Fridays from 5 to 10 PM, and Saturdays from 4 to 10 PM. The restaurant is closed on Tuesdays.

Pendleton

Raphael's Restaurant & Lounge, 233 SE 4th St., Pendleton, OR 97801, ☎ 503/276-8500, $$, serves Native American foods. Two other interesting eateries in Pendleton are **Crabby's Hole-in-the-Wall Kitchen**, 223 S. Main, Pendleton, OR 97802, $$, and **Crabby's Underground Saloon & Steak House**, 220 SW First St., Pendleton, OR 97801, ☎ 541/276-8118, $$.

Information Sources

US Department of the Interior, Bureau of Land Management, 100 Oregon St., Vale, OR 97918, ☎ 503/473-3144.

US Forest Service, 1550 Dewey Ave., Baker City, OR 97814, ☎ 503/523-6391.

Oregon Department of Fish & Wildlife, ☎ 800/233-3306, and the district offices in **Baker City**, ☎ 541/523-5832; **Enterprise**, ☎ 541/426-3279; **Heppner**, ☎ 541/676-5230; **John Day**, ☎ 541/575-1167; and **Pendleton**, ☎ 541/276-2344. Also under the jurisdiction of this department are the following wildlife areas: **Bridge Creek**, ☎ 541/276-2344; **Elkhorn**, ☎ 541/898-2826; **Ladd Marsh**, ☎ 541/963-4954; **Murderer's Creek**, ☎ 541/987-2843; and **Wenaha**, ☎ 541/828-7721.

Baker County Visitor & Convention Bureau, 490 Campbell St., Baker City, OR 97814, ☎ 541/523-3356 or 800/523-1235, is open seven days a week.

Grant County Chamber of Commerce, 281 W. Main St., John Day, OR 97850, ☎ 541/575-0547 or 800/769-5664.

Harney County Chamber of Commerce, 18 W. D St., Burns, OR 97720, ☎ 541/573-2636.

Hells Canyon National Recreation Area, 88401 Hwy 82, Enterprise, OR 97828, ☎ 503/426-4978; its **Snake River Office**, PO Box 699, Clarkston, WA 99403, ☎ 509/758-0616; **Riggins Office**, PO Box 832, Riggins, ID 83549, ☎ 208/628-3916.

LaGrande/Union County Chamber of Commerce, 2111 Adams Ave., La Grande, OR 97850, ☎ 503/963-8588 or 800/848-9969.

Lake County Chamber of Commerce, 513 Center St., Lakeview, OR 97630, ☎ 503/947-6040.

Milton-Freewater Area Chamber of Commerce, 505 Ward St., Milton-Freewater, OR 97862, ☎ 503/938-5563 or 800/228-6736, E-mail mfchamb@bmi.net, Web site business1.com/mforegon/.

Ontario Visitors & Convention Bureau, 88 SW 3rd St., Ontario, OR 97914, ☎ 503/889-8012 or 888/889-8012, E-mail ontvcb@micron.net.

Umatilla National Forest, 2517 SW Hailey Ave., Pendleton, OR 97801, ☎ 503/278-3716.

Wallowa-Whitman National Forest, 1550 Dewey Ave., PO Box 907, Baker City, OR 97814, ☎ 503/523-6391.

Wallowa County Chamber of Commerce, 107 SW 1st St., PO 427, Enterprise, OR 97828, ☎ 503/426-4622.

Wallowa Lake Tourist Committee, PO Box 853, Joseph, OR 97846, ☎ 503/432-1015.

Regions of Washington

Washington

The western portion of "The Evergreen State" abuts the coast, an alluring backdrop of mountains breaking the skyline to the east. It is where the bulk of Washington's industry is centered, where the majority of its population resides, and where most of its tourism is centered.

Central Washington is a stark contrast, dominated by the Cascade Mountains and an endless procession of national forests. Population is extremely sparse, thinly spread among a scattering of small, often colorful and historic, little communities.

Eastern Washington, sitting on the "back" side of the Cascades, is more moderate in temperature and heavily agricultural, given to miles and miles of wide open spaces.

No less an adventurer than Francis Drake arrived in the area, way back in 1578. Exactly two hundred years later, Capt. James Cook landed at Cape Flattery. Then it was George Vancouver, then Robert Gray.

It wasn't until 1872 that the San Juan Islands were finally awarded to the United States. In 1889, Washington was admitted to the Union.

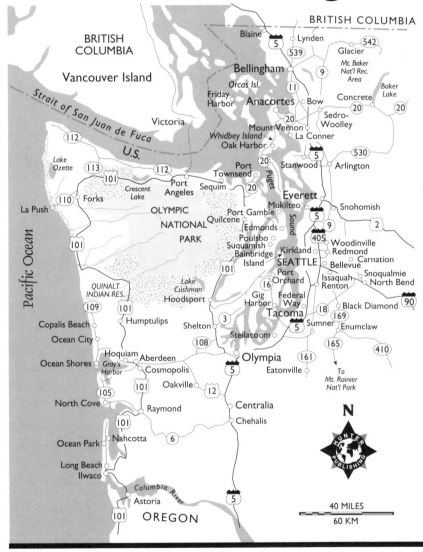

Coastal Washington

Greater Seattle and its neighbor to the north, Vancouver, British Columbia, are, without question, the major metropolitan centers of the Pacific Northwest. In these environs are the seats of government and the "heart" of business, banking, industry, and cultural activity.

What New York City and Montreal are to the eastern seaboard, Seattle and Vancouver are to the western seaboard.

Everywhere, the influence of the vast Pacific Ocean can be felt. It effects the weather. It provides the routes of commerce. It affords limitless opportunities for every sort of outdoor recreation. Its waters are the "life blood" of the Pacific Northwest.

Getting Around

Driving in Washington is often a challenge.

The signage can be poor, vague, and sometimes hidden behind a bush. Turning onto an intersecting roadway is often difficult because the signs frequently are located too close to the turn, not allowing drivers sufficient warning to move into the proper lane.

State law allows the use of tandem trucks, and some of them can be nearly half a block long. Passing one of them can be almost as unnerving as having one of them pass you... particularly when it occurs on anything less than a four-lane highway.

In some places (I-405 N in Bellevue is an example), the carpool lane is on the *right* side, rather than the left side – a practice that tends to defeat their purpose completely.

Washington drivers do rate highly in one particular: they are quick to stop for pedestrians in the crosswalks.

The mountains direct the flow of traffic primarily north to south, just as they do in California and Oregon.

The Redwood Highway (US 101) follows the Pacific coast north from the state line to South Bend, and then forsakes the ocean as it continues due north through Aberdeen. From there, it begins a slow loop around the Olympic Peninsula, continuing north to Quinault, angling west across a portion of the Quinault Indian Reservation to the sea, and then returning inland through the Olympic National Park to the little town of Sappho. At Sappho, the highway turns almost due east, passing through Port Angeles and Sequim (*Skwim*) to Gardiner, where it abruptly changes direction once again and heads south, paralleling the Hood Canal until it reaches Tumwater, just south of Olympia.

At Raymond, just past South Bend, Route 105 takes the more scenic, if considerably longer, coastal route, while US 101 crosses inland. It rejoins 101 in Aberdeen.

Similarly, Route 109 marches along the coastline just past Aberdeen until it reaches the tiny coastal village of Taholah on the Quinault Indian Reservation. Taking this route, there are few opportunities to return inland and rejoin US 101, and they require taking poorer, sometimes unpaved, roads.

In Sappho, on the northern part of the Olympic Peninsula, Route 113 continues northward for 10 miles and then links up with Route 112, which runs along the north coast of the peninsula from the Makah Indian Reservation on the west to the city of Port Angeles on the east, where the highway rejoins US 101.

Excluding the two roadways on the Olympic Peninsula (US 101 and Route 112), the opportunities to turn inland from the coastal region are pretty well thwarted by the Olympic Mountains *except in the south*, where Route 4 links Interstate 5 at Longview/Kelso with US 101 just short of Nemah.

A little farther north, Route 6 joins I-5 at Chehalis with US 101 in Raymond; and still farther to the north, US 12 leaves I-5 at Bucoda to join US 101 at Aberdeen.

At Elma, eastbound traffic on US 12 has the option of turning southeast toward Bucoda or continuing west-northwest on Route 8, joining US 101 just outside of Tumwater.

From Olympia northward, it is I-5 that carries the bulk of the traffic along Washington's coastal region. The highway passes through Tacoma, Seattle, Everett, Mount Vernon, and Bellingham en route to the Canadian border just past Blaine.

The slower and more scenic Route 9 roughly parallels I-5 from just outside Bothell into Canada, exiting the United States at the town of Sumas, opposite Abbotsford, British Columbia.

East-west highways in the northern half of Washington's coastal region include I-90, which runs from Seattle through the mountains to Ellensburg.

A bit farther north, US 2 takes a similar path from outside Everett to a point just north of Wenatchee.

And finally, Route 20, which joins the Olympic Peninsula with the San Juan Islands, returns to the mainland at Burlington and crosses the mountains eastward to Okanogan.

Railroads

Rail service remains a viable means of transportation in the major cities of the state.

The *Coast Starlight* (Amtrak), ☎ 800/USA-RAIL, Web site www.amtrak.com, travels between Los Angeles and Seattle.

For general information about other Amtrak routes or to make Amtrak reservations, ☎ 800/872-7245.

Airlines

Although every city of any significance is served by some type of airport, and an excellent network of interconnecting flights exists, the population centers of coastal Washington are served by just two "major" airports: **Olympia Airport**, 7643 Old Hwy 99 SE, Olympia, WA 98501, ☎ 360/586-6164, and **Seattle-Tacoma Airport**, 17801 Pacific Hwy South, SeaTac, WA 98158, ☎ 206/431-4645.

To reach SeaTac going southbound on I-5, take Exit 154 and follow the signs.

The **Arlington Airport**, ☎ 360/659-7491, has runways 5,300 and 3,500 feet long. **Bellingham Airport** is at the north end of Mitchell Way, just off I-5 at Exit 258. **Blaine Municipal Airport**, which has a 2,100-foot strip, is within a few blocks of the city center and adjacent to I-5. Swanson Field in **Eatonville** offers a 3,000-foot runway.

Elma has a small airport, while **Everett** and **Lynnwood** are served by the Snohomish County Airport (Paine Field), 3220 100th St. SW, Everett, WA 98208, ☎ 206/353-2110, fax 206/355-9883. **Gig Harbor** has the Tacoma-Narrows Airport, 1302 26th Ave. NW, Gig Harbor, WA 98335, ☎ 253/851-3544, and **Hoquiam** (*Ho-qwe-um*) utilizes the Grays

Harbor Airport (Bowerman Air Field), which has a 5,000-foot runway, a new terminal, and a new Instrument Landing System (ILS). The airfield at **Ilwaco**, ☎ 206/642-3143, has a 2,000-foot runway.

Oak Harbor has a small airport, and **Port Angeles** is served by Fairchild International Airport, ☎ 360/417-3433, at Laurdsen Boulevard on the west side of town, which has a 6,350-foot runway, a restaurant, and a comfortable passenger terminal.

Port Townsend has the Jefferson County International Airport, 310 Airport Rd., Port Townsend, WA 98368, ☎ 360/385-2323. **Puyallup** *(Pew-al-up)* is served by the Pierce County Airport (Thun Field), 16715 S. Meridian, Puyallup, WA 98373, ☎ 253/841-3779. The field in **Raymond**, ☎ 206/942-9954, has a 3,000-foot runway. Sequim Valley Airport is between Kitchen Dick Road and Carlsbord Road and between Spath Road and the Old Olympic Highway in **Sequim**, just north of US 101.

Shelton has a small airport, and **Snohomish** is served by Harvey Airfield, 9900 Airport Way, Snohomish, WA 98290, ☎ 360/568-1541. **Stanwood** utilizes Camano Island airfield, ☎ 206/629-4811, which has a 1,750-foot runway.

Ferries

What suburban rail lines are to Chicago and the subway is to New York, the water is to the region around Seattle.

The largest ferry system in the country, **Washington State Ferry**, 801 Alaskan Way, Pier 52, Coleman Dock, Seattle, WA 98104-1487, ☎ 206/464-6400 (Seattle), 604/381-1551 (Victoria), or 800/843-3779, carries over 23 million passengers a year aboard 25 vessels serving 10 routes. The line links historic towns and rural islands, the Kitsap and Olympic Peninsulas, and the US mainland with Victoria, BC, on Vancouver Island. It also goes to Lopez, Shaw, Orcas, and San Juan Island in the San Juan Islands. A fast passengers-only ferry is currently being built in Anacortes to transport people from Seattle to the communities on the west side of Puget Sound in a little over half an hour. **Victoria Express**, ☎ 360/452-8088 (Washington), 604/361-9144 (Canada) or 800/633-1589, operates out of Port Angeles, providing one-hour service between Port Angeles and Victoria, British Columbia.

Urban Transit

Metropolitan transportation in the major cities of Washington is excellent.

The Metro Transit Tunnel, completed in 1990, is a 1.3-mile underground roadway for buses only that runs beneath downtown Seattle. Inside the tunnel, the buses operate on electricity, then convert to diesel power on the surface streets and highways. Daily, about 31,400 people move through the tunnel.

> In **Olympia**, a free *Rider's Guide*, ☎ 360/786-1881, will help you get around on the intercity transit lines.

Touring

Beginning just north of the state line, Route 103 runs the length of a narrow peninsula to Leadbetter Point, a trip reminiscent of the drive along the Outer Banks on the east coast.

Aberdeen

Aberdeen claims to have the "third best climate in the US." Numerous sightings of Big Foot, the shy, hairy (or furry) nine-foot brute with footprints 13- to 16-inches long, have been reported over the years. (A neighbor with a bad hair day?)

Anacortes

Anacortes is a quaint little community in which colorful, cutout, life-size figures representing historic figures and various scenes of the town in the late 1800s have been attached to the sides of many buildings, providing a "picture" of the town's past.

Bainbridge Island

Bainbridge Island, four miles wide and 12 miles long, sits in Puget Sound. The island can be reached by **Washington State Ferry**, which leaves downtown Seattle hourly. The trip takes half an hour and you can take your car with you.

Bellevue

Bellevue is the home of Microsoft, the software giant headed by Bill Gates, said to be one of the world's richest men.

Hiking near Mount Baker (Washington Tourism Dev).

Hoquiam

Hoquiam, at the east end of Grays Harbor, has a magnificent viewing tower that overlooks the port.

Lynden

Lynden, a quaint town near the Canadian border, is designed to look like a little Dutch village. A small indoor shopping mall has a simulated Dutch canal passing through it, and a four-story "windmill" stands on the corner.

Mount Baker

Perpetually snow-capped 10,778-foot Mount Baker was called Komo Kulshan ("white and shining") by the early Indians. When Capt. George Vancouver first sailed into Puget Sound, the mountain was smoking and fuming.

Mukilteo

The first white settlement in Mukilteo (*Muck-ill-tay-oh*) was established in 1858. Nearly half a century later (1905), the population included 200 whites and 150 Japanese. A year after that (1906), the **Mukilteo Lighthouse** went into service. Access to the mainland is provided by a ferry terminal, ☎ 206/355-7308.

North Bend

North Bend will be recognized by some as the town in which the television series *Twin Peaks* was filmed. Particularly recognizable is the cafe on the southeast corner of North Bend Way and North Bend Boulevard, which often was featured in the series.

Oakville

Oakville was the last city in Washington to be robbed by a bandit on horseback.

Ocean Park

Ocean Park, on the two-mile wide, 28-mile long Long Beach Peninsula, began as a Methodist vacation camp. The region once was served by the narrow-gauge Clam Shell Railroad.

Ocean Shores

Ocean Shores is the most popular vacation destination in Washington, next to Seattle. Popular pastimes include beachcombing, bicycling, boating, birdwatching, clam digging, fishing, horseback riding, kite flying, swimming, storm-watching, surfing, sailboarding, tennis, and whale-watching.

Port Angeles

Port Angeles is the largest city on the North Olympic Peninsula. In the early days, the downtown portion of the city was under water every time there was a high tide. Peabody Creek gurgled where Lincoln Street and Front Street are now. In 1914, the creek was diverted and the streets were filled to raise them above tide level. This created an "underground city" made up of the buried first stories of the downtown businesses.

Port Angeles is a popular departure point for Canada. **Black Ball Transport**, 101 E. Railroad Ave., Port Angeles, WA 98362, ☎ 360/457-4491, fax 360/457-4493, Web site www.northolympic.com/coho, operates the *MV Coho*, a passenger-vehicle ferry, to Victoria, British Columbia. **Victoria Express**, ☎ 800/633-1589 (in Washington), 360/452-8088 (outside of Washington), or 604/361-9144 (in Canada), runs a passenger ferry.

Poulsbo

Poulsbo (originally Paulsbo, meaning "Paul's place"), has a strong Scandinavian flavor.

Quilcene

Quilcene in the Hood Canal area has the largest oyster hatchery in the world.

Seattle

Seattle has been the home of many prominent companies. **Nordstroms** was founded here. **Starbucks Coffee** began here in 1971. **The Boeing Company**, founded here in 1910, had become the world's leading manufacturer of commercial jet aircraft by 1960. Metro buses in the downtown area are all free. The Monorail can be boarded every 15 minutes at Westlake Center, 5th and Pine, and will get you to the Seattle Center in just 90 seconds.

In Seattle, the most recognizable landmark is the **Space Needle** at Broad Street and 5th Ave. North, ☎ 206/443-2111 or 800/937-9582, Web site www.spaceneedle.com, a holdover from the 1962 Seattle World's Fair. An observation deck near the 600-foot level provides sweeping views of the city and the harbor. A monorail, which operates every 15 minutes from 9 AM to 11 PM, links Seattle Center, where the Space Needle is located, to Westlake Center in downtown Seattle.

Sedro-Woolley

Sedro-Woolley evolved from a merger between the town of Sedro (originally Cook) and Woolley, named for its founder, Phillip Woolley. Through stubbornness, the towns wouldn't merge until 1898, and because neither town would agree to move its streets, the north-south streets of Sedro and Woolley do not align to this day.

Steilacoom

Steilacoom (*Still-a-cum*) gave Washington its first Protestant church, in 1853, its first library, in 1858, and its first jail, in 1858.

Whidbey Island

Whidbey Island, the longest island in the continental United States (50 miles) has 148 miles of shoreline and provides exciting views of the Cascade and Olympic mountains.

Adventures

A more perfect environment for outdoor activities would be hard to imagine, and the residents of coastal Washington and their out-of-town visitors are well aware of it. Boating, fishing, swimming – whatever the heart desires – it's all available along the coast of Washington.

Dense forests, towering mountain peaks, and roaring rivers are symbolic of central Washington. Endurance is the prime requisite when intent upon pursuing most outdoor activities. "Urban" sports are available, of course, but for the most part, visitors will find the hiking trails a little steeper, the boating a little more frenetic, and the surroundings a little more primitive than those to which they may have been accustomed.

Watersports take no back seat in eastern Washington, even if it is the "desert" region of the state. Boating, fishing, waterskiing – all of these and more are available east of the Cascades. Add to that the opportunity to go rockhounding, hiking, mountain climbing, paragliding, or virtually any other form of activity, and your search for new adventures will find no bounds.

■ On Foot

Hiking Trails

Two nice walks in **Aberdeen** are the **Chehalis River** boardwalk and the trails through **Stewart Park**.

The **Snohomish County Centennial Trail**, ☎ 206/339-1208, completed in 1994, runs from **Snohomish** to **Arlington** along the route of the 1889 Seattle Lakeshore Eastern Railroad and is available to walkers, cyclists, skaters, and horseback riders. It is staffed by an on-site trail ranger, ☎ 206/568-8434.

The **Snohomish** area offers some excellent hiking opportunities, including great views of a 300-foot waterfall at the end of an easy, well-maintained trail in **Wallace Falls State Park**, located on the north side of Route 2 east of Startup. From a trailhead 14.5 miles east of the Verlot Ranger Station, a one-mile hike leads to the **Big Four Ice Caves** at the base of Big Four Mountain, and somewhat strenuous three-mile hike leads to spectacular views from an old lookout atop **Mount Pilchuck**. Seven miles east of Granite Falls, on the right side of Mountain Loop Highway, is **Old Robe Trail**, which leads less than one mile to the abandoned old townsite of Robe.

Kanaskat-Palmer Recreation Area, Green River Gorge State Park, 23700 SE Flaming Geyser Rd., **Auburn**, WA 98002, is a 296-acre strip along a one-mile stretch of the Green River. Located 11 miles northeast of Enumclaw via Farman Road, the park offers hiking, camping, rafting, kayaking, and fishing.

Belfair State Park, NE 410 Beck Rd., **Belfair**, WA 98528, ☎ 206/275-0668, three miles west of town on WA 300, is a wonderful place for beach walking and saltwater swimming. The park has 3,000 feet of freshwater shoreline along Big Mission and Little Mission Creeks and over 3,700 feet of saltwater shoreline along the south end of Hood Canal.

Bellevue has many excellent hiking trails, including the **Sammamish River Trail**, which runs from Marymoor Park northward to Bothell and links the **Burke-Gilman Trail** to the north with the **Bridle Crest Trail** to the south. The Burke-Gilman Trail and the Sammamish River Trail constitute one of the longest uninterrupted urban trails in the country (12.1 miles).

The **Bellingham** area also maintains an exceptional number of trails, including the three-quarter mile **Arroyo Park Trail**; the three-tenths of a mile **Connelly Creek Trail**; the 1.5-mile **Cornwall Park Trail**; the mile-long **Haskell Fitness Trail**; the 2.6-mile **Lost Lake Trails**; the half-mile **Old Village Walking Route**; and the two-mile **Railroad Trail**.

Bug Lake Trail covers eight-tenths of a mile and provides fishing access to the lake, but it may be impassable during high water. A half-mile trail leads to **Sunset Pond**, which has good fishing and a number of unimproved trails that run along the pond's western and northern shores.

Interurban Trail, which covers 5.6 miles, follows the bed of a former railroad. **Lower Padden Creek Trail** climbs three short, steep hills for three-quarters of a mile up an old interurban rail line. The mile-long **South Bay Trail** follows the railroad right-of-way and affords a scenic view of the bay. Less than half a mile long, **Scudder Pond Trail** follows an old railroad bed to a pond that contains some beavers.

The half-mile **Lower Whatcom Creek Trail** leads to a bridge over a scenic creek below a waterfall. **Sehome Hill Arboretum** has 5.3 miles of mostly steep, unpaved trails passing through the woods.

Green River Gorge State Park, 2.5 miles south of **Black Diamond** and eight miles north of Enumclaw off WA 169, includes a number of different areas, only three of which are developed: Flaming Geyser, Nolte,

Hurricane Ridge, Olympic Peninsula (Washington Tourism Dev).

and Kanaskat/Palmer. The three cover 2,008 acres and include over 18 miles of river shoreline. Flaming Geyser is a popular take-out point for rafters, kayakers, and inner-tubers on the Green River, and an excellent place to fish for steelhead trout in the winter.

Good hiking can be found in a number of parks around **Concrete**, including **Ann Wolford Park**, three miles west of town on Route 20; **Grandy Lake**, five miles northeast from Route 20 on Baker Lake Road; **Howard Miller Steelhead Park,** in Rockport between Route 20 and the Skagit River; **Padilla Bay Shore Trail**, which begins at the Breazeale Interpretive Center; **Pomona Grange Park**, eight miles north of Burlington on Old Highway 99; **Sauk Park**, a quarter of a mile north of Lower Gov Bridge on Sauk Valley Road; and **Sharpe Park,** on Rosario Road at Fidalgo Island.

Beachcoming is very popular at three county parks near **Everett**: the 428-acre **Kayak Point**, the 105-acre **Meadowdale Beach**, and the 54-acre **Picnic Point**.

There also are a number of eye-pleasing waterfalls to be seen in **Snohomish County**. To reach **Alpine Falls**, a double-wide falls with a 50-foot drop, drive east out of Everett on US 2. About 2.5 miles from the Ranger Station at Mile Marker 49, park at the turnout just past the bridge crossing the Tye River on the south side and follow an unmarked but well-worn path. **Deception Falls** is east of Everett, about 6.6 miles east of the ranger station on US 2. The falls is on the south side of the road at Mile Marker 49. **Bridal Veil Falls**, east of Everett on US 2, is visible from the highway a quarter of a mile east of the Index turnoff.

Lord Hill Regional Park on 150th St. SE in **Everett** has hikers-only and all-users trails, plus nine small ponds and some wetlands. Wildlife seen there includes an occasional skunk, deer, bear, or bobcat.

There also are a number of interesting trails around **Forks**, including **Ruby Beach Trail**, a picturesque walk where hikers can see sea stacks, driftwood, tidal pools, caves, and multicolored cliffs while searching for garnets in the beach sands. At high tide, **Beach Trail 4** is the best beach for smelting, and at low tide a place to hear tidal pool talks by park rangers during the summer. **Beach Trail 6**, a good place to go beachcombing, is popular as a lookout point for whales, sea lions, and puffins in late spring. A Visitor Information Center at Kalaloch Ranger Station, ☎ 360/962-2283, can provide more information.

Queets Rain Forest, an excellent area for fishing, camping, and hiking, is 13 miles up a gravel road from Forks.

The **Hoh Indian Tribe**, 2464 Lower Hoh Rd., Forks, WA 98331, ☎ 360/374-6582, produces some interesting Indian crafts. On US 101, watch for mile post 188, then turn onto Lower Hoh Road and go 2.2 miles to the village.

From **Gold Bar**, follow the signs from First Street to 678-acre **Wallace Falls State Park**. There, a hike of three to four hours is needed to reach the falls. It's an additional one-third of a mile to reach the upper falls, where there is a spectacular 265-foot waterfall.

There is a colorful covered bridge on Route 4 southeast of **Grays River**.

The **Hood Canal** region provides many interesting sights to explore on foot. WA 104 crosses a floating bridge over the Hood Canal near the town of **Port Gamble**.

From the **Mary E. Theler Community Center**, East 22871 Hwy 3, PO Box 1445, Belfair, WA 98528, ☎ 360/275-4898, fax 360/275-3857, three trails lead into the 135-acre Theler Wetlands: the Alder/Cedar Swamp Trail, the Fresh Water Marsh Trail, and the South Tidal Marsh Trail.

There are two interesting walks around **Hoquiam**: a walking tour of the downtown historic district and the **Elton Bennet** nature walk. The **Grays Harbor National Wildlife Refuge** outside of Hoquiam is open daily during daylight hours. The best viewing times are the two hours before and the two hours after high tide, especially from mid-April through early May. On weekends, a shuttle bus occasionally runs from Hoquiam High School to the wildlife refuge trailhead (fee: 25 cents). More information about the refuge is available from Grays Harbor National Wildlife Refuge, c/o Nisqually National Wildlife Refuge, 100 Brown Farm Rd., Olympia, WA 98516, ☎ 360/532-5237 or 753-9467.

The 1,700-acre **Fort Canby State Park**, PO Box 488, Ilwaco, WA 98624, ☎ 360/642-3078, can be found two miles southwest of **Ilwaco** off US 101. A store is open during the tourist season, and there are four hiking trails. Beachcombing is excellent, especially after a storm. **Fort Canby**, originally built in 1875, was expanded and improved until the end of World War II. Tours of the park are offered. Popular pastimes include surf fishing, whale-watching, kite flying, bicycling, birdwatching, and camping. Offshore is the **Columbia River Bar**, sometimes called the "Graveyard of the Pacific." The **Cape Disappointment Lighthouse**, now the oldest lighthouse still in use on the West Coast, was built in 1856.

Because ships coming from the north could not see the Cape Disappointment Lighthouse, the **North Head Lighthouse** was built in 1898. The **Lewis and Clark Interpretive Center**, ☎ 360/642-3029, high above Cape Disappointment, is open daily from 10 AM to 5 PM.

In the **Issaquah** area, there are a number of places to go hiking in the **Tiger Mountain State Forest**. The easier hikes include **Busline Trail**, which passes Round Lake; **Around the Lake Trail**, which passes Tradition Lake; **Swamp Trail**, **Brink Trail**, and **Big Tree Trail**. More strenuous hikes involve **West Tiger Trail**, a 2.75-mile trek to the top of the mountain; **Tiger Mountain Trail** toward Preston; **Railroad Grade**, **Adventure Trail**, **Wetlands Trail**, **Lake Trail**, **Nook Trail;** and the steep **Section Line Trail**.

Lake Cushman State Park, N. 7211 Lake Cushman Rd., Hoodsport, WA 98548, ☎ 360/877-5491, is seven miles northwest of **Hoodsport** in the lower foothills of the Olympic Mountains. At the turn of the century, two resorts were located here in the Olympic National Park, and the area was a hunting and fishing paradise. Both resorts had closed by 1920. Roosevelt elk, blacktail deer, black bear, cougar, bobcat, river otter, and raccoon often are seen in the area.

The park covers 565 acres and is on the north side of Lake Cushman, which contains kokanee salmon, cutthroat trout, Dolly Varden trout, and rainbow trout. There is a boat ramp and an unguarded swimming beach. A dam, completed in 1926, increased the size of the lake from 400 acres to 4,000 acres.

Lake Cushman has many submerged bars, boulders, and stumps within a foot of the surface near shore, unmarked by buoys. Stay well away from shore except when landing. Traveling with the outboard in "tilt" position will help reduce damage to your craft if you hit an obstruction. Reduce speed when motoring through the Big Creek inlet, which is narrow and often congested with swimmers, sunbathers on floats, and other boats. Sailboats also should be alert when crossing Big Creek inlet, where the power lines are low enough for a mast to strike them.

Between April 1 and September 30, the park is open from 6:30 AM to dusk; between October 1 and March 31, it is open from 8 AM to dusk; and between December 1 and March 31, it is open only on weekends and holidays.

Lake Quinault and the **Quinault Rain Forest** are popular places to stop and explore. Lake Quinault covers six square miles and is 250 feet deep. A natural lake, it is used for swimming, canoeing, kayaking, sailing, birdwatching, and fishing. Steelhead trout populate the rivers; cutthroat trout are found in the lake.

Long Beach has 28 miles of uninterrupted beach. There is a boardwalk along much of the beach, and horseback riding, surf fishing, and storm-watching are all popular pastimes.

Buck Island (Al Borlin) City Park is formed at the junction of Skykomish River and Woods Creek in **Monroe**. It is accessible only by footbridge from Lewis Street Park or by auto via Simons Road. Camping is allowed only during the day, but the park has a sandy beach for swimmers, hiking trails, and some terrific river fishing.

The **Stevens Pass** area, 49 miles east of Monroe on Route 2, offers camping, hiking trails, streams, and waterfalls, but check at the ranger station before entering the area.

Walkers will find a number of interesting attractions in and near **Port Angeles**. The six-mile paved **Waterfront Trail** goes east from the Port Angeles pier for one mile and west onto Ediz Hook, where you can walk the beach. A map is available at the Chamber of Commerce.

Salt Creek County Park on the Strait of Juan de Fuca has tidepools, old harbor defense bunkers, and a beach on Crescent Bay. The park has hiking trails and can be used for camping. The Clallam County Parks &

Fair Department, 223 E. 4th St., Port Angeles, WA 98362, ☎ 206/417-2291, can provide more information.

In **Tumwater Falls Park**, PO Box 4098, **Tumwater**, WA 98501, ☎ 360/943-2550, the Deschutes River tumbles 82 feet into Capitol Lake. The 15-acre park contains half a mile of trails.

DID YOU KNOW?

*Visitors to **Port Hadlock** play a game called "Tracking the Dragon." Twelve "dragon tracks" have been placed in beautiful and interesting places throughout the county, and the object is to track the dragon by visiting each of those places. A free packet explaining the game can be obtained at the Chamber of Commerce.*

Maps & Guides

The Washington **Department of Fish & Wildlife**, 600 Capitol Way North, Olympia, WA 98501-1091, ☎ 360/696-6211, has produced a free pocket brochure called *A Guide to Ultimate Wildlife Watching* that is extremely helpful.

Washington State's **Parks & Recreation Commission**, 7150 Cleanwater Lane, PO Box 42650, Olympia, WA 98504-2650, ☎ 360/902-8500 or 800/233-0321, provides a free 8.5 x 14-inch sheet entitled *Trails in Washington State Parks*. The document lists the state's trails, provides a brief description of each, gives a phone number for obtaining more information, and shows the state laws that pertain to the use of the trails.

The **Interagency Committee for Outdoor Recreation**, 4800 Capitol Blvd., Tumwater, WA 98504-5611, ☎ 206/753-7140, has a slick-paper, pocket-size *Trails Directory* that contains an enormous amount of information.

A free brochure/map, *Mount Tahoma Trails*, is available from the Mount Tahoma Trails Assn., 30205 SR 706 (Whittaker's Bunkhouse), PO Box 206, **Ashford**, WA 98304. The Ashford area also supports a number of helpful telephone references: ☎ 360/569-2451 for trail conditions, ☎ 206/526-6677 for an avalanche forecast, and ☎ 206/526-6097 for the National Weather Service forecast.

The Visitor Center on **Bainbridge Island** has a free trail guide, *Bainbridge Island Forests & Trails*, that can be very helpful. **Weather Vane Tours**, PO Box 10584, Bainbridge Island, WA 98110, ☎ 206/780-5003, fax 206/842-0246, conducts guided tours of the island, Hood Canal, and the Olympic Peninsula.

Wildlife Viewing & Nature Parks

Bellingham is an excellent area for birdwatching. Some of the best sites are **Chuckanut Mountain**, **Lake Padden**, **Lake Terrell**, **Nooksack River**, **Red River Road**, **Schome Hill Arboretum** next to Western Washington University, **Samish Flats/Padilla Bay** near the towns of Bow and Edison, **Tennant Lake**, and **Whatcom Falls Park/Scudder's Pond**.

The area around **Blaine** is excellent for birdwatchers. Birdwatching also is popular in several county parks near **Everett**: Flowing Lake, Kayak Point, Lake Roesiger, Lord Hill, Meadowdale, six-acre Martha Lake, and Picnic Point. All but the last two have extensive nature trails.

Federation Forest State Park, 49201 Enumclaw-Chinook Pass Rd., **Enumclaw**, WA 98022, ☎ 206/663-2207, has the Catherine Montgomery Interpretive Center (ask for a free copy of *Birds of Federation Forest State Park*) and three nice hiking trails: the Naches Trail, the half-mile Fred Cleator Interpretive Trail East, and the mile-long Fred Cleator Interpretive Trail West. **Bowerman Basin Refuge** in Grays Harbor County is the nation's newest wetlands bird sanctuary. The annual **Grays Harbor Shorebird Festival**, Grays Harbor Audubon Society, PO Box 444, **Montesano**, WA 98563, ☎ 360/533-2619 or 495-3101, is held in April.

Birdwatching also is good at **Damon Point** (also known as Protection Island) near **Ocean Shores**, which is frequented by Snowy plovers, Brown pelicans, Peregrine falcons, and herons. The 1,000-acre **Oyehut Wildlife Preserve** also is located near Ocean Shores.

The **Columbian White-Tailed Deer National Wildlife Refuge** is north of **Cathlamet** on the way to Skamokowa.

Northwest Trek is a 635-acre wildlife park in **Eatonville** where the animals roam free. Visitors tour in trams, getting close to the bison, elk, moose, mountain goats, and other indigenous animals. The park has nature trails and a cafe, and is open daily from February through October plus weekends from November through January.

To reach the 413-acre **Spencer Island County Park**, one of the best spots in the **Everett** area to view birds and animals, start at Langus Riverfront Park. From there, take 4th Street SE and cross the historic Jackknife Bridge to reach the island.

South of **Quilcene** is the **Seal Rock Viewing Platform.**

The **Quinault Indian Nation Fish Hatchery** is at the west end of lake, and elk can often be seen in the Rain Forest. There is a half-mile interpretive loop trail, and the **Maple Glade Trail**, which follows the north shore of the lake. A 30-mile loop drive also is provided. Hiking and backpacking, with or without a guide, are permitted in the Rain Forest, as are lakeside camping, bicycling, and horseback riding. Further information can be obtained from the **Quinault Rain Forest Visitor Information Center**, 6084 US 101, Amanda Park, WA 98526, ☎ 360/288-2644.

For backcountry fishing trips, a Tribal guide is required. Access to the ocean beach also requires a Tribal pass. For details, contact Quinault Indian Nation, 1214 Aalis, Taholah, WA 98526, ☎ 360/276-8211.

Watch the tides carefully. The sand and ocean have been known to swallow entire cars and trucks!

Padilla Bay, near **Mount Vernon,** is the only National Estuarine Research Reserve in the state. It encompasses 11,000 acres of bay and nearly 200 upland acres. Visitors are likely to see jellyfish, anemone, ribbon worms, lugworms, amphipods (sand fleas), mud shrimp, helmet crab, Dungeness crab, shore crabs, bend-nosed clams, mud clams, littleneck clams, limpets, mud snails, lacuna snails, opalescent nudibranch, Taylor's sea hare, threespine stickleback, bay pipefish, starry flounder, sculpin, and gunnels, as well as gulls, herons, harbor seals, and river otters.

Padilla Bay trails include **Shore Trail**, a 2.25-mile diketop trail that follows the southeast shore of the bay. A one-way hike takes 40 minutes, and the trail, which is well marked with interpretive signs, is accessible to the handicapped. No motorized vehicles or horses are allowed, but cycling is OK.

Stay on the trail; soft muds can be dangerous.

A second trail, **Upland Trail**, covers eight-tenths of a mile and begins near the barn. The first half of the trail is paved for the convenience of those in need of a wheelchair, and the rest is gravel. An Upland Trail Guide is keyed to the numbered posts along the trail, and binoculars are available on loan. The hike takes 30 to 60 minutes.

Beazeale Interpretive Center, 1043 Bayview-Edison Rd., Mount Vernon, WA 98273, ☎ 360/428-1558, borders a large seagrass meadows. It includes indoor exhibits, saltwater aquaria, and a reference library. An observation deck a few hundred yards from the entrance, and a ramp provides wheelchair access. The Center is open Wednesday through Sunday from 10 to 5 except on state holidays. A staircase to the beach is open from April through October.

Around **Ocean Shores**, agate and shell hunting is good along six miles of beach. **Wynoochee Falls** is nearby.

Ledbetter Point State Park Natural Area, three miles north of Oysterville on Stackpole Road, has many hiking trails leading to ocean dunes, tidelands, ponds, forests, and a pristine bay shoreline. The park is for day-use only and the ocean dunes are closed from March 15 through August to protect the nesting sites of an endangered species, the Snowy plover.

Marymere Falls are 20 miles west of Port Angeles on US 101 at Storm King. A three-quarter-mile nature trail begins at the Lake Crescent Lodge or the Storm King Station and leads to the 90-foot waterfall.

The hills south of **Sequim** provide excellent hunting for deer, elk, and bear, while the shoreline is good for duck hunting. The Sequim lighthouse (1857) is the oldest lighthouse north of the Columbia River.

Potlatch State Park, Route 4, Box 519, **Shelton**, WA 98584, is on Annas Bay at the Great Bend of the Hood Canal, an ancient gathering place where the local Indian tribes once held their festivals ("potlatches"). Later, it was the site of a logging mill, and after that, a private resort. Oysters, mussels, cockles, and butter and littleneck clams can be gathered at low tide. Dungeness and red rock crab can be taken, along with shrimp. Deer and beaver usually occupy the area.

Fireman's Park, overlooking the Port of **Tacoma,** has the state's largest totem pole (105 feet). **Snake Lake Nature Center** is a 54-acre wetland habitat that includes some exciting walking trails and birdwatching.

Wolf Haven International, 3111 Offut Lake Rd., Tenino, WA 98589, ☎ 360/264-4695 or 800/448-9653, is one of the nation's leading advocates for the wolf. Hourly tours are conducted between 10 AM and 4 PM from

May and October and between 10 AM and 4 PM from October and April. The site is closed on Tuesdays. In addition to beachcombing and birdwatching, **Tokeland** offers fishing and crabbing off the dock.

Twanoh State Park, East 12190 Hwy 106, **Union**, WA 98592, ☎ 206/275-2222, is on Hood Canal, 12 miles east of Route 101. The campground is closed from October 1 to April 15, but limited day-use facilities are open year-round. The day-use area has a tennis court, hiking trails, and a concession stand that is open from Memorial Day to Labor Day. There also are a boat dock, two boat ramps, and 500 feet of swimming beach. In the fall and winter, the park is popular for smelt dipping, oyster picking, and clam digging.

Guided Hikes

Gerrie's Step On Tour Guide Service, 6995 Birch Bay Dr., **Blaine**, WA 98230, ☎ 360/371-2244 or 604/240-2960, fax 360/2960, takes tours throughout the county, to Seattle, and to Canada.

Deli Llama Wilderness Adventures, 1505 Allen Rd., **Bow**, WA 98232, ☎ 360/757-4212, conducts hiking and pack trips using llamas to do the toting.

Outlaw Tours, PO Box 613, **Deming**, WA 98244, ☎ 800/929-8029, E-mail outlawtour@aol.com, leads "Old West" guided tours, day trips, overnighters, and weekend trips.

Intertidal Beach Walks are conducted along Olympic Beach, Dayton Street, and Admiral Way in **Edmonds** from May through August by the **Beach Rangers**, ☎ 206/771-0227.

Peak 6 Tours, 4883 Upper Hoh Rd., Forks, WA 98331, ☎ 360/374-5354, leads hiking, camping, climbing, and biking expeditions. **Wooley Packers Llama Co.**, 5763 Upper Hoh Rd., Forks, WA 98331, ☎ 360/374-9288, takes pack trips into Olympic National Park. **Hoh Valley Adventures**, 62 Lindner Creek Lane, Forks, WA 98331, ☎ 360/374-4288, takes visitors on a hunt for "incredible edibles" – berries in the summer and mushrooms in the fall.

Maverick Tours, USA, 30716 40th Ave. East, Graham, WA 98338, ☎ 206/846-2602, hosts "Tea Hikes & Weekend Walks." A walking tour of **Puyallup** guides visitors to 15 pieces of outdoor sculpture positioned throughout the town. The **Granite Falls Sportsmen's Club** holds two annual Turkey Shoots, one on the Saturday before Thanksgiving and one on the Saturday before Easter. **Grays Harbor** has over 1,000 acres of cranberry bogs.

Issaquah Alps Trails Club, PO Box 351, Issaquah, WA 98027, ☎ 206/328-0480, takes guided day hikes to Cougar Mountain Regional Wildlife Park, Coal Creek Park, May Creek Park, Tiger Mountain, and other sites in the area.

Eastside Excursions, PO Box 186, Issaquah, WA 98027, ☎ 206/557-5534 or 498-7185, fax 206/557-3782, E-mail excursions@juno.com, leads two- to four-hour day trips and arranges special interest trips involving such topics as arts and crafts galleries, the wine country, microbreweries, biking, hiking, kayaking, fly fishing, Northwest heritage, and shopping. Trips often include visits to the eastside towns of Bothell, Woodinville, Redmond, Canation, Duvall, Renton, Black Diamond, Bellevue, and Kirkland.

Kit's Llamas, PO Box 116, **Olalla**, WA 98359, ☎ 206/857-5274, conducts day, overnight, and extended hikes into the Olympic Mountains with llamas. At **Llama Wilderness Pack Trips**, 4235 36th Ave. NE, Olympia, WA 98516, ☎ 206/491-LAMA, you can lease a llama or take a guided trip.

The entire village of **Oysterville** on the Long Beach Peninsula is listed on the National Register of Historic Places. A walking tour visits a pioneer cemetery and a historic one-room redwood schoolhouse on School Road east of Route 103. The school was built in the late 1850s, and the first teacher, Bethenia Owens, became the first female physician on the Pacific Coast. Children once played hooky from school in order to dig oysters, which they could sell to the crews on visiting schooners for 25 cents a bushel.

Olympic Mountaineering, 221 S. Peabody St., Port Angeles, WA 98362, ☎ 206/452-0240, rents packs, tents, stoves, and other equipment for campers, hikers, and backpackers. The store also has a climbing gym.

Jaywalking Tour Co., PO Box 45454, Seattle, WA 98145-0454, ☎ 206/517-5700, fax 206/517-4131, conducts tours including one called "High Tea on a Houseboat," a four-hour event held on Mondays between May and October.

DID YOU KNOW?

*In **Port Townsend**, white seagulls painted on the street point the way to the town's most scenic points. Guided historical sidewalk tours, ☎ 360/385-1967, also are provided.*

On Horseback

Washington State Horsemen, PO Box 1566, Yelm, WA 98597, ☎ 360/458-6300, produces a tabloid newspaper, *Canter*, which lists riding clubs throughout the state and shows how to contact them.

Riding

In **Bellevue**, horseback riding is allowed on **Bridle Crest Trail** and on **Sammamish River Trail**. **Peace Arch Equestrian Center**, 3545 Lynden Rd., Birch Bay, WA 98230, ☎ 360/366-4049, just south of **Blaine**, offers indoor and outdoor riding, one-hour guided trail rides, pony rides, day camps, and both Western- and English-style lessons. **Jorgenson Enterprises**, PO Box 129, **Duvall**, WA 98019, ☎ 206/788-5103, rents horses and horse-drawn carriages. They also arrange pack trips and wagon train excursions.

EZ Times Outfitters, 18703 State Route 706, **Elbe**, WA 98330, ☎ 360/569-2449, conducts guided trips by the hour or the day. In **Issaquah**, **Eliel Ranch**, ☎ 206/222-4625, and **Tiger Mountain Stables**, ☎ 206/392-5090, have horses for rent. Among the county parks around **Everett**, **Centennial Trail** and **Lord Hill Trail** are good places for horseback riding.

Party Ponies Pony Farm, ☎ 206/222-7724, in **Fall City** rents ponies, while **Horse Country-Ponies Too**, ☎ 360/691-7509, in **Granite Falls** rents both horses and ponies. **Seahorse Ranch**, 1181 State Route 109, **Hoquiam**, WA 98550, ☎ 360/532-6791, and **Chenois Creek Horse Rentals**, 620 Ocean Beach Rd., Hoquiam, WA 98550, ☎ 360/533-5591, both rent horses.

In **Neah Bay**, you can rent a horse at **Ray's Horseback Rides**, ☎ 206/645-2391; in **Ocean Shores**, at **Nan-Sea Stables**, ☎ 360/289-0194; in **Redmond**, at **Lori's Sammamish Stables**, ☎ 206/868-5293, or **Serenity Ranch**, ☎ 206/702-9373; and in **Renton**, at **Aqua Barn Ranch**, ☎ 206/255-4618. **Whatcom-Skagit Outfitters**, ☎ 360/595-1136, arranges day and overnight rides in **Sedro-Woolley**.

Horse Shows

The area surrounding **Enumclaw** is one of the largest thoroughbred horse breeding and boarding areas in America. **Fox Ridge Farm**, 42015 192nd Pl. SE, Enumclaw, WA 98022, ☎ 360/825-5144, fax 360/825-2057, E-mail fox@foxridgefarm.com, Web site www.foxridgefarm.com, breeds horses, and also operates a quaint little B&B.

During the spring and summer, a nearly endless string of horse-related events is scheduled at **Evergreen State Fairgrounds**, ☎ 206/794-7832, 883-8033, or 339-3309, fax 206/794-8027, in **Monroe**. In April, it's the **Washington State Hunter/Jumper Spring Nationals**. In May, the **Bits 'N Spurs 4H Horse Show**, the **Morgan Horse Show**, the **Pacific Northwest Hunter/Jumper Horse Show**, the **Pacific Northwest Quarter Horse Show**, and the **Pacific Northwest Paint Horse Show** are held. In June, the **Washington Reining Horse Clinic**, the **Cascade of Ponies and Mini-Horses**, and the **Northwest Miniature Horse Can Am Classic** are presented. In July, the **Pacific Northwest Paint Horse Show**, the **4H Horse Show**, and the **Puget Sound Quarter Horse Show** come along. In August, the **American Miniature Horse District Show** and the **County Fair Charity Horse Show** are staged. And in September, they have the **Washington State Hunter/Jumper Horse Show**, the **Pacific Northwest Quarter Horse Show**, and the **Draft Horse & Mule Extravaganza**. For a little variety, the **Llama Expo** is presented in July.

The **Daffodil Arabian Horse Show** is held each year at the Puyallup Fairgrounds, PO Box 430, **Puyallup**, WA 98371, ☎ 206/841-5045, Web site www.thefair.com.

Whidbey Island Percherons Carriage Co., 188 Percheron Lane, PO Box 1163, **Coupeville**, WA 98239, ☎ 360/678-6897 or 929-0194, offers horse-drawn carriage rides.

Rodeos

The **WRA Timber Bowl Rodeo**, ☎ 206/629-2842 or 360/436-1740, is held on the last full weekend in June on the grounds of the **Darrington Horse Owners Assn**. Activities include a rodeo dance for the women and a petting zoo for the kids.

Rodeo also is big around **Enumclaw**, where a PRCA rodeo is included in the **King County Fair**, ☎ 360/825-7777, held in July; the **NWGRA Rodeo** is held during the second week in August; and the **Enumclaw Junior Rodeo** is held during the last week in August.

The annual **Long Beach Rodeo** has been held at the Rodeo Grounds on Sandridge Road, Long Beach, WA 98631, ☎ 800/451-2542, in August for over 50 years. The annual **Black Hills Wranglers Rodeo** is held in **Oakville** each July.

The **Western Washington Fair**, ☎ 206/845-1771, held in **Puyallup** every September, includes a rodeo, name entertainment, rides, and a whole lot more. The fair has been held since 1900 and attracts 1.5 million visitors a year.

The town of **Roy** stages the **Roy Pioneer Rodeo**, ☎ 253/843-1113, each year; **Sedro-Wooley** presents the **Loggerodeo**, ☎ 360/855-1129 or 800/214-0800, each year; and **Silverdale** holds a rodeo in the Kitsap Pavilion, ☎ 360/871-7051 or 692-6153 each year. **Yelm**, ☎ 360/458-6608, holds its annual rodeo in July.

Races

Emerald Downs, 2300 Emerald Downs Dr., **Auburn**, WA 98001, ☎ 206/931-8400 or 888/931-8400, Web site www.seattleonline.com/emdowns, has a six-level stadium for thoroughbred horse racing. The 166-acre grounds includes a restaurant. Racing is presented Thursdays through Mondays from June 20 to November 4.

Another **Emerald Downs**, at 6329 S. 212th St., **Kent**, WA 98032, ☎ 206/395-3800 or 800/527-1133, fax 206/395-3022, provides thoroughbred horse racing. Tours of the stable area, ☎ 206/288-7711, are conducted on Saturdays.

Harbor Park Horse Races, are held on the Grays Harbor Fairgrounds in **Elma** each July.

■ On Wheels

Biking

Seattle is consistently ranked among the top 10 best cities in America for cycling. It has 30 miles of bike/pedestrian trails, 90 miles of signed bike routes, and 13 miles of bike lanes on the city streets. An estimated 4,000-8,000 people commute about the city by bicycle each day, depending on the weather. There even is a **Bicycle Hotline**: ☎ 206/522-BIKE.

Backcountry Bicycle Trails Club, PO Box 21288, Seattle, WA 98111-3288, ☎ 206/283-2995, can provide a lot of pointers on places you might want to go.

Tim Kneeland & Assocs., 200 Lake Washington Blvd., Suite 101, Seattle, WA 98122-6540, ☎ 206/322-4102 or 800/433-0528, fax 206/322-4509, E-mail timtka@aol.com, Web site www.kneeland.com/timtka/, arranges long-distance bike trips, including a 27-day, 1,689-mile ride from Victoria, British Columbia to Tijuana on the Mexican border south of San Diego.

You can get a free *Kitsap & Olympic Peninsula Bike Map* at the Visitor & Convention Bureau in **Bremerton**.

This & That, 748 Ocean Shores Blvd. NE, **Ocean Shores**, WA 98569, ☎ 206/289-0190, will rent you a bicycle built for two, while **O.W.W.**, Shores Mall on Chance-de-la-Mer, ☎ 206/289-3830, and **Mac's Rentals**, 206/289-4692, rents mopeds. **Olympic Outdoor**, ☎ 360/289-3736, will rent you a bike or a moped.

Pedal 'N' Pack, 120 E. Front St., **Port Angeles**, WA 98362, ☎ 206/457-1240, is the Olympic Peninsula's largest bike store. It will rent you a bicycle or a kayak, and arrange half-day or all-day tours.

Around **Port Hadlock**, **Fort Flagler State Park**, **Mystery Bay State Marine Park**, and **Old Fort Townsend State Park** off Route 20 are nice places to go biking.

Centennial Trail, a paved 50-mile stretch of abandoned railroad right-of-way, extends northward from Maple Avenue and Pine Street in **Snohomish** and follows the Machias Road to Lake Stevens. An extension in 1997 added nine more miles to the trail.

Three picturesque waterfalls are within a half-hour ride of **Quilcene**: Dosewallips, Rocky Brook, and Falls View.

 A free publication, *Washington State Traffic Data for Bicyclists*, is available from the Public Affairs Office, Washington State Department of Transportation, Transportation Building, Olympia, WA 98504-5201, ☎ 206/705-7277.

Rail Tours

Waterfront Streetcars, ☎ 206/684-2046, carries Seattle passengers between the Jackson Street Station, 5th Avenue and South Main Street, and the Broad Street Station at Pier 70 on Elliott Bay, on Australian-made streetcars. The streetcars run about every 20 minutes, seven days a week, and make nine stops. Transfers are free.

Bright yellow sandwich boards mark the boarding points for **Seattle Trolley Tours**, ☎ 206/626-5212. The trolleys are red, blue, or green according to route and go by every 30 minutes.

Lake Whatcom Railway, PO Box 91, **Acme**, WA 98220, ☎ 360/595-2218, offers an excursion on an old-fashioned steam train. The train leaves Wickersham Junction at 11 AM and at 1 PM on Saturdays, from July 5 through August 30.

Anacortes Railway, 7th Street and R Avenue, **Anacortes**, WA 98221, ☎ 206/293-2634, rides an 18-inch narrow-gauge track downtown and back, *for a fee of just one dollar*. Pulled by an old steam locomotive, the train has a plush interior that features private compartments and a marble fireplace. The train runs on Saturdays and Sundays from mid-June through Labor Day.

The *Spirit of Washington* dinner train, 625 S. 4th St., PO Box 835, **Renton**, WA 98057, ☎ 206/227-7245 or 800/876-7245, travels north from Renton to Woodinville and the Chateau Ste. Michelle Winery (the largest in the state). En route, the passengers dine on prime rib, salmon, chicken, or Dungeness crab crepes. After dinner, the passengers disembark for a tour of the winery and/or the tasting room, then go back to the train for their return. The round trip covers 45 miles. Dinner cruises are made daily; lunch trips are made only on Saturdays; and there is a brunch cruise on Sundays. Occasionally, the line schedules a murder mystery cruise in which the passengers attempt to unravel an intricately woven intrigue.

Mount Baker International Amtrak Service, ☎ 800/USA-RAIL, has resumed between Seattle and Vancouver. Using high-tech Spanish-built Talgo 200 trains, daily round-trips leave Seattle in the morning, arrive in Vancouver at mid-day, and return to Seattle in the early evening. Stops en route are made in Edmonds, Everett, Mt. Vernon/Burlington, and Bellingham. Discounts are offered to seniors and children.

Snoqualmie Valley Railroad Co., Railroad Ave., PO Box 459, **Snoqualmie**, WA 98065, ☎ 425/746-4025, operates the *Cascade Foothills Limited*, which makes weekend runs between North Bend and Snoqualmie from April to October. During the holiday season, the line runs a Santa train.

Off-Road Driving

A free pamphlet, *Off-Road Vehicle Recreation Information*, is available from the Snohomish County office in **Bremerton**.

Races

Auto races are held at **Seattle International Raceway**, 31001 144th Ave. SE, **Kent**, WA 98032, ☎ 253/631-1550, and at **Spanaway Speedway**, 16413 22nd Ave. E., **Spanaway**, WA 98387, ☎ 206/531-4249.

Evergreen Speedway, Evergreen State Fairgrounds, **Monroe**, WA 98272, ☎ 360/794-5917, holds auto races every Saturday night from April through September.

■ On the Water

Fishing

For general info about fishing, contact the **Washington State Department of Fish & Wildlife**, ☎ 360/902-2250.

Salmon anglers can access the Washington Department of Fisheries' **Salmon Hotline**, ☎ 206/976-3200, for 50 cents a call.

Around **Anacortes**, there are a number of excellent fishing sites, including **Egg Lake** and **Hummel Lake**. **Campbell Lake**, five miles south of town, covers 410 acres, has a boat launch, and is an excellent place to catch largemouth bass and spiny rays. The lake also contains yellow perch, brown bullhead, cutthroat trout, and rainbow. **Pass Lake**, six miles south of town, covers 98 acres, has a boat launch, and provides excellent fishing in the early spring and late fall. Fly fishing is all that is allowed on Pass Lake, which contains Atlantic salmon, rainbow trout, brown trout, and cutthroat trout.

A number of outstanding freshwater lakes can be found near **Bellingham**. **Lake Padden**, a 152-acre urban lake off Samish Way, is surrounded by a city park, has a boat launch and several fishing docks, and has a paved shoreside platform on the north side of the lake for the benefit of the handicapped. The lake contains rainbow trout, cutthroat trout, and kokanee salmon. **Silver Lake**, three miles north of **Maple Falls** on Silver Lake Road, covers 173 acres and is bordered on the south side by a county park where boat rentals are available. The lake contains rainbow trout, cutthroat trout, and eastern brook trout.

Toad Lake (aka Emerald Lake), five miles northeast of Bellingham off Britton and Hillside Roads, is quite small (29 acres), but it has a fishing dock on the southeast side and cartop boats are easily launched from the west end. Rainbow trout and kokanee can be taken here.

Cain Lake, 9.5 miles southeast of Bellingham, contains rainbow trout, largemouth bass, perch, and spiny rays. There is a launch ramp at the south end of the lake on Camp Two Road. **Fazon Lake**, 1.5 miles northwest of **Goshen** off East Hemmi Road, contains rainbow trout, largemouth bass, bluegill, cutthroat trout, and channel catfish. The 32-acre lake has a boat launch, but there is virtually no access to the water from shore due to heavy brush. There is a summer bluegill tournament for the kids at the lake, and some special regulations restrict fishing there.

Lake Samish, 6.5 miles southeast of Bellingham beside I-5, covers 814 acres and contains kokanee salmon, largemouth bass, perch, and cutthroat trout (14-inch minimum). The lake is being considered as the site of northwest Washington's first tiger musky fishery. There is a boat launch on the east side of the lake off East Lake Samish Drive. Fishing generally is best in early June and September.

Squalicum Lake, 6.5 miles northeast of Bellingham off Mount Baker Highway and Squalicum Lake Road, covers 33 acres and is open to fly fishing only. The lake contains cutthroat trout. **Lake Whatcom**, on the east edge of Bellingham off Lakeway Drive via Alabama Street or Electric Avenue, covers 5,003 acres and contains Eastern cutthroat trout, kokanee salmon, largemouth bass, smallmouth bass, and yellow perch.

Near **Concrete**, freshwater fishermen favor **Baker Lake**, six miles northeast of town. The 3,616-acre lake has a boat launch and is a popular place to fish for kokanee salmon in May and June and again in the fall, and for rainbow trout in early July. **Shannon Lake**, just north of **Concrete** on Baker Lake Road, is a 2,148-acre lake containing kokanee salmon, but it has a difficult boat launch. **Copalis Beach** offers good fishing for salmon, tuna, cod, and snapper.

Backman Park, two miles from **Darrington** on Darrington Clear Creek Road, is a two-acre county park that offers good river fishing. Darrington is bordered by the **Sauk** and **Stillaguamish Rivers**, both of which are good for steelhead trout, rainbow trout, cutthroat trout, and Dolly Varden trout. The **Skagit River**, 20 minutes north of town, is popular for steelhead trout and salmon from November through April.

Des Moines has a public fishing pier.

In **Edmonds**, anglers fish for salmon off a lighted 950-foot pier. From October to March, blackmouth salmon ranging from four to 20 pounds are caught here. In April, the catch usually includes small silvers, blackmouth, and some early spring salmon. Between July and September, the usual catch includes chinook and coho salmon.

Nolte State Park, 36921 Veazle Cumberland Rd., **Enumclaw**, WA 98022, centers around Deep Lake, once a private resort. The lake, located six miles northeast of Enumclaw on Route 410, is 100 feet deep and has two fishing docks, a boat launch, and a 200-foot swimming area (guarded Wednesdays through Sundays from mid-June to Labor Day). Cutthroat trout, rainbow trout, steelhead trout, bass, perch, catfish, walleye, and bluegill can be caught there, and there also is a 1.4-mile interpretive trail for hiking. The park is open from 6:30 AM to dusk between mid-April and October 1.

The county parks in **Everett** offer opportunities to do saltwater fishing, lake fishing, and river fishing. Lake fishing is available at **Flowing Lake, Lake Roesiger, Martha Lake,** and **McCollum**. River fishing can be found at **Backman**, on the Darrington Clear Creek Road two miles from Darrington, and at **Jordan Bridge** six miles north of Route 92 on Jordan Road. **Kayak Point, Meadowdale Beach,** and **Picnic Point** provide access to saltwater fishing.

Lake Terrell, five miles west of **Ferndale** off Mountain View Road, is a 438-acre lake that offers excellent fishing for spiny ray. The lake, which has a fishing dock and a boat launch along the western shore, also contains largemouth bass, yellow perch, cutthroat trout, and bullhead catfish.

Around **Grays Harbor**, there are 27 miles of interconnecting freshwater lakes and canals containing perch, bass, trout, walleye, and grayling. Close by, saltwater fishermen are able to catch tuna, salmon, ling cod, sea bass, halibut, whiting, Pacific cod, and red snapper. Dungeness crab, oysters, prawns, and shrimp also are available.

> 📖 Pick up a free copy of *Recreational Fishing Guide*, prepared by Grays Harbor Fisheries Enhancement Task Force, 2109 Sumner Ave., Suite 200, **Aberdeen**, WA 98520, ☎ 206/532-8812.

In Grays Harbor County, the **Humptulips River** also affords good fishing.

In **Ilwaco**, salmon can be caught from a charter boat or off the North Jetty. Sturgeon, bottom fish, and tuna also are present. The best sturgeon fishing generally occurs from mid-December through October. **Wiser Lake**, three miles southwest of **Lynden**, covers 123 acres and contains largemouth bass, brown bullheads, cutthroat trout, and sunfish. A boat launch is provided.

Buck Island City Park, near **Monroe,** provides salmon and steelhead trout fishing in the Skykomish River. Fishing also is available in nearby **Flowing Lake County Park** and **Lake Roesiger County Park**.

Big Lake, five miles southeast of **Mount Vernon** off Route 9, covers 545 acres and contains largemouth bass, crappie, yellow perch, and cutthroat trout. Nighttime bass fishing with topwater lures is especially good in the summer.

The 223-acre **Clear Lake** is three miles south of **Sedro-Woolley** off Route 9. It has a boat launch and contains rainbow trout, largemouth bass, yellow perch, cutthroat trout, and bullhead catfish. **Erie Lake**, a 111-acre lake four miles south of **Anacortes**, and **Heart Lake**, a 61-acre lake 2.5 miles south of town, both contain rainbow trout.

Oak Harbor is another good place to try your hand at catching rainbow trout. **Cranberry Lake** has been stocked with 6,000 four-pound rainbows; **Goss Lake** with 3,800 four-pound, 2,800 two-pound, and 140 large broodstock rainbows; **Lone Lake** with 7,500 four-pound and 1,700 two-pound rainbows; and **Deer Lake** with 7,800 four-pound, 2,000 two-pound, and 190 large broodstock rainbows.

Fishing in **Ocean Shores** is best near the North Jetty or on Protection Island near the marina. Crabbing is most productive near the marina at Damon Point. Those who wish to do their fishing from a boat can charter the *Midnight Star*, at Ocean Shores Marina, Ocean Shores, WA 98569, ☎ 206/289-2647, or rent their own from **Summer Sails**, ☎ 206/289-2884, on the Grand Canal at the south end of Pt. Brown Avenue.

From late January to early March, "black mouth" salmon can be taken at **Port Angeles**. Freshwater fishing also is good in this area, particularly at **Lake Crescent**, 17 miles west of town on US 101, which is 8.5 miles long and over 1,000 feet deep. (An old railroad grade along the north shore now serves as a biking and hiking trail.)

Anderson Lake State Park, off Route 19 near **Port Hadlock**, offers good fishing, hiking, and swimming. According to an Indian legend, a dragon named No-Qui-Klos (the demon) lived on an island in the lake long ago. The old people stayed safely away from the dragon, but they could clearly see the dragon's golden scales and iridescent purple eyes as he sunned himself on Tomanawos Rock.

There is a fishing dock in **Waterfront Park** in **Raymond**.

The **Mill Pond**, a former holding pond for logs, is now a refuge for fish and wildlife near **Snoqualmie**. From WA 202 eastbound or Meadowbrook Bridge westbound, take Mill Pond Road.

If you prefer to fish without the disruption of power boat traffic, try **Spada Lake** near **Sultan**. Power boats, swimming, and overnight camping are not allowed.

Around **Taholah**, the peak steelhead season runs from November to April; king and silver salmon, from September to November; sockeye salmon, from February to April; and summer-run king salmon, from May to August. Trout can be taken year-around.

Westport has the largest charter fishing fleet in Washington. **Advantage Adventures**, ☎ 360/268-9140 or 800/648-1520; **Catchalot Charters**, ☎ 360/268-0323 or 800/356-0323; **Coho Charters**, ☎ 360/

268-0111 or 800/572-0177; **Ocean Charters**, ☎ 360/268-9144 or 800/562-0105, fax 360/268-1223; **Deep Sea Charters**, ☎ 360/268-9300 or 800/562-0151; and **Westport Charters**, ☎ 360/268-9120 or 800/562-0157, all take on fishing excursions. Bait and tackle generally are included in the charter fee. The best season for tuna is generally July through October; for salmon, June through September; and bottom fishing, March through October.

Catching Squid & Shellfish

📖 Enjoy eating calamari? A free 36-page pocket guide, *The Tantalizing Squid*, is available from the **Washington Department of Fisheries** (address below). The booklet shows where, how, and when to catch squid; how to clean them; and how to cook them. Five recipes are included.

Good places to catch squid are the public fishing piers at **Port Angeles** from late June to the end of August; the piers at **Edmonds**, beginning about September; the piers at **Seattle**, particularly Elliott Bay, during October and November; the piers at **Des Moines** in late November and December; Les Davis Pier in **Tacoma** in late November and December; the piers at **Olympic** between January and February; and **Neah Bay** on the Olympic Peninsula in late May

📖 A free pocket brochure, *Shellfish in Washington*, is available from the **Washington Department of Fisheries**, 115 General Administration Building, Olympia, WA 98504.

Littleneck clams average three to four inches and have concentric rings with radiating ridges. Butter clams grow to six inches and have only concentric rings. Horse clams reach eight inches and are chalky-white in color with patches of yellow-brown. Geoducks (*gooie-ducks*), the world's largest burrowing clams, can weigh as much as ten pounds and live two to three feet beneath the sand.

Softshell clams grow to six inches in size and are chalky-white in color. They usually are found eight to 14 inches under the sand around river mouths and are harvested with long-tined rakes. Softshells are abundant in Port Susan, Skagit Bay, Grays Harbor, and Willapa Bay. Cockles, light brown in color with prominent, evenly spaced ridges, are found near the surface of sand-gravel beaches and can be harvested with an ordinary garden rake. They are most commonly used in chowder.

Razor clam digging is excellent at **Copalis Beach** in season. Those seeking Pacific razor clams should know that the daily limit is 15 clams per person. Both the north and south beaches of **Grays Harbor**, where there are over 50 miles of digging grounds, are popular. Low or minus tides are best.

Giant horse clams, steamers, and butterclams can be found in **Birch Bay**. A shellfish license is required. Clam digging is popular at **Kayak Point, Meadowdale Beach**, and **Picnic Point**, county parks in the **Everett** area.

Long Beach claims the world's longest beach – 28 miles of hard-packed sand – ideal for clam digging, as well as beachcombing, surf fishing, storm watching, jogging, and walking. The best clam digging in **Tokeland** is in North Cove. **Olympic Outdoor**, 773 Pt. Brown Ave. NW, **Ocean Shores**, WA 98569, ☎ 206/289-3736, rents clam gear.

A free map of the public shellfishing sites around **Sequim** is available from the Chamber of Commerce. The best place to find clams is in Dungeness Bay and along the south shore of Sequim Bay. The best crabbing can be found inside Dungeness Bay from Dungeness to Hulahala Point and on the north shore of Sequim Bay.

Dungeness crabs run from six to ten inches in size, have a grayish-brown back tinged with purple, and usually are associated with beds of eel-grass. Red rock crabs are smaller and have brick-red shells and black-tipped claws.

In **Hood Canal**, the shrimp season begins in late May.

Boating

The **Washington State Parks & Recreation Commission**, 7150 Cleanwater Lane, PO Box 42650, Olympia, WA 98504-2650, ☎ 360/902-8500 or 800/233-0321, provides a free pocket-sized brochure, *Your Guide to Marine Parks and Boat Moorage*, that boat owners will find useful.

Grays Harbor is the only deep-water port on the coast of Washington. There, the *Lady Washington* makes tall ship cruises out of **Aberdeen**.

Island Adventure Charters & Tours, PO Box 1718, **Anacortes**, WA 98221, ☎ 360/293-2428 or 800/465-4604, takes passengers whale-watching in the San Juan Islands. It also rents boats, charters salmon fishing trips, and schedules sunset cruises. The company is located at the foot of 11th Street in Slip 2 at the Cap Sante Marina. **ABC Yacht Charters**, 1905 Skyline Way, PO Box 129, Anacortes, WA 98221, ☎ 360/293-9533 or 800/426-2313, fax 360/293-0313, charters power cruisers and sailing yachts.

Orcas, San Juan Islands (Washington Tourism Dev).

For a small fee, you can take a self-guided tour of the **W.T. Preston**, a sternwheel snagboat moored at 703 R Ave., **Anacortes**. Snagging was the practice of clearing log jams from clogged waterways.

Adventure Pacific, 31607 44th Ave. South, **Auburn**, WA 98001, ☎ 206/939-8351 or 979-3230, charters half-day, full-day, sunset, and custom cruises through the San Juans on the *SV Chinook*.

Brisa Charters, ☎ 360/385-2309, offers sunset cruises out of **Port Townsend**, while **Sea Sport Charters**, PO Box 805, Port Townsend, WA 98368, ☎ 306/385-3575, hosts fishing and marine and wildlife tours. **Affordable Dreams**, PO Box 581, **Ferndale**, WA 98248-0581, ☎ 360/384-6945 or 800/354-8608, provides half-day, day, sunset, and overnight cruises as well as yacht vacations.

Family Charters, 12218 SE 192nd St., **Renton**, WA 98058, ☎ 206/915-0807 or 907/321-0603, will take you sightseeing, fishing, beachcombing, and exploring aboard the *Nip N Tuck*. **Sequim Bay Tours & Charters**, 2577 W. Sequim Bay Rd., **Sequim**, WA 98382, ☎ 360/681-7408, fax 360/681-7409, Web site www.northolympic.com/sequimbay, takes tours out of John Wayne Marina.

Island Mariner Cruises, #5 Harbor Esplanade, **Bellingham**, WA 98225, ☎ 206/734-8866, fax 360/734-8867, takes orca cruises through the 172 San Juan Islands every Saturday from May 28 through mid-September and every Monday and Wednesday during July and August.

The cruises leave at 10 AM and return about 5:30 PM. (Orcas, also called "killer whales," are not whales, but the largest members of the *dolphin* family. They travel in groups called "pods," a family cluster of about 30 animals, and are commonly sighted off the Washington coast.) There are three resident pods of orca (called J, K and L) residing in the San Juan Islands year-around.

Victoria-San Juan Cruises, 355 Harris Ave., #104, **Bellingham**, WA 98225, ☎ 360/738-8099 or 800/443-4552, makes daily round-trips aboard the *Victoria Star Two* to Victoria, BC, from mid-May through early October, making stops at Roche Harbor on San Juan Island. The return trip includes an all-you-can-eat salmon dinner. The cruise leaves the Bellingham Cruise Terminal at 9 AM, stops at Roche Harbor at 10:45 AM, and arrives in Victoria at 1 PM, returning to Bellingham by 8 PM.

Anchor Excursions, 723 14th St., **Bellingham**, WA 98225, ☎ 360/733-9078, allows passengers to join scientists aboard *The Snow Goose*, a 65-foot marine research vessel, on research cruises through the San Juan Islands. The company also charters island day-trips and three- to five-day adventures.

Northern Trading Voyages, 9067 Sunrise Rd., **Custer**, WA 98240, ☎ 800/326-3486, uses the *Northern Song*, an 80-foot luxury charter yacht to provide sightseeing, fishing, and gourmet dining cruises. The yacht contains four guest staterooms, each equipped with a private bathroom ("head") and shower.

Mosquito Fleet, 1724 W. Marine View Dr., **Everett**, WA 98201, ☎ 206/252-6800, 787-6400 (from Seattle), or 800/325-6722, leads whale-watching cruises. During the spring, summer, and fall, it also conducts three-hour tours of the "Everett Everglades," Puget Sound's largest wetland, aboard *The Heron,* a jet pontoon boat.

Another *Mosquito Fleet,* 73 Sidney, **Port Orchard**, WA 98366, ☎ 360/876-2300, provides a ten-minute boat trip that connects Port Orchard with downtown Bremerton. The fleet makes 76 crossings a day, and passengers can ride free on Saturdays and Sundays from June through October.

A sternwheeler, the *Snohomish River Queen,* ☎ 206/259-2743, takes scenic river cruises along the Snohomish River, from the Everett Marina on West Marine View Drive (behind the Chamber of Commerce office). The tours are conducted Tuesdays through Sundays during the peak season. Lunch, dinner, and Sunday brunch cruises are available.

Trophy Charters, PO Box 2444, **Friday Harbor**, WA 98250, ☎ 360/378-2110 or 317-8210, arranges fishing charters, provides a water taxi, conducts wildlife cruises, and sets up cruises to Canada.

North West Para-Sail, ☎ 371-3070 or 650-9459, is on Lake Whatcom in **Bellingham**. They'll tow you to a height of 600 feet above the lake, then bring you back to the boat – and you won't get your feet wet.

Swimming, Windsurfing & Whale-Watching

Believe it or not, there is a Waikiki Beach in Washington. It sits on a picturesque cove alongside the North Jetty in **Ilwaco** and is a great place to go swimming.

Olympic Coast National Marine Sanctuary, which includes the northern two-thirds of the Washington coast and extends 40 miles out to sea, is just the fourteenth such sanctuary in the United States.

Boom Town Enterprises, PO Box 5943, Bellingham, WA 98227, ☎ 360/319-9515, operates out of **Semiahmoo**. The firm takes customers sport fishing, whale-watching, and scuba diving around the San Juan and Canadian Gulf Islands. Good scuba diving is available in a 32-acre underwater park in **Edmonds**.

Windsurfing is popular in **Des Moines**, where camping, hiking, and beach activities also are popular in **Saltwater State Park**.

Marine Adventure Safari Camp, Island Institute, PO Box 661, **Vashon Island**, WA 98070, ☎ 206/463-6722, permits people to whale-watch, go kayaking, and snorkel from a private island in the San Juans. The 550-acre Spiden Island, which holds bighorn sheep, deer, elk, and 60 species of birds, is accessible by sea-plane from Seattle, Victoria, and Vancouver, or by boat from San Juan Island.

Kayaking

Kayaking is an extremely popular sport in coastal Washington, particularly in and around the San Juan Islands.

Around **San Juan Island**, you can take a kayak tour with **Crystal Seas Kayaking**, ☎ 360/378-7899; **Leisure Kayak Adventures**, ☎ 360/378-5992 or 217-8561; and **The Whale Museum Sea Kayak Tours**, ☎ 360/378-4710. Three-hour kayak tours conducted by **San Juan Excursions**, ☎ 360/378-6636 or 800-80-WHALE, leave Mariella Inn daily at 10 AM and 2 PM, while similar tours conducted by **San Juan Safaris**, ☎ 360/378-2155, leave Roche Harbor Resort, from mid-May through September.

Around **Orcas Island**, **Crescent Beach Kayaks**, ☎ 360/376-2464; **Orcas Kayak Rental**, ☎ 360/376-3767; **Shearwater Sea Kayak Tours**, ☎ 360/376-4699; and **Spring Bay Kayaking**, ☎ 360/376-5531, rent kayaks.

Eddyline Watersports Center, 1019 Q Ave., **Anacortes**, WA 98221, ☎ 360/299-2300; **Bainbridge Island Boat Rentals**, 528 Winslow Way West, **Bainbridge Island**, WA 98110, ☎ 206/842-9229, fax 206/842-9687; **Elakah! Kayak Tours**, PO Box 4092, **Bellingham**, WA 98227, ☎ 360/734-7270 or 800/434-7270; **NorthWest Experiences**, 1215 Dundee Dr., **Cosmopolis**, WA 98537, ☎ 360/532-9176; **Shearwater Adventures**, PO Box 787, **Eastsound**, WA 98245, ☎ 360/376-4699; **Upper Left-Hand Corner Kayak Tours**, 10823 NE 60, **Kirkland**, WA 98033, ☎ 425/828-4772; **Anacortes Kayak Excursions**, PO Box 1361, **La Conner**, WA 98257, ☎ 206/299-2954; **Black River Canoes & Kayaking Trips**, 15847 Littlerock Rd. SW, PO Box F, **Littlerock**, WA 98556, ☎ 360/273-6369; **Kayak Port Townsend**, 435 Water St., PO Box 1387, **Port Townsend**, WA 98368, ☎ 360/385-6240; **Olympic Outdoor Center**, 18971 Front St., PO Box 2247, **Poulsbo**, WA 98370, ☎ 360/697-6095; and **Outdoor Odysseys**, 12003 23rd Ave. NE, **Seattle**, WA 98125, ☎ 206/361-0717 or 800/647-4621, are among the many places you can rent a kayak, take lessons, and in many cases, schedule a guided kayaking tour.

Canoeing and kayaking are popular at **Flowing Lake, Kayak Point**, and **Lake Roesiger**, county parks close to **Everett**.

Whitewater Rafting

Whitewater rafting is another popular sport in this land of rushing rivers and spectacular waterfalls.

North Cascades River Expeditions, PO Box 116, **Arlington**, WA 98223, ☎ 360/435-9548 or 800/634-8433, makes whitewater rafting trips on the Methow, Skagit, Suiattle, Wenatchee, Green, Sauk, Tieton, White Salmon, and Skykomish Rivers.

Wildwater River Tours, PO Box 3623, **Federal Way**, WA 98063-3623, ☎ 206/939-2151 or 800/522-9453, conducts rafting trips on the Nisqually, Upper and Lower Skagit, Queets/Hoh, Yakima, Suiattle, Wenatchee, Tieton, Deschutes, Methow, Clackamas, Klickitat, White Salmon, Toutle, Green, Upper Cispus, and Skykomish Rivers.

Extreme Adventures, 5405 Upper Hoh Rd., **Forks**, WA 98331, ☎ 360/374-6366, guides scenic and whitewater floats on the Hoh River. **Uncle Dave's Guide Service**, 133 Lindner Creek Lane, Forks, WA 98331,

☎ 360/374-2577, and **Z's Guide Service**, 842 Clearwater Rd., Forks, WA 98331, ☎ 360/962-2140, also lead fishing trips and float trips on the Hoh.

The **Skykomish River** offers some outstanding whitewater rafting between **Gold Bar** and **Index** in the spring and early summer.

AAA Rafting, 860 Hwy 141, PO Box 203, **Husum**, WA 98623, ☎ 509/493-2511 or 800/866-RAFT, guides rafting trips on the White Salmon, Upper White Salmon, Deschutes, Wind, and Klickitat Rivers.

River Recreation, 13 211th Pl. SE, **Redmond**, WA 98053-7038, ☎ 206/392-5899 or 800/464-5899, arranges whitewater rafting trips on the Methow, Wenatchee, White Salmon, Klickitat, and Tieton Rivers in eastern Washington, as well as the Skagit, Skykomish, Nooksack, and Green Rivers in western Washington.

River Riders, PO Box 566, **Pateros**, WA 98846, ☎ 509/923-2351 or 800/448-RAFT; **River Rafting Adventures**, 464 Hwy 101 West, **Port Angeles**, WA 98362, ☎ 206/457-7011; **Wild & Scenic River Tours**, PO Box 22606, **Seattle**, WA 98122, ☎ 206/323-1220 or 800/413-6840; **Pacific Northwest Float Trips**, 1039 Sterling Rd., **Sedro-Woolley**, WA 98284, ☎ 360/856-5224 or 856-1107; and **River Riders**, PO Box 2887, **Woodinville**, WA 98072, ☎ 206/448-RAFT, are among the numerous other places where whitewater rafting trips can be arranged.

Ferry Rides

Automobile ferries leave **Mount Vernon**, 21 miles west of I-5 near Anacortes. The three-hour voyage terminates at Sidney on Vancouver Island, not far from Victoria, and makes stops en route at Lopez, Shaw, Orcas, and San Juan Island. Plan to arrive early because the ferries are often crowded.

The **Washington State Ferry System**, ☎ 206/464-6400 or 800/84-FERRY, which operates car and passenger ferries to San Juan Islands and Vancouver Island, leaves from **Anacortes**.

San Juan Island Shuttle Express, 355 Harris, #105, **Bellingham**, WA 98225, ☎ 360/671-1137, operates a ferry daily from late May through September. The ferry leaves the Bellingham Cruise Terminal at 9:15 AM, stops at Orcas Island at 10:30 AM, and arrives in Friday Harbor by 11:30 AM. It then departs Friday Harbor at 4 PM, stops at Orcas at 4:50 PM, and returns to Bellingham at 6:15 PM.

The Alaska Marine Highway, 355 Harris Ave., **Bellingham**, WA 98225, ☎ 360/676-8445, makes car and passenger ferry runs two to three times a week from the Bellingham Cruise Terminal through Alaska's

Inside Passage. **Lummi Island Ferry**, ☏ 360/671-3990, operates a car ferry across Bellingham Bay to Lummi Island. The crossing takes 10 minutes.

Victoria-San Juan Cruises offers a passengers-only link between **Bellingham** and Victoria, British Columbia via the San Juan Islands. Operating from late May to October, the narrated cruise includes a one-hour stopover in Roche Harbor on San Juan Island.

San Juan Island Shuttle Express, Bellingham Cruise Terminal, **Bellingham**, WA 98225, ☏ 360/671-1137 or 888/373-8522, Web site www.bluewater.com/sjise, conducts whale-watching cruises and private charters. The line offers a narrated daily passengers-only service to Friday Harbor on San Juan Island from late May through September that makes a brief stop on Orcas Island and a 4.5-hour layover in Friday Harbor.

Kitsap Harbor Tours, 290 Washington Beach Ave. #7, **Bremerton**, WA 98337, ☏ 360/377-8924, operates *M/V Admiral Pete,* an 82-passenger ferry that provides fast links between Bremerton, Keyport, and Poulsbo. The ferry departs every two hours between 10 AM and 4 PM. **Kitsap Transit**, 234 S. Wycoff Ave., Bremerton, WA 98312-4199, ☏ 800/501-RIDE, provides a link between bus and ferry boat connections.

Horluck Transportation Co., 73 Sidney Ave., PO Box 87, Port Orchard, WA 98366, ☏ 206/876-2300, operates a passenger ferry between Port Orchard and Bremerton seven days a week. Bicycles are welcome.

Victoria Clipper, 2701 Alaskan Way, Pier 69, **Seattle**, WA 98121, ☏ 206/448-5000, 250/382-8100, or 800/888-2535, fax 206/443-2583, Web site www.victoriaclipper.com, takes trips to the San Juan Islands as well as Vancouver and Victoria, BC. Three new high-speed catamarans reach Victoria's Inner Harbour in 2.5 hours, and a new turbojet makes the trip in less than two hours. The car ferry to Victoria operates from mid-May through mid-September and requires 4.5 hours to make the trip.

Gray Line, 720 S. Forest St., Seattle, WA 98134, ☏ 206/624-5813 or 800/426-7505, Web sites www.seattleonline.com/grayline or www.sightseeing.com, provides daily service between Seattle, Friday Harbor, and Vancouver and Victoria, BC aboard *The Northwest Explorer.*

From **Mukilteo**, a passenger/car ferry crosses from the mainland to the southern end of Whidbey Island.

Cruises

On the Pier Inn at Semiahmoo, **Blaine**, WA, ☎ 360/731-3500, takes whale and nature cruises aboard the 64-foot *Odyssey*. The excursions run from 9:30 to 5:30 on Saturdays from May through September. Additional trips are scheduled on Sundays during June, July, and August.

Lake Washington Cruises, ☎ 206/623-4252, leave **Kirkland**'s Marina Park for 1.5-hour cruises on Lake Washington at 1 and 3 PM from May 1 to May 28; at 11 AM and 1, 3, and 5 PM from May 29 through August; and from 1 and 3 PM during September. The cruises do not operate from October through April.

Viking Cruises, 109 N. 1st St., PO Box 327, **La Conner**, WA 98257, ☎ 360/466-2639, provides cruises aboard *The Viking Star* to look for whales throughout the San Juan Islands. **Protection Island Cruises**, ☎ 360/385-5582, sponsored by Port Townsend Marine Science Center, provides three-hour cruises from **Port Townsend** to explore Washington Coastal Refuge. **P.S. Express**, 431 Water St., Port Townsend, WA 98368, ☎ 360/385-5288, also conducts tours to see the orcas and to tour the San Juan Islands.

American West Steamboat Co., 601 Union St., Suite 4343, **Seattle**, WA 98101, ☎ 800/434-1232, uses the sternwheeler *Queen of the West* to cruise the Columbia, Willamette, and Snake Rivers. Similar cruises are available through **Great Rivers Cruises & Tours**, 601 Union St., Suite 4343, Seattle, WA 98101, ☎ 800/720-0012.

Argosy Cruises, Pier 55, Suite 201, Seattle, WA 98101, ☎ 206/623-4252, provides 1.5 and two-hour cruises on Lake Washington, 2.5-hour cruises through the locks, and cruises of the harbor. Casino cruises to Kiana and Suquamish Clearwater Casino leave Chandler's Cove on Mondays during the summer (discount coupons are available).

Catalyst Cruises, 515 S. 143rd St. South, **Tacoma**, WA 98444, ☎ 206/537-7678 or 800/670-7678, Web site www.cruise-nw.com, visits the San Juan Islands, the Gulf Islands in British Columbia, Johnstone Straits in Alert Bay, Campbell River, and other destinations with the *Sacajawea*.

Sailing enthusiasts will not be disappointed by the opportunities available throughout coastal Washington, either.

Crown Charters, 1015 Auburn Way South, Auburn, WA 98002, ☎ 253/939-0898 or 800/863-9908, charters sailing excursions. **Island Junkets**, 601 Briar Rd., **Bellingham**, WA 98225, ☎ 360/671-2908, fax 360/671-4110, E-mail stebb@pacificrim.net, Web site www.pacificrim.net/~stebb/~isljunkets.html, sails the San Juan Islands on a 46-foot, junk-rigged ketch.

Island Sailing Club, 2100 Carillon Point, **Ilwaco**, WA, 98033 ☎ 425/822-2470, offers sailboat lessons, rentals, and charters. The company also does business at 515 NE Tomahawk Island Dr., **Portland**, WA, ☎ 503/285-7765.

Let's Go Sailing, PO Box 31874, **Seattle**, WA 98103, ☎ 206/624-3931, E-mail obsession@afts.com, provides cruises aboard sailing ships. **Sailing in Seattle**, 1900 Westlake Ave. North, ☎ 206/298-0094, sets sail in the sloop *Whoodat* on Monday and Wednesday evenings at 7:30 and 10, and on Sundays at 1:30, 4, and 7:30.

Tall Ship Tours, Pier 55, Suite 201, Seattle, WA 98101, ☎ 206/682-4876, offers rides aboard the *Lady Washington,* built in 1989 as a reproduction of the 1787 vessel of the same name, which was the first American vessel to explore the Pacific Coast. "Early bird" cruises take place from 10 AM to noon. Two-hour sails are offered from 1 to 3 and from 3:30 to 5:30. Three-hour sunset sails also are available. The cruises leave Pier 54.

Lake Union Boat Rental, 2046 Westlake Ave. North, Suite 104, Seattle, WA 98109, ☎ 206/283-5532, rents a 21-foot, self-righting and unsinkable MacGregor sailboat.

The Vessel *Zodiac* Corp., PO Box 322, **Snohomish**, WA 98291-0322, ☎ 206/483-4088 or 325-6122, offers rides aboard a two-masted sailing schooner.

■ On Snow

Mount Baker Ski Area, 1019 Iowa St., **Bellingham**, WA 98226, ☎ 360/734-6771, fax 360/734-5332, is one of 13 ski sites throughout the state. The facility provides downhill and cross-country skiing, equipment rentals, lessons, and snowboarding. There are two rope tows and eight chairs, six doubles and two quads. Nine of the runs are easy, 11 are moderate, eight are difficult, and two are for experts only. A cafeteria is on the premises. To get a snow report: ☎ 360/671-0211 (from Bellingham), 206/634-0200 (from Seattle), or 604/688-1595 (from Vancouver, BC).

Mount Baker has the longest skiing season in the state (November through April), the most snow in the nation (an average of 595 inches per year), and a vertical drop of 1,500 feet.

Mini Mountain, 1900 132nd Ave. NE, **Bellevue**, WA 98004, ☎ 425/746-7547, has an indoor ski hill and provides skiing and snowboarding lessons.

246 ■ Coastal Washington

Mount Baker snowboarding (Washington Tourism Dev).

Club Vertical, Crystal Mountain Resort, One Crystal Mountain Blvd., **Crystal Mountain**, WA 98022, ☎ 360/663-2265, Web site www.snowlink.com/crystal, keeps its lifts open from 9 AM to 4:30 PM, Monday through Friday and from 8:30 AM to 4:30 PM on weekends and holidays. Night skiing is available from 4 PM to 8 PM on Fridays, Saturdays, Sundays, and holidays, from December through late March. Snowboarding is available. The resort also rents equipment and provides children's programs and day care. Condos, hotel-style lodgings, inns, and restaurants also are available. For a snow report: ☎ 206/632-3771 (from Seattle) or 206/922-1832 (from Tacoma).

An hour's drive east of Seattle is **Snoqualmie Summit** or "The Pass," where four downhill resorts with a combined 23 chairlifts serving 65 runs across 4,500 acres of mountainside are linked by a shuttle bus. There are two ski schools, **Snoqualmie Ski & Snowboard School**, PO Box 1068, Snoqualmie Pass, WA 98068, ☎ 206/236-PASS, and **Ski School Alpental**, PO Box 168, Snoqualmie Pass, WA 98068, ☎ 206/434-6364, fax 206/434-6334. **Snoqualmie Ski Area**, 425/236-1600, will provide a report on current snow conditions.

Ski Acres Ski & Snowboard School, 8206 NE 117th St., **Kirkland**, WA 98034, ☎ 425/823-2690, offers lessons.

Ski Lifts, 7900 SE 28th St., Suite 200, **Mercer Island**, WA 98040, ☎ 206/236-6141, fax 206/232-1721, E-mail thepass@ix.netcom.com, Web site www.snowlink.com/thepass, represents the Hyak, Ski Acres, Snoqualmie, and Alpental ski areas.

Hurricane Ridge is the choice skiing area around **Port Townsend**.

Terrene Tours, 117 32nd Ave. East, Seattle, WA 98112, ☎ 206/325-5569, fax 206/328-1937, plans ski trips.

■ In the Air

Shuttle Service

West Isle Air, ☎ 360/293-4691 or 800/874-4434, operates out of Anacortes Airport, two miles south of **Anacortes** at 12th and Oakes Ave. It flies single and multiengine aircraft, and has a regular schedule of flights to Friday Harbor, Lopez Island, Orcas Island, Seattle, Victoria, and Vancouver. Customers can fly to the islands and ride the ferry back free.

Horizon Airlines, ☎ 800/547-9308, provides daily service to Seattle, Portland, and Victoria, BC from Fairchild International Airport in **Port Angeles**.

Harbor Airlines, ☎ 360/675-8444 or 800/359-3220, an Alaska Airlines connection, flies the 40-minute route from Sea-Tac to Eastsound Airport on Orcas Island.

Sound Flight, Bellingham, at Terminal Floathaven on Lake Whatcom, ☎ 206/255-6500 or 800/825-0722, makes scheduled seaplane flights to the San Juan Islands and Victoria as well as flightseeing tours.

Air Shows

Concrete holds an Old-Fashioned Fly-In at Concrete Municipal Airport on the third weekend in May.

Blaine stages a free annual Airport Fair in late June, with planes and helicopters flying in and out all day. Arts and crafts and food also are featured.

A Radio-Controlled Model Aircraft Competition, sponsored by **International Miniature Aerobatic Club**, ☎ 360/805-0100, is held in **Arlington** each June, and the **Evergreen Soaring Club**, ☎ 360/772-3002, meets on weekends at the Arlington Municipal Airport. During the second week in July, the airport also hosts the third largest experimental air show in the country, the annual **NWEAA Fly-In**, ☎ 360/435-5857 or 435-3708. The annual **South Puget Sound Air Show**, ☎ 360/

754-0793, is held in **Tumwater** in early July, and an **International Air Fair** is held in **Everett** in mid-August.

Charters & Tours

Magic Air Tours, PO Box 223, **Eastsound**, WA 98245, ☎ 360/376-2733, makes scenic biplane flights out of Eastsound Airport on Orcas Island. **Summit Flights**, PO Box 822, **Eatonville**, WA 98328, ☎ 360/832-4000, makes scenic flights out of Swanson Field over Mt. Rainier from mid-May through September. **Conroy Flying Service**, 34 Airport Way, **Elma**, WA 98541, ☎ 360/482-2228, gives lessons and offers scenic flights over the area.

Snohomish County Airport (Paine Field) in **Everett** offers aircraft rentals and provides instruction. A museum of flight also can be found at the airport.

Alpha Aviation, 12233 80th Ave. NE, **Kirkland**, WA 98034-5800, offers charter flights.

Monroe Aviation, 13812 179th Ave. SE, **Monroe**, WA 98272, ☎ 360/794-9134, is located across from the fairgrounds. It provides scenic rides, charters, lessons, and rentals.

Port Townsend Airways, ☎ 360/385-6554, provides daily scenic flights out of Jefferson County Airport in **Port Townsend**.

Open-cockpit biplane flights are offered by **Galvin Flying Service**, ☎ 206/763-9706, out of Boeing Field, five miles south of **Seattle**. **Erickson Aviation's Scenic Air**, ☎ 206/764-1175 or 800/995-3332, also flies out of Boeing Field.

Island Air, ☎ 206/567-4994, located on Cove Road at Vashon Municipal Airport on **Vashon Island**, features scenic flights, including whale-watching from the air.

Evergreen Airways, 468 Dorothy Hunt Lane, **Sequim**, WA 98382, ☎ 360/683-7597, offers scenic and charter flights. Harvey Airfield in **Snohomish** charters helicopter and airplane rides.

Ludlow Aviation, ☎ 360/385-6554, located at Jefferson County Airport, **Port Townsend**, books charters, makes rentals, takes flights to SeaTac Airport, gives scenic flights, offers float plane service, and provides flight instruction.

Pegasus Air, ☎ 360/674-2542 or 800/294-2542, features scenic and float plane flights in **Poulsbo**.

Seaplane flights also are available from **Sound Flight**, PO Box 812, **Renton**, WA 98057, ☎ 206/255-6500 or 800/825-0722, which flies out of

Renton Municipal Airport, and **Northwest Seaplanes**, 860 W. Perimeter Rd., Renton, WA 98055, ☎ 425/277-1590 or 800/690-0086, fax 425/277-8831, which makes flights to the San Juan Islands.

Seattle Seaplanes, 1325 Fairview Ave. East, **Seattle**, WA 98155, ☎ 206/329-9638 or ☎ 800/637-5553, and **Kenmore Air**, 6321 NE 175th St., Seattle, WA 98155, ☎ 425/486-1257, 206/364-6990 or 800/543-9595, fax 425/485-4774, E-mail kenair@seattleonline.com, Web site www.kenmoreair.com, also provide float plane tours.

Ballooning

Hot air ballooning is popular in this region.

Vagabond Balloons, ☎ 360/466-1906 or 800/488-0269, offers rides in a hot air balloon in **La Conner**, as does **Over the Rainbow**, 14481 Woodinville-Redmond Rd., **Woodinville**, WA 98072, ☎ 206/364-0995. **Kent** hosts an **International Balloon Festival** each July.

The **Whatcom County Hot Air Balloon Festival**, International Folkdance Festival, and Civil War Re-enactment are held in Hovander Homestead Park in **Ferndale** on the second weekend in August.

Kite Flying

With near constant breezes off the ocean, it is no surprise that kite flying also is a popular pastime in this area.

World Kite Museum & Hall of Fame, 3rd St. NW & Boulevard, PO Box 964, **Long Beach**, WA 98631, ☎ 360/642-4020, honors the 2,500-year history of the kite. Admission to the museum is free. **Stormin' Norman's Kites & Clothing**, ☎ 360/642-3482 or 800/4-Stormin, on Pacific Highway, one block south of the main stoplight in **Long Beach**, gives free kite flying lessons and is open every day except Christmas. Long Beach's oldest kite shop, **Long Beach Kites**, 104 Pacific Ave. North, Long Beach, WA 98631, ☎ 360/642-2202, is open daily from 9 to 6 during the season and from 10 to 5 Friday through Monday during the off-season.

Ocean Shores also has a number of kite shops, including **Cutting Edge Kites**, 676 Ocean Shores Blvd. NW in Nantucket Mall, 98569, ☎ 206/289-0667; **Cloud Nine Kites**, 380 WA 115, 98569 ☎ 206/289-2221; **Ocean Shores Kites**, 172 W. Chance-a-la-Mer in the Ocean Shores Mall, 98569, ☎ 206/289-4103; **Winds Northwest**, just west of town on Damon Road, 98569, ☎ 206/289-4578; and **Salty's Kites**, 810 Pt. Brown Ave. NE, 98569, ☎ 206/289-3531.

In June, **Long Beach** holds a Stunt Kite Competition, and **Ocean Shores** hosts one of the state's largest Kite Festivals.

Westport has a Kite Festival in mid-July.

During August, **Long Beach** entertains the Washington State International Kite Festival, PO Box 387, Long Beach, WA 98631, ☎ 360/642-2353 or 800/451-2542, voted the best kite festival in the world. A $1,000 prize is awarded if any kite record listed in the *Guinness Book of World Records* is broken during the festival.

In September, **Copalis Beach** hosts the Up Your Wind Kite Festival on Pacific Beach. Competition includes precision, power pull, mystery ballet, night-lighted flying, and more.

Gliders, Paragliders & Parachutes

Alpha Soaring Adventures, ☎ 206/823-6214, provides glider flights out of the Arlington airport.

Tiger Mountain Para-Gliding, ☎ 206/467-5944, provides thrills around **Issaquah** (*Iss-a-quaw*), and **Lake Washington Parasail**, ☎ 425/822-SAIL, is located at the end of Kirkland Ave. in **Kirkland** Marina Park. **North American Paragliding**, ☎ 800/727-2354, E-mail napi@eburg.com, Web site www.fun2fly.com, and **Pier 57 Parasail**, ☎ 360/622-5757, are in **Seattle**.

Parachutes Over Snohomish, ☎ 360/568-5960 or 800/338-5867, operates out of Harvey Airfield, 30 minutes from downtown Seattle.

■ Cultural Excursions

Aberdeen

The *Lady Washington* **Museum**, 813 E. Heron St., PO Box 2019, Aberdeen, WA 98520, ☎ 360/532-8611 or 800/200-LADY, is housed in a full-scale, 170-ton replica of a ship built in Massachusetts in 1783. The original was sailed to the Pacific Northwest by Capt. Robert Gray, who discovered Grays Harbor and the Columbia River. The ship was later the first US vessel to make landfall in Japan. The replica was built in 1989, has 12 sails, and carries over 4,400 square feet of canvas. Dockside tours are conducted from 10 AM to 1 PM daily. Sailing times are from 2 to 5 PM daily and from 6 to 9 PM on Saturdays and Sundays.

Arlington

The **Festival of the River**, ☎ 360/435-2755, is celebrated by the Stillaguamish Tribe in River Meadow Park, Arlington, every August.

Bainbridge Island

Bainbridge Island Vineyards & Winery Museum, 7650 NE High School Rd., Bainbridge Island, WA 98110, ☎ 206/842-2773, conducts tours at Strawberry Hill Park. While in the area, take a walking tour of historic **Winslow** nearby.

Bellevue

Snoqualmie Falls Forest Theater & Family Park, PO Box 516, Bellevue, WA 98009, ☎ 425/222-7044, presents performances on Fridays and Saturdays at 8 PM and on Sundays at 3 PM. Dinner after the performances is optional.

Bellingham

> The Bellingham Visitors Center has a free four-color, pocket-sized brochure, *Outdoor Art in Bellingham, WA*, that can lead you on an interesting self-guided walk through town. While at the Visitors Center, ask for the free pocket-sized walking tour map *Fairhaven Historic District*, which will serve as a guide to the local landmarks in that part of town.

The **Mount Baker Theatre**, 104 N. Commercial, Bellingham, WA 98225, ☎ 206/734-6080, fax 206/671-0114, now the town's cultural center, is housed in a 1927 Moorish/Spanish-style movie theater and vaudeville palace. The theater is the oldest continuously operating movie palace in the northwest.

Mindport Exhibits, 111 Grand Ave., Bellingham, WA, ☎ 360/647-5614, is a free family-oriented museum featuring hands-on exhibits on science, art, nature, and humanity. The museum is open Wednesday through Sunday from 11:30 AM to 6 PM and on Friday to 8.

Marine Life Center, 1801 Roeder Ave. (Harbor Center), Bellingham, WA, ☎ 360/734-4597, is an outdoor exhibition that includes three large glass tanks containing local marine life. Exhibits include a touch tank and a simulated tide pool. The Center is open daily from 8 AM to dusk.

Big Rock Garden Park, 2900 Sylvan St., Bellingham, WA, ☎ 360/676-6985, formerly a private nursery overlooking Lake Whatcom, is open from April through October. **Sehome Hill Arboretum**, 25th Street, Sehome Hill, Bellingham, WA ☎ 360/676-6985, a 165-acre preserve above Western Washington University, has 3.5 miles of trails and an observation tower providing excellent views of town, the San Juan Islands, and Mt. Baker.

Fairhaven is a colorful turn-of-the-century section of Bellingham that has a busy ferry terminal and a large dock from which residents cast their "rings" for crabs. Early on, tents, gamblers, ministers, madams, and "glory girls" arrived in the town, and 2,000 cattle roamed the streets, along with a great many "pistol maniacs." The sheriff resigned in disgust after his wife complained of constantly having prisoners handcuffed to the iron cookstove in their kitchen. **Dirty Dan Harris'**, 1211 11th St., Bellingham, WA 98225, ☎ 360/676-1011, is a seafood, steak, and ribs restaurant that was named for the pioneer settler who created the town.

Blaine

Peace Arch, at the Canadian border just north of Blaine, celebrates two centuries of peace between the United States and Canada. Sitting in a 40-acre park, the white arch is designed in a Greek Doric style. Eighteen meters high and built of concrete, reinforced with steel, the arch was dedicated in September 1921 and a time capsule was sealed behind the cornerstone, to be opened in 2021. On the south side of the arch, the inscription reads "Children Of A Common Mother"; on the north side, "Brethren Dwelling Together in Unison." The arch receives 75,000 visitors daily. On the second Sunday in June each year, a "Hands Across the Border" celebration at the arch draws 10,000 people, mostly children, from Canada and the United States.

Carnation

The **Cam Lann Medieval Faire**, ☎ 425/788-1353, is held three miles north of Carnation on Saturdays, Sundays, and Labor Day from mid-July through September 1. The celebration includes "Armored knights, merrie minstrels, and old-world crafts."

Concrete

Forty-five-minute tours of the colorful little community of Concrete are conducted aboard a canopied, open-air pram, *The Sockeye Express*, ☎ 360/853-7009. The tours, which depart from the Camp 7 Museum, are offered between noon and 3 PM on weekends and holidays from Memorial Day through Labor Day.

Camp 7 Museum, 119 Railroad Ave., Concrete, WA, ☎ 360/853-7185, is an old logging camp. The museum is open from noon to 4 PM on Saturdays, Sundays, and holidays from the third weekend in May through the Labor Day weekend.

Copalis Beach

September brings the sand castle and sculpture competitions in Copalis Beach. Contestants vie for cash prizes.

Coupeville

Coupeville, one of the state's oldest settlements, has the **Island County Historical Museum** and the **1855 Alexander's Blockhouse**. **Fort Casey State Park**, a turn-of-the-century coastal defense network, has some huge old military pieces and a lighthouse. Nearby **Langley** is an artists' colony.

Deming

Mount Baker Vineyards, ☎ 360/592-2300, in Deming hosts tasting hours from 11 AM to 5 PM, Wednesday through Sunday. The vineyards are on Mount Baker Highway northwest of town.

Eatonville

Pioneer Farm Museum and Ohop Indian Village, 7716 Ohop Valley Rd., Eatonville, WA 98328, ☎ 206/832-6300, offers a 1.5-hour guided tour. The museum is closed during the winter.

NorthwesTrek Wildlife Park, 11610 Trek Dr. East, Eatonville, WA 98328, ☎ 360/832-6117 or 800/433-8735, Web site www.nwtrek.org, offers narrated bus tours of the park, in which animals roam freely. The tours are provided daily from 10 AM to closing on Friday, Saturday, Sunday, and selected holidays from March through October. The park is the venue for the annual (banana) Slug Festival held in early July.

Edmonds

Cascade Symphony Orchestra, PO Box 550, Edmonds, WA 98020, ☎Edmonds206/778-4688, stages six concerts from September through May. The performances are held at Puget Sound Christian College. **Edge of the World Theatre**, Firdale Village, Edmonds, WA 98020, ☎ 206/542-7529, performs in a 115-seat air-conditioned theater, and **Driftwood Players**, PO Box 385, Edmonds, WA 98020, ☎ 206//774-9600, presents five productions from September through June in the

Wade James Theatre. **Edmonds Historical Museum**, 118 Fifth Ave. North, Edmonds, WA 98020, ☎ 206/774-0900, is housed in an old Carnegie Library. There is no admission fee, and the museum is open on Tuesdays, Thursdays, Saturdays, and Sundays.

Enumclaw

The **King County Fair**, ☎ 360/825-7777, is held in Enumclaw in mid-July, and **Rainier Stage Co.**, 1751 Cole St., Enumclaw, WA 98022, ☎ 360/825-7529, presents live community theater.

Everett

Forest Park Animal Farm, Mukilteo Boulevard, Everett, WA, ☎ 206/257-8303, a free animal petting zoo, is open from 9 AM to 5 PM daily. **Boeing Aircraft Co.**, ☎ 206/544-1264, 342-4801 or 800/464-1476, Web site www.boeing.com, offers free 1.5-hour tours Monday through Friday, except for Memorial Day, the Fourth of July, Labor Day, Thanksgiving, and the December holiday season. Individuals need no reservations. Tour the world's largest building and see the assembly of such aircraft as the Boeing 747. **Everett Symphony**, ☎ 206/259-0382, has been performing for more than half a century. The season runs from September through June. **Everett AquaSox**, Everett Memorial Stadium, 3802 Broadway, Everett, WA 98201, ☎ 206/258-3673, provides the venue for the Frogs, a Class-A affiliate of the Seattle Mariners. The **Everett Giants** professional baseball team,, ☎ 206/258-0380, an affiliate of the San Francisco Giants, have a season that extends from mid-June to September 1.

Federal Way

Rhododendron Special Botanical Garden, PO Box 3798, Federal Way, WA 98063, ☎ 206/661-9377, is open between 10 AM and 4 PM daily except Thursdays from March through May, and between 11 AM and 4 PM daily except Thursdays and Fridays from June through February. The **Pacific Rim Bonsai** (*Bon-sigh*, Japanese for "a tree in a pot") **Collection**, Weyerhaeuser Co., 33663 Weyerhaeuser Way South, Federal Way, WA 98003, ☎ 206/924-5206, was created in 1989. The **Elandan Gardens**, ☎ 360/373-8260, in **Gorst,** also contain bonsai trees, some of which are over 1,000 years old.

Ferndale

At Gooseberry Point, just south of Ferndale, climb aboard the *Whatcom Chief* and cross Hale Passage to **Lummi Island**, a 10-minute trip.

Three times a year, the Lummi Indian potters, wood carvers, sculptors, jewelers, and garden artists open their studios for public tours. The annual **Lummi Stommish Water Carnival**, ☎ 360/734-8180, which features 11-man war canoe races, a salmon BBQ, and Indian dancing, is held in June.

Hovander Homestead Park, at the south end of Neilsen Road in Ferndale, has a turn-of-the-century farmhouse, a barn, and a mile of river beach. There are walking trails, fishing facilities, and a treehouse. Tours of the 60 acres are available between noon and 4 PM, Thursday through Sunday, from June through Labor Day. Each June, the **Scottish Highland Games** are played in this park.

Tennant Lake Natural History Interpretive Center, adjacent to Hovander Homestead Park at the south end of Neilsen Road, has a half-mile system of trails and boardwalks, plus a birdwatching tower and a Fragrance Garden. The 200-acre Center is open from Thursday through Sunday year-around.

Fort Lewis

Fort Lewis Military Museum, Building 4320, Main Street, Fort Lewis, ☎ 253/967-7206, was built as an inn by the Salvation Army in 1918. It is open from noon to 4 PM Wednesday through Sunday, but closed on federal holidays. Fort Lewis is the third largest military base in the nation.

Hoodsport

Hoodsport Winery, N. 23501 Hwy 101, Hoodsport, WA 98548, ☎ 360/877-9894, is open daily from 10 AM to 6 PM.

Ilwaco

During the winter, storms create monstrous breakers over the Columbia River Bar next to Ilwaco. The mouth of the Columbia River is notorious for its hazard to shipping. During the past 300 years, nearly 2,000 vessels and almost 700 lives have been lost there.

Nineteen murals are displayed on the sides of many buildings in Pacific County, including those in the cities of Long Beach, Seaview, and Ocean Park. Ilwaco has five.

Ilwaco Heritage Museum on Lake Street has a nice collection of Chinook Indian artifacts. **Fort Canby State Park** in Ilwaco contains the Lewis and Clark Interpretive Center, two lighthouses (Cape Disappointment and North Head), a US Coast Guard station, the Columbia

River Bar, a boat launch, and a couple of beaches. From the air, Cape Disappointment is shaped like a miniature Italy.

Issaquah

Gilman Village, 317 NW Gilman Blvd., Issaquah, WA 98027, ☎ 206/392-6802, fax 206/392-6283, is a fun place to shop. The village is a collection of old buildings, linked by a boardwalk and converted into an attractive mall that contains a variety of boutique shops. **Village Theatre**, 120 Front St. N., ☎ 206/392-2202, fax 206/391-3242, a 488-seat theater built in 1914, is the venue for live theater performances. **Boehm's Candies**, 255 NE Gilman Blvd., ☎ 425/392-6652, fax 425/557-0560, lets you watch as they make such delicious treats as hand-dipped chocolates and peanut brittle.

The **State Salmon Hatchery**, 125 W. Sunset Way, Issaquah, WA 98027, ☎ 206/392-1118, fax 206/392-3180, the birthplace of over six million Chinook and coho salmon each year, makes an interesting stop. Chum salmon are often called "dogs" because of the large canine teeth they develop during spawning, but they are also called "calicos" because of their bright spawning colors. Spawning pink males develop a large humped back and are often referred to as "humpies." At the hatchery, you catch the salmon swimming up Issaquah Creek to spawn during the season.

Cougar Mountain Zoological Park, 19525 SE 54th St., Issaquah, WA 98027, ☎ 206/391-5508, fax 206/392-1076, which handles threatened and endangered species, is also a teaching zoo. The facility is open between 10 AM and 5 PM, Wednesday through Sunday, from March through October; between 10 AM and 4 PM, Friday through Sunday, during November and February; and between 5 and 8 PM, Wednesday through Sunday, in December.

Long Beach & North Cove

There is a **Cranberry Museum** on Pioneer Road in Long Beach, and the **Furford's Cranberry Museum** is in North Cove.

Lynden

The Dutch-style community of Lynden celebrates Holland Days each year and has Sinterklaas festivals around Christmas. Both are characterized by Dutch Klompen dancing and authentic Dutch food. The town also hosts the **Northwest Washington Fair**, 1775 Front St., Lynden, WA 98264, ☎ 360/354-4111, in mid-August. The **Pioneer Museum**, 217 W. Front St., Lynden, WA 98264, ☎ 360/354-3675, has 20,000 square

Biking through tulips, near Mount Vernon (Washington Tourism Dev).

feet of exhibits and is open between 10 AM and 4 PM, Monday through Saturday.

Mount Vernon

In the spring, hundreds of acres of commercial bulb fields outside of Mount Vernon are ablaze with color.

Mukilteo

During August, Mukilteo hosts the annual **Lighthouse Festival** at the Rosehill Community Center, 304 Lincoln Ave., ☎ 206/355-2514.

Nahcotta

Willapa Bay Interpretive Center, ☎ 206/665-4547, on the breakwater east of the Ark Restaurant in Nahcotta, depicts the history of Washington's 150-year-old oyster industry. The Center is open between 10 AM and 3 PM on Fridays, Saturdays, Sundays, and holidays from May 1 through October 30. Admission is free.

Neah Bay

Makah Cultural & Research Center, PO Box 160, Neah Bay, WA 98357, ☎ 360/645-2711, is a museum containing artifacts from the Ozette archeological site, a cedar longhouse, and oceangoing canoes.

There is a craft shop and a book store. The center is open between 10 AM and 5 PM in the summer, but closed on Mondays and Tuesdays between September 16 and May 31.

Oak Harbor

In September, Oak Harbor hosts the **Artichokes & Art Festival** along the waterfront. Music, food, wine tasting, microbeers, an art show, and a beachfront BBQ are included in the three-day weekend celebration.

Ocean City

North Bend Historical Society, PO Box 1531, Ocean City, WA 98569, ☎ 360/289-3842, sits on the east side of Route 109 in a 1926 cabin built of logs that were hauled from the beach in a wheelbarrow by pioneer Dorothy Anderson. The museum is open during the summer. Admission is free.

Olympia

Self-guided tours of the **State Capitol**, 14th Street and Capitol Way, Olympia, WA 98507, ☎ 360/586-3460, are offered from Monday through Friday. The **Washington State Capitol Museum**, 211 W. 21st St., ☎ 206/753-2580, is open between 10 AM and 4 PM Tuesday through Friday and between noon and 4 PM on Saturday and Sunday. The museum is closed on Mondays and major state holidays. **Yahiro Japanese Garden**, ☎ 360/753-8380, is at 9th and Plum Street, and **Delbert McBride Ethnobotanical Garden**, ☎ 360/753-2580, is at 211 W. 21st Ave.

Priest Point Park, minutes from downtown Olympia, encompasses **Ellis Cove Trail**, which crosses several bridges, including a 300-foot bridge over Ellis Creek. The trail has boardwalks and a number of interpretive stations. **Lattin's Country Cider Mill**, 9402 Rich Rd. SE, ☎ 360/491-7328, can help quench your thirst, as can **Olympia Brewing Co.**, ☎ 360/754-5177, which conducts spring tours at 9:30 and 11:30 AM and at 1:30 and 3:30 PM, except on Sundays, Mondays, and holidays.

Port Angeles

Arthur D. Fiero Marine Laboratory, ☎ 360/452-9277 or 417-6254, is at the city pier at the foot of Lincoln Street in Port Angeles. There are touch tanks, and guided tours are available on request. The laboratory is open daily between 10:00 AM and 8:00 PM from mid-June through Labor Day. The **Chinese Tree of Heaven**, on Washington Street east of

Fillmore in Port Angeles, is said to have been a gift from the Emperor of China over 100 years ago.

Port Gamble

A little cluster of buildings near the waterfront in Port Gamble, largely centered around the General Store, ☎ 360/297-7636, includes a number of old residences, a 1903 butcher shop, the 1870 St. Paul's Episcopal Church, an 1856 cemetery, an 1853 community hall and post office, and an 1872 Masonic Temple. Above the General Store is **Of Sea & Shore Museum,** ☎ 360/297-2426, said to be the world's largest privately owned collection of sea shells.

Port Orchard

Log Cabin Museum, 202 Sidney Ave., Port Orchard, WA 98366, ☎ 360/876-3693, is located in a 1914 settler's cabin. Visitors to Port Orchard during March can participate in the annual seagull-calling contest.

Port Townsend

In Port Townsend, visitors go to North Beach to see the sunset, South Beach to watch the moon rise, and the east beaches in the mornings. For birdwatching, they go to Protection Island, and for entertainment, to the **Water Street Dinner Theatre**, 926 Water St., ☎ 306/385-2422. The town's **School of Wooden Boat Building** conducts tours.

Poulsbo

Suquamish Museum, PO Box 498, 15838 Sandy Hook Rd., Poulsbo, WA 98370, ☎ 360/598-3113, operated by descendants of Chief Seattle, presents two films, *The Eyes of Chief Seattle* and *Comes Forth Laughing*. The museum has a gift shop and a book store. Guided tours also are available.

A **Viking Fest** and **Medieval Faire** are held in Poulsbo in May, **Skandia Midsommarfest** in June, **Oktoberfest** in September, a **Lutefisk Dinner** in October, and a **Yule Fest** in December.

Raymond

Willapa Harbor Players presents three or more live theater productions per year in Hannan Playhouse on 9th Street in Raymond.

Seattle

Seattle has more equity theaters than any city except New York and Chicago and presents more theater performances each year than any city except New York. Foremost among its theater groups are **Meany Theatre**, University of Washington campus, ☎ 206/543-4880; **Annex Theatre**, 1916 4th Ave., ☎ 206/728-0933; **A Contemporary Theatre**, 700 Union St., ☎ 206/292-7676; **Bathhouse Theatre**, 7312 W. Greenlake Dr. North, ☎ 206/824-9108; **Cabaret de Paris**, 2nd Level, Rainier Square, 1333 8th Ave., ☎ 206/623-4111; **Empty Space Theatre**, 3509 Fremont Ave. North, ☎ 206/547-7500; **Fifth Ave. Musical Theatre**, 1308 5th Ave., ☎ 206/292-ARTS; **Intiman Theatre**, 201 Mercer St., ☎ 206/289-1900; **Northwest Actors Studio**, 1100 E. Pike St., ☎ 206/324-6328; **Northwest Asian-American Theatre**, 409 7th Ave. South, ☎ 206/340-1049; **Paramount Theatre**, 911 Pine St., ☎ 206/292-ARTS; **Seattle Children's Theatre**, the Charlotte Martin Theatre, Second Avenue North and Thomas Street, ☎ 206/441-3322; **Seattle Repertory Theatre**, Bagley Wright Theatre, Seattle Center, ☎ 206/443-2222; **Taproot Theatre Co.**, 204 N. 85th St., ☎ 206/781-9705; and **Unexpected Productions**, 1428 Post Alley, ☎ 206/587-2414.

Seattle!, musical tales from the great Northwest, is presented in the Museum of History & Industry's McEachern Theater, ☎ 206/324-1126 or 888/NWTALES. There is a discount for seniors and children.

Omnidome Theatre, Pier 59, Waterfront Park, Seattle, WA 98101, ☎ 206/622-1869 or 622-1868, fax 206/622-5837, is located next to the Seattle Aquarium and presents *The Eruption of Mount St. Helens* on a super-large screen.

Seattle also is one of only six cities in the United States to have a major symphony, a major opera, *and* a major ballet.

Free brown bag concerts are held in the downtown parks and plazas of Seattle nearly every lunchtime during the summer.

The CityPass provides a 50% discount at such attractions as Woodland Park Zoo, Space Needle, Pacific Science Center, Seattle Aquarium, Seattle Art Museum, and Museum of Flight. The books, good for seven days, are available at any of the attractions mentioned above.

Seattle Aquarium, Pier 59, Waterfront Park, Seattle, WA 98101, ☎ 206/386-4353 or 386-4320, Web site www.seattleaquarium.org, is located just below the Pike Place Market. It is open daily between 10 AM and 7 PM from Memorial Day to Labor Day and between 10 and 5 PM during the winter months.

Pike Place Market, stretched along four blocks of First Street parallel to Elliott Bay, was founded in 1907. Covering two square miles, the market is a mecca for fresh seafood, fruits, vegetables, fresh meats, organically grown produce, homemade baked goods, sauces and jams, herbs and spices, coffees and teas, wearing apparel, toys, and stuffed animals. It also contains crafts shops, a clinic, taverns, restaurants, florists, and curio shops. Sampling is encouraged. Two newspapers, *Market Fresh Newsletter*, published weekly, and *Pike Place Market News*, a monthly, keep customers apprised of upcoming events. One of the oldest outdoor markets in the country, it is open between 9 AM and 6 PM Monday through Saturday, and between 11 AM and 5 PM on Sunday.

Kingdome, 201 S. King St., Seattle, WA 98104-2832, ☎ 206/296-3100 or 296-3128, fax 206/296-3127, Web site www.metrokc.gov/stadium, the home of the Seattle Mariners baseball team and the Seattle Seahawks football team, is soon to be demolished in favor of a new stadium. As long as it's there, tours are available.

KeyArena, 305 Harrison St., Seattle, WA 98104, ☎ 206/283-DUNK, is the home of the Seattle SuperSonics basketball team.

Woodland Park Zoo, 5500 Phinney Ave. N., Seattle, WA 98103-4897, ☎ 206/684-4800, Web site www.zoo.org, is ranked one of the nation's 10 best. A 4.6-acre Elephant Forest features a tropical forest, a working Thai logging camp, and a temple. The zoo is open at 9:30 AM daily and closes at 6 PM from March 15 through October 30, and at 4 PM from October 31 through March 14.

Chinatown International District is at South Main Street and 7th Avenue South. **Chinatown Discovery**, PO Box 3406, Seattle, WA 98114, ☎ 206/236-0657, fax 206/583-0460, offers minitours and tours with dinner.

Tillicum Village, 2200 6th Ave., Suite 804, Seattle, WA 98121, ☎ 206/433-1244 or 800/426-1205, Web site www.seattleonline.com/tillicum, is located offshore on Blake Island. Visitors must take a boat over and back. While there, they see a replica Indian longhouse, watch Indians perform a skit that recreates some of their local lore, have a traditional baked salmon dinner, and witness some crafts demonstrations. **Blake Island State Park** has a nature trail, hiking trails, a ranger station, and camping facilities.

Underground Tour, 610 First Ave., Seattle, WA 98104, ☎ 206/682-1511 or 682-4646, Web site www.seattleonline.com/ugt, in Pioneer Square, conducts four to six tours of "underground Seattle" daily.

The **Water, Wings & Wine Tour**, ☎ 206-789-6498, Web site www.columbiawinery.com, leaves Pier 57 on the Seattle waterfront aboard a Gray Line bus Monday through Friday from 10:30 AM to 4:30 PM. After driving across a floating bridge to Woodinville, the participants tour the Columbia Winery and enjoy a wine-tasting. The bus then delivers the group to Kenmore Air, where they board a floatplane to take a bird's-eye view of the area en route to Chandler's Cove on Lake Union. At Chandler's Cove, they board an Argosy Cruises ferry for a narrated cruise back to the Seattle waterfront.

Wing Luke Asian Museum, 407 Seventh Ave. South, Seattle, WA 98104, ☎ 206/623-5124, fax 206/623-4559, displays exhibits that depict 10 Asian Pacific-American groups: Cambodians, Chinese, Filipinos, Japanese, Koreans, Laotians, Pacific Islanders, South Asians, Southeast Asian hill tribes, and Vietnamese. The museum, which recently celebrated its 30th anniversary, is open between 11 AM and 4:30 PM Tuesday to Friday and between noon and 4 PM Saturday and Sunday. It is closed on Mondays. **Seattle Asian Art Museum**, 1400 E. Prospect St., Seattle, WA 98104, ☎ 206/654-3255 or 625-8900, is in the old Seattle Art Museum building in Volunteer Park. Its Asian collection ranks among the top 10 outside of Asia, and the Japanese collection is one of the top five in the United States. The museum is open between 10 AM and 5 PM, Tuesday through Sunday, and Thursdays until 9. It is closed Mondays except on certain holidays.

Thomas Burke Memorial Museum, Memorial Way on the University of Washington campus, ☎ 206/543-5590, reflects the natural and cultural heritage of the Pacific region and has an outstanding Northwest Indian collection.

Seattle Scottish Highland Games Assn., PO Box 75685, Seattle, WA 98125-0685, ☎ 206/522-2541, fax 206/522-4403, E-mail scots4ev@sshga.org, Web site www.sshga.org, stages its competition each year in July. Food, clan tents, dog demonstrations, pipe-and-drum events, dancing competitions, and athletic competitions are included.

Lake Washington Ship Canal and **Hiram M. Chittenden Locks**, 3015 NW 54th St., Seattle, WA 98107, ☎ 206/783-7059, 783-7000, or 783-7001, include an eight-mile ship canal, two locks, and a 235-foot-long, 63-foot-high spillway. There is an interesting Visitor Center.

Lake Washington Ship Canal Fish Ladder, 3015 NW 54th St., Seattle, WA 98107, ☎ 206/783-7059 or 783-7001, Web site www.nps.usace.army.mil/opdiv/lwsc/lakewsc.html, includes a Visitor Center and a botanical garden. The best viewing for Chinook (king) salmon is from July to December, with the peak in the latter part of August. For coho (silver) salmon, it is August to December, with the peak in the latter part of September. For sockeye (red) salmon, from June to November, with the peak in July. And for steelhead trout, from mid-November to mid-April, with the peak in January. About the only time when one species or another isn't migrating is from mid-April to early June.

Carl S. English Jr. Botanical Garden, 3015 NW 54th St., Seattle, WA 98107, ☎ 206/783-7059, is at the Lake Washington Ship Canal Visitor Center. It contains over 500 trees, shrubs, and herbaceous plants. There is a quarter-mile self-guided tour, and an excellent descriptive brochure is available.

Sedro-Woolley

Woolley Prairie Buffalo Co., ☎ 360/856-0310 or 800/524-7660, fax 360/856-0310, in Sedro-Woolley raises bison, has a trading post, and conducts ranch tours on the *Prairie Schooner* (a large open-bed truck).

Sequim

Dungeness Recreation Area, at the entrance to Dungeness Spit in Sequim, is the longest natural sand hook in the nation, nicknamed "Shipwreck Spit." The 216-acre county park offers camping (for a fee), hiking, beachcombing, and good birdwatching. It is a six-mile hike to the lighthouse, built in 1892 (an entrance fee is collected at the trailhead). The campground, ☎ 360/683-5847, is open from February 1 to October 1. The gates to the park close at dark.

Olympic Game Farm, 1423 Ward Rd., Sequim, WA 98382, ☎ 360/683-4295 or 800/778-4295, fax 360/681-4443, Web site www.northolympic.com/gamefarm, exhibits exotic animals like a white rhino, grizzly bears, and jaguars. Its animals have appeared in films such as *Never Cry Wolf, Kid Colter, The Incredible Journey, Those Calloways, Life and Times of Grizzly Adams*, and *Nikki, Wild Dog of the North*, as well as the *Grizzly Adams* TV series. There is a "U-fish" pond and an animal petting area, and it is possible to either walk or drive through the property.

Erik's Edible Landscaping, 162 Creekside Dr., Sequim, WA 98382, ☎ 360/683-6684, produces apples, apricots, cherries, peaches, plums, pears, grapes, and berries. **Cedarbrook Herb Farm**, 1345 Sequim Ave. South, ☎ 360-683-7733, is open between 9 AM and 5 PM daily, and between 10 AM and 4 PM on Sunday, March through December 23.

John Wayne Marina, east of Sequim, is a 245-boat moorage that was donated by the legendary movie star, a frequent visitor to the area aboard his ship *Wild Goose*. The marina is located off W. Sequim Bay Road on Sequim Bay.

Shelton

In mid-June, the **Sa-Heh-Wa-Mish Pow Wow & Art Show** is held on the Mason County Fairgrounds in Shelton. Mushroom vendors have roadside stands along US 101 north of town in the autumn. There is a **Skokomish Tribal Center**, ☎ 206/426-4232, in town; the **Dalby Waterwheel**, built in 1922, is still working; and the 440-foot-high **Steel Arch Bridge** spans the Skokomish Gorge.

Silverdale

A memorial pole across from Kitsap Mall in Silverdale commemorates the Suquamish Indian Chief Kitsap (Kitsap Tyee) by depicting his life achievements. **Anna Smith Children's Park**, ☎ 360/692-6152, open from April through October, contains a Master Gardener Demonstration Garden and a small children's garden. **Kitsap County Indian Center & Trading Post**, 2222 Bucklin Hill NW, ☎ 360/692-7460, is open between 9 AM and 5 PM from Monday through Saturday.

Steilacoom

Steilacoom, Washington's oldest incorporated town (1854), once was the seat of Pierce County and a leading candidate for territorial capital. **Steilacoom Historical Museum**, Box 88016, Steilacoom, WA 93888-0016, ☎ 206/584-4133, includes 32 buildings and sites listed on the National Registry of Historic Places. The grounds may be covered in a self-guided walking tour or a driving tour. The museum is open between 1 and 4 PM on Fridays from November through February and between 1 and 4 PM Tuesday through Sunday the rest of the year, but it is closed during January and on legal holidays. The **Steilacoom Tribal Cultural Center & Museum**, 1515 Lafayette St., ☎ 206/584-6308, is open between 10 AM and 4 PM Tuesday through Sunday.

Sumner

Sumner is called "the rhubarb pie capital" of the United States and is the home of the **Manfred Vierthaler Winery**.

Suquamish

The Old Man House in Suquamish is the site of the original Suquamish Village and the largest longhouse in the Pacific Northwest. Suquamish also is the site of Chief Seattle's grave and of the **Suquamish Museum**, 15838 Sandy Hook Rd., ☎ 206/598-3311.

Tacoma

Point Defiance Zoo & Aquarium, 5400 N. Pearl St., Tacoma, WA 98407-3218, ☎ 206/591-5337, a zoo with over 5,000 animals and two aquariums, is in **Point Defiance Park** with the **Fort Nisqually Historic Site** (☎ 253/591-5339), a 700-acre park with a beach, gardens, nature trails, tennis, and swimming. **African American Museum**, 959 Market St., ☎ 206/274-1278, is open between 9:30 AM and 5 PM Monday through Saturday and between noon and 5 on Sunday.

Stadium High School off North 2nd Street in Tacoma, originally a luxury hotel with distinctive turrets and an incomparable setting, is now one of the Northwest's oldest and most colorful high schools. **Temple Theatre**, 47 St. Helen's Ave., ☎ 206/272-2042, an art deco theater built in 1926, houses Tacoma's largest performing arts theater, the state's largest ballroom, two additional ballrooms, five dining rooms, and convention and teaching facilities. Tours are offered.

The newly opened **Washington State History Museum**, 1911 Pacific Ave., Tacoma, WA 98402, ☎ 253/272-3500 or 888/238-4373, in the heart of downtown next to the Grand Union Station, contains 100,000 square feet of space. **Lakewold Gardens**, 12317 Gravelly Lake Dr. SW, Tacoma, WA 98499, ☎ 206/584-3360, are open between 10 AM and 4 PM daily except Tuesday and Wednesday from April through September, and between 10 AM and 3 PM Monday, Thursday, and Friday from October thru March.

The **Puyallup Tribal Museum**, ☎ 206/597-6200, is in Tacoma. The **Quinault Indian National Museum**, ☎ 360/276-8211, is in **Taholah**.

Tenino

Tenino once was famous for its sandstone quarries. Now, the 80-foot deep **Tenino Quarry** is the free town swimming hole during the summer.

Woodinville

Columbia Winery, 14030 NE 145th St., Woodinville, WA 98072, ☎ 206/488-2776, offers wine tasting and a gift shop in an "old" Victorian mansion.

Where to Stay

Island Lodgings

The many islands along the northern coast of Washington provide a plethora of charming, relaxing places in which to stay.

Outlook B&B, 608 H Ave., **Anacortes**, WA 98221, ☎ 293-3505, $$, provides a warm, homey atmosphere in the midst of the San Juan Islands.

On **Bainbridge Island**, comfortable accommodation can be obtained at **Island Country Inn**, 920 Hildebrand Lane NE, Bainbridge Island, WA 98110, ☎ 206/842-6861 or 800/842-8429, $$-$$$.

The Captain Whidbey Inn, 2072 W. Captain Whidbey Rd., **Coupeville**, WA 98239, ☎ 360/678-4097, fax 360/678-4110, $$-$$$, is a historic two-story log inn with 32 room, a full-service dining room, and a lounge. Three of the rooms are equipped with kitchens. There is no air conditioning, but on an island where the sea breezes are constant, it's never missed.

The Inn at Penn Cove B&B, 702 N. Main, Coupeville, WA 98239, ☎ 360/678-8000, $-$$, links two two-story Victorian homes with great views. Only six rooms are available for rent.

Rosario, One Rosario Way, **Eastsound**, WA 98245, ☎ 360/376-2222 or 800/562-8820, fax 360/376-2289, $$$$, is on Orcas Island in the San Juan Islands. Various packages are available.

Best Western Harbor Plaza, 33175 WA 20, **Oak Harbor**, WA 98277, ☎ 360/679-4567 or 800/927-5478, fax 360/675-2543, E-mail bestwest@whidbey.net, $$-$$$$, Whidbey's newest motor inn, is nine miles south of Deception Pass Bridge on Whidbey Island.

Acorn Manor Inn, 8066 WA 20, Oak Harbor, WA 98277, ☎ 360/675-6646 or 800/280-6646, fax 360/679-1850, $-$$, has a few kitchen units and provides a free island sightseeing bus.

MacKaye Harbor Inn, Rt. 1, Box 1940, **Lopez Island**, WA 98261, ☎ 360/468-2253, $$-$$$, is a B&B on a sandy beach in the San Juan Islands. Mountain bike and kayak rentals are available.

Mariella Inn & Cottages, 630 Turn Point Rd., **Friday Harbor**, WA 98250, ☎ 360/378-6868 or 800/700-7668, fax 360/378-6822, E-mail mariella@rockisland.com, Web site www.mariella.com, $$$-$$$$, is a serene inn on a serene island – Lopez Island in the San Juan Islands.

Bellingham

Although it may be somewhat less romantic, the mainland offers an equally diverse range of lodgings for those who, for whatever reason, cannot or do not wish to stay in the islands.

> The **Bellingham Chamber of Commerce**, 1801 Roeder Ave., Bellingham, WA 98225, ☎ 360/734-1330, fax 360/734-1332, chamber@bellingham.com/~chamber, can provide you with a free copy of *The Bed & Breakfast Guild of Whatcom County Welcomes You*, a guide to B&Bs in the area.

Hampton Inn, 3985 Bennett Dr., Bellingham, WA 98225, ☎ 360/676-7700 or 800/HAMPTON, fax 360/671-7557, $$-$$$, is convenient to the interstate and to the airport, yet away from the midtown traffic.

Blaine

Semi-ah-Moo, 9565 Semiahmoo Pkwy., Blaine, WA 98230-9326, ☎ 360/371-2000 or 800/770-7992, $$$-$$$$, is a four-star, four-diamond Wyndham resort. Condé Nast's Traveler Gold List for 1996 called it "one of the 500 best places to stay in the whole world." In 1995, *Links* magazine rated its Arnold Palmer golf course the "Best in the West." Guests have their choice of three restaurants. A spa, tennis, health club, sand beach, and pool are provided. Sailing, jetskiing, sea kayaking, parasailing, whale-watching, ice skiing, and children's programs are offered. A bike and hiking path runs through an adjacent 1,100-acre wildlife preserve. Boat tours to the San Juan Islands, sightseeing in Canada, and an evening dessert cruise also are available.

Everett

Marina Village Inn, 1728 W. Marine View Dr., Everett, WA 98201, ☎ 425/259-4040 or 800/281-7037, fax 425/252-8419, $$-$$$, is a two-story upstairs inn in Everett Marina Village. Its 26 rooms overlook either the Marina Village or Port Gardner Bay. A complimentary breakfast and morning newspaper are included in the rates. Restaurants are nearby.

Kirkland

Woodmark Hotel on Lake Washington, 1200 Carillon Point, Kirkland, WA 98033, ☎ 206/822-3700, fax 206/822-3699, $$$-$$$$, occupies a picturesque waterfront location.

La Conner

The Wild Iris, 121 Maple Ave., PO Box 696, La Conner, WA 98257, ☎ 360/466-1400 or 800/177-1400, fax 360/466-1221, E-mail wildiris@ncia.com, Web site www.ncia.com/~wildiris, $$$, is a Victorian B&B with a charming gourmet restaurant.

Ocean Shores

The Canterbury Inn, 643 Ocean Shores Blvd., PO Box 310, Ocean Shores, WA 98569, ☎ 360/289-3317 or 800/562-6678, fax 360/289-3420, Web site www.canterburyinn.com, $$-$$$, provides luxurious condominium units – 44 rooms with a balcony or patio, most with a fireplace. There are 12 two-bedroom units and 32 units have kitchens. All rooms have a coffeemaker, a microwave, and a refrigerator. The three-story building also provides a beach and an indoor pool.

Shilo Inn, 707 Ocean Shores Blvd. NW, Ocean Shores, WA 98569-9593, ☎ 360/289-4600 or 800/222-2244, fax 360/289-0738, Web site www.shiloinns.com, $-$$$, offers 113 deluxe suites with oceanfront balconies, a pool, a spa, a fitness center, steam, and a sauna. The lobby contains a 3,000-gallon aquarium, and the restaurant provides oceanfront dining.

Olympia

Ramada Inn Governor House, 621 S. Capitol Way, Olympia, WA 98501, ☎ 360/352-7700 or 800/272-6232, fax 360/943-9349, $$-$$$, provides 122 rooms with views of City Park or Capitol Lake. The eight-story hotel has a seasonally heated pool and a cocktail lounge. The restaurant is open from 6:30 AM to 9 PM, except Saturdays, when it is open from 7 AM to 10 PM. On the down side: a fee is charged for parking.

Port Angeles

Best Western Olympic Lodge, 149 Del Guzzi Dr., Port Angeles, WA 98362, ☎ 360/452-2993 or 800/528-1234, fax 360/452-1497, $$-$$$, sits next to a private golf course for added seclusion. The three-story building houses 106 rooms. Ask for a room that has a view of the Olympic Mountains and the Strait of Juan de Fuca.

Red Lion Bayshore Inn, 221 N. Lincoln, Port Angeles, WA 98362, ☎ 360/452-9215, $$-$$$, is just one block from the ferry terminal for ships to Victoria, BC.

Doubletree Hotel, 221 N. Lincoln, Port Angeles, WA 98362, ☎ 360/452-9215 or 800/547-8010, fax 360/452-4734, $$-$$$, always greets you with a freshly baked chocolate chip cookie and a free newspaper. Many of its 187 rooms have balconies and some have nice views of the harbor and the Strait. There is one two-bedroom unit. The two-story hotel is just a block from the center of town and the ferry terminal. There is a heated pool and a spa. The dining room and coffee shop are open from 5:30 AM to midnight, and there is a lounge.

Port Townsend

Port Townsend has a number of delightful 19th-century mansions that have been converted to lodgings. One such is the **Ann Starrett Mansion**, 744 Clay St., Port Townsend, WA 98368, ☎ 360/385-3205, fax 360/385-2976, $$-$$$$, now a historic B&B. There are 11 rooms in the 1889 Victorian house, with frescoed ceilings and a free-hung, three-tiered spiral staircase that leads to an unusual domed ceiling. The mansion has one two-bedroom unit. Down side: the mansion has three stories and no elevator... a possible deterrent. Also, there is street parking only.

The **F.W. Hastings House Old Consulate Inn**, 313 Walker, Port Townsend, WA 98367, ☎ 360/385-6753 or 800/300-6753, fax 360/385-2097, Web site www.oldconsulateinn.com, $$-$$$$, is another delightful 1889 Victorian mansion. It has eight rooms with excellent views of Admiralty Inlet and the Olympics. There are king beds, a gazebo hot tub, and a billiard room. Tea is served in the afternoon and there are complimentary evening beverages. Again, the three-story building has no elevator, there is street parking only, and the rooms have no telephones.

Maresa Castle, 7th and Sheridan, PO Box 564, Port Townsend, WA 98367, ☎ 360/385-5750 or 800/732-1281, fax 360/385-5883, Web site www.olympus.net/manresa, $$-$$$, has 40 rooms. The three-story building has an Edwardian cocktail lounge and an elegant Victorian restaurant that serves gourmet meals, including a delightful Sunday brunch.

Seattle

The city of Seattle operates a Hotel Hotline from April through October: ☎ 800/535-7071 (from the US) or ☎ 206/461-5882 (from outside the US)

Of the many in-town hotels, the most worthy of mention are **Best Western Executive Inn**, 200 Taylor Ave. N, Seattle, WA 98109, ☎ 206/448-9444 or 800/351-9444, fax 206/441-7929, E-mail executiveinn@uno.com, Web site usa.nia.com/bwexec, $$-$$$$; **Cavanaugh's Inn on Fifth Ave.**, 1415 Fifth Ave., Seattle, WA 98101, ☎ 206/971-8000 or 800/THE INNS, fax 206/971-8100, E-mail jdisalvo@cavanaughs.com, $$$-$$$$;

Crowne Plaza Seattle, 1113 Sixth Ave., Seattle, WA 98101, ☎ 206/464-1980 or 800/521-2762, fax 206/340-1617 or 223-3750, $$$-$$$$; **Four Seasons Olympic Hotel**, 411 University St., Seattle, WA 98101, ☎ 206/621-1700 or 800/821-8106 (in Washington), or 800/332-3442 (in US), fax 206/682-9633, Web site www.fshr.com, $$$$; **Hampton Inn**, 700 Fifth Ave. North, Seattle, WA 98109, ☎ 206/282-7700, fax 206/282-0899, $$-$$$; **Ramada Inn Downtown**, 2200 Fifth Ave., Seattle, WA 98121, ☎ 206/441-9785 or 800/2-RAMADA, fax 206/448-0924, $$-$$$; **Seattle Hilton**, 1301 Sixth Ave., Seattle, WA 98101, ☎ 206/624-0500 or 800/542-7700 (in Washington) or 800/426-0535 (outside Washington), fax 206/682-9029, $$$-$$$$; **Travelodge by the Space Needle**, 200 6th Ave. N., Seattle, WA 98109, ☎ 206/441-7878, fax 206/448-4825, $$-$$$; and **The Westin Hotel Seattle**, 1900 5th Ave., Seattle, WA 98101, ☎ 206/728-1000 or 800/228-3999, fax 206/728-2259, $$$$.

Two other in-town hotels are of special interest:

The **New Hotel Monaco**, 1101 Fourth Ave., Seattle, WA 98101, ☎ 206/621-1770 or 800/945-2240, fax 206/621-7779, $$$-$$$$, opened in late 1997. Each room in the 11-story hotel has a fax machine and two telephone lines. The restaurant is open from 7 to 10 AM, from 11:30 AM to 2 PM, and from 5:30 to 10 PM daily. Complementary evening beverages are served, guests receive a free newspaper... and if you ask for it when you make your reservation, they'll name a goldfish for you and place it in your room to greet you on arrival, including a bowl and fish food.

Sorrento Hotel, 900 Madison St., Seattle, WA 98104-9742, ☎ 206/622-6400 or 800/323-7500, fax 206/343-6155, $$$-$$$$, was designed in 1908 with a circular palm-lined courtyard, mission towers, and an Italian wishing well fountain. Amenities include twice-daily maid service, a complimentary paper, and a shiatsu massage.

For those who like to be near the airport, there is again a large selection from which to choose: **Doubletree Guest Suites**, 16500 Southcenter Pkwy., Seattle WA 98188, ☎ 206/575-8220 or 800/528-0444, fax 206/575-4743, $$$; **Hampton Inn Hotel**, 19445 International Blvd., Seattle, WA 98188, ☎ 206/878-1700 or 800/HAMPTON, fax 206/824-0720, $$; **Holiday Inn**, 17338 International Blvd., Seattle, WA 98188, ☎ 206/248-1000, fax 206/242-7089, $$-$$$; **Radisson Hotel Seattle Airport**, 17001 Pacific Hwy South, Seattle, WA 98188, ☎ 206/244-6000 or 800/333-3333, fax 206/246-6835, $$$-$$$$; **Seattle Airport Hilton Inn**, 17620 Pacific Hwy South, Seattle, WA 98188, ☎ 206/244-4800 or 800/445-8667, fax 206/248-4499, $$$; and **Seattle Marriott Hotel**, 3201 S. 176th St., Seattle, WA 98188, ☎ 206/241-2000, fax 206/248-0789, $$$-$$$$.

Sequim

Greywold Inn, 395 Keeler Rd., Sequim, WA 98382, ☎ 360/683-5889 or 800/914-WOLF, fax 360/683-1487, $$-$$$, is a delightful B&B that serves a scrumptious complimentary four-course breakfast in its French-country dining room.

Snoqualmie

The Salish Lodge, 6501 Railroad Ave. SE, PO Box 1109, Snoqualmie, WA 98065-1109, ☎ 206/888-2556 or 800/826-6124, fax 206/888-9634, $$$-$$$$, sits beside 268-foot Snoqualmie Falls. It has a spa of international proportions and an excellent dining room. Diversions include hiking and biking.

Snoqualmie Summit Inn, PO Box 163, **Snoqualmie Pass**, WA 98068, ☎ 206/434-6300 or 800/557-STAY, fax 206/434-6396, $$-$$$, can offer an outdoor heated pool, a jacuzzi, a sauna, skiing, hayrides, mountain biking, sleigh rides, hiking, fishing, and nature walks. Reminiscent of a ski lodge, it is a place for urbanites to cool off in the summer. Winter ski packages also are available.

Tacoma

In Tacoma, the Bed & Breakfast Assn. of Tacoma & Mt. Rainier, PO Box 7957, Tacoma, WA 98704, ☎ 253/593-6098 or 888/593-6098, Web site www.tribnet.com/bb/tacomainns, will field questions about accommodations, and **A Greater Tacoma**, 3312 N. Union Ave., Tacoma, WA 98407, ☎ 206/759-4088 or 800/406-4088, fax 206/759-4025, E-mail tacomabnbs@aol.com, provides a B&B reservation service.

Among the city's many in-town hotels are **Howard Johnson Inn-Tacoma**, 8702 S. Hosmer, Tacoma, WA 98444, ☎ 206/535-3100 or 800/446-4656, fax 206/537-6497, $$-$$$; **Ramada Hotel Tacoma Dome**, 2611 E. E St., Tacoma, WA 98421, ☎ 206/572-7272 or 800/228-5151, fax 206/572-9664, $$-$$$; and **Sheraton Tacoma Hotel**, Tacoma Convention Center, 1320 Broadway Plaza, Tacoma, WA 98402, ☎ 206/572-3200, fax 206/591-4105, $$-$$$$.

■ Camping

Washington State campground information can be obtained at ☎ 800/452-5687.

📖 A free brochure, *Special Places for Special Times RV & Camping Directory*, has been produced by the Washington Assn. of RV Parks & Campgrounds, PO Box 1646, Bothell, WA 98041, ☎ 206/298-2589.

The Washington State Parks & Recreation Commission has produced a free pocket-sized brochure, *Your Guide to Washington State Parks*, that lists the state park camping facilities and describes the features of each. Another brochure, *Cabins in Washington State Parks*, tells where and how to rent a cabin.

Western RV News, 56405 Cascade View Lane, Warren, OR 97053-9736, is a commercial monthly tabloid newspaper for RV aficionados.

The Convention & Visitors Bureau in **Bellingham** provides a free sheet listing all Whatcom County campgrounds.

Shady Pines Resort, PO Box 44, **Conconully**, WA 98819, ☎ 509/826-2287 or 800/552-2287, sits on the west shore of Conconully Reservoir. Lake and stream swimming and fishing, boat rentals, waterskiing, nature trails, and mushrooming are available, along with grouse, mule deer, and white-tail deer hunting in the fall. The resort is open from April 25 to October 31. **Conconully Lake Resort**, PO Box 131, Conconully, WA 98819, ☎ 509/826-0813, is on the upper lake. Lake and dock fishing, lake swimming, waterskiing, boating, a boat ramp, and a dock are available. Rowboats and motorboats may be rented. Hunting is permitted for grouse, mule deer, and white-tail deer.

Driftwood Acres Ocean Campground, 3209 State Rt. 109, PO Box 216, **Copalis Beach**, WA 98535, ☎ 360/289-3484 or 206/472-6914, occupies the banks of the Copalis River. Some choice hiking is readily available. The campground is open from Memorial Day to Labor Day.

Blueside Resort, 400041 Hwy 20, **Cusick**, WA 99119, ☎ 509/445-1327, faces onto the Pend Oreille River. It has a heated pool, a country store, and a playground, and features hunting as well as fishing for bass, perch, crappie, and rainbow trout.

Schafer State Park, W. 1365 Schafer Park Rd., **Elma**, WA 98541, ☎ 360/482-3852 or 800/233-0321, is on the East Fork of the Satsop River, 12 miles south of town. Pastimes include hiking and fishing, but the campsite is closed from October through March.

Snoqualmie River Campground, 34807 SE 44th Pl., PO Box 16, **Fall City**, WA 98024-0016, ☎ 206/222-5545, is close to Snoqualmie Falls. River swimming, boating, river fishing, and hiking are available.

Deer Lake Resort, 3908 N. Dee Lake Rd., **Loon Lake**, WA 99148, ☎ 509/233-2081, can offer a sandy beach, fishing, boating, swimming, hiking, and bicycling. There is a small grocery and a laundry, and fishing boats, paddle boats, and bicycles are available for rent.

In Mason County, there are a number of US Forest Service campgrounds, about which the Hood Canal Ranger Station, ☎ 360/877-5254, can supply more information. They include campgrounds at **Brown Creek**, Skokomish Valley Road and Forest Service Road 23; **Lena Creek**, eight miles west of Eldon on Forest Service Road 25; **Hamma Hamma**, six miles west of Eldon on Forest Service Road 25; **Big Creek**, nine miles northwest of Hoodsport via WA 119; **Coho Campground**, in the Wynoochee Dam area; **Lilliwaup Creek**, three miles northwest of Lilliwaup; and **Collins Campground,** on Duckabush Road.

There also are campgrounds in a number of Tahuya State Forest multiuse areas throughout Mason County, including Howell Lake Campground, Camp Spillman, Tahuya River Horse Camp, Aldrich Lake, Toonerville, and Twin Lakes.

Washington State Parks, ☎ 800/233-0321, can provide campsites in **Jarrell's Cove State Park**, on the northwest end of Harstine Island; **Lake Cushman State Park**, seven miles west of Hoodsport via WA 119; **Belfair State Park**, three miles west of Belfair via WA 300; **Schaffer State Park**, 12 miles north of Brady on Route 401; **Twanoh State Park**, eight miles west of Belfair on Route 106; and **Potlatch State Park**, 12 miles north of Shelton on Route 101.

Rainbow Cove RV & Fishing Resort, 512514 Clear Lake Rd., **Medical Lake**, WA 99022, ☎ 509/299-3717, sits in a cove on Clear Lake and is open from April to November. Fishing is permitted for rainbow trout, brown trout, and bass. There is a 10-foot fishing dock, a boat launch, a store with tackle, a cafe, and boat rentals are available.

NACO Little Diamond Preserve, 1002 McGowan Rd., **Newport**, WA 99156, ☎ 509/447-4813, offers a heated pool, a private fishing lake, and laundry facilities.

Deep Lake Resort, 12405 Tilley Rd. South, **Olympia**, WA 98512, ☎ 360/352-7388, has an old-time country store and a playground. Pedal boats, aqua bikes, and canoes are available for rent. Swimming, fishing, and hiking also are available. The lakeside resort is open from April 22 to September 30.

American Heritage Campground, 9810 Kimmie St. SW, Olympia, WA 98512, ☎ 360/943-8778 or 800/943-8778, is open from Memorial Day to Labor Day. It has a heated pool, a playground, a free kiddie farm, a laundry, a game room, and a convenience store. Daily wagon rides and movies are available.

Osoyoos Border RV Park, Rt. 1, Box 113, **Oroville**, WA 98844, ☎ 509/476-4159, features a boat ramp, a swimming area, fishing, and waterskiing. The park is open from April 1 through September 30.

Lyre River Park, 596 W. Lyre River Rd., **Port Angeles**, WA 98362, ☎ 360/928-3436, is located on the Lyre River and the Strait. Swimming, tubing, and fishing is permitted in the pond, the river, or the Strait.

Lake Quinault's Rain Forest Resort, Rt. 1, Box 40, **Quinault**, WA 98575, ☎ 360/288-2535 or 800/255-6936, is a lakeside resort.

Big Fir Campground & RV Park, 5515 NE 259th St., **Ridgefield**, WA 98842, ☎ 360/887-8970, is frequented by deer and rabbits. Fishing, boating, hiking, and swimming are popular pastimes, and there is a small store.

Lake Pleasant RV Park, ☎206/487-1785 or 800/742-0386, offers a pleasant wildlife habitat with hiking, fishing, and a playground close to **Seattle**. Take I-5 to I-405, Exit 26, and then travel one mile south on Bothell Highway.

Surfside Campland, PO Box 39, **Sekiu**, WA 98381, ☎ 360/926-2723, has views of the ocean, easy access to the beach, a paperback bookshop, and laundry facilities. Fishing, boating, hiking, kayaking, and biking are popular pastimes.

Minerva Beach Resort & Mobile Village, N. 21110 Hwy 101, **Shelton**, WA 98584, ☎ 206/877-5145, is located on 360 feet of waterfront along the Hood Canal. It offers a clubhouse and a driving range in addition to fishing, and has a laundromat, a dive shop, and a store. Oysters and clams are available in season.

Winona Beach Resort, 33022 Winona Beach Rd., **Valley**, WA 99181, ☎ 509/937-2231, fax 509/937-2215, is on a 450-acre lake with rainbow trout (the state record was set here), brown trout, bass, and perch. There also are a swimming beach, a fishing dock, pontoon boats, a boat launch, a country store, a snack bar, and a bait and tackle shop.

Where to Eat

Anacortes

La Petite, 3401 Commercial Ave., Anacortes, WA 98221, ☎ 360/293-4644, $$, located in Islands Inn, offers a "Dutch breakfast" that includes fresh-baked bread with butter and chocolate sprinkles, a soft-boiled egg, Dutch cheese, and ham.

Bellevue

Lisa's Tea Treasures Tea Room, 10687 NE Second St., Bellevue, WA 98004, ☎ 206/453-4832, fax 206/453-1424, $$, is reminiscent of a genuine English tea room, right down to the tea and scones. Delicious soups and other light fare are offered.

Black Diamond

Famous Black Diamond Bakery & Restaurant, 32805 Railroad Ave., Black Diamond, WA 98010, ☎ 360/886-2235, $$, has served the community since 1902. It is open daily from 7 AM to 5 PM, and is reputed to have the best bakery in western Washington. From the restaurant, it is possible to see Mount Rainier.

Bow

Chuckanut Manor, 302 Chuckanut Dr., Bow, WA 98232, ☎ 360/766-6191, $$-$$$, has a seafood smorgasbord on Fridays from 5 to 10:30 PM, and a champagne brunch on Sundays from 10:30 AM to 2:30 PM.

Cosmopolis

Cosmopolis is a good place to sample one of the Native American salmon bakes that are popular throughout the region.

Everett

Club Broadway, 1611 Everett Ave., Everett, WA 98201, ☎ 425/259-3551, $-$$, presents a live comedy/dinner show in the top floor Manhattan Room Restaurant between 5 and 9:30 PM on Fridays and Saturdays.

Friday Harbor

Mariella Inn & Cottages, 630 Turn Point Rd., Friday Harbor, WA 98250, ☎ 360/378-6868 or 800/700-7668, $$-$$$, offers luncheon and dinner cruises aboard the 65-foot wooden yacht *Arequipa*.

Gig Harbor

Time for a cold beer and a pizza, or maybe a burger? Darts? Pool? Try **Hy Iu Hee Hee**, 4309 Burnham Dr., Gig Harbor, WA 98335, ☎ 206/851-7885, $.

Kirkland

Yarrow Bay Grill, 1270 Carillon Point, Kirkland, WA 98033, ☎ 425/889-9052, fax 425/803-2982, $$$, has wonderful food and gorgeous waterfront views. A less expensive, more informal restaurant, Yarrow Bay Café, is downstairs.

La Conner

Mystic Sea Charters, 413 Morris St., La Conner, WA 98257, ☎ 360/466-3042 or 800/308-9387, Web site www.cyberspace.com/mbrunk/mystic.html, $$-$$$, provides Sunday brunch cruises aboard a 100-foot vessel from March 28 through October.

Champagne Charters, PO Box 969, La Conner, WA 98257, ☎ 206/466-4076, $$-$$$, offers brunch, lunch, and dinner cruises aboard *Champagne*, a 43-foot motor yacht.

Port Townsend

Manresa Castle, 7th and Sheridan, PO Box 564, Port Townsend, WA 98368, ☎ 360/385-5750 or 800/732-1281, fax 360/385-5883, $$-$$$, was built in 1892 as a private home. In 1927, the home was bought by Jesuits, expanded, and named after the Spanish town in which St. Ignatius founded the Jesuit Order. In 1968, the building was converted into a hotel.

Renton

Diamond Lil's, 321 Rainier Ave. South, Renton, WA 98055, ☎ 425/226-2763, $$, is an "old west" restaurant that serves lunch and dinner. It also has a lounge and a cardroom, ☎ 425/255-9037, where they play Texas Hold'em and Blackjack. The restaurant is open from 10 AM to 6 AM.

Seattle

Fine Food & Wine Tours, 1541 NE 88th St., Seattle, WA 98115, ☎ 206/523-7464 or 888/623-7464, fax 206/522-3342, E-mail epicure@wolfenet.com, will take you winin' and dinin' throughout greater Seattle.

The Spirit of Puget Sound, leaves Pier 70, Broad Street and Alaskan Way, **Seattle**, WA 98101, ☎ 206/674-3500 or 443-1442, Web site www.spiritcruises.com, $$$, for lunch, dinner, and moonlight party cruises in the harbor.

Oyster-lovers will be enraptured at **Elliott's Oyster House**, Pier 56, Seattle, WA 98101, ☎ 206/623-4340, fax 206/224-0154, $$. Oysters available at the restaurant include Penn Cove Selects from Penn Cove, WA; Quilcenes from Hood Canal; Shoalwaters from Willapa Bay; Kumamotos from Humboldt Bay; and Malaspinas and Evening Coves from British Columbia.

Mystery Cafe Dinner Theatre, 3rd and Pine Streets, Seattle, WA 98101, ☎ 206/324-8895, $$, stages its shows on Friday and Saturdays evenings at 8 PM. **Cabaret de Paris**, 4th and Union Streets, ☎ 206/623-4111, $$, presents comic musical revues in a dinner theater setting.

Space Needle Restaurant, Seattle Center, Seattle, WA 98101, ☎ 206/443-2111 or 800/937-9582, Web site www.spaceneedle.com, $$-$$$, occupies the 500-foot level on the famous landmark. Enjoy outstanding views of the city and the harbor as the revolving restaurant slowly turns while you dine. The restaurant serves breakfast, lunch, and dinner, and the elevator ride and access to the observation deck are free to diners.

Sequim

The Three Crabs, 11 Three Crabs Rd., Sequim, WA 98382, ☎ 360/683-4264, $$, features waterfront dining. In addition to the crab burger, the oyster sandwich, and the hali-wich (halibut), the restaurant serves a broad selection of local seafood plus steaks.

Stanwood

Into Norwegian food? Thousands of pounds of lefse (Norwegian potato pancakes or 'flatbread' made of grain flour and mashed boiled potatoes mixed with milk or water) are shipped out of **Scandia Bakery** in Stanwood each year.

Information Sources

Mount Baker-Snoqualmie National Forest, 21905 64th Ave. West, Mountlake Terrace, WA 98043, ☎ 206/775-9702.

Olympic National Forest, 1835 Black Lake Blvd. SW, Olympia, WA 98502-5423, ☎ 206/956-2300.

Olympic National Park, 600 E. Park, Port Angeles, WA 98362, ☎ 360/452-4501 or 452-0330.

Bainbridge Island Chamber of Commerce, 590 Winslow Way East, Bainbridge Island, WA 98110, ☎ 206/842-3700.

Bellingham/Whatcom Chamber of Commerce & Industry, 1801 Roeder Ave., Bellingham, WA 98225, ☎ 360/734-1330, fax 360/734-1332, E-mail chamber@bellingham.com/~chamber.

Bremerton Area Chamber of Commerce, 120 Washington Ave., PO Box 229, Bremerton, WA 98337, ☎ 360/479-3579.

Washington Coast Chamber of Commerce, PO Box 562, Copalis Beach, WA 98535, ☎ 206/289-4552 or 800/286-4552.

Enumclaw Area Chamber of Commerce, 1421 Cole St., Enumclaw, WA 98022, ☎ 360/825-7666.

Snohomish County Visitor Information Center, 101 128th St. SE, Suite 5000, Everett, WA 98208, ☎ 206/338-4437, 745-4133, or 888/338-0976.

Gig Harbor & Peninsula Chamber of Commerce, 3125 Judson St., PO Box 1245, Gig Harbor, WA 98335, ☎ 206/851-6865, fax 206/851-6881.

Lacey/Thurston County Chamber of Commerce, 701 Sleater-Kinney Rd. SE, Suite 7, Lacey, WA 98503, ☎ 360/491-4141.

Long Beach Peninsula Visitor's Center, PO Box 562, Long Beach, WA 98631, ☎ 360/642-2400 or 800/451-2542. (Ask for a free copy of *Southwest Washington's Coastal Vacationland*.)

South Snohomish County Chamber of Commerce, 3500 188th St. SW, Suite 490, Lynnwood, WA 98036, ☎ 206/774-0507.

Olympia/Thurston County Chamber of Commerce, 521 Legion Way, Olympia, WA 98507, ☎ 360/734-6320.

State Capitol Visitor Center, 14th and Capitol Way, Olympia, WA 98501, ☎ 360/586-3460, Web site www.youra.com/olympic_guide.html.

Olympic Peninsula Travel Assn., PO Box 625, Port Angeles, WA 98362-0112, ☎ 360/385-4938, fax 360/379-0151, E-mail thomasmc@waypt.com, Web site www.waypt.com/opta/opta.html.

North Olympic Peninsula Visitor & Convention Bureau, 338 W. First St., #104, PO Box 670, Port Angeles, WA 98362, ☎ 360/452-8552 or 460-1696, fax 360/452-7383, E-mail rick@northolympic.com, Web site www.northolympic.com.

Kitsap Peninsula Visitor & Convention Bureau, PO Box 270, Port Gamble, WA 98364.

Chamber of Commerce of Eastern Pierce County, 2823 E. Main St., Puyallup, WA 98372, ☎ 253/845-6755.

Seattle/King County Convention & Visitors Bureau, 520 Pike St., Suite 1300, Seattle, WA 98101. ☎ 206/575-1633 or 800/638-8613.

Shelton/Mason County Visitor Information, 230 W. Railroad Ave., PO Box 2389, Shelton, WA 98584, ☎ 360/426-8678, 426-2021, or 800/576-2021.

Tacoma-Pierce County Visitor & Convention Bureau, 906 Broadway, Tacoma, WA 98401, ☎ 206/627-2836, fax 206/627-8783.

Vashon-Maury Island Chamber of Commerce, PO Box 1035, Vashon, WA 98070, ☎ 206/463-6217.

Central Washington

When one thinks about central Washington, one thinks about the Cascade Mountain Range because that is the principle feature that dominates the region.

Although the range averages just 5,000-8,000 feet in elevation, it is punctuated by four magnificent peaks – Rainier at 14,411 feet, Adams at 12,276 feet, Baker at 10,778 feet, and the little-known Glacier Peak at 10,568.

Since its last eruption, Mount St. Helens has been reduced to an "insignificant" 8,364 feet.

Except for the southern region along the Columbia River Gorge, the population of this area is extremely sparse.

Getting Around

There are long stretches of highway throughout central Washington where the car radio can pick up no more than one radio station. In the extremely northern reaches, that station is often an affiliate of the Canadian CBC.

Highways running north and south are virtually limited to Interstate 5, a major link between Vancouver (across the Columbia River from Portland, OR) on the south to the Canadian border on the north. Short "linkages" running north and south carry little traffic, by and large.

Of the east-west arteries, WA 14 runs along the Columbia River on the north side of the gorge from Vancouver to Plymouth, a distance of 150 miles. Along the way, it passes through many tunnels and beside many stretches lined with lupine and other colorful wildflowers.

US 12 runs from Aberdeen on the west coast to the Idaho border at Clarkston on the east, passing through Chehalis and Morton on the way. The National Scenic Route runs between Mount St. Helens on the south and Mount Rainier on the north, traverses 4,500-foot White Pass, and wends its way through many miles of the pristine Gifford Pinchot National Forest toward the little community of Naches. It and Interstate 90 are, in fact, the only year-around routes passing through the Cascade Mountains.

Farther north, WA 419 takes a zigzag route from Enumclaw to Greenwater, then heads south through Cayuse Pass and Chinook Pass, following the American River to the Naches River, then southeast along the Naches River toward Yakima. The road is closed during the winter.

Still farther to the north, I-90 runs southeast through Snoqualmie Pass and along the Yakima River to Cle Elum.

US 2 from Index passes through Skykomish, Coles Corner, and Leavenworth on its way eastward toward Wenatchee, which sits on the northern portion of the great Columbia River, while the northernmost east-west trafficway, WA 20, leaves Newhalem and cuts through Northern Cascades National Park and the Okanogan National Forest on its way to the town of Winthrop and beyond.

Airports

Airports are as scarce as roadways in central Washington. None could be called a "major" transportation center, but they do provide a means of access to such centers if a need arises.

Three small airports are located east of Vancouver and north of Camas. Woodland has a small field, and there is a field just north of Toledo. Between Chehalis and Centralia lies another field, and there is another one just west of Bucoda. Morton, Packwood, and Rimrock have small airfields, and there are two near Cle Elum. Moving northward, there is an airfield at Easton, at Snoqualmie Pass, and at Skykomish. There is another field near Lake Wenatchee northwest of Plain, and there is one field north and another field southeast of Twisp.

Touring

Battle Ground was named for a battle that never was fought. In 1855, a group of Vancouver settlers sent a party to Battle Ground to check on the local Indians. Mysteriously, Chief Umtuch was killed, but the battle that many had feared was never waged.

Camas lily bulbs were a staple in the diet of the local Indians, hence the origin of the town named **Camas**. **Castle Rock,** on the Cowlitz River, is called the "Gateway to Mount St. Helens."

Chehalis is the seat of Lewis County, which once extended all the way north to Russian Alaska and as far south as the Cowlitz River. And yes – the county was named for Merriweather Lewis of Lewis and Clark fame.

The world's tallest single-tree totem pole stands in Marine Park in **Kalama**. The Port of Kalama on the Columbia River can accommodate large oceangoing vessels. **Kelso** is so named because it was founded by a native of Kelso, Scotland, It has been the county seat since 1889. A Bavarian theme runs throughout the town of **Leavenworth**. Indians referred to **Mount Adams** as Pahto. The U-Haul Co. got its start in the town of **Ridgefield**.

Central Washington

The Duck Brand Saloon built in **Winthrop** in 1891 is now the town hall. **Yacolt**, an Indian word describing spirits and other ghostly things, opened its first post office in 1895.

Adventures

■ On Foot

Hiking Trails

Appleton is virtually a ghost town, located on a gravel road west of Klickitat. The community hall, in use since 1912, is built entirely of logs.

The 90-mile Mount Tahoma Trail System near **Ashford** is popular for hiking, biking, and skiing. The **Lake Christine Trail** covers a distance of one mile; the **High Rock Lookout Trail** covers a mile and a half; and the **Glacier View Trail**, also covers a mile and a half.

Panther Creek Camp, north of **Carson** on Route 65, provides fishing and a horse camp as well as hiking, and the **Dog Mountain Wildflower Area**, east of town on Route 14, provides some marvelous hiking and sightseeing. **Conboy Lake Wildlife Refuge**, west of **Glenwood**

Hiking Dog Mountain, near White Salmon (Washington Tourism Dev).

off Glenwood Road, has an interpretive wildlife trail and offers some excellent views of Mount Adams. The **Ice House Bird Sanctuary** is east of **Klickitat** on WA 142. **Alpine Guide Service**, ☎ 800/548-5011, in **Leavenworth** conducts half-day, all-day, and overnight hiking and climbing adventures.

Obviously, **Mount Baker** provides opportunities for all sorts of outdoor activities. Hiking, camping, and backpacking probably top the list. A Visitor Information Center at Snoqualmie Pass can provide a great deal of useful information.

Some of the easier hikes in the Glacier-Nooksack Area of the Mount Baker Ranger District are the quarter-mile **Horseshoe Bend Nature Trail** loop, for which the trailhead is across from the Douglas Fir Campground on Route 542; the mile-and-a-half **Damfino Lake Trail**, reached from the trailhead at the end of Canyon Creek Road (Forest Service Road #31) off Route 542; and another quarter-mile loop, **Picture Lake Trail**, accessed by a trailhead at Heather Meadows just before the ski area. The latter is wheelchair accessible.

More difficult hikes in the same area include the six-mile round trip along **Excelsior Pass Trail**, from the same trailhead as the Damfino Lakes Trail; the four-mile round trip **Heliotrope Ridge Trail**, reached from a trailhead on Glacier Creek Road (Forest Service Road #39), nine miles east of Glacier off Route 542; another four-mile round trip, the **Twin Lakes Trail**, reached by turning onto Twin Lakes Road (Farm Service Road #3065) just east of the Shuksan Maintenance Complex, 14 miles east of the Glacier Public Service Center (park at the Tomyhoi Lake trailhead sign); and a 3.5-mile round trip, the **Table Mountain Trail**, accessed at Artist Point at the end of Route 542.

In the **Baker Lake** area, there are half a dozen easy hikes that should be of interest. **Shadow of the Sentinels Nature Trail**, a half-mile loop trail that is wheelchair accessible, can be reached from a trailhead just beyond the Komo Kulshan Guard Station on Baker Lake Highway (Forest Service Road #11) off WA 20. **Blue Lake Trail**, which covers a mile-and-a-half round trip, can be accessed from a trailhead on Forest Service Road #1230 off the Baker Lake Highway. **Elbow Lake Trail**, a three-mile round trip, starts at the end of Forest Service Road #12 off Baker Lake Highway. **East Bank Trail** covers eight miles, starting at Forest Service Road #1107, reached by crossing Baker Dam on Forest Service Road #1106. **Baker River Trail** covers five miles round trip and begins from a trailhead on Forest Service Road #1168 near the end of Baker Lake.

Two trails in the Baker Lake area are a bit more difficult. To hike the **Dock Butte Trail**, which covers three miles round trip, follow the directions to reach the Lake Trail, then take the spur trail to the right. To take the **Anderson-Watson Lakes Trail**, a five-mile round trip, follow the directions to East Bank Trail but continue on Forest Service Road #1107 until you can turn left onto a spur (#1107022).

There are many easy trails in the area of WA 20. To reach **Trail of the Cedars**, a quarter-mile loop, turn at the Newhalem General Store (Mile Post 121) and look for the trailhead at the end of the road. **Ladder Creek Falls Trail**, a half-mile loop, begins across the bridge by the Gorge Powerhouse at mile post 121. **Thunderwoods Nature Trail**, a 1.8-mile loop, starts at mile post 130 off Thunder Creek Trail by way of the south loop at Colonial Creek Campground. **Happy Creek Forest Walk**, which is wheelchair accessible and covers only a third of a mile, begins on the south side of the highway between Mile Posts 134 and 135, just beyond the Ross Lake Overlook. **Rainy Lake Trail**, also wheelchair accessible, covers two miles round trip and begins on the south side of the highway between Mile Posts 157 and 158 at the Rainy Pass Day Use Area. A high-clearance vehicle may be required to cover the last several miles to the trailhead for **Slide Lake Trail**, a 2.5-mile round trip. Turn south off WA 20 onto Route 530 at Rockport and then turn onto Forest Service Road #16. The trailhead will be on the right side of the road a little more than 20 miles off Route 530.

Mount Rainier trails (Washington Tourism Dev).

More difficult trails off WA 20 include **Sauk Mountain Trail**, a 4.2-mile round trip. Turn north off WA 20 onto Forest Service Road #1030 just west of Rockport State Park. Follow that road for about seven miles to a small spur road that curves to the right, where there is a parking lot and the trailhead. To find **Lake Ann Trail**, a 3.5-mile round trip, follow the directions to reach Rainy Lake Trail. For the trailhead for **Blue Lake Trail**, a four-mile round trip, go about three miles east of the Rainy Pass area near mile post 161 and watch for the sign on the south side of the road. **Cutthroat LakeTrail**, a four-mile round trip, is off

Cutthroad Lake Road, which is about four miles east of the Washington Pass Overlook, around mile post 167.

Another prime hiking area is **Mount Rainier National Park**, established in 1899. The park contains over 300 miles of trails and has more than 27 named glaciers. It is the fifth largest park in the United States and the nation's fifth oldest national park. The 14,410-foot mountain is the highest in the Cascade Mountain range. (Park headquarters, ☎ 360/569-2211; roads and weather: ☎ 360/569-2211.)

Among the more popular trails are **Wonderland**, 92 miles long; **Rampart Bridge**, a 4.5-mile loop; **Comet Falls**, 1.6 miles long; **Skyline**, a five-mile loop; **Pinnacle Peak**, which covers just one mile; **Snow Lake**, a mile and a quarter long; **Box Canyon**, a half-mile loop; **Grove of the Patriarchs**, a 1.5-mile loop; **Silver Falls**, a 2.2-mile loop; **Naches Loop**, covering 3.2 miles; **Sourdough Ridge**, two miles long; and **Burroughs Mountain**, a seven-mile loop.

Rainier Mountaineering, ☎ 206/569-2227 (June through September) or 206/627-6242 (October through May), leads guided summit climbs.

Mount St. Helens, located southwest of Mount Rainier and west of Mount Adams, is yet another prime hiking region. This area drew special attention when it suffered a 4.1 earthquake on 20 March 1980, followed by two months of billowing steam and ash and then a 5.0 eruption on 18 May that caused the north side of the mountain to give way and devastated an area of 156 square miles.

The final stretch of WA 504, which takes visitors to within five miles of the volcano's stricken north side, opened in May 1997, but may be closed occasionally if heavy winter snows make the road hazardous.

A WORD TO THE WISE

Mount St. Helens Climbing Hotline: ☎ 206/750-3961.

Mount St. Helens Adventure Tours, 14000 Spirit Lake Highway, PO Box 149, **Toutle**, WA 98649, ☎ 360/274-6542, guides parties onto the mountain.

Trout Lake is just south of **Mount Adams**. Northwest of town and north of Route 88 is **Sleeping Beauty**, according to legend a sleeping Indian princess who was turned into a mountain. Northwest of town near the junction of Routes 88 and 8851 is **Langfield Falls**, popular for the area's view, waterfalls, and huckleberry picking. And south of town off Route 60, a gravel road, is a 12,500-acre lava bed and an area that is popular for hiking, camping, and fishing.

Columbia River Waterfront Trail, a four-mile trail beginning at the Captain Vancouver Monument in **Vancouver** and going up-river to Tidewater Cove, passes a seven-foot bronze statue of a 19th-century Chinook Indian chief, passes Old Apple Tree Park, and passes Marine Park, where Henry Kaiser built his "Liberty Ships" during World War II.

Woodland, a gateway to the southern slopes of Mount St. Helens, is choice hunting country. Game includes elk, deer, pheasant, duck, geese, grouse, and rabbit.

■ On Horseback

Horse Shows

Chehalis hosts a number of annual events related to horses. The **Horse Leader's Council Horse Show** is held in the Southwest Washington Fairgrounds 4-H Arena, ☎ 360/736-6072, in June. The **Bit-n-Spur Show & Clinic**, ☎ 360/736-6072, and the **Saddle Pals Horse Show**, ☎ 360/736-6072, are held in the same arena in July and August, respectively.

Riding

Riders enjoy traveling through 213-acre **Iron Horse State Park** at the foot of Fourth Street in **South Cle Elum** as well as riding the **John Wayne Pioneer Trail** from the fir and pine forests near Easton to the rolling farmlands and canyons of the Upper Yakima River Valley nearby. **Happy Trails**, PO Box 32, **Easton**, WA 98925, ☎ 509/656-2634 or 925-9428, arranges one- to five-day wagon train trips, pack trips, sleigh rides, hay rides, horse rentals, and pony rides.

 Backcountry Horsemen of Washington, PO Box 563, **Leavenworth**, WA 98826, ☎ 509/763-3470, has produced *Backcountry Equipment Check List*, a publication that contains a great deal of useful backcountry information. Get a free copy at the Chamber of Commerce.

Early Winters Outfitting & Saddle Co., HCR 74, Box B6, **Mazama**, WA 98833, ☎ 509/996-2659 or 800/737-8750, offers horseback riding, pack trips, and overnighters.

Rodeos

Rodeos are popular in this region too. The **Lewis County Roundup Rodeo**, ☎ 360/330-2088, is held in July. The **Thunder Mountain Pro Rodeo** is held in **Longview** as a part of the annual Cowlitz County Fair. **Winthrop Rodeo Days**, ☎ 509/996-2435, are staged on the **Winthrop** Rodeo Grounds on Memorial Day and Labor Day.

On Wheels

Rail Tours

Lewis & Clark Railway Co., 1000 E. Main St., **Battle Ground**, WA 98604, ☎ 206/687-2626 or 503/227-2626, runs from Battle Ground to Moulton Falls, a 2½-hour trip along the Lewis River, across wooden trestles and steel bridges, past waterfalls, and through a 340-foot tunnel. The train leaves at 10 AM on Tuesdays and at 1:30 PM on weekends between April and Father's Day (in June); at 10 AM and 1:30 PM on Independence Day, Memorial Day, and Labor Day; at 1:30 PM on Saturday and Sunday of the Memorial Day weekend; and at 10 AM on Tuesdays and 1:30 PM on weekends from mid-June to mid-September. Weekend dinner trains also are scheduled. Call for the winter schedule (November through March).

Chehalis-Centralia Railroad, 1945 S. Market Blvd., **Chehalis**, WA 98532, ☎ 360/748-9593, operates on weekends from May 24 to Labor Day, making two 12-mile round trips daily. Extended excursions to Ruth can be taken on occasion, and dinner trains are scheduled on some weekends. Although the ticket office is located in Centralia, passengers board the train in Chehalis.

Mt. Rainier Scenic Railroad, PO Box 921, **Elbe**, WA 98330, ☎ 360/569-2588, fax 360/569-2438, makes a 14-mile, hour-and-a-half trip from Elbe to Mineral Lake every weekend from Memorial Day through the end of September. The train departs at 11 AM, 1:15 PM, and 3:30 PM. A dinner train leaves at 1 PM on Sundays during the spring, at 5:30 PM on Saturdays in the summer, and at 1 PM on Sundays in the fall.

Puget Sound Railway Historical Assn., PO Box 459, **Snoqualmie**, WA 98065, ☎ 425/746-4025, operates trains on Saturdays and Sundays from early April until the Labor Day weekend, plus a holiday season 'Santa Train.' The excursion runs between Snoqualmie and North Bend, departing Snoqualmie at 11 AM, noon, and 1, 2, 3, and 4 PM, and departing North Bend at 11:30 AM and 12:30, 1:30, 2:30, and 3:30 PM. A "Santa Train" is run in December.

Shuttle & Van Tours

Rainier Overland, 31811 WA 706, Ashford, WA 98304, fax 360/569-2033, E-mail overland@mashell.com, operates a daily minivan shuttle to Mount Rainier. **Custom Tailored Tours**, 2921 NE Littler Way, **Vancouver**, WA 98662, ☎ 360/256-0536 or 800/391-5761, conducts half- and all-day tours in a six-passenger van.

■ On the Water

Windsurfing

Bingen is one of the most popular places to go windsurfing on the Columbia River. **White Salmon** and **Swell City**, just west of White Salmon, also are very popular spots for windsurfing.

Home Valley, just east of **Carson** on the Columbia River, is a good spot for beginning windsurfers.

Vancouver Lake Sports, 8002 NW Hwy 99, Box 199, **Vancouver**, WA 98665, ☎ 360/573-1212, specializes in rentals and lessons for windsurfing, kayaking, and paddle boats. Located in Vancouver Lake Park, the store is open between 1 and 8 PM daily from June through August. Windsurfing lessons are provided in conjunction with the Columbia Windsurfing Academy.

Columbia Gorge Windsurfing Assn., PO Box 182, **Hood River**, OR 97031, ☎ 541/386-9225, can provide a great deal of useful information.

Rafting & Kayaking

Phil Zoller's Whitewater Adventure, ☎ 509/493-2641 or 800/266-2004, can arrange rafting trips in the **Bingen** area.

Windsurfing the Columbia River Gorge
(Washington Tourism Dev).

The 16-mile stretch of the Yakima River between **Cle Elum** and Thorp makes a nice three- to four-hour trip on a rubber raft or in a canoe, both of which are available for rent in Cle Elum.

Chinook Expeditions, PO Box 324, **Index**, WA 98256, ☎ 360/793-3451 or 800/241-3451, handles float tours. **Alpine Adventures**, 894 Hwy 2, Clocktower Blvd., PO Box 253, **Leavenworth**, WA 98826, ☎ 509/782-7042, 548-4159, or 800/926-7238, Web site www.leavenworth.or/~alpineadventures, guides whitewater rafting excursions and overnight trips, and **Osprey Rafting Co.**, ☎ 509/548-6800 or 800/743-6269, leads whitewater rafting trips, rents inflatable kayaks, and gives lessons.

White Water Adventures, 38 Northwestern Lake, **White Salmon**, WA 98672, ☎ 509/493-2641 or 800/366-2004, takes three whitewater rafting trips daily in the Columbia River Gorge. The journeys depart at 9 AM, 12:30 PM, and 3:30 PM.

Fishing

Excellent fishing can be found in **Lake Merwin**, a crescent-shaped body of water backed up behind the dam in **Ariel**. There are two fish hatcheries in the area, the **Lewis River Hatchery** at 4404 Lewis River Rd., and the **Speelyai State Hatchery** at 11001 Lewis River Rd.

Outlet Creek and Falls, east of **Glenwood** off the Glenwood-Goldendale Road, is a good fishing site and offers a marvelous viewpoint for the Klickitat River Gorge. The **Leidle Campground** southeast of town on that same road is a popular launching point for rafts and kayaks.

At the junction of the White Salmon River and Rattlesnake Creek, the region around **Husum** has some scenic waterfalls and is a widely used site for rafting and kayaking. **Northwestern Lake Park and Dam,** between Underwood and Husum off WA 141, is particularly popular for fishing, boating, and camping, and **BZ Corners**, north of Husum on the White Salmon River, is a choice spot for whitewater rafting and kayaking.

There is good fly fishing in the Kalama River, and the town of **Kalama** has a boat ramp and a 222-slip marina. The ruins of *Leona,* a sternwheeler sunk in 1912, can be seen 50 feet west of the town bridge in **La Center**. **Lake Chelan**, a 55-mile-long glacial lake, offers some outstanding fishing, and **Lyle**, on the Columbia River near the mouth of the Klickitat River, affords excellent canoeing, fishing, boating, and surfing.

Gorge Lake, 2.5 miles northeast of **Newhalem** in the North Cascades National Park, is a 210-acre lake with a boat launch and a good supply of rainbow and cutthroat trout. **Ross Lake**, an 11,674-acre impound 9.5 miles northeast of town, has campsites on the eastern shore, but the boat launch at the north end of the lake is accessible only from British Columbia, Canada. Ross contains rainbow, cutthroat, brook, and Dolly Varden trout, but all bull trout and Dolly Varden trout must be released during the season from July through October.

Northwest Guide Service, Mile Post 0.21 R Woodard Creek Rd., **Skamania**, WA 98648, ☎ 509/427-4625, will show you where the big ones are. **Trout Lake**, at the junction of WA 141 and Glenwood Road, is a great place for hunting, camping, and fishing.

Fishing for trout, steelhead, salmon, smelt, walleye, kokanee, and sturgeon is often superb in the Lewis and Columbia Rivers near **Woodland**.

■ On Snow

There are a number of Snow Phones to make decision making easy in central Washington. These include **Alpental-Ski Acres-Snowqualmie-Hyak**, ☎ 206/236-1600; **Crystal Mountain**, ☎ 206/634-3771; **49° North Ski Area**, ☎ 509/458-9208; **Mission Ridge Ski Area**, ☎ 800/374-1693; **Mount Baker Ski Area**, ☎ 360/671-0211; **Ski Bluewood**, ☎ 509/382-4725; **Stevens**

Sleigh ride at Mountain Springs Ranch, Leavenworth
(Washington Tourism Dev).

Pass Ski Area, ☎ 360/634-1645; and **White Pass Village**, ☎ 509/672-3100.

Greenwater Skis, Hwy 410, **Greenwater**, WA 98022, ☎ 360/663-2235, sits on the edge of Snoqualmie National Forest and will help arrange skiing trips and either sell or rent you some skis.

There are 100 miles of groomed snowmobile trails and four snow parks around **Leavenworth**, ☎ 509/548-7914. **Nordic Village**, ☎ 509/548-5807, has 40 kilometers of groomed cross-country ski trails and 1.5 kilometers of lighted tracks, arranges guided back country tours, has rentals, and provides lessons. **Bavarian Village**, ☎ 509/548-5807, a mile from town, features downhill skiing and has two rope tows.

Methow Valley skiing around **Winthrop** involves 175 kilometers of cross-country trails, snowmobiling, and a Ski Rodeo, ☎ 509/996-3287, held in late December.

■ In the Air

Dallesport, the airport serving The Dalles, OR, is located on the Washington side of the Columbia River. The **Chehalis-Centralia** airport has a 5,000-foot runway. The **Methow Valley State Airport**, ☎ 509/997-6962, is in **Winthrop**.

Pearson Field near **Vancouver** is the oldest operating airfield in the United States. A dirigible landed there in 1905 and the first airplane landed there in 1911. The world's first nonstop transpolar flight left Moscow and landed here on 20 June 1937, while Gen. George C. Marshall was the commanding officer of Vancouver Barracks. The **Chkalov Monument** at 1109 E. 5th St. in Vancouver commemorates this event.

M.J. Murdock Aviation Center (Pearson Air Museum), 1105 E. 5th, Vancouver, WA 98661, ☎ 360/694-7026, is open between noon and 5 PM from Wednesday through Sunday.

Vancouver Aviation, 101-A E. Reserve St., **Vancouver**, WA 98661, ☎ 206-695-3821, schedules scenic flights over Mount St. Helens.

Blue Bird Helicopters, ☎ 360/238-5326, takes scenic trips over Mount St. Helens out of **Cougar**.

Winthrop celebrates an **Air Balloon Festival**, ☎ 509/996-2125, in late February.

Pitt, southwest of Klickitat on WA 142, is a good site for hang gliding. Camping, hunting, and fishing also are popular in this area.

The **North Cascades Smokejumper Base**, ☎ 509/997-2031, in **Winthrop** is called "the birthplace of the Smoke Jumper." Visitors are welcome from June through September.

Kelso hosts the **Three Rivers Air Show** each August.

■ Cultural Excursions

Ariel

It was in the neighborhood of Ariel that the mysterious D.B. Cooper parachuted from an airplane with a fortune in stolen loot. The search is still on for $200,000 of the money that has never been accounted for. It also is in Ariel that the **Northwest Coast Indian Culture** holds its annual spring "Masks, Myths and Magic" program.

Battle Ground

The 388-acre **Moulton Falls County Park** near Battle Ground, 10 miles northeast of Battle Creek on NE Lucia Falls Road, is a stopping place for the Lewis & Clark Railway. A footbridge overlooks the falls. Fishing, hiking, and swimming are popular pursuits.

Battle Ground State Park, NE 244th St., ☎ 360/687-4621 or 800/452-5687, has a lake that was formed from the crater of an extinct volcano. Located three miles northeast of Battle Ground on WA 502, the park has a boat launch and provides for fishing, swimming, camping, hiking, and horseback riding.

Bingen

Bingen, in the area of Mount Adams, is noted for its wineries, one of which, **Mont Elise Vineyards**, WA 14, Bingen, WA, ☎ 509/493-3001, has produced varietal wines since 1975. The **Gorge Heritage Museum**, 202 E. Humboldt St., Bingen, ☎ 509/493-3573, is housed in a 1911 Methodist church.

Chehalis

Claquato Church on Stern Road in Chehalis is one of the oldest churches in the state. Nearby, the **John R. Jackson House State Historic Site** at Jackson's Prairie, a small 1845 log cabin, was an important meeting place during the organization of the Washington Territory, a stopover for pioneer travelers, and once served as the Jackson County Courthouse.

Cle Elum

When Theron Stafford, owner of the Stafford General Mercantile Store, placed the first telephone call from Cle Elum on April 5, 1901, there were fewer than 800,000 telephones in the entire United States. When Mayor Ray Owens placed the town's first dial telephone call on September 18, 1966, there were over 96 million. Today, the town recognizes that accomplishment at the **Cle Elum Historical Telephone Museum**, 221 E. First St., ☎ 509/674-5702. The museum is open between 9 AM and 4 PM from Tuesday through Friday and between noon and 4 PM on Saturdays, Sundays, and Mondays from Memorial Day to Labor Day. Cle Elum means "swift water" in the Kittitas Indian language.

Husum

The **Charles Hooper Family Winery**, PO Box 215, Spring Creek Rd., Husum, WA 98623, ☎ 509/493-2324, welcomes visitors.

Kalama

Kalama, named for a native Hawaiian who married the daughter of a Nisqually Indian chief and settled the area, has the largest single-tree totem pole in the world, a 149-foot specimen that sits in Marine Park. The town also had the first fish hatchery in the state, since replaced by two newer hatcheries. Some 100 antique dealers have shops along North First Street, and **Pyramid Breweries**, 110 W. Marine Dr., ☎ 360/673-2962, offers informal tours and tastings.

Kelso

Cowlitz County Historical Museum, 405 Allen St., Kelso, WA 98626, ☎ 360/577-3119, is open between 9 AM and 5 PM Tuesday through Saturday and between 1 and 5 PM on Sunday. The **Kelso Visitor & Volcano Information Center**, 105 Minor Rd., ☎ 360/577-8058, which is open daily between 9 AM and 5 PM, has a 15-foot scale model of Mount St. Helens and the Toutle River Valley, which is explained in a recorded narrative.

La Center

Salishan Vineyards, North Fork Road, La Center, WA, ☎ 360/263-2713, are open between 1 and 5 PM on Saturdays and Sundays from May through December.

Longview

One of the largest planned cities in America, Longview is where the pioneer settlers met in 1852 at a place now called the **Monticello Convention Site** to petition for a separate territory north of the Columbia River, a petition that was granted the following year. Near the downtown Civic Center is **Nutty Narrows Bridge**, a 60-foot sky-bridge designed to provide squirrels with a safe passage over Olympia Way. Tours of the **Port of Longview** are available. **Charles W. Bingham Forest Learning Center**, ☎ 360/414-3439, features exhibits provided by Weyerhaeuser Co. and is open daily between 10 AM and 7 PM from May through October.

Mount St. Helens

Mount St. Helens, 207 Fourth Ave. North, Kelso, WA 98626, ☎ 360/577-3137, E-mail cc2rism@teleport.com, operates the **Hoffstadt Bluffs Visitor Center**, 27 miles east of I-5 at Exit 49. The center has a restaurant and is open year-around. **Mount St. Helens Cinedome Theater**, 1239 Mount St. Helens Way NE, Castle Rock, WA 98611, ☎ 360/274-8000, displays a 25-minute film about the 1980 eruption on a large screen and with "trembling seats" every 45 minutes from May through October beginning at 9 AM. The **Mount St. Helens Observatory** opened in April 1997.

Randle

Layser Cave was discovered on Lone Tree Mountain near Randle by Tim Layser in 1982. The cave, apparently undisturbed for 7,000 years until it was found, contained stone tools and animal bones. A 20-minute video, *Layser Cave: Silent Voice Vital Clues*, can be borrowed from the Randle Ranger Station, ☎ 206/497-7565.

Ridgefield

Ridgefield National Wildlife Refuge, ☎ 360/887-4106, near Ridgefield, contains over 3,000 acres of ponds, fields, and pastures. The two-mile self-guided Oaks-to-Wetlands Wildlife Foot Trail gives access to fishing, hiking, and opportunities to view deer, beaver, otter, and birds. No off-road vehicles are allowed.

Roslyn

Roslyn is a one-time mining community that began with the discovery of coal in the 1880s and peaked around 1910 with a population of 4,000. The **City Hall** was built in 1903 as a YMCA that had many advanced features for its time, including a gym, a bowling alley, and a swimming pool. **Brick Tavern**, the oldest (1898) operating saloon in the state, has a running-water spittoon. Both the **Mt. Pisgah Presbyterian Church** and the **Immaculate Conception Catholic Church** are over a century old, and the latter was featured in Stanley Kramer's 1978 movie *The Runner Stumbles,* starring Dick Van Dyke, Kathleen Quinlan, Beau Bridges, and Maureen Stapleton. Other scenes were shot in Brick Tavern, which also played a major role in the story line of TV's *Northern Exposure*. Twenty-five separate ethnic and fraternal lodge cemeteries are on the mountainside west of town. The **Roslyn Museum**, 203 Pennsylvania Ave, ☎ 509/649-2776, is open daily between 1:00 and 4:00 PM.

Snoqualmie

Northwest Railway Museum, 38625 SE King St., PO Box 459, Snoqualmie, WA 98065-0459, ☎ 425/746-4025, is open between 10 AM and 5 PM daily from July 1 to Labor Day and between 10 AM and 5 from Thursday through Monday the rest of the year.

Vancouver

Vancouver also has a rail museum: **SP&S Railway Museum**, 1511 Main St., Vancouver, WA 98668, ☎ 503/244-8822, which is open between 1 and 5 PM Tuesday through Saturday.

Fort Vancouver National Historic Site, 1501 E. Evergreen Blvd., Vancouver, WA 98668, ☎ 360/696-7655, is a reconstructed fort near the Columbia River. There is a Visitor Center, you can tour a blacksmith's shop and see a vintage garden, and you can taste fresh-baked bread made in frontier ovens.

Vancouver Barracks (not to be confused with Fort Vancouver) was a part of **Camp Vancouver**, built in 1849. Phillip Sheridan, Ulysses S. Grant, George C. Marshall, and Omar Bradley all served at Camp Vancouver during their careers. **Officers' Row**, ☎ 360/693-3103, contains 21 Victorian-era homes built for US Army officers between 1850 and 1906. The first house built was constructed for the commanding officer, and although Grant was the quartermaster, not the commanding officer, when he served there in the 1850s, the house has been known as the **Grant House** since Grant's presidency. Although Grant never lived in the house, he did visit it often. The house served as an officers' club for 25 years, after the **George C. Marshall House**, an 1886 Queen Anne, replaced the Grant House as the commanding officer's home. From 1936-38, Marshall was the commanding officer here and lived in the house.

Old Apple Tree Park, Columbia Way east of I-5 in Vancouver, contains the Old Apple Tree, "great grandfather of the Washington apple industry." Planted in 1826, the tree still bears fruit.

White Salmon

Mount Brook and **Snowden** are ghost towns northeast of White Salmon on Route H1000. Mount Brook has a schoolhouse that dates from 1910, and the one in Snowden dates from 1915.

Winthrop

Winthrop captures the feeling of the Old West with rows of false-fronted buildings, wooden sidewalks, and old-fashioned street lights along the main street. "The Castle," now the **Shafer Museum**, is the former home of pioneer Guy Waring, whose roommate at Harvard was Owen Wister, author of *The Virginian*, America's first western novel. Wister wrote the novel while honeymooning in Winthrop. Other local points of interest are **Methow Wildlife Area**, ☎ 509/996-2559; **Pearrygin State Park**, ☎ 509/996-2370; and **White Buck Museum** on Riverside Avenue, ☎ 509/996-3505.

Woodland

The 1876 **Cedar Creek Grist Mill**, ☎ 360/225-9552, located on Grist Mill Road off NE Cedar Creek Road, occupies the south side of Lewis River 10 miles east of Woodland and is still in operation. The mill is open on weekends in the summer, and volunteers demonstrate the way wheat is ground into flour. The **Lewis River** has dozens of picturesque waterfalls. **Ape Cave** is the longest lava tube in the US (12,810 feet), but you'll need a flashlight or a lantern if you want to see it. The 5.5-acre **Hulda Klager Lilac Garden**, ☎ 360/225-8996, is open from dawn to dusk daily. The best displays occur during the last week in April and the first week in May.

Yacolt

The red brick city hall in Yacolt has a classic Old West jail that is open on weekdays.

Where to Stay

Ashford

Nisqually Lodge, 31609 State Route 706, Ashford, WA 98304, ☎ 360/569-8804, fax 360/569-2435, $-$$, is near the entrance to Mt. Rainier National park.

Mount Rainier Guest Services, PO Box 108, Ashford, WA 98304, ☎ 206/569-2275, Web site www.mashell.com/rainier.guest/guestsv.html, manages both the Paradise Inn and the National Park Inn. **Paradise Inn** provides views of Mt. Rainier and Nisqually Glacier, and is open from late spring through early fall. The inn features open-beamed cathedral ceilings, hand-crafted Indian rugs, parquet wood floors, and a Sunday brunch that is served between 11 AM and 2:30 PM from June to October. **National Park Inn** in Longmire, renovated in 1990, is smaller than Paradise Inn and acts as a ski center during the winter.

Leavenworth

Alpen Rose Inn, 500 Alpine Pl., Leavenworth, WA 98826, ☎ 509/548-3000 or 800/582-2474, fax 509/548-7332, $-$$, is a small hotel with 40 rooms. The three-story inn has an elevator and a small heated pool in season. A full breakfast and evening desserts are provided.

Linderhof Motor Inn, 690 Hwy 2, Leavenworth, WA 98826, ☎ 509/548-5283 or 800/828-5680, fax 509/548-6616, $-$$, has 32 rooms including 10 two-bedroom units and some family units with kitchenettes. The rooms have fireplaces, in-room spas, a seasonal swimming pool, and a complimentary continental breakfast.

Enzian Motor Inn, 590 Hwy 2, Leavenworth, WA 98826, ☎ 509/548-5269, fax 509/548-5269, $$-$$$, has 104 rooms. Nine units have a fireplace and a spa, and two have a fireplace only.

Longmire

National Park Inn, PO Box 108, Longmire, WA 98304, ☎ 360/569-2275, fax 360/569-2275, Web site www.guestservices.com/rainier, $-$$, is six miles from the southwestern entrance to Mount Rainier. The two-story facility has just 25 rooms. The restaurant, Paradise Inn, is open from 7 AM to 8 PM daily.

Packwood

Cowlitz River Lodge, 13069 US 12, Packwood, WA 98361, ☎ 360/494-4444, fax 360/494-2075, $-$$, is located near Mount St. Helens.

■ Camping

Washington State Park information: ☎ 800/452-5687.

National Campground Reservation System: ☎ 800/280-2267.

Forest Service campgrounds in central Washington normally are open from May 1 through mid-October.

A number of campgrounds are located in the **Columbia River Gorge** area. **Beaver** is located 12.2 miles north off Route 14 on Wind River Hwy at **Carson**, and provides opportunities for fishing, hiking, and mushroom picking. **Goose Lake**, 20 miles north of Route 14 near **Willard**, features good fishing and a lava bed. Also near Willard on Route 18 is **Moss Creek**, another good fishing site, and **Oklahoma**, which offers both fishing and hiking. **Panther**, on Wind River Highway near Carson, can provide fishing, hiking, and sightseeing opportunities. Another park on Wind River Highway near Carson is **Paradise Creek**, popular for fishing, hiking, wildlife viewing, and sightseeing. **Peterson Prairie** is on Route 24 seven miles west of Trout Lake, and offers berry picking as well as hiking.

Eco Park, 14000 Spirit Lake Hwy, PO Box 149, **Toutle**, WA 98649, ☎ 360/274-6542, fax 360/274-8437, is the world's first tent-and-breakfast. The park has 90 acres of trails. The operators are survivors of the Mount St. Helens eruption, where they owned the Spirit Lake Lodge, which was lost in the eruption.

Where to Eat

Leavenworth

Andreas Keller Bavaria Haus, 829 Front St., PO Box 694, Leavenworth, WA 98826, ☎ 509/548-6000, $-$$, occupies a downstairs location (keller means "cellar" in German) and advertises the town's "most authentic" Bavarian food. It's a great place to have Mittagessen (lunch) on wieners, bratwurst, knackwurst, and Bauernteller. Live music is often offered. *Guten Appetit!*

Longview

The Rutherglen Mansion, 420 Rutherglen Rd., Longview, WA, ☎ 360/425-5816, $$, sits 600 feet above the Columbia Valley and affords great views of the river, the town, and Mount St. Helens. Try the Champagne salmon, an eight-ounce salmon fillet, baked and topped with champagne pippin sauce.

Vancouver

Hidden House, 100 W. 13th St., Vancouver, WA, ☎ 360/696-2847, $$, serves lunch from Monday through Friday and dinner from 5 PM, Tuesday through Sunday. Located in a charming 1885 house, the restaurant serves such tempting appetizers as Smoked Treasures of the Sea – salmon filet and mussels served with bagels and cream cheese – and such equally mouth-watering dinners as Cuervo Prawns – black tiger prawns sauteed with fresh lime and garlic, then flashed with dark tequila.

Sheldon's Cafe at the Grant House, 1101 Officer's Row (Evergreen Blvd.), Vancouver, WA, ☎ 360/699-1213, $$, serves entrees representing various geographical regions: New England, the Northwest, the Midwest, and the South.

Information Sources

To order maps of the Washington and Oregon National Forests, Wilderness Areas, and Ranger Districts, contact **Mount Baker-Snoqualmie National Forest**, 21905 64th Ave. West, Mountlake Terrace, WA 98043, ☎ 206/775-9702. Wilderness Areas in the Mount Baker-Snoqualmie National Forest extend over 140 miles along the western slopes of the Cascade Mountains from the Canadian border to the northern boundary of Mt. Rainier National Park.

State Parks & Recreation Commission, 7150 Clearwater Ln., Olympia, WA 92504, ☎ 360/902-8500 or 800/233-0321.

Outdoor Recreation Information Center, 222 Yale Ave. N, Seattle, WA 98109, ☎ 206/470-4080 or 800/365-2267.

Tourism Lewis County, 500 NW Chamber of Commerce Way, Chehalis, WA 98532, ☎ 360/748-8885 or 800/525-3323, fax 360/748-8763.

Vancouver/Clark County Visitors & Information Bureau, 404 E. 15th St., #11, Vancouver, WA 98663, ☎ 360/693-1313 or 800/377-7084.

Mount Adams Chamber of Commerce, PO Box 449, White Salmon, WA 98672, ☎ 509/493-3630.

Mount Adams Ranger Station, 2455 Hwy 141, Trout Lake, WA 98650, ☎ 509/395-3400

Mount Rainier, PO Box 108, Ashford, WA 98304-0109, ☎ 360/569-2275, fax 360/569-2770, Web site www.mashell.com/rainier.guest/gustsv.htrol.

Winthrop Forest Service & Visitor Center, ☎ 509/996-4000, fax 509/996-4060, E-mail fsinfo@methow.com.

Norse Peak is in the White River Ranger District, 857 Roosevelt Ave. E, Enumclaw, WA 98022, ☎ 360/825-6585. **Clearwater** also is in the White River Ranger District. **Alpine Lakes** is in the Skykomish Ranger District, 74920 NE Stevens Pass Hwy, PO Box 305, Skykomish, WA 98288, ☎ 360/677-2414; the North Bend Ranger District, 42404 SE North Bend Way, North Bend, WA 98045, ☎ 206/888/1421; the Cle Elum Ranger District, 803 W. 2nd St., Cle Ulum 98922, ☎ 509/674-4411; and the Leavenworth Ranger District, 600 Sherbourne, Leavenworth 98826, ☎ 509/548-6977.

Glacier Peak is in the Darrington Ranger District, 1405 Emmens St., Darrington, WA 98241, ☎ 360/436-1155; the Mount Baker Ranger District, 2105 Hwy 20, Sedro Woolley, WA 98284, ☎ 856-5700; the Lake Wenatchee Ranger District, 22976 St. Hwy 207, Leavenworth 98826, ☎ 509/763-3103; the Entiat Ranger District, 2108 Entiat Way, PO Box 476, Entiat 98822, ☎ 509/784-1511; and the Chelan Ranger District, 428 W. Woodin Ave., Rt. 2, Box 680, Chelan 98816, ☎ 509/682-2576.

Henry M. Jackson is in the Skykomish Ranger District and the Darrington Ranger District. **Noisy-Diobsud** is in the Mount Baker Ranger District; **Boulder River**, the Darrington Ranger District; and Mount Baker, the Mount Baker Ranger District.

Information about the **Columbia River Gorge** and its neighboring communities is available from a number of sources, including **Columbia River Gorge Visitors Assn.**, PO Box 1037, Stevenson, WA 98648,

☎ 800/98-GORGE; **Columbia Gorge Interpretive Center**, 990 SW Rock Creek Dr., Stevenson, WA 98648, ☎ 509/427-8211; and **Columbia River Gorge Commission**, PO Box 730, White Salmon, WA 98672, ☎ 509/493-3323.

Information about **Mount St. Helens** can be obtained from **Mount St. Helens National Volcanic Monument**, 42218 NE Yale Bridge Rd., Amboy, WA 98601, ☎ 360/750-3903 or 750-3900; **Mount St. Helens National Volcanic Monument Visitor Center**, 3029 Spirit Lake Hwy, Castle Rock, WA 98611, ☎ 206/274-2103 or 274-2100; and **Mount St. Helens National Volcanic Monument Visitor Center**, 5304 Spirit Lake Hwy, Toutle, WA 98649, ☎ 206/274-7988.

Gifford Pinchot National Forest, 10600 NE 51st Circle, Vancouver, WA 98682, ☎ 360/891-5000, encompasses **Randle Ranger District**, Randle, WA 98377, ☎ 360/497-7565; **Wind River Ranger District**, Carson, WA 98610, ☎ 509/427-5645; **Packwood Ranger District**, Packwood, WA 98361, ☎ 360/494-5515; and **Mount Adams Ranger District**, Trout Lake, WA 98650, ☎ 509/395-2501.

Eastern Washington

Eastern Washington is agricultural country from the wheat fields in The Palouse to the seemingly endless farmlands that lie between Wenatchee and Spokane, and thence to the ranching country in the Okanogan Highlands.

The southern region is largely a vast basaltic plateau, created from lava flows and sculpted by the runoff of the last Ice Age. The mountains in the northern region, the Kettles and the Selkirks, are an extension of the northern Rockies.

The most prominent feature in the region, however, is the Columbia River, which flows south out of Canada until it reaches the mighty Columbia River Gorge, which constitutes Washington's border with Oregon, and then heads westward to the sea.

Although the Columbia River flows for more than 600 miles through the United States, dams have turned the once-turbulent river into a series of slack-water lakes. The only stretch that continues to flow freely is the 51-mile portion between Richland and the Priest Rapids Dam, known locally as the Hanford Reach.

Getting Around

From the Oregon border to the south, US 395 knifes across southeastern Washington to Spokane and then turns northward to the Canadian border.

US 195 runs inside the state's eastern border between southwestern Idaho and Spokane.

I-90 goes east from Ellensburg to Spokane and the Idaho state line, merging with US 395 near Ritzville.

US 2 crosses the Cascades and enters eastern Washington at Wenatchee, where it briefly turns northward and then continues in an easterly direction to Spokane.

US 97 heads north from the Columbia River Gorge, merges with I-82 near Toppenish, separates itself again at Ellensburg, and winds its way erratically northward to the Canadian border. The route parallels the old Cariboo Trail, which carried cattle between Pasco and Canada during the 1860s and later served the adventurers attracted by the Gold Rush.

I-82 links I-84, which parallels the Columbia River Gorge on the Oregon side of the border, and I-90 at Ellensburg.

Airports

With sparsely populated cities spread well apart, eastern Washington is well suited to air transportation. Consequently, many relatively small communities have landing fields and most of them have a charter service of some sort that makes it possible to get to a major air center rather quickly.

Brewster has an airport three miles from town on Route 97 North that has 5,000 feet of lighted runway.

Pangborn Memorial Airport on Grant Road in **East Wenatchee** provides daily commercial airline service.

Eastern Washington

Chelan Airways, Box W, **Chelan** (*She-LAN*), WA 98816, ☎ 509/682-5555, has an air taxi, charters flightseeing excursions, provides biplane rides, and flies a floatplane into the isolated little town of Stehekin.

The **Electric City/Grand Coulee** area has an airport, and there are others in **Ephrata**, in **Goldendale**, and north of **Kauspel** in Pend Oreille (*Pond-er-ray*).

Kettle Falls has a field, as does **Laurier** at the Canadian border.

Moses Lake has two airports, including Grant County Airport (formerly Larson Air Force Base), which has the second longest runway west of the Mississippi River (13,500 feet) and is the fourth busiest airport in the state.

The **Omak** Municipal airport has a 4,650-foot paved and lighted runway. The **Othello** airport has a 4,000-foot paved and lighted runway. The Tri-Cities Airport in **Pasco** is just off 4th Avenue.

Ferry County Airport, six miles northeast of **Republic**, has a 3,500-foot paved and lighted runway.

Spokane International Airport is the second largest field in the state and handles over 100 flights per day.

Methow Valley State Airport is in **Twisp**, and **Walla Walla** has two air fields.

Yakima Municipal Airport is located off W. Washington Avenue.

Railroads

Rail service also is available in this part of Washington. Both the Burlington Northern and the Union Pacific make regular stops in **Spokane**, for example.

Touring

Brewster

It was just north of Brewster that John Jacob Astor's Pacific Fur Co. established its first American post in Washington in 1811.

Where **Chelan** now stands, the Indians had a winter village called Yenmusi `Tsa ("rainbow robe"). Later, the Army's Camp Chelan was built here. Lake Chelan is the third deepest lake in the United States.

Cheney

Eastern Washington University is based in Cheney.

Colfax

Colfax, the seat of Whitman County, is in the southeastern portion of the state, known as The Palouse (from the French pelouse, meaning "green grassland"). The name also applied to a tribe of Indians and a river, and the spotted horses ridden by the Indians became known as Palouse or Palousey horses. In time, a "Palousey" became known as an Appaloosa.

The town of Colfax was named for Schuyler Colfax, who was vice president of the United States during President Grant's first administration (1869-73).

Ellensburg

Ellenburg was known as Robbers Roost in the 1870s. The community of **Ephrata** calls itself the "Land of Contagious Smiles."

George

George was named for... well... it IS George *Washington*, isn't it? Every Fourth of July, the town produces what they claims to be the world's largest cherry pie.

Kennewick

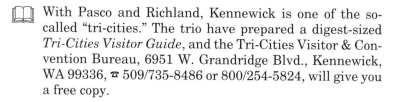 With Pasco and Richland, Kennewick is one of the so-called "tri-cities." The trio have prepared a digest-sized *Tri-Cities Visitor Guide*, and the Tri-Cities Visitor & Convention Bureau, 6951 W. Grandridge Blvd., Kennewick, WA 99336, ☎ 509/735-8486 or 800/254-5824, will give you a free copy.

Kettle Falls

The area around Kettle Falls is famous for its orchards, which produce cherries, apricots, peaches, nectarines, prune plums, and apples. Grapes, raspberries, and blackberries also come from the area. As you enter the town, there's a sign that says: "Kettle Falls: 1256 Friendly People and One Grouch." That kinda tells you something.

When Grand Coulee Dam was built between 1939 and 1941, Kettle Falls and other communities along the Columbia River were forced to evacuate. Many of the people moved to nearby Meyers Falls, four miles away, which has since been renamed Kettle Falls. Apparently, the grouch didn't want to move.

Moses Lake

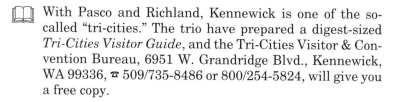 Moses Lake has prepared a useful digest-sized book called *Moses Lake: Washington's Great Escape Visitor's Guide*. Once more, the Chamber of Commerce, 324 S. Pioneer Way, Moses Lake, WA 98837, ☎ 509/765-7888 or 800/992-6234, will be happy to give you a free copy.

Odessa

Odessa is in a region of eastern Washington known as the "scablands."

Pateros

Pateros, where the Methow River joins the Columbia River, was settled in 1884, but it was inundated in 1966 by the waters behind Wells Dam that formed Lake Pateros.

Pullman

Pullman is surrounded by yellow fields of rapeseed, which is used to make a cooking oil.

Ritzville

Ritzville has prepared a pocket-sized brochure that provides a map and directions for a self-guided tour. Ask the Chamber of Commerce for a free copy.

Soap Lake

Soap Lake, the "City of Mineral Waters," located on the last lake in the Coulee chain, 50 miles south of the dam, was called Smokiam (healing waters) by the Indians.

Spokane

Spokane (*Spo-can*), the biggest city in the region, derived its name from an Indian word meaning "children of the Sun." Often called "the Lilac City," the town hosts a **Lilac Festival**, ☎ 509/326-3339, each spring. In 1910, Father's Day was founded here by Sonora Smart Dodd, and President Woodrow Wilson proclaimed the day a national holiday in 1916.

Toppenish

Toppenish, "Where the West Still Lives," has 40 murals scattered throughout town, giving rise to the name "The City of Murals."

Twisp

Twisp (a modification of the Indian word *T-wapsp*, meaning "yellow jacket" or *Twistsp*, "the sound of a buzzing wasp") is the sunflower capital of the state.

Union Gap

Union Gap, the first municipality in Yakima County and the county seat until 1887, was known by the Indians as Pahoticute ("place where two mountain heads come together"). Early settlers called it Two Buttes, but after the Civil War, a federal survey party called it Union Gap. In 1883, the town was incorporated as Yakima City, but when some of the residents wouldn't sell their land to the Northern Pacific Railroad, the railroad laid out a new townsite, which it called North Yakima. In 1917, North Yakima became Yakima, and Yakima City once more became Union Gap.

Walla Walla

Walla Walla is the home of Walla Walla sweets, one of the sweetest tasting onions in the world.

Wenatchee

Wenatchee took its name from the Indian word Wat-Nat-Chee, meaning "robe of the rainbow."

Yakima

 In Yakima, the Yakima Valley Visitors & Convention Bureau, 10 N. 8th St., Yakima, WA 98901-2515, ☎ 509/575-1300 or 800/221-0751, fax 509/575-6252, can provide you with a free booklet called *Circle Tours*, which describes 12 day-trips through the surrounding area.

Adventures

■ On Foot

Hiking

 Turnbull National Wildlife Refuge, South 26010 Smith Rd., **Cheney**, WA 99004, ☎ 509/235-4723, is laced with trails on which bicycles and motorized vehicles are not permitted. The refuge is open during daylight hours only and a small fee is charged. **Blackhorse Lake**, **Kappel Lake**, and **Pine Lakes**, ☎ 509/235-4723, are all within the refuge.

Clearwater and Snake River National Recreational Trail consists of 16 miles of paved, landscaped pathways that connect **Clarkston** with Lewiston, ID, across the river. **Apple Capital Recreational Loop** is an 11-mile paved hiking and biking trail that runs along both sides of the Columbia River near **East Wenatchee**.

The Pinnacles, a geological feature on which mountain climbers like to practice, is in **George**. Across a chasm from The Pinnacles is "the disappearing waterfall."

Brooks Memorial State Park, Rt. 1, Box 136, **Goldendale**, WA 98620, is 13 miles north of town off US 97. The park has 45 campsites, good fishing, and nine miles of hiking trails. Beaver frequent the Klickitat River, and the town has an **Environmental Learning Center** (for more information, contact the Washington State Parks & Recreation Commission, 7150 Clenwater Lane, KY-11, Olympia, WA 98504-5711, ☎ 360/902-8600).

The 600-acre **Columbia River Park** near **Kennewick** has 5.5 miles of waterfront with nature trails and hiking/biking trails.

Kettle Falls is a prime area for rockhounding. It also boasts 35 challenging hiking trails, two interpretive trails, 25 backpacking trails, and two natural history trails in the area. Peregrine falcons are often seen and, during the winter, bald eagles. Within the Kettle Falls Ranger District, US Forest Service, 555 W. 11th St., Kettle Falls, WA, ☎ 509/738-6111, there are more than 50 miles of trails, their most recent improvement being the extension of **Hoodoo Canyon Trail #17**, which is open to hikers and mountain bikers, through the canyon to Trout Lake Campground, increasing the length of the trail from 1.7 miles to 4.7 miles.

Paradise Llama Ranch, ☎ 509/982-2404, popular among backpackers and hikers, is located 12 miles north of Odessa. **Omak** is a good place to go mushroom hunting in the spring.

With 12 national parks within a day's drive, **Spokane** is a great place from which to take day-trips. The Visitor Center can supply you with a free pocket-sized brochure, *Spokane Area Hiking*, that describes 13 hikes in the area. The 37-mile **Centennial Trail** follows the Spokane River from the 100-acre Riverfront Park to Coeur d'Alene, ID.

Sherman Park in **Union Gap** has some nature trails, and the **Yakima Greenway Path** is a 10-mile walking/biking system of paths that includes **Noel Pathway** between Sarg Hubbard and Sherman parks, **Jewett Pathway** between Nob Hill and Valley Mall Boulevard, and **Plath Path** along the Naches River.

A pleasant path runs from **Rooks Park** to Cambridge Drive (College Place) in **Walla Walla**. The path can be used for either hiking or biking.

> The Chamber of Commerce can provide you with a free pocket-sized brochure produced by the City Parks & Recreation Department, *Parks in Walla Walla*, that names and locates all of the town's parks and describes their facilities.

Boulder Cave on US 410 (Chinook Pass Highway) near **Yakima** is a 25,000-year-old basalt formation with an accessible entry. **Cowiche Canyon Conservancy**, PO Box 877, Yakima, WA 98907, a secluded basalt and andesite canyon northwest of town, has an unpaved trail along a former railway bed that crosses Cowiche Creek 11 times. From January through March, hundreds of elk feed in the **Oak Creek Wildlife Recreation Area** nearby.

> The Lake Chelan Chamber of Commerce, 102 E. Johnson, PO Box 216, **Chelan**, WA 98816, ☎ 509/682-3503 or 800/4CHELAN, fax 509/682-3538, has a free pocket-sized brochure, *Chelan County PUD* [Public Utility District] *Park Guide*, that describes 15 parks between Chelan and Wenatchee.

■ On Horseback

Rodeos

Head 'em up; move 'em out. Move 'em out; head 'em up. During rodeo season, it's never hard to find some action in this part of the Rawhide Country.

Spokane kicks off the festivities with the **Wrangler Pro Classic**, ☎ 509/325-7328 or 800/325-7328, held in the Arena each February. In March, **Walla Walla** picks up the pace with the annual **Community College Rodeo**. In mid-April, there's the **Gonzaga University Rodeo**, ☎ 509/328-4220, at the Fairgrounds in **Spokane** (for those who remember, Gonzaga was where Bing Crosby went to school). Also in April, the **Keller Junior Rodeo** is staged in **Keller**.

Grand Coulee hosts a rodeo on the second weekend in May; **Arden** has the annual **Old Timers Rodeo,** and **Springdale** stages the **Frontier Days Pee-Wee Rodeo**, ☎ 509/258-4548, in mid-May; and **Kennewick** holds not one, but *two* **Mexican Rodeos**, ☎ 509/586-9211, in May at the Benton-Franklin Fairgrounds.

On the first weekend in June, **Barrel Derby Days** are held in **Curlew**. The following weekend, the annual **Alder Creek Pioneer Picnic & Rodeo** is held in **Cleveland**. In mid-June, there's a **PRCA Rodeo**, ☎ 509/684-4849, at the Northeast Washington Fairgrounds in **Colville** and a **PWRA Rodeo**, ☎ 509/775-3387, at the Ferry County Fairgrounds in **Republic**.

The **Glenwood Rodeo Association**, ☎ 509/364-3427, has been staging rodeos on the Glenwood Rodeo Grounds since 1934. Their **"Ketchum Kalf" NPRA Rodeo** is held there every Father's Day weekend.

Also scheduled in June are the annual **Yakama All-Indian Rodeo** in **White Swan** and the **PWRA Rodeo**, ☎ 509/447-5812, in **Newport**. Newport also hosts an annual **Junior Rodeo**, ☎ 208/437-2095 or 437-2365, in mid-July.

Chesaw holds its rodeo on the Fourth of July, and the annual **Toppenish Pow Wow & Rodeo**, PO Box 127, **Toppenish**, WA 98948, ☎ 509/865-3262 or 865-5313, also is held on the Fourth of July. The Toppenish event is held on the rodeo grounds on South Division Street and includes a Pioneer Fair, an Indian Village, and a parade. The **Eagles Junior Rodeo** is staged in Toppenish during mid-July.

The **Wrangler Round-Up Junior Rodeo**, ☎ 509/775-2091, held at the Ferry County Fairgrounds in **Republic**, also is held in mid-July, and **Kennewick** stages two **Mexican Rodeos** at the Benton-Franklin Fairgrounds in July.

A rodeo is held on the **Cheney** Rodeo Grounds, ☎ 509/235-4848, on the second weekend in July. **Manson**'s **Junior Rodeo** and **WRA Rodeo** are held in July. **Springdale**'s **Frontier Days Rodeo & Celebration**, ☎ 509/258-4548, is held in July, and **Chelan** hosts its annual rodeo on the last weekend in July.

Come August, there's the **Pend Oreille County Fair & Rodeo**, ☎ 509/445-1367, 445-1128, or 445-1258, in **Cusick**; the **Grant County Fair & Rodeo** in **Moses Lake**; and the **Lincoln County Fair & Rodeo** in **Odessa**.

The **Omak Stampede & World Famous Suicide Race**, Box 2028, Omak, WA 98841, ☎ 826-1983, 826-1002, or 800/933-6625, is held on the town's Stampede Grounds on the second weekend in August. It includes a 100-tepee Indian encampment, Indian costumes and dancing, the Indian stick game (a form of gambling), and a "suicide race" that has been featured on TV's *Ripley's Believe It of Not*, in Disney's 1989 film *Run, Appaloosa, Run*, and on ESPN's *Amazing Games,* in 1992.

Ellensburg has barrel racing and roping competitions on the Fairgrounds throughout the year, but the **Ellensburg Posse/KCF Junior Rodeo** is held in August and the **Kittitas County Fair & Ellensburg Rodeo**, 512 N. Poplar, PO Box 777, Ellensburg, WA 98926, ☎ 509/962-7639, 800/426-5340, or 800/637-2444, fax 509/962-7830, started in 1923, is held every Labor Day weekend. **Walla Walla** holds its **Frontier Days Parade & Rodeo** on Labor Day weekend also, and **Goldendale** stages the **Klickitat County Fair & Rodeo** on the fourth weekend in August.

Othello hosts the **Adams County Fair and PRCA Rodeo** every summer.

The annual **Benton-Franklin County Fair & Horse Heaven Round-Up Rodeo** is held on the County Fairgrounds in **Kennewick** each August. The city also stages twice-a-month **Tri-County Barrel Racing** competitions from April through September.

Pro West Rodeo hits **Newport** in September, the same month the **Southeastern Washington Fair & Rodeo** is held in **Walla Walla** and the **Central Washington State Fair & Rodeo**, ☎ 509/248-7160, comes to **Yakima**.

Horse Shows & Races

A wide variety of other events related to horses can be found throughout eastern Washington throughout the year. **Panorama Gold Cup Horse Show**, ☎ 509/738-2819, is held on the Northeast Washington Fairgrounds in **Colville** in late June. The **Cusic Classic Horse Show**, ☎ 509/447-2401, occupies the Pend Oreille County Fairgrounds in **Cusick** in July.

Ellensburg keeps its fairgrounds occupied with an **Appaloosa Horse Show** in May, two **Posse Youth Horse Shows** in June and July, a **4-H Horse Show** in August, and the **4-H Open Horse Show** in October.

Quarterhorse and thoroughbred horse racing is conducted from February through May and again in September and October at **Sundown Racetrack** on the Benton-Franklin County Fairgrounds, 1500 S. Oak St., **Kennewick**, ☎ 509/586-9211 or 582-5434. Kennewick also conducts **Finely Saddle Club Horse Events** in April and October, a **4-H Merit Horse Show** in May, and a **Miniature Horse Show** in August.

Reardon presents the annual **Mule Days**, ☎ 509/796-4703, at the end of May.

Ferry County Fairgrounds, ☎ 509/775-3387, in **Republic** hosts a **Draft Horse Show** in mid-July, a **4-H Horse Show** in August, and a **Cattle Roundup** in October.

In **Spokane**, **Playfair Racing**, East Main and North Altamont Streets, ☎ 509/534-0505, presents horse races from mid-August to December. At the Spokane Fairgrounds, the **Inland Northwest Paint Horse Show**, ☎ 509/448-6019, is held in April; the **Inland Empire Arabian Show**, ☎ 509/238-6597, is held in May; the **Inland Empire Quarter Horse Show**, ☎ 509/ 466-6340, is held in June; and the **Inland Empire Tennessee Walker Horse Show**, ☎ 509/244-3671, is held in August.

Rock'n Tomahawk Ranch, 2590 Upper Green Canyon Rd., **Ellensburg**, WA 98926, ☎ 509/962-2403, offers guided horse rides.

The **Heritage College Polo Tournament** in **White Swan** is held in mid-September. Horse racing is conducted by the Apple Tree Racing Assn. at **Yakima Meadows**, Yakima Fairgrounds, PO Box 213, **Yakima**, WA 98907, ☎ 509/248-3920, and the town also hosts an annual **Dressage Summer Classic**, ☎ 509/865-2244.

Riding

Indian Canyon Riding Stables, 4812 W. Canyon Dr., Spokane, WA, ☎ 509/624-4646, can rent you a horse. In **Toppenish**, a horse- or mule-drawn wagon will take you on a tour of the town's murals.

During the last weekend in April, **Twisp** stages the **Back Country Horsemen's Spring Ride**, and **North Cascades Outfitters**, ☎ 509/ 997-1015, provides horseback rides. There is a **Spring Race Meet**, ☎ 509/527-FAIR, at the fairgrounds in **Walla Walla,** and the community stages a number of horse shows each year.

North Western Lake Riding Stables, ☎ 509/493-4965, is located off Route 141 on Lakeview Drive in **White Salmon**. Open daily from 8 AM to sunset, the stables offer horse rides, pack trips, and access to trails in the adjoining Gifford Pinchot National Forest.

■ On Wheels

Auto Racing

Stock car races are held on alternating weekends during the summer in **Republic**, and the **Roving Gambler's Motorcycle Rally**, ☎ 509/775-3387 or 775-2704, is held in late May.

Spokane Raceway Park, 101 N. Hayford Rd., Spokane, WA 99204, ☎ 509/244-3663, offers drag and stock car racing every Saturday from May through September.

The annual **Wheelin' Walla Walla Weekend**, 33 E. Main St., Suite 213, **Walla Walla**, WA 99362, ☎ 509/529-8755, is held in September. The three-day event is limited to the first 400 entries, and is judged according to the car's year of manufacture, whether the car is custom or modified, sports car, best street rod, best muscle car, best paint, best engine, and farthest traveled. There also are categories of competition for motorcycles.

Yakima Speedway, 1600 Pacific Ave., **Yakima**, WA 98901, ☎ 509/248-0647, presents auto racing on a half-mile paved oval. **Renegade Raceway**, Parkato Road, **Wapato**, WA 98951, ☎ 509/877-4621, is a quarter-mile paved drag strip.

Biking

The Chamber of Commerce in **Chelan** can provide a free pocket-sized brochure, *Lake Chelan Public Trails*, prepared by the Public Trails Committee, PO Box 402, Chelan, WA 98816, that details the biking and hiking trails throughout the area. Similarly, the Chamber of Commerce in **George** can give you a free brochure called *The Greatest Dam Tour in the World* to guide you on a nice day trip past Grand Coulee Dam, seven Columbia River dams, and a host of other sights along the way.

The Visitor Center in **Spokane** has a free pocket-sized brochure, *Spokane Area Biking*, that describes six excellent rides throughout the region.

The Benton-Franklin Regional Council, PO Box 217, **Richland**, WA 99352, ☎ 509/943-9185, has published a *Tri-Cities Bicycle Guide Map* that can be obtained free of charge at the Chamber of Commerce.

The **Yakima Greenway**, which runs along the Yakima River, is an excellent trail for biking.

Wagons & Motorcycles

An hour-and-a-half **Conestoga Wagon Tour**, ☎ 509/865-2898, is offered in **Toppenish**.

Seven motorcycle trails can be found in the **Kettle Falls** area.

Rail Tours

The **Lions Excursion Train**, ☎ 509/446-4708, leaves the **Ione** depot at 11 AM, 1 PM, and 3 PM one weekend each month from Father's Day weekend (June) through October.

Toppenish Simcoe & Western Railroad, Toppenish Train Depot, ☎ 509/865-1911 or 575-4859, offers a 20-mile round trip from Harrah to White Swan. Special runs are made on the Fourth of July and Harrah Days, charters are available, and the line has a Pumpkin Run at Halloween and a Santa Train in December.

Yakima Valley Rail & Steam Museum, 10 Asotin Ave., PO Box 889, **Toppenish**, WA 98948, ☎ 509/865-1911 or 575-4821, fax 509/877-2996, has a variety of interesting exhibits for rail buffs.

Yakima Electric Railway Museum, 306 W. Pine St., PO Box 649, **Yakima**, WA 98907, ☎ 509/575-1700, features both guided and self-guided tours. The museum also has a trolley that goes through town, follows the roadside through the orchards north of town, crosses the Naches River, traverses the cliffs of Selah Gap, passes Convict's Cave, and descends into the town of Selah. The hour and 40-minute round trip includes a half-hour layover in Selah. The rides leave Yakima at 10 AM, noon, 2 PM, and 4 PM on Saturdays, Sundays, and holidays from early May to mid-October. Evening rides are offered at 7 PM on July and August weeknights.

■ On the Water

Rafting

All Rivers Adventures, PO Box 12, **Cashmere**, WA 98815, ☎ 509/782-2254 or 800/743-5628, guides whitewater rafting trips.

Four Seasons Outfitters, PO Box 1779, **Chelan**, WA 98816, ☎ 509/682-4571, 800/642-7334 (US), or 800/447-2651 (Canada), fax 509/682-3650, arranges raft adventures, day tours, night tours, and drift fishing excursions. Kayak rentals are available at **Don Morse Park** in Chelan.

 *In June 1997, two-time Olympic kayaker Richard Weiss (33) drowned on the White Salmon River near Trout Lake after going over a 15-foot waterfall. Weiss lived in nearby Hood River, OR, and was wearing a life jacket and a helmet at the time of his accident. Be careful!*

Hells Canyon near **Clarkston** is North America's deepest gorge, and is a popular place to go whitewater rafting, jet boating, sailing, windsurfing, kayaking, and waterskiing. **Beamers Hells Canyon Tours & Excursions**, 1451 Bridge St., Clarkston, WA 99403, ☎ 509/758-4800 or 800/522-6966, E-mail excursions@hellscanyontours.com, Web site www.hellscanyontours.com, offer day-trips traveling 100 miles up the Snake River to Rush Creek, overnight trips, mail runs, evening dinner cruises, and boat-and-float combinations. Their tours begin on the dock behind Quality Inn, 700 Port Dr., Clarkston.

AAA Rafting, 860 Hwy 141, PO Box 203, **Husum**, WA 98623, ☎ 509/493-2511 or 800/866-7238, guides whitewater rafting trips on the White Salmon, Deschutes, Wind, and Klickitat Rivers.

Rafting by Phil's, 1244 Hwy 141, **White Salmon**, WA 98672, ☎ 509/493-2641, takes whitewater rafting trips between April and September, with daily launches at 10 AM and 2 PM.

> The US Army Corps of Engineers has produced a free pocket-sized brochure, *Lower Snake River Recreation Guide,* that highlights recreational areas along the river between Lake Sacajawea and Clarkston. Contact Walla Walla District Corps of Engineers, Walla Walla, WA 99362-9265, ☎ 509/552-6711.

Cruises & Ferry Rides

The Tour Boat, PO Box 1119, **Chelan**, WA 98816-1119, ☎ 509/682-8287 or 800/243-0820, offers day or overnight trips, camping/hunting trips, dinner or picnic trips, and cruises, including an hour-and-20-minute cruise to Stehekin, from the Lake Chelan Marina.

Lake Chelan Boat Co., PO Box 186, Chelan, WA 98816, ☎ 509/682-2224 or 682-4584, operates *Lady of the Lake* for long scenic cruises and *Lady of the Lake II* and *Lady Express* for shorter trips. The longest trip leaves Chelan at 8:30 AM, arrives in Stehekin at noon, spends 90 minutes there, and then returns to Chelan at 6 PM.

Stehekin is an isolated community at the far end of Lake Chelan, 55 miles from Chelan and reachable only by boat, by airplane, or on foot. It has a public dock, a restaurant, a campground, a post office, a ranger station, and a visitor center. *Lady of the Lake* docks there, and Chelan Airways has established a floatplane moorage there. Wenatchee National Forest has produced a free pocket-sized brochure, *Discover Lake Chelan*, that outlines an extensive self-guided boat tour of the lake, along with a walking tour of Stehekin.

Gifford operates a free ferry across the Columbia River to Wilbur between 6:30 AM and 9:30 PM. **Keller** also operates a free ferry across Lake Roosevelt to Inchelium between 6 AM and 11 PM.

Columbia River Journeys, 303-D Casey Ave., PO Box 26, **Richland**, WA 99352, ☎ 509/943-0231, charters 4.5-hour cruises aboard a 26-passenger, shallow-draft river boat. Morning cruises leave daily at 8 AM from May through October. Afternoon cruises leave daily at 3 PM from July through Labor Day.

Lady of the Lake on Lake Chelan (Washington Tourism Dev).

Fishing

A number of outstanding fishing lakes can be found near **Cheney**. **Amber Lake**, which is 12.5 miles from town via Mullinix Road and Pine Springs Road, contains cutthroat and rainbow trout. **Badger Lake**, ☎ 509/235-2341, 10.5 miles from town, contains smallmouth bass as well as cutthroat and rainbow trout. **Chapman Lake**, ☎ 509/523-2221, is 12 miles from town via Cheney-Plaza Road, and holds kokanee salmon, largemouth bass, and rainbow trout. **Clear Lake**, ☎ 509/299-3830 or 299-3717, located eight miles from town via Salnave Road and Clear Lake Road, is popular for crappie, brown trout, largemouth bass, and rainbow trout. **Fish Lake**, ☎ 509/456-4730, in Fish Lake County Park only 3.3 miles from town via Cheney-Spokane Road, offers fishing for brook and German brown trout. **Fishtrap Lake**, ☎ 509/235-2284, 20 miles from town; **Hog Lake**, 18 miles from town; and **West Medical Lake**, ☎ 509/299-3921, 11.5 miles from town, all contain rainbow trout. **Medical Lake**, ☎ 509/299-7781, in Waterfront Park, holds German brown trout and largemouth bass. **Rock Lake** is 28 miles from town via Cheney-Plaza Road and Rock Lake Road and provides crappie, German brown trout, largemouth bass, and rainbow trout. **Silver Lake**, ☎ 509/ 299-7273 or 299-3223, contains German brown trout, largemouth bass, and rainbow trout. **Williams Lake**, ☎ 509/235-5212 or 235-2391, only 12 miles from town, has cutthroat, kamloops, and rainbow trout.

Lake Roosevelt has 630 miles of public coastline. Around **Davenport**, visitors can use one of 16 public boat ramps, enjoy six sandy beach campgrounds, and go houseboating, windsurfing, waterskiing, fishing, or hiking.

Potholes Reservoir, 18 miles southwest of **Moses Lake**, offers some of the best bass fishing in the state. Crappie, trout, walleye, and perch also are available. The lake, which is at the west end of O'Sullivan Dam, the longest earthen dam in the United States (3.5 miles), has over 120 miles of shoreline and covers 25,000 acres. **Cascade Water Rentals**, 8138 Scott Rd. NE, Moses Lake, WA 98837, ☎ 509/766-7075, rents fishing boats, canoes, pedal boats, and Sea Doos. **Mar Don Resort**, 800 O'Sullivan Dam Rd., **Othello**, WA 99344-9623, ☎ 509/346-2651, 765-5061, or 800/416-2736, fax 509/346-9493, also rents boats, provides guides, and offers fishing from the dock. Ice fishing is popular during January and February.

There are 237 lakes around **Omak** in Okanogan County.

An annual bass tournament is held on **Lake Pateros**, and **Alta Lake State Park**, near the town of **Pateros**, can provide fishing, boating, swimming, and camping opportunities. The 100-acre lake, located three miles north of town on Route 153, also has an 18-hole golf course and horses for hire.

Soap Lake contains rainbow trout, salmon, and "spiny ray fish," while nearby **Lake Lenore** is stocked with cutthroat trout. Anglers in **Spokane** are extremely fortunate because there are 75 lakes within a 50-mile radius of town. **Rotary Lake**, near **Union Gap**, has fishing piers for the disabled.

Races

The annual **Pend Oreille Poker Paddle**, ☎ 509/447-5812, is a two-day event that involves canoeing along the Pend Oreille River between **Dalkena** and **Ione**, stopping at designated points to pick up a playing card. The team with the best poker hand at the end of the event wins the contest. Held in July, the celebration also includes a BBQ.

Hydroplane races are held near Columbia River Park in **Kennewick** during July and August, and the **State Western Circuit Limited In-**

board **Hydroplane Races** are held the third weekend in August on **Lake Pateros**.

Houseboating

Houseboating on Lake Roosevelt is a popular pursuit around **Kettle Falls**. There are 15 beaches in the area and seven lakes that are open to fishing in the Kettle Falls Ranger District. Floating on the Kettle River also is popular, and Lake Roosevelt has an annual walleye tournament. **Lake Roosevelt Vacations & Marina**, PO Box 340, Kettle Falls, WA, ☎ 509/738-6121 or 800/635-7585, rents boats. (Knowing the level of the lake is particularly important during the spring drawdown. To learn the current lake level, ☎ 800/824-4916.)

■ On Snow

Snowmobiling

The **Brewster** area has the **Loup Loup Ski Bowl** for downhill skiing and various trails for cross-country skiing and snowmobiling. Ice skaters work out on **Alta Lake**.

The Chamber of Commerce in **Chelan** can provide a four-page brochure prepared by the Lake Chelan Snowmobile Club that includes maps of the Grade Creek/Black Canyon and Devil's Backbone snowmobile areas. Also ask for a free copy of the pocket-sized brochure *Echo Nordic Trails*, which identifies cross-country ski trails on Echo Ridge.

Skiing

The **Wenatchee** area also can claim 50 miles of groomed snowmobile trails in town, ☎ 509/663-3208, and 125 additional miles of groomed snowmobile trails on both sides of Lake Chelan, ☎ 509/682-2576 or 800/4CHELAN, as well as two full-size ice skating rinks in **Wenatchee Riverfront Park**, ☎ 509/664-5994 or 664-5980.

The **Chelan** golf course provides five kilometers of groomed cross-country trails; the **Chelan-Douglas County Riverfront Park**, ☎ 509/664-5980, has another 10 kilometers; and **Bear Mountain Ranch Nordic Center**, ☎ 509/682-5444, six miles south of town, has 55 kilometers more. **Lake Chelan Nordic Skiers**, ☎ 800/4CHELAN, in Echo Valley, 12 miles northwest of town, can offer another 35 kilometers of cross-country ski trails, plus 500 feet of vertical downhill skiing.

The **49° North Ski Area** 10 miles from **Chewelah** can offer both skiing and snowboarding. The facility has four chair lifts and is equipped for night skiing.

Around **Clarkston**, people go downhill skiing in the **Blue Mountains** and cross-country skiing in **Field Springs State Park**. **Conconully**, ☎ 800/422-3048, has 100 miles of groomed snowmobile trails and six snow parks. In addition to **Ski Bluewood**, Box 88, N. Touchet Rd., ☎ 509/382-4725, which has 22 major ski runs, a halfpipe for snowboarders, two triple chairlifts, and one platterpull, the **Dayton** area has the new **Skyline Ski Basin**, which is in the Blue Mountains 21 miles south of town.

The **Tri-City Americans**, 7100 W. Quinault, Kennewick, WA 99336, ☎ 509/736-0606, is a minor league hockey club.

The **Kettle Falls** Ranger District has five trails (55 miles) of groomed snowmobile trails and three cross-country ski trails. The free downtown **Municipal Ice Skating Rink** in **Moses Lake** is open from mid-November through late February. **Omak** has two downhill ski areas, 175 kilometers of groomed cross-country trails, snowmobile trails, and ice skating and ice fishing capabilities.

Loup Loup-South Summit snow park, ☎ 509/997-5334, provides **Oroville** with 20 kilometers of cross-country trails and 1,200 feet of vertical downhill skiing with two pomas and one rope tow. The cross-country trails are open daily, and the downhill facilities are open from Wednesday through Sunday, plus holidays. Nearby, **Sitzmark**, ☎ 509/485-3323, provides six kilometers of groomed cross-country ski trails; facilities for sledders and tubers; and 650 feet of vertical downhill skiing with one chair, one poma, and one rope tow.

Desert Ski Club, PO Box 623, **Richland**, WA 99352, ☎ 509/946-4FUN, can steer out-of-towners to the best places for winter outdoor fun. **Spokane** skiers participate in the **Langlauf**, a 10K classic citizens' Nordic ski race on Mount Spokane, ☎ 509/922-7130, in early February. There are five kilometers of groomed cross-country trails in **Stehekin**, ☎ 509/682-2224. Backcountry touring also is available.

Near **Walla Walla**, **Spout Springs Fun Machine & Snow Co.**, ☎ 503/382-4725, provides downhill and cross-country skiing from late November through April. The facility sports two chairlifts, one I-bar, one rope tow, a snowmobile trail, cross-country trails, a ski school, equipment rental, a restaurant (open Friday through Sunday), a lounge, and a nursery. Night skiing also is available.

The **Mission Ridge Ski Area**, PO Box 1668, **Wenatchee**, WA 98807, ☎ 509/663-7631 or 663-3200, Web site www.missionridge.com, is 12 miles outside of town on the east side of the Cascade Mountains. It has 33 runs, four double chairlifts, two tows, night skiing, cross-country skiing, snowboarding, a restaurant, and a rental shop. The winter snow line: ☎ 800/374-1693.

Near **Winthrop**, **North Cascades Heli-Ski**, ☎ 509/996-3272 or 800/422-3048, covers 350,000 acres with 80 designated downhill runs ranging from 1,500 to 4,000 feet of vertical drop. **Sun Mountain Lodge**, ☎ 800/572-0493, offers 60 kilometers of groomed cross-country trails plus opportunities for skating, rentals, a hotel, a restaurant, and a lounge.

■ In the Air

Ballooning

Hot air ballooning and balloon-related events are celebrated in eastern Washington by the **Harvest Festival & Balloon Rally**, ☎ 509/786-3177, held in **Prosser** each September, and the **Walla Walla Hot Air Balloon Stampede**, 29 E. Sumach, PO Box 644, Walla Walla, WA 99362, ☎ 509/525-0850, Web site www.bmi.net/wwchamb, held the second weekend in May. Free balloon flights are offered in Howard-Tietan Park during the Walla Walla event.

Gliding, Hang Gliding & Paragliding

Other popular outdoor adventures are hang gliding and paragliding. **Chelan Butte** near the town of **Chelan** offers perfect conditions for both. In 1994, Chelan hosted the 1994 Women's World Hang Gliding Championships. Parasailing also is available over Lake Chelan. **North American Paragliding**, PO Box 4, **Ellensburg**, WA 98926, ☎ 800/727-2354, can give you a chance to enjoy the action.

A glider club is based at **Pangborn Memorial Airport** in **East Wenatchee**, and gliders are available at the **Ephrata Airport** in **Ephrata**.

Kites

Kite flyers in **Chelan** enjoy testing their skills at **Old Mill Park**. **Kennewick** hosts an annual **Kite Festival** each April, and **Pasco** holds one at the Preston Winery in early May.

Air Shows

The **Pangborn-Herndon Memorial** in **East Wenatchee** commemorates the first nonstop flight across the Pacific from Misawa, Japan to East Wenatchee in 1931. The **Tri-Cities International Air Show** is held at the Tri-Cities Airport in **Pasco** each September. **Bergstrom Aircraft**, ☎ 509/547-6271, is located at the Tri-Cities Airport in Pasco and provides an around-the-clock, year-around charter service. In **Twisp**, the annual **Kiwanis Fly-In Breakfast** takes place at the Methow Valley State Airport.

Pearson Air Museum, 1105 E. 5th, **Vancouver**, WA 98661, ☎ 360/694-7026, is in historic Central Park. Pearson Field is the oldest operating airfield in the United States (1905). The museum, which contains a cockpit simulator, is open between noon and 5 PM from Wednesday through Sunday.

The **Walla Walla Airfair** is held each June in **Walla Walla**. At Walla Walla Airport, **Mountain States Aviation**, ☎ 509/525-2180, conducts sightseeing flights over Palouse Falls, Hells Canyon, the Blue Mountains, Mount St. Helens, and more.

Yakima also hosts an annual **International Air Fair**, ☎ 509/248-0246, which takes place in mid-July. **Noland-Decoto Flying Service**, 2810 W. Washington Ave., Yakima, WA 98903, ☎ 509/248-1370, fax 509/248-1375, provides air aficionados with scenic flights, charters, and lessons.

■ Cultural Excursions

Bridgeport

Fort Okanogan interpretive center in Bridgeport portrays the history of the Hudson's Bay Co. in this area that once was one of their trading posts. The Hudson's Bay Co. was incorporated in May 1670 and once owned and governed much of North America, and still is the largest retail concern in Canada.

Burbank

McNary National Wildlife Refuge, ☎ 509/547-4942, is a quarter-mile north of US 12 near Burbank and covers 3,600 acres. Fishing is allowed from February through September.

Cashmere & Chelan

Cashmere has a restored main street with a Western theme, an Indian museum, and a pioneer museum. Chelan, a community bedecked with murals, has an interesting historical museum.

Colfax

There are a number of interesting sights in Colfax. The largest chainsaw sculpture in the world, the **Codger Pole**, commemorates a 1938 football game that was replayed by the same players on the same field *50 years later*. In **Palouse Falls State Park**, 65 miles out of town, the spectacular falls tumble 198 feet.

Colville

Keller Heritage Center, 700 N. Wynne St., Colville, WA 99114, includes a museum, the 1910 Keller House, Colville's first schoolhouse, a farmstead cabin, a trapper's cabin, a pioneer machinery museum, a sawmill, a blacksmith shop, the Graves Mountain Lookout, and some magnificent gardens.

Coulee City & Dry Falls

Coulee City, the oldest town in the county, was a regular stop on the Caribou Trail. Nearby Dry Falls, although now dry, once was the largest waterfall ever, measuring 400 feet high and 3.5 miles wide.

Curlew

There are two interesting gravesites in Curlew, that of Chief Tonasket and that of Ranald MacDonald (no, not Ronald McDonald), an early pioneer.

Ellensburg

Children's Activity Museum, 400 N. Main, Ellensburg, WA 98926, ☎ 509/925-6789, is open daily except Monday and Tuesday from June through August, between 10 AM and 5 PM Thursday through Saturday from Sept through May, and between 1 and 5 PM on Sundays the rest of the year. **Laughing Horse Summer Theatre**, ☎ 509/963-3400, presents live performances during July and August. **Central Washington University** has a charming Japanese Garden and a **Chimpanzee & Human Communication Institute**, where you can meet Washoe at a "Chimposium" and watch her and her family communicate by means of human sign language.

Ephrata

Columbia National Wildlife Refuge in Ephrata has a scenic 22-mile driving loop. The **Columbia County Historical Museum**, 742 Basin St. North, ☎ 509/754-3334, includes a Pioneer Village with over 28 buildings. Also of passing interest is the **Grant County Courthouse**, built in 1917, that is heated geothermally with water from a local hot spring.

George

"The Gorge," a natural amphitheater in George, provides live summertime entertainment.

Goldendale

Goldendale Observatory State Park, 1602 Observatory Dr., Goldendale, WA 98620, ☎ 509/773-3141, holds the largest telescope in the country that is available for public viewing. The 24.5-inch reflecting telescope is open year-around. More than a dozen telescopes are available for public use between 2:00 and 5:00 PM and between 8:00 PM and midnight Wednesday through Sunday from April through September; between 1:00 and 5:00 PM and 7:00 and 9:00 PM on Saturdays, and between 1:00 and 5:00 PM on Sundays the rest of the year. **Stonehenge**, east of Maryhill, is a replica of England's Stonehenge that overlooks the Columbia River from atop a 600-foot bluff. **Horsethief Lake State Park**, 15 miles south of town on Route 14, occupies the site of a former Indian village in which many of the petroglyphs are still visible. **Presby Mansion Museum**, 127 W. Broadway, PO Box 86, Goldendale, WA 98620, ☎ 509/773-4303, occupies a 1903 mansion and is open daily between 9 AM and 5 PM from April through October. It is stuffed with interesting household items from the turn of the century, including coffee mills and branding irons.

Grand Coulee Dam

At Grand Coulee Dam, the largest concrete structure in the world, a new laser light show, the largest in the world, is shown on the dam's 10-acre spillway nightly from Memorial Day through September. Tours of the dam also are available, and the **Colville Confederated Tribes Museum**, ☎ 509/633-0751, is of considerable cultural interest.

Kennewick

> There are 23 wineries within a 50-mile radius of Kennewick. The Chamber of Commerce has a free pocket-sized brochure, *Tri-Cities Area Winery Guide*, that describes and locates each winery. For more specifics, contact the **Tri-Cities Winery Assn.**, ☎ 509/588-6716.

East Benton County Historical Museum, 205 Keewaydin Dr., PO Box 6964, Kennewick, WA 99336-0602, ☎ 509/582-7704, has a stunning petrified wood floor, and Indian petroglyphs recovered from the Columbia River in 1939 are located on the grounds. The museum is open between noon and 4 PM from Tuesday through Saturday.

Kennewick's **Mid-Columbia Symphony**, 615 Columbia Center, PO Box 65, ☎ 509/735-7356, provides a lively program of live music throughout the season.

Richland

Ye Merrie Greenwood Players, 6015 W. 20th Ave., ☎ 509/783-7727, has presented a **Renaissance Faire** in Richland's Howard Amon Park for more than 10 years. The Faire is held on a weekend in late June.

Kettle Falls

An 1847-48 hand-hewn chapel, **St. Paul's Mission**, stood along the shores of Lake Roosevelt near Kettle Falls. Abandoned in 1862, the mission has since been restored. The **Kn-Kanna-Xwa Celebration**, held there on the fourth Sunday in July, features a traditional Indian baked salmon dinner.

A self-guided historical tour of Kettle Falls has been prepared by students in the high school World History Class and is available at the Chamber of Commerce. The town holds an annual **Ciderfest** on the first Saturday in October.

The toll-free **Gifford Ferry**, 25 miles south of Kettle Falls, travels to Inchelium. **Meyers Falls**, south of Kettle Falls on the Colville River, is where the first patented flour in the United States was milled in 1816.

Marcus

Marcus, five miles north of Kettle Falls on Route 25, once was a community of 3,000 people. It was one of many communities forced to moved above the 1,310-foot level when Lake Roosevelt was formed, and now sits in a pine forest on a high plateau overlooking the lake. During the spring drawdown of the lake, it is possible to walk the streets of Old Marcus, where sidewalks, foundations, and street signs still remain.

Mead

Cat Tales, N. 17020 Newport Hwy, Mead, WA, ☎ 509/238-4126, is a zoo specializing in big cats from around the world. Tours are available.

Metaline Falls

Pend Oreille County is the home of Kalispel Indians, Gardner Caves, Indian Caves (Manresa Grotto), the Devil's Well, numerous waterfalls, 55 lakes, and 48 streams. The turn-of-the-century **Washington Hotel** in Metaline Falls is now an art gallery.

Moses Lake

Free summertime entertainment is provided on most Saturdays between the Fourth of July and Labor Day at a lakeside amphitheater, **Centennial Theatre**, ☎ 509/766-9240, located at Dogwood and 4th Streets in McCosh Park in Moses Lake.

Schiffner Military Museum, ☎ 509/765-6374, in Moses Lake is open by appointment. A guided tour takes three hours.

Nespelum

Nespelum, 102 miles northwest of Spokane, is the burial place of the Nez Percé warrior Chief Joseph, best known for his pronouncement at the close of the Nez Percé War: "From where the sun now stands, I will fight no more forever." The **Chief Joseph Memorial** stands in **Omak**.

Omak

Omak has a 560-seat **Performing Arts Center** where various live performances are held.

Othello

Hunter Hill Vineyards, 2752 W. McManamon Rd., Othello, WA 99344, ☎ 509/346-2736, is open daily between 11 AM and 5:30 PM.

Pasco

Franklin County Historical Museum, 305 N. Fourth Ave., Pasco, WA 99301, ☎ 509/547-3714, charges no admission fee. It also arranges a number of tours and day trips. The museum is open between 1 and 5 PM from Tuesday through Friday and between 10 AM and 5 PM on Saturday.

Tri-Cities Stadium off Road 68 and north of I-182 in Pasco is the home of the **Tri-City Posse** baseball team, 6200 Burden Rd., ☎ 509/547-6773, a part of the Western Baseball League. The 4,000-seat stadium also is used for concerts, exhibits, shows, and other sporting events. **Columbia Basin College of Performing Arts**, 2600 N. 20th, ☎ 509/547-0511, presents live theater at least four times per academic year.

Pateros

Pateros holds the **Apple Pie Jamboree** in the town park on Lake Pateros on the third weekend in July.

Pullman

The night-lighted **Bryan Hall Clock Tower** at Washington State University in Pullman is a city landmark. **Marmes Rock Shelter**, where the remains of the earliest known inhabitants of the Western Hemisphere were found, is located at the confluence of the Palouse and Snake Rivers near **Lyons Ferry State Park**, ☎ 509/646-3252. The **Palouse River** has three waterfalls, one of which is higher than Niagara Falls (198 feet). **Kamiak Butte County Park**, 10 miles north of town on WA 27, sits on a 3,360-foot butte named for Kamiakin, a Yakima Indian chief.

Richland

The **Hanford Museums of Science & Industry**, 825 Jadwin, Richland, WA 99352, ☎ 509/376-6374, is an atomic science museum. It is open between 8 AM and 5 PM Monday through Friday and between 9 AM and 5 PM on Saturday.

The Richland Players, 608 The Parkway, PO Box 603, Richland, WA 99352, ☎ 509/943-1991, is a community theater that has performed such plays as Tennessee Williams' *The Night of the Iguana*, Ferenc Molnar's *The Play Is the Thing*, and Neil Simon's *Chapter Two* for more than 50 seasons. Richland also sustains the **Mid-Columbia Regional Ballet**, 1405 Goethals, ☎ 509/946-1531, and the **Richland Light Opera**, PO Box 112, ☎ 509/946-0504.

Soap Lake

Soap Lake presents a **Greek Festival**, ☎ 509/246-0659, in June that involves a Greek dinner, dancing, a parade, a minicarnival, and a flea market.

Spokane

Spokane's Skywalk System connects 13 blocks of buildings, keeping shoppers out of the weather and the traffic. Sports fans will enjoy visiting Spokane for its hockey (**Spokane Chiefs**, ☎ 509/328-0450), baseball (**Spokane Indians**, ☎ 509/535-2922), and dog racing (**Coeur d'Alene Greyhound Park**, ☎ 800/828-4880).

Spokane also sustains a great many theatrical performances. **Interplayers**, 174 S. Howard, ☎ 509/455-7529, produces seven live productions from October through June. **Magic Lantern Theatre**, 123 S. Wall, ☎ 509/838-4919, offers foreign, art, and quality domestic films upstairs in the Atrium Building. **Rogue Players**, ☎ 509/327-9907, is a community theatre that stages four productions a year. **Spokane Civic Theatre**, 1020 N. Howard St., ☎ 509/325-2507, presents live theater year-around. The **Spokane Symphony**, ☎ 509/326-3136, performs in the Spokane Opera House. **Riverfront Park**, ☎ 509/456-4386, located on an island in the Spokane River, has an IMAX theatre, rides, and a historic carousel. From Riverfront Park, it is possible to cross a walking bridge to a century-old flour mill.

The **Camas Days Celebration**, a Native American pow wow and encampment, is held on the **Spokane Indian Reservation**, ☎ 509/489-3912, near Spokane every May.

Toppenish

Yakama Indian National Cultural Center, 280 Buster Rd. (Route 97), PO Box 151, Toppenish, WA 98948, ☎ 509/865-2800, fax 509/865-6101, includes a museum, a restaurant, a gift shop, a library, and a theater. During the summer, the hours are 9 AM to 6 PM. During the autumn, the Center is open between 9 AM and 5 PM. Also worth checking out are the **Yakama Indian Nation Tourism Office**, ☎ 509/865-5121, fax 509/865-7570.

Yakima Valley produces 75 percent of the country's hops and the United States provides 25 percent of the world's total supply; therefore it is only natural that the valley sustains the nation's only hop museum. The **American Hop Museum**, 22 S. B St., Toppenish, WA 98948, ☎ 509/865-4677, is open between 11 AM and 4 PM from April through October.

Heritage Cultural Center Theater, Route 97, Toppenish, ☎ 509/865-3262, presents old-fashioned melodrama in late July and early August.

Union Gap

Union Gap has an interesting 1865 Pioneer Graveyard, and the Old Town Mill, established in 1869, continues to grind wheat into flour in the old natural way.

Usk

The annual **Salish Fair**, ☎ 509/445-1147, held at the Kalispel Ceremonial Grounds in Usk each August, includes Indian dancing, stick games, a buffalo BBQ, and crafts.

Vantage

Ginko Petrified Forest in Vantage has an Interpretive Center. **Wanapum Dam**, south of town on Route 243, has an Indian museum and a fish-viewing room.

Walla Walla

The first **Fort Walla Walla**, a Hudson's Bay Co. trading post called Fort Nez Percé, is now under water. A tablet on the old Liberty Theater, located on Main Street between First and Colville Avenues, marks the site of the second Fort Walla Walla, established in 1856. The **Fort Walla Walla Museum**, 755 Myra Rd., ☎ 509/525-7703, located 45 miles northeast of Pendleton, OR, includes a pioneer village with 14 original and replica buildings and is open between 10 AM and 5 PM every day but Mondays from April to October.

A marker off Stanton Street at the entrance to the campus amphitheater indicates the site at which thousands of Nez Percé, Yakama, Cayuse, Walla Walla, and Paulouse Indians attended a great council organized by Gov. Stevens in 1855. Learning of a plot to kill the white people, Nez Percé leader Hol-Lol-Sote-Tote (called Chief Lawyer) moved his lodge and his family into the white men's camp to protect them from the attack.

Walla Walla Little Theatre, ☎ 509/529-3683, offers live entertainment, and **Walla Walla Symphony**, Cordiner Hall, Park Street and Boyer Avenue, ☎ 509/520-8020, is the oldest continuously operating symphony west of the Mississippi River.

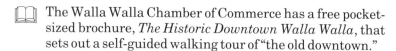 The Walla Walla Chamber of Commerce has a free pocket-sized brochure, *The Historic Downtown Walla Walla*, that sets out a self-guided walking tour of "the old downtown."

In July, Walla Walla celebrates the annual **Sweet Onion Harvest Fest**. Walla Walla sweets (onions) don't bite or cause your eyes to burn. If you buy one, look for a round shape, an elongated neck, and a dry, paper-thin skin. The onions can be stored in a cool, ventilated location for three to six weeks.

Twin Sisters, 30 miles west of Walla Walla, are two basalt pillars. Cayuse Indian legend says that Coyote, an animal spirit, turned two beautiful Indian sisters into stone during a fit of jealousy.

On Route 12 seven miles west of Walla Walla, **Whitman Mission**, ☎ 509/529-2761, commemorates the lives of Marcus and Narcissa Whitman, who journeyed west in 1836 to begin a Protestant mission among the Cayuse Indians. When the Oregon Trail began introducing more settlers during the 1840s, the Indians killed the Whitmans and 11 others. The locations of the original buildings are indicated at the site, and there are regular pioneer demonstrations, films, and displays that depict the era.

Look southwest from the **Frenchtown Mission Church** marker on Route 12, nine miles west of Walla Walla, to see where Chief Peu-Peu-Mox-Mox of the Walla Wallas was slain and the Battle of Walla Walla was concluded in 1855. On the north side of the highway, a granite marker and a wooden cross atop a hill mark the Frenchtown Cemetery.

L'Ecole No. 41 Winery, 41 Lowden School Rd., Lowden, WA, ☎ 509/525-0940, a dozen miles west of Walla Walla, produces wine in the cellar of the historic old Frenchtown school. Tours are conducted between 11 AM and 4 PM from Wednesday through Sunday. By appointment, you can arrange to have dinner there.

A Christmas pow-wow is held in the **Wapato** Longhouse, ☎ 509/865-5121.

Wellpinit

The **Alex Sherwood Memorial Center Museum**, ☎ 509/258-4581, is operated by the Spokane Tribe in Wellpinit. **Rocky Reach Dam** north of **Wenatchee** on US 97 has a museum full of Indian relics.

Wenatchee

Wenatchee hosts a **Fasching** (*fah-shing*), a sort of German Mardi Gras, during one of the weekends in February.

White Swan

Fort Simcoe State Park Heritage Site, 5150 Fort Simcoe Rd., White Swan, WA 98952, ☎ 509/874-2372, was the site of an 1856 military fort and later an Indian Agency. Four officers' quarters are still standing, and there is an Interpretive Center that is open between 9 AM and 4 PM Wednesday through Sunday from April through September.

Numerous Indian celebrations and competitions are held in the White Swan Pavilion on the Yakama Indian Reservation, ☎ 509/865-5121.

Winthrop

Winthrop is an interesting "Old West" town.

Yakima

Yakima Bears baseball, 810 W. Nob Hill Blvd., Yakima, WA 98902 ☎ 509/457-5151, a Dodgers affiliate, may be as intriguing for its food as for its home runs. Fans can order a Single (a jumbo hotdog or hamburger, chips, and a soft drink), a Double (a grilled chicken sandwich or super-hotdog, chips, and a soft drink), a Triple (a foot-long kielbasa or large burger, chips, and a soft drink), or a Home Run (a T-bone steak, potato salad, and a soft drink). The cost includes admission and a scorecard.

The **Yakima Sun Kings**, 1001 S. Third St., ☎ 509/248-1222, are a CBA basketball franchise.

 Yakima Valley Wine Growers Assn., ☎ 800/258-7270, has prepared a free pocket-sized brochure, *Yakima Valley Wine Tour*, which is a guide to the wineries throughout the region, and the Chamber of Commerce has a free pocket-sized brochure, *Yakima Walking Tours*, that recommends two routes to guide you through the town and point out the historic highlights.

You can have a soda at an art deco soda fountain from the 1930s at **Yakima Valley Museum**, 2105 Tieton Dr. (Franklin Park), Yakima, WA 98902, ☎ 509-248-0747. The museum is open between 10 AM and 5 PM Monday through Friday and between noon and 5 PM Saturday and Sunday. The museum also has a 2,500-square-foot hands-on learning center, **Children's Underground**, that is open between 1:00 and 5:00 Wednesday through Sunday.

World Famous Fantastic Museum, 15 W. Yakima Ave., Yakima, WA 98902, ☎ 509/575-0100, contains over 10,000 antique toys, pedal cars, and Hollywood artifacts. The attraction is open daily between 10 AM and 6 PM.

Washington's Fruit Place Visitor Center, 105 S. 18th St., Yakima, WA 98901, ☎ 509/576-3090, has samples, exhibits, a gift shop, and complimentary fruit samples. The center is open between 10 AM and 5 PM Monday through Saturday and between noon and 4 PM on Sundays from Memorial Day to Labor Day. Winter hours are between 10 AM and 5 PM Monday through Friday.

Yakima Area Arboretum, ☎ 509/248-7337, on Nob Hill Boulevard an eighth of a mile east of I-82 (Exit 34), fills 40 acres with a Japanese Garden, the Jewett Interpretive Center, a gift shop, and a library. There is no admission fee and the arboretum is open daily from dawn to dusk.

Where to Stay

Kennewick

Ever dream of running your boat right up to a dock outside your hotel? You can at **Ramada Inn Clover Island**, 435 Clover Island, Kennewick, WA 99336, ☎ 509/586-0541 or 800/2RAMADA, fax 509/586-6956, $$-$$$. The four-story hotel (nice views from the top floor) contains 149 rooms and has a heated pool, a boat dock, a cocktail lounge, and an around-the-clock dining room.

Moses Lake

Best Western Hallmark Inn & Conference Center, 3000 Marina Dr., Moses Lake, WA, ☎ 509/765-9211 or 800/235-4255, $$-$$$, bills itself as the only resort hotel on **Moses Lake**. The inn features a restaurant, a cocktail lounge, a spa, an outdoor pool, tennis courts, and boat docks. It also rents kayaks.

Republic

K Diamond K Guest Ranch, 404 Hwy 21 South, Republic, WA 99166, ☎ 509/775-3536, $$, offers its guests an outstanding variety of activities: hiking, biking, horseback riding (they have 30 horses), rockhounding (at the Stonerose fossil digs), range shooting (nearby), off-road driving, hunting, cross-country skiing, snowmobiling, and birdwatching. Guests also can go fishing in San Poil River, right on the ranch, or in Curlew

Lake nearby, both of which contain rainbow trout. Guests stay in a log ranch home and can ride in genuine western roundups (the ranch runs 200 head of cattle).

Richland

Shilo Inn, 50 Comstock St., Richland, WA 99352-4499, ☎ 509/946-4661 or 800/222-2244, fax 509/943-6741, $$, is on the banks of the Columbia River adjacent to a paved walking and biking path. **Hampton Inn**, 486 Bradley Blvd., ☎ 509/943-4400 or 800-HAMPTON, $$-$$$, is Richland's newest inn and a neighbor of the Shilo Inn.

Soap Lake

The Inn at Soap Lake, 226 Main Ave. East, PO Box 98, Soap Lake, WA 98851, ☎ 509/246-1132, sits on the lake and rents paddle boats and canoes. The inn has a lovely garden courtyard.

Walla Walla

Whitman Motor Inn, 107 N. Second, Walla Walla, WA 99362, ☎ 525-2200, $-$$$, is conveniently located, comfortable, and nicely staffed.

■ Camping

Grand Coulee Dam National Recreation Area, North District Office, South 1230 Boise Rd., Kettle Falls, WA 99141, ☎ 509/738-6266, provides many campsites, but there is a 14-day limit on stays and a fishing license is required to fish in Lake Roosevelt. The campsites include Gifford, Cloverleaf, Bradbury Beach, Haag Cove, Kettle Falls, Marcus Island, Kamloops, Kettle River, Summer Island, Evans, and Snag Cove.

Colville National Forest, Kettle Falls Ranger District, Kettle Falls, WA 99141, ☎ 509/738-6111, keeps office hours between 7:30 AM and 4 PM Monday through Friday. Campsites in the district are located at Lake Ellen, Trout Lake, Canyon Creek, Sherman Pass, Davis Lake, Pierre Lake, Elbow Lake, and Summit Lake. Boat-in campsites along the north shore of **Lake Chelan** include Mitchell Creek, site of a disastrous fire in 1970 that destroyed 42,280 acres; between Camas Creek and Coyote Creek, a popular winter range for deer; Safety Harbor Creek, a haven from strong winds and the site of two tremendous fires in 1970 and 1972; Prince Creek, site of an enormous flood in 1948 that wiped out a ranger's cabin, barn, dock and campground; Fish Creek, home of

Moore's Inn, the first hotel on the upper lake (1889); and Purple Creek at Stehekin Landing.

The south shore of Lake Chelan also offers a selection of campsites: one between Little Big Creek and Big Creek; one between Big Creek and Corral Creek, nearly opposite the deepest point in the lake (1,486 feet); two at Graham Harbor Creek; one at Domke Creek near Domke Falls; two at Refrigerator Harbor; one between Lightning Creek and Devore Creek near Bridal Veil Falls and Castle Peak, which in the autumn are covered with brilliant yellow larch trees; and one at Devore Creek and Weaver Point. Daisy Weaver's homestead was the setting for the sheep ranch in Elizabeth Taylor's 1944 movie *The Courage of Lassie*. There are two other campsites on the south side of the lake at Lucerne, a staging area for those headed to Holden or the Glacier Peak Wilderness beyond: (1) a hike-in campsite at Domke Lake, and (2) a nine-mile hike-in to campsite up Railroad Creek past the old Holden townsite. Holden was a mining company town that served the needs of the largest copper mine in the state. The mine and village were closed in 1957, and when no buyer could be found for the buildings, they were donated to the Lutheran Church in 1960.

For useful information regarding camping in the **Umatilla National Forest**, which straddles the Oregon-Washington state line, contact the forest office, 2517 SW Hailey Ave., Pendleton, OR 97801, ☎ 503/276-3811, or the district offices in Pomeroy or Walla Walla and ask for the pocket-sized brochure *Camping on the Umatilla National Forest*. Penland Lake Campground, five miles off Forest Road 53, sits at lakeside; Bull Prairie Campground, three miles off WA 207, affords fishing, hiking, and nonmotorized boating on a 24-acre lake; North Fork John Day Campground, 10 miles west of Granite on the Blue Mountain Scenic Byway (Forest Road 52), has some facilities for horses; Bear Wallow Campground along WA 244 between Ukiah and La Grande is adjacent to Bear Wallow Creek and has a quarter-mile interpretive trail; Jubilee Lake Campground has a 2.8-mile trail; Umatilla Forks Campground, between the North and South Forks of the Umatilla, offers fishing and hiking; Tucannon Campground is on Forest Road 47; and Teal Spring Campground is on Forest Road 40.

At the **Yakama Indian Nation Cultural Heritage Center & RV Park Resort**, PO Box 151, **Toppenish**, WA 98948, ☎ 509/865-2800 or 800/874-3087, fax 509/865-7570, visitors can rent a tipi, hook up their own RV, or pitch a tent.

In the **Tri-Cities** area, there are Corps of Engineers campgrounds at Charbonneau Park, Fishhook Park, and Hood Park, all along the river northeast of Pasco, and at Windust Park near Lower Monumental Dam.

A free pocket-sized descriptive brochure is available from the Walla Walla District Corps of Engineers, Walla Walla, WA 99362-9265, ☎ 509/552-6711.

Fort Walla Walla Park Campground, 1530 Dalles Military Rd., **Walla Walla**, WA 99362, ☎ 509/527-3770, is a 65-acre nature preserve with self-guiding walking trails. Security patrols are provided, there is a bicycle track and an old cavalry and Indian cemetery, and there is an amphitheater in which concerts and plays are presented periodically.

Where to Eat

Cheney

Klink's on the Water, 18617 W. Williams Lake Rd., Cheney, WA, ☎ 509/235-2391, $, is at Williams Lake Resort and has a cabinlike atmosphere. The restaurant is closed in the winter.

Conconully

Sit 'n Bull Saloon, 308 Main St., Conconully, $-$$, has a colorful western atmosphere.

Goldendale

For a gourmet meal, try **Highland Creeks Resort**, 2120 Scenic Hwy 97, Goldendale, ☎ 509/773-4026, $$-$$$, where you can enjoy oven-baked Cornish game hen with wild berries and toasted hazelnut sauce, bourbon barbecued baby back ribs, or broiled rainbow trout with smoked bacon and sweet onion relish.

Newport

Diamond Lodge, 1261 S. Shore Rd., Newport, ☎ 509/447-LAKE, $$, is located on Diamond Lake and serves such unusual delights as raspberry BBQ ribs and creole-style oysters.

Omak

Hopefully, you have never had to stand in a true breadline, but eating in **The Breadline Cafe**, 102 Ash St., Omak, ☎ 509/826-5836, $$, might be something of a treat. The restaurant has homemade bread and desserts, a full bar, a soda fountain, and espresso. The cafe is open for breakfast and lunch on Sunday and Monday, and for breakfast, lunch, and dinner from Tuesday through Saturday.

Spokane

C. I. Shenanigans, 322 N. Spokane Falls Court, ☎ 509/455-5072, $$-$$$, serves seafood and steak.

At **Glover Mansion**, 321 W. 8th Ave., ☎ 509/459-0000, $$, ask about the crepes of the day.

A favorite at **Windows of the Seasons**, W. 303 N. River Dr., ☎ 509/328-9526, $$-$$$, is honey-smoked halibut with honey lime *beurre blanc*, a delicate butter sauce.

The Otter, 104 S. Freya, ☎ 509/534-5329, $$, is located in Tapio Center and serves steak-and-prawns or steak-and-salmon.

Innovative food and uncommonly low prices are to be found at **Ripples on the River**, N. 700 Division, ☎ 509/326-5577, $$. Some examples: Chinese wonton salad, blackberry brandy ribeye, and bleu scampi – tiger prawns sauteed in garlic, herbs and lemon juice, then finished with bleu cheese and creamy Asiago cheese.

A great place for lunch (and the kids will love it) is **Heroes**, N. 4750 Division, ☎ 509/326-1349, $, in the North Town Mall. Their innovative burgers include a BBQ bacon burger and a Swiss mushroom burger.

Hobart's, E. 110 4th Ave., ☎ 509/838-6101, $$, serves such mouthwatering favorites as breast of duck with wild mushrooms and Coquille Saint Jacques.

Try **Hilary's at the Stockyards Inn**, 3827 E. Boone, ☎ 509/534-1212, $$, where the appetizers include escargot and stuffed mushrooms and they serve such entrees as ostrich picatta or stir-fry, raspberry chicken, pecan halibut, and sherried oysters.

Toppenish

Liberty Theatre, 211 S. Toppenish Ave., Toppenish, WA 98948, ☎ 509/865-5995 or 865-7573, is a dinner theater that conducts backstage tours. Built as a vaudeville theatre in 1915, the building was purchased by Howard Hughes in 1930, when Toppenish had four movie theaters, 32 bars, and 13 houses of ill repute and was the entertainment center of the county.

Information Sources

Colville National Forest, 765 S. Main St., Colville, WA 99114, ☎ 509/684-3711.

Grand Coulee Dam Area Chamber of Commerce, 306 Midway, PO Box 760, Grand Coulee, WA 99133-0760, ☎ 509/633-3074 or 800/268-5332.

Kettle Falls Chamber of Commerce, PO Box 119, Kettle Falls, WA 99141, ☎ 509/738-2300 or 738-6514.

Okanogan National Forest, 1240 Second Ave. South, PO Box 950, Okanogan, WA 98840, ☎ 509/826-3275.

Spokane Area Convention & Visitors Bureau, 926 W. Sprague, Suite 180, Spokane, WA 99204, ☎ 509/624-1341, fax 509/623-1297, Web site www.spokane-areacvb.org.

Tri-Cities (Kennewick, Richland, and Pasco **Visitor & Convention Bureau**, 6951 Grandridge Blvd., PO Box 2241, Kennewick, WA 99302, ☎ 800/254-5824, fax 509/783-9005, Web site www.owt.com/tcvcb.

Walla Walla Area Chamber of Commerce, 29 E. Sumach, PO Box 644, Walla Walla, WA 99362, ☎ 509/525-0850 or 800/743-9562, fax 509/522-2038.

Wenatchee National Forest, 301 Yakima St., PO Box 811, Wenatchee, WA 98807, ☎ 509/662-4335.

Greater Yakima Chamber of Commerce, PO Box 1490, Yakima, WA 98907-1490, ☎ 509/248-2021, fax 509/248-0601, E-mail yakimachamber@efcom.com.

Southern British Columbia

With an area of 948,596 square kilometers, British Columbia is larger than any state in the continental United States and bigger than Germany, France, Austria, and Switzerland *combined*.

To most Americans, the British way of spelling words and the numerous British expressions used in Canada can be somewhat amusing. Center, for example, becomes centre; harbor, harbour; and blessed, blest. Schedule is pronounced *shed-yule*, and groups of Indians are referred to as "bands," rather than "tribes."

(In passing, it should be pointed out that the Canadians are somewhat sensitive to the way in which the citizens of the United States have commandeered the word "American." They consider themselves Americans too, as do the citizens of Mexico, our other North American neighbors.)

Canadians celebrate a few holidays that are unfamiliar to most Americans: Victoria Day, which falls on 24 May if that happens to be a Monday – otherwise it's on the first Monday just prior to the 24th; British Columbia Day, which is the first Monday in August; and Canada Day, the first of July.

Canadians love their sports as we do, but few Americans are familiar with some of the traditional British/Canadian sports such as cricket, curling, and lacrosse. The rules of Canadian football, of course, bear only a passing resemblance to those of the US game.

Prices in Canada tend to be somewhat higher than we are used to in the United States, but we do benefit somewhat from a favorable rate of exchange, commonly about $1.15 Canadian to the US dollar. Many find it beneficial to use a credit card instead of cash in Canada because card companies generally get a better rate of exchange than tourists are likely to find in many Canadian hotels, restaurants, retail stores, and banks.

Save the receipts for your expenditures while you are in Canada because you can get a rebate on the seven percent GST tax that you pay on many of your purchases. A free brochure, *Goods and Services Tax Refund*, explains the Canadian tax refund policy and contains a copy of the necessary application form. The brochure is available at most chambers of commerce and visitor's centres, or you can simply ask for one at any border crossing.

Canadians use the metric system for virtually everything. This can be somewhat confusing to those who are driving there for the first time. To estimate mileage, begin with the number of kilometers involved, multiply it by six, and then drop the last digit. Example: 25 km x 6 = 150. Dropping the final digit (6) leaves you with 15. To be precise, 25 kilometers equals 16 miles, but 15 is close enough for most purposes.

MPH Conversion

25 km/hr	16 mph
40 km/hr	26 mph
50 km/hr	33 mph
60 km/hr	40 mph
80 km/hr	53 mph
100 km/hr	66 mph

Gasoline (petrol) is sold by the litre, which is an amount slightly less than a quart. To approximate the price of gasoline *per gallon* in Canada, it is necessary to multiply the price *per litre* by four. For example: If you pay 57 cents per litre for gasoline in Canada, it will be costing you roughly $2.28 per gallon (0.57 x 4 = 2.28)... but also bear in mind that you have paid for it in *Canadian*, rather than *American* dollars, which may make you feel a *wee* bit better about the transaction.

Victoria & Vancouver Island

The Oregon Treaty of 1846 set the 49th parallel as the border between Canada and the United States, but it left Vancouver Island in the hands of the British even though a part of the island is below the 49th parallel. The capital city of British Columbia, Victoria, sits on the southern tip of the island, due west of Anacortes, WA, a popular resort town in the San Juan Islands.

Vancouver Island became a British crown colony in 1849. The mainland portion of the province did not become a colony until 1858; the two were not united until 1866.

Isolated from the eastern regions of Canada, the residents of British Columbia strongly considered joining the United States in the 1860s, but in 1871, the Canadian government kept them pacified with the promise of a transcontinental rail link – a promise that was not fulfilled until 1885.

In 1993, British Columbia's Kim Campbell became the first female Prime Minister of Canada.

Getting Around

Because Victoria sits on the southeastern tip of an island, it should be no surprise to discover that the area contains few roads. The island's major trafficway follows the eastern shoreline, which parallels the Strait of Georgia, Johnstone Strait, and Queen Charlotte Strait as it heads northward. Trans Canada Route 1 and its extension, Route 19, run from Victoria to Port Hardy, from which it is possible to take a gravel road the rest of the way to the northernmost tip of the island in Cape Scott Provincial Park.

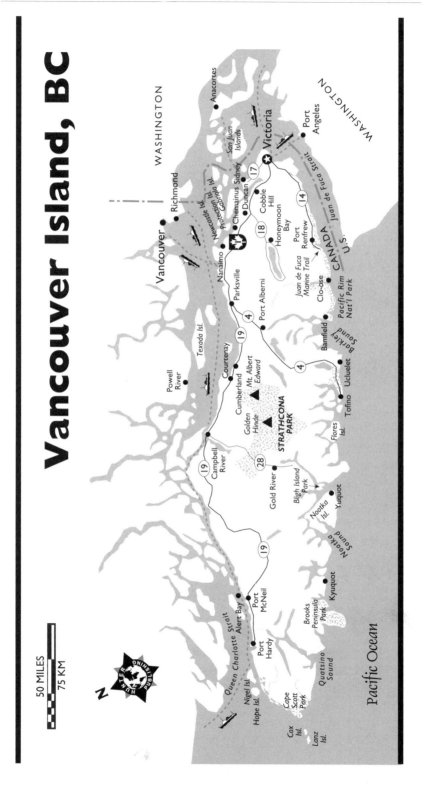

Route 17 runs due north out of Victoria to Swartz Bay on the tip of a short peninsula, while Route 14 heads west from the city to Sooke and Port Renfrew along the Juan de Fuca Marine Trail.

Few roads cross the island from east to west. Nearest to Victoria is Route 18, which heads west to Youbou on the north side of Cowichan Lake and Honeymoon Bay on the south side. A bit farther north, Route 4 cuts across the island to Long Beach and Tofino. Finally, Route 28 passes between Crown Mountain and Elkhorn Mountain en route to Gold River and the Muchalat Inlet.

What the island lacks in roadways, waterways are more than adequate to replace.

BC Ferries, 1112 Fort St., Victoria, BC V8V 4V2, ☎ 250/386-3431 or 888/233-3779, fax 250/381-5452, Web site www.bcferries.bc.ca, serves Vancouver, Victoria, Nanaimo, and other British Columbia west coast routes including the Queen Charlotte Islands, the Inside Passage, and the Discovery Coast Passage. The ferries provide links to Galiano Island, Mayne Island, Saturna Island, Pender Island, and Salt Spring Island in the Southern Gulf Islands, and to Swartz Bay, Tsawwassen, Nanaimo, Duke Point, Gabriola Island, Langdale, Horseshoe Bay, Bowen Island, Earls Cove, Battery Bay, Comox, Powell River, and Texada Island on the Sunshine Coast.

Victoria Line, 185 Dallas Rd., Victoria, BC V8V 1A1, ☎ 604/480-5544, 800/683-7977 (US), or 800/668-1167 (Canada), fax 604/480-5222, Web site victoria-line.bc.ca, a car and passenger ferry, lands at Ogden Point in Victoria and at Pier 48 in Seattle.

Touring

Alert Bay, on Cormorant Island, can be reached by a car/passenger ferry, ☎ 250/956-4533, that travels to and from Port McNeill six times a day.

Bamfield, which is on the north end of the West Coast Trail, sits on the south side of Barkley Sound. It can be reached only by a gravel road from Port Alberni or by boat (the *MV Lady Rose,* which also originates in Port Alberni). The inlet acts as the town's main street, and a local water taxi shuttles people between the west and east sides of town. Houses, resorts, and stores are interconnected by boardwalks. There is good fishing in the area, and Brady's Beach is just a short walk from town.

The **Campbell River** is on Discovery Passage opposite Quadra Island – two hours from Nanaimo by highway.

Called "The City of Totems," **Duncan** has 41 of the gigantic icons on display throughout the town. The world's largest (in terms of diameter) is 24 feet tall and seven feet around. A trail of yellow footprints on the sidewalk helps you to make a self-guided tour of the totems, five of which stand in the Court House complex on Government Street.

Gabriola Island, northernmost of the Gulf Islands, is a 20-minute ferry ride from Nanaimo. The ferries run every hour between 6 AM and 10:45 PM.

Metchosin is in an area noted for beachcombing and for a number of nearby petroglyphs.

Port Alberni is billed as the "Salmon Capital of the World."

Salt Spring Island is one of the Gulf Islands. A ferry links it to Swartz Bay from Fulford Harbour, to Tsawwassen from the end of Long Harbour Road, and to Crofton from Vesuvius. (For information regarding the ferry, ☎ 604/669-1211 in Vancouver; 604/386-3431 in Victoria; or 604/537-9921 on Salt Spring Island.)

The **Sheringham Point Lighthouse** is at Sooke.

Ucluelet (from *Nuu Chah Nulth,* the Indian term for "people with a safe landing place") has quiet coves, sandy beaches, interesting tidepools, sea lions, whales, and 240 species of birds.

Adventures

Over 16.5 million acres of British Columbia have been committed to 406 provincial parks, 131 ecological parks, and six national parks, providing ample recreational opportunities for everyone.

The protected waterways between Vancouver Island and the mainland, particularly the Strait of Georgia, afford outstanding sailing and superb salmon fishing.

One of Canada's great attractions is the "laid back" attitude of its people, nearly all of whom seem to have an inborn realization that there is more to life than the 9-5 grind. Indeed, there is perhaps no city of comparable size in the entire world that has such a wealth of outdoor recreational opportunity at its very door-step than Vancouver. Cultural activities are not ignored there, either.

Canadians enjoy their watersports, their skiing, their hiking and biking... and they are quite willing to share those things with everyone concerned. You will find a visit there to be most congenial in every respect.

■ On Foot

Outfitters

Big Bear Rentals, 2250 N. Island Hwy, Campbell River, BC V9W 2G8, ☎ 250/286-8687, guides wilderness tours. It also rents jet-skis, boats, scooters, kayaks, ATVs, and snowmobiles.

River City Adventures, 850 12th Ave., Campbell River, BC V9W 6B5, ☎ 250/287-7715 or 800/567-6511, fax 250/287-7573, E-mail venture@oberon.ark.com, Web site www.ark.com/venture/index.html, leads groups interested in seeing grizzly bears, watching killer whales (orcas), or going salmon fishing.

Hiking Trails

Cape Scott Provincial Park, on the north end of Vancouver Island, can be reached only on foot. The nearest settlement is **Holberg**. Trails, primitive and often muddy, lead to San Josef Bay, Eric Lake, Fisherman River, Hansen Lagoon, Nissen Bight, Nels Bight, Experiment Bight, Guise Bay, and Cape Scott. Sights along the way include the Henry Ohlsen home, store, and post office (1908-1944) on the trail to San Josef Bay; the wharf at the south end of Eric Lake; a wooden cart, Caterpillar tractor, and collapsed tool shed on the north side of the trail near the Spencer farm; a building believed to have been a store during World War II, located on a short path off the trail to Guise Bay; the ruins of two cabins used as World War II barracks, on a short trail off Guise Bay Beach; the Cape Scott Lighthouse, built in 1960; and two sets of sea stacks, one on San Josef Bay and one near the lighthouse. For more information, contact BC Parks District Manager, Box 479, Parksville, BC V9P 2H4, ☎ 604/248-3931 or 755-2483, fax 604/248-8584.

Rusted tools, nails, unstable buildings, and old wells can be hazardous.

Cathedral Grove, in MacMillan Provincial Park, has well-marked trails through the last accessible forest of giant fir trees in British Columbia. **Della Falls**, reached by taking an 11-mile trail, is the highest waterfall in North America and the eleventh highest in the world. Denman and Hornby Island, a 15-minute ferry ride from Buckley Bay, offers good beachcombing, hiking, and swimming.

There is good hiking west of **Duncan** along the Cowichan River and east of town near Mount Tzouhalem. Gold River, home of the British Columbia Speleological Association, provides an interesting cave, **Upana Cave,** and three good places to test your skills at mountain climbing: Kings Peak, Elkhorn Mountain, and Crest Craggs.

Goldstream Provincial Park has numerous good hiking trails. Try Arbutus Loop, Arbutus Ridge Trail, Gold Mine Trail, Gold Mine Trail North, Lower Goldstream Trail, Upper Goldstream Trail, and Prospectors' Trail. Nature trails in the park include Arbutus Trail, Bridge Trail, Lower Falls Trail, and Marsh Trail.

Canadian Underworld Tours & Adventures, Box 86, R.R. 4, South Wellington, **Nanaimo**, BC V9R 5X9, ☎ 250/753-8587, Web site www.island.net/~bribis/, conducts wild cave tours around Cowichan Lake, Port Alberni, and Port McNeill. **Horn Lake Caves**, near Nanaimo, is called "one of the finest spelunking experiences in North America," and offers guided tours on a first-come, first-served basis between 10 AM and 4 PM during July and August. English River Falls, a riverfront park, has with trails that lead to waterfalls and a number of inviting pools.

Newcastle Island Provincial Marine Park, on a 306-hectare island just off Nanaimo, is adjacent to Protection Island and provides numerous hiking trails. The island was mined for coal between 1853 and 1883. Sandstone was quarried there between 1869 and 1932, and in 1910, Japanese fishermen established a settlement on the west side of the island, where they built a saltery and a shipyard, which they continued to operate until 1941. In 1931, the Canadian Pacific Steamship Co. operated a resort on the island that had a dance pavilion, a tea house, a soccer field, a wading pool, and picnic areas. The *Charmer* (later replaced by the *Princess Victoria*) was tied to a dock and used as a floating hotel. Today, the island can be reached only by a foot-passenger ferry, ☎ 604/753-5141 or 391-2300. During the summer it leaves the wharf at Mafeo-Sutton Park behind the Civic Arena north of downtown Nanaimo.

Alpine Trail in **Parksville** leads to a lookout on Mount Arrowsmith, and there are waterfalls in the Englishman River and Little Qualicum Falls Provincial Parks nearby. **Eagle Adventures**, Box 5196, Port Hardy, BC V0N 2P0, ☎ 250/949-7788, conducts guided wilderness walks and hosts a traditional salmon bake.

Little Qualicum Falls Provincial Park has a trail that goes around ravines and past spectacular waterfalls, including Little Qualicum Falls. Camping is permitted along the Little Qualicum River.

On **Salt Spring Island**, an easy two-kilometer trail that starts half a kilometer up Sunset Drive off Vesuvious Bay Road and follows Duck Creek. Numerous other trails lead out of Beaver Point Park, nine kilometers from the Fulford ferry terminal at the end of Beaver Point Road, and the adjacent Ruckle Provincial Park. The mountainous south end of the island, where Mount Tuam and Mount Bruce can be found, is for the more experienced hiker.

Around **Sooke**, tidepooling, beachcombing, and hiking are popular along the Kludahk Trail, in Juan de Fuca Marina Park, and in East Sooke Park.

South Cowichan, an hour north of Victoria, has numerous hiking/biking trails, including Burnt Bridge, which follows the Koksilah River along Renfrew Road; Cobble Hill Mountain Trail and Quarry Wilderness Park on Cobble Hill Road; Galloping Goose Trail off Sooke Road; Kerry Park Trails behind the Kerry Park Recreation Centre; Koksilah Provincial Park; Old Baldy Mountain and East Shawnigan Lake; the trails around the lake in Spectacle Lake Provincial Park; Manley Creek Park; Mill Bay Nature Park on Holling Road; and Old Mill Commercial Park in East Shawnigan.

Petroglyphs can be found around Sproat Lake Provincial Park, 15 kilometers west of **Port Alberni**, and the lake is the home base for the largest fire-fighting aircraft in the world, the Martin Mars Waterbombers. **Strathcona Provincial Park** provides numerous hiking trails, including Kwai Lake, Hairtrigger Lake Loop, Circlet Lake, Croteau Lake Loop, Cruickshank Canyon View, Comox Glacier, Mount Becher, Elk River, Crest Mountain, Marble Meadows, and Flower Ridge. Three trails lead to some lovely waterfalls: Della Falls, Phillips Ridge, and Upper Myra Falls.

You can take a water taxi from Tofino to **Meares Island**, where a trail winds through a forest of giant trees. At **Ucluelet**, there are trails around Terrace Beach, and a chance to see a lighthouse on Amphitrite Point. Galloping Goose Regional Trail leads 26 kilometers through View Royal, Colwood, Metchosin, and Sooke.

Midnight Sun Adventure Travel, 550-777 Royal Oak Dr., PO Box 355, **Victoria**, BC V8X 4V1, ☎ 800/255-5057, fax 250/652-8308, E-mail midsun@islandnet.com, arranges small group tours that travel in minivans, plus campouts of one to 14 days. **Bird's Eye View Walking**

Tours, Box 8145, Victoria, BC V8W 3R8, ☎ 250/592-9255, fax 250/386-2237, will take you on a hiking adventure.

Lantern Tours in the Old Burying Ground, PO Box 40115, Victoria, BC V8W 3N3, ☎ 250/598-8870, adds a touch of the eerie to an evening's stroll. The tours start at 9 PM nightly during July and August. Similar events are offered by **Murder, Ghost, & Mayhem Walking Tours**, 78 San Jose Ave., ☎ 250/385-2035; **Victoria's Haunted Walk & Other Tours**, 103-2647 Graham St., ☎ 250/361-2619; and **Victoria Bobby Walking Tours**, 874 Fleming St., #414, ☎ 250/995-0233.

Victorian Garden Tours, 1770 Milton St., Victoria, BC V8P 3B1, ☎ 250/721-2797, fax 250/721-3906, steers you to the city's most beautiful gardens, while **Eco Tours, Inc.**, 3198 Ilona Place, Victoria, BC V9B 5C8, ☎ 250/474-7463 or 800/665-7463, fax 250/474-4713, E-mail ecotours@oceanside.com, Web site www.oceanside.com/oceanside/ecotours/, sets up four- and seven-day hikes, cruises, yacht outings, and ski trips.

The **West Coast Trail**, ☎ 250/728-3234 or 726-7721, is located between **Bamfield** and **Port Renfrew**. The 77-kilometer track was constructed for shipwrecked sailors and requires strength and stamina. Allow a minimum of five days to make the hike. (For more information, contact The Superintendent, Pacific Rim National Park, Box 280, Ucluelet, BC V0R 3A0.)

■ On Horseback

Horseback riding is superb along the Chemainus River southeast of Chemainus. Equally enjoyable are the rides east of Maple Bay near Maple Mountain and Sansum Narrows. A new indoor arena, Arbutus Meadows, is in Nanaimo.

As you ride on the beach in Newcastle Island Provincial Marine Park, you can see rare champagne-colored raccoons. **Salt Spring Guided Rides**, ☎ 250/537-5761, conducts half-hour to two-hour rides seven days a week on Salt Spring Island.

Woodgate Stables, 915 Mt. Maxwell Rd., Saanichton, ☎ 250/652-0287, is on Derrinburg Road just off East Saanich Road. English riding, Western riding, lessons, pony rides, and tours are available.

Celebration Carriage Services, ☎ 250/655-3672, takes groups of six people or fewer on a tour of Sidney in a horse-drawn carriage. **Sandown Harness Raceway**, ☎ 250/656-1631, features harness racing on Saturdays and Sundays during July and early August.

Tallyho Horsedrawn Tours, 2044 Milton St., Victoria, BC V8R 1N9, ☎ 250/383-5067, fax 250/595-2625, takes one-hour carriage tours of the city beginning outside the Parliament buildings and across from the Wax Museum. The tours leave every 20 minutes between 10 AM and 5:30 PM from April 4 to June 5 and from September 2 to October 4, and every 15 minutes between 9:30 AM and 7 PM from June 6 to September 3. Similar horse-drawn carriage tours are offered by **Victoria Carriage Tours**, 251 Superior St., ☎ 604/383-2207 or 389-2286, fax 604/383-2207, and by **Black Beauty Line**, ☎ 604/361-1220.

Canadians are as fond of their rodeos as Americans. Indeed, one of the world's largest is the annual Calgary Stampede, held in Calgary, Alberta. In British Columbia, Coombs hosts an annual **Bull-O-Rama** in mid-May on the Coombs Rodeo Grounds, ☎ 250/248-1009; South Cowichan holds the **Kerry Park Rodeo** in Mill Bay each May; and Victoria stages the **Luxton Pro Rodeo** on the Luxton Fair Grounds, Sooke and Luxton Roads, ☎ 250/478-2759 or 478-6390, in mid-May.

■ On Wheels

Tours & Motor Home Rentals

Adventures West Tours, PO Box 775, Station A, Campbell River, BC V9W 6J3, ☎ 604/923-6113, fax 604/923-6119, takes groups in minivans to watch whales and bears. **Salt Spring Tours**, ☎ 604/537-4737, fax 604/537-1846, conducts minivan and bus tours of Salt Spring Island.

Big Boy's Toys, 6862 Mart Rd. (Island Hwy), Lantzville, BC V0R 2H0, ☎ 250/390-2345 or 800/492-2869, fax 250/390-2334, rents 19- to 27-foot air-conditioned motor homes.

Racing

Cassidy Speedway, ☎ 250/245-5545, offers auto racing – mini-stocks, sprint cars, and stock cars – every Saturday night at 7:30 from April through October at a raceway seven miles south of Nanaimo. **Saratoga Speedway**, ☎ 250/337-5024, 337-8106, or 923-2982, also features auto racing on a track between Courtenay and Oyster River from April through September. Take Hamm Road east to Macaulay Road and turn right.

Cycling

Cycling is popular on Vancouver Island, where the auto traffic is light, and a ring road on Gabriola Island is also very popular with cyclists.

Chain Reaction Bicycle Sales, ☎ 250/754-3309, in Nanaimo rents bikes. So do **Spoke Folk**, 104 McPhilips Ave., Salt Spring Island, ☎ 250/539-4664; **True Value Hardware**, 2488 Beacon Ave., Sidney, ☎ 250/656-8611; and **Sports Rent**, 611 Discovery St., Victoria, ☎ 250/385-7368.

Rail Tours

Two Spot, a **fully restored steam locomotive** operated by Alberni Pacific Ltd. in Port Alberni, provides hourly rides during on summer weekends. The train leaves the E&N Railway Station near Harbour Quay. VIA Rail, ☎ 250/383-4324 or 800/561-8630, provides day excursions for railroad fans.

■ On the Water

Diving & Whale-Watching

National Geographic magazine has said that the scuba diving around Vancouver Island is "second only to the Red Sea." Winter, when underwater visibility can extend up to 130 feet, is the best season for diving.

Diving off Cape Scott Provincial Park on the north end of the island is particularly fruitful for those wishing to explore **shipwrecks**. The wrecks of *Magic Mac* (1892) and *Galiano* (1918) are in Scott Channel. Off Cape Scott are the *Hermit* (1892) and *Louisa Down* (1868). West of Cape Scott is the *Northolm* (1943). *Black Barnacle* (1938) is in Guise Bay, *Flayberg* (1897) is in Hansen Bay, and *Cape Scott I* (1910) went down west of Lowrie Bay. *Consort* (1860) and *Henry Dennis* (1892) are in San Josef Bay.

Scuba diving also is good in Maple Bay southeast of **Crofton**, and while Gabriola Island offers an excellent variety of watersport opportunities, the scuba diving and kayaking are superb. **Gabriola Sands Provincial Park** on Ricard Road has sandy beaches that are ideal for swimming. **Sandwell Provincial Park** has a fine pebble beach at the end of Strand Road. **Drumbeg Provincial Park** on Stalker Road provides trails, rocky and pebble beaches, tidal pools, and great swimming. **Orlebar Point** on Berry Point Road has rocky beaches, good swimming, great views, and some fine diving. **High Test Adventures**, ☎ 250/977-7823 or 247-9753, conducts diving and photo tours.

Campbell River Snorkel Tours, PO Box 62, **Campbell River**, BC V9W 4Z9, ☎ 350/286-0030, conducts underwater tours during salmon runs. **Exta Sea Charters**, 6209 Scollos Pl., **Nanaimo**, BC V9V 1K9, ☎ 250/756-0544, fax 250/758-4897, schedules scuba diving, kayaking, sightseeing, and wildlife-viewing charters, as do **Clavella Adventures**, Box 866, ☎ 250/753-3751, fax 250/755-4014, E-mail clavella@nanaimo.ark.com; **Ocean Explorers Diving**, 1956 Zorkin Rd., ☎ 250/753-2055, fax 250/753-2004, E-mail oceanex@islandnet.com; **Sundown Diving**, 22 Esplanade, ☎ 250/753-1880 or 888/773-3483, fax 250/753-6445, E-mail sundown@nanaimo.ark.com; and **Emerald Coast Adventures**, Box 971 Sta. A, ☎ 250/755-6946, fax 250/722-3394.

Dorcas Point Charters, Box 12 Schooner House, 3521 Dolphin Dr., **Nanoose Bay**, Vancouver Island, BC V0R 2R0, ☎ 250/468-7144 or 800/468-7144, offers group charters as well as picnics, kayaking, hiking, and wildlife cruises. They also charter cruises to nearby Jedediah Island.

In **Parksville**, **Beachcomber Excursions**, French Creek Harbor, ☎ 250/248-8538, books diving expeditions aboard the 41-foot *MV Terry Wayne*. Two other Parksville companies that charter diving parties are **Dorcas Point Charters,** Schooner Cove Marina, ☎ 250/468-7144 or 800/468-7144, and **Pacific North Scuba Diving**, 240 Dogwood St., ☎ 250/248-9681.

AK Trips & Charters, PO Box 1620, **Port Hardy**, BC V0N 2P0, ☎ 250/949-7952, fax 250/949-6040, and **Catala Charters**, 6170 Hardy Bay Rd., Box 526, Port Hardy, BC V0N 2P0, ☎ 250/949-7560, are the place to book a diving charter in Port Hardy.

Around **Port McNeill**, the place to line up a dive is either **Sun Fun Divers**, 1697 Beach Dr., Port McNeill, BC V0N 2R0, ☎ 250/956-2243, or **Starline Water Tours**, Fort McNeill Marina, ☎ 250/949-0373, Web site www.marlin.travel.com.

Scuba diving also is good in Telegraph Cove and in the region around **Ucluelet**.

For lessons and equipment rental around **Victoria**, contact either **Ocean Centre**, 800 Cloverdale Ave., ☎ 250/475-2202, or **Frank White's Scuba Shop**, 2537 Beacon Ave, Sidney, or 1855 Blanshard St., Victoria, ☎ 604/656-9202 or 385-4713. The latter also can arrange for a dive on the *McKenzie* or the *G.B. Church*, both nearby shipwrecks.

Headwind Charters, Box 319, **Alert Bay**, BC V0N 1A0, ☎ 250/974-2032 or 800/947-2031, schedules trips for whale-watching, sight-seeing, kayak transport, and camping trips. **Seasmoke/Sea Orca Expeditions**, ☎ 250/974-5225 or 800/668-6722, also conducts whale-watching trips.

Marine Wildlife Tours, PO Box 124, **Campbell River**, BC V9W 5A7, ☎ 604/286-3474 or 800/660-9747, conducts tours to the Discovery Islands and provides a "rare chance to observe bald eagles capturing fish right beside the boat." **King Salmon Adventure**, Discover Harbour Marina, ☎ 604/644-4999, accommodates four to six people for two- to five-day fishing trips aboard a 45-foot Bayliner motor yacht, or will take up to nine people on a day's cruise/fishing excursion. **River City Adventures**, 850G 12th Ave., ☎ 604/287-7715 or 800/567-6511, takes people on trips to watch grizzly bears as well as whales. Fishing and ocean or river kayaking also are available.

Nootka Sound Service, PO Box 57, **Gold River**, BC V0P 1G0, ☎ 250/283-2325 or 283-2525, fax 250/283-7582, provides transportation to the communities of Mooyah Bay, Yuquot, Tahsis, Kyuquot, Chamiss Bay, and Fair Harbour, while passing Bligh Island, Strange Island, Bodega Island, Catala Island, Union Island, Whiteley Island, Hohoae Island, and Moketas Island.

Canoeing in Vancouver (Graham Osborne).

Alberni Marine Transportation, PO Box 188, **Port Alberni**, BC V9Y 7M7, ☎ 250/723-8313 or 800/663-7192, fax 250/723-8314, rents canoes and kayaks. Between 8 AM and 5 PM from Monday through Friday, the company also carries passengers, freight, mail, and charters to Bamfield, Ucluelet, and Broken Islands.

Tri-Island Ferry, ☎ 250/956-4533, transports cars and passengers between Port McNeill, Alert Bay, and Sointula.

Prince of Whales Ocean Tours, ☎ 250/656-8788, takes whale-watching tours out of **Saanich**, and **Stubbs Island Whale Watching**, PO Box 7, **Telegraph Cove**, BC V0N 3J0, ☎ 250/928-3185, 928-3117, or 800/665-3066, fax 250/928-3102, E-mail stubbs@north.island.net, Web site north.island.net/~stubbs/, conducts four- to five-hour orca-watching tours daily from mid-June to mid-October.

Coastline Charters, Box 105, **Bamfield**, BC V0R 1B0, ☎ 250/728-3217, guides fishing trips on Barkley Sound. **Bamfield Fishing Charters**, ☎ 250/728-3286, offers similar services.

Tula Girl Charters, Box 44, **Sointula**, BC V0N 3E0, ☎ 250/973-6002 or 974-8133, provides kayak transport, nature studies, beachcombing expeditions, whale-watching, and fishing trips. **Sooke Coastal Explorations**, 7815 Dalrae Place, Sooke, BC V0S 1N0, ☎ 250/642-2343, takes whale-watching cruises.

Ocean Pacific Whale Charters, Box 590, **Tofino**, BC V0R 2Z0, ☎ 604/725-3919, takes whale-watching groups aboard the *M/V Lady Selkirk*. The trips depart at 11 AM and 1:30 PM from March 1 to April 30, and at 10 AM and 1:30 PM from May 1 to October 15. **Nootka Charters**, ☎ 604/725-3318; **Seaside Adventures**, ☎ 250/725-2292 or 888/332-4252; **Cypre Prince Tours**, ☎ 250/725-2202 or 800/787-2202; **Jamie's Whaling Station**, ☎ 250/725-3919 or 800/667-9913; and **Remote Passages Zodiac Adventures** ☎ 250/725-3330 or 800/666-9833, also take whale-watching trips out of Tofino.

Subtidal Adventures, 1950 Peninsula Rd., Box 78, **Ucluelet**, BC V0R 3A0, ☎ 604/726-7336 or 726-7061, takes tours, provides a water taxi service, arranges private charters, drops off campers, and leads whale-watching trips during the season. The grey whale migration runs from March through May.

From **Victoria**, **Seacoast Whale Watching Expeditions**, 45 Songhees Rd., ☎ 250/383-2254; **Springtide Charters**, 950 Wharf St., ☎ 250/658-6016, or 4336 Crownwood Lane, ☎ 250/658-6016 or 800/470-3474; **Seaker Adventure Tours**, 950 Wharf St., ☎ 250/480-0244 or 800/728-0244; **Victoria Marine Adventure Centre**, 950 Wharf St.,

☎ 250/995-2211 or 800/575-6700; **Spy Hoffer Whale Watching**, 950 Wharf St., ☎ 250/388-6222; and **Victoria Harbour Charters**, 950 Wharf St., ☎ 250/381-5050, will all take you whale-watching. **Island Boat Rentals**, 950 Wharf St., ☎ 250/995-1661, rents kayaks, canoes, and fishing boats. **Ocean Wind Water Springs**, 5411 Hamsterly Rd., ☎ 250/658-8171, will help you go windsurfing.

Fishing

Trout fishing and windsurfing are popular at Cameron Lake, and there is a campground on the lake with a good swimming beach.

Campbell River has Canada's only saltwater fishing pier, and fishing charters can be arranged through **Blue Water Charters**, 2321 South Island Pkwy., ☎ 604/923-3499; **Top Guides**, PO Box 20025, ☎ 250/287-4475, fax 250/287-3435; **Harry MacDonald**, 632 Erickson Rd., ☎ 250/923-2236, fax 250/923-5744; **Calypso Charters**, 384 Simm's Rd., ☎ 250/923-2001 or 287-0542, fax 250/923-5121; **Megan Cruising**, 738A Beaver Lodge Rd., ☎ 250/286-9610; **Sea Blue Salmon Charters**, 623 Holm Rd., ☎ 250/923-6079; **Aqua Vets**, 180 S. Thulin St., ☎ 250/287-4833 or 830-7039; **Silver King**, PO Box 351, ☎ 250/286-0142 or 800/811-7455, fax 250/286-3639; and **C.R. Moonshadow Charters**, 569 S. Alder St., ☎ 604/287-3153 or 287-6091, fax 604/287-3453.

By renting boats by the hour or the day, **Campbell River Sportfishing Rentals**, 1231 Spruce St., Campbell River, BC V9W 3L6, ☎ 250/287-7279, fax 250/287-2353, Web site oberon.ark.com/~crfish, makes it possible for you to go fishing on your own.

The largest of the Discovery Islands, **Quadra** is a 10-minute ferry ride from Campbell River. **Discovery Charters**, PO Box 48, **Quathiaski Cove**, BC V0P 1N0, ☎ 250/285-3146 or 800/668-8054, fax 250/285-3034, conducts fishing charters around Quadra, the western shore of which is studded with steep slopes covered with starfish and anemones. The *HMCS Columbia,* an antisubmarine destroyer launched in 1956 and decommissioned in 1974, was sunk there recently to create an artificial reef.

Denverlene, 1784 Dogwood Ave., **Comox**, BC V9M 2X3, ☎ 250/339-5137, Web site mars.ark.com/~denverle/, offers fishing charters.

Around **Gabriola Island**, fishing charters can be scheduled with **Fish Witch Salmon Charters**, ☎ 250/247-8512; **Silver Blue Charters**, ☎ 250/247-8807 or 755-6150, fax 250/247-9700; **Crowsnest Sailing**, ☎ 250/247-8961; **Blackbeard Charters**, ☎ 250/290-8540 or

247-8934; **Sea-Er Charters**, ☎ 250/247-9708; and *Lucky Lou Charters*, ☎ 250/247-8455.

In **Goldstream Provincial Park**, salmon travel the Finlayson Arm and run into the Goldstream River from the Pacific Ocean. The runs occur from October through December.

End of the Line, Box 64, **Holberg**, BC V0N 1Z0, ☎ 800/447-9322, charters fishing trips and rents boats.

Codfather Charters, 1-6465 Hardy Bay Rd., **Port Hardy**, BC V0N 2P0, ☎ 250/949-6696, and **Lead-On Adventure Co.**, PO Box 937, Port Hardy, BC V0N 2P0, ☎ 250/949-5977, both charter fishing trips, as do **Dixon Charters**, Box 1005, **Port McNeill**, BC V0N 2R0, ☎ 250/956-4887 or 974-8300, and **Sure Hit Charters**, PO Box 587, Port McNeill, BC V0N 2R0, ☎ 250/956-3474 or 949-1291.

In **Saanich**, fishing trips can be scheduled through **Sunrise Salmon Charters**, ☎ 250/656-5570, and on Salt Spring Island through **Salt Spring Marine Rentals**, ☎ 250/537-9100 or 800/334-6629.

In **Sidney**, **Affordable Fishing Charters**, ☎ 250/655-8817, arranges fishing trips from the Main Dock at Port Sidney Marina, and **Island Moorings**, ☎ 250/655-8987, offers the same service at Van Isle Marina.

Magic Dragon Charter Tours & Fishing, Box 410, **Sointula**, BC V0N 3E0, ☎ 250/974-8080, conducts fishing, exploring, and whale-watching excursions between February 1 and December 10. Five lakes that afford excellent fishing in **Strathcona Provincial Park** are Douglas Lake, McKenzie Lake, Gold Lake, Bedwell Lake, and Price Creek/Cream Lake.

Ucluelet provides choice salmon fishing from April to October. **Quest Charters**, PO Box 487, Ucluelet, BC V0R 3A0, ☎ 250/726-7532, fax 250/726-7531, guides fishing charters on Barkley Sound and the surrounding area.

Juan de Fuca Sportfishing Centre, 110-2244 Sooke Rd., **Victoria**, BC V9B 1X1, ☎ 604/391-9952, and **Reel Action Fishing Charters**, 961 Haslam Ave., ☎ 250/478-1977, offer fishing charters. **Cheanuh Marina**, 4901 E. Sooke Rd., ☎ 604/478-4880, fax 604/478-3585, takes anglers to nearby Beechy Head, Trapshack, and Secretary Island, and **Above & Below Charters**, PO Box 8089, ☎ 604/361-4321 or 361-5067, not only arranges fishing charters but videotapes your adventure.

Boating

Do-it-yourselfers can rent kayaks and fishing boats at **Brentwood Inn Boat Rentals**, 7172 Brentwood Dr., **Brentwood Bay**, BC, ☎ 250/652-3151, and **Brentwood-Port Side Marina**, 789 Saunders Lane, ☎ 250/652-2211, rents 16- to 27-foot sailboats by the hour, day or week.

The **Broken Group Islands**, centered in Barkley Sound, include more than 100 islands and islets that afford excellent kayaking action.

In the Gulf Islands, **Gulf Island Kayaking**, R.R. #1, **Chemainus**, Galiano Island, BC V0N 1P0, ☎ 250/539-2442, E-mail kayak@gulfislands.com, Web site www.seakayak.bc.ca.tour, conducts kayaking tours. **Esquimalt Lagoon** near Colwood has a nice sandy beach for swimming. **Desolation Sound Yacht Charters**, 101-1819 Comox Ave., Comox, BC V9M 3L9, ☎ 604/339-7222, fax 604/339-2217, operates charters on both power and sail boats.

Tree Island Kayaking, 3050 Comox Rd., **Courtenay**, BC V9N 2L3, ☎ 250/339-0580, and Comox Valley Kayaks, 2020 Cliffe Ave., ☎ 250/334-2628 or 888/545-5595, offer kayak rentals, lessons, and tours. **Big Island Inflata-Boats**, 2703 Kilpatrick Ave., Unit J, ☎ 250/897-1169, rents tenders, sport boats, specialty boats, and life rafts. **Sunstar Yachts**, 2020 Pine Pl., ☎ 250/338-2520, offers cruises aboard the 45-foot yacht *Affinity I*.

On **Gabriola Island**, **Gabriola Cycle & Kayak**, ☎ 250/247-8277, rents kayaks, while Silva Bay Boatel & Store, ☎ 250/247-0186, fax 250/247-0184, not only rents boats, but sells fishing tackle and bait. **Kayaking Centre**, 2755 Departure Bay Rd., **Nanaimo**, BC V9S 3W9, ☎ 250/758-2488, rents kayaks, provides lessons, and conducts tours. **Alpha-Wave Adventures**, Argyle Pier, 5425 Argyle St., **Port Alberni**, BC V9Y 7M7, ☎ 250/723-0026, rents kayaks and canoes, provides lessons, and guides kayaking, hiking, and camping tours to the Broken, Deer, and Chain Group Islands.

Saltspring Kayaking, 104 McPhilips Ave., **Salt Spring Island**, BC V8K 2T5, ☎ 250/653-4222, and **Sea Otter Kayaking**, 1186 North End Rd., ☎ 250/537-5678, E-mail kayaking@saltspring.com, Web site www.islandnet.com/~wtaylor/seaotter.html, make guided day, sunset, and full-moon kayak paddles. Kayaks also can be rented from **Island Escapades**, 118 Natalie Lane, ☎ 250/537-2571 or 888/KAYAK-67, fax 250/537-2532.

Robson Bight Charters, Box 99, **Sayward**, BC V0P 1R0, ☎ 250/282-3833 or 800/658-0022 (BC only), fax 250/282-3833, takes charters aboard the 56-foot motor yacht *Le Caique* from June through October.

In **Sidney**, boat rentals can be arranged through **Sea-Trek Sports**, 9813 3rd St., ☎ 250/656-9888; **Bosun's Charters**, 2240 Harbour Rd., ☎ 250/656-6644 or 800/226-3694, fax 250/656-4935; and **Gulf Islands Cruising School**, Canoe Cove Marina, 2300 Canoe Cove Rd., ☎ 250/656-2638 or 800/665-2628, fax 259/656-6433. Charters can be scheduled through **Seaquest DSV Adventures**, 591 Braemar Ave., R.R.#2, ☎ 250/655-9256, fax 250/655-3771, E-mail seaquest@tnet.net, Web site www.bctravel.com/seaquest.html, and **The Island Cruising Group**, 9851 Seaport Place, ☎ 800/663-5311, E-mail islandcruise@commercial.net, Web site www.commercial.netvaultisland. **Sidney Harbour Shuttle**, ☎ 604/385-1998, provides a water bus, leads a wildlife tour, and takes waterfront cruises that leave every hour from the town pier at the foot of Beacon Avenue; from Blue Peter Pub, 2270 Harbour Rd.; and from Canoe Cove Marina.

Aquarium

Marine Ecology Station, Pier 66, R.R. #1, Cowichan Bay Road, **Cowichan Bay**, BC V0R 1N0, ☎ 250/748-4522, fax 250/748-4410, Web site www.island.net/~mareco/, has a hands-on aquarium that is open between noon and 5 PM daily in the summer and on the weekends during the fall and spring.

■ On Snow

Skiing and snowboarding are popular on **Mount Washington** near Campbell River.

In **Courtenay**, the **Snow Phone** is ☎ 250/338-1919, and the **Ski & Surf Shop**, 333 5th St., ☎ 250/338-8844, will rent you skis and/or a snowboard. **Forbidden Plateau**, ☎ 250/334-4744, has ski lifts (which are open for the use of hikers between Wednesday and Sunday in the summer). **Mount Washington Resort**, Box 3069, Courtenay, BC V9N 5N3, ☎ 250/338-1386, fax 250/338-7295, Web site www.vquest.com/alpine/, features both downhill and cross-country skiing during the winter and hiking in the summer.

Mount Arrowsmith also provides downhill and cross-country skiing in the winter and hiking and climbing in the summer. **Strathcona Provincial Park** offers good skiing at Mount Washington and at Wood Mountain Ski Park on the Forbidden Plateau.

■ In the Air

E&B Helicopters, 2595 Island Hwy, PO Box 1000, **Campbell River**, BC V9W 6Y4, ☎ 250/287-4421, fax 250/287-4352, offers sight-seeing tours of an hour or more for one to three passengers. The tours include whale-watching flights. **CoVal Air Ltd.**, PO Box 1451, ☎ 250/287-8371, fax 250/287-8366, provides sightseeing and fishing excursions in aircraft equipped with either wheels or floats.

Hang gliding is popular at Mount Prevost Park southwest of **Crofton** and northwest of Duncan. **SuperScenic Flight**, PO Box 19, Gold River, BC V0P 1G0, ☎ 250/283-2255, conducts flights for whale-watching, hiking, fishing, and exploring the coastal beaches.

Seair, ☎ 800-447-3247, flies three scheduled flights daily between the Gulf Islands and Vancouver with stops at Ganges Harbour, Montague Harbour, Lyall Harbour, Bedwell Harbour, Telegraph Harbour, and/or Miner's Bay. Scenic tours and seaplane charters also can be arranged.

Harbour Air Seaplanes, ☎ 250/537-5525 or 800/665-0212, makes eight scheduled flights between the Gulf Islands, Vancouver, and northern British Columbia on weekdays and four flights on weekends and holidays. Scenic tours and seaplane charters also can be arranged.

CFB Comex Air Force Museum, Lazo, BC V0R 2K0, ☎ 250/339-8162, is open between 10 AM and 4 PM Wednesday through Sunday and on holidays from June to August, and on Saturdays, Sundays, and holidays in the winter.

Bungy Zone, 35 Nanaimo River Rd., PO Box 399, Station A, Nanaimo, BC V9R 5L3, ☎ 250/755-1266 or 800/668-7771, fax 250/755-1196, Web site www.com/bungy, is North America's only legal bridge jump site.

Baxter Aviation, ☎ 250/754-1066 or 800/661-5599, operates out of the Nanaimo Seaplane Terminal, conducting flights for whale-watching, exploring glaciers, sightseeing, and seeing the Gulf Islands.

Nanaimo Airport, ☎ 604/245-2157, fax 604/245-4308, E-mail ycd4@mail.island.net, Web site www.island.net/~ycd/, offers an average of 15 scheduled flights daily to Vancouver.

Air Rainbow, Box 520, Port McNeill, BC V0N 2R0, ☎ 250/956-2020, fax 250/956-2025, schedules chartered flights.

Harbor Air Seaplanes, 4760 Inglis Dr., Richmond, BC V7B 1W4, ☎ 250/385-2203, fax 250/385-2234, E-mail harbour@harbour-air.com, Web site www.harbour-air.com, is based on the inner harbour at Wharf Street beside the Victoria Regent Hotel. Their fleet takes passengers from Victoria to Vancouver in 35 minutes and arranges aerial tours and charters. The company has other locations in Vancouver and Prince Rupert.

On Salt Spring Island, hang gliders leave 589-meter Mount Bruce and land in Fulford Valley.

In Sidney, tours and flight training are provided by **Victory Flying Club**, 101-1852 Canso Rd., Sidney, BC V8L 5B5, ☎ 250/656-4321, fax 250/655-0910. Also of interest to aviation enthusiasts is **BC Aviation Museum**, 1910 Norseman Rd. (Victoria International Airport), Sidney, BC, ☎ 250/655-3300.

Contrails, 101-19 Bastion Square, Victoria, BC V8W 1J1, ☎ 250/361-4745, specializes in gifts for aviators.

■ Cultural Excursions

Brentwood Bay

Perhaps the most popular single attraction on Vancouver Island is **Butchart Gardens**, 800 Benvenuto Ave., Brentwood Bay, BC V8M 1J8, ☎ 250/652-4422 or 652-5256, fax 250/652-3883, E-mail butchartgardens.bc.ca, which has 50 acres of gorgeous flower gardens on a private 130-acre estate. The gardens are open daily, including holidays, at 9 AM. A dining room, ☎ 250/652-8222, is on the grounds.

Also located in Brentwood Bay are the **Butterfly Gardens**, 1461 Benvenuto Ave., PO Box 190, Brentwood Bay, BC V8M 1R3, ☎ 250/652-3822, fax 250/652-4683, Web site victoriabc.com/attract/butterfly.htm, where you can explore some gardens amid hundreds, if not thousands, of free-flying butterflies. The attraction is open daily at 9 AM.

Two other sights are nearby. **Dominion Astrophysical Observatory**, 5071 W. Saanich Rd., ☎ 250/363-0030, is open between 9:15 AM and 4:30 PM daily and between 7 and 11 PM on Saturday evenings from April through October, while the **Institute of Ocean Sciences**, 9860 W. Saanich Rd., ☎ 250/363-6518, conducts tours at 11 AM on Mondays and Wednesdays by appointment.

Chemainus, a former mill town, bills itself as the "world's largest outdoor art gallery." The colorful little town contains 32 murals and six outdoor sculptures.

Cobble Hill

Cherry Point Vineyards, 840 Cherry Point Rd., R.R. 3, Cobble Hill, BC V0R 1L0, has a tasting room and an art gallery on its spacious grounds.

Parksville

Butterfly World, ☎ 250/248-7026, is in Coombs near Parksville and Qualicum Beach on the Alberni Highway as you head towards Cathedral Grove. It is open between 10 AM and 6 PM daily. Goats nibble on the grass roof of the nearby market.

Courtenay

Sid Williams Civic Theatre, 442 Cliffe Ave., Courtenay, BC, ☎ 250/338-2420, a 450-seat downtown theater, presents live performances year-around, and the **Courtenay & District Museum**, 360 Cliffe Ave., ☎ 250/334-3611, fax 250/334-4277, is open between 10 AM and 4:30 PM daily from May through August and daily except Sunday and Monday in the winter.

Cumberland

Cumberland Museum, 2680 Dunsmuir Ave., Box 258, Cumberland, BC V0R 1S0, ☎ 250/336-2445, contains a replica of an old mine. The museum is open between 9 AM and 5 PM daily from May to September and daily except Sunday in the winter.

Duncan

Duncan has a number of interesting sights. **Cowichan Native Village**, 200 Cowichan Way, ☎ 250/746-8119, fax 250/746-4143, Web site www.cowichan.org, is on the Cowichan River. There are crafts demonstrations, plus a cafe, a restaurant, a gift shop, a mid-day salmon BBQ, and a show. Summer hours (May to mid-October) are from 9:30 AM to 5 PM daily. Winter hours (mid-October to May) are from 10 AM to 4:30 PM daily.

British Columbia Forest Museum, 2892 Drinkwater Rd., R.R. 4, Duncan, BC V9L 3W8, ☎ 250/715-1113, fax 250/715-1170, which is open from April to October, occupies 100 acres and operates an old steam train.

World of Wonders, PO Box 20010, Duncan, BC V9L 5H1, ☎ 250/748-7620, a wildlife theme park, is four kilometers south of town off Bench

Road. It includes a walk-through aviary and a petting park. The attraction is open daily between 10 AM and 7 PM in the summer.

Gabriola Island

Each May, Gabriola Island has an **outhouse race**. Contestants do not run *to* the outhouse, but *with* the outhouse. The race is followed by a BBQ, a beer garden, and a dance.

Nanaimo

Sealand of Nanaimo, 1840 Stewart St., Nanaimo, BC, ☎ 250/754-1723, allows you to explore octopus grottos and wolf eel dens, study sharks and alligators, and take a safari through a tropical jungle. The attraction is open daily from 10 AM.

Parksville

Emerald Forest Bird & Reptile Garden, 1420 Alberni Hwy, Parksville, BC V9P 2G5, ☎ 604/248-7282, fax 604/248-1146, is open between 10 AM and 5 PM from May 14 to June 14, between 10 AM and 8 PM from June 15 to September 15, and between 10 AM and 3 PM from September 16 to May 13.

Port Alberni

In Port Alberni, the Harbour Quay has a clock tower that affords lovely views of the port and Mount Arrowsmith. In July, the **Nuu Chah Nulth Indian Games** are conducted there.

Sidney

Sidney Marine Mammal Historical Museum, 9801 Seaport Place, Sidney, BC V8L 1Y2, ☎ 250/656-1322, fax 250/656-2847, can answer your questions about whales, seals, and other marine mammals, while the **Friends of Sidney Museum**, 2538 Beacon Ave., ☎ 250/656-2140, has a gift shop that specializes in items relating to whales.

Victoria

Victoria not only is the capital of British Columbia, but it is a "City of Gardens." In addition to the gardens, **Thunderbird Park** is ornamented with a number of totem poles. **Royal British Columbia Museum**, 675 Belleville St., ☎ 250/387-5745, 387-3701, or 800/661-5411, fax 250/356-8197, Web site rbcml.rbcm.gov.bc.ca, conducts eco-tours for children, day trips, and over-nighters (write Uniglobe Travel, 1672

Douglas St., Victoria, BC V8W 2G6, or ☎ 250/386-3311, for a catalog). The museum is open daily between 9 AM and 5 PM except on Christmas and New Year's Day. **Craigdarroch Castle**, 1050 Joan Crescent, ☎ 250/592-5323, fax 250/592-1099, E-mail ccastle@islandnet.com, a 39-room mansion dating from 1890, is open between 9 AM and 7:30 PM in the summer and between 10 AM and 5 PM during the off-season.

Fort Rodd Hill National Historic Park, 603 Fort Rodd Hill Rd., Victoria, BC V9C 2W8, ☎ 250/478-5849, fax 250/478-2816, E-mail fort_rodd@pch.gc.ca, is in the Colwood district of the capital city. A fort in the 1890s, the site now hosts concerts every Sunday during July and August. The park itself is open between 10 AM and 5:30 PM daily from March 1 to October 31. **Fisgard Lighthouse**, ☎ 250/478-5849, the oldest working lighthouse on the west coast (1860), is open to the public between 10 AM and 5:30 PM daily from March 1 to October 31.

Victoria's **Chinatown**, Fisgard and Cormorant Streets, once was the largest such community in Canada. Spanning Fisgard Street is Tong Ji Men (Gate of the Harmonious Interest), and Fan Tan Alley, named for the popular Chinese game, Fan Tan (to turn over and spread out), is Victoria's narrowest, and until 1908, when the manufacture and sale of opium was outlawed, was the site of the Kwong Lee and Tai Soong opium factories.

Royal London Wax Museum, 470 Belleville St., ☎ 604/388-4461, fax 604/388-4493, E-mail khl@pinc.com, is a wax museum with a difference. Yes, Charlie Chaplin, John Wayne, and Marilyn Monroe are included in the exhibits, but so are explorer John Franklin, figures from the Mad Hatter's Tea Party and other children's stories, Queen Victoria, Charles Dickens, and Rudyard Kipling.

Kids will love the 155-acre **Beacon Hill Children's Farm,** Circle Drive, Beacon Hill Park, ☎ 250/381-2532. English Village and Anne Hathaway's Cottage, 429 Lampson St., ☎ 250/388-4353 or 800/663-6106, is a full-scale replica furnished with authentic 16th-century antiques. It is open between 9 and 9 during the summer and between 10 AM and 5 PM during the off-season.

Crystal Garden, 713 Douglas St., ☎ 250/381-1277 or 381-1213, fax 250/383-1218, displays a number of endangered tropical plants, butterflies, 75 species of exotic birds, the world's smallest monkeys, and some koi fish. There is also a restaurant and *six* gift shops. The garden is open between 8 AM and 11 PM daily. **Horticulture Centre of the Pacific**, 505 Quayle Rd., ☎ 250/479-6162, features some magnificent gardens.

Pacific Undersea Gardens, 490 Belleville St., ☎ 250/382-5717, fax 250/382-5210, is a theater on the bottom of the sea. Located opposite the Parliament buildings, the gardens produce a live scuba diving show.

September through May is the season for **Victoria Symphony**, 846 Broughton St., ☎ 250/386-6121 or 385/6515. **SummerFest** is held during July and August. **Kaleidoscope Theatre**, 520 Herald St., ☎ 250/383-8124, is a professional theater geared specially for young audiences and their families.

Maritime Museum of British Columbia, 28 Bastion Square, ☎ 250/385-4222, fax 250/382-2869, located in an historic 1899 building, is open between 9:30 AM and 4:30 PM daily.

The **Victoria Shamrocks Lacross Club**, ☎ 250/361-0506, plays its matches in Memorial Arena.

Where to Stay

Two reservations services that may be useful are **Canadian Gulf Islands Reservation Service**, ☎ 250/539-2930, E-mail reservations@gulfisland.com, Web site www.multimedia.bcit.bc.ca/b&b, and the **Tourism British Columbia Accommodations Program**, 1117 Wharf St., PO Box 9830, Stn. Prov. Govt., Victoria, BC V8W 9W5, ☎ 250/387-6309, fax 250/387-9406.

Campbell River

Anchor Inn, 261 Island Hwy, Campbell River, BC V9W 2B3, ☎ 250/286-1131 or 800/663-7227, fax 250/287-4055, E-mail anchor.inn@access.cn.camriv.bc.ca, Web site www.vquest.com/anchor, $-$$, has an oceanfront location and three oceanfront restaurants. The inn also arranges fishing, whale-watching, hiking, snorkeling, and diving excursions. **Austrian Chalet**, 462 South Island Hwy, ☎ 604/923-4231 or 800/667-7207, fax 604/923-2840, $-$$, can offer salmon fishing and skiing in addition to accommodations. **Painter's Lodge Holiday Resort**, 1625 McDonald Rd., ☎ 250/286-1102 or 800/663-7090, fax 250/598-1361, E-mail obmg@pinc.com, $-$$$, will put you up while you're whale-watching, mountain biking, or snorkeling with the salmon in the river. **Seascape Resort**, PO Box 92, ☎ 604/285-3450, fax 604/285-2101, $$-$$$, is located on Quadra Island, where its waterfront location overlooks Gowlland Harbour, and April Point, PO Box 1, ☎ 604/285-2222, fax 604/285-2411, also is located on Quadra Island.

Nanaimo

Dorchester Hotel, 70 Church St., Nanaimo, BC V9R 5H4, ☎ 604/754-6835 or 800/661-2449, fax 604/754-2638, $$, is a Best Western affiliate. The **Coast Bastion Inn**, 11 Bastion St., ☎ 250/753-6601 or 800/663-1144, fax 250/753-4155, $$, has a downtown waterfront location, a restaurant, and a lounge. **Pepper Muffin Country Inn B&B**, 3718 Jingle Pot Rd., ☎ 250/756-0473, fax 250/756-0421, E-mail pog@island.net, $$-$$$, is on the Millstone River and provides a shuttle service to the airport, the ferries, and town, while **Long Lake Inn**, 4700 North Island Hwy, ☎ 250/758-1144 or 800/565-1144, fax 250/758-5832, $$-$$$, has lakeside rooms and suites, and has facilities for guests to rent canoes and paddle boats.

Parksville

Gray Crest Seaside Resort, 1115 E. Island Hwy, Parksville, BC V9P 2E2, ☎ 800/663-2636, $$-$$$, rents waterview condominiums on Rathtrevor Beach.

Port Hardy

God's Pocket Resort, Box 130, Port Hardy, BC V0N 2P0, ☎ 250/949-9221, $$-$$$, is a rustic waterfront resort in a small cove on Hurst Island, Queen Charlotte Strait. Fishing and scuba diving packages are available.

Victoria

Best Western Carlton Plaza Hotel, 642 Johnson St., Victoria, BC V8W 1M6, ☎ 250/388-5513 or 800/663-7241, fax 250/388-5343, $$-$$$, has 103 rooms including six two-bedroom units and 42 rooms with kitchens. The seven-story building has a nice downtown location and a restaurant that is open from 7 AM to 10 PM daily. **Best Western Inner Harbour**, 412 Quebec St., ☎ 250/384-5122, 800/528-1234, or 888/383-BEST, fax 250/384-5122, $$$, has just 74 rooms, including one two-bedroom unit. Rooms have private balconies, there is a heated outdoor pool, and a complimentary continental breakfast is included in the rates. The eight-story hotel is near Parliament and the downtown shopping district.

Embassy Inn, 520 Menzies St., Victoria, BC V8V 2H4, ☎ 250/382-8161 or 800/268-8161, fax 250/382-4224, Web site travel.bc.ca/e/embassy, $$-

$$$, is a three- and four-story hotel adjacent to Parliament. It has 103 rooms, including 15 efficiencies and 36 with kitchens. Rooms in the older wing have nice views of the inner harbour, while rooms in the newer wing have balconies. There is a heated pool and an on-site restaurant.

The "dowager queen" of Victoria's hotels is **The Empress**, 721 Government St., Victoria, BC V8W 1W5, ☎ 250/384-8111 or 800/441-1414, fax 250/381-4334, E-mail cdick@emp.mhs.compuserve.com, Web site www.vvv.com/empress, $$$-$$$$. Located just north of Parliament and facing the inner harbor, the historic grand old hotel is bedecked in ivy. There are 482 rooms, including 12 two-bedroom units and five three-bedroom units, on seven floors. High tea, served in the lobby, is a local tradition (don't even *think* about going without a reservation). The hotel has a heated indoor pool, an exercise room, an excellent restaurant, and a cocktail lounge.

Ocean Pointe Resort, 45 Songhees Rd., Victoria, BC V9A 6T3, ☎ 604/360-2999 or 800/667-4677, fax 604/360-1041, $$$-$$$$, has 250 large, nicely-decorated rooms, 35 of which have kitchens. There is a heated indoor pool, a racquetball court, two lighted tennis courts, a fitness center, a dining room, a restaurant, and a cocktail lounge. The 17-story **Executive House Hotel**, 777 Douglas St., ☎ 250/388-5111 or 800/663-7001, fax 250/385-1323, $$-$$$$, provides 179 rooms, including three two-bedroom units, 81 units with kitchens, and 21 efficiencies. There is a health club and a fine restaurant, Barkley's Steak & Seafood.

Smaller and more intimate is the **Bedford Regency**, 1140 Government St., Victoria, BC V8W 1Y2, ☎ 250/384-6835 or 800/665-6500, fax 250/386-8930, $$$-$$$$, a 40-room, European-style hotel that is strongly service oriented. Some rooms have fireplaces. High tea is served in the afternoon. Garrick's Head Pub, one of Victoria's oldest pubs, and the Red Currant Cafe are on-site. The hotel is downtown, facing Eaton's Centre.

Admiral Motel, 257 Belleville St., Victoria, BC V8V 1X1, ☎ 250/388-6267, fax 604/388-6267, Web site www.admiral.bc.ca, $-$$$, is an owner-operated, 29-room place with a convenient downtown location, but no restaurant.

■ Camping

Tuta Marina and Campgrounds, PO Box 765, **Gold River**, BC V0P 1G0, ☎ 250/283-7550, is open from May (Victoria Day) to September (Labor Day), but from May to July 1, it is open only on weekends.

Brannen Lake Campsites, 4220 Biggs Rd., **Nanaimo**, BC V9R F4R, ☎ 250/756-0404 or 390-4119, $$-$$$, can offer lake access, swimming, and hayrides in addition to its campsites.

Big Tent RV Park, 745 E. Island Hwy, **Parksville**, ☎ 250/248-6249, and Junction Service Campground, 2611 Port Alberni Hwy, Port Alberni, ☎ 250/723-2606, can offer camping accommodations in their respective regions.

Thetis Lake Campground, 1938 Trans Canada Hwy, **View Royal**, ☎ 604/478-3845, fax 604/478-6151, has swimming, a grocery, and a laundry on its 12-acre grounds.

> **British Columbia Motels, Campgrounds & Resorts Assn.**, 3003 St. John's St., Suite 209, **Port Moody**, BC V3H 2C4, ☎ 604/299-7676, publishes the informative annual *Super Camping*. The publication is available free of charge at most visitor's centres.

> *The RV Times*, a bimonthly magazine produced by Sheila Jones Publishing, 3378 Douglas St., Unit 109, **Victoria**, BC V8Z 3L3, ☎ 250/475-8860, fax 250/475-8861, E-mail rvtimes@island.net, also is distributed free of charge.

Where to Eat

Chemainus

The **Waterford Inn & Restaurant**, 9875 Maple St., Chemainus, ☎ 250/246-1046, $$, provides solid waterfront fare.

Duncan

Skinny Piggs, 28 Station St., Duncan, ☎ 250/746-8024, $-$$, located downtown, half a block from the train station, offers fresh bread baked daily and has a comfortable, sunny patio. **Stinky's**, 8-5777 Trans Canada Hwy, Duncan, ☎ 250/746-7743, $$, serves lunch from 11 AM and dinner from 5 PM. **Filthy McNasty's**, 14 Commercial St., Nanaimo, ☎ 250/753-7011, $$, serves breakfast, lunch, and dinner.

Protection Island

Dinghy Dock Pub, ☎ 250/753-8244 or 753-2372, $$, Canada's only floating pub, is located on Protection Island, a 10-minute ferry ride from Nanaimo, and offers beautiful views of Nanaimo and the harbor.

Victoria

Olde England Inn, 429 Lampson St., Victoria, ☎ 250/388-4353, $$$, serves candlelit dinners daily from 5:30 PM in the atmosphere of an old English manor house. Try the Yorkshire pudding. **Camille's**, 45 Bastion Square, ☎ 250/381-3433, $$, offers candlelight dinners in a century-old brick building.

Rebecca's, 1127 Wharf St., ☎ 250/380-6999, $$, provides outstanding harbour views.

Three- to four-hour **sunset dinner cruises** are available aboard the *SS Beaver*, ☎ 250/384-8116, or the *Pride of Victoria*, 1175 Beach Dr., ☎ 250/592-3474 or 598-4556.

Information Sources

British Columbia has a new *Discover British Columbia* information line: ☎ 800/663-6000.

Campbell River Tourism, PO Box 482, **Campbell River**, BC V9W 5C1, ☎ 250/286-1616 or 800/463-4386, fax 250/286-8336, E-mail crtour@vquest.com, Web site www.vquest.com/crtourism/.

Comox Valley Chamber of Commerce, 2040 Cliffe Ave., **Courtenay**, BC V9N 2L3, ☎ 250/334-3234, fax 250/334-4908, E-mail info@tourism.ark.com, Web site www.tourism-comox-valley.bc.ca.

District of North Cowichan Tourism Committee, PO Box 278, **Duncan**, BC V9L 3X4, ☎ 250/746-7101, fax 250/746-4133.

Tourism Nanaimo, Beban House, 2290 Bowen Rd., **Nanaimo**, BC V9T 3K7, ☎ 250/756-0106 or 800/663-7337, fax 250/756-0075, E-mail info@tourism.nanaimo.bc.ca, Web site tourism.nanimo.bc.ca.

Parksville Travel InfoCentre, PO Box 99, **Parksville**, BC V9P 2G3, ☎ 604/248-3613, fax 604/248-5210.

Alberni Valley Chamber of Commerce, Site 215, C-10, **Port Alberni**, BC V9Y 7L6, ☎ 250/724-6535.

Port Hardy and District Chamber of Commerce, Box 249, **Port Hardy**, BC V0N 2P0, ☎ 250/949-7622, fax 250/949-6653.

Sooke Travel Info Centre, Box 774, **Sooke**, BC V0S 1N0, ☎ 250/642-6351, fax 250/642-7089, E-mail ibj@sookenet.com, Web site www.sookenet.com/sooke/sooke.html.

Greater Victoria Visitors & Convention Bureau, 1175 Douglas St., #710, **Victoria**, BC V8W 2E1, ☎ 250/953-2033 or 800/663-3883, fax 250/382-6539.

Tourism Vancouver Island, 302-45 Bastion Square, Victoria, BC V8W 1J1, ☎ 250/382-3551, fax 250/383-3523, E-mail tavl@islands.bc.ca., Web site www.islands.bc.ca.

Vancouver & Environs

Vancouver is just 141 miles north of Seattle – an easy 2.5-hour drive down Interstate 5. And what Seattle is to Washington, Vancouver is to British Columbia – a business center, a banking center, a population center, a center of commerce and industry. It is the third largest city in all of Canada, but it should *not* be confused with the provincial capital. That distinction belongs to the city of Victoria, which sits on Vancouver *Island*, across the Strait of Georgia from the *city* of Vancouver.

Vancouver is steeped in the traditions of the British Isles. For example, lawn bowling is a favorite pastime, and suburban Port Coquitlam has a golf and country club named Carnoustie. Yet the people of Vancouver are distinctive in their own right. Vancouver is an *international* city – a place where people of every nationality mix freely on the streets throughout the day and the retail stores offer wide selections of merchandise from all over the world.

Getting Around

From the United States, take I-5 to the border, then follow Route 99 into the city, crossing the Fraser River near Delta, passing Vancouver International Airport on Sea Island, and going through Stanley Park before the highway crosses over Burrard Inlet into the community of West Vancouver.

Inside the Canadian border, TransCanada 1 travels northwest from Abbotsford, crosses the Fraser River northeast of Route 99, and passes through the suburbs of New Westminster and Burnaby, before it crosses Burrard Inlet east of Route 99 and enters the community of North Vancouver.

Severe traffic jams often occur throughout Greater Vancouver during rush hour, even at the major border-crossing points. On a busy day, re-

Vancouver (Bob Leong).

entry to the United States at the Peace Arch may take as long as an hour.

Airports

Greater Vancouver has a number of airports, including ones in Abbotsford, Clearbrook, Hope, and Squamish.

Langley Municipal Airport, ☎ 604/534-7330 or 671-2665, has lighted runways and handles 81,000 take-offs and landings each year.

Pitt Meadows Airport, ☎ 604/465-8977, is on Baynes Road south of Ford Road. It has three runways, the longest of which covers 1,310 meters, and there also is a seaplane access with a float dock along the Fraser River. Daily flights are provided to Victoria, and charter flights, helicopter rides, flying lessons, parachute lessons, and sightseeing excursions are available.

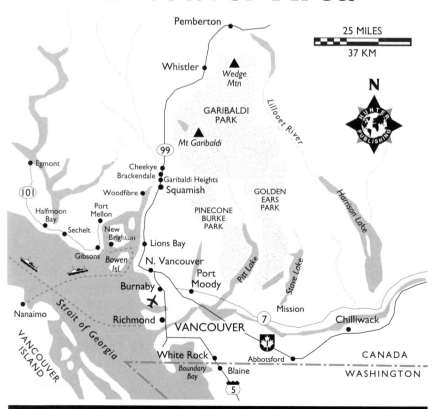

Vancouver International Airport is the region's major airfield, of course, and **Helijet Airways**, 4520 Agar Dr., Vancouver International Airport, Richmond, BC V7B 1A3, ☎ 604/273-1414, 273-4688, or 800/665-4354 (250/382-6222 in Victoria), fax 604/273-5301, serves downtown Vancouver, downtown Victoria, and Seattle.

Touring

The **Albion Ferry**, ☎ 604/660-8770, on River Road near 240th Street in **Albion**, shuttles vehicles and passengers to Fort Langley seven days a week between 5 AM and 2 AM. During daylight hours, two 24-vehicle ferries make the trip back and forth about every 15 minutes.

Ft. Langley, a recreated Hudson's Bay Company fort, produces reenactments of frontier life in the region. The village of Fort Langley, running along Glover Road from 88th Avenue to 96th Avenue, is a favorite among antique collectors.

New Westminster is Western Canada's oldest city. **Coquitlam**, a city of 100,000 people, has more than 70 parks covering over 3,000 acres. **Port Coquitlam**, known locally as "Poco," is about half that size. **Port Moody**, the terminus of Canada's first transcontinental rail line (completed 4 July 1886), celebrates **Golden Spike Days** in late June and early July each year. **Richmond** is located on Lulu Island, the largest of 14 islands that sit in the mouth of the Fraser River.

In 1910, there were seven permanent residents in the writers' and artists' colony of **White Rock** on Semiahmoo Bay, not far from the International Peace Arch. Today there are 17,500.

Adventures

■ On Foot

Hiking Trails

Rapidly moving toward completion, the **TransCanada Trail** will cross Canada from Victoria, British Columbia on the west to Prince Edward Island on the east and from Calgary, Alberta on the south to the North Sea. The trail will be available for hiking, cycling, horseback riding, snowmobiling, and cross-country skiing.

Mill Lake & Centennial Park, at Mill Lake Road and Emerson Street in **Abbotsford**, has nature trails, a fitness track, a wildfowl refuge, and an outdoor swimming pool. **Monkey Mountain**, 34100 S. Fraser Way, #3, ☎ 604/864-2917, maintains a 9,000-square-foot indoor rock climbing gym.

Mundy Park, in the southwestern part of **Coquitlam**, occupies 435 acres, has a number of hiking trails, and has two lakes. **Minnekhada Regional Park**, in the northeastern part of town, with trails, wildlife, and a marshland, is an excellent place for birdwatching.

Reifel Bird Sanctuary, six miles west of **Ladner**, occupies 850 acres of Westham Island. The sanctuary is operated by the nonprofit, nongovernment British Columbia Waterfowl Society. Two regional parks also are nearby: **Boundary Bay** and **Deas Island**. Deas Island has trails that pass Burrvilla, an old Victorian home; Inverholme, a one-room schoolhouse; and the Delta Agricultural Hall.

The **Langley** area also has some interesting regional parks worth exploring. **Campbell Valley** has foot and horse trails to the slow-moving Little Campbell River. **Aldergrove Lake Regional Park**, 272nd Street and 8th Avenue, has hiking trails, horse trails, and a swimming pond. **Glen Valley Regional Park**, 272nd Street and River Road, has trails and some opportunities for fishing.

Other parks around **Langley** include **Fort Langley Community Park**, at Nash and St. Andrews; **Douglas Park**, 206th Street and Douglas Crescent; **City Park**, 207th Street and 48th Avenue; **Brydon Park**, 198th Street and 53rd Avenue; **Buckley Park**, 196th Street and 48th Avenue; **Nicomekl Park**, 208th Street and 54th Avenue; **Linwood Park**, 201A Street and Michaud Crescent; **Nicholas Park**, 209th Street and 50A Avenue; **Alice Brown Park**, 20011 44th Ave.; **Langley Prairie**, 20060 Fraser Hwy; and **Simonds Park**, 20190 48th Ave. Thirty-acre **Noel Booth Park**, 202nd Street and 36th Avenue, has trails, lakes, and streams; 41-acre **Williams Park**, 238th Street and 66th Avenue, contains a lovely little brook; in **Sendall Gardens**, 201A Street and 50th Avenue, there are a botanical garden, a nature trail, and a lot of pheasants; **Portage Park**, 204th Street and 51st Avenue, has a quarter-mile fitness track; **Hunter Park**, 199th Street and 45A Avenue, has a number of trails; **Uplands Park**, 4471 207A St., has a jogging track; and **H.D. Stafford Park**, 20441 Grade Crescent, also has a jogging track.

📖 A free booklet, *Explore Our Trails*, is available from the Chamber of Commerce in **Mission** and includes 15 maps of trails in the area. Also ask for *Visit Our Wildlife in Mission* for some birdwatching hints.

Easy trails near Mission include **Devil's Lake Trail**, which follows a gravel road for four kilometers from the west end of Staves Dalls Dam; **Hayward Lake Trail**, leaving Dewdney Trunk Road at Stave Falls Dam and circling the Beaver Pond; a somewhat more difficult trail that follows an old railway line along the west side of Hayward Lake; **Rolley Lake Trail**, off Bell Street north of Dewdney Trunk Road and northwest of Stave Falls, which is an old logging trail that goes around the lake and past a waterfall; **Saunders Pond Trail**, which follows Saunders Road off Richards Avenue; and **Lane Creek Trail**, which goes from the library parking lot in town (Second Avenue and Welton Street), follows Lane Creek, and terminates at a small playground on the corner of Seventh Avenue and Murray Street.

A 1.5-kilometer trail leaves the West Canyon parking lot near Mission and leads to Lake Viewpoint, where a waterfall can be seen during the wet season.

Trails of slightly greater difficulty around Mission include the **Fraser River Heritage Park Trail**, which goes from the east end of 5th Avenue to Westminster Abbey; the **Bear Mountain Trail**, which follows a forestry road at the end of Saunders Street into the Mission Municipal Forest; the **Stave Lake Trails** that travel along the west side of the lake from Burma Road off Dewdney Trunk Road; and two trails at **Davis Lake**, one that follows a rough logging road at the north end of the lake and another, steeper trail that leaves Sylvester Road just after it turns to gravel and leads past a number of waterfalls.

Three challenging trails can be found in the area around Mission: the Rolley Falls Trail, the Steelhead Mountain Trail, and the Hoover Lake Trail.

To take the **Rolley Falls Trail**, start on Bell Street north of Dewdney Trunk Road near Stave Falls and follow the easy lakeside trail eastward to a wooden bridge. Do not cross the creek for 15 minutes, then take one of the rough, unmarked trails that follow the creek eastward.

To reach **Steelhead Mountain**, take Cardinal Street to Johnson Street and turn right. Go 1.5 miles and then right on Campbell (Cambel) Street. Stay left at the fork, and climb the ridge west of Hatzic Valley, a one-hour trip. From there, you can see six major peaks: Blanshard Needle, Golden Ears, Crickmer, Robie Reid, Judge Howay, and Mount St. Benedict.

Hoover Lake Trail begins at the yellow gate across Dewdney Trunk Road from the municipal garbage dump. The 3.7-kilometer trail follows an old logging road. Stay left at the first main junction, then follow a rustic trail to the shore of the lake.

Many of the better trails near Mission, east of Vancouver, can be found in **Golden Ears Provincial Park**, north of Mission and 48 kilometers east of Vancouver (a free pocket-sized brochure containing a map and descriptions of the trails is available from Golden Ears Provincial Park, Box 7000, Maple Ridge, BC V2X 7G3, ☎ 604/463-3513, fax 604/463-6193). A hiking and horse trail, the **Menzies Trail** runs from the Park Headquarters to the Gold Creek parking lot. Navigating the **Mike Lake Trail**, a hiking and horse trail that runs from Mike Lake to the main corral, takes about two hours. The 1.2-kilometer **Incline Trail**, another hiking and horse trail, runs from Mike Lake to the fire access road. The **Lower Falls Trail**, for hikers only, goes from the Gold Creek parking lot to Lower Falls, which are 10 meters high.

Other interesting trails in Golden Ears Provincial Park include a 2.5-kilometer loop that involves going outbound on the **Lookout Trail** and returning on the **Loop Trail**; the **Spirea Nature Trail**; and the **Alouette Valley Trail**, a horse and hiking trail that links Mike Lake Trail and Menzies Trail. If you take the strenuous **Alouette Mountain Hiking Trail**, look for snow into late June, expect to spend at least five hours, and be sure to carry sufficient water. In **Pitt Meadows**, a trail in **Maple Ridge Park** follows the Alouette River bordering the park. There are trails and fish ponds in **Rieboldt Park**; **Centennial Peace Park** contains a short walking trail, a bandstand, and a pond; and **Allco Park** has both foot and riding trails.

PoCo Trail in **Port Coquitlam** winds through the city's natural and residential areas along the Coquitlam River. It is accessible from several points throughout the city and gives access to fishing, swimming, and exploring as well as hiking.

There are hiking trails at **Buntzen Lake** and **Foreshore Park** in **Port Moody**. **Belcarra Regional Park**, a 15-minute drive from town, covers 2,848 acres (making it 3.5 times the size of Stanley Park in Vancouver) and contains 15 kilometers of trails leading to Jug Island or across the floating walkway in Sasamat Lake.

Dyke Trails in **Richmond** consist of 50 kilometers of interconnecting trails for hiking and biking. The 65-acre **Minoru Park** downtown contains trails, swimming pools, a fitness complex, some lakes, the Pierrefond Gardens, the Gateway Theatre, and the Minoru Chapel. The 200-acre **Richmond Nature Park**, 11851 Westminster Hwy, ☎ 604/

273-7015, has nature trails and a boardwalk that leads around a pond. In **Iona Regional Park and Beach**, at the mouth of the Fraser River's North Arm, one can walk and cycle along a 4.5-kilometer jetty and beachcomb for driftwood.

A free pocket-sized brochure describing **Garibaldi Provincial Park** near **Squamish** is available from the BC Parks District Manager, Alice Lake Provincial Park, Box 220, Brackendale, BC V0N 1H0, ☎ 604/898-3678, fax 604/898-4171. The 195,000-hectare wilderness is located 64 kilometers north of Vancouver and includes Lake Garibaldi, which is 300 meters deep. Snow may last until late July, so the best time to visit is late July, August, or early September. Route 99 runs past the west side of the park.

The **Diamond Head Area**, which includes Mount Garibaldi, can be accessed north of Squamish. It also includes Atwell Peak (a volcanic pinnacle), the Opal Cone, Garibaldi Névé, and Mamquam Lake.

The **Black Tusk Area** is accessed between Alice Lake Park and Brandywine Falls Park, 37 kilometers north of Squamish. It includes the Black Tusk, Helm Glacier, the Sphinx, Garibaldi Lake, the Table (a flat-topped mesa), and Sentinel Glacier. A trail leads to a shoulder below the Black Tusk, but the isolated volcanic peak should be approached only by experienced and properly equipped climbers. The last 100 meters of the climb must be made by means of a chimney and should be ascended very carefully. Beware of falling rocks.

The **Cheakamus Lake Area** is accessed between Brandywine Falls Park and Whistler and includes the glacier-fed Cheakamus Lake. About halfway to the lake, a side trail leading to Black Tusk Meadows drops down to Cheakamus Creek, where there is a cable car crossing. Two people are required to move the cable car. On the other side of the creek, the trail switchbacks upward and then follows Helm Creek to the Upper Lakes and the meadows.

Accessed from **Whistler**, the **Singing Pass Area** includes views of two mountain ranges and the Cheakamus Glacier. Wildflowers are prevalent in the late summer, and there are two interesting trails, one that follows Fitzsimmons and Melody Creeks and another that leads to Russet Lake.

The **Wedgemount Lake Area** can be reached north of Whistler. Glacial Lake is circled by the Wedgemount and Armchair Glaciers, and there is a beautiful view of a 300-meter waterfall at Wedgemount Creek. Mountain goats are often seen.

Surrey also provides a great number of good hiking trails. **Sunnywide Acres Urban Forest**, which runs along both sides of 24th Avenue between 140th and 148th Streets, has more than three kilometers of trails. **Elgin Heritage Park** on the Nicomekl River at Crescent Road near 137th Street contains the interesting 1890s Stewart Farmhouse. **Crescent Park**, near Crescent Road and 128th Street, has 5.5 kilometers of hiking trails and some nice horse trails. **Redwood Park**, on 16th Avenue east of 176th Street, is located on a former tree farm where the inhabitants once lived in a treehouse, since rebuilt.

Other nice walking/hiking regions near Surrey include **South Surrey Athletic Park** off 148th Street on either side of 20th Avenue; **Centennial Park** off North Bluff Road near 142nd Street; **Semiahmoo Park** in the 15700 block of 8th Avenue; **Tynehead Regional Park**, bounded by 96th Avenue, Route 1, and 176th Street; and **Blackie Spit** at Crescent Beach. The city has a free map that outlines the Crescent Beach walking tour, which passes 15 heritage sites.

Stanley Park, 2099 Beach Ave., **Vancouver**, ☎ 604/681-1141, is a lovely place to walk, and **Landsea Tours**, 830 Clark Dr., Vancouver, BC V5L 3J7, ☎ 604/255-7272, fax 604/254-8968, E-mail landseatours@ orca.bc.ca, sets up excursions by bus, boat, or seaplane, as well as on foot.

Cypress Provincial Park, 12 kilometers from Vancouver via the Lions Gate Bridge, affords breathtaking views of Vancouver to the south, Mount Baker to the southeast, the Gulf Islands to the southwest, and Vancouver Island to the west. Accessed via a road off Routes 99 and

Along the Vancouver Coast (Graham Osborne).

1, the park allows primitive camping, and mountain bikes are allowed on the main access road and on designated trails.

A free pocket-sized brochure describing and illustrating the area is available from the BC Parks District Manager, 1610 Mount Seymour Rd., North Vancouver, BC V7G 1L3, ☎ 604/924-2200, fax 604/924-2244.

Numerous hiking trails traverse the park. **Black Mountain Loop** skirts several mountain lakes, and side trips lead to the Yew Lake viewpoint and the Vancouver lookout. The several **Lodge Trails** that can be found around Hollyburn Lodge (now closed) include Old Forks Trail, which runs south to the Cypress Parkway, Grand National Trail, Jack Pratt Trail, Sitzmark Trail, Telemark Trail, and Burfield Trail. **Hollyburn Mountain Trail** covers six kilometers. **Yew Lake Trail**, an easy 45-minute loop, is an interpretive trail that runs from the ticket office, passes some small lakes, and returns to the Black Chairlift. **Howe Sound Crest Trail** is a rugged 30 kilometers hike that should be attempted only by experienced, well-equipped hikers.

Baden-Powell Centennial '71 Trail, which covers 41.7 kilometers between Horseshoe Bay and Deep Cove along the North Shore Mountains, has two sections that pass through Cypress Provincial Park. One section runs from Horseshoe Bay to Cypress Bowl, a six-hour hike that goes from the north end of Eagleridge Drive off Route 1 to Eagle Ridge, the steepest part of the trail; crosses Black Mountain; and then descends into the Cypress Bowl Ski Area. The other section requires a hike of about 3.75 hours from the ski area parking lot at Cypress Bowl, follows the Burfield Trail to Hollyburn Lodge, and then goes along Blue Gentian Lake and Lawson Creek to the British Properties.

Trails near Cypress Provincial Park include **Brothers Creek Trail**, which runs from the Baden-Powell Trail on the south, follows along Brothers Creek, and extends to Blue Gentian Lake on the north; **Skyline Trail**, which goes from Cypress Parkway on the west to the Baden-Powell Trail on the east; and **Seaview Walk**, which begins at Route 1 south of Marine Drive and just north of Route 99, parallels Marine Drive to Cranley Drive just east of Nelson Creek, and then takes Cranley south to rejoin Marine Drive.

The back country wilderness is extremely rugged and dangerous. Grizzly bears, black bears, and cougars inhabit the area. Exercise extreme caution.

White Rock provides some outstanding opportunities for birding. **Serpentine Fen** off Mud Bay is a 240-acre sanctuary with several viewing towers. Located off King George Highway at 44th Avenue, the sanctuary is open daily from 7 AM to dusk. Other choice sites are **Blackie Spit** at Crescent Beach, **Boundary Bay** just west of Mud Bay, and the 850-acre **Reifel Bird Sanctuary** on Westham Island in the Delta, 30 minutes from town.

■ On Horseback

Rodeos

For rodeo, residents of southwestern British Columbia turn to Exhibition Park, ☎ 604/888-2891, in **Abbotsford** for the **Let'er Buck Rodeo** in late January and **Let'er Buck Bull, Broncs, Bares & Cabaret** in March and April. **Cloverdale** is the home of Canada's second largest rodeo (for this year's date, contact the Chamber of Commerce). **Langley** hosts the **Little Britches Rodeo**, ☎ 604/882-1395 or 530-5981, for children between the ages of two and 18 in the Langley Riders Arena.

Horse Shows

Rusty Spurs 4-H Invitation Horse Show, ☎ 604/864-9848, takes place in **Abbotsford**'s Exhibition Park in April. **Horse Council of British Columbia**, 5764B 176th St., **Cloverdale**, publishes a compilation of more than 400 horse-related businesses and activities in the Cloverdale area.

Riding

With over 6,000 horses in the area, horses are a $40 million a year industry in **Langley** and the town claims to be the "Horse Capital of British Columbia." There are miles of riding trails near town, and both **Campbell Valley Riding Stables**, ☎ 604/534-7444, and **EXP Horseback Adventures**, ☎ 604/533-7978, can provide lessons and guided trail rides. **Langley 204 Pub & Trail Rides**, ☎ 604/533-7978, offers lessons, one- and two-hour trail rides, and *pub rides*, while **Misty Morning Acres**, 21144 4th Ave., ☎ 604/532-3940 or 800/538-2112, features riding, but only for those who spend the night in their B&B.

Thunderbird Equestrian Centre, ☎ 604/888-1511, hosts the **Quarter Horse Trade Show & Bazaar** and the **Hunter Jumper Show** in Langley each March. Other Hunter Jumper Shows are held there in May, July, and August, and the **Fort Langley Grand Prix**, a jumping competition, is held there in August. August is **Langley Horse Festival Month** and features various competitions and demonstrations.

In **Maple Ridge**, riders can go to **Golden Ears Riding Stables**, 13175 232nd Ave., ☎ 604/463-8761, to rent a horse, take a lesson, or arrange a trail ride. Similar services are available from **Maple Ridge Equi-Sports Centre**, 21793 132nd Ave., ☎ 604/467-5616; **Mustang Stables**, 22947 132nd Ave., ☎ 604/467-9287; and **Timberline Ranch**, 22351 144th Ave., ☎ 604/463-9278.

In **Mission**, guided trail rides and half-day or all-day trips can be arranged at **McConnell Creek**, 35779 Hartley Rd., ☎ 604/462-0345. The 7.3-kilometer **Alouette Mountain Horse Trail** in Golden Ears Provincial Park makes an interesting ride as it follows the fire access road through the forest and passes a "blowdown" area caused by Typhoon Freda in 1962. **Mission Horse Club**, 9457 Stave Lake St., ☎ 604/826-3967 or 467-9420, is extremely active throughout the summer with a program of games, shows, and other horse-related activities.

There are 160 kilometers of pastoral riding trails between **Pitt Meadows** and **Maple Ridge**, and Horseman's Park in Pitt Meadows has a number of additional riding trails. In **Port Coquitlam**, lessons and trail rides can be arranged with **Sady Baggen-Mueller**, Devon Road and Lincoln Avenue, ☎ 604/985-0493 or 318-0413.

Narrated one-hour horse-drawn tours of Stanley Park in **Vancouver** are offered by **AAA Horse & Carriage**, ☎ 604/681-5115. The tours leave the lower zoo parking lot every 30 minutes between 10 AM and 5 PM daily from July 1 to Labour Day, and between 10:30 AM and 4 PM from the day after Labour Day to October 15 and during May and June.

Racing

Thoroughbred racing is featured on Wednesdays and Fridays at 6:15 PM, and on Saturdays, Sundays, and holidays at 1:15 PM from mid-April through October. The races are held in **Vancouver**'s **Exhibition Park**, ☎ 604/254-1631.

■ On Wheels

Motor Home Rentals

Motor homes, vans, camper vans, and minivans can be rented at **Candan RV Rentals**, 20257 Langley Bypass, **Langley**, BC V3A 6K9, ☎ 604/530-3645 or 800/922-6326, fax 604/530-1696, E-mail candan@direct.ca; at **Go West**

Campers, 1577 Lloyd Ave., North Vancouver, BC V7P 3K8, ☎ 604/987-5288 or 800/661-8813, fax 604/987-9620, E-mail inform@go-west.com; and at **CanaDream**, 13541 73rd Ave., Surrey, BC V3W 2R5, ☎ 604/572-3220 or 800/461-7368, fax 604/572-0278.

Biking

Bikers can rent equipment at **STP Bike & Board**, 27082 Fraser Hwy, **Aldergrove**, ☎ 604/856-3171; at **Wenting's Cycle Shop**, 33272 1st Ave., Mission, ☎ 604/826-1411; and at **White Rock Cycle**, 1465 Johnston Rd. (152nd St.), White Rock, ☎ 604/531-8111.

Brookswood BMX Track, 42nd Avenue and 208th Street, **Langley**, ☎ 604/533-0084, can offer some exciting biking. Be sure to wear protective gear. Bikes are permitted on the trail between the parking lot and Elfin Lakes in the Diamond Head Area of Garibaldi Provincial Park near **Squamish** and on the trail from the parking lot to Singing Creek in the Cheakamus Lake Area, but they may not be taken up on the cable car.

Auto Racing

Auto racing is provided at **Mission Raceway Park**, PO Box 3421, **Mission**, BC V2V 4J5, ☎ 604/826-6315, fax 604/820-1244.

Railroads

Railroad buffs will enjoy **West Coast Railway Heritage Park**, Box 2790, Station Terminal, **Vancouver**, BC V6B 3X2, ☎ 604/898-9336. Located a half-mile west of Route 99 on Centennial Way, the park is open daily between 10 AM and 5 PM from May to October. **BC Rail**, PO Box 8770, Vancouver, BC V6B 4X6, ☎ 800/663-8238, fax 604/984-5505, Web site www.bcrail.com/bcr, conducts rail tours from North Vancouver to Squamish, Whistler, Pemberton, Lillooet, Kelly Lake, Clinton, Exeter, Williams Lake, and Quesnel to Prince George.

Vancouver Trolley Co., 4012 Myrtle St., **Burnaby**, BC V5C 4G2, ☎ 604/451-5581 or 888/451-5581, fax 604/451-9590, Web site www.vancouvertrolley.com, offers a full circuit of 16 popular locations throughout town for a single fare. The sights include Gastown, Canada Place, the Art Gallery, the Aquarium, and Science World.

Harbour Cruises, #1 North Foot of Denman St., **Vancouver**, BC V6G 2W9, ☎ 604/688-7246, 299-9000, or 800/663-1500, fax 604/687-5868, offers a boat-train day trip. The train goes from North Vancouver to Squamish through Horseshoe Bay, Lions Bay, Porteau Cove, and Britannia Beach along Howe Sound; then passengers return by boat to Coal Harbour and Vancouver. **Alpine Adventure Tours**, PO Box 48903, ☎ 604/683-0209, fax 604/683-6037, schedules day trips and overnighters by boat, train, and bus to Whistler and back.

■ On the Water

Rafting

The best rafting in southwestern British Columbia can be found on the Cheakamus, Squamish, Chehalis, Chilliwack, and Fraser Rivers, and on the Green River north of Whistler.

From May through September, whitewater rafting can be arranged on the Chilliwack, Lillooet, Fraser, and Thompson Rivers through **Frontier River Adventures**, 927 Fairfield Rd., **Vancouver**, BC V7H 2J4, ☎ 604/929-7612. Similar rafting adventures can be planned through **Hyak River Rafting**, 1975 Maple St., #204-A, Vancouver, BC V6J 3S9, ☎ 604/734-8622 or 800/663-7238 (☎ 206/382-1311 in Seattle), fax 604/734-5718, E-mail hyak@lightspeed.bc.ca, and through **REO Rafting Adventures**, 612-1200 W. Pender St., Vancouver, BC V6E 2S9, ☎ 604/684-4433 or 800/736-7238, fax 604/684-9536. **Nahatlatch River Escort**, 535 Thurlow St., #355, Vancouver, BC V6E 3L2, ☎ 604/686-4438

Vancouver river rafting (Hyak Wilderness Adventures).

or 800/736-7238, will arrange kayak and horseback tours as well as rafting trips.

Fishing

Fraser Valley Trout Hatchery, 34345 Vye Rd., **Abbotsford**, BC V2S 4N2, ☎ 604/852-5444, manages an extremely interesting Visitor Centre including a "living stream" containing many species of freshwater fish and a walk-in beaver house. A 12-minute slide show, *A Freshwater Fish Tale*, is presented, and there are fishy computer games to be played. The center is open daily between 10 AM and 5 PM during the summer, and between 10 AM and 3 PM in the winter, but it is closed during December and January.

Mill Lake and Centennial Park, on Mill Lake Road off Bourquin Crescent in Abbotsford, offers trout fishing as well as majestic views of Mount Baker, walking trails, and some outstanding birdwatching. Spring and fall are the best seasons for the rainbow trout fishing. No power boats are allowed.

Between July and October, steelhead trout and chinook salmon fishing is good in the **Fraser River** around the Mission bridge.

In **Morris Lake**, the cutthroat and rainbow trout fishing is best in the spring and fall. Coho salmon also are taken in the fall, and during the winter, an occasional steelhead will be caught.

Rolley Lake, about 13 kilometers northwest of **Mission**, contains cutthroat, Dolly Varden, and rainbow trout, plus some brown bullhead. Action is best in the spring and fall. No power boats are allowed.

In **Stave Lake** north of **Ruskin**, anglers catch cutthroat, rainbow, and Dolly Varden trout as well as kokanee salmon. The lake is hazardous, however, due to submerged snags, floating logs, cold water, and high winds. The south end of the lake can be reached at Staves Falls north of Ruskin.

Five kilometers of the **Stave River** from Ruskin Dam to the Fraser River are fishable. Whitefish action is good in the spring, and spring salmon are often taken at the mouth of the river in the spring and summer. Fall is the best season for catching cutthroat and Dolly Varden trout or coho salmon, while the steelhead strike best in the winter.

Sumas River produces good fishing for coho salmon, sturgeon, and Dolly Varden, cutthroat, and steelhead trout in the spring and fall. Coho salmon production in this river is best from mid-September to December. On the **Vedder River**, some whitefish are taken from April to September, coho salmon from mid-September to December, and steelhead trout from December to March. **Weaver Creek**, 10 kilometers northeast of Harrison Bay, offers some exciting steelhead fishing from December to March.

Derby Beach Regional Park in **Langley** has one of the best fishing bars on the Fraser River. Salmon can be taken right off the banks there.

Around **Mission**, there are a number of places to go fishing for a fee (if less adventuresome than do-it-yourself fishing, this at least is a good way to squeeze a fishing trip when you're on a tight schedule). **Bent-Rod Trout Park**, 10358 Dewdney Trunk Rd., ☎ 604/820-4029, has three ponds stocked with rainbow trout, rents fishing tackle, has hiking trails, and allows camping. It is Located just 53 kilometers east of Vancouver and is open between 9 AM and 7 PM daily. **Sun Valley Trout Park**, 31395 Silverdale Ave., ☎ 604/826-6471, fax 604/826-7818, has four ponds on 35 acres that are stocked with trout 11 inches long and larger. It too rents equipment and allows camping, and is open daily from 10 AM to dusk. **Rainbow Trout Creek Farm**, 31474 Townshipline Ave., ☎ 604/826-5640, has two ponds stocked with 12- to 24-inch fish. Rods, reels, and bait are furnished free, and the staff cleans your fish. All for a $1 admission fee. The farm is open six days a week between 9 AM and dusk, excluding Wednesdays.

Ever tie into a hundred-pound sturgeon? An excellent sturgeon hole is opposite the Tourist InfoCentre in **Mission**.

Another fishing hotspot is **Slaughter Bar** at the end of Newton Road in **Dewdney**, where you can spincast for cutthroat trout, coho salmon, and spring salmon or catch sturgeon on the upper side of the bar. **Strawberry Island**, halfway down Nicomen Trunk Road on Nicomen Island near Mission, is good for steelhead trout, sturgeon, and salmon. **McDonald's Landing**, at the end of McDonald's Road, and **Deroche Landing**, at the end of Deroche Landing Road, have salmon and cutthroat trout. **Bowman's Bar**, a midriver bar between Dewdney Landing and McDonald's Landing, has steelhead and cutthroat trout, salmon, and sturgeon. **Deroche Bar** (Wing Dam) is located on Athey Road in Deroche (go down the third lane off the river dike) and provides good fly fishing for steelhead trout, cutthroat trout, and salmon between the channels.

At the end of Athey Road in **Deroche**, turn right to Deroche Dump Slough or turn left and then take the second right to Queen's Bar. Between those two sites and Queen's Island is another good fishing spot, the midriver **Mosquito Bar**, where cutthroat trout can be taken in the middle channel and salmon and steelhead trout can be taken in the main channel.

The midriver **Mountain Bar**, located at the foot of Bell Mountain, may be the most productive salmon hole on the Fraser River, but you'll need a boat. **Calamity Point**, off the mouth of the Harrison River, and **Island 22** in the Harrison River also are good for salmon. Good salmon catches also are taken off **Kilby Beach** and the railway bridge near Mission.

The bridges on Route 7 at **Dewdney** and **Nicomen** usually provide good coho salmon and trout fishing, and there are some deep holes for trout and salmon on the trail along Inch Creek (aka Suicide Creek and Norrish Creek) 10 kilometers east of Mission via Hawkins Pickle Road.

Hatzic Lake, six kilometers east of **Mission** on Route 7, contains cutthroat trout, rainbow trout, and black crappies. **Hatzic Slough**, three kilometers east of Hatzic on Route 7 (or to reach the south side of the slough, take Dyke Road), has rainbow and cutthroat trout. **Lake Errock**, 31 kilometers east of Mission on Route 7, has rainbow and cutthroat trout, coho salmon, brown bullhead, and squawfish. **Whonnock Lake** contains rainbow and cutthroat trout as well as black crappie, and boats are available for rent during the peak season.

Garden Bay, Madeira Park, and Irvine's Landing are located on **Pender Harbour**, which has some excellent salmon fishing.

The lakes in **Garibaldi Provincial Park** can provide some outstanding fishing, too. Rainbow trout are taken in **Mamquam Lake** in the Diamond Head Area during the summer and early fall, and in **Barrier Lake, Garibaldi Lake**, and **Lesser Garibaldi Lake** in the Black Tusk/Garibaldi Lake Area. Rainbow trout and Dolly Varden also can be taken in the Cheakamus Lake Area.

Fort Langley Marina at the end of Church Street on the Fraser River in **Langley** has a boat ramp, rents boats, and provides access to the Bedford Channel and the river. In **Mission, Mission Marine**, 6971 Bridge St., ☎ 604/826-0425 or 556-8826, also rents fishing boats, while **Fraser Valley Outdoor Adventures**, 8944 Hammond St., ☎ 604/826-3181 or 888/826-3862, fax 604/826-3181, E-mail fvoa@mindlink.bc.ca, arranges fishing trips, fishing trips solely for women, and Indian interpretive trips. **Southview Marine Services**, 34043 Richards Ave., ☎ 604/826-6387 or 240-6955, accepts fishing charters on the *MV Waylin Myth*, which can sleep four to six people.

Kanaka Creek Park offers the opportunity for canoeing and kayaking in the **Pitt Meadows** area, and there are steelhead trout, cutthroat trout, and coho salmon below Cliff Falls. Nearby, **Golden Ears Provincial Park** has facilities for swimming, water-skiing, and boat launching. Canoe and paddle boat rentals also are offered at **Whonnock Lake Park**, and during the summer, canoes can be rented at **Pitt Lake**. Although no power boats are allowed, **Rolley Lake Park** makes swimming, sailboarding, sailing, and canoeing possible, and there is a 65-acre campground and a loop trail that encircles the lake.

Reed Point Boat Rentals, 850 Barnet Hwy, **Port Moody**, BC, ☎ 604/931-8211 or 931-2477, rents boats by the hour or day and offers a special discount on weekdays.

In **Stevenson**, **Westin Bayshore Yacht Charters**, ☎ 604/691-6936, fax 604/691-6960, takes clients salmon fishing in the Strait of Georgia and Howe Sound, and in **Vancouver**, **Vancouver Sportfish Center**, 1525 Coal Harbour Quay, ☎ 604/689-7108 or 329-0910, does the same. **Sewell's Marine Group**, 6685 Nelson Ave., **West Vancouver**, BC V7W 2B2, ☎ 604/921-3474 or 800/661-8933, fax 604/921-7027, arranges fishing charters in Queen Charlotte Strait aboard the **MV Charlotte Explorer**. **Maple Leaf Adventures**, 3055 Cassiar Ave., **Abbotsford**, BC V2S 7G9, ☎ 604/240-2420, fax 604/850-7259, charters four- to 11-day trips aboard the schooner **Maple Leaf**.

Westwind Tugboat Adventures, 1160 Holom Ave., **Burnaby**, BC V5B 3V6, ☎ 604/270-3269, fax 604/270-8865, provides deluxe accommodations and serves fabulous food aboard an 85-foot west coast tug. The tug takes eight to 12 guests per week to remote fjords with calm water where they can fish for salmon, go beachcombing, go clam-digging, and look for eagles, whales, and porpoises.

Boundary Ventures, 14025 Nico Wynd, #8, **Crescent Beach**, ☎ 604/535-9212, charters the 58-foot *Virgin Trader*.

In **New Westminster**, **The Fraser River Connection**, ☎ 604/525-4465, cruises the Fraser River from the Westminster Quay to Fort Langley with the paddlewheeler *Native*. The cruises are offered from June to September, and sunset dinner cruises also are available.

Pacific Rim Yacht Charters, 8031 River Rd., **Richmond**, BC V6X 1X8, ☎ 800/675-5800, Web site www.lionsgate.com/webtown/pacrim, rents drive-yourself 32- to 58-foot diesel yachts.

Tzoonie Tours, PO Box 222, **Sechelt**, BC V0N 3A0, ☎ 604/885-0351, offers day cruises along the Sechelt inlet aboard the *MV Tzoonie*. The ship also is available for custom tours and for use as a water taxi.

The River Queen, ☎ 604/274-9565, tours **Steveston Harbour** from Fisherman's Wharf, Steveston, every hour on the half-hour between 10:30 AM and 6:30 PM from May through October, weather permitting.

The **Sunshine Coast Marine Parks** – Halkett Bay Marine Park, Plumper Cove Marine Park, Buccaneer Bay Marine Park, Simson Marine Park, and Smuggler Cove Marine Park – offer all sorts of watersport opportunities. **Halkett Bay Marine Park**, occupying a sheltered site on the east side of Gambier Island in Howe Sound, is great for kayaking. Kayaking and fishing are popular at **Plumper Cove Marine Park**, on the northwest side of Keats Island in Howe Sound. The park is accessible by taking the passenger ferry from Langdale to Keats Landing and then walking two kilometers to the park, which has campsites, trails, a wharf, mooring buoys, and a pebble beach for swimming and beachcombing. **Buccaneer Bay Marine Park**, at the southern tip of North Thormanby Island in the Strait of Georgia, has a broad sandy beach accessible by dinghy and limited on-shore development. Kayaking, swimming, and fishing are popular there. **Simson Marine Park**, on South Thormanby Island in the Strait of Georgia, has a pebble beach, but no development, and is popular primarily for kayaking and fishing. **Smuggler Cove Marine Park**, an all-weather anchorage on the south side of Sechelt Peninsula near Secret Cove on the Strait of Georgia, can be accessed on foot via a 1.3 kilometers trail from a parking lot off Route 101. The park has five walk-in campsites, a pit toilet, and a boat launch, and offers good hiking and fishing.

Similarly, a string of **Sunshine Coast Provincial Parks** accommodates many enjoyable outdoor activities. BC Parks, Garibaldi/Sunshine Coast District Manager, Box 220, Brackendale, BC V0N 1H0, ☎ 604/898-3678, can provide you with a free pocket-sized brochure describing their features. **Roberts Creek**, east of Vancouver on Route 101, has a boat launch and is widely used by swimmers and fishermen. **Porpoise**

MV Britannia (Harbour Cruises Ltd).

Bay Provincial Park, at the south end of Sechelt Inlet, offers swimming, kayaking, fishing, camping, and hiking trails. Take East Porpoise Bay Road northeast of town. **Sargeant Bay Provincial Park**, north of Vancouver, has a sandy beach and makes a good base for canoeing, kayaking, sail-boarding, scuba diving, bay fishing, and swimming.

Garden Bay Provincial Park, 37 kilometers north of **Vancouver**, is accessible by car or boat. There is a dinghy dock, and the park is used for swimming, fishing, and kayaking. **Sechelt Inlets Recreation Area** features kayaking, camping, hiking, beach, swimming, fishing, and scuba diving.

Cruising & Diving

During the summer, **Vancouver** Parks & Recreation operates a beach information hotline: ☎ 604/738-8535.

Aqua Bus, ☎ 604/689-5858, operates a ferry service to Granville Island, leaving Vancouver's Burrard Bridge daily between 7 AM and 10 PM.

MV Britannia, ☎ 604/688-7246 or 800/663-1500, cruises the coast from Vancouver to Squamish from Wednesday through Sunday at 9:30 AM between June and September. Passengers may take the boat round-trip, go to Squamish by boat and return by train, or go to Squamish by train and return by boat.

Starline Tours, ☎ 604/522-3506, fax 604/930-0556, provides Fraser River eco-tours, a six-hour tour to Pitt Lake, a bus/boat trip to Harrison Lake, and cruises on the Fraser River from New Westminster to Stevenson. **Blue Pacific Yacht Charters**, 1519 Foreshore Walk, Granville Island, Vancouver, BC V6H 3X3, ☎ 604/682-2161 or 800/237-2392, fax 604/682-2722, will take you out on a yacht, while **Cooper Boating Center**, 1620 Duranleau St., Granville Island, Vancouver, BC V6H 3S4, ☎ 604/687-4110, fax 604/687-3267, claims to have British Columbia's largest selection of sailboats for charter.

Scuba lessons, equipment rentals, and guided trips can be arranged at **Diving Locker**, 2755 Lougheed Hwy, #20, **Port Coquitlam**, BC, ☎ 604/942-4838, fax 941-4837, and at **Ocean Pro Divers**, 3189 King George Hwy, #2, **Surrey**, BC, ☎ 604/538-5608.

On Snow

Skating

Ice skating and hockey. What could be more Canadian? **Matsqui Recreation Centre**, 3106 Clearbrook Rd., **Abbotsford**, BC, ☎ 604/855-0500, offers year-around hockey and skating. In **Aldergrove**, **Aldergrove Arena**, ☎ 604/856-8221, provides ice skating and skate rentals.

"Planet Hollywood" on ice, **Planet Ice**, 2300 Rocket Way, **Coquitlam**, BC, ☎ 604/941-9911, has an ice arena, a fitness club, a sports bar, and a grill. Ice skating and skate rentals are available at **Langley Civic Centre**, ☎ 604/530-1323, and at **Langley Twin Rinks**, ☎ 604/532-8946. Ice skating and hockey are offered at **Cam Neely Arena**, 11963 Haney Place, **Maple Ridge**, BC, ☎ 604/467-7349, from fall to spring. **Pitt Meadows Arena Complex**, 11465 Bonson Rd., **Pitt Meadows**, BC, ☎ 604/465-5877, has two NHL-sized ice rinks, where skating and hockey classes are available, and the premises include a sports bar and restaurant.

Skiing

Want to ski or hike on a glacier? **Alpine Adventure Tours**, PO Box 48903, **Vancouver**, BC V7X 1A8, ☎ 604/683-0209, fax 604/683-6037, will fly you there in a plane equipped with landing skis.

Hemlock Valley, ☎ 604/797-4411, located 45 minutes east of **Mission**, provides downhill and cross-country skiing. Downhill skiing is available at 8,668-acre **Mount Seymour Provincial Park**.

Near **North Vancouver**, skiing is available in Cypress Park, at Grouse Mountain, and at Mount Seymour. **Grouse Mountain**, 6400 Nancy Greene Way, ☎ 604/984-0661 or 980-9311, fax 604/984-6360, can accommodate skiing and snowboarding. Rental equipment, lessons, and night skiing are available. There are 22 runs, a sky ride, and a chair ride; and the new Peak Chalet has a bar, a gift shop, a number of fireplaces, the Theatre in the Sky, and three restaurants. Tandem paragliding, hiking, guided 25-kilometer mountain biking tours, and helicopter tours can be arranged. Snowphone: ☎ 604/986-6262. **Mount Seymour**, 1700 Mt. Seymour Rd., ☎ 604/986-2261 or 872-6616, provides lessons, rentals, a cafeteria, and snowboard and snowshoe slopes. Snowphone: ☎ 604/879-3999.

Cypress Provincial Park can provide winter tobogganing, snowshoeing, and skiing via **Cypress Bowl Recreation**, Box 91252, **West Van-**

couver, BC V7V 3N9, ☎ 604/926-5612 (alpine) or 922-0825 (Nordic). The facility has three chairlifts and a double rope-tow. Snowmobiling is offered on designated trails, and there are several well-maintained cross-country trails. Lessons and rentals are available, and a cafeteria and lounge are on-site.

■ In the Air

Abbotsford International Air Show, ☎ 604/328-JETS or 852-8511, held at the Abbotsford Airport on the second weekend in August, features a performance by the Canadian Air Force Snowbirds, a group similar to our own Blue Angels. A trade show and symposium held during the International Air Show, **Airshow Canada**, ☎ 604/852-4600, is staged every other year on the odd-numbered year (1999, 2001, etc.).

The **Sevenoaks Shopping Centre** in Abbotsford hosts the annual **Flight Begins Festival**, a paper plane competition that encourages participants, mostly children, to make and fly their own paper airplanes.

Hope stages an annual skydiving competition in August.

At **Langley** Municipal Airport, the **Canadian Museum of Flight & Transportation**, 5333 216th St., is open daily between 10 AM and 4 PM. **Helicopter Canada**, ☎ 604/532-7822, provides flights or lessons in helicopters or airplanes to aviation enthusiasts in Langley.

Balloonists also flourish in Langley, where **Fantasy Balloon Charters**, ☎ 604/530-1974 or 533-2378, offers 1.5-hour champagne flights. **Balloons Above the Valley**, ☎ 604/533-2378, and **Pegasus Ballooning**, ☎ 604/533-2701, provide similar services.

Glacier Air, Box 2014, Squamish, BC, V0N 3G0, ☎ 604/898-9016 or 800/265-0088, fax 604/898-1553, provides sightseeing and ski plane landing flights.

Baxter Aviation, 2-1239 Coal Harbour Rd., Vancouver, BC V6G 2W6, ☎ 604/688-3097 or 800/661-5599 (604/683-6525 in Nanaimo), E-mail info@baxterair.com, Web site www.baxterair.com, offers float plane adventures such as whale-watching and transport for kayakers; they can also arrange and bungy jumping.

Cultural Excursions

Abbotsford

The **MSA Museum**, 2313 Ware St., ☎ 604/853-0313, is located in Abbotsford's 1920 Trethewey House, which was built of local fir. It is the site of an annual Medieval Fair, staged in mid-August. **Clayburn Village**, north of Abbotsford on the Abbotsford-Mission Highway and then right on Clayburn Road, is a secluded little brick village on the site of an old brick plant. The Clayburn Village Store, ☎ 604/853-4020, was established in 1912 and has a tea shop that serves fresh currant scones with real Devonshire cream and local jam. The store is open Tuesday through Saturday between 9 AM and 5:30 PM and on Sundays between noon and 5. In a similar vein, **Kilby Historic Store & Farm**, ☎ 604/796-9576, located off Lougheed Highway east of the Harrison River, is a restored 1920s store and farm outbuildings and includes a restaurant that is open between 10:00 AM and 7:00 PM from May through October.

A colorful boardwalk circles **Mill Lake** near Abbotsford.

Aldergrove

Greater Vancouver Zoological Centre, 5048 264th St., Aldergrove, BC V4W 1 N7, ☎ 604/856-6825 or 857-9005, fax 604/857-9008, exhibits 115 exotic species on 120 acres. A miniature train, "Safari Express," takes visitors on a 20-minute narrated tour of the grounds, which are open daily between 8 AM and dusk.

Britannia Beach

BC Museum of Mining, Box 188, Route 99, Britannia Beach, BC V0N 1J0, ☎ 604/688-8735 or 896-2233, fax 896-2260, exhibits 2,000 square feet of photographs and artifacts. A gravity-fed plant is capable of processing 7,000 tons of ore per day. Visitors can go on a tour, have an underground adventure and a real hard-rock mining experience, and pan for gold. The museum is open from May 11 to October 13.

Fort Langley

Fort Langley National Historic Site, 23433 Mavis St., PO Box 129, Fort Langley, BC V1M 2R5, ☎ 604/888-4424, fax 604/888-2577, E-mail fort_langley@pch.gc.ca, the "Birthplace of British Columbia," can be reached by road or by means of the Albion Ferry, ☎ 604/467-7298. The historic village is on Fraser River near the town of Langley, and was established in 1827. In the 1850s, it became a Hudson's Bay Co. trading post. The site is open daily between 10 AM and 4:30 PM.

Langley

Domaine de Chaberton Estates Winery, 1064 216th St., Langley, BC, ☎ 604/530-1736, offers tours at 2 and 4 PM on Saturdays and Sundays during the spring and summer. The winery is open Monday through Saturday between 10 AM and 6 PM and on Sunday between noon and 5 PM, but closed on Sundays during January and February.

Maple Ridge

St. John the Divine Anglican Church, 21299 River Rd., Maple Ridge, was built in 1859 and is the oldest church in British Columbia.

Mission

The **Xá:ytem Longhouse Interpretive Centre**, 35087 Lougheed Hwy, Mission, BC V2V 6T1, operated by the Sto:lo Elders, is at Xá:ytem (formerly called Hatzic Rock), British Columbia's oldest dwelling site. Said to be older than the Pyramids or Stonehenge, the place is an important spiritual site for the Sto:lo. The center is open between 10 AM and 4 PM from June to September.

An annual **Mission Indian Friendship Centre International Society Pow Wow** is held in Fraser River Heritage Park, ☎ 604/826-1281, fax 604/826-4056, in Mission in mid-July. Dancers and drum performers come from across North America to participate in the event, now 25 years old. A much newer festival, the **Stratford-on-the-Fraser Shakespearian Festival** is held in July.

Westminster Abbey, 34224 Dewdney Trunk Rd., Mission, ☎ 604/826-8975, a Benedictine monastery, is open for visits on Sundays between 2 and 4 PM and on weekdays between 1:30 and 4 PM. Mass is sung at 10 AM on Sunday and at 6:30 AM on weekdays.

Fraser River Heritage Park, PO Box 3341, Mission, BC V2V 4J5, ☎ 604/826-0277, is on the site of the former St. Mary's Mission and Indian Residential School, which was founded by the Oblates of Mary Immaculate in 1861. It was the first and largest mission in the Pacific Northwest. Although the school buildings and grotto were torn down in 1965, the school foundations and the Oblate remain and the grotto has been rebuilt. The park is open daily from 8 AM to dusk, and the Blackberry Kitchen is open daily between 10 AM and 4 PM. Summer twilight concerts are held every Wednesday evening between 7 and 8, and the snack bar stays open between 6 and 9 on those occasions. To reach the park, go east on 5th Avenue off Stave Lake Street.

New Westminster

A great fire in September 1898 destroyed nine-tenths of downtown New Westminster, excluding only the Queens Hotel and the Burr Block, both at 4th Street and Columbia. "The Royal City," once had the second largest Chinatown in British Columbia and now has a lovely riverside boardwalk. The Community Centre, 65 E. 6th Ave., ☎ 604/527-4640, houses the **Canadian Lacrosse Hall of Fame**, which is open year-around. **Samson V Maritime Museum**, ☎ 604/527-4640 or 522-6894, located on Westminster Quay, exhibits the last steam-powered paddlewheeler to operate on the Fraser River and is open Wednesday through Sunday between noon and 5 PM from June to Labour Day and on Saturdays, Sundays, and holidays between 1 and 5 PM from Labour Day through May. The **Museum of the Royal Westminster Regiment**, 530 Queens Ave., ☎ 604/526-5116, housed in the old Armoury, is open Tuesdays and Thursdays between 10 AM and 3 PM, and on Thursday evenings between 7 and 10 PM year-around.

North Vancouver

North Vancouver, across Lions Gate Bridge from Vancouver, boasts of another unusual span, **Capilano Suspension Bridge**, 3735 Capilano Rd., ☎ 604/985-7474, fax 604/985-7479, a 450-foot link across the 230-foot-deep Capilano River gorge. The 15-acre forest park contains a 200-foot waterfall, illuminated on summer evenings, and a restaurant. There also are totem poles and life-sized Indian carvings. From Vancouver, take Exit 14 off Route 1 and then go 1.2 miles north on Capilano Road. The park is open every day but Christmas. Summer hours are from 8 AM to dark, and winter hours from 9 AM to 5 PM.

Grouse Mountain, 6400 Nancy Greene Way, North Vancouver, BC V7R 4K9, ☎ 604/984-0661, has a restaurant, a sky ride, hiking trails, horse-drawn sleigh rides, chair rides, and helitours. There also is a multimedia presentation, *Our Spirit Soars*. The attraction is open every day between 9 AM and 10 PM.

Richmond

In Richmond, the Buddhist **Kuan Yin Temple**, 9160 Stevenson Hwy, ☎ 604/274-2822, is "the most exquisite example of Chinese palatial architecture in North America." Admission is free.

South Surrey

Crocodiles in Canada? Yes, at the **Rain Forest Reptile Refuge Society**, 1395 176th St., South Surrey, ☎ 604/538-1711.

Stevenson

Garry Point Park in Stevenson occupies 44 acres and is very popular with kite-flyers. There is a Fishermen's Memorial in the park, and the town's annual Salmon Festival is held there. The park was known by the Salish Indians as the "place of churning waters."

Stevenson also houses the **Japanese-Canadian Culture Centre**, 4111 Moncton St., and the **Stevenson Museum**, 3811 Moncton St., ☎ 604/271-6868, which was floated to its current site and served (in 1905) as Richmond's first branch of the Northern Bank. The museum charges no admission and is open year-around from Monday to Saturday between 9:30 AM and 1 PM and between 1:30 and 5 PM.

Vancouver

As one would expect, Vancouver has a great many sites to see.

Queen Elizabeth Park, off Cambie Street and W. 33rd Avenue, occupies the highest point in town, 492-foot Little Mountain. It contains an arboretum, a sunken gardens, a quarry garden, tennis courts, and putting greens. It is always open and there is no charge for admission. **Bloedel Floral Conservatory**, ☎ 604/872-5513 or 874-8008, is under a triodetic dome inside the park. The conservatory houses free-flying birds and a fish pond, and it is open, excluding Christmas, between 9 AM and 8 PM from Monday through Friday and between 10 AM and 9 PM on Saturdays and Sundays from April through September; and daily between 10 AM and 5 PM during the rest of the year.

Stanley Park, ☎ 604/257-8531, an outstanding in-town park, has 50 miles of roads and trails, a children's zoo (open daily between 11 AM and 4 PM), a rose garden, a miniature steam railway (which operates daily between 11 AM and 5 PM from May to September, weather permitting), totem pole displays, and pony rides (running between 11 AM and 4 PM daily from mid-June through Labour Day). In July and August, an open-air theatre is conducted in Malkin Bowl. **Vancouver Aquarium**, PO Box 3232, Vancouver, BC V6B 3X8, ☎ 604/268-9900 or 685-3364, fax 604/631-2529, Web site www.vanaqua.org, is located in Stanley Park and contains over 8,000 marine animals. The aquarium is open every day.

The Lookout! Viewing Deck in the Harbour Center Tower, 555 W. Hastings, ☎ 604/689-0421, fax 604/685-7329, provides enthralling 360-degree views from a circular deck 553 feet above the ground. The 12-minute multiimage show, *Once in a World, Vancouver*, is included in the admission fee, and there is a revolving restaurant inside the tower.

BC Sports Hall of Fame & Museum, 777 Pacific Blvd., ☎ 604/687-5520 or 687-5523, is open between 10 AM and 5 PM from Tuesday through Sunday. **Science World**, 1455 Quebec St., ☎ 604/268-6363, Web site www.scienceworld.bc.ca, shows Omnimax films, has a 3D laser theatre, and presents special exhibitions. It is open between 10:00 AM and 5:00 PM Monday through Friday and between 10:00 AM and 6:00 PM on Saturdays and Sundays. **BC Sugar Museum**, ☎ 604/253-1131, offers guided tours and admission is free. The museum is open between 9:00 AM and 4:00 PM Monday through Friday. Go to the foot of Rogers Street north of Powell Street and cross the tracks.

Gordon Southam MacMillan Observatory, 1100 Chestnut, ☎ 604/738-2855, is open daily from dusk to 11 PM during July and August, and on Fridays and Saturdays the rest of the year. Laser light shows and other educational programs are offered at the Observatory's **H.R. MacMillan Planetarium**, ☎ 604/738-7827. Admission to the Observatory is free, but programs in the Planetarium require payment of a fee.

Holy Rosary Cathedral, 646 Richards St., ☎ 604/682-6774, contains eight bells that are hung in a rare English manner. The bells are rung at 7:30 PM on Tuesdays and at 10:30 AM on Sundays. The cathedral is open between 6 AM and 6 PM on Monday through Friday and between 7 AM and 8 PM on Saturdays and Sundays. **St. Andrew's-Wesley Church**, 1012 Nelson St., ☎ 604/683-4574, a Gothic structure with many stained glass windows, is open between 10 AM and 3 PM Monday through Friday from mid-May through Labour Day. Sunday services are conducted at 11 AM and 7 PM.

Gastown, an interesting section of mews, courtyards, and Victorian buildings founded in 1867, is located on Water Street near the waterfront. Vancouver's **Chinatown**, on E. Pender Street between Carrall and Gore Streets, is Canada's largest and the second largest on the North American continent.

Dr. Sun Yat-Sen Classical Chinese Garden, 578 Carrall St., ☎ 604/689-7133 or 662-3207, is in the heart of Chinatown. Modeled on the city of Suzhou during the Ming Dynasty (1368-1644), the garden includes four main elements – buildings, rocks, plantings, and water – that reflect the Taoist philosophy of yin and yang. Tours are available. The garden is open daily between 10 AM and 7:30 PM from mid-June to mid-

September, between 10 AM and 6 PM from May to mid-June, and between 10 AM and 4:30 PM the rest of the year.

Van Dusen Botanical Garden, 5251 Oak St., ☎ 604/299-9000, 878-9274, or 266-7194, covers 55 acres and offers tours at 2 PM every Sunday and on other afternoons between April and October. A gift shop and a restaurant are on the grounds.

A 70-acre **Botanical Garden**, 6804 SW Marine Dr., ☎ 604/822-9666, is located on the University of British Columbia campus. It includes the E. H. Lohbrunner Alpine Garden, an Asian garden with blue Himalayan poppies, a winter garden, and a 16th-century Physick garden. **Nitobe Memorial Garden**, also on the university campus off NW Marine Drive, is one of best Japanese gardens in North America. A tea garden has been integrated into the landscaping. The garden is open between 10 AM and 6 PM daily from mid-March to mid-October and between 10 AM and 2:30 PM Monday through Friday during the remainder of the year.

Two marvelous museums also can be found on the campus of the university. **Museum of Anthropology**, 6393 Northwest Marine Dr., ☎ 604/822-3825 or 822-5087, is open during the summer (Victoria Day through Labour Day) between 10 AM and 5 PM daily and until 9 PM on Tuesdays. During the winter, the museum is closed on Mondays, but is open between 11 AM and 5 PM from Wednesday through Sunday and until 9 PM on Tuesdays. **M. Y. William Geological Museum**, ☎ 604/822-5586, is on the university's West Mall. It includes exhibits of minerals and fossils, including an 80-million-year-old Lambeosaurus dinosaur. The museum is open between 8:30 AM and 5:30 PM Monday through Friday, and admission is free.

Vancouver Maritime Museum, 1905 Ogden Ave., ☎ 604/257-8300, has a Children's Maritime Discovery Centre that is open daily between 10 AM and 5 PM from May through September and between 10 AM and 5 PM Tuesday through Sunday from October through April. **St. Roch National Historic Site**, next to the museum, displays a ship that was built in 1928 to transport supplies to and conduct patrols for the Royal Canadian Mounted Police. During World War II, the ship became the first vessel to travel from the Pacific to the Atlantic via the Arctic's treacherous Northwest Passage. When the ship returned to Halifax in 1944, it became the first to complete a round-trip through the Northwest Passage.

White Rock

White Rock features a 1,559-foot pier which, along with Marine Drive and some hillside residences, appeared in the movie *Knight Moves*. The white, 487-ton rock that gave the town its name was mentioned by Spanish explorers as early as 1791. One legend claims that the son of Sea God fell in love with a Cowichan princess and took her to his father's home, but both of the young man's parents were saddened that he had fallen in love with a mortal so they rejected the young girl. At that, the son of Sea God picked up a white rock, threw it, and said: "Where this stone lands will be our home." The stone landed on the shore of what is now known as Semiahmoo Bay, where the young couple made their home and raised a mighty, peace-loving tribe called the Semiahmoo.

You can have your picture taken with a real Mountie on the Marine Drive (8th Avenue) promenade near the train station, the pier, and White Rock on Sundays between 1 and 2 PM on the West Beach and between 2 and 3 PM on the East Beach (weather permitting), but only from May through August. Contact Mike Lane of the RCMP, ☎ 604/541-5113.

Where to Stay

Harrison Mills

In Harrison Mills, there is a farm-style B&B with private bathrooms, a billiards room, a library, a hot tub, and a sauna: **Harrison Mills Country House**, 828 Kennedy Rd., Box 59, Harrison Mills, BC V0M 1L0, ☎ 604/796-0385 or 800/551-2511, fax 604/796-2214, $$$.

Langley

Another charming bed-and-breakfast, **Misty Morning Acres**, 21144 4th Ave., Langley, BC V2Z 1T6, ☎ 604/532-3940 or 800/583-2112, fax 604/530-6651, $$-$$$, offers trail rides and caters to special functions.

New Westminster

New Westminster has two attractive places to stay, **Royal Towers Hotel & Casino**, 6th St. & Royal Ave., New Westminster, BC V3M 1J4, ☎ 604/524-3777 or 800/663-0202, fax 604/524-6673, $-$$, and the pricier **Inn at Westminster Quay**, 900 Quayside Dr., New Westminster, BC

V3M 6G1, ☎ 604/520-1776 or 800/663-2001, fax 604/520-5645, $$$-$$$$.

Richmond

Not to be outdone, Richmond offers *three* excellent places to rest and relax. **Radisson President Hotel & Suites**, 8181 Cambie Rd., Richmond, BC V6X 3X9, ☎ 604/276-8181 or 800/333-3333, fax 604/276-8136, $$$-$$$$, is a 12-story hotel with 184 rooms, that has a dining room (open between 6:30 AM and 10 PM), a cocktail lounge, a heated indoor pool, and an exercise room. Located five minutes from the airport and 15 minutes from the heart of town, the hotel adjoins a scenic ocean walk and provides its guests with complimentary coffee and tea. **Delta Vancouver Airport Hotel & Marina**, 3500 Cessna Dr., Richmond, BC V7B 1C7, ☎ 604/278-1241 or 800/268-1133, fax 604/276-1975, $$-$$$, occupies nine acres overlooking the Fraser River. Its 415 rooms fill 10 stories, and there is a heated pool, an exercise room, a dining room, a coffee shop, and a cocktail lounge in addition to the trendy The Pier restaurant, ☎ 604/276-1962. **Delta Pacific Resort**, 10251 St. Edward's Dr., Richmond, BC V6X 2M9, ☎ 604/278-9611 or 800/268-1133, fax 604/276-1121, $$-$$$, spaces its 460 rooms among three separate guest towers. The resort has a landscaped courtyard; three heated pools, one indoors; four indoor, lighted tennis courts; two squash courts; and a health club. There are two dining rooms plus the Suehiro Japanese Steakhouse, ☎ 604/278-9611, which is housed in an authentic samurai house surrounded by Japanese gardens.

Vancouver

Vancouver is literally bursting with outstanding hotels, and it is not difficult to find one that will suit your tastes and pocketbook. **Best Western Chateau Granville**, 1100 Granville St., V6Z 2B6, ☎ 604/669-7070 or 800/663-0575, fax 604/669-4928, $$$-$$$$, offers 144 rooms, each with a balcony or a patio, on 15 floors. It has an excellent downtown location, a restaurant that is open from 7 AM to 10 PM, and a cocktail lounge. **Blue Horizon Hotel**, 1225 Robson St., V6E 1C3, ☎ 604/688-1411 or 800/663-1333, fax 604/688-4461, $$-$$$, has 214 spacious rooms, a small heated indoor pool, an exercise room, a restaurant that is open between 6:30 AM and 10 PM, and a cocktail lounge. **Holiday Inn Vancouver Downtown Hotel & Tower Suites**, 1110 Howe St., V6Z 1R2, ☎ 604/684-2151 or 800/465-4329, fax 604/684-4736, $$$-$$$$, provides 243 rooms, including 18 efficiencies. Its seven stories also contain a heated indoor pool, an exercise room, a restaurant that is open between 6:30 AM and 11 PM, and a cocktail lounge. One drawback: the hotel requires a minimum stay of five nights.

Hyatt Regency Vancouver, 655 Burrard St., Vancouver, BC V6C 2R7, ☎ 604/683-1234 or 800/233-1234, fax 604/689-3707, $$$-$$$$, offers 644 rooms on 34 floors plus a small heated pool, an exercise room, a dining room, a coffee shop, and two lunch buffets.

The Westin Bayshore, 1601 W. Georgia St., V6G 2V4, ☎ 604/682-3377 or 800/228-3000, fax 604/687-3102, $$$-$$$$, places 517 rooms amid four acres of luxurious gardens. The hotel has a dining room, a restaurant that is open between 6:30 AM and 11 PM, and a cocktail lounge, in addition to the on-site Trader Vic's, ☎ 604/682-3377. There also are two heated pools, one indoors, and an exercise room. Bike rentals also are available. The 23-story **Pan Pacific Hotel Vancouver**, 300-999 Canada Place, ☎ 604/662-8111, fax 604/891-2861, E-mail pphsales@panpacific-hotel.com, $$$$, occupies a lovely waterfront location not far from Gastown. It has 506 rooms, a heated pool, paddle tennis, a spa, a running track, and three restaurants and lounges. Try the Five Sails restaurant, ☎ 604/662-8111, for harbour views and excellent cuisine.

Those who are traveling on a budget might enjoy the brand-new **YMCA Hotel/Residence**, 733 Beatty St., Vancouver, BC V6B 2M4, ☎ 604/681-5830, fax 604/681-2550, E-mail ywcavan_hotel@bc.sympatico.ca, $-$$, in the heart of downtown. At the other end of the scale, the **Metropolitan Hotel Vancouver**, 645 Howe St., Vancouver, BC V6C 2Y9, ☎ 604/687-1122 or 800/323-7500, fax 604/689-7044, $$$$, located across the street from the Pacific Mall, is 18 stories tall and has 197 rooms plus a heated indoor pool, a racquetball court, a health club, and a sports court.

■ Camping

Near **Langley**, camping facilities are available in **Aloha Trailer Park & Campground**, ☎ 604/856-2366; **Livingstone Campsite & Trailer Park**, ☎ 604/882-3880; **Lombardy Campsite**, ☎ 604/888-2244; and **Fort Camping**, ☎ 604/888-3678.

One of largest campsites in the province is at **Alouette Lake** in Golden Ears Provincial Park near **Mission**.

Numerous camping sites can be found in **Garibaldi Provincial Park** near **Squamish**. In the **Diamond Head Area** are Red Heather Campground, Elfin Lakes Campground, and Mamquam Lake. In the

Black Tusk/Garibaldi Lake Area, camping is restricted to two sites: Taylor Meadows and the west end of Garibaldi Lake. In the

Cheakamus Lake Area, there are primitive campsites at Singing Creek and at Castle Tower Creek at the west end of the lake (accessible only by boat). The **Singing Pass Area** provides camping at the northwest end of Russet Lake, where there also is a hut and a pit toilet. Similar facilities can be found in the **Wedgemount Lake Area**.

In **Surrey**, camping facilities can be found at **Bayside Campground**, 16565 Beach Rd., ☎ 604/531-6563.

Where to Eat

New Westminster

The Old Bavaria Haus, 233 6th St., New Westminster, BC V3M 6G1, ☎ 604/524-5824, $$, serves everything from schnitzel to seafood – even vegetarian meals, if you wish. Outdoor dining is available in the summer. The restaurant is open from 5 PM, Tuesday through Sunday. **Starlight Tours**, Westminster Quay, New Westminster, BC V3M 6G1, ☎ 604/522-3506, conducts dinner cruises.

Richmond

Charthouse Restaurant, 3866 Bayview St., #200, Richmond, BC V6X 1S1, ☎ 604/271-7000, $$, provides waterfront dining on Stevenson Harbour. Lunch and dinner are served daily, and a brunch is served between 11 AM and 3 PM on Saturdays and Sundays. Patio dining is available seasonally.

Stevenson

Cottage Tea Room, 100-12220 2nd Ave., Stevenson, BC, ☎ 604/241-1853, $$, provides homemade soups, sandwiches, and fresh-baked pies, scones, and pastries daily between 9 AM and 5 PM.

Vancouver

A great waterfront seafood restaurant in Vancouver is **Bridges**, ☎ 604/687-4400, $$, which is located on the west side of Granville Island and open daily. **Amorous Oyster**, 3236 Oak St., ☎ 604/732-5916, $$, serves lunch Monday through Friday and dinner every day.

White Rock

Want some honest-to-goodness British food? **Yorkshire Rose**, 15238 Russell Ave., White Rock, BC V4A 4Z2 ☎ 604/531-3980, $$, has the whole thing: Penguin Bars, British canned goods, British pop, and mushy peas.

Information Sources

Vancouver, Coast & Mountains Tourism Region, 1755 W. Broadway, #204, Vancouver, BC V6J 4S5, ☎ 604/739-9011 or 800/667-3306, fax 604/739-0153, E-mail vcm_tourism@mindlink.bc.ca., Web site supernatural.bc.ca.

Vancouver Tourist Information Centre, Plaza Level, 200 Burrard St., Vancouver, BC V6C 3L6, ☎ 604/683-2000 or 800/663-6000, fax 604/682-6839.

Inland BC

For the reader's convenience, we have divided our traveler's guide to southwestern British Columbia into three parts, as you may have noticed. The first part deals with the capital city of Victoria and Vancouver Island, upon which Victoria sits. The second part deals with the great metropolitan area of Greater Vancouver. This, the third part, attempts to cover all that is left in the large but thinly populated southwestern corner of British Columbia.

Getting Around

The roads in British Columbia go up mountains, down mountains, and around mountains. They twist through mountain passes and along wild, rushing rivers. They are lovely... they get the job done... but *they are anything but straight*.

One of the main thoroughfares on the western side of the province, where it essentially runs east and west, is TransCanada Highway 1. But as it heads east, Route 1 abruptly goes northbound at Hope, follows the Fraser River as it passes through Hell Gate Canyon, and at Cache Creek, with equal abruptness, heads east once again, moving through Kamloops and Revelstoke toward Banff National Park and the province of Alberta, just beyond.

Roughly paralleling the US border just north of the Washington state line, Route 3 twists, turns, winds, and climbs through a countryside dotted with campgrounds, where it links the cities of Princeton, Oliver, Osoyoos, Grand Forks, and Salmo, each progressively farther from the great metropolitan area that is Vancouver.

Only two other east-west highways exist between Route 1 on the north and Route 3 on the south. Route 97C links Route 5 (at Merritt on the west) with Route 97 (near Kelowna on the east), while Route 6 wanders between Route 97 (at Vernon on the west) with Route 23 (at Nakusp on the east), before it turns south to the Washington border.

The major north-south highway is Route 5, which cuts north-northwest from Hope to TransCanada Highway 16 just outside of Jasper National Park. Route 97 begins near Osoyoos at the US border and runs northward through Kelowna, Kamloops, and beyond.

Airports

The distances are great and the communities, generally speaking, are small, making the airplane a useful mode of transportation.

Castlegar, 100 Mile House, 108 Ranch, Kamloops, Penticton, Powell River, Revelstoke, Salmon Arm, Squamish, and Texada Island all have small airports. Chilliwack Municipal Airport sustains a lighted, paved, 3,900-foot runway, and the Kelowna Airport provides 27 scheduled flights daily, along with 24-hour customs service and a restaurant/lounge.

Kootenay Airways serves the communities of **Cranbrook**, ☎ 604/426-3762, fax 604/426-4050, and **Grand Forks**, ☎ 604/442-5866, fax 604/442-2665.

Canadian Regional Airlines serves **Kelowna**, ☎ 604/765-4510, 763-6620, or 800/665-1177, and **Penticton**, ☎ 250/493-2900, 493-0436 or 800/667-7000. **AirBC**, ☎ 250/493-6662, also serves Penticton.

Pacific Coastal Airlines, 7576 Duncan St., Powell River, BC, ☎ 604/483-2107 or 800/663-2872, serves **Powell River, Port Hardy**, **Rivers Inlet**, **Hakai Pass**, and **Bella Bella** along the coast north of Powell River out of Vancouver (☎ 604/273-8666). **Suncoast Air**, 7494 Duncan St., Powell River, BC V8A 1W7, ☎ 604/485-2915, also provides an air taxi service.

Touring

When a large tree in **Hope**'s Memorial Park fell victim to root rot in 1991, Pete Ryan, a local chainsaw artist, proposed turning the situation into a positive event by making the stump of the tree into a carving that depicts a bald eagle with a salmon in its talons. Since then, two dozen additional chainsaw carvings have been created throughout the town, earning Hope the title of "Chainsaw Carving Capital" of British Columbia. (The Chamber of Commerce can provide you with a free map that shows the locations of these carvings.)

Another Hope resident, Andrew McCulloch, was such an ardent fan of William Shakespeare's plays that he once rowed a dinghy from **Hope** to **Seattle** and back across Puget Sound *just to see a Shakespearean play*. McCulloch gave added substance to his fondness for Shakespeare when, as chief engineer of the Kettle Valley Railway, he named the stations along the rail line through Coquihalla Pass Othello, Lear, Jessica, Portia, Iago, Romeo, and Juliet. Today, many of those names can still be seen on signs, bridges, and interchanges along the Coquihalla Highway (Route 5).

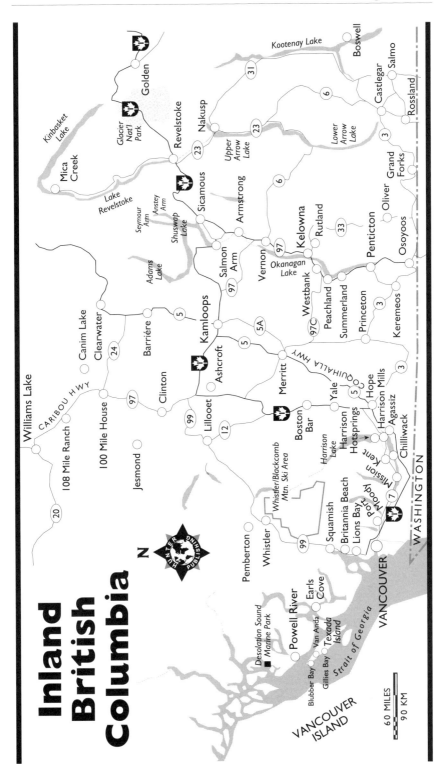

Kelowna, which sits on the banks of Okanagan Lake, was completely isolated except by water until 1925, when the railroad finally arrived. From 1913 to 1932, there was considerable speculation about oil in the region and two oil wells were drilled, but after a great deal of time and money was invested in the search, no oil was found.

Okanagan Lake has its own version of the Loch Ness monster, Ogopogo, the modern name for a creature that the Indians called N'ha-a-itk. Animal sacrifices were made to the Indian's "Devil of the Lake," which is said to have a snakelike body with several humps, a green outer skin, and a very large head. The creature has been called a demon fish, snake, sea serpent, Big Lake Devil, oar fish, and giant sturgeon, but the modern name of Ogopogo was adopted from a music hall song of the 1920s. When, in 1926, the government said that a new ferry was being built for Okanagan Lake, it announced that the ferry would be equipped with "monster-repelling devices."

Thanks to the discovery of gold, **Lillooet** was the largest city west of Chicago and north of San Francisco in the 1860s.

The **Nicola Tribal Association**, Nicola Valley, ☎ 604/378-4235, fax 604/378-9119, administers the Cook's Ferry, Coldwater, Lower Nicola, Nooaitch, Shackan, Siska, and Upper Nicola bands of the Nlaka'pamux Indian Nation.

Eighty miles northwest of Vancouver, **Powell River** had the first paper mill in Western Canada. It also was the first town in British Columbia to have dial telephones.

Texada Island, the largest and most industrialized of the Gulf Islands, shelters three small communities – Van Anda, Blubber Bay, and Gillies Bay. Regular ferry service runs between Powell River and Texada, and the island's Shelter Point Park offers excellent camping opportunities.

Adventures

■ On Foot

Hiking Trails

Agassiz offers three interesting trails for hiking and walking: Nature House Walk, Cemetery Mountain Loop, and Nancy's Trail. Inquire at the Tourist Centre for a free map and directions.

Bridal Veil Falls Provincial Park is located 100 kilometers east of Vancouver beneath Mount Cheam. A creek flows through the park, under the freeway, and into Cheam Lake Regional Nature Park before it empties into the Fraser River. The park's 122-foot falls are the fifth highest in all of Canada.

In **Burnaby**, Railway Trail parallels Hayward Lake Reservoir from the Recreation Area Warden's office to a parking lot located off Wilson Road near Ruskin Dam. A short interpretive trail also runs around the pond by the Warden's office.

The **Canim Lake** area has some lovely hikes at Whale Lake and around Deception Falls, Mahood Falls, and Canim Falls.

Some of the easy hiking/biking trails around **Castlegar** are the 1.5-kilometer Selkirk Trail, the 6-kilometer Kinnaird Pipeline Trail, the 5-kilometer Brilliant Dam Trail, and the 2-kilometer Merry Creek Trail, which offers a nice view of the Columbia River and passes the remains of an early homestead. Intermediate trails include the 1- to 5-kilometer Beaver Trails, the 17-kilometer Robson Loop, the 85-kilometer CPR Rail Grade, and the 18-kilometer Fairview Loop. The 5-kilometer Viewpoint Trail is for advanced hikers.

Trails in the **Chilliwack Forest District** include Denham Trail, a 2-kilometer trail that encircles Weaver Lake; Eaton Lake Trail, a steep 6.5-kilometer trail that leads to a large alpine lake; Radium Lake Trail, a 6-kilometer trail that leads to a small alpine lake and an old cabin; Post-Greendrop Trail, that leads past one medium-size alpine lake to another, set deep in a narrow valley; Devil's Lake Trail, a short 0.33-kilometer trail that leads to a small lake; Rolley Falls Trail, a 2-kilometer trail that passes two sets of falls and provides nice views of Stave Lake; and Hoover Lake Trail, 3.8 kilometers of road and trail that leads to Hoover Lake.

There's a half-hour loop trail at the **Chilliwack River Fish Hatchery**, and both **Weaver Creek** and **Cheam Lake Wetlands Regional Park** are good places to hike and look for wildlife. The **Rotary Vedder River Trail** runs 5 kilometers along the north dike of the Vedder River between Vedder Road and Sumas Prairie Road.

> 📖 Ask the Chilliwack Chamber of Commerce, 44150 Luckakuck Way, Chilliwack, BC V2P 4P1, ☎ 604/858-8121 or 800/567-9535, for a free copy of the pocket-sized *Forests in Action: A Self-guided Tour of Vedder Mountain*.

British Columbia Backcountry Adventures, 45138 Wells Rd., Chilliwack, BC V2R 1H6, ☎ 604/858-0507, fax 604/824-0005, E-mail bcba@rapidnet.net, Web site www.ntonline.com/biz/bcba, conducts rock climbing, hiking, rafting, mountain biking, caving, and mountaineering excursions.

Wells Gray Park, near **Clearwater**, offers hiking, mountain biking, birdwatching, wildlife-viewing, fishing, whitewater rafting, kayaking, horseback riding, canoeing, boat tours, waterfalls, and camping. **Helmcken Falls** also are located in the Clearwater area.

Cultus Lake Provincial Park has some exciting hiking trails that include the two-hour Teapot Hill Trail, accessed by a Trailhead near the Honeymoon Bay group site; the two-hour Seven Sisters Trail from Entrance Bay to the Clear Creek campgrounds; and the three- to four-hour Edmeston Road-Road 918 Trail that connects the north and south ends of the park. There also are two nice nature trails in the park: the Giant Douglas Fir Trail that begins 150 meters west of the entrance to Delta Grove Campground on Columbia Valley Highway, and the half-hour Maple Bay Trail, a self-guided interpretive trail that starts at the Maple Bay parking area.

The **Harrison Hot Springs Hiking Group**, ☎ 604/796-3425 or 796-2084, invites visitors to join them on their Wednesday hikes. The group sometimes hikes on the weekends too.

There are three nice hikes around **Hope**. To reach the medium-difficulty, two-mile **Landstrom Ridge Trail**, cross the Fraser River Bridge going north on Route 1 and take the Route 7 exit west. Park at the west end of the weigh scales, cross the railroad tracks, and look for the Trailhead on the left. The trail offers nice views of Hope and the Fraser River from four lookouts near the summit. Getting to the easy, five-mile **Kettle Valley Railway Trail** requires driving east from Hope on Kawkawa Lake Road to the cemetery, turning right onto Kettle Valley Road, and following that road to the end. The section of the trail from Myra Road to Little White Road is 12 kilometers long, passes over 18 trestles and through two tunnels, and requires about four hours to hike each way. No vehicles are permitted. Finding the **Nicola Trail** requires driving east on Kawkawa Lake Road, following the signs to the Othello Tunnels, then leaving your car in the parking lot as you walk through the tunnels to a kiosk that marks the trail. The five-mile trail, of medium difficulty, goes over the mountain, then returns to the parking lot, providing great views of the Coquihalla River and the canyon.

Tours through the forests around **100 Mile House** include the Dry Belt Forestry Tour and the 99 Mile Demonstration Forest Tour. Ask for a free map at the Chamber of Commerce office.

To reach **Black Knight Mountain Trail** take Route 97 north from Kelowna and turn right at the junction with Route 33. About eight kilometers east of Rutland, turn left onto Pyman Road and keep to the right. You can either drive or hike the road (about 6.5 kilometers long) to a forest lookout tower at the top.

The **Kettle Valley Railway Trail** railbed passing through horseshoe-shaped Myra Canyon is good for both hiking and biking. The comfortable level-grade trail runs along a trackbed carved into the mountainside (the tracks were removed in 1992). There are 18 trestles and two short tunnels in an 8-kilometer loop of the canyon. Part of the railway was built in the early 1900s. Take McCulloch Road north to June Springs, then follow June Springs to the Little White Forest Service Road. From the end of the pavement, it is about four kilometers to the parking lot at the end of Little White where the trail begins.

To find **Wild Horse Canyon**, follow Lakeshore Road to the end, approximately 16 kilometers south and west of town. Park on the right; the trail is on the left. Walk for about three kilometers, cross a creek, and then continue on an uphill road for another five kilometers to the canyon. Another interesting trail leads to **Wrinkley-Face Cliffs**. Follow Route 97 past the road to Beaver Creek Falls and look for an old logging road going off to the left. Follow that road northeast to the cliffs. **Crux Climbing Center**, 2-1414 Hunter Court, ☎ 604/860-7325, can get you ready to do some climbing.

Okanagan Llama Expeditions, 118 Timberline Rd., ☎ 604/764-0225, arranges llama treks and overnight camping trips from April to October.

Easy to moderate hiking trails in the Manning Provincial Park include the nine-kilometer **Lightning Lake Loop Trail**, the 12-kilometer **Lightning Lake Chain Trail**, a short trail that follows the shoreline of Lone Duck Bay, the 4.6-kilometer **Similkameen West Trail**, the 5.4-kilometer **Similkameen East Trail**, the 2.7-kilometer **Little Muddy Trail**, the 12-kilometer **Castle Creek/Monument 78 Trail**, the nine-kilometer **Strawberry Flat/Three Falls Trail**, the 7.6-kilometer **North Gibson Trail**, the 7.6km **South Gibson Trail**, and the 21-kilometer **Heather Trail**.

Fairly strenuous trails through the park include the 15-kilometer **Windy Joe Mountain Trail**; the 12-kilometer **Pacific Crest Trail**, the beginning of the 4,000-kilometer trek to Mexico; the **Monument 83 Trail**, that goes 16 kilometers one way and passes Pasayten Pete's grave and a 1920s Forest Service log cabin; the eight-kilometer **Poland Lake Trail**; the 29-kilometer **Bonnevier Trail**; the 19.5-kilometer

Grainger Creek Trail that leads to a camping area at the north end of Nicomen Lake; and the 5.6-kilometer **Skagit Bluffs Trail**.

Strenuous trails through the park include the 29-kilometer **Frosty Mountain Loop Trail**; the 20.4-kilometer **Skyline I Trail**, where the wild-flowers peak from mid-July to mid-August; and the 12.5-kilometer **Skyline II Trail**.

In the **Cascade Recreation Area** are three other interesting trails. The **Dewdney Trail** was one of the first trade routes between the interior of British Columbia and the Pacific coast. Constructed by Edgar Dewdney in 1860 at the request of Governor Douglas, the trail travels 36 kilometers one way, requiring a hike of 14 to 16 hours or a two-day trip on horseback. The **Whatcom Trail**, originally built in 1858, covers 17 kilometers one way and is a strenuous six- or seven-hour hike. The **Hope Pass Trail** is also strenuous and requires a hike of six or seven hours to cover 17 kilometers one way, along with the need to beware of and yield to the logging trucks.

> A free pocket-sized brochure describing hiking facilities in the park is available from BC Parks, Manning Provincial Park, Box 3, Manning Park, BC V0X 1R0, ☎ 250/840-8836, fax 250/840-8700.

The **Powell River** Chamber of Commerce has a free visitor's map that lists and maps 25 good hikes ranging from easy one-hour hikes to challenging eight-hour hikes.

Nearly complete is the **Sunshine Coast Trail** that will ultimately extend 180 kilometers from Saltery Bay on the south to Sarah Point, land's end on the north. Over 120 kilometers already have been completed. (The Visitors Bureau can provide you with an information packet about the trail.)

From **Squamish**, it is a nice hike to **Shannon Falls**, where the water tumbles 1,300 feet into Howe Sound. Choice climbing also can be enjoyed in this area, where 200 routes lead up the granite monolith known as the Stawamus Chief, and there are such other climbs as the Apron, 400 meters north of the Chief; Smoke Bluffs, which overlooks the downtown area; and the Malamute. In the winter, this area is the home of more than 3,000 bald eagles.

Three excellent walking trails can be found near **Summerland**. The 3-kilometer **Don Agur Trail** can be reached from Milne Road at the gates to Giant's Head Park. The 4.5 kilometers **Peach Orchard Loop**, accessed at a trailhead at Peach Orchard Beach, goes south along the Rotary Walkway below Lakeshore Drive and passes the racquet club, the trout hatchery, and the yacht club as you head to Butler Street. The end of Butler Street starts what is locally known as the Gulch Trail, and you will cross two small bridges as you border Route 97 for a short distance, then turn right onto Bristow Road. Following Bristow, you cross Solly Road and go to the end of the cul-de-sac. There, the trail cuts into the hillside to the left, swings down, and then returns to Peach Orchard Road. Lakeshore Drive, Peach Orchard Beach, and the trailhead are just down the hill. To take the six-kilometer **Lakeshore Loop**, go to the Peach Orchard Beach trailhead and head north along the lakeshore to Crescent Beach. There, take Slater Road to the left until you reach Whitfield Road. Go south along Whitfield to Huddlestone Road and turn right. Continue on to Dosbery Road, then turn south again to the intersection of Dosbery and Switchback Road. Follow Switchback Road, which joins Peach Orchard Road across from the campground, and take Peach Orchard Road down the hill to Lakeshore Drive, where you should turn right and return to the Peach Orchard Beach trailhead.

East of **Tappen**, close to Herald Provincial Park on Sunnybrae Road, is a short trail that leads to **Margaret Falls**. Swimming is available nearby.

Taking a self-guided walking tour of **Trail** is a pleasant experience (ask for a free map at the Chamber of Commerce). You can dig your own opals in Canada's first opal mine. **Okanagan Opal**, PO Box 298, **Vernon**, BC V1T 6M2, ☎ 250/542-5173, fax 250/542-7115, offers day-trips on weekends and holidays from June 1 to September 30.

Rockhounding

Chilliwack offers some excellent rockhounding. Agate, jasper, basalt, and obsidian can be found along the Fraser River banks, and the local jade has a "mutton fat" color, dull off-white on the outside and turquoise, brown, or pink on the inside.

Around **Shuswap Lake**, there is good rockhounding for blue-grey and banded agate, crystalline geodes, and amethyst on Squilax Mountain near Chase, the Enderby Cliffs, and Mount Ida near the Salmon Arm.

Wildlife Viewing

Know Mountain, a nature park that offers great views of the city, a nature pavilion, a pond, and good hiking trails is at the north end of Ellis Street in **Kelowna** (Salish for "grizzly bear"). **Okanagan Mountain Provincial Park**, at the end of Lakeshore Road in Kelowna, is a rugged wilderness park with good hiking, trail riding, and biking trails. Good hiking trails for birders can be found in **Woodhaven Nature Conservancy Park** at the end of Raymer Road in Okanagan Mission.

Manning Provincial Park is 224 kilometers east of Vancouver on two major rivers, the Skagit and the Similkameen. Nature trails in the park include the short **Beaver Pond Trail**, 500 meters east of the Visitor Centre, which can provide good birdwatching in May and June; the equally short **Rein Orchid Trail**, off a parking lot on Gibson Pass Road, along which orchids and other bog flora can be seen from June through July; the half-hour **Sumallo Grove Trail**; the 45-minute **Canyon Trail**, which leaves the Coldspring Campground and follows both sides of the Similkameen River; and the one-kilometer **Paintbrush Trail** that passes through meadows that are in peak bloom from mid-July to early August.

Monck Provincial Park, ☎ 604/378-2111, is 22 kilometers northeast of **Merritt**. Park personnel conduct daily talks, slide shows, and nature walks.

Pocket Desert, southeast of **Oliver** on Black Sage Road or Route 97, both of which are paved, displays a variety of desert flora and fauna including burrowing owls and rattlesnakes.

The **Osoyoos** area is noted for its good birding. Uncommon finds may include the Canyon wren, White-headed woodpecker, Western bluebird, Lazuli bunting, Chukar partridge, Lewis woodpecker, and Sage thrasher.

Lions Nature Park along Mission Creek in **Rutland** has some nice trails. Mission Creek is a major spawning stream for kokanee salmon and has a novel fish ladder. The annual salmon run extends from mid-September to mid-October. **Salmon Arm** has 1,000 kilometers of shoreline, most of which is ideal for hiking and biking as well as swimming and boating.

> Ask the **Salmon Arm & District Chamber of Commerce**, Box 999, Salmon Arm, BC V1E 4P2, ☎ 604/832-6247, fax 604/832-8382, for a copy of *Shuswap Pathways: A Trail Guide*.

■ On Horseback

Rodeos

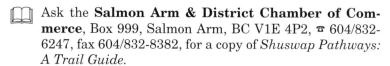

Whether you pronounce it *ROAD-ee-oh* or *road-AY-oh*, rodeo is a part of the culture throughout the Pacific Northwest.

In **Armstrong**, the **Kinsman Rodeo** is held each August. During the second week in September, it's time for the **Interior Pro-**

vincial **Exhibition & Stampede**, ☎ 604/546-9406, British Columbia's largest agricultural fair as well as a rodeo. And throughout the year, the **Agriplex** is the venue for numerous horse events involving quarter horses, Arabians, Icelandic horses, miniatures, and paints.

In **Ashcroft**, the **Ashcroft Stampede** reaches the Rodeo Grounds, ☎ 604/989-1300, each June. By September, it's time for the **North Thompson Fall Fair & Rodeo** in **Barriere**.

The **High School Rodeo** is held in **Chase** each May along with an annual **Horse & Rider Poker Run**. In September, the town hosts the **Chase Creek International Equestrian Events**.

The annual **Chilliwack Exhibition & Rodeo** is held on the Exhibition Grounds in **Chilliwack** every August.

Clinton has three annual rodeo-related events, the **Ball & Rodeo** in May, and the **Williams Lake Stampede** and the **Anahim Lake Stampede**, both of which are held in July.

At **100 Mile House**, a **Little Britches Rodeo** is held in May, while **Kamloops** hosts the **Kamloops Cowboy Festival** in March and the **Indoor Pro Rodeo** in April. The **Black Mountain Rodeo** is held on the Black Mountain Rodeo Grounds in **Kelowna** each May while the Ranch & Country Club in **Logan Lake**, ☎ 604/523-6925 or 523-6843, hosts both the **Jackpot Rodeo & Craft Fair** in June and the **Little Britches Rodeo** in August. Another **Little Britches Rodeo**, ☎ 604/378-5193, is held in June at the Nicola Valley Fairgrounds in **Merritt**, which also serves as the venue for the **Nicola Valley Fall Fair & Pro Rodeo**, ☎ 604/378-4314, presented on the Labor Day weekend.

Powell River holds the **Sidewinder Rodeo**, ☎ 604/485-4701 (contact the Chamber of Commerce for the date). In July **Pritchard** stages the **Pritchard Community Association Rodeo**, ☎ 604/989-1300; **Summerland** hosts the **Trail Riders Rodeo** on the Summerland Rodeo Grounds; and the **Shuswap Rodeo** is held on the **Salmon Arm** Fairgrounds, ☎ 604/832-2762. In September, the **BCRA Championship Rodeo** also is held in **Salmon Arm**.

Riding

Simply riding a horse is equally popular in this part of Canada.

Lo-Bo Ranch Trail Rides, ☎ 604/867-8865, fax 604/867-9764, provides ranch and alpine rides in the **Boston Bar** area. **Crystal Waters Guest Ranch**, Box 100, **Bridge Lake**, BC V0K 1E0, ☎ 250/593-4252, fax 250/593-0052, is a working cattle ranch where guests can participate in all of the ranch activities while staying in private, heated log cabins.

In May, June, and July, **Chilliwack** hosts the **Chariot & Chuckwagon Races**, and every September, the "Koolah" horse events. Horses can be rented at the **Island 22 Campground & Equestrian Centre**, ☎ 604/792-5567, or at **Matsqui Trail Stables**, ☎ 604/826-0806, just outside Matsqui Village.

Trophy Mountain Buffalo Ranch, Box 1768, R.R. 1, **Clearwater**, BC V0E 1N0, ☎ 250/674-3095, fax 250/674-3131, can accommodate horseback riding and camping. Visitors to **Big Bar Guest Ranch**, Box 27, Clearwater, ☎ 250/459-2333, E-mail bigbar@mail.netshop.net, and **EV Ranch Resort**, PO Box 16, **Jesmond-Clinton**, BC V0K 1K0, ☎ 250/459-2386 or 800/253-8831, fax 250/459-0086, Web site www.evranch.com, can engage in horseback riding, sleigh riding, hiking, river rafting, fishing, canoeing, skiing, skating, or cross-country skiing.

In **Cultus Lake**, you can rent a horse at **Cultus Lake Riding Stables**, 36 Columbia Valley Hwy, ☎ 604/858-5649. **Douglas Lake Ranch**, General Delivery, **Douglas Lake**, BC V0E 1S0, ☎ 250/350-3344 or 800/663-4838, fax 250/350-3336, Web site www.douglaslake.com, is Canada's largest working cattle ranch and it conducts daily trail rides, guided overnighters, and ranch tours. There are 12 private lakes, campgrounds, and a general store on the premises.

In **Greenwood**, **Lind Valley Vacations**, ☎ 250/445-6585, arranges trail rides, wagon rides, wagon trips, and overnight pack trips. **The Hills Guest Ranch**, C-26 108 Ranch, **100 Mile House**, BC V0K 2E0, ☎ 604/791-5225, fax 604/791-6384, offers horseback riding, hayride parties, and cowboy breakfast rides.

An exciting feature of mid-July is the annual **Nicola Valley-to-Kamloops Cattle Drive**, PO Box 1332, Kamloops, BC V2C 6L7, ☎ 250/372-7075 or 800/288-5850, fax 250/372-0262, E-mail cattledr@mail.netshop.net, Web site www.netshop.net/cattledr, a genuine holdover from the days of the Old West.

At **Kelowna**, horseback riding is available at Idabel Lake Resort, Eight Mile Ranch, and B&B Stables. **Saddle Ridge Ranch**, ☎ 250/491-8813; **Lake Okanagan Resort Stables**, ☎ 250-769-2634; and **Mandy & Me Trail Riding**, ☎ 250/769-5735, also offer trail rides, while **Catchahorse Trail Rides**, ☎ 250/212-2844, arranges one-hour to all-day rides at Big White Ski Resort. **Advanced Trail Rides & Pack Trips**, ☎ 250/707-3013, advertises "bed, bale and breakfast" and can arrange a ride over mountain trails. **Mt. Boucherie Riding Stables**, ☎ 250/769-5274, provides one- to three-hour rides, pony rides, day trips, camping trips, and BBQs.

In **Keremeos**, go to **Similkameen Adventure Ranch**, ☎ 250/499-6166, for horseback riding, rock climbing, rappelling, mountain biking, canoeing, hiking, and almost anything else. **Tunkwa Lake Resort**, PO Box 196, **Logan Lake**, BC V0K 2B0, ☎ 604/523-9697, has daily trail rides. **Keefer Lake Wilderness Resort**, ☎ 250/549-7858, arranges pack trips in the **Lumby** area.

Manning Provincial Park contains numerous horse trails. From a staging area in the Monument 78/83 parking lot, the **Castle Creek Trail** provides a 20-kilometer ride, while the **Monument 83 Trail** covers 32 kilometers. Riders staging at the Cascade Recreation Area take the 72-kilometer **Dewdney/Whipsaw Trail**. Those choosing to ride the 47-kilometer **Cayuse Flats/Hope Pass Trail** or the 11.2-kilometer **Skagit Bluff Trail** start at the staging area at Cayuse Flats. The Strawberry Flats parking lot is the staging area for the 16-kilometer **Poland Lake Trail** and the 7.6-kilometer **North Gibson Trail**. Four nice trails begin at the staging area in the Beaver Pond parking lot: the 4.6-kilometer **Similkameen West Trail**, the 5.4-kilometer **Similkameen East Trail**, the 24-kilometer **Pacific Crest Trail**, and the 15-kilometer **Windy Joe Trail**. The six-kilometer **Little Muddy Trail** starts in a staging area at the Manning Park Corral.

Winding River Guest Ranch, Box 2838, **Merritt**, BC V0K 2B0, ☎ 250/378-6534, is on Route 8, 15 miles west of town. It offers 200 miles of wilderness trails and can provide trail rides, guided overnighters, hay rides, and three-day pack trips. **A-P Western Guest Ranch**, ☎ 250/378-6520, also can arrange trail rides in the Merritt area.

Copper Mountain Ranch, ☎ 250/449-2234, is an English riding camp in **Midway**.

Horses can be rented from **Wolf Creek Riding Stables**, ☎ 604/498-3259, 5.5 kilometers from **Oliver** on McKinney Road, and from **Southern Pines Stables**, ☎ 604/498-2399, which are located eight kilometers northwest of town. **Indian Grove Riding Stables**, ☎ 604/498-4478 or 495-7555, conducts trail rides at 9 and 11:30 AM and 4 and 6:30 PM daily. Day rides are offered between 9:30 AM and 7:30 PM, and horseback pack trips also are available. The stables are located near **Osoyoos** (from the Osoyoos Lake bridge, go half a mile east, then turn left onto 45th Street).

Apex Mountain Guest Ranch, ☎ 250/492-2454, fax 250/490-8537, is 20 minutes west of **Penticton** on Green Mountain Road. Guided trail rides, one- to six-day pack trips, and a children's riding camp are available there, and in the winter, cross-country skiing.

Harrison Horseback Riding, 7850 Nixon Rd., Rosedale, BC V0X 1X0, ☎ 604/794-0102 or 793-5013, offers scenic rides, pony rides, BBQ rides, and Sunday breakfast rides daily from April through September. A gymkhana is held each June on the **70 Mile House** Riding Grounds, ☎ 604/456-2233, and harness racing is presented at Sandown Park in **Sidney** from June to September. Around **Summerland**, the **Stiefelknecht Ranch**, ☎ 250/494-0506, is the place to go when you're in the mood for a trail ride.

In **Vernon**, trail rides can be arranged at **Bobslide Park** or **Silver Star Mountain Resort**, ☎ 604/542-0104, fax 545-4927; at **Aspen Grove Equestrian Center**, ☎ 604/545-9470; and at **Lone Pine Ranch**, ☎ 250/549-2209.

■ On Wheels

Biking

Bicycle outings can be booked with **Turtle Island Cycling Tours**, RR 1, C79, **Jarvis-Armstrong**, BC V0E 1B0, ☎ 604/546-8525 or 800/661-6338, fax 604/542-2353, and **Desert Pedal Mountain Bike & Rafting Adventures**, Box 844, **Ashcroft**, BC V0K 1A0, ☎ 250/453-9602, E-mail dpedal@mail.netshop.net, Web site www.netshop.net/~dpedal.

Gravel Travel, 9708 Williams St., **Chilliwack**, BC V2P 5G7, ☎ 800/429-2533, schedules mountain biking day-trips. (They'll send you a complimentary video on request.) In **Kamloops** guided biking tours also can be arranged through **Full Board Bike Store**, 414 Seymour St., ☎ 250/314-1888, fax 250/851-2553; **Crazy Moon Enterprises**, ☎ 250/578-2651; and **Sun Peaks Resort**, ☎ 250/578-7842 or 800/807-3257.

In **Kelowna**, bike tours to Kettle Valley Trestles can be arranged by **Okanagan Bicycle Tours**, ☎ 800/991-3233. When you book a tour with **Vintage Cycle Tours**, 4847 Parkridge Ave., ☎ 604/764-7223, the price includes a helmet, a bike, a water bottle, and a picnic.

In **Falkland**, mountain bikers like to ride up the Chase-Falkland Road to see the Pillar, a 90-foot column of rock and clay that rises above Pillar Lake. **Gerick Cycle & Sports**, 702 Baker St., ☎ 250/354-7717, rents canoes and kayaks as well as bicycles in **Nelson**, while **Simoka Wheels**, Oliver Mini-Mall, ☎ 604/498-0876, offers the same service in **Oliver**. (While in Oliver, pick up a copy of the International Bicycling & Hiking Society Trail's map at the Chamber of Commerce.)

Sun Country Cycle, 533 Main St., ☎ 250/493-0686, can rent you a mountain bike or provide a trail guide in **Penticton**, while **Taws Cycle & Sports**, 4597 Marine Ave., ☎ 604/485-2555, rents both bikes and tents in **Powell River**. Some of the more interesting bike trips out of Powell River include the **Inland Lake Trail**, a 13-kilometer loop that passes some nice swimming sites; the moderate eight-kilometer **Suicide Creek Loop**, which passes waterfalls and goes over some bridges along Suicide Creek; and the **Bunster Hills Loop**, a steep, four- to five-hour, 34-kilometer ride that provides great views of Okeover Inlet and Georgia Straight. Sunshine Coast Forest District, 7077 Duncan St., can provide descriptions of mountain bike trails throughout the Powell River area.

There is a 56-kilometer loop trail on **Texada Island** that ranges from intermediate to advanced in difficulty and features side trips to Bob's Lake and Shingle Beach.

Sunoka Adventure Tours, RR #3, Dale Meadows Road, **Summerland**, BC V0H 1Z0, ☎ 250/494-8346 or 800/431-3344, Web site adventures.summerland.net, arranges one- to seven-day mountain biking, canoeing, and hiking tours and also will provide for self-guided adventures.

In **Vernon**, **Skedaddle Tours**, ☎ 604/764-0990 or 800/663-4431, plans mountain bike day-trips, air-biking trips from the top of Kettle Valley Railway, and heli-boat biking trips. **Olympia Cycle & Sky**, 3102 31st Ave., Vernon, BC V1T 2H1, ☎ 604/542-9684, rents bikes and cross-country skis.

Day Trips & Off-Road Trips

The drive from **Hope** to **Boston Bar** is enhanced by the necessity to pass through seven tunnels along the TransCanada Highway. The first is the 286-meter **Yale Tunnel**, which is encountered 1.5 kilometers east of Yale. The 146-meter **Saddle Rock Tunnel** is named for a saddle-shaped rock in the Fraser River below. **Sailor Bar Tunnel** is 292 meters long; **Alexandra Tunnel**, 290 meters; **Hell's Gate Tunnel**, 100 meters; and **Ferrabee Tunnel**, 100 meters.

DID YOU KNOW?

***China Bar Tunnel**, at 610 meters one of the longest in North America, was named for the gold-bearing sand bar in the Fraser River below, where Chinese prospectors once retrieved a fortune by reworking a supposedly exhausted area that their white comrades had abandoned for "more promising" sites.*

Off-roaders can rent four-wheelers, motorcycles, trailers, and other outdoor gear at **Interior Motorcycle**, 142 Tanquille Rd., ☎ 604/554-2321, in **Kamloops**; at **McScoot's Scooter & Motorcycle Rentals**, ☎ 604/763-4668, in **Kelowna**, where "scootin's a hoot"; at **Moguls Offroad Go-Karts**, 2681 Kyle Rd., ☎ 604/769-4331, in **West Kelowna**; and at **The Great Canadian Motor Corp.**, ☎ 250/837-6500 or 800/667-8865, in **Revelstoke**.

Races

Auto races are held at **Mission Raceway Park** in **Chilliwack** at the west end of the Mission Bridge on Route 11.

Train Rides

In **Summerland**, the **Kettle Valley Steam Railway**, ☎ 250/494-8422, fax 250/494-8452, E-mail kvr@summer.com, provides an evening that includes a BBQ dinner, a confrontation with outlaws, western dancing, and wine tasting. Transportation can be arranged from Penticton (☎ 604/494-9597 or 800/862-9155) or from Kelowna (☎ 604/763-5355).

■ On the Water

Fishing

Kent Outdoors, 7032 Cheam Ave., ☎ 604/796-0006, arranges fishing charters in **Agassiz**. **Jones Boys Boats**, ☎ 604/353-7717, fax 353-2911, and **Woodbury Resorts & Marina**, ☎ 604/353-7717, rent boats and schedule fishing charters around **Ainsworth**. **Shuswap Marina**, ☎ 604/675-2250, rents boats in **Blind Bay**.

King Jigger Charters, 375 Ptarmigan Place, **Campbell River**, BC V9W 7B2, ☎ 250/923-7084, 287-0136, or 287-6221, fax 250/923-3340, charters fishing trips. **Canim Lake Resort**, Box 248, Canim Lake, BC V0K 1J0, ☎ 250/397-2355, fax 250/397-2607, E-mail canim@canim.com,

Web site www.canim.com/clr/canim.htm, provides guides for kokanee salmon, rainbow trout, lake trout, and ling cod outings. At **Castlegar**, the 400-kilometer-long **Arrow Lakes** provide excellent boating, sailing, and fishing.

Fishing takes many forms around **Chilliwack**. In the **Fraser River**, anglers catch salmon, steelhead, and sturgeon (the sturgeon can be taken on a catch-and-release basis only). Along the Chilliwack, Fraser, and Chehalis Rivers, winter steelhead are most prevalent from December to April. **Chilliwack Lake Provincial Park**, where kokanee salmon run best in July and August but rainbow, cutthroat, and Dolly Varden trout can be taken year-around, also provides good camping and hiking. **Lindeman Lake**, a 1.6-kilometer hike from Chilliwack Lake along Post Creek Centennial Trail, can produce some great rainbow trout.

Osprey Fly Fishing Adventures, PO Box 974, **Cranbrook**, BC V1C 4J6, ☎ 250/426-6805 or 800/779-8338, arranges float trips, including trips on float tubes. **Silver River Boat Tours**, Village Mall, **Harrison Hot Springs**, BC, ☎ 604/796-5506 or 556-1884, schedules fishing charters, ecotours, scenic tours, and history tours. **Live Action**, 2469 E. TransCanada Hwy, **Kamloops**, BC, ☎ 604/374-4520, rents aluminum fishing boats with gas or electric motors and 24-ft. pontoon boats.

Bear Lake, 22 kilometers from **Kelowna** on a good road, is a good place to go fly fishing for trout in the two-pound range.

The **Powell River** Chamber of Commerce has a visitor map that indicates the area's best fishing sites, including the north end of Texada Island; Harwood Island; the spot where Powell Lake enters Malaspina Strait; places off Elephant, Culloden, Scotch Fir, Black, and Myrtle Points; and places off Ball and Alexander Points on Hardy Island. **Blue Eyes Charters**, 5366 Larch Ave., Powell River, BC V8A 4M5, ☎ 604/483-4198, will take you out to try some of them.

Water sports are central to the activities in the **Sunshine Coast Provincial Parks** north of Greater Vancouver in the vicinity of Powell River. Kayaking, swimming, boat launch, fishing, and camping are available at **Okeover Arm**, which sits on the waterfront adjacent to a wharf. **Saltery Bay** offers a beach and a boat launch from which to go swimming, fishing, scuba diving, and camping. Traveling north on Route 101, visitors to the park at Saltery Bay must take a 16-kilometer car ferry from Earls Cove. Jervis Bay, near the park, enjoys good fishing from April through late fall.

Malaspina Charters, 4008 Joyce Ave., **Powell River**, BC V8A 2Z5, ☎ 604/485-6386, *guarantees* that you will catch salmon on one of its four-hour charters. **BellBoy Charters**, Beach Gardens Marina, 7074 Westminter Ave., Powell River, BC V8A 1C5, ☎ 604/485-2608, fax 604/485-2343, Web site www.coc.powell-river.bc.ca, charters fishing trips aboard the 33-ft. Trojan *Bushmills*. **Kaptain Wave Charters**, ☎ 604/483-1057, also books charters for sports fishing, beachcombing, and sightseeing.

Fred's Custom Tackle, Site 3, Comp. 8, 5616 Vedder Rd., **Vedder Crossing**, BC V2R 3N7, ☎ 604/858-7344, fax 604/858-7307, guides fishing trips for salmon, steelhead, and sturgeon.

The four arms of **Shuswap Lake** form a rather haphazard H. All four arms converge at Cinnemousun Narrows, where there is a provincial park with a 1.5-kilometer hiking trail and a campground. The lake contains kokanee and lake trout, Dolly Varden, rainbow trout, and ling (burbot).

The **Main Arm** of the lake offers **Horseshoe Bay**, which has a maximum depth of 107 meters, and two provincial parks. **Shuswap Lake Provincial Park** has a visitor center that is open from June through September, a swimming beach, and a boat launch ramp, but the overnight mooring of boats is not permitted. **Roderick Haig-Brown Provincial Park** experiences a major run of sockeye salmon to the river's spawning beds in October of every fourth year. In 2002, one of the "peak years," trained staff will present *A Salute to the Salmon* explaining the event.

The **Salmon Arm** of Shuswap Lake has a number of interesting features including Aline Hill, Hermit Bay, Hungry Cove, Paradise Point, and Tillis Beach. At **Marble Point**, a nice trail leads past an abandoned mine shaft. While the Salmon Arm reaches a maximum depth of 131 meters, an appendage, **Mara Lake**, has a maximum depth of 49 meters, a nice beach, and a boat ramp. Once again, there are two provincial parks on this arm of the lake, **Sunnybrae Provincial Park**, which offers swimming, and **Herald Provincial Park**, which sits on the site of the old Herald homestead. Reinecker Creek wanders through Herald Park and a short wooded trail leads to Margaret Falls. The park also contains a campground, a sandy beach, and a boat launch ramp.

Anstey Arm, the most secluded arm of the lake, reaches a depth of 119 meters. Nonetheless, shallow sandbars require a cautious approach and one should not beach a boat for an extended period of time without allowing for a drop in the level of the lake. A trail leads to **Hunakwa Lake**, and other popular attractions include Four Mile Creek, the Rendezvous Picnic Site, and Twin Bays.

The **Seymour Arm** contains the deepest point in the lake (162 meters) at a point about four kilometers north of Woods Landing. At **Albas**, a trail passes a series of waterfalls. Other sights include Beach Bay, Cottonwood Beach, Encounter Point, Fowler Point, Nielsen Beach, Two Mile Creek, Woods Landing, and Wright Creek. **Silver Beach Provincial Park**, at the head of the arm, allows visitors to explore the site of old Seymour City. Shallow bars occur in front of the park's main beach, and a safer, deeper approach and mooring can be found along the shore toward Bughouse Bay to the ridge eastern part of British Columbia.

Kanata Wilderness Adventures, Box 1766, **Clearwater**, BC V0E 1N0, ☎ 250/674-2774, fax 250/674-2197, E-mail kanata@mail.netshop.net, Web site www.profiles.net/kanata.htm, handles canoeing, boating, biking, hiking, rafting, fishing, trail riding, dog sledding, skiing, van touring, and snowmobiling expeditions. In **Clearwater**, **Interior Whitewater Expeditions**, ☎ 604/674-3727, will take you on a three-hour, one-day, or two-day whitewater rafting trip on the Clearwater River. **Shuswap River Adventures**, Box 938, **Enderby**, BC V0H 1V0, ☎ 250/838-7370, fax 250/838-7317, conducts 45-minute tours of the river with a 10-passenger boat.

Boating

📖 **BC Hydro**, 6911 Southpoint Dr., **Burnaby**, BC V3N 4X8, can provide you with a pocket-sized *Stave Lake Reservoir Boater's Guide* and a similar brochure, *Hayward Lake Reservoir Recreation Area*, for the neighboring impound.

Chilliwack River Rafting Adventures, 49704 Chilliwack Lake Rd., **Chilliwack**, BC V4Z 1A7, ☎ 604/824-0334 or 800/410-7238, fax 604/872-3187, E-mail river_rafting@mindlink.bc.ca, can set you up for river rafting, and **Purple Hayes School of Kayaking**, 4552 McFaul Rd., Chilliwack, BC V2R 4N2, ☎ 604/858-2888, will tend to your kayaking interests.

Alpine Rafting Co., PO Box 2446, **Golden**, BC V0A 1H0, ☎ 250/344-6778 or 888/599-5299 and **Whitewater Voyageurs Ltd.**, PO Box 183, ☎ 250/344-7335 or 800/667-7238, fax 250/344-7808, both book whitewater rafting trips. **Reo Rafting Adventure Resort**, ☎ 800/736-7238, in Fraser Canyon, 90 minutes from **Harrison Hot Springs**, offers whitewater rafting trips, nature hikes, rock climbing, horseback riding, campsites, BBQs, and float trips.

Lytton is called the "Rafting Capital of Canada," although it also is popular for fishing, gold panning, rockhounding, birdwatching, hiking on the Stein Trail, and swimming. **Kumsheen Raft Adventures**, Hwy 1,

PO Box 30, ☎ 250/455-2296 or 800/663-6667, fax 250/455-2297, will help to arrange whitewater rafting trips on the Thompson River from May to October. The company also handles requests for rappelling, rock climbing, mountain biking, and trail riding adventures.

Rivers & Oceans Unlimited Expeditions, 333 Baker St., **Nelson**, BC V1L 4H6, ☎ 250/354-2056 or 800/360-7238, fax 250/354-2056, E-mail rivers@netidea.com, organizes whitewater rafting expeditions and also rents rafts, kayaks, bicycles, and canoes.

Around **Revelstoke**, two-hour whitewater rafting adventures leaving at 10:30, 1:30, and 4:30 can be booked through **Apex Raft Co.**, ☎ 888/232-6666, and **Wet 'n' Wild Adventures**, ☎ 250/344-6546 or 800/668-9119, handles kayak tours, ATV tours, jet boat rides, and camping trips. One- and two-day rafting trips can be scheduled through **Ryan's Rapid Rafting**, PO Box 129, **Spences Bridge**, BC V0K 2L0, ☎ 250/458-2479 or 800/665-7926.

Rafting and jet boating trips ranging from two hours to two days are scheduled on the Green, Brikenhead, Elaho, and Lillooet Rivers by **Whistler River Adventures**, Box 202, Whistler, BC V0N 1B0, ☎ 604/932-3532 or 888/932-3532, fax 604/932-3559, E-mail raftnjet@whistler.net. **Canadian River Expeditions**, 9571 Emerald Dr., #301, ☎ 604/938-6651 or 800/898-7238, fax 604/938-6621, arranges expeditions that last for six to 12 days. **Extreme Whitewater & Guide Service**, PO Box 201, ☎ 604/894-2311 or 800/606-7238, will arrange raft, kayak, or boogie board outings.

Fraser River Raft Expeditions, Box 10, **Yale**, BC V0K 2S0, ☎ 604/863-2336 or 800/363-RAFT, fax 604/863-2355, schedules whitewater rafting or combination rafting-and-horseback riding trips.

Chilliwack Lake is popular for swimming, boating, canoeing, kayaking, rafting, fishing, and hiking.

Cultus Lake Provincial Park has boat launching ramps, a marina, campsites, horse trails, nature trails, and hiking trails. Swimming and windsurfing are popular there. **Lakeside Marina**, 3175 Columbia Valley Hwy, **Cultus Lake**, BC, ☎ 604/858-4284, rents boats and jet skis. A free pocket-sized brochure is available from BC Parks District Manager, Box 10, Cultus Lake, BC V0X 1H0, ☎ 604/858-7161 or 858-4515 (gatehouse), fax 604/858-4905.

In **Osoyoos**, **Gateway Marine Rentals**, ☎ 604/495-7231, is located next to the Oasis Campsite and rents SeaDoos, ski boats, pedal boats, aqua bikes, and pontoon boats. The store is open from 8 AM to 9 PM daily. In **Penticton**, you can rent a kayak from **Coyote Cruises**, 215 Riverside, ☎ 604/492-2115.

Powell River, the second shortest river in Canada, connects **Powell Lake** and the ocean. Powell Lake has layers of salt water trapped at the bottom – the oldest trapped sea water yet discovered anywhere in the world. Powell River is the gateway to good kayaking opportunities in Copeland Islands Marine Park; in Okeover Inlet; near Willingdon Beach and Gibsons Beach; and in Hotham Sound. **Powell River Sea Kayak**, 5233 Powell Pl., ☎ 604/483-2410, rents kayaks and gives kayaking lessons. **Edgehill Store**, 5206 Manson Ave., ☎ 604/483-3909, rents canoes.

The magnificent – and demanding – **Powell Forest Canoe Route** starts at the south end of Lois Lake and passes through Horseshoe, Dodd, Windsor, and Goat Lakes to Lake Powell and the marina at Wildwood. There are portages between Lois Lake and Horseshoe Lake (1.7 kilometers); between Horseshoe Lake and Dodd Lake via Little Horseshoe Lake and Beaver Lake (two kilometers); between Dodd Lake and Windsor Lake (0.7 kilometers); and between Windsor Lake and Goat Lake (2.4 kilometers). The trip involves 80 kilometers of canoeing and 10.7 kilometers of portaging. Although the trail can be accessed from either end, the portaging is easier when you go from Lois Lake to Powell Lake.

Windsurfing

Harrison Lake is a typical mountain lake, prone to strong thermal winds that begin to blow from the southwest about noon each day throughout the summer. For that reason, the lake provides excellent opportunities for windsurfing.

EXERCISE EXTREME CAUTION because the winds may reach as much as 25-30 knots and create waves over three feet high.

There are boat launches on the lake near Rendall Park in town, at the Green Point day-use area in Sasquatch Provincial Park, and in Kilby Park, but there are no facilities at the lake, so bring plenty of gas. Swimmers will find nice sandy beaches in Marine Park at Rainbow Falls in Cascade Bay, at Cogburn Creek on the east side, at Eagle Falls on the west side, and in Long Island Bay. **Castaway Charter Corp.**, Box 28, Harrison Hot Springs, BC V0M 1K0, ☎ 604/796-8398, provides day cruises on the lake with departures at 1:30 and 4 PM. **Harrison**

Watersports, 6069 Rockwell Dr., ☎ 604/796-3513 or 795-6775, also provides tours.

Cruising

A delightful two-hour cruise up the Thompson River on the sternwheeler *Wanda Sue*, ☎ 604/374-7447, goes from **Kamloops** to **Dallas**. The cruise is offered at 6:30 PM from Monday through Friday, at 1:30 PM on Saturday, and at 1:30, 3:30, and 6:30 PM on Sunday during May and June. An additional 1:30 PM cruise is offered on weekdays during July and August.

MV Fintry Queen, 210 Bernard Ave. (at the lake), **Kelowna**, BC, ☎ 604/763-2780, provides daily dining and dancing cruises aboard a rebuilt sternwheeler in season. Lunch cruises are offered from noon to 2 PM, six days a week. **Sparky's Watersport Rentals**, 1310 Water St., ☎ 604/862-2469, will take you parasailing.

Lund Water Taxi, Government Harbour, **Lund**, BC, ☎ 604/483-9749, serves Savary Island, leaving Lund at 7:45 AM and 4 PM year round. There is good swimming around Savary Island and Harwood Island.

Pitt Lake, outside **Pitt Meadows,** is the world's largest freshwater tidal lake. A ferry service out of **Powell River** transports passengers to Comox (an hour and a quarter trip), Sechelt (50 minutes), and Texada Island (35 minutes).

Destiny Charters, 6865 Gerrard St., Powell River, BC V8A 1S4, ☎ 604/485-9616, fax 604/485-5832, provides day and overnight packages as well as sightseeing tours to Desolation Sound. **BRD Charters**, Beach Gardens Marina, 7074 Westminster Ave., Powell River, BC V8A 1C5, ☎ 604/355-2319, 240-6929, or 485-3004, fax 604/355-2255, takes customers cruising, fishing, and/or sightseeing aboard the 45-foot cruiser *Marjatta*. **Spirit Winds Sailing Charters**, 7236 Field St., Powell River, BC V8A 1S8, ☎ 604/485-5873, schedules charters by the day, the week, or even longer, either barefoot or skippered.

The Company of Discoverers, Box 45, **Proctor**, BC V0G 1V0, ☎ 250/229-4415, fax 250/229-4520, takes a cabin cruiser out of Balfour to tour Kootenay Lake. **Kootenay Kayak Co.**, ☎ 250/229-4949, E-mail kayak@awinc.com, arranges one- to five-day guided kayak tours.

In **Sicamous**, **Shuswap Lake Ferry Service**, Box 370, ☎ 604/836-2200, cruises Shuswap Lake aboard the *Phoebe Ann* paddlewheeler daily except Sundays during July and August. In **Sorrento**, both **Shuswap Marina** on Blind Bay Road, ☎ 604/675-2250, and **Boat World**, ☎ 604/675-2321, four miles west of town, rent boats. **Stampede**

Marine & Storage, 13415 Lakeshore Dr., **Summerland**, BC, ☎ 250/494-8449 or 809/6231, fax 250/494-8499, also rents boats.

A Place To Be Tours & Travel, 4801 27th St., **Vernon**, BC V1T 4Z1, ☎ 604/545-7949 or 800/661-3766, fax 604/549-4252, rents powerboats and yachts. It also books canoeing, heli-hiking, horseback riding, gold panning, hiking, skiing, and snowmobiling tours.

Houseboating

Canada's large lakes, such as **Shuswap Lake** near **Sicamous** (Indian for "thin in the middle"), are ideal for houseboating. Indeed, Sicamous calls itself the "Houseboat Capital of Canada."

Shuswap has 620 miles of shoreline. Ta'Lana, the legendary Roaring Water Bear, is said to live in a subterranean cavern beneath the lake at Copper Island, the only island in the main arm of the lake. Accessible only by boat, Copper Island has a number of good hiking trails and is a good place to go rockhounding. Mule deer are often seen there in the summer.

Twin Anchors Houseboat Rentals, 101 Martin St., PO Box 318, **Sicamous**, BC V0E 2V0, ☎ 250/836-2450 or 800/663-4026, fax 250/836-4824; **Bluewater Houseboats**, Box 248, ☎ 800/663-4024; **Foggy Valley Rentals**, 918 Riverside Ave., ☎ 250/836-3500; and **Sun 'n' Fun**, Box 68, ☎ 250/836-2282 or 800/663-4028, all rent houseboats on Shuswap Lake. Foggy Valley Rentals can even rent you a floating party hot tub to tow behind your houseboat.

Kaslo Shipyard Co., Box 449, **Kaslo**, BC V0G 1M0, ☎ 250/353-2686 or 800/554-1657, rents houseboats on Kootenay Lake. In **Kelowna**, both **Okanagan Motor Sport Rental**, ☎ 604/862-7330, and **Okanagan Water Toyz**, ☎ 604/769-JET2, rent houseboats. **Salmon Arm Bay**, PO Box 1480, **Salmon Arm**, BC V1E 4P6, ☎ 800/665-7782, rents houseboats.

At the Okanagan Lake Marina, **Okanagan Boat Charters**, 291 Front St., **Penticton**, BC V2A 1H5, ☎ 250/492-5049 or 800/524-2212, fax 250/492-3911, rents houseboats by the day, the weekend, or the week. The company also rents powerboats and sailboats, and operates the *Casabella Princess*, a 48-passenger paddlewheeler.

Thrills & Spills Outdoor Adventure, 2140 Boucherie Rd., **Westbank**, BC, ☎ 604/768-3260, rents houseboats as well as fishing boats, jet skis, and canoes. They'll also take you parasailing.

Scuba Diving

Jacques Cousteau rated British Columbia second only to the Red Sea for scuba diving, and Powell River claims to be the diving capital not only of British Columbia but for all of Canada. Visibility often exceeds 100 feet.

In the winter, the largest species of octopus – four to six feet long – lives here. Steller's sea lions and harbor seals become your diving buddies. Wolf eels, whose jaws can exert 2,000 psi of pressure, sufficient to bite through a sea urchin or powder an oyster shell, sit on your arm like gentle kittens. A nine-foot bronze statue of a mermaid, said to be the world's finest underwater statue, sits in 60 feet of water in Mermaid Cove at Saltery Bay Provincial Park.

Excellent wall dives can be experienced at Iron Mines, Lund, and Vivian Island, and there are three wrecks to dive upon, the *Gulf Stream* at Dinner Rock, the *Capilano* west of Vivian Island, and the *Shamrock,* a steam-powered oceangoing vessel off the tip of Vivian Island. Soon, the government plans to sink a 360-foot destroyer to form an artificial reef.

The Chamber of Commerce in **Powell River** (☎ 604/485-4701, fax 604/485-2822, E-mail prvb@prcn.org) has a visitor map that lists and maps 20 top scuba diving sites.

Among the **Sunshine Coast Provincial Parks**, some excellent scuba diving can be enjoyed. **Musket Island Marine Park** at Jervis Inlet occupies a small undeveloped island in Blind Bay south of Hardy Island (anchor with care). Also in Jervis Inlet, the **Harmony Islands Marine Park**, a chain of small undeveloped islands in Hotham Sound, can provide some anchorage in the event of stormy winter weather. In the Desolation Sound Area, **Copeland Islands Marine Park** encompasses a group of small islands northwest of Lund that can provide anchorage, walk-in campsites, fine kayaking, swimming, and fishing as well as scuba diving. **Teakerne Arm Marine Park**, also in the Desolation Sound Area, is in Lewis Channel on the side of Redonda Island and, although undeveloped, offers two special features, the 30-meter Cassel Falls and a hike to Cassel Lake, a pleasant place to swim. **Desolation Sound Marine Park,** at the confluence of Malaspina Inlet and Homfray Channel, is British Columbia's largest marine park. It offers more than 60 kilometers of shoreline, several small islands, numerous small bays, and many snug coves, plus a number of good trails and small lakes. Major anchorages are Prideaux Haven, an area with islands and small coves; Tenedos Bay, east of Mink Island in Homfray Channel; and Grace Harbour, a large bay in Malaspina Inlet.

Three other Sunshine Coast Provincial Parks include **Roscoe Bay Marine Park**, a small fjord on the east side of West Redona Island with tent sites and a hiking trail that leads to Black Lake; **Walsh Cove Ma-**

rine Park, on the east side of West Redona Island north of Roscoe Bay Marine Park on the Waddington Channel, where the rock cliffs are adorned with ancient petroglyphs; and **Princess Louisa Marine Park**, voted "the most scenic natural anchorage in the world," where Chatterbox Falls is at the head of the inlet.

> A free pocket-sized brochure is available from BC Parks District Manager, Garibaldi/Sunshine Coast District, Box 220, Brackendale, BC V0N 1H0, ☎ 604/898-3678. Also ask for a copy of *Coastal Marine Parks of British Columbia*.

Good Diving & Kayaking, Box 47, **Lund**, BC V0N 2G0, ☎ 604/483-3223, rents scuba gear and provides instruction.

■ On Snow

Skiing

Hemlock Resorts, Comp 7, Hemlock Valley Site, R.R. 1, **Agassiz**, BC V0M 1A0, ☎ 604/797-4411, can provide cross-country and downhill skiing, a snowboard halfpipe, a disabled skiers program, night skiing, tobogganing, lessons, equipment rentals, child care, a cafeteria, a bistro, and a charming fireplace lounge. For a ski report: ☎ 604/918-0002.

Castlegar has a number of fine skiing facilities in the area. **Red Mountain Ski Resort**, Box 670, **Rossland**, BC V0G 1Y0, ☎ 250/362-7700 or 800/663-0105, fax 250/362-5833, utilizes two mountains 42 kilometers from town and recently added two triple chairs. Snow phone: ☎ 250/362-5500. **Blackjack** is 42 kilometers from town near Red Mountain. **Whitewater Ski Resort**, Box 60, **Nelson**, BC V1L 5P7, ☎ 250/354-4944 or 800/666-9420, fax 250/354-4988, just 19 kilometers from Nelson and 62 kilometers from Castlegar, has the best steeps, deeps, bowls, and Nordic skiing. Snow phone: ☎ 250/352-7669. **Salmo**, two kilometers southeast of the community of Salmo and 39 kilometers from Castlegar, offers night skiing in a field that provides a 1,100-foot vertical drop. **Paulson Cross-Country Ski Trails**, offering 45 kilometers of cross-country ski trails, is 20 kilometers west of town along Route 3.

Grand Forks has the Phoenix Ski Hill; **Hemlock Valley**, the Hemlock Valley Ski Area; **Kamloops**, the Tod Mountain Ski Area; **Lac la Hache**, the Mt. Timothy Ski Hill & Snowboard Park; **99 Mile**, the 99 Mile Recreation Area for cross-country skiing and motocross; **Penticton**, the Apex Alpine Ski area; and **Revelstoke**, downhill skiing on Mt. MacKenzie as well as cross-country skiing on Mt. McPherson.

There are a number of fine skiing facilities near **Kelowna,** too. In fact, **Big White Ski Resort**, Box 2039, Station R, Kelowna, BC V1X 4K5, ☎ 250/765-3101, 765-8888, or 800/663-2772, fax 250/491-1484 or 765-1822, E-mail bigwhite@silk.net, Web site www.bigwhite.com, is British Columbia's second largest ski resort. Located 45 minutes from town, the resort has 92 ski runs on 2,075 skiable acres, and a new high-speed quad chairlift.

Silver Star Mountain, ☎ 604/542-0224 or 800/663-4431, Web site www.silverstarmtn.com, just 90 minutes from Kelowna, has 84 runs covering 2,500 vertical feet. Skiing, tubing, tobogganing, 25 kilometers of trails for cross-country skiing, summer roller skiing, roller blading, cycling, and mountain biking are available.

Heliskiing
(TLH Heliskiing, Vernon BC).

Apex Alpine Resort, ☎ 800/663-1900, is 120 kilometers south of Kelowna, near Penticton. It has 45 ski trails and a 660-meter descent, and the 1,120 acres are served by five lifts. One snowboarding halfpipe also is available.

Selkirk Wilderness Skiing, 1 Meadow Creek Rd., **Meadow Creek**, BC V0G 1N0, ☎ 250/366-4424 or 800/799-3499, fax 250/366-4419, provides some excellent skiing. **Nicola Nordic Ski Club**, Box 1499, **Merritt**, BC V0K 2B0, can provide a map of the Kane Valley ski trails. So can the Ministry of Forests, Bag 4400, Hwy 5A and Airport Road, Merritt, BC V0K 2B0, ☎ 604/378-8400.

Kootenay Helicopter Skiing, Box 717, **Nakusp**, BC V0G 1R0, ☎ 250/265-3121 or 800/663-0100, fax 250/265-4447, transports skiers into the Selkirk and Monashee Mountains aboard a chopper.

Retallack Alpine Adventures, Box 347, **New Denver**, BC V0G 1S0, ☎ 800/330-1433, fax 250/358-2777, has just 11 double rooms with private baths to offer, along with a restaurant, a bar, and a sauna. Sitting in the Selkirk Mountains between New Denver and Kaslo, the facility offers snow cat skiing and touring, cross-country skiing, and ski and bike rentals.

Cat Powder Skiing, 1601 W. 3rd St., Box 1479, **Revelstoke**, BC V0E 2S0, ☎ 250/837-5151 or 800/991-4455, fax 250/837-5111, guides Snowcat skiing expeditions. **Red Mountain**, ☎ 604/362-7384 or 800/663-0105, seven miles from **Trail**, has established 75 runs with a 2,900-foot vertical descent for downhill and cross-country skiing on two separate mountains. **Silver Star Mountain**, PO Box 2, **Silver Star Mountain**, BC V0E 1G0, ☎ 604/542-0224 or 800/663-4431, fax 604/542-1236, has 400 hectares of skiable terrain with a vertical drop of 760 meters. There are 80 runs and eight lifts, but hiking, horseback trail riding, mountain biking, and roller blading also are popular.

Crystal Mountain, ☎ 250/768-5189, is just 15 minutes from **Westbank**. You can ski both day and night, and if it's your birthday, you can ski free. Snow phone: ☎ 250/768-3753. **Telemark Ski Club** has a facility on Last mountain Road nearby with 32 kilometers of trails for cross-country skiing. **Whistler**, Canada's most renowned alpine resort, offers skiing on Blackcomb Mountain and on Whistler Mountain.

Snowmobiling

Snowmobiling also is popular in this part of Canada.

Around **Merritt**, people go snowmobiling at Thynne Mountain, Honeymoon, Lundbom Lake/Marquart Lake, Mount Henning, 10K, Helmer Lake, Stoyoma Mountain, Juliet Creek, Iron Mountain, and Murray Lake. **M.R. Merritt Rentals**, 1121 McFarlane Way, Unit 103, ☎ 250/378-5452, fax 250/378-6762, rents snowmobiles.

In the **Revelstoke** area, people go snowmobiling in the Inverness Range north of town, at Frisby Ridge, at Boulder Mountain, at Mt. Hall, and at McCrae Peak. Two-, three-, and five-hour guided tours on snowmobiles are offered at **Silver Star Mountain**, ☎ 604/558-5575 or 800/663-4431.

Hockey & Dog Sledding

Of course, there are other winter sports besides skiing and snowmobiling. Over the Christmas holidays, **Chilliwack** hosts an annual Pee Wee Hockey Jamboree. **Falkland** hosts the annual International Dog Sled Races. **100 Mile House** features the Jack Gawthorn Memorial Dog Sled Race every winter, and **Wells** has an International Dog Sled Race & Winter Carnival every winter.

■ In the Air

In February, **Vernon** hosts the annual Hot Air Balloon Fiesta, ☎ 604/545-2236, and in October, **Armstrong** stages the Armstrong/Spallumcheen Hot Air Balloon Rendezvous at the Highland Park School, ☎ 604/546-8155. **Skywalker Balloons**, 16709 Maki Rd., **Winfield**, BC V0H 2C0, ☎ 604/766-2804 or 766-3744, enables two to five passengers to take a champagne flight in a hot air balloon. Flights usually lift off shortly after dawn or about an hour before sunset. In **Kelowna**, **Stardust Ballooning**, ☎ 604/868-8382, also offers balloon rides.

There are 20 established paragliding sites in the **Chilliwack** area (for more information: ☎ 604/858-2300). **Mescalito Adventure Co.**, ☎ 604/858-2300, can get you started. **Sun Wind Paragliding**, 3009 Weststyle Rd., **Kamloops**, BC, ☎ 250/579-2005, also handles paragliding adventures.

Want to go up in a helicopter? **Mike Wiegele**, Heli-Ski Village, Box 159, **Blue River**, BC V0E 1J0, ☎ 250/673-8381 or 800/661-9170, fax 250/673-8464, uses a helicopter to take you sightseeing, mountain biking, horseback riding, or swimming. In **Hell's Gate**, **Rainbow Heli-Tours**, ☎ 888/887-9792, offers helicopter tours, and in **Kelowna**, it's **Canadian Helicopter Tours**, ☎ 604/542-6000. In **Revelstoke**, CMH Heli-Skiing & Heli-Hiking, ☎ 604/762-7100 or 800/661-0252, fax 604/762-5879, who will deliver you to your ski run or trailhead in a helicopter.

Glacier Air, Box 2014, **Squamish**, BC V0N 3G0, ☎ 604/898-9016 or 800/265-0088, offers flightseeing tours as well as ski plane landings on the glaciers.

Vancouver Soaring Assn., ☎ 604/521-5501, schedules glider flights every weekend out of **Hope** Airport. Interested parties should be at the airport before 11 AM.

Hell's Gate Airtram, Box 129, **Hope**, BC V0X 1L0, ☎ 604/867-9277, fax 604/867-9279, crosses the Fraser River rapids, a 502-foot ride. Located 35 minutes north of town on TransCanada Highway 1, the facility also includes a restaurant and a factory producing 30 flavors of fudge.

Air Southwest, 1-46244 Airport Rd., **Chilliwack**, BC V2P 1A5, ☎ 604/792-1123, fax 604/792-3114, provides charter flights, scenic flights, aerial photography, and adventure air tours out of the Chilliwack Municipal Airport. An annual Flight Fest is conducted at the Chilliwack Municipal Airport, 8550 Young St., ☎ 604/792-3430, in either August or September.

Kamloops sponsors an International Airshow each August.

Air-Hart Floatplane Tours, Box 24078, Lake Front PO, **Kelowna**, BC V1Y 9P9, ☎ 250/769-8060 or 470-4181, offers 20-minute, half-hour, and one-hour tours as well as a glacier tour, an air-biking tour, and Fly N' Dine tours aboard a De-Havilland Otter airplane that leaves the Grand Okanagan Resort.

CFB Comox Air Force Museum, CFB Comox, **Lazo**, BC, ☎ 250/339-8162, is devoted to Comox and West Coast aviation history. It is open between 10 AM and 4 PM from Wednesday through Sunday and on holidays from June to August, and on Saturdays, Sundays, and holidays during the winter.

Nelson Mountain Air, ☎ 250/354-1456, schedules charters, provides lessons, and rents aircraft at the **Nelson** Airport on Lakeside Drive. There is a float plane base at Wildwood Marina in **Powell River**, while **Shuswap Air**, ☎ 604/832-8830 or 800/663-4074, offers sight-seeing and charter flights in **Salmon Arm**. The community airport in Salmon Arm also sponsors an Air Affair, ☎ 604/832-6691, each June. **Mountain Spirit Aviation**, ☎ 604/898-5161, arranges fishing charters, lake tours, aircraft rentals, flight lessons, and float plane services out of the **Squamish** Airport.

■ Cultural Excursions

Agassiz

Agassiz-Harrison Museum, 6947 #7 Hwy, on the grounds of the Federal Research Station in Agassiz, ☎ 604/796-3545, is open daily between 10 AM and 4 PM from May 17 to September 14. It is housed in the oldest wooden railroad station still existing in British Columbia (102 years old). An 1892 horse barn and an arboretum planted in 1892 also are on the grounds.

Boswell

The Glass House on Kootenay Lake near Boswell, ☎ 250/223-8372, was built from over half a million discarded embalming fluid bottles. Tours are offered daily from May to October.

Britannia Beach

On the Sea-to-Sky Highway #99 in Britannia Beach, the **British Columbia Museum of Mining**, ☎ 604/688-8735, offers an underground train and an interesting video show.

Castlegar

In 1908, a group of pacifist emigrants from Russia, the Doukhobors, moved into Ootischenia Valley in the Grand Forks area near Castlegar. They planted orchards and gardens; built sawmills, a pipe works, and jam factories; and prospered. **Doukhobor Village Museum**, ☎ 604/365-6622, represents a reconstructed Doukhobor community (in 1943, the jam factory in nearby Brilliant was destroyed by arsonists). **Verigin's Tomb** is that of Peter Verigin, an early Doukhobor leader. **Doukhobor Suspension Bridge**, visible from the highway, was built in the early 1900s.

Bighorn sheep are often seen in **Syringa Park** in Castlegar. **Chase** stages the **Squilax Pow Wow** each July.

Chilliwack

Chilliwack, known as "The City of Festivals," hosts a **Chilliwack Pow-Wow** at the Ag-Rec Centre in mid-May. Also worth visiting are **Minter Gardens**, ☎ 604/794-7191 (April through October), 792-3799 (November through March), or 888/646-8377, fax 604/792-8893, Web site www.minter.org, which are open from April through October.

Creston

Near Creston is the 17,000-acre **Creston Valley Wildlife Area**, ☎ 250/428-3259, which is an excellent place for hiking, biking, birdwatching, canoeing, and fishing. An Interpretive Centre is open from the end of April to Thanksgiving.

Cultus Lake

The **Cultus Lake Indian Festival**, ☎ 604/858-0826, is held on the Main Beach at Cultus Lake on the first weekend in June from noon to 6 PM both days. Festivities include dining on BBQ salmon, the native princess contest, and war canoe races. Admission is not charged, but there is a parking fee. In Cultus Lake Park is a 30-foot totem pole erected in 1992 in honor of the late Chief Malloway.

Hope

Tashme, a Japanese internment camp during World War II, 14 miles east of Hope, housed 2,300 Japanese-Canadians between 1942 and 1945. The buildings are now a part of the Sunshine Valley recreational home community. **Friendship Garden**, a Japanese garden next to the District Hall in Hope, was built in 1991 in memory of the Tashme prisoners.

On 9 January 1965, Johnson Peak southeast of Hope collapsed, filling the bottom of Nicolum Creek valley to a depth of 200 feet and obliterating Outram Lake. Triggered by a minor earthquake, the slide engulfed three vehicles and their four passengers, two of whose bodies have never been found. A 15-minute drive east of town on Route 3 leads to a pullout from which the damage created by the slide can clearly be seen.

At certain times of the year, a large white cross suddenly appears on the side of a mountain south of Hope. The cross results from snow that is lodged in natural formations on the mountainside. Some people refer to the apparition as Holy Cross Mountain.

Many films have been made in the Hope area. In 1981, the first Rambo movie, *First Blood*, was filmed there in its entirety. *Shoot To Kill*, starring Sidney Poitier, Tom Berenger, and Kirstie Alley, was filmed there in part. So were Paramount's *Fire With Fire*; *K-2*, which was shot in Fraser Canyon; *White Fang*, based on a Jack London novel; and *Far From Home: Adventures of Yellow Dog*, Disney's 1993 remake of an "Old Yeller" film.

Visitors to Hope can see some of the areas that were shown in these films. Water Avenue near Gardner Chevrolet-Olds is where Sheriff Tesle dropped off Rambo. The railroad tracks at Third Avenue is where Rambo attempted to escape from the police on a stolen motorcycle. The north side of Wallace Street in front of Cheyenne's Sports and the Alpenhaus Restaurant is where Rambo rode his stolen motorcycle down the sidewalk. And Hudson Bay Street, especially where it intersects with Fifth Avenue, is where Rambo drove with the police in hot pursuit. The Othello-Quintette tunnels, created for the one-time Kettle Valley Railway, were seen not only in *First Blood*, but in *Shoot To Kill* and *Far From Home: Adventures of Yellow Dog*. There is a photo board in town where you can have yourself photographed as "Rambo."

Kamloops

Kamloops Indian Band, 315 Yellowhead Hwy, Kamloops, BC V2H 1H1, ☎ 250/828-9700, fax 250/372-8833, is a band of Indians, not a musical combo. Their three-day **Kamloops Pow Wow** is held in Kamloops every August.

Kelowna

Kelowna has a number of magnificent gardens. **Kasugai Gardens**, a Japanese garden and tea house, is behind City Hall, the Kelowna Museum, and Memorial Arena, north of either Queensway Avenue or Water Street. **Butterfly World Botanical Gardens**, ☎ 604/769-4408, are at 1190 Stevens Rd. **Geert Maas Sculpture Gardens**, 250 Reynolds Rd., ☎ 604/860-7012, include an indoor gallery and studio. **Parrot Island**, 1160 Stevens Rd., ☎ 604/769-6911, offers a "tropical island" adventure punctuated with tropical birds and plants, which includes an opportunity to hold a baby parrot.

A community fixture for 40 years, the **Okanagan Symphony Orchestra**, PO Box 1120, Kelowna, BC V1Y 7P8, ☎ 250/763-7544, fax 250/763-3553, attracts a variety of guest artists. Also serving Kelowna is the **Sunshine Theatre**, a professional regional theatre, and the **Kelowna Community Theatre**.

For anyone who thought that California is the only place on the West Coast to grow grapes and produce fine wines, a stop in Kelowna will convince them otherwise. Most of the wineries are open for tours and tastings. **Calona Vineyards**, 1125 Richter St., ☎ 604/762-9144, "British Columbia's original winery," is open seven days a week. **Cedar Creek Estate Winery**, 5445 Lakeshore Rd., ☎ 250/764-8866, has lovely grounds with gardens and a view of Okanagan Lake. **Gray Monk Estate Winery**, 1055 Camp Rd., ☎ 604/766-3168, just north of town in Okanagan Centre, is Canada's northernmost winery. **House of Rose Vineyards**, 2270 Garner Rd., ☎ 250/765-08702, bills itself as "Kelowna's farm winery" and is open between 10 AM and 5:30 PM daily during the summer (May 15 to October 15) "or year round till 9 PM by finding Vern, Russ or Aura on the farm." Each of the vineyard's wines bears the name of a different rose. **Quail's Gate Estate Winery**, 3303 Boucherie Rd., ☎ 250/769-4451 or 800/420-9463, fax 250/769-3451, is open between 10 AM and 6 PM during the summer. **Summerhill Estate Winery**, 4870-D Chute Lake Rd., ☎ 250/764-8000 or 800/667-3538, E-mail summerhill.silk.net, is an "organic vineyard" open daily between 10 AM and 6 PM.

Also of interest to the oenophile will be **The Wine Museum**, 1304 Ellis St., Kelowna, BC V1Y 1Z8, ☎ 250/868-0441, fax 250/763-5722. Among their exhibits: a 3,000-year-old clay drinking horn that was unearthed in Iran.

C-West Okanagan Tours, ☎ 205/763-5355 or 800/667-9898, conducts guided tours of the Kelowna-area wineries.

If you're into apples... I mean, REALLY into apples... visit the **BC Orchard Industry Museum**, 1304 Ellis St., Kelowna, BC V1Y 1Z8, ☎ 604/763-0433, fax 604/763-5722. Built in 1917 of locally made brick, the museum is open between 10 AM and 5 PM Monday to Saturday from July through August, and Tuesday to Saturday from September through June.

Keremeos

The Grist Mill, R.R. 1, Upper Bench Road, Keremeos, BC V0X 1N0, ☎ 604/499-2888, an 1877 water-powered grist mill, now combines a tea room, gardens, store, and craft workshops. The mill is open from mid-May to early October.

Lillooet's **Hangman's Tree** is where justice was dispensed by "Hanging Judge" Sir Matthew Baillie Beghie, British Columbia's version of Judge Roy Bean. Also of interest is a 1913 suspension bridge, one of the few remaining in British Columbia. In the 1980s, the bridge was replaced by the Bridge of the 23 Camels, named after the ill-fated beasts of burden that were used during the gold rush.

Okanagan Falls

Okanagan Falls also has a number of interesting and welcoming wineries. **Wild Goose Vineyards & Winery**, Lot 11, Sun Valley Way, ☎ 604/497-8919, is open daily between 10 AM and 5 PM. **Le Comte Estate Winery**, Green Lake Rd., ☎ 604/497-8267, fax 604/497-8073, and **Hawthorne Mountain Vineyards**, Green Lake Road, ☎ 250/497-8267, fax 250/497-8073, Web site www.hmvineyard.com and www.lecomte.com, keep the same hours.

If you still haven't had your fill of wineries, pop over to **Oliver** and sample a few more. **Okanagan Vineyards**, 11 Road West, ☎ 604/498-6663, produces Chardonnay, Carbernet sauvignon, Merlot, Johannisberg riesling, Gewurztraminer, and Pinot Noir. **Gehringer Brothers Estate Winery**, Road No. 8, Hwy 97S, ☎ 604/498-3537, is open daily between 10 AM and 5 PM. **Hester Creek**, Road No. 8 south of town on Hwy 97, ☎ 250/498-4435, hosts a tasting between 10 AM and 5 PM. Other local wineries include **Inkameep Vineyards**, Tucelnuit Road, ☎ 604/498-3552; **Domaine Combret Estate Winery**, Road No. 13, Box 1170, ☎ 604/498-8878, fax 250/498-8879; **Tinhorn Creek Vineyards**, R.R. #1, Site 58, Comp 10, ☎ 250/498-3743, fax 250/498-3228; and **Divino Estate Winery**, Road No. 8, ☎ 250/498-3537.

Peachland

In Peachland, **Chateau St. Claire Estate Winery**, Trepanier Bench Road, ☎ 604/767-3113, and **Hainie Vineyards Estate Winery**, 5355 Trepanier Bench Rd., ☎ 604/767-2525, enjoy company.

Penticton

Okanagan Adventure Co., 1330 Water St., Penticton, BC, ☎ 604/494-9597 or 800/667-9898, conducts half-day guided tours of the local wineries.

Okanagan Game Farm, ☎ 250/497-5405, fax 250/497-6145, exhibits 120 species of animals from around the world at its compound five miles south of Penticton on Route 97. The game farm is open daily from 8 AM to dusk.

Powell River

Patricia Theatre in Powell River is the oldest continuously running movie theatre in British Columbia – and it still employs an organ player who entertains prior to the start of the movie.

Rossland

There's a real gold mine in Rossland, **Le Roi Gold Mine**, Hwys. 22 & 3B, ☎ 250/362-7722. You can try your hand at gold panning there, too. Tours are offered between 9:30 AM and 3:30 PM from mid-May to mid-September, and there is a tea room on the premises.

Summerland

Two more nice wineries can be found in Summerland. **Sumac Ridge Estate Winery**, 17403 Hwy 97, ☎ 250/494-0451, Web site www.sumacridge.com, has daily tours and tastings, and its Web site offers a great deal of interesting and useful information about wines. **Scherzinger Vineyards & Winery**, 7311 Fiske St., RR #2, S68, C13, ☎ 250/494-8815, is open for tours and tastings between 10 AM and 6 PM daily from April to October.

Vernon

The O'Keefe Ranch, ☎ 604/542-7868, is located 12 kilometers north of Vernon. An historic mansion, the 1889 St. Anne's Church, farm animals, a general store, and a restaurant are open to tourists.

You can dig your own opals nearby at **Okanagan Opal**, Hwys. 97 & 97A, ☎ 604/542-5173 or 542-1103, five miles north of town. Tours of the opal mine, which is open from June 1 through September 30, are available.

Westbank

Thirsty? There still are two more wineries to try: **Mission Hill Winery**, 1730 Mission Hill Rd., Westbank, BC V4T 2E4, ☎ 604/768-7611, and **Gray Monk Estate Winery & Vineyards**, Okanagan Centre, Winfield, BC, ☎ 604/766-3168 or 800/663-4205, fax 604/766-3390.

Yale

Yale Museum, General Delivery, Yale, BC V0K 2S0, ☎ 604/863-2324, fax 604/863-2495, E-mail prospect@uniserve.com, Web sites at heritage.gov.bc.ca and www.octonet.com/~prospect/yale.html, occupies an 1868 house and conducts guided tours of a former Gold Rush town. The museum is open from mid-April to mid-October.

Where to Stay

Chilliwack

Best Western Rainbow Country Inn, 43971 Industrial Way, Chilliwack, BC V2R 1A9, ☎ 604/795-3828 or 800/665-1030, fax 604/795-5039, $-$$, is a two-story inn with 74 rooms. Features include countryside and mountain views, a heated indoor pool, a restaurant, and a cocktail lounge. **Holiday Inn Chilliwack-Downtown**, 45920 First Ave., Chilliwack, BC V2P 7K1, ☎ 604/795-4788 or 800/520-7555, $-$$, is a downtown high-rise (nine stories) with a waterfront location. It has 110 rooms, a heated indoor pool, a restaurant, and a cocktail lounge.

Jesmond-Clinton

Big Bar Guest Ranch, PO Box 27, Jesmond-Clinton, BC V0K 1K0, ☎ 604/459-2333 or 395-7101, $$$, has 12 guest rooms and two log cottages. Amenities include a hot tub, billiard room, fireside lounge, and video room. Riding, cross-country skiing, fishing, canoeing, hiking, swimming, mountain biking, and gold panning are available.

Harrison Mills

Rowena's Inn on the River, 14282 Morris Valley Rd., Harrison Mills, BC V0M 1L0, ☎ 604/796-0234, 800/661-5108, or 888/ROWENAS, $$$$, occupies 160 acres on the Harrison River. Lunch and dinner are served year-around. **The Harrison Hot Springs Hotel**, ☎ 604-796-2244 or 800/663-2266, fax 604/796-9374, $$$, sits on the south shore of the lake. The eight-story building has 303 rooms, including 34 two-bedroom units, and bungalows also are available. Facilities include indoor hot mineral pools, two tennis courts, a boat dock, a marina, a health club, a playground, and a nine-hole golf course. The Copper Room is open from 6 to 10 PM daily, with live entertainment and big-band dancing until midnight.

108 Mile Ranch

The 108 Resort, Box 2, 108 Mile Ranch, BC V0K 2Z0, ☎ 250/791-5211, fax 250/791-6537, E-mail 108rst@netshop.net, $$$, is a Best Western affiliate that provides golf, horseback riding, tennis, swimming, canoeing, biking, hiking, cross-country skiing, tobogganing, dog sledding, sleigh riding, and snowmobiling on a 650-acre spread. **The Hills Health Ranch**, Hwy 97 N, ☎ 250/791-5225, fax 250/791-8394, E-mail thehills@netshop.net, $$$, can furnish a spa, horseback riding, skiing, dog sledding, and hay rides.

Jandana Ranch

Horse lovers will enjoy Jandana Ranch, General Delivery, **Pinantan Lake**, BC V0E 3E0, ☎ 250/573-5800, 371-1232, or 800/573-5881, Web site www.mwslutions.com/jandana, $$. The ranch has its own schedule of events, covering horse care, dressage, and a hunter/jumper clinic. A half-hour drive from **Kamloops**, take Route 5 north to Paul Lake Road and turn right, then turn left (north) at Pinantan Lake onto Botta Road.

Kelowna

Lake Okanagan Resort, 2751 Westside Rd., Kelowna, BC V1Y 8B2, ☎ 604/769-3511 or 800/663-3273, fax 604/769-6665, $$$-$$$$, provides lakeside kitchenettes, condos, and chalets. It also features a restaurant, golf, tennis, hiking, horseback riding, a beach, a marina, swimming, and waterskiing. **Casa Loma Resort**, 2777 Casa Loma Rd., ☎ 604/769-4630 or 800/771-5253, fax 604/769-6388, $$$-$$$$, has 900 feet of sandy beach, a laundry, and tennis courts. Accommodations include cottages, townhouses, and apartment condos. **Best Western Inn-Kelowna**, 2402 Hwy 97 N, ☎ 604/860-1212 or 800/667-9210, fax 604/860-0675, $-$$, is a two-story inn with 99 rooms. It is adjacent to a golf course and has a heated outdoor pool that is enclosed in the winter, a tennis court, a restaurant, and a pub. **Eldorado Hotel**, 500 Cooks Rd., ☎ 604/763-7500, fax 604/861-4779, $$$, is a lakeside hotel with a dining room, boat rentals, and a waterski school.

Definitely upscale is **The Grand Okanagan**, 1310 Water St., Kelowna, BC V1Y 9P3, ☎ 604/763-4500 or 800/465-4651, fax 604/763-4565, $$$-$$$$, a 10-story lakeshore property with 205 rooms, including 36 two-bedroom units and two three-bedroom units. It is within walking distance of the beach; offers city, lake, and mountain views; and has a heated pool, a marina, an exercise room, and two restaurants.

Penticton

Best Western Inn at Penticton, 3180 Skaha Lake Rd., Penticton, BC V2A 6G4, ☎ 250/493-0311 or 800/668-6746, fax 604/493-5556, $$-$$$, is a two-story facility with 69 spacious rooms, 15 with kitchens, including two two-bedroom units and seven efficiencies. There is a beautiful courtyard with a comfortable BBQ area, and there are two heated pools, one indoors. **Clarion Lakeside Resort**, 21 Lakeshore Dr., ☎ 604/493-8221 or 800/663-9400, fax 604/493-0607, $$-$$$, is a six-story building with 204 rooms, a heated indoor pool, two tennis courts, an exercise room, and a boat dock.

Revelstoke

3 Valley Gap Motor Inn, Box 860, Revelstoke, BC V0E 2S0, ☎ 250/837-2109, fax 250/837-5220, $$-$$$, is open from mid-April through mid-October. It offers a restaurant, a sandy beach, a theater, guided ghost town tours, a heated indoor pool, and a laundromat.

Vernon

Prestige Inn Vernon, 4411 32nd St., Vernon, BC V1T 9G8, ☎ 604/558-5991, fax 604/558-5996, $$$, is a two-story building with 62 spacious rooms, one two-bedroom unit with a kitchen, a whirlpool, and a washer/dryer. There is a heated indoor pool and an exercise room. **Castle on the Mountain**, 8227 Silver Star Rd., ☎ 250/542-4593 or 800/667-2229, fax 250/542-2206, $$$, is a year-around B&B.

Whistler

Whistler Village Inns, 4429 Sundial Pl., Box 970, Whistler, BC V0N 1B0, ☎ 800/663-6418, fax 604/932-3487, $$$-$$$$, sits in the heart of town at the base of the Blackcomb and Whistler Mountains. There are

87 rooms, most with fireplaces and balconies, that include 65 units with kitchens. The three-story inn also has a heated pool. **Delta Whistler Resort**, Box 550, ☎ 604/932-7332, 932-1982, or 800/515-4050, Web site www.delta-whistler.com, $$$$, is an eight-story facility with 292 rooms, many of which have fireplaces and balconies. There are a heated pool, a steamroom, two lighted tennis courts, and four golf courses. Available activities include mountain biking, hiking, heli-skiing, snowmobiling, and 28 kilometers of cross-country trails. Gondolas carry guests into the Blackcomb and Whistler Mountains, and the resort has been designated the top-rated ski resort in North America.

■ Camping

Campgrounds abound in Eastern British Columbia. For more information, contact **Discover Camping**, ☎ 800/689-9025, where a new service enables you to reserve a campsite at any of 42 provincial parks by telephone.

Castlegar RV Park & Campground, 1725 Mannix Rd., **Castlegar**, BC V1N 3R8, ☎ 604/365-2337, has laundry facilities and a couple of interesting walking trails.

In the **Chilliwack** area, **Chilliwack RV Park & Campground**, Rt. 3, Hack Brown Rd., ☎ 604/794-7800, and **Sweltzer Creek Campsite**, 4070 Soowahli Rd., ☎ 604/858-4603, each have convenience stores. For more specific information about different areas within the region, contact Fraser Valley Regional District, ☎ 604/792-5000; Cultus Lake Parks Board, ☎ 604/858-3334; Village of Harrison Hot Springs, ☎ 604/796-2171; District of Kent (Agassiz), ☎ 604/796-2235; Hope Recreation Commission, ☎ 604/869-5913; or BC Parks-Fraser Valley District, ☎ 604/824-2300

Sunnyside Campground, 3405 Columbia Valley Hwy in **Cultus Lake Provincial Park**, ☎ 604/858-5253, provides a laundromat, 24-hour security, swimming, fishing, a boat launch, and a convenience store.

Bigfoot Campgrounds, 670 Hot Springs Rd., Box 113, **Harrison Hot Springs**, BC V0M 1K0, ☎ 604/796-9767 or 800/294-9907, fax 604/796-8452, E-mail bigfoot@uniserve.com, features night security, a camp store, a laundry, and a mini-golf course.

Coquihalla Campsite, 800 Kawkawa Lake Rd., Box 308, **Hope**, ☎ 604/869-0719, has riverfront sites and 24-hour security plus a convenience store and laundry facilities.

100 Mile Village Campground is on Horse Lake Road east of Route 97 at **100 Mile House**.

The **Kelowna** area provides campsites at **Billabong Beach Resort**, 29-2065 Boucherie Rd., ☎ 250/768-5913; **Marina Village Campground**, 2035 Campbell Rd., ☎ 250/769-0571; and **Todd's Tent Town & TV**, 3976 Beach Ave., Peachland, ☎ 250/767-2344 or 767-6644.

In **Penticton**, **Easy Go Holidays RV Rentals**, 198 Ellis St., ☎ 250/493-7991, rents RVs.

Campsites in the **Powell River** area are available at **Seabreeze Cabins & Campground**, Route 101, ☎ 604/487-9534, and at **Willingdon Beach Campground**, 4845 Marine Ave., ☎ 604/485-2242.

In **Squamish**, **Klahanie Campground & RV Park**, ☎ 604/892-3435, is on Route 99.

Summerland has a number of nice campgrounds. **Cedarbrook Campground**, ☎ 604/494-0911, is on Route 97 at the south end of town. **Lakeshore Tent & RV Park**, 15419 Lakeshore Dr. N., ☎ 604/494-8149, has stores, a nightly campfire, and a safe, sandy beach. **Peach Orchard Campground**, 6321 Peach Orchard Rd., ☎ 604/494-9649, has tennis courts and is located near two beaches.

Dutch's Tent & Trailer, 15408 Kalamalka Lake Rd., **Vernon**, BC V1B 1Y9, ☎ 604/545-1023, enjoys a creekside location and has a laundry, an arcade, and a mini-golf course.

Where to Eat

Kelowna

Kelly O'Bryan's Neighborhood Restaurant has two locations in Kelowna: 262 Bernard Ave., ☎ 250/861-1338, and 105 Hwy 33W, ☎ 250/491-7669, $$. **Rose's Waterfront Pub**, 1352 Water St., ☎ 250/860-1141, $$, in the Grand Hotel, features a lakefront patio, live music, and a dance floor.

Merritt

In Merritt, the **Black Bull Pub**, 245 Ponderosa Ave., ☎ 604/523-6451, $$, celebrates "Appy" hour between 4 and 6 PM daily.

Penticton

Two of the favorites in Penticton are **Granny Bogner's Restaurant**, 302 Eckhardt Ave. West, ☎ 604/493-2711, $$, and **the Historic 1912 Restaurant**, ☎ 604/497-6868, $$, located five miles south of town at Pioneer Village in Kaleden.

Powell River

The Little Tea Pot, 4582 Willingdon Ave., Powell River, ☎ 604/485-5955, $$, an "olde English tea house," is open seven days a week between 10 AM and 8 PM during the summer.

Information Sources

Castlegar & District Chamber of Commerce & Business Information Centre, 1995 6th Ave., Castlegar, BC V1N 4B7, ☎ 604/365-6313, fax 604/365-5778, E-mail cdcoc@knet.kootenay.net.

High Country Tourism Assn., 1490 Pearson Pl., #2, **Kamloops**, BC V1S 1J9, ☎ 250/372-7770 or 800/567-2275, fax 250/828-4656, E-mail hcta@tourvan01.tbc.gov.bc.ca., Web site travel.bc.ca/region/high.

Kelowna Visitors & Convention Bureau, 544 Harvey Ave., Kelowna, BC V1Y 6C9, ☎ 250/861-1515 or 800/663-4345, fax 250/861-3624, E-mail kelownachamber@awinc.com.

Merritt & District Chamber of Commerce, 2099 Garcia St., PO Box 1649, Merritt, BC V1K 1B8, ☎ 250/378-5634, fax 250/378-6561.

Nakusp & District Chamber of Commerce, ☎ 250/265-4234 or 800/909-8819, fax 250/265-3808.

Kootenay Country Tourist Assn., 610 Railway St., **Nelson**, BC V1L 1H4, ☎ 250/352-6033 or 800/661-6603, fax 250/352-1656.

Penticton Information Centre, 185 Lakeshore Dr. West, Penticton, BC V2A 1B7, ☎ 250/492-4103 or 800/663-5052, fax 250/492-6119, Web site www.aim.awinc.com.

Powell River Visitors Bureau, 4690 Marine Ave., Powell River, BC V8A 2L1, ☎ 604/485-4701, fax 604/485-2822, E-mail prvb@prcn.org.

Princeton & District Chamber of Commerce, PO Box 540, Princeton, BC V0X 1W0, ☎ 250/295-3103, fax 250/295-3255.

Revelstoke Visitor Information Centre, 206 Campbell Ave., Revelstoke, BC

Squamish & Howe Sound District Chamber of Commerce, 37950 Cleveland Ave., Squamish, BC, ☎ 604/892-9244, fax 604/892-2034.

Trail & District Chamber of Commerce, 843 Rossland Ave., Trail, BC V1R 4S8, ☎ 250/368-3144, 368-3312, or 800/56-EVENT, fax 250/368-3990, E-mail tcoc@ciao.trail.bc.ca.

Index

100 Mile House, BC, 406, 411, 439
108 Mile Ranch, BC, 436
Abbotsford, BC, 372, 378, 382, 389, 390
Aberdeen, WA, 211, 215, 237, 250
accommodations, 117; British Columbia, 363-365, 396-398, 435-438; California, 40-41, 74-75, 89; Oregon, 122-123; price scale, 9; Washington, 266, 298-299, 332-333. *See also* camping
Adel, OR, 176
Agassiz, BC, 404, 416, 425, 429
air adventures: British Columbia, 358-359, 389, 428-429; California, 68-69, 88; Oregon, 118, 158-159, 195; Washington, 247-250, 292-293, 321-322
airports: British Columbia, 358, 370-371, 401-402, 428-429; California, 36, 45, 88; Oregon, 127, 195; Washington, 209-210, 247, 281, 292, 303-305
Albany, OR, 158, 171
Aldergrove, BC, 380, 390
Alert Bay, BC, 343, 351-352
Alton, CA, 21, 25
Anacortes, WA, 211, 231, 232, 237-238, 266, 275
aquariums, 121, 357. *See also* zoos
Arcata, CA: adventures, 24, 25, 26, 32, 33, 35; sightseeing, 17-18, 36-37
Ariel, WA, 293
Arlington, WA, 215-216, 241, 247, 251
Armstrong, BC, 410-411, 428
Ashcroft, BC, 411, 414
Ashford, WA, 283, 298
Ashland, OR, 135, 141, 151, 154, 160, 166, 171
Astoria, OR, 96, 101, 102, 105, 113, 119-120, 124, 125
Auburn, WA, 216, 229, 238, 244
Aurora, OR, 127
auto races: British Columbia, 349, 380, 416; Oregon, 189; Washington, 231-232, 313-314
auto touring: British Columbia, 343, 370, 371, 401, 415; California, 16-20, 27-28, 47-49, 57-58, 80-83, 85-86; Oregon, 96-99, 106-109, 127-135, 144-145; Washington, 211-215, 281, 305-308

Bainbridge Island, WA, 211, 251, 266
Baker City, OR, 176, 181, 183, 184, 189, 195-196, 201
Baker Lake, 284-285
ballooning, 68, 158-159, 195, 249, 321, 389, 428
Bamfield, BC, 343, 348, 353
Bandon, OR, 101, 102, 107, 111-112, 116, 118, 124
Banks, OR, 135
baseball, 327, 328, 331
Battle Ground, WA, 281, 288, 293
beachcombing, 100-101, 217, 218, 219
bed and breakfast directory, 10
Belfair, WA, 216
Bellevue, WA, 211, 216, 227, 245, 251, 275
Bellingham, WA: accommodations, 267; adventures, 216, 222, 232-233, 238-239, 240, 244; camping, 272; sightseeing, 251-252; skiing, 245
Bend, OR: accommodations, 166; adventures, 135-136, 141, 148, 150, 151, 155, 157-158, 158, 189; sightseeing, 144, 159, 160-161
Big Foot, 70
biking: British Columbia, 350, 380, 414-415; California, 28, 58-59, 86; Oregon, 109, 145-146, 188-189; safety, 5; Washington, 229-230, 314
Bingen, WA, 289, 293
Black Diamond, WA, 216-217, 275
Blaine, WA, 222, 225, 244, 247, 252, 267
boating: British Columbia, 356-357, 419-423; California, 34, 35-36, 64-66; Oregon, 115-116, 148-153, 190-193; safety, 5-6; Washington, 237-245
Boswell, BC, 429
Bow, WA, 225, 275
Brentwood Bay, BC, 356, 359
breweries, 38, 146-147, 258, 294
Brewster, WA, 303, 305
Bridgeport, WA, 322
Britannia Beach, BC, 390, 430
British Columbia, 339-340; history and geography, 2-3, 341, 367, 371; information sources, 367-368, 400, 440; inland area, 400-441; maps, 342, 370, 403; Vancouver (city) area, 368-400; Victoria and Vancouver Island, 339-368
Brookings, OR, 96, 102-103, 115, 118, 124
Brookings Harbor, OR, 122
bungy jumping, 68, 358

Burbank, WA, 322
Burnaby, BC, 405, 419
Burney, CA, 46, 53, 60, 64, 68, 69
Burns, OR, 176, 184, 196

California: history and geography, 1-2, 13-14, 44; information sources, 43-44, 78, 91; maps, 14, 45, 81; north-central, 44-91; northeastern, 79-91; northern coast, 13-43
Campbell River, BC, 349, 351, 352, 354, 357, 358, 363-364, 416
camping: British Columbia, 365-366, 398-399, 438-439; California, 41-42, 76-77, 89; Oregon, 124-125, 169-171, 200-202; safety, 9; Washington, 271-274, 299, 333-335
Cannon Beach, OR, 101, 103, 108, 117, 118, 122
canoeing and kayaking: British Columbia, 356-357, 419-421; California, 64-66; Oregon, 116, 148, 151-152; safety, 5-6; Washington, 240-241, 289-290
Canyon City, OR, 196
Cape Arago, 104, 106-107
Cape Blanco, 106
Carnation, WA, 252
carriage tours, 29, 57, 348-349
Cascade Recreation Area, 408
Cashmere, WA, 315, 323
Castlegar, BC, 405, 417, 425, 430, 438
Cave Junction, OR, 166-167
caves: British Columbia, 346; California, 51, 53, 54; Oregon, 133, 136, 137, 162, 295; Washington, 310, 326
Charleston, OR: adventures, 101, 102, 104, 111-112, 113, 116, 117; camping, 124; sightseeing, 107
Chehalis, WA, 281, 287, 288, 293-294
Chelan, WA, 304, 311, 315, 316-317, 319, 321, 323
Chemainus, BC, 366
Cheney, WA, 308, 311, 317-318, 335
Chico, CA, 46, 50, 66, 69
Chilliwack, BC: adventures, 405-406, 409, 412, 414, 417, 419, 428; auto races, 416; camping, 438; hockey, 427; sightseeing, 430
Chiloquin, OR, 161
clam-digging and crabbing, 34, 111-112, 223, 224, 236-237
Clarkston, WA, 309, 316, 320
Clearwater, BC, 406, 412, 419
Cle Elum, WA, 290, 294
climbing, 105, 286, 346. *See also* hiking and backpacking
Cobbie Hill, BC, 360
Colfax, WA, 305-306, 323

Columbia River Gorge, 129-132, 152-153, 299
Colville, WA, 311, 312, 323
Colville National Forest, 333-334
Conconully, WA, 272, 335
Concrete, WA, 217, 233, 247, 252-253
Condon, OR, 184, 190
Coos Bay, OR, 110, 120, 124
Copalis Beach, WA, 250, 253, 272
Coquitlam, BC, 371, 372
Corvallis, OR, 129, 151
Cosmopolis, WA, 275
Cottage Grove, OR, 132, 142, 159, 191
Coupeville, WA, 228, 253, 266
Courtenay, BC, 360
covered bridges, 141-143
crabbing. *See* clam-digging and crabbing
Cranbrook, BC, 402, 417
Crater Lake National Park, 132-133
Crescent City, CA: accommodations, 40; adventures, 21, 24, 25, 31, 34, 35; dining, 42; sightseeing, 19, 23, 26, 37-38
Creston, BC, 430
Crofton, BC, 350, 358
cruises: British Columbia, 380-381, 384-385, 387, 422-423; Oregon, 133, 152-153; Washington, 237-240, 244-245, 316-317
Cultus Lake, BC, 412, 420, 430
Cultus Lake Provincial Park, 406, 438
Cumberland, BC, 360
Curlew, WA, 311, 323
Cusick, WA, 272, 311, 312
Cypress Provincial Park, 376-377, 388-389

Dallas, OR, 132
Dalles, The, OR, 168
Darrington, WA, 228, 233
Davenport, WA, 318
Deming, WA, 225, 253
Depoe Bay, OR, 98, 112, 113, 117
Des Moines, WA, 233, 240
Diamond Lake, OR, 156, 167
dining: British Columbia, 366, 399-400, 439-440; California, 42-43, 77-78, 90-91; Oregon, 125, 171-173, 202; Washington, 275-277, 299-300, 335-336
diving, 34, 64-66, 350-354, 387, 424
dog racing, 328
dog sledding, 158, 427
Douglas Lake, BC, 412
Duncan, BC, 344, 346, 360-361, 366
Dunsmuir, CA, 46, 47, 50, 56, 65, 69, 74

Eastsound, WA, 248, 266
East Wenatchee, WA, 303, 321
Eatonville, WA, 222, 248, 253

Echo, OR, 196-197
Edmonds, WA, 225, 233, 240, 253-254
Elbe, WA, 227, 288
Elgin, OR, 180, 182, 184, 190, 191, 201
Elkton, OR, 115
Ellensburg, WA, 306, 312, 313, 321, 323
Elma, WA, 248, 272
Enterprise, OR, 182, 195
Enumclaw, WA, 222, 227, 228, 233-234, 254
Ephrata, WA, 304, 321, 324
Etna, CA, 51-52, 56, 67, 69
Eugene, OR, 142, 156, 161-162, 164, 172
Eureka, CA: accommodations, 40; dining, 42-43; fishing, 31, 32, 35; rodeo, 26; sightseeing, 16, 17, 24, 25, 38
Everett, WA: accommodations, 267; adventures, 217-218, 223, 227, 234, 237, 239; dining, 275; sightseeing, 248, 254

Falkland, BC, 414, 427
Fall City, WA, 227, 272
Fall River Mills, CA, 69
Federal Way, WA, 241, 254
Ferndale, CA, 22, 38-39
Ferndale, WA, 234, 238, 249, 254
ferries: British Columbia, 343, 344, 353, 371, 404, 422; Washington, 210, 242-243, 316-317
fishing: British Columbia, 354-355, 382-387, 416-419; California, 31-33, 60-64, 86-87; Oregon, 111-115, 149-151, 190-193; Washington, 232-237, 290-291, 317-318
Florence, OR: accommodations, 122; adventures, 104, 105, 110, 114, 115-116, 117; camping, 124; sightseeing, 107-108, 118, 121
flowers. *See* trees and flowers
food. *See* dining
Forks, WA, 225, 241
Fort Bragg, CA, 24, 26, 30, 31, 39, 41, 42-43
Fort Jones, CA, 70
Fort Langley, BC, 371, 390-391
Fort Lewis, WA, 255
Fortuna, CA, 17, 23, 26
Fossil, OR, 184, 201
fossils, 179
Frenchglen, OR, 195, 197
Friday Harbor, WA, 240, 266, 276

Gabriola Island, 350-351, 354-355, 356, 361
Galice, OR, 133
Garberville, CA, 21, 26, 32
gardens: British Columbia, 348, 359, 362-363, 393, 394, 395, 430, 431, 432;

California, 39; Oregon, 120, 121, 132; Washington, 251-252, 254, 257, 258, 263, 265, 297, 332
Garibaldi, OR, 98, 113, 124
Garibaldi Provincial Park, 375, 384, 398
Gearhart, OR, 118
gemstones. *See* mines and mining; rockhounding
geodes, 139-140, 178-180
George, WA, 306, 309, 324
ghost towns, 134, 186-188, 297
Gig Harbor, WA, 276
Gleneden Beach, OR, 123
Glenwood, WA, 290, 311
gliding, 68, 159, 250, 321, 428
gold. *See* mines and mining; rockhounding
Gold Bar, WA, 218, 242
Gold Beach, OR, 98, 104, 105, 106, 115, 116, 123
Goldendale, WA, 304, 312, 324, 335
Gold River, BC, 352, 365
Goose Lake, OR, 177
Grand Coulee, WA, 304, 310
Grand Coulee Dam, 333
Grand Forks, BC, 402, 425
Grants Pass, OR, 133, 143-144, 152
Greenhorn, OR, 177
Greenwater, WA, 292
Gulf Islands, 356, 358

Haines, OR, 184, 202
Hakai Pass, BC, 402
Halfway, OR, 182, 190, 194, 199-200
Hammond, OR, 113, 124
hang gliding, 69, 118, 159-160, 195, 292, 321, 358, 359
Happy Camp, CA, 46, 49, 55, 57, 70, 76
Harrison Hot Springs, BC, 417, 419, 421-422, 438
Harrison Mills, BC, 396, 436
Hells Canyon, 177, 189, 190, 316
Heppner, OR, 182, 184, 191, 201
Hermiston, OR, 184
hiking and backpacking: British Columbia, 345-348, 371-378, 404-409; California, 50-56, 84; Oregon, 100-105, 133, 135-139, 181-183; safety, 4-5; Washington, 215-226, 283-287, 308-310. *See also* beachcombing
Hiouchi, OR, 98
hockey, 320, 327, 328, 427
Holberg, BC, 345, 355
Hood River, OR, 139, 156, 159, 171, 172, 289; accommodations, 167
Hoodsport, WA, 219, 255
Hoopa, CA, 39, 41

Hope, BC, 402, 406-407, 415, 428, 431, 438
Hoquiam, WA, 212, 218-219, 227
Hornbrook, CA, 64, 71
horseback riding: British Columbia, 348-349, 378-379, 411-414; California, 26-27, 56-57, 84; Oregon, 105-106, 140-141, 183-186; safety, 5; Washington, 227, 287-288, 313
horse shows and rodeos: British Columbia, 349, 378, 410-411; California, 26, 56-57; Oregon, 106, 140, 183-185; Washington, 227-229, 287, 288, 310-313
houseboating, 153, 319, 423
hunting, 24, 84, 103, 180, 182
Husum, WA, 242, 290, 294, 316

Ilwaco, WA, 219, 234, 240, 245, 255-256
Index, WA, 242, 290
Indian festivals and ceremonies, 38-39, 49, 329, 391, 430, 431-432
Indian museums, 39, 40, 257-258, 264, 324, 328, 329, 330
Indian reservations, 19, 39, 83, 177, 198, 404
Indian villages, 177, 264
Irrigon, OR, 193
Island City, OR, 194
Issaquah, WA, 219, 226, 227, 256

Jacksonville, OR, 133-134
Jandana Ranch, BC, 436
Jesmond-Clinton, BC, 435
jetskiing, 5-6, 64-66, 116
John Day, OR, 183, 184, 191, 197
Johnstonville, CA, 80, 82, 90
Jordan Valley, OR, 177, 183, 191, 197
Joseph, OR, 177, 182, 183, 184, 193, 197-198

Kalama, WA, 281, 290, 294
Kamloops, BC: adventures, 412, 414, 417, 425, 428, 429; sightseeing, 411, 422, 431-432
kayaking. *See* canoeing and kayaking
Kelowna, BC: accommodations, 436-437; adventures, 412, 414, 417, 423, 426, 428, 429; airport, 402; camping, 439; dining, 439; sightseeing, 404, 411, 422, 432-433
Kelso, WA, 281, 294
Kennewick, WA, 306, 310, 312, 318, 320, 325, 332
Keremeos, BC, 413, 433
Kettle Falls, WA, 304, 306, 309, 315, 319, 320, 325, 333
Kirkland, WA, 244, 246, 248, 267, 276

kite flying, 118, 249-250, 321
Klamath, CA, 39
Klamath, OR, 98
Klamath River, 33, 61-63, 66, 76

La Center, WA, 295
La Conner, WA, 244, 249, 268, 276
lacross, 363
LaGrande, OR: adventures, 154, 180, 181, 182, 191; airport, 195; sightseeing, 118, 178, 183, 184
Lake Almanor, 80
Lake Cushman State Park, 219
Lakehead, CA, 64-65
Lake Oswego, OR, 147
Lakeview, OR, 157, 159, 180, 183, 195
Langfield Falls, WA, 286
Langley, BC: accommodations, 396; adventures, 372, 378-379, 380, 382, 384; camping, 398; sightseeing, 371, 389, 391
La Porte, CA, 83
Lassen National Forest, 87-88, 90, 91
Laurier, WA, 304
Lazo, BC, 429
Leavenworth, WA, 281, 290, 291, 292, 298, 299-300
Lebanon, OR, 134
Lewiston, CA, 60-61
lighthouses, 106-109, 219, 344, 362
Lincoln City, OR, 98, 99, 100, 104, 114, 124
llama farms and pack trips, 143-144, 226, 407
Logan Lake, BC, 411, 413
Long Beach, WA, 228, 237, 249, 250, 256
Longmire, WA, 298
Longview, WA, 295, 300
Lopez Island, 266
Lumby, BC, 413
Lund, BC, 422, 425
Lynden, WA, 212, 256-257
Lytton, BC, 419-420

Manning Provincial Park, 407-408, 410, 413
Maple Ridge, BC, 391
maps, list of, xiv (in front section)
Marble Mountain Wilderness, 63
Marcus, WA, 325-326
McArthur, CA, 56
McCloud, CA, 51, 59, 61, 67, 71, 74, 76
McKinleyville, CA, 19, 26
Medford, OR, 133-134, 137, 158, 171
Merritt, BC, 410, 411, 413, 426, 427, 439
Metaline Falls, WA, 326
Milton-Freewater, OR, 182, 183, 192

mines and mining: British Columbia, 390, 430, 434, 435; California, 27, 55-56, 69, 70; Oregon, 136-137, 186-187
Mission, BC: adventures, 373-374, 379, 380, 382, 383, 384, 388; camping, 398; sightseeing, 391-392
Modoc National Forest, 83, 91
Monroe, WA, 220, 228, 234, 248
Montague, CA, 46, 53, 56-57, 59
Moses Lake, WA, 304-305, 306, 311, 318, 320, 326
motorcycle trails, 315
motor home rentals, 349, 379-380
mountain biking. *See* biking
Mount Baker, 212, 284
Mount Hood, 129, 134, 144, 147, 155-156, 157
Mount Rainier, 286-287, 289
Mount Shasta: adventures, 50-51, 56, 60, 61, 65, 66, 67; airport, 46; sightseeing, 47-48, 57
Mount St. Helens, 134, 286, 287, 295
Mount Vernon, WA, 224, 234, 257
movie sets, 16
Mt. Shasta, CA, 59, 65, 66, 75, 77-78
Mukilteo, WA, 212, 257
museums: British Columbia, 358, 359-363, 390-396, 429-435; California, 37-40, 69-74, 88-89; Oregon, 119-122, 160-166, 195-199; Washington, 250-265, 293-296, 322-331
music. *See* theater and music
Myers Flat, CA, 39

Nahcotta, WA, 257
Nanaimo, BC, 346, 350, 356, 358, 361, 364, 366
Neah Bay, WA, 227, 257-258
Nelson, BC, 414, 420, 425, 429
Nespelum, WA, 326
Newberg, OR, 143, 159, 167-168, 171
Newcastle Island, 346
Newport, OR: adventures, 100, 104, 114, 116; camping, 124; dining, 125; sightseeing, 98, 106, 108, 117
Newport, WA, 273, 312, 335
New Westminster, BC, 371, 392, 396-397, 399
North Bend, WA, 213
North Vancouver, BC, 392
Nyssa, OR, 183, 192

Oak Harbor, WA, 235, 258, 266
Oakridge, OR, 141, 192
observatories, 394
Ocean City, WA, 258
Ocean Park, WA, 213

Ocean Shores, WA, 213, 222, 224, 230, 235, 237, 249, 268
Odessa, WA, 307, 311
off-road vehicle touring, 5, 28-29, 58, 109-110, 188, 231, 415-416
Okanagan Falls, BC, 433
Okanagan Lake, 404
Oliver, BC, 410, 413, 414
Olympia, WA, 258, 268, 273-274
Omak, WA, 305, 311, 320, 326, 335-336
Ontario, OR, 198, 201
Oregon: central, 126-174; coastal, 93-204; eastern, 174-204; history and geography, 2-3, 93-94, 126, 174, 176-178; information sources, 126-174, 173-174, 203-204; maps, 93, 97, 128, 163, 164, 175
Orick, CA, 16, 19, 25, 26, 27, 40
Orleans, OR, 123
Oroville, WA, 274, 320
Osoyoos, BC, 413, 420-421
Othello, WA, 305, 326
Oysterville, WA, 224, 226

Padilla Bay, 223-224
paragliding and parachuting, 250, 321, 389, 428
Parksville, BC, 351, 360, 361, 364, 366
Pasco, WA, 305, 326-327
Pateros, WA, 242, 318, 327
Pendleton, OR, 181, 184-185, 198-199, 200, 201, 202
Pend Oreille, WA, 304, 311, 318
Penticton, BC: accommodations, 437; adventures, 413, 415, 423, 425; airport, 402; camping, 439; dining, 440; sightseeing, 434
Pilot Rock, OR, 193
Port Alberni, BC, 344, 347, 350, 353, 356, 361
Port Angeles, WA, 213; accommodations, 268-269; adventures, 220-221, 224, 226, 230, 235; camping, 274; sightseeing, 258-259
Port Coquitlam, BC, 371, 374
Port Gamble, WA, 259
Port Hadlock, WA, 230, 235
Port Hardy, BC, 346, 351, 364, 402
Portland, OR: accommodations, 168; adventures, 137-138, 152, 158; dining, 172-173; sightseeing, 146-147, 152-153, 159
Portland, WA, 245
Port McNeill, BC, 351, 358
Port Moody, BC, 371, 374
Port Orchard, WA, 239, 259
Port Orford, OR, 99, 100, 101, 104, 110, 117, 125

Port Townsend, WA, 238, 244, 248, 259, 269, 276
Poulsbo, WA, 214, 248, 259
Powell River, BC: adventures, 408, 415, 417-418, 421, 424, 429; airport, 402; camping, 439; dining, 440; sightseeing, 404, 411, 422, 434
price scale: accommodations, 9; restaurants, 9
Prineville, OR, 139-140, 147
Protection Island, 367
Pullman, WA, 307, 327
Puyallup, WA, 228-229

Quilcene, WA, 214, 223
Quinault, WA, 223, 274
Quincey, CA, 89

races. *See* auto races; dog racing; horse shows
rafting: British Columbia, 381-382, 419-420; California, 35-36, 57, 64-66; Oregon, 116, 151-152, 189-190; safety, 5-6; Washington, 241-242, 289-290, 315-316
railroads: British Columbia, 350, 380-381, 416; California, 29, 59; Oregon, 110, 127, 147-148, 189; Washington, 209, 230-231, 288-289, 305, 315
Randle, WA, 295
Ravendale, CA, 89
Raymond, WA, 235, 259
Red Bluff, CA, 46, 71
Redding, CA, 46, 50, 56, 60, 64-65, 68, 72-73
Redmond, OR, 147-148, 150, 158, 159
Redwood state parks, 21, 22, 25
Reedsport, OR, 99, 104, 114, 115, 116, 117, 124
Renton, WA, 238, 248-249, 276
Republic, WA, 305, 311, 313-314, 332-333
restaurant price scale, 9
Revelstoke, BC, 420, 425, 427, 428, 437
Richland, OR, 183, 192
Richland, WA, 317, 320, 325, 327, 333
Richmond, BC, 371, 374-375, 392, 397, 399
Ridgefield, WA, 274, 295-196
Ritzville, WA, 307
road condition phone numbers: California, 15
rockhounding: British Columbia, 409; California, 55-56, 80; Oregon, 100-101, 139-140, 178-180; safety tips, 140
rodeos. *See* horse shows and rodeos
Roslyn, WA, 296
Rossland, BC, 425, 434

Salem, OR, 134-135, 158, 165-166, 168, 173
Salmon Arm, BC, 411, 423, 429
Salmon River, 76-77
Salt Spring Island, 344, 347, 349, 350, 355, 356, 359
Samoa, CA, 41, 42-43
Sasquatch, 18-19, 70
scuba diving. *See* diving
Seaside, OR, 99, 104-105, 108, 112, 115-116, 118, 124, 125
Seattle, WA: accommodations, 269-270; biking, 229-230; camping, 274; cruises, 244, 245; dining, 277; sightseeing, 214, 226, 248, 249, 260-263; transportation, 230, 231
Sedro-Woolley, WA, 214, 227, 234-235, 263
Sequim, WA, 224, 237, 238, 248, 263, 271, 277
Shelton, WA, 224, 264, 274
Shuswap Lake, BC, 409, 418-419, 422-423
Sidney, BC, 350, 357, 359, 361, 414
skating, 157-158, 388
skiing: British Columbia, 388-389; California, 66-69, 87-88; Oregon, 154-157, 194; Washington, 245-247, 291-292, 319-321
Smith River, 33-34
Snohomish, WA, 215-216, 230, 245, 248
Snoqualmie, WA, 231, 235, 246, 271, 288-289, 296
snowboarding. *See* skiing
snowmobiling, 68, 157, 194, 319, 427
snow sports: British Columbia, 357, 388-389, 425-427; California, 66-68, 87-88; Oregon, 154-158, 194; safety, 8-9; Washington, 245-247, 291-292, 319-321
Soap Lake, WA, 307, 328, 333
Sointula, BC, 353, 355
South Cowichan, BC, 347
Spokane, WA: adventures, 309, 310, 313, 314, 320; airport, 305; dining, 336; sightseeing, 307, 328
Squamish, BC, 375, 380, 389, 408, 428, 429, 439
squid catching, 236
St. Helens, OR, 134-135, 150
Standish, CA, 80
Stanwood, WA, 277
Steilacoom, WA, 214, 264
Stevenson, BC, 393, 399
storm-watching, 117
Sultan, WA, 235
Summerland, BC, 408-409, 414, 415, 416, 423, 434, 439

Sunshine Coast Parks, 385-387, 417, 424
Suquamish, WA, 264
surfing, 34, 117
Surrey, BC, 375-376
Susanville, CA, 82, 84-87, 89, 90, 91

Tacoma, WA, 224, 244, 265, 271
Tenino, WA, 224-225, 265
tepees, renting, 200-201
Texada Island, 404, 415
theater and music, 120; British Columbia, 360, 363, 434; California, 37-40; Oregon, 160, 161, 197, 198; Washington, 251, 253, 256, 259, 260, 265, 323, 325, 326, 327, 328, 329, 331
thundereggs. *See* geodes
Tillamook, OR: adventures, 103, 106, 111-112, 115, 117, 118; camping, 124; sightseeing, 108, 110, 121-122
Toppenish, WA: adventures, 307, 311, 313, 314, 328-329; camping, 334; dining, 336
tours. *See* auto touring; carriage tours; cruises; off-road vehicle touring; railroads; wagon tours
Trail, BC, 409, 427
trams, 118, 195
TransCanada Trail, 371-372
transportation: British Columbia, 341-343, 369-371, 401-402; California, 15-16, 44-45, 79-80; Oregon, 95-96, 126-127, 174-175; Washington, 207-211, 248-249, 280, 281, 303-305
trees and flowers, 25-26. *See also* gardens; wildlife watching
Trinidad, CA, 27, 40, 41
Trinity Center, CA, 46, 49
trolleys, 147, 195, 380
Troutdale, OR, 159, 168-169
Tulelake, CA, 46, 49, 54, 63, 65, 68
Tumwater, WA, 221, 248
Twisp, WA, 307, 313

Ucluelet, BC, 347, 351, 353, 355
Ukiah, OR, 199, 201
Umatilla, OR, 199
Umatilla National Forest, 201-202, 334
Union, OR, 183, 184, 193, 202
Union Gap, WA, 308, 309, 318, 329

Vale, OR, 180, 184, 193, 194, 199
Vancouver, BC: accommodations, 397-398; adventures, 376, 379-382, 385-389; dining, 399; sightseeing, 393-395
Vancouver, WA, 287, 289, 296-297, 300, 322
Vancouver Island, 341-368
Vantage, WA, 329
Vashon Island, WA, 240, 248
Vernon, BC, 414, 415, 434-435, 437, 439
Victoria, BC, 364-365; adventures, 347-348, 349, 350, 351, 353-354, 355; sightseeing, 343, 361-363
vineyards. *See* wineries and vineyards

wagon tours, 141, 200, 314
Waldport, OR, 112, 115-116, 124
Walla Walla, WA: accommodations, 333; adventures, 310, 312, 314, 320; camping, 335; sightseeing, 308, 322, 329-330
Warm Springs, OR, 161, 168-169
Warrenton, OR, 105, 114, 193
Washington, 205-337; central, 279-302; coastal Washington, 207-279; eastern, 302-337; history and geography, 3, 205-206, 279-280, 281, 283, 302, 305-308; information sources, 278-279, 300-302, 337; maps, 206, 282, 304
water sports: British Columbia, 350-357, 384-387, 416-425; California, 29-36, 64-66; Oregon, 111, 116-117, 148-153, 189-193; safety, 5-8; Washington, 232-245, 289-291, 315-319
Weaverville, CA, 46, 49, 55, 60, 64-65, 67, 73, 75
Weed, CA, 46, 54, 59, 65, 68, 73, 75
Wellpinit, WA, 330
Wenatchee, WA, 308, 319, 321, 330
Westbank, BC, 423, 427, 435
Weston, OR, 190, 194
Westport, WA, 235-236
whale-watching: British Columbia, 350-354, 357, 358; California, 29-31; Oregon, 101, 117; Washington, 240
Whidbey Island, 214
Whistler, BC, 420, 427, 437-438
White Rock, BC, 371, 377-378, 380, 396, 400
White Salmon, WA, 290, 297, 313, 316
White Swan, WA, 313, 331
whitewater classification chart, 6
wildflowers. *See* trees and flowers; wildlife watching
wildlife watching: British Columbia, 350-354, 357, 358, 361, 362, 409-410, 430; California, 6-8, 23-25, 29-31, 50-56, 83; Oregon, 101-102, 117, 137, 138, 180-181, 193; Washington, 219, 222-226, 295, 310, 322. *See also* trees and flowers
Willow Creek, CA, 18, 22, 27, 35, 76
Winchester Bay, OR, 105, 107, 115, 123

windsurfing: British Columbia, 421-422; Oregon, 116-117, 149, 193; safety tips, 117; Washington, 240, 289
wineries and vineyards: British Columbia, 360, 391, 432, 433, 434; Oregon, 143; Washington, 251, 255, 261-262, 264, 265, 293, 294, 295, 325, 326, 330
Winthrop, WA, 283, 292, 297, 321
Woodinville, WA, 249, 265
Woodland, WA, 287, 291, 297

Yachats, OR: accommodations, 123; adventures, 100, 105, 111-112; camping, 124, 125; sightseeing, 99, 107, 122

Yacolt, WA, 283, 297
Yakima, WA, 305, 308, 310, 312, 313, 314, 322, 331-332
Yale, BC, 420, 435
Yreka, CA: accommodations, 75; adventures, 51-53, 54, 55, 59, 64, 68; dining, 77-78; sightseeing, 48, 57, 58, 73-74
yurts, 124

zoos: British Columbia, 361, 362, 390; California, 69; Washington, 256, 260, 261, 263, 265, 326. *See also* aquariums

Adventure Guides from Hunter Publishing

ALASKA HIGHWAY

2nd Edition, Ed & Lynn Readicker-Henderson
"A comprehensive guide.... Plenty of background history and extensive bibliography." *Travel Reference Library on-line*
Travels the fascinating highway that passes settlements of the Tlingit and the Haida Indians, with stops at Anchorage, Tok, Skagway, Valdez, Denali National Park and more. Sidetrips and attractions en route, plus details on all other approaches - the Alaska Marine Hwy, Klondike Hwy, Top-of-the-World Hwy. Color photos.
400 pp, $16.95, 1-55650-824-7

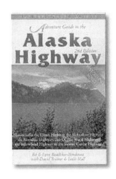

BAHAMAS

2nd Edition, Blair Howard
Fully updated reports for Grand Bahama, Freeport, Eleuthera, Bimini, Andros, the Exumas, Nassau, New Providence Island, plus new sections on San Salvador, Long Island, Cat Island, the Acklins, the Inaguas and the Berry Islands. Mailboat schedules, package vacations and snorkeling trips by Jean-Michel Cousteau. The best accommodations and restaurants, local customs and cuisine, entertainment, nightlife, gambling, along with tips on sailing, kayaking, fishing, diving, hiking, horseback riding.
350 pp, $14.95, 1-55650-852-2

EXPLORE BELIZE

4th Edition, Harry S. Pariser
"Down-to-earth advice.... An excellent travel guide." *Library Journal*
Extensive coverage of the country's political, social and economic history, along with the plant and animal life. Encouraging you to mingle with the locals, Pariser entices you with descriptions of local dishes and festivals. Maps, color photos.
400 pp, $16.95, 1-55650-785-2

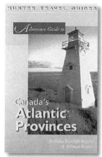

CANADA'S ATLANTIC PROVINCES
Barbara Radcliffe Rogers & Stillman Rogers
Pristine waters, rugged slopes, breathtaking seascapes, remote wilderness, sophisticated cities, and quaint, historic towns. Year-round adventures on the Fundy Coast, Acadian Peninsula, fjords of Gros Morne, Viking Trail & Vineland, Saint John River, Lord Baltimore's lost colony. Photos.
672 pp, $19.95, 1-55650-819-0

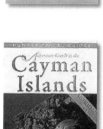

CAYMAN ISLANDS
Paris Permenter & John Bigley
The only comprehensive guidebook to Grand Cayman, Cayman Brac and Little Cayman. Encyclopedic listings of dive/snorkel operators, along with the best sites. Enjoy nighttime pony rides on a glorious beach, visit the turtle farms, prepare to get wet at staggering blowholes or just laze on a white sand beach. Color photos.
224 pp, $16.95, 1-55650-786-0

COLORADO
Steve Cohen
Adventures in the San Juan National Forest, Aspen, Vail, Mesa Verde National Park, the Sangre De Cristo Mountains, Denver, Boulder, Telluride, Colorado Springs and Durango, plus scores of smaller towns and attractions. Invaluable advice from a resident author who knows the state intimately.
256 pp, $15.95, 1-55650-842-

COASTAL ALASKA & THE INSIDE PASSAGE
3rd Edition, Lynn & Ed Readicker-Henderson
"A highly useful book." *Travel Books Review*
Using the Alaska Marine Highway to visit Ketchikan, Bellingham, the Aleutians, Kodiak, Seldovia, Valdez, Seward, Homer, Cordova, Prince of Wales Island, Juneau, Gustavas, Sitka, Haines, Skagway. Glacier Bay, Tenakee. US and Canadian gateway cities profiled.
400 pp, $16.95, 1-55650-859-X

COSTA RICA

3rd Edition, Harry S. Pariser

"... most comprehensive... Excellent sections on national parks, flora, fauna & history."
CompuServe

Incredible detail on culture, plants, animals, where to stay & eat, as well as practicalities of travel. E-mail and Web site directory.
560 pp, $16.95, 1-55650-722-4

HAWAII

John Penisten

Maui, Molokai, Lanai, Hawaii, Kauai and Oahu are explored in detail, along with many of the smaller, less-visited islands. Full coverage of the best diving, trekking, cruising, kayaking, shopping and more from a Hawaii resident.
420 pp, $16.95, 1-55650-841-7

EXPLORE THE DOMINICAN REPUBLIC

3rd Edition, Harry S. Pariser

Virgin beaches, 16th-century Spanish ruins, the Caribbean's highest mountain, exotic wildlife, vast forests. Visit Santa Domingo, revel in Sosúa's European sophistication or explore the Samaná Peninsula's jungle. Color.
340 pp, $15.95, 1-55650-814-X

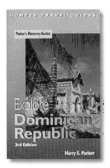

FLORIDA KEYS & EVERGLADES

2nd Edition, Joyce & Jon Huber

"... vastly informative, absolutely user-friendly, chock full of information..." Dr. Susan Cropper
"... practical & easy to use." *Wilderness Southeast*
Canoe trails, airboat rides, nature hikes, Key West, diving, sailing, fishing. Color.
224 pp, $14.95, 1-55650-745-3

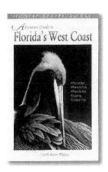

FLORIDA'S WEST COAST
Chelle Koster Walton
A guide to all the cities, towns, nature preserves, wilderness areas and sandy beaches that grace the Sunshine State's western shore. From Tampa Bay to Naples and Everglades National Park to
Sanibel Island.
224 pp, $14.95, 1-55650-787-9

GEORGIA
Blair Howard
"Packed full of information on everything there is to see and do." *Chattanooga Free Press*
From Atlanta to Savannah to Cumberland Island, this book walks you through antique-filled stores, around a five-story science museum and leads you on tours of old Southern plantations.
296 pp, $15.95, 1-55650-782-8

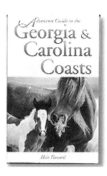

GEORGIA & CAROLINA COASTS
Blair Howard
"Provides details often omitted... geared to exploring the wild dunes, the historic districts, the joys... " *Amazon.com Travel Expert*
Beaufort, Myrtle Beach, New Bern, Savannah, the Sea Islands, Hilton Head and Charleston. Restaurants, hotels, shopping, what to see and do, plus the best fishing, hiking, diving, canoeing, and more.
288 pp, $15.95, 1-55650-747-X

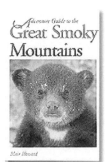

GREAT SMOKY MOUNTAINS
Blair Howard
"The take-along guide." *Bookwatch*
Includes overlapping Tennessee, Georgia, Virginia and N. Carolina, the Cherokee and Pisgah National Forests, Chattanooga and Knoxville. Scenic fall drives on the Blue Ridge Parkway.
288 pp, $15.95, 1-55650-720-8

HIGH SOUTHWEST
2nd Edition, Steve Cohen
"Exhaustive detail... [A] hefty, extremely thorough & very informative book." *QuickTrips Newsletter*
"Plenty of maps/detail - an excellent guide." *Bookwatch*
Four Corners of NW New Mexico, SW Colorado, S Utah, N Arizona. Encyclopedic coverage.
376 pp, $15.95, 1-55650-723-2

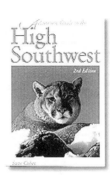

IDAHO
Genevieve Rowles
Snake River Plain, the Owyhee Mountains, Sawtooth National Recreation Area, the Lost River Range and the Salmon River Mountains. Comprehensive coverage of ski areas, as well as gold-panning excursions and activities for kids, all written by an author with a passion for Idaho.
352 pp, $16.95, 1-55650-789-5

THE LEEWARD ISLANDS
Antigua, St. Martin, St. Barts, St. Kitts, Nevis, Antigua, Barbuda
Paris Permenter & John Bigley
Far outdistances other guides. Recommended operators for day sails, island-hopping excursions, scuba dives, unique rainforest treks on verdant mountain slopes, and rugged four-wheel-drive trails.
248 pp, $14.95, 1-55650-788-7

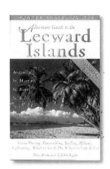

NEW HAMPSHIRE
Elizabeth L. Dugger
The Great North Woods, White Mountains, the Lakes Region, Dartmouth & Lake Sunapee, the Monadnock region, Merrimack Valley and the Seacoast Region. Beth Dugger finds the roads less traveled.
360 pp, $15.95, 1-55650-822-0

NORTHERN FLORIDA & THE PANHANDLE
Jim & Cynthia Tunstall
From the Georgia border south to Ocala National Forest and through the Panhandle. Swimming with dolphins and spelunking, plus Rails to Trails, a 47-mile hiking/biking path made of recycled rubber.
320 pp, $15.95, 1-55650-769-0

ORLANDO & CENTRAL FLORIDA
including Disney World, the Space Coast, Tampa & Daytona
Jim & Cynthia Tunstall
Takes you to parts of Central Florida you never knew existed. Explore wildlife refuges and forests, pristine canoe trails and some of the Southeast's best dive sites. Where to stay, where to eat, what to do. Photos.
300 pp, $15.95, 1-55650-825-5

MICHIGAN
Kevin & Laurie Hillstrom
Year-round activities, all detailed here by resident authors. Port Huron-to-Mackinac Island Sailboat Race, Isle Royale National Park, Tour de Michigan cycling marathon. Also: canoeing, dogsledding and urban adventures. Includes transportation details, history, flora & fauna, campgrounds, outfitters, and full trail descriptions.
360 pp, $16.95, 1-55650-820-4

NEVADA
Matt Purdue
Adventures throughout the state, from Winnemucca to Great Basin National Park, Ruby Mountain Wilderness to Angel Lake, from Cathedral Gorge State Park to the Las Vegas strip. Jeeping, hiking, boating in Lake Tahoe or Lake Meade. Take your pick!
250 pp, $15.95, 1-55650-842-5

NORTHERN CALIFORNIA

Lee Foster & Mary Lou Janson

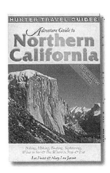

Waves lure surfers to Santa Cruz; heavy snowfall attracts skiers to Lake Tahoe; scuba divers relish Monterey Bay; horseback riders explore trails at Mammoth Lake. Travel the Big Sur and Monterey coasts, enjoy views of Yosemite and savor Wine Country. Resident authors.
360 pp, $15.95, 1-55650-821-2

PUERTO RICO

3rd Edition, Harry S. Pariser

"A quality book that covers all aspects... it's all here & well done." The San Diego Tribune
"... well researched. They include helpful facts... filled with insightful tips." The Shoestring Traveler
Crumbling watchtowers and fascinating folklore enchant visitors. Color photos.
344 pp, $15.95, 1-55650-749-6

SIERRA NEVADA

Wilbur H. Morrison & Matt Purdue

California's magnificent Sierra Nevada mountain range. The Pacific Crest Trail, Yosemite, Lake Tahoe, Mount Whitney, Mammoth Lakes, the John Muir Trail, King's Canyon and Sequoia - all are explored. Plus, excellent historical sections. An adventurer's playground awaits!
300 pp, $15.95, 1-55650-845-X

SOUTHEAST FLORIDA

Sharon Spence

Get soaked by crashing waves at twilight; canoe through mangroves; reel in a six-foot sailfish; or watch as a yellow-bellied turtle snuggles up to a gator. Interviews with the experts - scuba divers, sky divers, pilots, fishermen, bikers, balloonists, and park rangers. Color photos.
256 pp, $15.95, 1-55650-811-5

SOUTHERN CALIFORNIA
Don & Marge Young
Browse an art festival, peoplewatch at the beach, sportfish near offshore islands and see world-class performances by street entertainers. The Sierras offer a different adventure, with cable cars ready to whisk you to their peaks. A special section covers daytrips to Mexico.
400 pp, $16.95, 1-55650-791-7

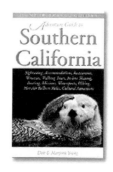

TEXAS
Kimberly Young
Explore Austin, Houston, Dallas/Ft. Worth, San Antonio, Waco and all the places in-between, from Dripping Springs to Marble Falls. Angle for "the big one" at Highland Lakes, or try some offshore fishing. Tramp through the Big Thicket or paddle on Lake Texoma. Photos throughout.
380 pp, $15.95, 1-55650-812-3

VIRGIN ISLANDS
4th Edition, Harry S. Pariser
"Plenty of outdoor options.... All budgets are considered in a fine coverage that appeals to readers." *Reviewer's Bookwatch*
Every island in the Virgins. Valuable, candid opinions. St. Croix, St. John, St. Thomas, Tortola, Virgin Gorda, Anegada. Color.
368 pp, $16.95, 1-55650-746-1

VIRGINIA
Leonard Adkins
The Appalachian Trail winds over the state's eastern mountains. The Great Dismal Swamp offers biking, hiking and canoeing trails, and spectacular wildlife. Skyline Drive and the Blue Ridge Parkway - popular drives in spring and summer. Photos.
420 pp, $16.95, 1-55650-816-6

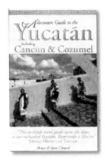

THE YUCATAN including Cancún & Cozumel
Bruce & June Conord
"... Honest evaluations. This book is the one not to leave home without." *Time Off Magazine*
"... opens the doors to our enchanted Yucatán." Mexico Ministry of Tourism
Maya ruins, Spanish splendor. Deserted beaches, festivals, culinary delights.
376 pp, $15.95, 1-55650-792-5

Send for our complete catalog. All Hunter titles are available at bookstores nationwide or direct from the publisher.

ORDER FORM				
Yes! Send the following *Adventure Guides*:				
TITLE	ISBN #	PRICE	QUANTITY	TOTAL
		SUBTOTAL		
SHIPPING & HANDLING (United States only)				
(1-2 books, $3; 3-5 books, $5; 6-10 books, $8)				
ENCLOSED IS MY CHECK FOR				

NAME:
ADDRESS:
CITY, STATE, ZIP:
PHONE:

Make checks payable to Hunter Publishing, Inc. and mail with order form to: Hunter Publishing, Inc., 239 South Beach Rd., Hobe Sound FL 33455; ☎ 561/546-7986; Fax 561/546-8040.

VISIT US ON THE WORLD WIDE WEB

http://www.hunterpublishing.com

You'll find our full range of travel guides to all corners of the globe, with descriptions, reviews, author profiles and pictures. Our **Alive Guide** series includes guides to *Aruba, Bonaire & Curaçao, St. Martin & St. Barts, Cancún & Cozumel* and other Caribbean destinations. **Romantic Weekends** guides explore destinations from *New England* to *Virginia, New York* to *Texas*. **Charming Small Hotel Guides** cover Italy, Venice, Tuscany, Spain, France, Britain, Paris, Germany, Switzerland, Southern France, New England, Austria and Florida - all in full color. Hundreds of other books are described, ranging from *Best Dives of the Caribbean* to *Battlefields of the Civil War* and *The African-American Travel Guide*. Books may be purchased on-line through our secure credit card transaction system or by check.

We Love to Get Mail

This book has been carefully researched to bring you current, accurate information. But no place is unchanging. We welcome your comments for future editions. Please write us at: Hunter Publishing, 130 Campus Drive, Edison NJ 08818, or e-mail your comments to hunterpub@emi.net.